D0138229

most current ed.
GRL
11/2012

DISCARDED

The Routledge Dictionary of Anthropologists

The Routledge Dictionary of Anthropologists provides a Who's Who of anthropologists from the birth of the discipline in the nineteenth century to the present day. Over three hundred of the most influential and significant figures in world anthropology are discussed, from the precursors of anthropology, such as Darwin, through celebrated figures such as Evans-Pritchard and Margaret Mead, to lesser-known and more controversial names such as Arthur Maurice Hocart and Carlos Castaneda. The entries provide details of each anthropologist's life and work, theories and publications.

The fourteen chapters are arranged by national traditions and schools of thought, and cover a wide geographical area including the United Kingdom, the United States, Europe, Latin America and Asia. Each section includes a brief history of the national school under review and places the anthropologists within the framework of their peers and the key thinkers who influenced their thought.

The Routledge Dictionary of Anthropologists features:

- Chapters arranged by national traditions
- An introduction to each section outlining the prominent features of the anthropological movements
- Cross-references of names and schools of thought
- A thorough index to assist in locating entries quickly and easily
- Selected bibliographies at the end of each chapter

Written by an experienced social anthropologist, *The Routledge Dictionary of Anthropologists* will prove indispensable for students of the discipline and those with an interest in ethnology and sociology.

To my mother

The Routledge Dictionary of Anthropologists

Gérald Gaillard

Translated by Peter James Bowman

Routledge
Taylor & Francis Group

LONDON AND NEW YORK

NOV 2 2 2004

First published in French (*Dictionnaire des ethnologues et des anthropologues*) 1997
by Armand Colin
21 rue du Montparnasse, F 75283 Paris, Cedex 06, France

First published in English 2004
by Routledge
11 New Fetter Lane, London EC4P 4EE

Simultaneously published in the USA and Canada
by Routledge
29 West 35th Street, New York, NY 10001

Routledge is an imprint of the Taylor & Francis Group

© 1997 Armand Colin Publisher
Chapters II, IX, X and XI © 2004 Armand Colin Publisher
© Translation 2004 Routledge

Typeset in Galliard by RefineCatch Limited, Bungay, Suffolk
Printed and bound in Great Britain by
TJ International Ltd, Padstow, Cornwall

British Library Cataloguing in Publication Data
A catalogue record for this book is available from the British Library

Library of Congress Cataloging in Publication Data
A catalog record for this book has been requested

ISBN 0–415–22825–5

Contents

General remarks and acknowledgements

It gives me pleasure to offer to students, colleagues, and possibly also the general reader, a work containing biographies of a large number of ethnologists and anthropologists and a brief institutional history of each of the national traditions. Suggestions for further reading are given in the extensive chapter bibliographies.

In introducing the work, I must explain its limitations. For obvious reasons I have had to be selective in my inclusion of authors and brief in my discussion of their works, and in the cases of some of the national traditions I have only been able to point to a few salient features. With rare exceptions anthropologists of what is generally called the Western world are excluded. This will not please everyone; my reason for this policy is that, although the discipline today probably produces more investigations of the 'here' than the 'there', this book treats primarily of a period in which the former were scarce, and most often belonged more properly to sociology or human geography or history than to anthropology.

The second limitation concerns the number of authors treated. Although the book contains a fairly large number, I should have liked to include more. The selection process has necessarily been determined by my incomplete knowledge of the discipline, but has also been partly subjective. I have had to make choices, and apologize to readers whose choices would have been different. One objective criterion was age, and I decided that Tim Ingold, Arjun Appadurai, Rayna Rapp, Bruno Latour and many others were too young for inclusion. In some instances I have had to abandon the idea of including a particular scholar quite simply because even extensive research, letters and telephone calls failed to yield enough material for an entry. I have made requests for curricula vitae, which some authors have been kind enough to provide, and to them I must apologize for having, in all cases, used only a fraction of the information they supplied. As the reader has no access to these sources, I have referred to them simply as 'correspondence with the author'.

As an Africanist with a deep attachment to Africa, where I grew up, I greatly regret not having been able to gather sufficient material for a chapter on African anthropologists. Given the state of the documentary evidence, the task of reconstructing the dynamic of research centres such as Lagos, Dakar, Abidjan, Cairo, Bissau and Nairobi would have defeated me. Furthermore, although Jomo Kenyatta published his Malinowski-supervised Ph.D. *Facing Mount Kenya: The Tribal Life of the Gikuyus* in 1938, most African anthropologists belong to the younger generation. The continent's intellectuals long rejected anthropology, seeing it as the 'child of colonialism', and even thereafter its development was hindered by financial difficulties. It is nonetheless worth recalling that a Pan-African Anthropological Association was established in 1988.

I have made use of most of the classic works on the prosopography and history of the

---

discipline as well as several dictionaries and encyclopaedias, all of which are listed below and subsequently cited in abbreviated form. Titles cited fully in the text of an entry are not repeated in the bibliography beneath it. References to works which have not been published in English translation are given in the original language in the bibliographies and in both languages in the entries.

I should like to thank Sabine Gaillard-Starzmann for carefully reading the typescript before it was passed on to the translator, and for sharing my life for so many years. At different stages of my work I have benefited in various ways from the help of Jonathan Benthall, Chris Beyers, Clara Carvalho, Mariza Corrêa, Tony Chapman, Robert Deliège, Youssouf Diallo, Mary O'Donnell, Beverley Emery, Scarlett Epstein, Carlos Fausto, Thomas Fillitz, Andre Gingrich, Isabelle Henrion-Dourcy, Adam Jones, Nicolas Journet, Sergei Kan, Mori Kyoko, Adam Kuper, Françoise Lestage, Peter Limb, John Middleton, Sidney Mintz, Marc Poncelet, George W. Stocking, Marilyn Strathern, William C. Sturtevant, Julie Velarde, Douglas White, Eric Wolf, Jan de Wolf, Katsuhiko Yamaji, and Filippo Zérilli. None of them, of course, necessarily agrees with my presentation, but their assistance has been invaluable. I should also like to thank my colleagues at the University of Lille I, whose spirit of professional co-operation has been exemplary. I am grateful to Routledge, particularly to Victoria Peters and above all to Julene Barnes, who have been encouraging and understanding. Finally my thanks go to my translator Peter James Bowman for embarking on his lengthy task, and to the past, present and future students whose serious-mindedness, enthusiasm and determination give real meaning to my duties as a teacher.

As well as the limitations consciously imposed on this work, there are doubtless a number of unintentional and regrettable omissions. I apologize for these and for the errors of fact which always creep into a book of this sort. To all those who would wish not to criticize but to condemn this work, I reply with an extract from a letter Eric Wolf wrote to me after receiving the French edition. He had been kind enough to read the American chapters in draft form, and his widow Sydel Silverman has authorized me to quote this passage: 'I am just coming back home after surgery and hoping to write quickly, both to thank you very much for sending me your *Dictionnaire des ethnologues et des anthropologues*, and to say how useful it has been for me. I am preparing a lecture for the EASA meeting in Frankfurt in September on the topic of anthropology's relations to the institutional, national and international contexts in which it finds itself; and your *Dictionnaire* proves to be invaluable for this endeavour' (27 March 1998). Thank you Eric Wolf.

FREQUENTLY USED SOURCES

A. Aguirre, ed., 1982, Conceptos clave de la anthropologia cultural, Madrid, Daimon. T. Barfield, ed., 1997, The Dictionary of Anthropology, Oxford, Blackwell. A. Barnard and J. Spencer, eds, 1996, Encyclopedia of Social and Cultural Anthropology, London and New York, Henry Holt. P. Bonte and M. Izard, eds, 1991, Dictionnaire de l'ethnologie et de l'anthropologie, Paris, PUF. J.O. Brew, ed., 1968, One Hundred Years of Anthropology, Cambridge, Mass., Harvard UP. Regna Darnell, 2001, Invisible Genealogies. A History of Americanist Anthropology, The University of Nebraska Press. M. Harris, 1968, The Rise of Anthropological Theory, London, New York, Routledge. Sol Tax, ed., 1975, Fifth inter-national directory of anthropologists, Chicago. Ute Gacs, ed., 1988, Women Anthropolo-gists: A Biographical Dictionary, New York, Westport. G. Gaillard, 1988, Eléments pour servir à la constitution d'une histoire de l'anthropologie française de ces trente dernières années, EHESS, 10 volumes. G. Gaillard, 1990, Répertoire de l'anthropologie française, 1950–1970, Paris, CNRS, 2 vols. F. Gresle et al., 1990, Dictionnaire des Sciences Humaines, Paris, Nathan. W. Hirschberg, Christian F. Feest, Hans Fischer, Thomas Schweizer, eds, 1988, Wörterbuch der Völkerkunde, Berlin, Reimer. H. Kuklick, 1991, The Savage Within. The Social History of British Anthropology 1885–1945, London, Cambridge. A. Kuper, 1973, Anthropology and Anthropologists, London and New York, Routledge. A. Kuper and J. Kuper, eds, 1985, The Social Science Encyclopedia, London and New York, Routledge. A. Kuper, 1988, The Invention of Primitive Society, New York, Harper and Row. D. Levinson and M. Ember, eds, 1996, Encyclopedia of Cultural Anthropology, New York, Henry Holt and Company. T. L. Mann, ed., 1988, Biographical Directory of Anthropologists born before 1920, New York and London, Garland. C. Seymour-Smith, 1986, Macmillan Dictionary of Anthropology, London and Basingstoke, Macmillan Press. D.L. Sills, ed., 1968–1979, International Encyclopedia of Social Sciences, New York. G.W. Stocking, 1987, Victorian Anthropology, New York, The Free Press. G.W. Stocking, ed., 1983-, History of Anthropology, 9 vols to date, London, Wisconsin UP. G.W. Stocking, 1995, After Tylor. British Social Anthropology, 1888–1951, London, Athlone. G.W. Stocking, 2001, Delimiting Anthropology, Wisconsin UP. F.W. Voget, 1975, A History of Ethnology, New York, Holt, Rinehart and Winston. C. Winter, ed., 1991, International Dictionary of Anthropologists, New York and London, Garland.

Note

This translation is based on the author's revision and updating of the original French text (published in 1997). Chapters II, IX, X and XI are new chapters written and translated specifically for the English edition. The author has also updated and amended the bibliographies for the English edition.

Abbreviations

AA	*American Anthropologist*
AAA	American Anthropological Association
AISEA	Associazione Italiana per le Scienze Etno-Antropologiche [Italian Association for Ethnological and Anthropological Sciences]
AMNH	American Museum of Natural History
AMNHP	American Museum of Natural History Press
ARBE	*Annual Report of the Bureau of Ethnology* (to the Secretary of the Smithsonian institution)
ASA	Association of Social Anthropologists of the UK and the Commonwealth
AT	*Anthropology Today*
CA	*Current Anthropology*
CERM	Centre d'études et de recherches marxistes [centre for Marxist study and research]
CFRE	Centre de formation à la recherche ethnologique [training centre for ethnological research]
CNRS	Centre national de la recherche scientifique [national centre for scientific research]
DEA	Diplôme d'Etudes Approfondies [diploma of further studies]
DES	Diplôme d'études supérieures [diploma of advanced studies]
EFEO	Ecole française d'Extrême-Orient [French school of the Far East]
EHESS	Ecole des hautes études en sciences sociales [school of higher studies in the social sciences]
ENA	Ecole nationale d'administration [national school of administration]
ENFOM	Ecole nationale de la France d'Outre-Mer [national school for French overseas territories]
ENS	Ecole normale supérieure [advanced standard school]
EPHE	Ecole pratique des hautes études [practical school of higher studies]
FAO	Food and Agricultural Organization
HOA	*History of Anthropology* (published by University of Wisconsin Press)
IAI	International African Institute
IFAN	Institut français d'Afrique noire [French Institute for Black Africa]
INALCO(V)	Institut national des langues at civilisations orientales (vivantes) [national institute for (modern) oriental languages and civilizations]
INED	Institut national d'études de développement [national institute for development studies]

INI	Instituto Nacional Indigenista [national indigenist institute]
IRSAC	Institut pour la recherche scientifique en Afrique Centrale [institute for scientific research on Central Africa]
JRAI	*Journal of the Royal Anthropological Institute*
JSA	*Journal de la Société Asiatique*
LSE	London School of Economics
ORSTOM	Office de la recherche scientifique et technique des territoires Outre-Mer [bureau for overseas scientific and technical research]
PUV	Presses Universitaires de France
RAI	Royal Anthropological Institute
RAIN	*RAI News*
RCP	Recherches coopératives sur programme (part of CNRS) [programme-based cooperative research]
SOAS	School of Oriental and African Studies
SVD	Societas Verbi Divini [Society of the Divine Word]
UCLA	University of California at Los Angeles
UCPAAE	*University of California Publications in American Archeology and Ethnology*
UNESCO	United Nations Educational, Scientific and Cultural Organization

I

The nineteenth century and the evolutionists

ORIGINS AND FORERUNNERS

The beginnings of anthropology and ethnology are many and various; thinkers such as Rousseau, Ferguson and Desmoulin, as well as **Herder**, **Edwards**, **Pritchard**, **Virchow**, **Lyell** and **Darwin**, are all associated with the discipline's earliest development. And this is no arbitrary list of names. It was Herder who created the genre of *Volkskunde*, and from it *Völkerkunde*. *Volkskunde* (science of the nation (cf. p. 41)) looks only at the popular traditions and cultural practices of the Germanic peoples, their *Kultur* (a term he 'introduced into modern discourse' (Kuper, 1999: 31)), whereas *Völkerkunde* is a form of geographical ethnology. Pritchard, Edwards and Virchow were the founders of the first British, French and German ethnological societies respectively. Finally, in a work aimed at students, an introduction to what Kroeber has called 'the prodigious decade' (1861–1871) would be incomplete without a reminder of the role of Darwin, or indeed without some mention of Lyell and, in his wake, the establishment of geology as the precondition of evolutionist ideas.

As with many other disciplines, the study of anthropology was initially pursued within learned societies, and only later were museums provided by the state and professorships endowed by universities. First the Ethnological Society of Paris was founded in 1839, followed in 1843 by the Ethnological Society of London as an offshoot of the Quaker-dominated Aborigines Protection Society, itself founded in 1837 (Chapman, 1985: 21). The Ethnological Society of Paris did not survive the 1848 revolution, while the Ethnological Society of London merged in 1871 with its rival the Anthropological Society of London to form the Anthropological Institute of Great Britain and Ireland, which in turn became the Royal Anthropological Institute (which now publishes *Man* and *Anthropology Today*). After the demise of the Ethnological Society of Paris, France saw the appearance of a Society of American and Oriental Anthropology, which became the Ethnographical Society of Paris in 1859 at the behest of L. de Rosny. At a meeting held on the same day, Broca founded the Anthropological Society of Paris, which, unlike the Ethnographical Society, was intended to concentrate entirely on physical anthropology. This is an unusual instance because the Anthropological Society of Washington (1859), the Berlin Society of Anthropology, Ethnology und Prehistory (1869), the Anthropological Institute of Great Britain and Ireland (1871) and the Italian Ethnological Society (1871) were all concerned as much with physical as with social and cultural anthropology, as much with linguistics as with prehistory and archaeology. The Anthropological Society of Vienna (*Anthropologische Gesellschaft in Wien*), founded in 1870 and located in the *Naturhistorisches Museum*, undertook to reconstruct the history of the Austrian race ('*Österreichische Rassenlehre*'), and it still combines the various parts of what was known as *Völkerkunde* in the nineteenth century: ethnology, physical anthropology, archaeology, geography and prehistory ('*Ur- und Frühgeschichte*').

The fundamental debate during this period set monogenists against polygenists. Drawing on biblical narrative, monogenism stated that the various races descended from Adam and that peoples were dispersed after the episode of the Tower of Babel. Current differences between races could be explained in terms of environmental influences which caused degeneration in some of them. Conversely, for polygenists each race was a separate species (some authors identified more than twenty). Noting that the 'Blacks' in Herodotus were identical with those of their own day, and insisting that environmental factors could not effect redundancy modifications in the physical human structure, polygenists asserted that races remained essentially unchanged. Because of the perceived association between moral and physical characteristics, races were held to differ radically and, in a sense, ontologically in their capacity for civilization.

Following the victory of evolutionism and the affirmation of the fundamental psychic unity of mankind (Bastian) without reference to theories of degeneration and biblical myth, a new set of questions arose. With the exception of Lyell, who closes our consideration of the discipline's beginnings, the writers treated below are generally thought of as anthropologists or as ethnographers. And yet they are as much descendants of the ancient voyagers or of Montesquieu, Concordet and Comte, as of Cuvier, Boucher de Perthes, Lamarck or Darwin. Regrettably, there is not the space here to deal with even such prominent names as T. Waitz, A. Lang, C. Letourneau, W. Ellis, E. Hartland, and others besides. For the same reason, and despite the enormous importance of their works, neither Durkheim nor Spencer (basically sociologists) are treated here.

Herder, Johann Gottfried (1744–1803)

Born in Mohrungen in East Prussia, Johann Gottfried Herder studied literature, law, philosophy and theology before becoming a pastor. He wrote more than thirty books, all strongly influenced by the thought of Kant and Lessing, including *Fragmente über die neuere deutsche Literatur* [*Fragments on Recent German Literature*] (1767) and other essays of literary criticism. In 1774 his *Auch eine Philosophie der Geschichte zur Bildung der Menschheit* [*A New Philosophy of History for the Education of Humanity*] took the field 'against the uniform universalism of the Enlightenment (. . .) Each cultural community, or *Volk*, expresses in its own way an aspect of humanity' (Dumont, 1991: 23). He also introduced into modern discourse the word *Kultur*, taken from the Latin of Cicero. But it is the publication in 1778 of *Stimmen der Völker in Liedern* [*The Voices of Peoples in Their Songs*] a collection of German folksongs, which makes him a precursor of anthropology. For Herder, popular songs, fables, and legends construct the cultural identity of a people. This is considered to be the founding work of *Volkskunde*, or 'science of the nation' (cf. p. 41), and of ethnological and folkloric studies in Germany. These ideas were exported from Germany when A. **Bastian** transmitted them to **Boas**, the father of much of American anthropology. Herder died in Weimar in 1803, but his work was carried forward by the Brothers Grimm, who collected Germanic myths from all the nations of Northern Europe (*Deutsche Mythologie*, 1836).

Humboldt, Alexander von (1769–1859)

A Prussian baron born in Berlin, Alexander von Humboldt was without doubt one of the last savants to have possessed an overview of all the learning of his day, including mathematics, chemistry, philosophy, astronomy, meteorology and botany. There was hardly a subject on which he did not write. He studied at the universities of Frankfurt-an-der-Oder and Göttingen and became an engineer and then a state councillor responsible for mines. At his mother's death in 1796, Humboldt inherited a fortune which allowed him to give up paid employment and realise his dream to travel. From 1799 to 1804 he journeyed to the Spanish colonies in the Americas; he stayed in Venezuela, Cuba, Mexico, followed the Orinoco upstream, crossed the equator, and entered Peru. Before returning to Europe he travelled to the USA, where he met Thomas Jefferson. From 1808 to 1827 Humboldt lived in Paris, where he wrote most of the thirty volumes (fourteen of them on botany) of his *Voyage to the Equinoctial Regions of the New World, undertaken in 1799, 1800 . . . by A. de Humboldt and Aimé Bonpland*, which appeared between 1807 and 1834. In 1827 he returned to Berlin, where Frederick William III of Prussia entrusted him with leading a commission for the advancement of scholars and artists. During this period he gave his famous lectures on the cosmos (1828) and travelled to Russia and Central Asia (1829). The rest of his life was divided between his writings and various diplomatic missions.

As well as the geographical aspect of his journey to the Americas (including his discovery of the point of confluence of the Amazon and Orinoco rivers), Humboldt observed the diversity of the native Indian populations, which he believed had originated from Asia 20,000 years ago. He made a study of their economic life and customs, described monuments in Mexico and Peru, and drew up a chronology of the European conquest.

Philippe Descola says of him:

When he studied a phenomenon as a geologist or botanist, he always related it to other observable phenomena in the same environment and to historical and sociological factors, and always then sought to clarify the relationships he had established by comparing them with analogous sets of relationships in other parts of the world. A. von Humboldt followed the same practice in his investigations into American Indians of the Orinoco and of the high plateaux of the Andes and Mexico: far from seeing them as amiable or repulsive beings who made suitable subjects for philosophical parables, he endeavoured to show how their development was determined by land, climate and vegetation, but also by migrations, exchanges of goods and ideas, interethnic conflicts and the vicissitudes, even if only indirectly felt, of Spanish colonization. He intuitively felt, in other words, that the natural history of humanity was inseparable from the human history of nature.

[*Leçon inaugurale*, Paris: Collège de France, 2001]

Humboldt's brother, Karl Wilhelm, became a minister and was one of the founders of modern linguistics.

Edwards, William (1776–1842)

Born the son of a planter in the British colony of Jamaica, William Edwards studied medicine at Bruges and then at Paris (1814). In 1829, after a number of minor works, he published a text entitled *Des caractères physiologiques des races humaines considérées dans leurs rapports avec l'histoire. Lettre à M. Amédés Thierry* [*The Physiological Characteristics of the Human Races Considered in Relation to History. Letter to M. Amédés Thierry*]. A polygenist, Edwards took issue with J. C. **Pritchard**'s monogenist idea that different races emerge as a result of conditioning by climate or of particular lifestyles. Using a concept of 'human mass', he sought to explain how the effects of racial interbreeding, brought about most notably by migrations (which he called 'invasions'), were eliminated by sheer force of numbers.

Hence races remain stable and self-identical, and those existing in the present can be found in identical form in the classical texts of antiquity, so that notions of race and nation are more or less interchangeable. In 1839 Edwards founded the Ethnological Society of Paris and set it the task of determining the moral characteristics of races.

Pritchard, James Cowles (1786–1848)

James Cowles Pritchard first studied medicine at Edinburgh, and then, having forsaken Quakerism for Anglicanism, continued his studies at Cambridge and Oxford (at the time Anglican confession was a condition for admittance to many universities). A number of texts he published while working as a general practitioner in Bristol culminated in 1813 in *Researches into the Physical History of Man*. This work develops a monogenic conception of mankind's earliest appearance. In Stocking's view, Pritchard turned the biblical paradigm into an ethnological paradigm in which linguistics, culture and physical differences were all linked (**Stocking**, 1973). In 1843 Pritchard published *The Natural History of Man*, in which the monogenist thesis is taken up again and further developed. Racial differences are explained in terms of degeneration or evolution, factors conditioned less by physical environment than by lifestyle adopted. Pritchard constructs a typology in which these lifestyles are seen as stages of civilization corresponding to racial types: hunter–gatherers, nomadic cultivators, and farmers. The coarser races have the capacity for successful self-transformation (including physical self-transformation) when they acquire settled living patterns and moral norms. Pritchard was based in London between 1845 and 1848, and became president of the Ethnological Society of London, which had been formed in 1837.

Lyell, Charles (1797–1875)

Although Charles Lyell was neither ethnographer, nor ethnologist, nor yet anthropologist, a dictionary of these disciplines must make mention of his *Principles of Geology*, published in 1830–1833, and his *Ancient Existence of Man as proven by Geology, with additional Remarks on Theories relative to the Origins of Species by Variation*, published in 1863. The former work proposes for the first time a gradualist history of the planet. This dissents from the calculations of the Church, which on the basis of biblical chronology asserted that the world had been created 4,000 years ago, and also from the then dominant catastrophist theories, which explained the presence of fossil remains in terms of the Great Flood (thus assuming the existence of antediluvian animal life). Lyell demonstrates in this work that traces of life in the deepest geological strata are very rare, and that above these are found the vestiges of fish and reptiles, followed by those of birds and quadrupeds, and that only then, seemingly belatedly, do human remains first appear. **Darwin** took careful note of Lyell's conclusions, became his friend, and from 1842 confided to him the broad outlines of his own theories. Lyell's second book is a popularized presentation of the work of Boucher de Perthes, Lamarck and Darwin. It also contains a theory, later taken up by Teilhard de Chardin, which conceives of evolution as a process by which spirit progressively takes precedence over matter. Together with the American botanist A. Gray and the Englishmen A. Wallace, T. Huxley, the archaeologist J. **Lubbock** and the sociologist H. Spencer, Lyell formed a clique which, though not in agreement on all matters (Darwin rejected Spencer's extrapolations on social Darwinism), gave evolutionism scientific respectability.

Darwin, Charles (1809–1892)

Charles Darwin was no more an anthropologist or ethnologist than Lyell, but a naturalist, and it was as such that he undertook his voyages aboard the *Beagle* between 1831 and

1836. Darwin's boat ranged along the coasts of Brazil, Patagonia, the Galapagos Islands and Tahiti, as well as Australia, allowing him to gather the materials he would use for *On the Origin of Species by Means of Natural Selection, or the Preservation of Favoured Races in the Struggle for Life*, which appeared in 1859 after Darwin had already produced a number of other publications. This work poses the by then classical problem of evolution and develops the theory of natural selection. Darwin clarified and developed his thoughts in 1871 in *The Descent of Man, and Selection in Relation to Sex*. In the face of hostility from religious circles, he was able to draw on an immense body of scientific proofs which his predecessors, notably Lamarck, had not provided. His work turned the scientific thinking of his day upside down and exerted a profound influence on the social sciences. Darwin gave monogenism a scientific foundation and replaced the notion of theological purpose with that of utility, in the sense of advantage, and this proved to have applications to all of reality, possibly including social reality.

Virchow, Rudolf (1821–1902)
Rudolf Virchow was appointed to professorships of medicine at the universities of Würzburg (1849) and Berlin (1856). When, in 1865, **Boas** became an assistant curator at the *Völkerkundemuseum*, founded by A. **Bastian**, he worked under the supervision of Virchow, who taught him museology and the impor-

tance of statistical measurement. When Boas later wrote his obituary for the journal *Science* (no.16: 441–445), he portrayed him as the founder of modern German physical anthropology. Virchow's early interests were in phrenological perspectives on 'cretinism', but, as he became struck by physical variation in the human body, his attention turned to races and to prehistoric skulls, and thence to prehistory itself, which brought him closer to the folklorists. Virchow's most significant achievement was to see through the institutionalization of anthropology in Germany. He participated very actively in the founding of the German Society of Anthropology and the Berlin Society of Anthropology, Ethnology and Prehistory, and also in the establishment of the *Archiv für Anthropologie*. Through the impetus he provided, these societies became the centre of activity of German anthropology. The first of the three was dedicated above all to a study, carried out in schools across the whole country, of the physical characteristics of Germans, such as hair and eye colour and build; in this way maps were drawn up which permitted historical hypotheses. Virchow then followed the same procedure for Eastern Europe. According to Boas, while Virchow held skull shapes to be true ethnic characteristics (there were thus Slav skulls and German skulls), he nevertheless maintained that these physical types did not correspond to linguistic or cultural types (Boas, 1902).

MUSEOLOGISTS AND EVOLUTIONISTS

From the Renaissance onwards all manner of cabinets of curios were assembled, containing natural objects such as minerals and shells as well as objects later classified as ethnographic, and these collections are generally considered to have been the germ from which museums grew. However, the British Museum, founded in 1753 as the first of the great museums of the Western world, contained no such collection, and it was not until the beginning of the nineteenth century that what one might call ethnographic and anthropological artefacts were brought together in special collections. Thus began the 'museum period' of anthropology, extending from the 1840s to 1890 (see **Sturtevant**), during which museums became the institutional homeland of anthropology, well before universities opened their doors to the subject.

In briefly outlining this history I should like to stress the role growing national consciousness played in the development of museums. In Denmark the National Museum, founded in 1816, used a periodization comprising three ages of ancient history in the presentation of its anthropological exhibits, which were set out as a separate ethnographical collection in 1840. In Russia, the colonization of the interior gave the Academy of Sciences of Petrograd the opportunity in 1836 of endowing a museum exhibiting artefacts taken from the different populations of the empire. In the Netherlands, the Japanese collection of the diplomat and geographer P. F. B. von Siebold, on display from 1837, formed the basis for the establishment of the very important *Rijksmuseum voor Volkenkunde* in Leiden, which saw its role as assisting in the process of colonial expansion (Siebold, 1843). In Germany the ethnographic collections of the Royal Prussian Cabinet of Art were gathered together and entrusted to the Museum of Antiquities in Berlin in 1829, allowing it to open a department of ethnology in 1856, and in 1868 A. **Bastian** transformed this department into the *Königliches Museum für Völkerkunde* (Royal Ethnological Museum). In the following year Leipzig endowed a *Kulturhistorische Sammlung*, based in large part on the acquisition of the collection of G. **Klemm**, and in Dresden a Museum of Anthropology and Ethnography was opened in 1874, followed by a similar institution in Hamburg in 1877.

In Austria-Hungary, the geologist Ferdinand von Hochstetter (1829–1884), who devoted himself to ethnology following his exploratory mission on the ship *La Novara*, submitted a plan in 1876 for the founding of the *Naturhistorisches Museum* (Museum of Natural History). This idea won the Emperor's approval, and so the museum was formed from the collections of the *Zoologisches Hofkabinett* (1852), whose contents included the ethnographic items in the Emperor's *Hofnaturalienkabinett*. The museum contained an anthropology and ethnography department comprising three sections: anthropology, prehistory and ethnography; this department filled six halls when the museum was formally opened in 1884. Hochstetter was succeeded by Franz Hegel (1853–1931), and then by the Americanist Fritz Röck (1879–1953), who also considerably augmented the department's collection, but it was not until 1920 that the *Völkerkundemuseum* (Ethnographical Museum) was granted its own display area. Between 1870 and 1890 Sweden, Switzerland and Belgium endowed ethnographical museums. In Portugal the Geographical Society of Lisbon, founded in 1875, endowed a Museum of Ethnography, while the University of Coimbra inaugurated a professorship of anthropology, human palaeontology and prehistoric archaeology in 1885. Attached to this professorship were a laboratory and a collection of artefacts. In Italy L. Pigori created the Prehistoric and Ethnographic Museum in 1874 following the holding of the International Congress of Anthropology and Archaeology in Rome three years earlier. In Spain Dr Pedro Gonzáles Velasco was financially ruined by the building of an edifice dedicated, in his words, 'to the glory of anthropological science', and which was inaugurated by the King in 1875 (Romero de Tejada, 1992: 13). In France, a chair in the anthropology of contemporary and extinct human societies was endowed in 1858, to which the prehistoric, anthropological and ethnographical collections of the Natural History Museum were attached. The next important step was taken on the occasion of the Paris Universal Exhibition by T. Hamy, who added the holdings of the Naval Ministry and American items from the Louvre to these collections to create the *Musée d'ethnographie du Trocadéro*, which was opened in 1878. In 1938 this new collection was moved to a new home and became the *Musée de l'Homme*. In Great Britain the rich ethnographical collections of Henry Christy were acquired by the British Museum on his death in 1865, and soon afterwards General **Pitt Rivers** offered his collections of weaponry and prehistoric, anthropological and ethnographical artefacts to Oxford University, which however did not formally accept them until 1883. A condition of the gift was that the collection should conserve its evolutionist presentation, the donor's idea being that a 'succession of ideas' could be retraced through the objects.

In the USA the major new foundations were the National Museum of Washington, linked to the Smithsonian Institution, and the Peabody Museum of Archeology and Ethnology. M. Peabody, who had made his fortune in the import-export business, had opened a museum in London in 1850, and his archaeologist nephew suggested he open another at Harvard. When this museum duly opened in 1866, its management was entrusted first to J. Wyman, a naturalist working on Amerindian prehistory, and then to F. **Putnam** in 1874. The museum acquired rich holdings by purchasing European collections (such as that of the Frenchman G. de Mortillet). In 1895, the American Museum of Natural History, founded in 1869, opened an anthropological section, also curated by Putnam.

Bastian, Adolf (1826–1905)

Born in Bremen, Adolf Bastian studied law at the University of Heidelberg and medicine in Berlin and Prague. He was engaged as a naval doctor after obtaining a doctorate in 1851, and then spent almost twenty years travelling around Africa, America and Asia, and later he returned alone to Asia to study Buddhism. In 1859 he published *Ein Besuch nach San Salvador* [*A Visit to San Salvador*], in which he describes his voyage along the southwestern coast of the African continent. In 1860 he published the three volumes of *Der Mensch in der Geschichte: Zur Begründung einer psychologischen Weltanschauung* [*Man in History: Towards the Establishment of a Psychological World View*]. He reviewed all 'primitive' religious phenomena, and asserted that the savage makes no distinction between subjective and objective worlds. Bastian travelled to the Far East for four years in 1861, and this journey yielded his six-volume *Peoples of East Asia*, published between 1866 and 1871. In 1868 he was appointed curator of the ethnographical collections of the new Museum of Berlin, and put out the watchword: 'Above all, we must purchase in large quantities so as to save the products of savage civilization from destruction, and accumulate them in our museums'. It was in order to gather such items that he made a fresh journey to South America in 1871. After his return he published *The Civilized Countries of Ancient America* (3 volumes) between 1878 and 1899. Having become the president of the University of Berlin, he opened the world's most extensive ethnography department there in 1886. Together with **Virchow** he founded the Berlin Society of Anthropology, Ethnology and Prehistory, which published the *Zeitschrift für Ethnologie*. Bastian undertook further travels to Turkistan, India, Java and Bali, and, back in Germany, planned a further voyage which was to have taken him to Malaysia and Jamaica. However he only got as far as Port of Spain, where he died in 1905. From 1860 onwards he deduced from similarities he had observed between different cultures an *Elementargedanke* – or elementary psychic unity – of humanity, which endures the modifications imposed upon it by the constraints of the ecological environment. Bastian used this concept to oppose the absolute domination of diffusionist theories, and it had a profound influence on the early career of **Boas**, who worked as his assistant.

Pitt Rivers, Augustus (1827–1900)

Born [Augustus Lane Fox] in Yorkshire, Pitt Rivers studied at the Royal Military Academy and then pursued a career in the army. In the 1850s he served in Malta, Turkey and the Crimea, where he was given particular responsibility for training recruits in the use of new weapons. It appears that a visit in 1851 to the Great Exhibition of the Works of Industry of All Nations led him to expand his collection of guns to include all forms of weaponry and then other ethnographical artefacts. Back in London, he joined the Ethnological Society of London in 1861. In 1862 he discovered the work of **Darwin** (Thompson, 1977: 113), and applied his theories to artefacts. In 1870 he made a gift of his enormous collection to Oxford University, which still has a Pitt Rivers Museum. The contents of the collection, of which **Tylor** became the first curator, were divided along naturalist principles into classes, subclasses and varieties. The proposition underlying this arrangement was that artefacts could be understood in the same way as biological species and classified according to a schema of cultural evolution. The aim was to retrace a 'succession of ideas' by progressing from the simplest to the most complex objects. The terms of the donation stipulated that the collection must conserve the evolutionist presentation chosen by the donor, who in 1880 inherited the name Pitt Rivers from an uncle (following a testamentary stipulation). Included in the inheritance was an immense estate, and its new owner used its resources to pursue archaeological research, of which he was one of the pioneers in Great Britain. He later became secretary to the committee which produced the first *Notes and Queries for Travellers, Ethnologists and other Anthropological Observers* (1874) (Stocking, 1987: 258). Among his most important works is *The Clash of Culture and the Contact of Races: An Anthropological and Psychological Study of the Laws of Racial Adaptability, with Special Reference to the Depopulation of the Pacific and the Government of Subject Races* (London: Routledge, 1927). His most important articles have been collected by J. L. Meyers under the title *The Evolution of Culture and Other Essays* (Oxford, 1906).

THE PRODIGIOUS DECADE

In parallel with the advent of museology emerged a new mode of thinking known as evolutionism. Embracing almost the entirety of contemporary learning, evolutionists sketched out a notion of linear human evolution, in which so called 'primitive' societies constituted a stage anterior to their own, modern society. Often this is all that is known of the evolutionists, and judgements of them are therefore severe. Their theories are often described as erroneous and, worse, as racist. It is necessary to revise this hasty judgement and acknowledge that evolutionists built from scratch a new edifice of knowledge, sweeping away creationism and, almost unanimously, defending the idea of the unity of the human race. Finally and most importantly, they constructed human history as a history of progress.

As Kuper writes, a distinction must be made between two phases of evolutionism (Kuper, 1988). The first phase was that of the jurists who questioned the origins of law. As the modern society of the nineteenth century was defined in terms of the boundaries of the state, monogamous family relations and private property, it was assumed that primitive (and thus original) society was ordered by blood links, and was sexually promiscuous and communist. During the years 1870–1880 the dwindling power of the Church allowed questions relating to the sources and nature of beliefs and religion to take precedence over questions concerning juridical institutions and their origins. Evolutionists drew on ethnographic considerations regarding totemism, particularly recently discovered Australian totemism. **Tylor** and **Frazer** were the champions of this second phase. Although this mode of thought long remained current in the discipline, the period of its dominance closed in monumental fashion with the publication in 1912 of Durkheim's *Elementary Forms of Religious Life*. The key operative term of evolutionists was 'survival'.

The great classics on the history if this period are Burrow 1966, Hays 1958, Kuper 1999, Stocking 1995.

THE INDO-EUROPEANISTS

The beginnings of Indo-Europeanism can be traced back to a paper given by the British Orientalist Sir William Jones to the Royal Asiatic Society of Calcutta in 1798, which asserted for the first time that the affinities between Greek, Sanskrit and ancient Persian could not be fortuitous. The German linguist Franz Bopp went on to prove the validity of this observation and substantiate the thesis of a common language and civilization. Within the context created by this new paradigm were developed the disciplines of linguistics and comparative grammar, and also mythological, religious and archaeological studies, all infused with the rapidly spreading influence of evolutionist thought.

Bachofen, Johannes Jakob (1815–1887)

Born in German-speaking Switzerland, Johannes Jakob Bachofen studied law in Berlin, Paris and Cambridge, and in Rome took up the fledgling subject of archaeology. In 1844 he was appointed professor of Roman law at the University of Basel. In 1851 he published a *History of the Romans* in which he made use of mythical narratives. In so doing he revived an approach rejected ever since the publication in 1738 of L. de Beaufort's *Considerations on the Uncertainty of the First Five Centuries of Roman History*, which held that myths could not be used in historical scholarship. Bachofen proposed the rehabilitation of myths, which, he argued, only make sense when interpreted (hence the episode of the Rape of the Sabine Women is to be seen not as historical fact, but as a myth charged with the memory of the origins of exogamy). Using this approach, Bachofen gave a series of lectures in Stuttgart in 1856 on the 'Rights of Women'. In 1859 he published *The Funeral Symbolism of the Ancients*, and in 1861 *The Maternal Law*. Drawing essentially on Roman laws and Greek myths, the latter work posits a reign of mothers, or gynaecocracy, in ancient human society, a system subsequently undone by male vanity.

In Bachofen's view, human society was originally characterized by an 'Aphroditic' promiscuity, which he sees as linked symbolically to a 'swamp-like fertility'. Women revolt against this state, and the idea of female descent then becomes established. The first form of marriage is instituted under the reign of the earth-mother goddess (the *Tellurische Urmutter* attested by steatopygous statues). This matriarchy purportedly contains three orders: first, a kinship matriarchy – the Lycians, according to Herodotus, named a child not after its father, as did the Greeks, but exclusively after its mother, and they used the mother's social rank alone to determine a child's class; second, a legal matriarchy – in the treaty of alliance concluded between Hannibal and the Gauls, arbitration in unresolved questions is granted to Gallic mothers; and third, the religious matriarchy – the sacrifice of virgins demonstrates that female sacrifice was considered more agreeable to the divinity.

The motivation for the passage from 'swamp-like fertility' to matriarchy is twofold. On the one hand is the urge natural in women, especially mothers, to devote their efforts to developing their practical faculties and enhancing material well-being. At the same time they are worn nearly to death by male lustfulness and feel, sooner and more deeply than men, the imperative need for a settled lifestyle and a better developed moral code. The first stage towards matriarchy involves offerings to an Aphroditic hetaerism before rather than during marriage. The second phase brings the constitution of a special caste of sacred courtesans, with extensive possessions which they contribute in the form of a dowry. In the final stage, the family is obliged to provide the dowry. At this point the phase of Amazonism is entered with its inhumanely rigid code attributable to women's resentment over the outrages they have previously suffered. Matriarchy is symbolically related to the night, the moon, the left, earthly depths and Amazonism. In reaction against Amazonism, the next era of human society sees the development of a new form of marriage under male hegemony. This era is linked to the sun, the right, the day and the mind. The *Oresteia* of Aeschylus, and particularly the pursuit of the Erinyes, provides Bachofen with an illustration for the passage from matriarchy to patriarchy and from the laws of subterranean forces to a new law of 'Jupiter the Olympian', for the victory of the 'metaphysical principle' over the 'physical principle', and for the passage from the religion of the earth-mother to that of celestial deities. He repeatedly insists that each stage is superior to that which preceded it, and that it is under women's leadership that humanity makes its first great step towards civilization.

In 1870 Bachofen published his last big work, *Die Sage von Tanaquil* [*The Legend of Tanaquil, or Rome and the Triumph of Patriarchy over Oriental Gynaecocracy*], which develops the same argument. From the phrases quoted above it is clear that *The Maternal Law* is poetic in tone, and **McLennan** calls its author a mystic.

Maine, Sir Henry Sumner (1822–1888)
Henry Sumner Maine studied Roman law at Cambridge University and then taught the subject there from 1847. In 1850 he was called to the Bar and at the same time took up journalism. One of the great issues of the day was India; the crown annexed Punjab in 1849, followed by a number of other territories, and, even before the dissolution of the East India Company in 1858, the question arose of the form to be taken by future British rule in the colony. While utilitarians, following J. Bentham, proposed a dirigiste but reforming code, Maine joined the Whig party in opposing the extension of universal suffrage and defending an aristocratic mode of government.

Maine's continued preoccupation with these questions is evident in his writings. After completing a lecture series on Roman Law (*Roman Law and Legal Education*, 1856), he produced his *Ancient Law: Its Connection with the Early History of Society and it Relations to Modern Ideas*, published in 1861. Drawing on the Old Testament and classical sources, he asserted that human beings were originally members of a family or 'corporate group', ruled by a despotic patriarch who possessed indivisible property. For Maine, patriarchal authority then establishes the basis for more extensive groups, which initially function as autonomous units within larger federations. In the course of time abandoned and vagrant children are adopted by these groups, and territorial associations gain in importance while the principle of local patriarchal authority is rapidly weakened. Societies based on kinship are thus ultimately replaced by small state units with territorial foundations, in which the individual is constituted as a legal entity. The transition from blood to soil, from status to social contract is, in Maine's view, the most significant revolution in human history.

Maine's undertaking was at once theoretical and purely empirical, and as such it founded a science of man opposed to the philosophy of Rousseau (who declared, 'Let us begin by getting rid of all the facts'), and also to that of Hobbes, which was used as a model for all the theories of natural law in the classical age and for all those versions of the social contract which, in their varying modalities, put forward the view that primary social relationships were based on contracts binding individuals with one another. Hobbes, Rousseau and even Bentham present the individual as born free and master of his destiny, and the state as a constructed entity. Unlike them, Maine sees the earliest societies as organised around families, not individuals. These societies were unified by status rather than contracts, with a 'despotic patriarch' ruling over a family made up exclusively of males (a situation Maine found among Southern slaves and in India).

Maine must be seen as one of the thinkers of Indirect Rule because of the way he felt obliged to take a stance on the question of the governance of India, where the substitution of agnation by territoriality had not yet taken place. In 1861 he was appointed to the Council of India, in 1862 he became an advisor to the Viceroy of Calcutta and in 1864 vice-chancellor of Calcutta University. He returned to Oxford as a professor in 1869, and in 1871 he gave a lecture series entitled *Village Communities of the East and West, to which are Added Other Lectures, Addresses and Essays*, in which he attempted to study the evolution of castes. In 1875 he published his *Lectures on the Early History of Institutions* and *The Effects of Observation of India on Modern European Thought*. He died in Cannes in 1888.

The most durable of his works is *Ancient Law*, which A. **Kuper** (1988) considers even more important than Darwin's theory as a common source for evolutionists. Although most of his ideas have since been rejected, Maine raised questions which were to preoccupy his rivals and successors for half a century. With his categories blood/soil and status/contract he constructed a typological opposition which is found in **Morgan** ('*societas*'/'*civitas*'), in Tönnies ('*Gemeinschaft*'/'*Gesellschaft*'), and in Durkheim ('*solidarité organique*'/'*solidarité mécanique*'), and which endures right up to the distinction of British Functionalists between 'lineal-segmentary societies' and 'state societies'.

Müller, Friedrich Max (1823–1900)

Born in Dessau in Germany, Friedrich Max Müller studied first at Leipzig (1841) and then at Berlin (1843), where he read philology and Orientalism with F. Bopp. In 1844 he published *Hitopadesa: A Collection of Ancient Indian Myths translated for the First Time from Sanskrit into German*. After spending a year in Paris in 1845 studying comparative religion with E. Burnouf, he emigrated to England in 1846. In 1850 he took up a position at Oxford University, where he spent the rest of his career, becoming professor of comparative philology in 1868. In 1856 his *Essay in Comparative Mythology* appeared, setting the course for his research into religious anthropology, which was crowned by success with the publication of his *Introduction to the Science of Religion* in 1873.

Rather as **Morgan** had done in the case of kinship, Müller looked at religion using the philological model of comparative analysis of languages, seeking answers to three questions: 'What is religion?', 'What are its origins?', and 'What are the laws of its historical development?'. This was the first time that the 'science of religion' was given a clear identity as a scholarly discourse. It is worth remembering that the publication by Renan of *The Life of Jesus* in 1863 cost him his professorship at the *Collège de France*, and that the encyclical *Quanta Cura*, followed by *Syllabus*, issued by Pius IX in 1864, condemned the study of the history of religion for transforming the sacred into an object of knowledge like any other. Müller advanced the idea of a genealogy of the world's religions, and gained considerable notoriety by reviving the study of comparative mythology. His works are still essential reading despite the blemish of his enthusiasm for the theme of sun worship and the myths derived from it, which he saw as constituting a primary religious principle. Müller is also known for his translation of Kant's *Critique of Pure Reason* into English.

THE EVOLUTIONISTS

Klemm, Gustav (1802–1867)

In 1843 Gustav Klemm published the first part of his *Allgemeine Kulturgeschichte der Menschheit* (*General History of Human Culture*), of which the tenth and final volume appeared in 1852. In this work he propounds the idea that the development of human societies is divided into three phases: savagery (*Wildheit*), bondage (*Zahmheit*), and freedom (*Freiheit*). The differences between the first two phases are technical and social; gathering is succeeded by farming and livestock rearing, and human hordes are succeeded by tribal groups which recognize a sacerdotal form of authority in their leaders. The second phase also sees the earliest use of writing, but only in the third phase, in which authority is secularized, can the potential of writing be fully exploited, thereby permitting man's inventive capacity to flourish. Klemm distinguishes between two racial types, active and passive. The active races originate from somewhere in Central Asia and are most eminently represented by the Germanic race. They submit the passive races (Mongoloid and Negroid races, Egyptians, Finns, Hindus) and in doing so permit them to develop. According to **Lowie**, Klemm anticipates the Tylorian definition of culture by identifying it as a collection of 'customs, information and skills, domestic and public life in peace and war, religion, science and art' (Lowie, *The History of Ethnological Theory*, 1937: 12). Moreover, as Harris notes, **Tylor** would make 'an extensive use of [his] ethnographic compilation' (Harris, *The Rise of Anthropological Theory*, 1968: 144). From the 1830s Klemm built up a large collection of ethnographic artefacts which later formed the basis of the Museum of Leipzig's collection.

Morgan, Lewis Henry (1818–1881)

Lewis Henry Morgan was born in Aurora in New York State, and in his university years in the 1840s he developed an interest in the Iroquois, a 'confederation' of five different nations living by Lake Erie. In 1844 he became a lawyer and defended one of the Iroquois clans, the Senecas, against the Ogden Kand Company, which sought to dispossess them of land belonging to their reserves. The company had in effect bought the signatures of a number of their chieftains in order to acquire plots of land for $3.50 rather than the stipulated $35. Morgan got up a petition which was sent to the US Senate and prevented the ratification of this treaty of cession. While it is true that Morgan spent time in the field and that in 1846 he was admitted by the Seneca to the Falcons of the Tonawanda clan (E. **Parker**'s clan) under the name Ta-ya-da-o-wuh-kuh ('between the two'), the legend, propagated by **Engels** (1884) and then by **Tylor** (1897: 262) and L. **White** (1961), of a man who spent the larger part of his life amongst the American Indians must be questioned. The investigation carried out by Trautmann (1987) and

E. Tooker (*AA*, 1992: 358–59) reveals that Morgan lived amongst the Iroquois about a dozen times for a week or two, so for about four months in total. He benefited above all from the help of an Iroquois law student called E. Parker. Morgan became a federal official for Indian questions, and in 1879 was the first anthropologist to be elected president of the American Association for the Development of Science.

Morgan's first article, a study of the visions of an Indian shaman, appeared in 1844. At the same time he began a voluminous ethnographical correspondence with Gallatin, the president of the Historical Society of New York, and was given immediate encouragement by **Schoolcraft**. In 1850 he wrote a report on Indian collections belonging to universities in New York State, and in 1851 he published *League of the Ho-de-no-saunee, or Iroquois*, in which he described in minute, purely ethnographical detail the history, dance, religion, leadership principles, material culture and marriage customs of the Iroquois confederation. His investments in railways and mining made him a prosperous man of business, without detracting from his status as a man of science. In 1857, at the request of the American Association for the Development of Science, he published an article on the 'System of Iroquois Kinship', and another on the 'Laws of Descent among the Iroquois'. Morgan died in Rochester in 1881.

It was in 1859 that Morgan discovered that other Indians (the Ojibwa) of a different language family from that of the Iroquois, with a quite distinct lexis and grammar, nonetheless adhered to the same formal kinship naming conventions. As he later wrote: 'Every term of relationship was radically different from the corresponding term in the Iroquois; but the classification of kindred was the same. It was manifest that the two systems were identical in their fundamental characteristics' (1871: 3). This discovery can be said to mark the beginnings of the study of kinship. In line with the polygenic view current at the time, Morgan suggests that this formal correspondence between different vocabularies points to a common system which must have existed before the Amerindians were dispersed over the American continent. This thinking emerges clearly in a paper he gave entitled 'System of Consanguinity of the Red Race in its Relations to Ethnology', which proposes a systematic comparison of the various Indian kinship nomenclatures. At the annual congress of the American Academy of Arts and Sciences he went further by advancing the thesis that the discrepancy between existing family relationships and the naming system used for them results from the survival at a terminological level of forms of relationships which had a real existence in earlier times but have since disappeared. Terminologies are thus 'fossils', or what **McLennan** calls 'symbols', or what Tylor, whose term has been adopted by the discipline, calls 'survivals'. If the Amerindians originated from Asia, it follows that their system should be found in other peoples descended from the same source, and from 1859 onwards a missionary in India, Dr H. W. Scudder, provided Morgan with indications of the existence of the Amerindian system among the Tamils of Southern India.

In 1860 Morgan approached religious organizations via the Smithsonian Institution and, thanks to the support of the Secretary of State, was permitted to distribute a questionnaire to government officials and missionaries in all four corners of the world. He sent out a few hundred questionnaires and received 48 replies, and to these he added information he had gathered himself to give a total of 139 examples. In 1871 his *Systems of Consanguinity and Affinity of the Human Family* was published by the Smithsonian Institution. This is the first ever comparative study of systems of kinship, and in it Morgan asserts that 'all forms of consanguinity presented in the tables belong to one of two types, the descriptive and the classificatory'

(1871: 7). The latter, which corresponds to various sorts of group marriage, comprises a principal Indo-European form and two subordinate forms: the Malayan (of which the Hawaiian form is typical) and the Eskimo. The classificatory system is a survival from the era of sexual promiscuity, when it was impossible to determine the identity of a person's father, uncle, brother and nephew. As civilization advanced, a distinction was introduced between different members of one family: this is the descriptive type. The descriptive type resulting from monogamous marriage characterizes the family groupings of Aryans (in whom the Roman form of consanguinity is typical), Semites, and Uralians (who also display the divergent model of the Chinese family).

It is important to remember that Morgan did not conceive his book as being concerned with the study of kinship systems, but as taking the field under the banner of a then new discipline of philology or the 'science of language', whose principal methods had been codified by F. M. **Müller**. That Morgan saw his work as contributing to this new discipline is made clear by the way information is presented. Were it a book on kinship, Dravidian systems would take a marginal place alongside those of the American Indians, but Morgan adds details of their geography, philology and physical anthropology so as to resolve the question of the history of the human family.

Systems of Consanguinity and Affinity of the Human Family was warmly received by **Darwin**, **Lubbock**, **Maine** and **Spencer**, but rejected by McLennan. After its publication Morgan travelled to Europe, where he met these intellectual luminaries (and was granted a papal audience). On his return to the USA, and under the influence of British intellectuals, he expanded his field of investigation by taking in the history of institutions and proposing to piece together the history of the 'arts of subsistence' (i.e. techniques of production), forms of property, family life

and statehood for the whole of mankind. This came to fruition in *Ancient Society, or Researches into Human Progress from Savagery to Civilization via Barbarism*, published in 1877.

Morgan employed and popularized the categories of savagery, barbarism and civilization, and he subdivided the first and second into three stages: lower, intermediate and higher. The lower stage of savagery starts with the beginnings of the human race and lasts until the invention of fire, and it now no longer exists. At the intermediate stage of savagery the use of language is established, property is held in common ownership and sexual promiscuity has yet to give way to a family structure; this stage is held to be illustrated by the Australian Aborigines. The invention of the bow and arrow takes place during higher savagery (represented by the Athabaskan Indians of Canada), and pottery is developed during lower barbarism (the Iroquois). It is only when these stages have been succeeded by civilization that monogamy becomes established and alphabets are used.

Morgan does not clearly define the causes of this evolution, which could be attributed to technical inventiveness, growth in intelligence or morality, or even demographic expansion. One can see how such a typology was open to a variety of criticisms, for example by failing to account for a society which practises monogamy but knows nothing of farming.

Ancient Society was well received by Maine, and **Bachofen** dedicated his last book to Morgan. Darwin accepted Morgan's findings but questioned the idea of primitive sexual promiscuity, while McLennan attacked Morgan for opposing the theory of abduction. The book was enthusiastically read by Marx and Engels, and *The Origins of the Family, Private Property and the State*, published by Engels in 1884, took up Morgan's schema and invested it with economic determinism. As a result of this interpretation of his text, Morgan (who married his pious cousin Mary Steele – apparently the only love of his life, founded an orphanage for girls, and accepted Darwinian evolutionism while denying its applicability to the human race) gained notoriety as a 'red'. Scientific attacks on him by F. **Boas** and his followers, especially R. **Lowie**, banished him from ethnological tradition until L. **White** and then E. **Leacock** restored him to his rightful place. Finally, E. **Terray** has attempted to show (1969) that the factual truth of the correspondences suggested by Morgan was in fact less important to him than setting out a model to explain modes of production and their infrastructures and superstructures.

It is perhaps also worth stressing that Morgan rejected the thesis that savages are the degenerate vestiges of earlier civilizations, and that his entire project, bolstered by an evolutionist procedure, is informed by a conviction that the various societies of the 'human family' constitute a unity which transcends the diversity of civilizations and cultures. For him, the history of mankind is one in its source, its experience and its progress.

Engels, Friedrich (1820–1895)

Born in Barmen as the son of a textiles manufacturer, F. Engels joined the ranks of the Left Hegelians in Berlin, where he met Marx in 1842 and became the co-founder of Marxism. Although the place and importance of Engels's work in anthropology is debatable, mention must be made of his *Origins of the Family, Private Property and the State*, published in 1884, which was inspired by his reading of **Morgan**'s *Ancient Society*. He takes up Morgan's data (and some of his factual errors) in summarized form, to which notes are added from Marx's reading of evolutionist texts. In his reading of Morgan's work, Engels presents the development of the forces of production as the motor of every facet of social life, sets out the genesis of social classes, and insists that the existence of societies as states is only transitory. It is

also worth noting that in the preface to the second edition (1895) the description of the theoretical positions taken by various foundational thinkers of evolutionism constitutes the best account of debates of this period.

McLennan, John Ferguson (1827–1881)

Born in Scotland as the son of an insurance agent, J. F. McLennan obtained his MA in 1849 and then began studies at Trinity College, Cambridge. He spent the years from 1853 to 1855 in literary circles in London. In 1857 he composed the 'Law' article for the eighth edition of the *Encyclopaedia Britannica* (vol. 13: 253–279) and was called to the Bar; he continued to practise until 1870, the year he became a member of the Ethnological Society of London. Between 1857 and 1865 he published articles on a range of subjects including law and Scottish art, and, most significantly, in 1863 wrote a general review of publications relating to India entitled 'Hill Tribes in India' (1863, *North British Review*, no. 38: 392–422).

In 1865 A. and C. Black published *Primitive Marriage*, in which McLennan, like **Bachofen** but without knowing his work, put forward a thesis of primitive matriarchy as the first stage of human society. In seeking to prove this he began by investigating the existence of bride capture rites, which 'fulfil a contract' within a marriage ceremony, and which are encountered in a great variety of periods and locations (from Spartans to Romans, from Hindus to North Europeans). McLennan rejects the psychological hypothesis that this rite can be explained in terms of 'feminine modesty', stating that 'women in these coarse tribes are customarily depraved and exposed to scenes of depravity from their tenderest infancy' (1970 (1865): 12). He suggests instead that bride capture rites accompanying a marriage ceremony should be interpreted as a 'symbol' of the really existing practice of abduction. This 'symbol' is a fossil of the social world, 'just as the discovery of a fossilised fish in hillside rock forces us to conceive of the whole surrounding country as having been under water' (1970 (1865): 19). He remarks that 'the Dorians who invaded Greece were probably not accompanied by their wives and children', that among 'Caribs and other cannibal nations, male captives become a means of subsistence whereas women are kept as spouses or items of luxury', and finally that in New Zealand, Fiji and other Pacific islands 'the object of intertribal wars was the acquisition of women for marriage and of men as food' (1970 (1865): 36). McLennan deduces from all this that the system used by certain tribes entailed capturing women – of necessity women from other populations – in order to marry them. The word he uses to define this compulsion is 'exogamy', the principle prohibiting marriage within the tribe, and this is set against the opposing principle of 'endogamy' (1970 (1865): 23). Exogamy and bride capture are associated because relations between savage tribes are characterized by war and general hostility (1970 (1865): 57), and because 'the restriction on marriage within the group is connected with the relative scarcity of women caused by the ancient practice of killing female infants, which results in polyandry within the state and the capture of women outside it' (1970 (1865): 58). First discovered in India in 1857, the practice of female infanticide is also found in Graeco-Latin mythology and is explained by the fact that 'sons were a source of strength, both for defence and in the search for food, while daughters were a source of weakness' (1970 (1865): 58).

According to McLennan, 'the union between the sexes in early times was probably free, transitory and to a degree promiscuous' (1970 (1865): 67), and men held women in common ownership like other goods, but as a 'scarce commodity', and women were thus provided with several husbands. An individual was related to a group rather than to other individuals, because the fact that his mother's identity was certain while his father's was not engendered a 'system of kinship by women only' (1970 (1865): 64). McLennan distinguishes between two stages of polyandry (the terms polyandry and polygeny derive, like polygamy, from botany, and were coined by Linnaeus). In the first stage the husbands of a single wife are not necessarily related, and he says that the 'Blacks and Cossacks provide examples of this.' Subsequently, feelings of close family ties and the establishment of kinship through women led to the formation of groups composed of 'the sons of a single mother', as in Tibet and amongst the ancient Bretons (McLennan citing Caesar).

In the following stage, a wife would be chosen by the eldest of a set of brothers, and all her children would belong to him. This form is already agnatic in that it introduces the principle of 'kinship through men'. The practice of compulsory marriage between a man and the widow of his deceased elder brother (known as the levirate, although McLennan does not use this term) is attested in ancient times amongst the Hebrews, Mongols and numerous other peoples. This practice derives in McLennan's view from polyandry, and is followed by further stages of polygamy before the monogamous couple finally becomes predominant.

As well as the evolutionist schema it proposes, *Primitive Marriage* advances the notion of universal 'rites of capture' and the concepts of symbol, exogamy and endogamy. It is worth noting that H. **Spencer** took issue with McLennan's schema by asserting in 1895 that any shortage of women would be offset by high levels of mortality in men.

In 1866 McLennan published 'Kinship in Ancient Greece' in *The Fortnightly Review* (vol. 4) in order to demonstrate that the schema set out in *Primitive Marriage* is applicable to the literature on Ancient Greece. In a footnote he makes his first mention of totemism as a stage through which all societies have passed. In 1868 he wrote the 'Totem' entry in the first supplement to *Chamber's Encyclopaedia* (pp. 753–754), and in 1869–1870 he developed this topic in three instalments of an article entitled 'The worship of animals and plants', published by *The Fortnightly Review*. The word 'totem' comes from the word 'ototeman', meaning 'he is of my family', in Ojibwa (an Algonkan language), and it was first used by J. Lang in 1791 to describe the relationship existing in a society between a set of animals (or plants) and a human group. McLennan looked into totemism in Australia and America and defined it, in a still well-known formulation, as fetishism plus exogamy and matrilineal filiation. He concluded that it formed an evolutionary stage which all of mankind has since moved beyond. He explored themes and ideas already present in *Primitive Marriage* in another article, 'The Levirate and Polyandry' (*The Fortnightly Review*, 1877, vol. 27, 694–707), which gathers ethnographic examples to prove that the levirate is a development from polyandry, and also in 'Exogamy and Endogamy' (*The Fortnightly Review*, 1877, vol. 27, 884–895), in which he seeks to clarify the meanings of these two terms, which he felt had become opaque in Spencer's hands. McLennan died in 1881 while he was working on a book entitled *The Patriarchal Theory*, in which this theory was attacked; this final work was edited by his younger brother and published in 1888.

Tylor, Sir Edward Burnett (1832–1917)

Tylor was born in Camberwell near London into a Quaker family which owned a copper smelting works. He went to school in Tottenham, but could not study for a degree as admittance to universities was restricted to members of the Anglican Church. In 1855, when he was 23 years old, a dangerous tubercular condition led doctors to prescribe a sunny climate for him. He travelled to the Antilles and Mexico in the company of the amateur archaeologist and Darwinian H. Christy. Tylor returned from Mexico committed both to evolutionist thought and to archaeology. In 1860 he published an account of his journey, *Anahuac or Mexico and the Mexicano ancient and modern*, in which he comments on the persistence of slavery in Cuba, describes Mexico and provides meticulous details of its ruins, and also includes a history of the Aztecs. After his marriage to a fellow Quaker, A. Fox, he set up home in Oxford, where he remained for the rest of his life.

In 1865 Tylor published *Researches into the Early History of Mankind and the Development of Civilisation* (3rd edn 1878), which maintains the thesis of the psychic unity of the human race. The book opens with a reflection on sign language as used by the deaf-and-dumb, and goes on to investigate the ethnography of this mode of communication. He writes: 'Gesture-language, a natural mode of expression common to all mankind [...], is good evidence of similarity in the mental processes communicated to the outside world. As the gesture-language appears not to be specifically affected by differences in the race or climate of those who use it, the shape of their skulls and the colour of their skins, its evidence, so far as it goes, bears against the supposition that specific differences are traceable among the various races of man, at least in the more elementary processes of the mind' (Tylor, 1964 (1878): 46–47). Enriched by pre-Columbian evidence, Tylor traces the evolution of the process of symbolization in graphic representation and in the earliest writing. He takes up the categories of savagery, barbarism and civilization, delimited respectively by a use of stone tools and gathering, the practice of farming and metallurgy, and the first development of writing. All the same, his thought differs from unilinear evolutionism because he sees the increasing complexity of a single trend, namely that 'there has been from age to age a growth of man's power over nature' (Tylor, 1964 (1878): 166), as running in parallel with the succession of various cultures, some of which must 'degenerate' ('which explains how they are met in their current state' (Tylor, 1964 (1878): 166)). As **Fabian** has shown, it is Tylor's unwillingness to break free from the evolutionist idea of a single natural temporality which necessitates this recourse to notions of cultural degeneration (or decline) (Fabian, 1983).

Tylor proposes a division between 'myths of observation', which record facts, and 'pure myths', which are products of fiction (Tylor, 1964 (1878): 168). He notes themes which the myths of America and those of Oceania and Asia hold in common (Tylor, 1964 (1878): 231), but takes a cautious line on the question of the diffusion process, stating that 'unless coincidences exceed the limits of ordinary probability, it is more prudent to register particular phenomena as belonging to independent traditions' (Tylor, 1964 (1878): 148).

McLennan had already used the word 'symbol' to designate 'fossilised usages and social representations', but it is to Tylor that we owe the more durable term 'survival'. Derived like McLennan's term from geology, the 'survival' provides vestigial evidence from which a complete picture of ancient society can be reconstructed. The institution of couvade, in which a husband plays the wife's role (sometimes going as far as to simulate giving birth) is an example of a 'survival from the time when matrilineal and patrilineal descent were still struggling for predominance, and the husband endeavoured to attract his child to himself and his line' (Tylor, 1889: 260).

In the two volumes of his *Primitive Culture* (1871), Tylor takes up the word 'culture' as used by German historians, and defines it as 'a complex whole encompassing knowledge, beliefs, art, morality, laws and any other arrangements and customs acquired by man' (Tylor, 1871: 1). This constitutes a radical break with the more restricted use of the word and generates the first definition of anthropology as the 'science of culture'. The accent is placed on the study of folklore, legends, superstitions and myths as the most precious repositories of the past. The second volume is devoted entirely to the origins and evolution of religion, which Tylor had already considered in 'The Religions of Savages', published by *The Fortnightly Review* in 1866. He suggests that the principle of separating spirit from flesh, image from reality, introduces a duality which is resolved by the notion of the soul understood as a phantasmagorical double, as a universal human reaction to such phenomena as death, dreams, visions and mirror images. 'Savages', who are as imaginative as children, are unable to distinguish clearly between the real and the imaginary. Tylor gives such beliefs definition by adopting the term 'animism' from Stahl, who used it specifically to mean the identification of the cognizant soul with the vital principle, and to indicate that man is immersed in nature 'animated' by supernatural forces and beings which he must win over. This theory of the origins of religious feeling offers an alternative to the 'naturism' of F. M. **Müller** and the 'manism' of H. Spencer. The next stage would be the ascribing of doubles to animals as well as humans, as attested by the placing of horses or cats in tombs, and then to objects (an object's double would be used in the next world by the deceased). The cult of manes, divine or daemonic creators of souls, is a further stage leading to a belief in souls existing in certain individuals and ancestors (the cult of saints in modern religions would be a survival of the latter). This is followed by the cult of spirits, known as fetishism, before souls are ascribed to objects (idolatry). With polytheism, and before the appearance of monotheism, naturally occurring phenomena become spirits of nature. Tylor's evolutionism involved him in controversy with supporters of the clergy, who saw an unbridgeable gap between primitive religions and the religion of civilized man.

Such was the success of *Primitive Culture*

that Tylor, not yet forty, was elected as a member of the Royal Society, and in 1875 he was granted an honorary degree by Oxford University. From 1878 he introduced diffusionism into his thinking by comparing the Hindu game of Pachisi with the Mexican Patolli. He continued this line of enquiry in 1898 by turning his attention to resemblances between Mexican games and those of South-East Asia. He soon concluded, in a phrase that has remained famous, that 'civilisation is a plant which has more often propagated itself than grown'. In 1881 Tylor published *Anthropology: An introduction to the study of man and civilisation*, which the journal *American Anthropologist* in 1917 called the first handbook of anthropology (R. **Lowie**, 1917: 263), and which **White** as late as 1960 describes as 'still one of the best introductions to the discipline' (White, 1960: iii). In this work Tylor reviews all fields of culture – technological, social, aesthetic – and closes with reflections on the entry of the world into modern civilization which, in bringing about revolutionary transformations, risks destroying good things without replacing them with better. This is why knowledge derived from anthropology could serve to 'guide us in our duty of leaving the world better than we found it', the phrase with which he finishes the book (Tylor, 1960 (1881): 275).

When the Pitt Rivers Museum, which aimed to display the evolution of mankind, was established at Oxford University in 1883, it was placed under the charge of Tylor, who was appointed to a lectureship at the University. In 1885 he returned to Mexico and travelled as far as the territory of the Pueblo Indians. He introduced statistical method into anthropology in his article 'On the Methods of Investigating the Development of Institutions applied to Laws of Marriage and Descent', published in 1889 in volume 18 of the *Journal of the Royal Anthropological Institute* (pp. 245–272). After declaring that the discipline needed a

method comparable to 'the operations of mathematics, physics, chemistry and biology', applied to 'the formation of laws of marriage and descent' (1889: 245), Tylor suggested that correlations (what he called 'adherences') be established in matters of residence, descent and couvade for 350 societies. He begins by looking at the practice of avoidance, a barbarian etiquette stipulating that a husband and his in-laws should neither look upon nor speak to one another (1889: 246), which he relates to types of residence. In this way, in cases of a husband's settling permanently in his wife's family (65 cases out of 350), while the law of numbers would produce only nine cases of avoidance, in fact there are fourteen. Conversely, where the husband takes his wife into his own family (141 cases out of 350), one would expect to find eighteen cases of avoidance between him and his in-laws, whereas there are actually only nine (1889: 247). Having linked avoidance to type of residence, Tylor turns to the practice of naming parents after the child, for which he coins the term 'teknonymy'. He finds that this phenomenon correlates closely to 'residence of the husband with his wife's family' and to 'the practice of ceremonial avoidance by the husband of the wife's relatives, occurring fourteen times where accident might have given four' (1889: 248). Having demonstrated that 'adherences' are not matters of simple statistical chance, Tylor uses graphs showing different customs in conjunction in an attempt to discern the phases of their development. Consequently, the adherence of the levirate and couvade to the three stages he calls 'maternal', 'maternal–paternal' and 'paternal' (terms he says he prefers to 'matriarchal' and 'patriarchal' (1889: 252)) would indicate that couvade belongs not to the 'maternal stage', but, 'arising in the maternal–paternal, at once takes its strongest development of twenty cases; in the paternal the number falls to eight cases, leading to the inference that here it is only kept up in dwindling survival' (1889: 255). A comparison with ties of adoption in the ancient world shows that couvade must have preceded true patrilineality. The fact, as Tylor tells us, that the 'maternal' stage exhibits neither the inheritance of widows nor couvade can be taken to prove that it comes before the 'paternal' stage, for otherwise such customs would have survived (1889: 257). Finally, Tylor demonstrates the much larger correlation existing between cross-cousin marriage, classificatory terminologies and exogamy. We may recall his well-known remark that populations were faced with 'the simple practical alternative between marrying-out and being killed out', which is a recasting of a biblical verse: 'then will we give our daughters unto you, and we will take your daughters to us, and we will dwell with you, and we will become one people' (Tylor, 1889: 267). Without coming to any conclusions about the relationship between exogamy and totemism, Tylor establishes the correlation between the dual organization of exogamy and the classificatory naming system, between types of residence and avoidance taboos, and between couvade and an intermediate social organization which can be called 'maternal–paternal'. The fundamental objection to this raised by Galton, known as 'Galton's problem', is that its validity would only be ascertainable if traits engendered independently had been separated from those acquired by diffusion.

In 1891 Tylor became the first president of the Anthropological Society (later the Royal Anthropological Society). Furthermore he contributed to the writing of the research guide *Notes and Queries on Anthropology*, of which the first edition was published in 1874. In 'The Matrilineal Family System', published in 1896 by the journal *Nineteenth Century* (XL: 81–96), he examined psychological aspects of kinship. Having taught at Oxford University since 1884, Tylor was appointed professor of anthropology in 1896 (at the age of 64) after con-

fessional restrictions governing appointments were relaxed. He remained in this post until 1909, was given a knighthood in 1912, and died on 2 January 1917.

Lubbock, Sir John (1834–1913)

Naturalist and botanist, then prehistorian, anthropologist and politician, John Lubbock was born in London in 1834. He was elected a member of the Royal Society in 1857 and became one of **Darwin**'s most ardent defenders and faithful disciples. In 1864, as president of the Royal Anthropological Society and of the Ethnological Society of London, he gave a series of lectures on man in ancient times, which he published in the following year in modified form as *Prehistoric Times, as Illustrated by Ancient Remains and the Manners and Customs of Modern Savages* (London, 1869). Having noted that stone tools found in the deepest deposits were cruder than others, he introduced the terms Palaeolithic (early stone age) and Neolithic (later stone age).

In 1870, based on the same lecture series, he published *The Origins of Civilisation and the Primitive Condition of Man: The Mental and Social Condition of Savages* (ed. by Peter Rivière, Chicago, 1978). He opposed theories of degeneration still predominant in the Anglican Church of the time and built up a picture of the evolution of religious ideas. In order, these are atheism (the absence of an idea), totemism (defined as the cult of natural objects), shamanism (higher deities accessible to magician-shamans), idolatry (gods accessible to men), and monotheism (a single divinity). The book also supports the thesis that moral and intellectual progress accompanies technical development. This belief in human progress led to Lubbock's involvement in politics. He was elected to Parliament as a Liberal in 1870, and subsequently joined the Liberal-Unionists (1880–1900). He published *The Use of Life* (1894), which was translated into fifteen languages and sold more than 250,000 copies. He also undertook pioneering research into social insects (ants and bees). Lubbock was elevated to the peerage as Baron Avebury in 1899, published *Marriage, Totemism and Religion* (London, 1911), and died on 13 May 1913.

Smith, William Robertson (1846–1894)

Born the son of a minister in the Church of Scotland in 1846, William Robertson Smith studied Hebrew at Aberdeen and Edinburgh, where he became associated with McLennan. In 1870 he himself became a church minister and also professor of Hebrew at Aberdeen. Under the influence of German thought he proposed a philological reading of the text of the Bible and established scholarly criticism of its sources. He composed the 'Bible' entry in the ninth edition of the *Encyclopaedia Britannica* (1870), which led to his suspension by the church for having denied that the biblical text was written under divine inspiration. While the ecclesiastical tribunal deliberated on his fate, Smith spent two years learning Arabic and travelled to Italy, Egypt and the Middle East in search of traces of matriarchy and totemism. The tribunal's verdict of April 1880 delivered only a reprimand, but Smith's fate was sealed by another article he published soon afterwards in the *Journal of Philology*, in which he examined zoolatry amongst the Arabs of the Old Testament, considering the social functions of beliefs rather than their theological aspect, and regarding the evolution of religious ideas as historically determined, but without enquiring into their veracity; this article led to his dismissal from the ministry in 1881. He then succeeded S. Baynes as editor-in-chief of the *Encyclopaedia Britannica*, and in 1883 Cambridge University offered him a lectureship in Arabic which had become vacant after its previous incumbent had been murdered in the Sinai. His *Kinship and Marriage in Early Arabia* (Cambridge UP) was published in 1885. A forerunner of the ideas of Durkheim, Smith thought of religion as rooted in the moral life of a collective and concentrated on public rites (particularly totemic feasts) and beliefs rather than theological questions. In 1888 he was invited to give a lecture course in Aberdeen, and this was published the following year as *Lectures on the Religion of the Semites* (1889). Smith's reflections on sacrifice and the periodical consumption of totemic animals are of momentous importance for the development of anthropology. He developed tuberculosis in about 1888 and died in 1894.

Frazer, Sir James George (1854–1942)

James George Frazer was born in Glasgow into a cultivated family of Presbyterians. His father, D. Frazer, a pharmacist who built his own chemical factory, was the author of two books on the history of his region. After studying at Glasgow University, Frazer went up to Trinity College, Cambridge, in 1874, and there studied law to please his father and classical literature to please himself. In 1879 he gained a doctorate with a thesis on Plato, and then took a teaching position. Apart from an interlude at Liverpool University, where a chair of sociology and anthropology was created for him in 1907 but which he filled for only one year, he passed his life in Cambridge. He made it clear that it was his reading of **Tylor**'s *Primitive Culture* and the influence of W. R. **Smith** which gave him his vocation. Following a meeting with Smith, Frazer turned to folklore and anthropology, and they inspired what was to become a substantial and extraordinarily celebrated work.

At Smith's request Frazer wrote a number of entries, including 'Taboo' and 'Totemism', for the ninth edition of the 24-volume *Encyclopaedia Britannica* (begun in 1875 and completed in 1888). He spent seven months on these articles, which became far too long for their purpose. On Frazer's behalf Smith asked for a dispensation from the publisher Black, who then suggested publishing the articles in book form, and so Frazer's *Totemism and Exogamy* (4 volumes) appeared in 1887 and subsequently went through four revised editions. The book expounds the hypothesis that mankind, in ignorance of the biological processes of reproduction, attributes it to a totem; this replaces explanations in terms of phases of family structure (matriarchy, patriarchy) with a dynamic of religious thought. Thus couvade is not analysed, as it was by Tylor, as a mode of asserting agnatic rights over children and as a survival in patriarchal regimes, but in terms of homeopathic magic and contagious magic, which became Frazer's main operative concepts.

Frazer believed he had discovered two intellectual laws: the law of similarity, by which like engenders like (thus drawing an injured animal inflicts injury on a real animal); and the law of contact or contagion, by which treatment of matter detached from a whole (for example hair and nail cuttings) continues remotely to exert an influence on that whole.

While successive editions of this work were appearing, Frazer embarked on his life's major work, *The Golden Bough*, of which the first edition was published in two volumes in 1890. The work's title was inspired by a painting by the English artist Turner, which is described at the opening of the book: 'Who does not know Turner's picture of the Golden Bough? The scene, suffused with the golden glow of imagination in which the divine mind of Turner steeped and transfigured even the fairest natural landscape, is a dream-like vision of the little woodland lake of Nemi'. The subject of the painting is the Roman myth of the slave who breaks off a branch of the sacred tree and then murders the priest of the Lake of Nemi and takes his place. Frazer's consideration of the sacred tree and the sacred grove leads him to study the meaning of the sacrifice of the divine priest-king, associated with fertility and nature, who must be put to death when his powers begin to decline. This stage is succeeded by another in which, instead of the divine king himself, a scapegoat is sacrificed, and this restores his strength. A second edition, appearing in 1900 in three volumes, was given the fuller title of *The Golden Bough: A Study of Comparative Religion*, and it contained data taken from *The Native Tribes of Central Australia* by **Spencer** and **Gillen**. The publication of a third edition of *The Golden Bough* began in 1911, and when it was completed in 1915 it had expanded to twelve volumes.

Frazer's general schema follows A. Comte's three stages. The first of these is the magical stage, in which man believes he is able to dominate nature through empathy. This gives way (albeit incompletely) to the religious stage, in which man recognizes his weakness and puts himself in the hands of the gods. Finally, in the stage of civilization, man effects a separation between science and those areas where he is powerless. Mixing ethnography with European folklore, mythology with classical history, Orientalism with biblical narrative, *The Golden Bough* brings together the totality of contemporary knowledge. This synthesis is served up by Frazer in an easily digestible form for a large readership. In the preface to the 1890 edition he described his intention to order his material in an artistic manner so as to appeal to readers who might have balked at a more rigorously logical and systematic presentation. In 1892 he even published an abridged version in one 900-page volume with all references removed. Striving for popular success is not easily compatible with academic status, and Frazer's work did not meet with scholarly approval. **Lowie** justified his brief mention of it by describing its author as 'a savant, but not a thinker' (Lowie, 1937: 102). In 1918 Frazer published *Folklore in the Old Testament*, which was, he said, intended to follow in the footsteps of W. R. Smith, and in which he reads the Old Testament in the light of a critique of the myths and folklore of all peoples. Frazer was given a knighthood in 1914. In 1931 he began to lose his sight. He died in Cambridge in 1941, and his French wife, who had worked as his agent, died just a few hours later following a heart attack (Ackerman, 1987: 308).

SELECT BIBLIOGRAPHY

Ackerman, R.E. (1987) *J.G. Frazer: His Life and Work*, Cambridge, New York: Cambridge University Press.

——(1991) *The Myth and Ritual School: J.G. Frazer and the Cambridge Ritualists*, New York: Garland Publishing.

Adler, E. (1968) *Herder und die deutsche Aufklärung*, Vienna, Frankfurt: Europa Verlag.

Augstein, H.F. (1999) *James Cowles Prichard's Anthropology. Remaking the Science of Man in Early Nineteenth Century Britain*, Amsterdam and Atlanta: GA.

Balfour, H. *et al.* (1994; 1st edn 1907) *Anthropological Essays Presented to Edward Burnett Tylor in Honour of his Seventy-Fifth Birthday*, London: Routledge.

Beidelman, T.O. (1974) *William Robertson Smith and the Sociological Study of Religion*, Chicago, London: University of Chicago Press.

——(1987) 'Smith, W. Robertson', in M. Eliade (ed.) *The Encyclopedia of Religion*, New York, Macmillan, vol.13, pp.366–367.

Bieder, R.E. (1986) *Science Encounters the Indian, 1820–1888: The Early Years of American Ethnology*, Norman and London: University of Oklahoma Press.

Blanckaert, C.L. (1988a) 'On the origins of French ethnology: W. Edwards and the doctrine of race', in G.W. Stocking (ed.) *Bones, Bodies, Behavior: Essays on Biological Anthropology*, *HOA*, vol.5: 18–56.

——(1988b) 'Story et History de l'anthropologie', *Revue de Synthèse*, 3(4): 451–469.

Boas, F. (1902) 'Rudolf Virchow's Anthropological Work', *Science*, 16: 441–445, September.

Bohannan, P. (1964) 'Introduction' to E.B. Tylor, *Early History of Mankind*, University of Chicago Press: pp. v–xvii.

Burrow, J.W. (1966) *Evolution and society: a study in Victorian social theory*, London: Cambridge University Press.

Chapman, W.R. (1981, 1985) 'Arranging ethnology: A.H.L.F. Pitt-Rivers and the typological tradition', in Stocking, G.W. (ed.) *Objects and others. Essays on Museums and Material Culture*, *HOA* vol.3: 15–48.

Cocks, R.C.J. (1988) *Sir Henry Maine: A Study in Victorian Jurisprudence*, Stocking, G.W. (ed.) *Objects and others. Essays on Museums and Material Culture*, Cambridge: Cambridge University Press.

Diamond, A. (ed.) (1991) *The Victorian Achievement of Sir Henry Maine: A Centennial Reappraisal*, New York, Cambridge: Cambridge University Press.

Dörmann, J. (1965) 'Was J.J. Bachofen Evolutionist?', *Anthropos*, 60: 1–48.

Dorson, R.M. (1955) 'The eclipse of solar mythology', *Journal of American Folklore*, 63: 393–416 and in T.A. Sebeok (ed.) *Myth: A Symposium*, Bloomington, pp.14–38.

Douglas, M. (1978) 'Judgments on James Frazer', *Daedalus*, 107: 151–164.

Downie, R.A. (1969; 1st edn 1940), *James George Frazer. The Portrait of a Scholar*, London: Watt.

Dumont, L. (1983, 1986) Essays on individualism: Modern ideology in Anthropological perspective, Chicago: University of Chicago Press.

——(1991, 1994) *Germany Ideology: From France to Germany and Back*, Chicago: University of Chicago Press.

Edwards, W. (1829) *Des caractères physiologiques des races humaines considérées dans leurs Rapports avec l'histoire. Lettre à M. Amédés Thierry*, Paris: Compère Jeune.

——(1844) *Recherches sur les langues celtiques*, Paris: Imp. National.

——(1845) *De l'influence réciproque des races sur le caractère national: Mémoires de la Société ethnologique de Paris*, no.2.

Fabian, Johannes (1983) *Time and the other: how anthropology makes its object*, New York: Columbia University Press.

Feaver, G. (1969) *From Status to Contract: Biography of Sir Henry Maine (1822–1888)*, London & Harlow: Longmans.

Fiedermutz-Laun, A. (1970) *Der kulturhistorische Gedanke bei Adolf Bastian*, Wiesbaden: F. Steiner.

Firth, R. (1963) *Introduction to Ancient Law*, Boston: Beacon Press.

Frazer, J.G. (1898) *Pausanias's Description of Greece*, 6 vols, London: Macmillan.

——(1905) *Lectures on the Early History of the Kingship*, London: Macmillan.

——(1913–1924) *The Belief in Immortality and the Worship of the Dead*, London: Macmillan.

——(1920, 1968) *The Magical Origin of Kings*, London: Dawsons.

——(1926) *The Worship of Nature*, London: Macmillan.

——(1930) *Myths of the Origin of Fire*, London: Macmillan.

——(1933–1936) *The Fear of the Dead in Primitive Religion*, 3 vols, London: Macmillan.

——(1938–39) *Anthologia Anthropologica*, 4 vols from the manuscript of Sir J.G. Frazer arranged and edited by R.A. Downie, London: Percy Lund Humphries.

Freud, S. (1912, 1998) *Totem and Taboo*, New York: Dover Publications.

Goldenweiser, A. (1937) 'Bastian, Adolf' in E.R.A. Seligman (ed.) *Encyclopedia of the Social Sciences*, New York, vol.2, pp.476.

Gruber, J.W. (1968) 'Lubbock, John', in D.L. Sills (ed.) *International Encyclopedia of the Social Sciences*, vol.9: 487–88.

Hays, Hoffman Reynolds (1958) *From Ape to Angel. An informal history of social anthropology*, Alfred A. Knopf: New York.

Héran, F. (1989) 'Une question de généalogie: la théorie de la segmentation' (On Maine), in M. Ségalen, *Anthropologie Sociale et ethnologie de la France*, Louvain-la-Neuve: Peeters, pp.231–237.

Hildebrandt, H.J. (1988) *Johann Jakob Bachofen: a Bibliography of the Primary and Secondary Literature, with an Appendix on the State of the Matriarchal Question*, Aachen: Herodot.

Izard, M. (1991) 'Le Bachofen de Walter Benjamin', *Gradhiva*, 10: 89–93.

Izard, M. and Belmont, N. (1991) 'Frazer, James George', in P. Bonte and M. Izard (eds) *Dictionnaire de l'ethnologie et de l'anthropologie*, Paris: Presses universitaires de France, pp.298–299.

Johnstone, W. (ed.) (1995) *W.R. Smith: Essays in Reassessment*, Sheffield: Sheffield Academic Press.

Jones, R.A. (1984) 'R. Smith and J. Frazer on religion: two traditions in British social anthropology', in Stocking (ed.), *Functionalism Historicized, HOA*, vol.2: 31–58.

Jorion, P. (1980) 'Un ethnologue proprement dit' (on Pritchard), *L'Homme*, 20(4): 119–128.

Koepping, K.P. (1985) *Adolf Bastian and the Psychic Unity of Mankind: The Foundations of Anthropology in Nineteenth Century Germany*, St. Lucia, London and New York: Queensland University Press.

Kuper, A. (1985) 'The development of L.H. Morgan's evolutionism', *Journal of the History of the Behavioral Sciences* 21: 3–22.

——(1988) *The invention of primitive society: transformations of an illusion*, London, New York: Routledge.

——(1997) 'On human nature: Darwin and the anthropologists' in Treich *et al.* (eds) *Nature and Society in Historical Context*, Cambridge: Cambridge University Press, pp.274–290.

——(1999) *Culture. The Anthropologists' Account*, Cambridge, MA: Harvard University Press, (chap. I on Herder).

Leach, E.R. (1966) 'Frazer and Malinowski: on the founding fathers', *CA*, 7: 560–576.

Leopold, J. (1980) *Culture in Comparative and Evolutionary Perspective: E.B Tylor and The Making of Primitive Culture*, Berlin: Reimen.

Leuser, C. (1996) *Theologie und Anthropologie: Die Erziehung des Menschengeschlechts bei J.G. Herder*, Frankfurt: Lang.

Lowie, R. (1917) 'E.B. Tylor', *AA*, 19: 262–268.

——(1937) *The History of Ethnological Theory*, New York: Farrar & Rinehart.

McLennan, J.F. (1865, 1975) *Primitive Marriage; an Inquiry into the Origin of the Form of Capture in Marriage Ceremonies*, ed. with intro. by Peter Rivière, Chicago: University of Chicago Press.

Malinowski, B. (1944) 'Sir J.G. Frazer. A biographical appreciation', in *A Scientific Theory of Culture and Other Essays*, Chapel Hill: North Carolina University Press.

Marett, R.R. (1936) *Tylor*, London: Chapman.

Mason, O.T. (1902) 'Rudolf Virchow', *AA*, 4: 568–571.

Morgan, L.H. (1851) *League of the Ho-dé-no-sau-nee, or Iroquois*, Rochester (reissued in a facsimile edition with an introduction by W.N. Fenton in 1962 by Corinth Books, Secaucus).

——(1868) *The American Beaver and his Works* (reissued in facsimile in 1970 by B. Franklin, New York).

——(1871, 1997) *System of Consanguinity and Affinity of the Human Family* (introduction by E. Tooker), Lincoln: University of Nebraska Press.

——(1st 1877, 1965) *Houses and House-life of the American Aborigines*, (introduction by P. Bohannan), Chicago: Chicago University Press.

——(1993) *Lewis Henry Morgan, the Indian Journal 1859–1862*, L.A. White ed., New York: Dover Publication.

Müller, F.M. (1847) *Meghadüta. Der Wolkenbote, dem Kälidäsa nachgedichtet*, Königsberg: A. Samter Verlag.

——(1861–1864, 1987) *Lectures on the Science of Language*, New Delhi: Cosmo Publications.

——(1878, 1882, 1997) *Lectures on the Origin and Growth of Religion*, London: Routledge.

——(1897) *Contributions to the Science of Mythology*, 2 vols, London, New York: Longmans.

——(1899, 1977) *The Six Systems of Indian Philosophy*, New York: AMS Press.

Müller, G.A. (1900) *The Life and letters of the R.H.F Max Müller*, 2 vols, Oxford: Oxford University Press.

Opler, M. (1962) 'Integration, evolution and Morgan', *CA*, vol.2: 478–489.

Orenstein, H. (1968) 'The ethnological theories of Henry Summer Maine', in *AA*, vol.70: 264–276.

Peters, E.L. (1968) 'Smith, W. Robertson', in D.L. Sills (ed.) *International Encyclopedia of the Social Sciences*, vol.14: 329–335.

Prichard, J.C. (1819) *An Analysis of the Egyptian Mythology*, London: Arch.

——(1822) *A Treatise on Diseases of the Nervous System*, London: Arch.

——(1831) *The Eastern Origin of the Celtic Nations Proved by a Comparison of their Dialects with the Sanskrit, Greek, Latin and Teutonic Languages. Forming a Supplement to Researches into the Physical History of Mankind*, London: Arch.

Quiñones Keber, E. (2001) 'A. de Humboldt' in *Oxford Encyclopaedia of Mesoamerican Cultures*, ed. D. Carrasco, 3 vols, Oxford: Oxford University Press.

Read, C.H. (1913) 'Lord Avebury', *Man*, 13: 97–99.

Redfield, R. (1950) 'Maine's Ancient Law in the light of primitive societies', *Western Political Quarterly*, 2: 574–579.

Reimer, C. and Rivière, P. (1973) 'Tylor', in *Encyclopaedia Universalis*, vol.16, pp.441–442, Paris.

Resek, C. (1960) *Lewis Henry Morgan: American Scholar*, Chicago, London: University of Chicago Press.

Rivière, P. (1970) 'Introduction' to *Primitive Marriage*, pp. vii–xlvii, Chicago, London: University of Chicago Press.

Romero de Tejada y Picatoste, P. (1992) *Un templo a la ciencia. historia del Museo Nacional de Etnología*, [Madrid]. Ministerio de Cultura, Dirección General de Bellas Artes y Archivos.

Service, E.R. (1981) 'The mind of Lewis H. Morgan', *CA*, 22: 25–43.

Siebold, Philipp Franz Balthasar von (1843) *Lettre sur l'utilité des Musées ethnographiques, et sur l'importance de leur création dans les états européens qui possèdent des colonies*, Paris: Benjamin Duprat.

Sommer, A. (1990) 'William Frederic Edwards: "Race" als Grundlage europäischer Geschichtsdeutung?', in G. Mann (ed.), *Die Natur des Menschen. Probleme der physischen Anthropologie und Rassenkunde (1750–1850)*, New York and Stuttgart: Fischer Verlag.

Sonderegger, P.A. (2002) *Jenseits der rassistischen Grenze*, Frankfurt, Berlin: Peter Lang.

Stagl, J. (1989) 'J.J. Bachofen's Mother Right and its consequences', *Philosophy of the Social Sciences*, 19: 183–200.

Steiner, K. (1905) 'Gedächtnisrede auf Adolf Bastian' in *Zeitschrift für Ethnologie*, 37: 236–249.

Stern, B.J. (1931) *Lewis Morgan: Social Evolutionist*, Chicago: University of Chicago Press.

Stocking, G.W. (1963) 'Matthew Arnold, E.B. Tylor, and the uses of invention', *AA*, 65: 783–799.

——(1965) 'Cultural Darwinism and philosophical idealism in Tylor' in *Southwestern Journal of Anthropolgy*, 81: 130–147.

——(1968, 1982) *Race, Culture, and Evolution, Essays in the History of Anthropology*, New York: Free Press.

——(1971) 'What's in a name? The origins of the Royal Anthropological Institute 1837–1871', *Man*, 6: 369–390.

——(1973) 'From Chronology to Ethnology. J. Cowles Prichard and British Anthropology 1800–1855', introduction to the reissue of J.C. Prichard, *Researches into the Physical History of Man*, Chicago: University of Chicago Press, pp. ix–lx.

——(1987) *Victorian anthropology*, New York: Free Press and Oxford: Maxwell Macmillan.

——(ed.) (1994) *Collected Works of E.B. Tylor*, London: Routledge, 8 vols.

——(1995) *After Tylor: British social anthropology, 1888–1951*, Madison: University of Wisconsin Press.

Stoczkowski, W. (2002) *Explaining Human Origins*, Cambridge: Cambridge University Press.

Terray, E. (1969, 1972) *Marxism and 'Primitive' Societies: Two Studies* (on Morgan), New York: Monthly Review Press.

Thompson, M.W. (1977) *General Pitt-Rivers. Evolution and Archaeology in the Nineteenth Century*, Bradford, Mooraker Press.

Tooker, E. (1992) 'Lewis Morgan and his contemporaries', *AA*, 94: 357–376.

Trautmann, T.R. (1987) *Lewis Henry Morgan and the Invention of Kinship*, Berkeley, CA: University of California Press.

Tylor, E.B. (1881) 'J.F. Mc Lennan', *Academy*, 2 July, p.20.

——(1889, 1994) *Primitive culture; researches into the development of mythology, philosophy, religion, language, art and custom*, London: Routledge.

——(1878, 1994) *Researches into the early history of mankind and the development of civilization*, London: Routledge.

Vincent, J. (1996) 'Morgan, Lewis Henry', in A. Barnard and J. Spencer (eds) *Encyclopedia of Social and Cultural Anthropology*, London: Routledge, pp.381–382.

Voigt, J.H. (1967, 1981) *Max Müller. The Man and His Ideas*, Calcutta: KLM Private.

White, L.A. (1940) *Pioneers in American Anthropology: the Bandelier-Morgan letters 1873–1883*, 2 vols, Albuquerque: University of New Mexico Press.

——(1957) *How Morgan Came to Write 'Systems of Consanguinity and Affinity'*, Papers of the Michigan Academy of Sciences, Arts, and Letters, no.42: 257–268.

——(1960) 'Introduction', to Tylor, *Anthropology*, Ann Arbor: University of Michigan Press

——(1964) 'Introduction' to L.H. Morgan *Ancient Society*, Cambridge, MA: Harvard University Press.

Zammito, J.H. (2002) *Kant, Herder, and the Birth of Anthropology*, Chicago: University of Chicago Press.

II

Field workers and early informants

Throughout the nineteenth and early twentieth centuries, anthropologists constructed evolutionist schemata using information gathered from the texts of classical antiquity (Cato, Caesar, Herodotus, Plutarch, Tacitus, Xenophanes, etc.), to which an ever-growing body of ethnographic data was gradually added. Important early nineteenth-century expeditions included the voyage of Nicolas Thomas Baudin from Le Havre to the South Sea Islands, begun in 1800 (J. Jamin and J. Copans, *The Origins of French Anthropology: Memoranda of the Society for the Observation of Man in Year VIII*, Paris, 1979), and the mission undertaken by Meriwether Lewis and William Clark in 1804 to explore the Missouri River and follow its distributaries downstream to the Pacific Ocean. In the USA further expeditions followed that of Lewis and Clark, many of them outside US territory. The most important of these was the Wilkes Expedition to the South Pacific of 1837–1842. Important institutional developments in America were **Schoolcraft**'s founding of the Algic Society in 1832, the creation by Albert Gallatin of the American Ethnological Society in 1842, and the establishment of the Smithsonian Institution in 1846. In London, the *Asiatic Journal* first appeared in 1816, and in 1823 the Royal Asiatic Society of Great Britain and Ireland was founded as a focus for interest in the religious institutions, costumes, languages, literatures and arts of Asia. The Society published a journal and also monographs devoted to Oriental subjects, and expanded with the establishment of a Bombay branch in 1841 and a Ceylon branch (at Colombo) in 1845. The year 1843 saw the emergence of the Anthropological Institute of Great Britain and Ireland, which later gained a royal charter. The British Crown annexed Punjab in 1849, dissolved the East India Company in 1858, and imposed indirect rule. In the same period J. D. Cochrane crossed Siberia on foot, R. Caillié reached Timbuktu, and J. L. Burckhardt and R. F. Burton wrote accounts of their celebrated voyages to Arabia and the Orient. In his *Systems of Consanguinity and Affinity of the Human Family*, published in 1871, **Morgan** was able to present the kinship nomenclatures of most of what he calls the 'branches of the human family' on every continent, failing to do so only in the cases of the 'Negroid nations' and the Aborigines of Australia (1871: 467). While Sub-Saharan Africa was still little documented by the beginning of the twentieth century, Australia had already been extensively studied by the end of the nineteenth. After having been rather unsuccessfully colonized by British convicts from 1788 onwards, the Australian continent saw an inrush of thousands of immigrants drawn by the discovery of gold in New South Wales. Some of these would take an interest in the Aborigines and supply a rich ethnography of their social structures, of which they were both the first and last scientific witnesses (L. R. Hiatt, *Arguments about Aborigines: Australia and the Evolution of Social Anthropology* (Cambridge: Cambridge UP, 1996)). Names not treated below include such writers on Australia as R. H. Matthews, C. Strehlow

---

and A. Kremer, as well as the precursors of British Africanist anthropology: M. Kingsley (1862–1900), who wrote *Travels in West Africa* (1897) and *West African Studies* (1899); C. Kingsley Meek (1885–1965), a colonial administrator best known as the author of *The Northern Tribes of Nigeria* (1925); and R. Rattray (1881–1938), author of the celebrated *Ashanti* (1923).

Schoolcraft, Henry Rowe (1793–1864)
Born in Guilderland in New York State, Henry Rowe Schoolcraft was appointed as a government geologist in 1820, and in 1822 he became a government official for Indian affairs and made his home by the Saint Mary River, which connects Lakes Michigan and Huron. Amongst other things he was charged with ensuring that the peace between the Chippewa and the Sioux was kept. He struck up friendly relations with the Chippewa, took a Chippewa wife, and, turning his back on geology, became an ethnographer and a protector of American Indians, whose case he tirelessly pleaded. In 1832 Schoolcraft set up the Algic Society dedicated to research on Amerindian languages and customs. In 1839 he published two volumes of myths and legends entitled *Algic Researches*, followed by *Notes on the Iroquois* (1847) and *Oneonta: The Indian in his Wigwam* (1848). Between 1851 and 1858 his magnum opus appeared: *Historical and Statistical Information Respecting the History, Condition and Prospects of the Indian Tribes of the USA, Collected and Prepared under the Direction of the Bureau of Indian Affairs*; this six-volume work contained everything known about the American Indians at the time. In 1851 Schoolcraft published his *Personal Memoirs of a Residence of Thirty Years with the Indians*, and he was also the author of many other works.

Parker, Ely (1828–1895)
An Iroquois American Indian and son of a Seneca chief of the Tonawanda clan, Ely Parker studied law and made the acquaintance of **Morgan**, becoming his friend and his first and principal informant. He fought in the Civil War and was made a brigadier by Ulysses Grant, and he also became a commissioner in the Bureau of Indian Affairs and Grand Sachem of the Iroquois League.

Howitt, Alfred L. W. (1830–1908)
Alfred L. W. Howitt was born into a family of writers who left London for Australia in 1852 in search of gold. Their hopes were soon dashed and they returned to England, but Howitt himself stayed behind in Australia, where he turned herdsman and then explorer. He was appointed by the government to lead an operation to rescue a geographical mission lost in the desert, but found only a single survivor who had been picked up by Aborigines. His admiration for their ability to survive in an environment in which civilized men were doomed to perish led him to begin studying the Aborigines. The authorities made him an administrative commissioner working with the Kurnai, and during this period he read **Fison**'s works and met Fison himself. Together they wrote *Kamilaroi and Kurnai: Group-Marriage and Relationship and Marriage by Elopement, Drawn Chiefly from the Usage of the Australian Aborigines*, published in 1880, which showed that the Kamilaroi were matrilineal and the Kurnai patrilineal. Seeing the community for which he was responsible dwindle, as a result of alcoholism, venereal disease and tuberculosis, from 1,500 to 400 members in about thirty years caused Howitt to give up his post in despair and become an inspector of mines. In 1901 he retired from this position and in 1904 published *The Native Tribes of South East Australia*.

Codrington, Robert Henry, Reverend (1830–1922)

Born in Wroughton in England, Robert Henry Codrington studied at Wadham College, Oxford, and was ordained an Anglican clergyman in 1855. In 1860 he was appointed to the diocese of New Zealand and then to St Barnabas, where he was given responsibility for the Anglican mission school. Working mainly in the Solomon Islands and in the northeast of the New Hebrides, Codrington became the first linguist and ethnographer of Melanesia. He produced numerous articles and a translation of the Bible, but his major works were *The Melanesian Language* (1885) and a collection entitled *The Melanesians: Studies in their Anthropology and Folklore* (1891). He is remembered above all as being the first to report on the Polynesian notion of 'Mana', a force prevailing across the universe which impregnates inanimate objects and imposes its stamp on certain human beings, who, he says, then exist on the edge of the spirit world. He defines Mana a 'force distinct from physical strength which acts for better or for worse and which it is highly beneficial to harness and control' (1891).

Fison, Lorimer, Reverend (1832–1907)

Born in Barningham, England, Lorimer Fison studied at Gonville and Caius College, Cambridge, but left without a degree and moved to Australia as a gold prospector in 1856. For two years he searched in vain, and then, after the death of his father, he became a Methodist missionary. He was posted to Fiji and lived there from 1864 to 1871 and from 1875 to 1884, also acting as **Morgan**'s informant for this part of the world from 1869. He wrote an article on the matrimonial systems and kinship terminologies on the islands of Fiji and Tonga, published in the *Journal of the Anthropological Institute*, and a collection of stories (*Tales of Old Fiji*, London, 1904). Back in Australia in 1871, he began working on the customs of the Kamilaroi Aborigines, and collaborated with A. L. W. **Howitt** from 1873. After a number of articles the two men published *Kamilaroi and Kurnai: Group-Marriage and Relationship and Marriage by Elopement* (1880), which provides the first description of the dualist system in Australia. Under Morgan's influence the authors interpreted orgiastic rites as a survival of group marriage. This work was one of the main sources of Durkheim's *Elementary Forms of Religious Life*. Fison gave up anthropology after having published several more articles but maintained an active correspondence with **Tylor** and **Frazer** and offered advice to younger researchers such as **Spencer** and **Gillen**.

Kropotkin, Pyotr Alekseyevich (1842–1921)

Born in Moscow into a family of princely rank and schooled in elite institutions, Pyotr Alekseyevich Kropotkin served as a military geographer and geologist in Siberia, and then undertook an exploration of Finland. Despite having made a name for himself with his publications, he abandoned scientific pursuits for politics in 1871 and became a major anarchist leader. He was imprisoned in both Russia and France, and then settled in England, where he remained until the revolution of 1917. On the basis of an analysis of various societies, his central thesis was that social evolution is determined by functional co-operation rather than, as social Darwinism would have it, by competition (*Mutual Aid*, 1902). Kropotkin met **Radcliffe-Brown** prior to his admission to Cambridge University and exerted a certain fascination over him; later Radcliffe-Brown would claim that he owed the anarchist ideas of the early part of his career to the Russian.

Miklukho-Maclay, Nicolai Nicolaevich (1846–1888)

Born into a family of the minor nobility in a village in the province of Novgorod, Miklukho-Maclay studied at the University of St Petersburg and became a revolutionary under the influence of the democratic ideas of Zerishevsky. This led to his expulsion from university, and he completed his studies in the natural sciences and political economy at the universities of Heidelberg, Leipzig and Jena. Maclay then worked as assistant to the Darwinian zoologist Ernst Haeckel, and accompanied him in 1867 to the Canary Islands, Sicily and the Red Sea. Back in Russia in 1868, he became closely associated with the zoologist, ethnographer and physical anthropologist Karl von Baer, who took a monogenist approach. Maclay wished to ascertain what links existed between Papuans and the rest of mankind, and to this end the Russian Geographical Society agreed to convey him New Guinea. He arrived there in September 1871 accompanied by a Polynesian servant, who died soon afterwards, and a Swedish mariner named Will Olsen (**Radcliffe-Brown** recruited a Swedish sailor of the same name for his Australian expedition of 1910). He dwelt for fifteen months in a hut just outside a Papuan village near Astrolabe Bay, and bit by bit won the trust and learnt the language of the villagers, who on his first arrival had attacked him with spears. Caring little for questions of religion and social organization, he directed all his attention to problems pertaining to physical anthropology. In December 1871 a boat sent by the Grand Duke Konstantin, president of the Geographical Society, arrived in New Guinea to pick Maclay up, and after a visit to the Negritos of the Philippines, he was set down in Java, where he spent seven months at the invitation of the Governor of the Dutch East Indies. In 1874 he set off anew and settled on the southeast coast of New Guinea, and there the raids on the island's population by slave traders led him to take his first public stand. Maclay subsequently carried out research on the Malaysian Peninsula, measuring the skulls of Aboriginal Negritos, and then arrived in Singapore in 1875. In February 1876 he returned to Astrolabe Bay

in an attempt to prevent, as he put it, 'the terribly pernicious consequences for the black population of their encounter with European colonisation' (quoted by Tumarkin, 1982: 25). He travelled via Yap Island, where he took notes, and sojourned in Astrolabe Bay from June 1876 to November 1877. Before departing he assembled the chiefs to warn them against other white men who might arrive in the area. Back in Australia Maclay married the granddaughter of a Scottish savant, but he set off again in 1879 for the Solomon Islands and the New Hebrides, and on his return journey visited the Trobriand Islands. In 1882 he returned to Russia after a vain attempt to persuade the British to institute Papuan self-government, which he would have served as a counsellor ('There was the late-nineteenth-century fantasy of the White man who became the ruler and god of the primitive people' (Webster, 1984: 348, quoted by **Stocking** 1991: 231)). Equally unsuccessful were his protests against the German annexation of the Maclay Coast. His final journey took him back to Australia to be reunited with his family, and he finished his life in St Petersburg preparing his manuscripts for publication. Maclay has entered legend as the White Papuan, and in 1947 the Institute of Ethnography of the Soviet Academy of Sciences was renamed the Nicolai Miklukho-Maclay Institute.

Hunt, George (1854–1933)

A half-caste American Indian born in British Columbia, G. Hunt was raised by the Kwakiutl. He acted as interpreter during Johan Jacoben's expedition of 1881–1883. He was trained by F. **Boas**, whom he met in 1886, and became his principal collaborator (Boas never mastered Kwakiutl). Hunt posted him regular reports, and L. **White** has written that Hunt and W. H. Tate (Boas's second informant) were responsible for 4,000 of the 10,000 pages of Amerindian texts published by Boas.

Gillen, Francis James (1856–1912)
An Irishman who emigrated to Australia, Francis James Gillen found work as a telegraphy agent responsible for transmissions between the north and south of the continent. He was based at Charlotte Waters in the barren centre of the country, where he was also charged with protecting the Aborigines. Lacking a university education, Gillen nonetheless spent twenty years amassing observations on the Arunta, the Warramunga and the Luritja. W. B. **Spencer**, a professor at Melbourne University, met him while on a mission to the interior of the territory. Together they spent some months with the Arunta and then crossed the continent, and they co-authored *The Native Tribes of Central Australia* (1899) and *The Northern Tribes of Central Australia* (1904). From their examination of totemic classes they deduced that the Aborigines practised multiple marriages. They are remembered for their descriptions of the impressive Aboriginal initiation ceremonies (notably those of the Arunta), and also for stating the importance of totemism in Australia and of 'alcheringa' or dream time.

Spencer, Sir William Baldwin (1860–1929)
Born in Manchester, W. B. Spencer studied biology and zoology at Oxford University, where he then worked under **Tylor**'s influence on the classification of the Pitt Rivers collections. After submitting his thesis he found a position as professor of zoology at Melbourne University (1887–1919). During an expedition in 1894 in search of a newly-discovered marsupial mole, Spencer met F. J. **Gillen** and studied the Aborigines with him. Together they published *The Native Tribes of Central Australia* in 1899, followed in 1904 by *The Northern Tribes of Central Australia*. Spencer went on alone to write two travel works, *Across Australia* (1912) and *Wanderings in Wild Australia* (1928). He left his university chair in 1919 to become

a government official with responsibility for indigenous populations. Later, in 1927, he published *The Arunta: A Study of a Stone Age People* (London, 2 vols), which he co-signed with F. J. Gillen, who had died in 1914. Having decided to retrace **Darwin**'s voyage, he died in Tierra del Fuego in 1929.

Junod, Henri-Alexandre (1863–1934)
Born near Neuchâtel in Switzerland in 1863, H.-A. Junod studied theology and then worked as a missionary in Mozambique and South Africa, where he lived almost uninterruptedly from 1880 to 1923. He wrote a number of works, and is best known for his *Life of a South African Tribe*, first published in 1912 and republished in a revised and expanded version in 1927 (2 vols). One of the first truly scientific ethnographic studies, this book describes systematically all aspects of Bantu life on the basis of the questionnaire prepared by J. **Frazer**. Junod's work inspired **Lévy-Bruhl** as well as **Lowie** and **Radcliffe-Brown**, whose appointment to the Cape he nonetheless opposed.

Nimuendajú, Curt Unkel (1883–1946)
Born in Jena in Germany, Curt Unkel Nimuendajú (known simply as Nimuendajú) moved to Brazil in 1903 without having been to university. He lived in São Paolo and, from 1913, in Belém. From 1905 he was in contact with the American Indians and made ever longer and more frequent stays amongst them, until in 1906 they performed a ceremony naming him Nimuendajú. It was not until 1914 that his first article appeared in the *Zeitschrift für Ethnologie*. As the foremost specialist on the Apapocuva-Guaraní, Tukuna, Kaingang, Apinaye and Canela Indians, the 'Malinowski of Brazil', as **Cardoso de Oliveira** called him (Interview with M. Corrêa, *CA*, 32 (1991): 334–343)), was employed by the Paulista Museum and by various government departments. He took charge of exploration, cartography, pacification, ethnology and archaeology,

all areas in which he produced significant work, especially by means of his contribution to the *Handbook of South American Indians* edited by **Steward**. Despite warnings from doctors that another period living in the Amazonian forest would have fatal consequences for his already declining health, he set off again but died among the Tukuna Indians of Brazil on 10 December 1945.

Ishi (?–1916)

In 1961 Theodora Kroeber (Krakow 1897–1979) published the life story of Ishi, the last of the Yana American Indians of California, under the title *Ishi in Two Worlds: Biography of the Last Wild Indian in North America*. The book relates an inside view of the rapid destruction of Ishi's world after the first encounter with Whites who had come to speculate for gold. The massacre of the Yahi reduced their numbers to a mere handful, and in the end Ishi remained as the sole survivor of his people. He took flight and lived off the land for a while, but eventually gave himself up in 1911. At first he was imprisoned, then placed in a psychiatric asylum until A. **Kroeber** and Waterman secured his release. Before his death in 1916 Ishi spent five years as an attendant in the Berkeley Museum. The book fed into the American anti-Establishment movement of the 1960s, and also the American Indian cultural renaissance. The ethics of the relationship of Kroeber (and that of anthropology in general) with Ishi have become topics of discussion in recent times (Nancy Rockefeller and Orin Starn, 'Ishi's Brain', *Current Anthropology*, vol.40 (1999):

413–415). Notable contributions to this discussion include the publication in *Anthropology News* (vol.40, (7 October 1999): 3–6) of two items by Kroeber's children (one by U. K. Le Guin, a renowned writer of futuristic fiction), together with a global summing-up by George M. Foster.

Valero, Helena (1928–?)

In 1939 a group of Yanoáma attacked a White family and abducted Helena Valero, a girl of eleven able to read and write. She lived with the Yanoáma until 1961, and during this time was married twice and bore four sons. She was recovered by a Venezuelan forester and entrusted to the Salesian mission, where she gave a full and unvarnished account of her adventure recorded onto tape by Ettore Biocca, a doctor working for the Italian National Research Council. Biocca retold Valero's story in his *Yanoáma: The Narrative of a White Girl Kidnapped by Amazonian Indians*, which was published in Italian in 1965, in French in 1968 and in English in 1970. Valero's acculturation provided the most vivid testimony to date on the living patterns of the Yanoáma at this time. For although she spoke a great deal of herself, her sufferings and her integration into her new life, her staggering account gave a good idea of the social formation of the group. Her reminiscences placed particular emphasis on endocannibalistic and shamanic rituals, the almost constant state of war, the 'circulation' of women, and lastly on interpersonal relations within a Yanoáma group and the political relations between group members and their chief.

THE CAMBRIDGE UNIVERSITY EXPEDITION TO THE TORRES STRAITS AND OXFORD AND CAMBRIDGE RESEARCHERS

'On the eve of the 1898 Expedition to the Torres Straits, British anthropology was in search of self-definition [. . .] it was struggling for legitimacy in the academy while lacking both recognisable boundaries and a unifying paradigm' (Herle and Rouse, 1998: 1). Under the leadership of the zoologist and ethnologist A. C. **Haddon**, the expedition brought together the following men: W. H. **Rivers**, a physician and psychologist; Charles S. Meyers and W. McDougall, both former students of Haddon and Rivers and both physicians, the first interested in the sense of hearing and music and the second specializing in the sense of touch; Sidney H. Ray, a primary school teacher with a passion for the study of Oceanic languages, who was responsible for linguistic research; Anthony Wilkin, another of Haddon's students, who had acquired archaeological experience in Egypt and who became the expedition's photographer, as well as being responsible under Haddon's direction for construction techniques and land tenure; and finally Charles G. **Seligman**, a physician specializing in tropical diseases. The expedition set off in March 1898 and arrived on 22 April 1898 in the Torres Straits, where it remained until October of that year. British New Guinea became the expedition's base for the first months, before most of its members left to spend several months in Borneo. The results of the expedition were set out in a report which ran to six volumes, and which was not fully published until thirty-five years later (1901–1935: vol.1: General ethnography (including geography and history), 1935; vol.2: Physiology and psychology, 1901, 1903; vol.3: Language, 1907; vol.4: Arts and crafts, 1907; vol.5: Sociology, magic and religion of the Western Islanders, 1904; vol.6: Sociology, magic and religion of the Eastern Islanders, 1908). The expedition also yielded several hundred photographs, a short ethnographical film, cylinder records and a rich harvest of indigenous artefacts, although it was twenty years before some of the cases were opened (Hays, 1958). An interesting discovery in the research was that the performances of Papuans in psychological tests were on a par with those of undergraduates at Cambridge University who served as the control group, which ran counter to the conventional wisdom concerning the racial aspect of modes of perception (the largest differences concerned eyesight, which was better in the Papuans than in Europeans). But the expedition also established that differences did not derive from biological inheritance, but were products of learning, and that perceptions of space and colour were thus culturally conditioned (see **Kuklick** 1991: 146–148). Finally, it was during this expedition that Rivers invented the 'genealogical method' and the signs which are used to describe kinship to this day. 'Indeed, it is just as appropriate to describe the Torres Straits Expedition as the culmination of a tradition of research as it is to see it as a revolutionary break', writes Kuklick (Ibid. 140). The emphasis placed on direct observation and first-hand collection of data 'provided the basis for the development of intensive fieldwork as the essential methodology of anthropology – the "ethnographic method"' (Herle and Rouse, 1998: 15), and 'marks a clear break in anthropology between the amateur and antiquarian of the nineteenth century, and the development of the professional anthropologist who combines field-based observation with theoretical analysis' (Ibid. 17).

Haddon, Alfred Cort (1855–1940)

Alfred Cort Haddon was born in London as the son of a printer. In 1874 he began studying zoology at Cambridge University and, after a brief period as curator in the Cambridge Museum, took a teaching position at the Royal College in Dublin in 1880. With Huxley's help he obtained financial support for a visit to the Torres Straits to pursue studies of coral reefs and their fauna (1888–1889). He spent his evenings among the Papuans, and on his return published several articles followed by two books: *The Decorative Art of British New Guinea* (1894) and *Evolution in Art* (1895), an important work recognized as his main contribution to theory. As of 1894 Haddon taught physical anthropology part-time at Cambridge, obtaining a science Ph.D. in 1897, and, thanks to **Frazer**'s help, was chosen two years later to lead the group expedition to the Torres Straits (1898–1899). There he concentrated on surveying, the study of decorative art, and collecting 'customs', and he made a particular effort to reconstruct ancient ceremonies and collect myths. While resuming his teaching in Dublin he was also, again thanks to Frazer's support, appointed to a part-time lecturing position in the ethnology department of London University in 1904. He went on to become reader in ethnology between 1909 and 1926, but it was not until 1933 that a chair was endowed for him. Haddon directed the publication of the expedition report, and himself mainly wrote on the Sarawak and the Papuans, following a classical diffusionist perspective by making human migration his primary interest. He also deserves recognition for producing one of the first histories of the discipline, *History of Anthropology* (with A. H. Quiggin, 1910, revised edition 1934), which brings together the development of prehistory, linguistics, ethnology, and physical anthropology. He carried out a further investigation in the Torres Straits in 1914.

Rivers, William Halse R. (1862–1922)

Born at Hope Hall near Bramham Park in Yorkshire, William H. R. Rivers studied medicine and then neurology, developing a strong interest in psychology in around 1890. He was appointed reader in physiology and experimental psychology at Cambridge University in 1897. In 1898–1899 he took part in the Cambridge University Torres Straits Expedition, during which he carried out psychological tests, relating particularly to eyesight, on the indigenous populations he encountered. His knowledge of Galton's work led him to think it would be useful to establish a relationship between these

tests and genealogical investigations. Thus he invented the 'genealogical method', which permitted the organized collection of kinship nomenclatures. Rivers set this approach out theoretically in *The Genealogical Method of Anthropological Inquiry* (1910), in which he devised a descriptive language which is still in use, thereby generating the second revolution in kinship studies following **Morgan**'s innovations of forty years earlier. With the help of a grant from the Percy Stade Trust, Rivers travelled to India in 1901–1902 to study a polyandric society there and to test **McLennan**'s hypotheses regarding the evolution of family structures; this became *The Todas* (London: Macmillan, 1906). One outcome of these experiments was that he became an opponent of evolutionist hypotheses, and in a statement made to the British Association for the Advancement of Science in 1911 he formally allied himself with diffusionist theories. In 1907 he went to Melanesia, and by 1910 was already able to publish *The History of Melanesian Society*, which developed a thesis drawing on the pan-Egyptianist theories of **Smith**. In this work Rivers interprets the two exogamous halves of the Melanesian peoples as deriving from two distinct population strata, with a dark-skinned people having been invaded by an originally light-skinned people. This second group he held to have introduced a megalithic Egyptian civilization, which then regressed as it was culturally absorbed. While the notion of Egyptian origin is fanciful, the book provided contemporaries with a very useful picture of Melanesian cultures.

Alongside his anthropological work Rivers continued his psychological researches, and in 1903 founded the *British Journal of Psychology* (with James Ward). He also carried out experiments on nerve regeneration in collaboration with H. Head. While working as a psychiatrist during the First World War he developed an interest in psychoanalysis and tried to develop a psychologized anthropology, but his premature death brought this undertaking to a halt, to be replaced by those of **Malinowski** and **Radcliffe-Brown**. It should also be noted that 'he is as well remembered in literary history – as Siegfried Sassoon's doctor during First World War and as the subject of a remarkable trilogy of novels by the British writer Pat Barker – as in anthropology' (Barnard and Spencer, 1996: 588).

Seligman, Charles Gabriel (1873–1940)
Born in London, Charles Gabriel Seligman studied medicine with pathology as his specialism (1896), and then took part at his own expense in the Cambridge University Torres Straits Expedition (1898–1899), in which he was in charge of the study of illnesses and traditional medicine. Back in London he resumed his research into pathology at St Thomas's Hospital, but returned into the field in 1904 at the head of the Major Cooke Daniels Ethnographical Expedition to New Guinea (named after its wealthy American sponsor). There Seligman collected the materials he needed to write *The Melanesians of British New Guinea* (London, 1910), a vast and pioneering work of comprehensive classification for this part of the world. In 1905 he married Brenda Z.

Salamon, who thereafter worked as his collaborator. The Seligmans travelled to the Veddas of Ceylon (Sri Lanka) in 1906, and in 1911 Seligman published *The Veddas*, a description of this Ceylonese population, which was considered particularly primitive although it cultivated yams. In 1909 he made his first visit to the Sudan, to which he devoted his attention from then on (1909–1910, 1911–1912, 1921–1922), and he collected substantial documentation from the Shilluk people on their view of the divinity of kings (according to which the king, as the central point in the cosmos, must be killed once his powers start to decline). After already having worked at the London School of Economics (LSE) as a part-time lecturer, Seligman was professor there between 1913 and 1934, and his students included **Malinowski**, **Evans-Pritchard**, **Firth**, **Nadel** and **Fortes**. He played an important role by assigning Malinowski to 'verify the pertinence of Freudian hypotheses to his Trobriand fieldwork' (Pulman, 1991: 660), but the novelty of the approach developed by his protégé from 1922, also at the LSE, would soon overshadow Seligman's own work.

SELECT BIBLIOGRAPHY

Anonymous, (1923) Article on Codrington in *AA*, 25: 130.

Baldus, H. (1946) 'Curt Nimuendajú', *AA*, 48: 238–243.

Barnard A, and Spencer, J. (1996) *Encyclopedia of Social and Cultural Anthropology*, London: Routledge.

Berman, J. (1996) 'The culture as it appears to the Indian himself: Boas, George Hunt, and the methods of ethnography', in G.W. Stocking (ed.) *Volksgeist as Method and Ethic*, *HOA*, 8: 215–257.

Berthoud, G. (1985) 'Entre l'anthropologie et le missionnaire: la contribution d'H-A. Junod (1863–1934)' in *Le Visage multiplié du monde: quatre siècles d'ethnographie à Genève*, Geneva: Musée d'Ethnographie, pp.59–74.

Bieder, R. E. (1991) 'Schoolcraft, H.', in C. Winter, p.622.

Briggs, C. and Bauman, R. (1999) 'The foundations of all future researches: F. Boas, G. Hunt, Native American texts and the construction of modernity', *American Quarterly*, 51(3): 479–528.

Butinov, (1971) 'A nineteenth-century champion of anti-racism in New Guinea (on Maclay)', *Unesco Courier*, November: 24–27.

Cannizzo, J. (1983) 'George Hunt and the invention of Kwakiutl culture', *Canadian Review of Sociology and Anthropology*, 20: 44–85.

Codrington, R.H. (1885, 1974) *The Melanesian Language*, Amsterdam: Philo Press.

——(1891, 1972) *The Melanesians: Studies in their Anthropology and Folklore*, New York: Dover Publications.

Firth, R. (1975) 'Seligman's contribution to Oceanic anthropology', *Oceania*, 45: 472–482.

Fortes, M. (1941) 'C.G. Seligman', in *Man*, 41: 1–6.

——(1974) 'C.G. Seligman', in *International Encyclopedia of the Social Sciences*, D.L. Sills (ed.), vol.14: 159–162.

Francillon, M. (1991) 'Fison, L.', in C. Winter, pp.201–202.

Fraser, D. (1971; 1957) 'The discovery of primitive art', in C. M. Otten, *Anthropology and Art*, New York: AMNHP, pp.20–39.

Frazer, J. (1907) 'Fison and Howitt', *Folklore*, 20: 144–180.

Freeman, J.F. (1965) 'Religion and personality in the anthropology of H. Schoolcraft', *Journal of the History of the Behavioral Sciences*, 1: 301–313.

Gathercole, P.W. (1977) 'Cambridge and the Torres Straits', *Cambridge Anthropology*, vol.3: 22–31.

Gillen, F.J. (1995) *Gillen's First Diary: Adelaïde to Alice Springs March to June 1875*, Adelaïde: Wakefield Press.

Haddon, A.C. (1895) *Evolution in Art*, London: W. Scott.

——(1898) *The Study of Man*, London: Bliss.

——(1901) *Head Hunters, Black, White and Brown*, London: Methuen.

——(1911) *The Wanderings of the Peoples*, Cambridge: Cambridge University Press.

——(1912) *The Races of Man and their Distribution*, Cambridge: Cambridge University Press.

Haddon, A.C. and Bartlett, F.C. (1922) 'Obituary of W.H.R. Rivers', *Man*, 22: 97–103.

Haddon, A.C., Evans-Pritchard, E.E., Firth, R., Malinowski, B. and Shapera, I. (eds) (1934) *Essays Presented to C.G. Seligman*, London.

Hays, Hoffman Reynolds (1958) *From Ape to Angel. An informal history of social anthropology*, Alfred A. Knopf: New York.

Herle, A. and Rouse, S. (eds) (1998) *Cambridge and the Torres Strait: Centenary Essays on the 1898 Anthropological Expedition*, Cambridge: Cambridge University Press.

Herskovits, M.J. (1941) 'C.G. Seligman', *AA*, 43: 437–439.

Hilliard, D.L. (1981) 'Codrington, R.H.', in R.D. Craig and F.P. King (eds) *Historical Dictionary of Oceania*, Westport: Greenwood Press, p.55.

Jacob, J-P. (1991) 'Junod Henri-Alexandre', in C. Winter, pp.332–333.

Junod, H-P. (1934) *H-A. Junod: missionnaire et savant*, Lausanne: Mission Suisse dans l'Afrique du sud.

Juillerat, B. (1991) 'Rivers William Halse', in P. Bonte and M. Izard (eds) *Dictionnaire de l'ethnologie et de l'anthropologie*, Paris: Presses universitaires de France, pp. 634–635.

Kroeber, T. (1961, 1976) *Ishi in Two Worlds: Biography of the Last Wild Indian in North America*, Berkeley: University of California Press.

Kuklick, H. (1991) *The Savage Within: The Social History of British Anthropology, 1885–1945*, New York and Cambridge: Cambridge University Press.

——(1996) 'British anthropology', in A. Barnard and J. Spencer, *Encyclopedia of Social and Cultural Anthropology*, London: Routledge, pp.76–79.

——(1997) 'Rivers, W. H. R.', in Barfield, T. (ed.) *Dictionary of Anthropology*, Oxford, Cambridge MA: Blackwell, pp.412–413.

Kuper, A. (1988) *The Invention of Primitive Society: Transformations of an Illusion*, London and New York: Routledge.

Langham, I. (1981) *The Building of British Social Anthropology: W.H.R. Rivers and his Cambridge Disciples in the Development of Kinship Studies, 1898–1931*, Dordrecht, Boston and London: Reidel.

Lonergan, D. (1991a) 'Codringon, R. H.', in C. Winter, pp.116–117.

——(1991b) 'Haddon, A.C.' in C. Winter, pp.260–261.

——(1991c) 'Hunt, G.' in C. Winter, pp.317–318.

——(1991d) 'Seligman, C.G.' in C. Winter, pp.629–630.

Marett, R.R. and Penniman, T.K. (eds) (1931, 1979) *Spencer's Last Journey*, New York: AMS Press.

——(1932) *Spencer's Scientific Correspondence*, Oxford University Press.

Mauss, M. (1923) 'W.H.R. Rivers', in *Oeuvres*, Paris, Minuit, vol.3: 465–472.

Michaelson, S. (1996) 'Ely Parker and Amerindian voices in ethnography', *American Literary History*, 8(4): 618–638.

Moore, D. (1984) *The Torres Strait Collections of A. C. Haddon*, London: British Museum Press.

Mulvaney, D.J. (1991) 'Spencer, W.B.', in C. Winter, pp.653–654.

Mulvaney, D.J. and Calaby, J.H. (1985) *So Much That is New: Baldwin Spencer (1860–1929), a Biography*, Melbourne University Press.

Mulvaney, J., Morphy, J. H. and Petch, A. (eds) (1997) ' *"My Dear Spencer": The Letters of F.J. Gillen to Baldwin Spencer'*, South Melbourne: Hyland House.

Nimuendajú, C.U. (1914) 'Die Sagen von der Erschaffung und Vernichtung der Welt als Grundlagen der Religion der Apapocuva-Guaraní', *Zeitschrift für Ethnologie*, 46: 284–403.

——(1939, 1967) *The Apinayé*, trans. Lowie, Oosterhout: Anthropological Pub.

——(1942, 1979) *The Serénte*, trans. Lowie, New York: AMS Press.

——(1946) *The Eastern Timbira*, trans. Lowie, Berkeley: University of California Press.

——(1952) *The Tukuna*, trans. Lowie, Berkeley: University of California Publications in American Archaeology and Ethnology.

Nimuendajú, C.U. and Lowie, R. (1937) 'The dual organization of the Rambókamekra (Canella) of Northern Brazil, Menasha', *AA*, 39: 635–582.

Parker, A.C. (1919) *The Life of General Ely S. Parker, Last grand sachem of the Iroquos and General Grant's military secretary*, New York: Buffalo Historical Society.

Pereira, N. (1946) *Curt Nimuendajú sintesa de uma vida e de uma obra*, Belém: Para.

Perry, R. J. (1978) *'Radcliffe-Brown and Kropotkin: the heritage of anarchism in British social anthropology'*, Berkeley, Kroeber Anthropological Society Papers, no.51 and 52.

Petch, A. (1996) *Correspondence between the Anthropologists F.J. Gillen and W. Baldwin Spencer*, University of Oxford, Pitt Rivers Museum.

Poignant, R. (1996) 'Royal Anthropological Institute', in Levinson and Ember, pp.1124–1125.

Pulman, B. (1989) 'Aux origines du débat anthropologie et psychanalyse, Seligman (1873–1940)', *Gradhiva*, 6: 35–50.

——(1990) 'Introduction' to 'Anthropologue et missionnaire avant la rupture: Une conférence de W.H.R. Rivers', *Gradhiva*, no.7: 73–87.

——(1991) 'Seligman, Charles Gabriel', in P. Bonte and M. Izard (eds) *Dictionnaire de l'ethnologie et de l'anthropologie*, Paris: Presses universitaires de France, p. 660.

Quiggin, A.H. (1942) *Haddon, the Headhunter: A Short Sketch of the Life of A.C. Haddon*, Cambridge University Press.

Quiggin, A.H. and Fegan, E.S. (1940) 'A.C. Haddon, 1855–1940', *Man*, 40: 97–100.

Riese, B. (1991) 'Nimuendajú, Curt' in C. Winter, pp.507–508.

Rivers, W.H.R. (1910, 1914) *The History of Melanesian Society*, 2 vols, Cambridge: Cambridge University Press.

——(1968, 1914), *Kinship and Social Organisation*, London: Athlone Press.

——(1922a) *History and Ethnology*, London: Society for Promoting Christian Knowledge.

——(ed.) (1922b, 1972) *Essays in the Depopulation of Melanesia*, New York: AMS Press.

——(1922c) *Instinct and Unconscious*, a contribution to a biological theory of the psycho-neuroses, Cambridge: Cambridge University Press.

——(1926) *Psychology and Ethnology*, London: Routledge and Kegan Paul.

Seligman, C.G. (1930, 1960) *Races of Africa*, London: Oxford University Press.

——(1934) *Egypt and Negro Africa: A Study in Divine Kingship*, London: Routledge.

Seligman, C.G. and Seligman, B.Z. (1932), *Pagna Tribes of the Nilotic Sudan*, London: Routledge.

Sentinella, C.L. (ed.) (1975) *Mikloucho-Maclay: New-Guinea Diaries, 1871–1883*, Madang, PNG: Kristen Press.

Slobodin, R. (1978) *W.H.R. Rivers*, New York: Columbia University Press.

——(1991) 'Rivers, W.H.R.' in C. Winter, pp.283–284.

Stern, B. (1930) 'Selections from the letters of Lorimer Fison and A.W. Howitt to L.H. Morgan', *AA*, 32: 257–279; 419–453.

Stocking, G.W. (1983) 'The ethnographer's magic: fieldwork in British Anthropology from Tylor to Malinowski', in Stocking *Observers Observed: Essays on Ethnographic Fieldwork*, *HOA*, 1: pp.70–121.

——(1992) 'Maclay, Kubary, Malinowski: archetypes from the dreamtime of anthropology' in G.W. Stocking, *The Ethnographer's Magic and Other Essays in the History of Anthropology*, Madison: University of Wisconsin Press, pp. 212–276.

——(1995) *After Tylor: British Social Anthropology, 1888–1951*, Madison: University of Wisconsin Press.

Tippett, A.R. (1983a) 'L. Fison: his place in the history of the Church in the Pacific', *Church History*, Sydney, 3: 1–30; 122–48.

——(1983b) 'L. Fison: inventory of material known to exist', *Church History*, Sydney, 3: 149–181.

Tumarkin, D. (1982) 'Miklouho-Maclay: nineteenth century Russian anthropologist and humanist', *RAIN*, 51: 4–7.

——(1988) 'Miklouho-Maclay: A great Russian scholar and humanist', Moscow Academy: *Social Sciences*, 19: 175–189.

Tumarkin, D. (ed.) (1982) *N. Miklouho-Maclay's Travels to New Guinea: Diaries, Letters, Documents*, Moscow: Science Academy.

Urry, J. (1993) *Before Social Anthropology: Essays on the History of British Anthropology*, Chur, Switzerland: Harwood Academic Publishers.

Walker, A.R. (1986) *The Toda of South India: A New Look*, Delhi: Hindustan Pub.

Webster, E.M. (1984) *The Moon Man : A Biography of Nikolai Miklouho-Maclay*, Berkeley: University of California Press.

III

The turn of the century

The diffusionist schools

Diffusionism holds that the phenomenon of diffusion of cultural elements forms the principle by which civilizations develop. Inspired by museological techniques for the classification of artefacts and the analysis of stylistic affinities, diffusionist methods acquired definition in Germany at the beginning of the twentieth century and won a large following in the USA and Great Britain after the First World War. In this way the label 'diffusionism' came to be applied to three principal currents of thought, each corresponding to a 'national' tradition. The first, German tradition, known as *Kulturgeschichte* (cultural history), was conceived by its adherents as a discipline unto itself, and the Cologne geographer F. **Graebner** is considered to be its founder. The second, American tradition was initiated in part by **Boas** and took the form of historical particularism, and it was practised by, among others, the first generation of Boas's students. American diffusionism, typified by the work of. C. **Wissler**, was moderate and had geographically limited ambitions. The third, British tradition led to the movement's climax in the hyperdiffusionism of G. E. **Smith** and W. J. **Perry**. Using various types of evidence these writers tried to prove that the origin of all cultures was to be found in ancient Egypt, whereas until then neither evolutionary theory nor visions of the psychic unity of mankind could account for where and when it happened.

For all their extreme diversity, diffusionists shared one common position. From the turn of the twentieth century it was clear that the ethnographical data accumulated were too contradictory to permit the view of unilinear evolution to be coherently maintained. What diffusionists would call 'cultural traits' already existed in evolutionist terms as 'survivals', although these were far rarer (for they involved explaining phenomena which seemed strange to the Western mind: teknonymy, the levirate, kinship nomenclature, etc.) and were isolated from their contexts (as relics and testimonies of earlier times).

Those who identified errors in evolutionist schemata were then faced with the problem of how to organize and present ethnographical data in a more apt manner. If the final version of **Frazer**'s *Golden Bough* now makes for rather embarrassing reading, it is less because of its thesis of the spiritual evolution of mankind or its factual errors than because it gives the impression of an immense list of exotic curiosities grouped under various headings (e.g. sixty consecutive pages are devoted to examples of naming taboos and dozens of pages to examples of sympathetic magic). The evolutionist argument is but a tenuous thread linking one chapter to the next, and the question with which the work opens is a mere pretext for the following twelve volumes. It is not raised again until the last chapter of the work, where it is treated in a few short lines.

The new findings of the diffusionists were located at the nexus of three factors: the cultural trait, the complex culture area or circle, and the cultural centre. Their use of these concepts permitted diffusionists to account for the entirety of ethnographical information by addressing a new problematics (that of diffusion). The ablest of them could thus conceive of a 'proliferating' history which did not ignore involutions and seeming discrepancies (for example among technical phenomena themselves or between technical and social phenomena).

In speaking of the passage from evolutionism to diffusionism, one must make mention of the enormous progress made by linguistics, archaeology and physical anthropology. But the tide of new information they provided was not all beneficial. The findings of linguistics and archaeology gave spurious authority to hare-brained fancies based on homophonies and homologies. As for physical anthropology, its use of measuring instruments (taken farthest by the Frenchman Paul Broca) in combination with the notion of averages opened the way for a determination of racial types based on scientific methods. The lowest point was reached in the associations made between race, language and culture. The American Boas must be given credit for delivering anthropology from a fatal temptation by demonstrating the separateness of these categories throughout his work, and a similar effect was achieved by Durkheim's creation of a 'primitive sociology' from which physical anthropology was banished.

GERMAN SCHOLARS AND THE *KULTURKREIS*

Ethnology and anthropology in German-speaking countries were divided between *Volkskunde* (science of the nation), initially dedicated to the study of Germanic cultures and inseparable from the rise of nationalism, and the exotically connoted *Völkerkunde* (science of nations), which was associated from its origins with the diffusionist tradition and contained a significant element of geography. **Herder** (1744–1803) is generally considered the father of *Volkskunde* and Alexander von **Humboldt** (1769–1859) the father of *Völkerkunde*. For reasons explained in the preface, we shall consider only the latter discipline. In 1868 A. **Bastian** transformed the ethnology department of the Berlin Museum of Antiquities into a Museum of Ethnology; in 1869 the city of Leipzig endowed a *Kulturhistorische Sammlung*; in 1874 a Museum of Anthropology and Ethnography opened in Dresden; Hamburg followed suit in 1877; and at the turn of the century Willy Foy (1873–1929) opened the Museum of Cologne. Lastly, in Vienna a department of anthropology and ethnology was created as part of the Museum of Natural History in 1884. From the moment they opened all these institutions became bases for research activity which went far beyond the study of artefacts. It was Bastian who established *Völkerkunde* as an academic discipline, and B. Ankermann (1859–1943) and above all **Graebner** who gave currency to the idea of the *Kulturkreis*. A specifically 'national' feature, as **Dostal** and Gingrich have noted, was that 'evolutionism did not play any significant role in late nineteenth-century German-speaking anthropology' (Dostal and Gingrich, 1996: 264). There is no doubt that the *Museum für Völkerkunde* in Berlin was Germany's most active centre of anthropological research until Nazi rule, and it sent a large number of missions into exotic regions. Important figures who worked at this museum include the Americanist E. Seler (1849–1922) from 1844 until his death; the Americanist and then Oceanian K. von **Steinen** (1855–1929) from 1890; Graebner from 1899 to 1906; Ankermann (1859–1943) until the end of his life; K. T. **Preuß** (1869–1938) from 1895 until his death; W. Lehmann (1878–1939) from 1903 to 1909; W. Krickeberg (1885–1963) from 1906 until his retirement; **Baumann** from 1921 to 1938; E. Brauer (1895–1942) until he fled to Palestine; and

Leonhard **Adam** (1891–1960). Meanwhile, at the University of Berlin, Felix von Luschan (1854–1924) occupied the anthropology chair from 1909 to 1922, and the ex-missionary Westermarck taught from 1908 in the Seminar for Oriental Languages and in 1925 obtained the chair in African languages and cultures. The Africanist and linguist Carl Meinhof (1857–1944) was offered the post of *Ordentlicher Professor* when the University of Hamburg was established in 1919. At the Museum of Cologne J. E. Lips (1895–1950) worked as Graebner's assistant and then succeeded him in 1928. He also created an anthropology department at the University of Cologne in 1927 and was appointed professor there in 1930. A member of the Social Democratic Party, Lips fled to the USA in 1934.

Ratzel, Friedrich (1844–1904)

Born in Karlsruhe, Friedrich Ratzel studied zoology and geography and then became the American correspondent of the *Kölnische Zeitung* (a Cologne daily), visiting the USA, Cuba and Mexico. From 1875 he taught in the sciences faculty of the University of Munich, where he was appointed professor in 1880, and then at the University of Leipzig between 1886 and 1904. His best-known work is *Völkerkunde*, published in three and subsequently two volumes (1885, 1886, 1888, new edition 1894–1895), which first appeared in English translation in 1896. Although more than one of its volumes is taken up with descriptions of races and sub-races, Ratzel does maintain the thesis of a unity of the human race, with each different type seen as more or less dependent on its natural environment. However, certain types (the *Kulturvölker*) have emancipated themselves from nature more than others (the *Naturvölker*). Ratzel conceives the history of mankind in terms of his theory, already present in his *Anthropogeographie* (1882), of an evolution from the monogamous family attached to a plot of land via the polygamous family to the clan and then the state. His contribution to anthropology has been well summarized by **Lowie** (1937: 123) in three major points: first, he offered the earliest complete delineation of the geographical distribution of different peoples; second, although he did not invent the principle of diffusion (already used by **Tylor** and **Pitt-Rivers**), he provided a theory for it; and third, a strong environmentalist, he advanced moderate propositions on the subject of determinism rather than exaggerating its weight.

Ratzel's theory can be summed up in two principles: first, the world is a small place; and second, the same places have been passed through many times, causing repeated cultural diffusion. In this way the spatial distribution of similar material elements of culture can be explained in terms of previous migration from a few centres. Ratzel examines in diffusionist terms the distribution of artefacts of material culture (for example the bow and arrow in Africa) and deduces from this a *Formkriterium* (a formal type allowing comparison). Other aspects of his work admit of more unfortunate interpretations. Nations and states possess a sum of 'energy for living' (*Lebensenergie*) determined by type (especially maritime or continental), and are born, grow old and die in a 'living space' (*Lebensraum*). The task of the geographer and politician is to discover the laws governing these developments and to acquire a sense of space (*Raumsinn*). While it is easy to imagine what became of such ideas, it would however be wrong to conclude that Ratzel had a racist cast of mind. It would be more accurate to see in him a German with a romantic longing for the expanses of American and Chinese territory awaiting colonization (*Die chinesische Auswanderung*, 1876). From *Anthropogeographie* (1882) onwards he asserts that contemporary peoples are all products of intermixing and that this promotes progress. Thus he held that the exploitation of territories bordering Hudson Bay was made possible by the union of European trappers and Amerindian peoples, and the same could be said for humid zones of the union of Amerindians and Black slaves.

Frobenius, Leo Viktor (1873–1938)
Born in Berlin as the son of an officer, Leo Viktor Frobenius worked in an export business in Bremen and at the same time read **Bastian** and **Ratzel**. In 1893 he was made an assistant in Bremen's Municipal Museum of Trades and Primitive Peoples, and then moved to Leipzig to study with Ratzel. To the maps designed by Ratzel showing the distribution of types of bow, Frobenius added details of other material items (shields, projectiles, musical instruments, etc.) which could be viewed in terms of quantity, and this led him to propose the concept of the *Kulturkreis*. He made use of the enormous quantities of data he had assembled in *Die Masken und Geheimbünde Afrikas* (1898) [trans. *The Voice of Africa*, 2 vols, 1968] and *The Origin of African Civilizations* (Washington, Smithsonian Report for 1898) [extended trans. of *Der Ursprung der afrikanischen Kulturen*, 1899–1901]. He scraped together enough money to finance an expedition to the Yoruba region only to see the British occupy the kingdom of Benin and remove its bronze sculptures (1898). With a small sum granted by the Museum of Hamburg he undertook his first mission to the Congo, bringing home eight thousand artefacts. On the strength of this success Frobenius organized another expedition, supported this time by the Museum of Hamburg, the Museum of Leipzig and the Ministry of the Colonies, and this was followed by a series of further missions to Africa up to 1916. His research was then interrupted by the war, but he resumed it between 1925 and 1933, travelling to North, East and West Africa. During his excavation of a site in Nigeria in 1910, he discovered statuettes of polished stone, terracotta and bronze which reminded him of Hellenistic sculptures. These discoveries led him to make connections between African civilizations and the Mediterranean. He also brought to light the rupestrian paintings of the Bushmen. Frobenius used the wide range of material he had catalogued as the basis for the Institute of Cultural Morphology, which he founded in Munich in 1922 and then transferred to the University of Frankfurt in 1925 (it became the Frobenius Institute after his death). From 1925 he taught at Frankfurt, eventually gaining a professorship in 1932. In 1934 he founded the Ethnographical Museum of Frankfurt and a journal entitled *Paideuma*. He died in 1938 in Biganzolo (Italy).

Frobenius took up Spengler's idea that both natural and cultural processes are isomorphic, each being constituted of birth, life and death. Like biological organisms, cultures pass through a cycle which determines their successive stages, from infancy to maturity and thence to decline. In this way they resemble organisms, living through a *Paideuma* (soul) which animates each of their limbs and gives meaning to their working. He gives this theory its fullest formulation in *The Destiny of Civilizations* (Munich, 1924). Frobenius wrote an immense amount, and some of his work still awaits publication. He was also the first to divide Africa into four culture areas.

Graebner, Robert Fritz (1877–1934)
Born in Berlin, Robert Fritz Graebner studied history, found work as an assistant curator in the Royal Ethnological Museum of Berlin in 1899, and in 1901 defended his thesis. He was employed by the museum to compile a catalogue of its collections, and his observation of similarities between items was inspired by the technique of **Ratzel**. In a lecture given to the Berlin Society of Anthropology, Ethnology and

Prehistory in 1904, he proposed the notion of *Kulturkreislehre*, already used by Frobenius in 1898, to designate the way small islands of original culture generated complex cultural units by means of diffusion. In so doing he used three criteria: form (independent of matter or function), quantity and continuity (the distance through which an object has been diffused). From 1907 he worked in the Museum of Cologne, which had opened in 1906, where he founded the journal *Ethnologica*. In 1911 his postdoctoral thesis was accepted and he published *Methode der Ethnologie*, the bible of German diffusionism. In this work he rejects any attempt to determine the source and diffusion of a single object, and instead of this approach he posits the constitution of a *Kulturkreis* (culture circle) comprising a whole set of associated elements (e.g. Polynesia, head restraint and scraper), and this became the central concept of the Viennese school. Borrowing is never automatic, and some societies are more apt to borrow than others, operating selectively and often modifying the object borrowed to the extent that it is unrecognizable. But the elementary prudence of this theory, deriving from the conviction that human beings have little capacity for invention, did not prevent Graebner indulging in some rather fanciful notions. One such was his refusal to accept the idea that the civilizations of Mexico and Peru originated separately, and another was his connection between the so-called 'bow' culture of Melanesia and that of Neolithic Central Europe on the grounds that both featured houses built on piles, rectangular plots of land, the same sorts of pottery, and finally identically shaped spoon handles and axes (Graebner, 1923: 464). Like **Malinowski** and others, Graebner was in Australia attending the International Congress of Anthropological Sciences when war broke out in the summer of 1914. Graebner was the only scholar to be kept in semi-captivity for five years for having concealed certain documents. On his return to Germany he taught at the University of Bonn, becoming a professor there in 1921 and director of the Museum of Cologne in 1925. He ceased working after suffering a heart attack in 1928.

THE VIENNA SCHOOL OF CULTURAL-HISTORICAL ETHNOLOGY

The peculiarity of the ethnological tradition of Austria is that the country never possessed colonies, and that research was instead stimulated by missions undertaken to enrich the collections of the royal family. In 1884 the Museum of Ethnography (*Völkerkunde-museum*) was opened in Vienna, acquiring its own building in 1920 (see Museologists and Evolutionists, pp. 5–8), and it owed much of its collection to voyagers such as A. Bernatzik.

In 1892 Michael Haberlandt (1860–1940), an assistant curator in the anthropology and ethnography department of the museum, was appointed as a *Privatdozent* in ethnography at the University of Vienna. He was joined in 1901 by the Africanist and Orientalist Wilhelm Hein (1861–1903). Rudolf Pöch (1870–1921), a physician who gained a postdoctoral degree in anthropology and ethnology in 1910, was appointed in 1913 to the first chair in the discipline, which still incorporated both physical anthropology and ethnology. Otto Reche succeeded Pöch after his death.

The year 1870 saw the founding of the journal *Mitteilungen der Anthropologischen Gesellschaft in Wien* (see Ch. 1, Origins and Forerunners pp. 1–4). In 1875 the Missionary

Society of the Divine Word (*Societas Verbi Divini* – SVD) was founded in the Austrian Tyrol by the Salesian Fathers. Father Wilhelm **Schmidt**, who in 1895 was appointed professor in the St Gabriel of Mödling Seminary near Vienna, gave a strong impetus to ethnographical studies accompanying religious proselytization, and in 1906 he founded the journal *Anthropos: Internationale Zeitschrift für Völker- und Sprachenkunde*. He taught linguistics at the University of Vienna from 1900 and ethnology from 1912, and in 1921 was made a *Privatdozent*. The focus provided by Father Schmidt and *Anthropos*, and by the concepts of the *Kulturkreis* and *Kulturkreislehre*, inspired such missionaries and anthropologists as Fathers **Gusinde**, **Koppers** and **Schebesta**. Soon one could speak of a Viennese school of ethnology (*Wiener Schule*). A major symposium on totemism held in 1914 allowed this new school to demonstrate its international credentials (with contributions by F. **Boas**, W. R. **Rivers**, J. **Swanton** and others).

Koppers was appointed *Dozent* at the University of Vienna in 1928 and occupied the first chair devoted entirely to ethnology. In 1929 an Institute of Ethnology (*Institut für Völkerkunde*) was installed in the Hofburg (imperial palace) close to the Museum of Ethnology, with Koppers as its director. Schmidt taught there while keeping his professorship at the SVD's seminary of St Gabriel. With the *Anschluss* (1938) and the war, the institute remained in Vienna but the journal *Anthropos* and its contributors (including Father Schmidt) took refuge in Switzerland, while **Heine-Geldern**, another important diffusionist, chose exile in the USA.

Father Schmidt took up the notion of *Kulturkreise* but considerably modified the methods associated with it (particularly as regards the criteria held to be relevant), and with the agreement of Koppers made the *Kulturkreislehre* the foundation of the Viennese school. The school's aim was to bring to light a cultural history of societies without writing, using not regional histories but *Kulturkreise* (culture circles), and allowing a relational chronology to be established on the assumption that such societies were constituted in large part from elements borrowed from other cultures. One of the dominant features of the school was its bias against **Morgan**'s evolutionism, which it considered too materialistic.

Schmidt, Wilhelm, Father (1868–1954)
Born in Hörde in Westphalia, Wilhelm Schmidt joined the Society of the Divine Word (*Societas Verbi Divini* – SVD) in 1883 and was ordained in 1892. Between 1893 and 1895 he studied Semitic languages at the University of Berlin and was then appointed professor at the St Gabriel of Mödling Seminary near Vienna. He became a member of the Anthropological Society of Vienna and published in *Mitteilungen der Anthropologischen Gesellschaft in Wien*, making a name for himself from 1899 with his work on Austronesian languages. Working with the testimonies of travellers, missionaries and anthropologists, and carrying forward the work of **Graebner**, Schmidt attempted to reconstruct 'original civilizations', or *Urkulturen* in **Herder**'s term. The non-specializing hunter–gatherers of the *Urkultur* supposedly spread from specific geographical centres (*Kulturkreise*), dividing themselves as they did so into primary circles with specialized features, such as hunter–fishermen, either totemic or exogamous, patrilineal nomadic herdsmen and exogamous matrilineal cultivators. These primary circles then split again into secondary circles which combined features of these different groups. Schmidt's major work is *Der Ursprung der Gottesidee* [The Origin of the Idea of God] (Münster, 12 volumes published between 1912 and 1955), which studies the genesis of the idea of the divine

and provides a description of religious images. In making and analysing connections between religions, and in his examination of ethnographical data, particularly relating to the Pygmies, Australians and other hunter–gatherers, Schmidt sought to demonstrate the universality of the idea of the divine and a primordial monotheism (*Urmonotheismus*). This explains why he first sent researchers (**Schebesta**, **Koppers**, **Gusinde**) to societies belonging to primitive *Kulturkreise*. He conjectured that monotheism degenerated in the hands of nomadic priests and then disappeared. Schmidt taught at the University of Vienna from 1910 and became a *Privatdozent* there in 1921. His first courses were entitled: 'The early development of society (marriage, family, clan state, cultural groups)', and 'Introduction to the history and method of ethnology' (Henninger, 1956: 36). The main founder of the Viennese ethnological school, Schmidt in 1906 also established the journal *Anthropos*, which was largely sustained with texts written by missionaries of various nationalities whose active collaboration had been sought (Le Roy, 1906: 10). He founded the *Anthropos-Institut* at St Augustin near Bonn in 1932, and directed the Lateran Papal Ethnology Museum between 1927 and 1939. Although mildly anti-Semitic himself, he took refuge in Switzerland when the Nazis seized power in Austria in 1938 (Conte and Essner, 1995), becoming a professor at the University of Fribourg in 1941. He gave up his directorship of the *Anthropos-Institut* in 1950 and died in Fribourg in 1954.

Koppers, Wilhelm, Father (1886–1961)

Born in Menzeln in Germany, Wilhelm Koppers studied at the Salesian Institute of St Gabriel of Mödling near Vienna. He was an ordained priest when he joined the journal *Anthropos* in 1913, and after gaining a doctorate in 1921 he became its editor-in-chief in 1923. He carried out investigations amongst the Fuegians in 1921–1922 (1924)

(according to **Schmidt** the Fuegians, together with the Pygmies, represented the least deformed 'original cultures'), and then with Schmidt co-authored *Völker und Kulturen* (Regensburg), the bible of the Viennese school. From 1924 Koppers taught at the University of Vienna, was made a *Dozent* in 1928 and director of the Institute of Ethnology on its foundation in 1929. Koppers was alone among German-speaking anthropologists in attacking Nazi precepts, most notably in an article of 1935 in which he criticizes the idea that the Indo-Germanic race originated in the north and shows how it in fact migrated from the east, particularly from Turkey. He lost his post in 1938 and travelled among the Bhil in India (*Die Bhil in Zentralindien*, Vienna, 1948). In 1940 he joined the *Anthropos-Institut* based in Fribourg (Switzerland), and after the war directed the Ethnological Institute of the University of Vienna (*Institut für Völkerkunde*) until his retirement in 1957, providing it with vigorous impetus but also recognizing the failure of the *Kulturkreislehre* project. He was the supervisor of **Kluckhohn**'s thesis (Fuchs, 1991: 360).

Gusinde, Martin, Father (1886–1969)

Born in Breslau, Martin Gusinde was sent by the SVD as missionary and teacher to Santiago in Chile in 1912. He completed four journeys to Tierra del Fuego (1918–1924), and is rumoured to have been initiated during the second of these. On his return to Europe in 1924 **Koppers** took him to the International African Congress at the Hague and then encouraged him to submit his thesis, entitled 'Einige Resultate meiner Expeditionen durch das Feuerland' (1924). He worked in Rome and then became **Schmidt**'s assistant. With **Lowie**'s support he was invited to the USA in 1928 and visited the American Indian reserves. He then successfully defended his postdoctoral thesis 'Ethnologie der Naturvölker Amerikas' in 1930. From 1949 he was visiting professor at the Catholic University of Washington. He is best remembered as an ethnologist of the Selknam, the Alakaluf and the Yamana, of which only about two hundred remained at the time of his visits to Tierra del Fuego.

Schebesta, Paul Joachim, Father (1887–1967)

Born at Peterwitz in Germany, Paul Joachim Schebesta studied at the Salesian Institute of St Gabriel of Mödling near Vienna. He was ordained a priest in 1911 and sent as a missionary to Mozambique, where he carried out ethnographic and linguistic investigations, submitting his results to the journal *Anthropos* (1919). He formally joined the Viennese school in 1918, acted as the guiding force behind *Anthropos* between 1920 and 1923, and gained a doctorate in 1926.

After a period with the Mbuti Pygmies on his first African visit, he conducted research among the Semang of Malaysia to test a number of historical and cultural hypotheses (1924–1925, 1939), and then returned to the Pygmies (1929–1930, 1934–1935), visited the Negritos of the Philippines (1938–1939) before returning again to the Pygmies (1949–1950, 1954–1956). Schebesta produced some rather speculative theoretical models which sought to determine the most ancient *Kulturkreise* and, above all, to show that an original monotheism degenerated into polytheism, but more importantly he became the foremost specialist on the hunter–gatherer populations he studied, submitting them to ethnographic and above all to linguistic study for the first time. He taught at both St Gabriel of Mödling and the University of Vienna.

THE BRITISH: DIFFUSIONISM AND HYPERDIFFUSIONISM EVOLUTIONISM AND DIFFUSIONISM

Marett, Robert Ranulph (1866–1943)

Born on Jersey, Robert Ranulph Marett studied law at Oxford University and joined the Jersey Bar in 1891, but gave this up in favour of a teaching post offered to him in the same year by Exeter College, Oxford. Initially he specialized in moral philosophy, but after early work on primitive morality his interest turned to the study of religion and magic. He became a disciple of **Tylor**, whose theories on the origins of religions he developed (*The Threshold of Religion*, 1909), while also reproaching both him and Lang for the assumption of reflectiveness in their theory of the origins of religious feeling. For Marett, a savage reflecting on the nature of dreams, doubles and hallucinatory experiences was harder to imagine than one who was subject to immediate, non-intellectualized fears of particular phenomena. Hence he constructed a theory, which he called Pranimism, that the origins of

religion were in physiological and emotional experiences (such as instinctive horror and violent passion). He made great play of the notion of *Mana* as a force, and this allowed him to put forward a minimal definition of religious sentiment. In 1909 Marett founded the Anthropological Society of Oxford, and in 1910 succeeded Tylor as a reader at Oxford University. Between 1912 and 1915 he devoted himself to archaeology and gained a science doctorate in 1913, after which he became rector of Exeter College.

Hocart, Arthur Maurice (1883–1939)

Born near Brussels as the son of a pastor, Arthur Maurice Hocart read history from 1902 to 1906 at Exeter College, Oxford, where he was a fellow student of **Evans-Pritchard**, and then briefly studied philosophy and psychology at the University of Berlin. In 1908–1909 he took part in the mission to the Solomon Islands led by P. S. Trust, assisted by W. **Rivers**. Thanks to **Haddon**'s support, he became a headmaster in the Lau Islands in Fiji from 1909 to 1912. In 1912 a bursary from Oxford University enabled him to concentrate on ethnography and carry out research in Fiji, Wallis, Samoa and Tonga. He returned to Oxford in 1914, but it was not until after the war that he had the opportunity to study languages (Sanskrit, Tamil, Pali). Between 1915 and 1919 he served in the light infantry. In 1921 he was appointed director of the British Archaeological Mission to Ceylon, concentrating particularly on restoration. He returned to England for health reasons in 1928 and married his nurse E. Graham Hearn in 1930. He taught at University College London as a colleague of **Smith** and **Perry** in 1932–1934, and then succeeded Evans-Pritchard in the chair of sociology at the University of Cairo, where he died of an infection contracted in Upper Egypt in 1939.

Hocart produced five books among almost two hundred publications. The essential characteristic of his work was its reconstruction of the history of culture and social institutions using the methods of **Tylor** and **Frazer**, despite the fact such approaches had been abandoned by the current and even part of the previous generation (Rivers or **Seligman**). Almost fifteen years after the publication of **Malinowski**'s *The Argonauts* in 1922, Hocart produced *Kings and Councillors* (1936), which is doubtless his best-known work. Completely original, this contribution sought the origins of the state in rituals of life and fertility, for 'it is clear that the king's *raison d'être* is not to coordinate, but to be head of the ritual' (Hocart, 1970 (1936): 137). He held that towns emerged not for defensive or commercial reasons, as authors like H. Pirenne had suggested, but as centres of cults and divine worship. Institutions were then established free of any deliberate intention (Hocart, 1970 (1936): 299). If Hocart's style is rather unaccommodating (particularly the way he overloads his writing with examples), his texts are nonetheless enriched by the innumerable reflections he weaves into them.

HYPERDIFFUSIONISM

The beginnings of hyperdiffusionism can be dated from 1911. In this year Elliot **Smith** published *Ancient Egyptians and their Influence upon the Civilization of Europe* (London), in which he asserted that the discovery of copper spread from Egypt around the world, and with it a megalithic Egyptian culture was disseminated to the Atlantic and Mediterranean seaboards. He reiterated this argument at the Congress of the British Association and broadened it to take in Asiatic, American and Oceanian monuments. At the same time **Rivers** announced his own conversion to ethnology, which at the time was synonymous with diffusionism. While the London School of Economics became the centre for **Seligman** and for the functionalism of **Malinowski**, University College London became the home of hyperdiffusionism with the appointments of Elliot Smith in 1919 and W. J. **Perry** in 1924. At the beginning of the 1920s, hyperdiffusionism enjoyed great popular acclaim bolstered by a succession of archaeological discoveries. As Kuklick notes, it is significant that 'the *Encyclopaedia Britannica* commissioned Elliot Smith to write the article on anthropology for its 1922 volumes; the author of the entry in the 1910 edition had been E. B. **Tylor**, and Bronislaw Malinowski would be selected in 1926' (Kuklick, 1991: 130). However, although Rivers made it known in 1915 that he was a supporter of heliolithic theory (**Stocking**, 1995: 213), nonetheless 'the president of the Royal Anthropological Institute had a difficult time preventing Elliot Smith's resignation in 1922 as a protest against alleged censorship of his ideas' (Kuper, 1973: 4), and when in 1927 the Rockefeller Foundation decided not to give Elliot Smith additional funds for anthropological research, one could say that the scholarly community saw functionalism as the only truly scientific form of anthropology (Kuklick, 1991: 211).

Smith, Sir Grafton Elliot (1871–1937)

Born in Grafton (Australia), G. E. Smith studied medicine at Sydney, where he became an assistant anatomist and published a number of articles on the neurology of marsupials. In 1896 he moved to London and then worked in a physiology laboratory at Cambridge University. In 1900 he was offered the first chair in anatomy at the University of Cairo. He returned to England in 1909 as professor at the University of Manchester with a reputation as a world expert on the cerebral evolution of primates (later Raymond Dart would study under him). **Rivers**'s journey to Egypt in 1901 led Elliot Smith towards anthropology by prompting him to study the remains of the ancient Egyptians (Kuklick, 1993 (1991): 128). In 1903 he carried out research into techniques of mummification, and then led an enquiry into the evolution of the physical characteristics of the ancient Egyptians which had to be completed before dozens of burial places disappeared under water as a result of the construction of a dam: this work involved excavating 20,000 tombs. Elliot Smith became the first to X-ray the royal mummies (*The Royal Mummies*, Cairo, 1912), an achievement which gained him wide public recognition. Appointed to the chair of anatomy at the University of Manchester in 1909, he made comparisons of Malay skulls contained in British collections with those of Egyptian mummies, and argued that the practices associated with their deformation were the products of diffusion. In 1911 he published *The Ancient Egyptians and their Influence upon the Civilization of Europe* (London), soon followed by *The Migrations of Early Cultures* (1915), in which he asserts that mummification, encountered in several parts of the world (including among the Papuans of the Torres Straits) is too complex to have been discovered several times, and advances the thesis that Egypt is the source of all cultures. Given man's uninventiveness, only exceptional circumstances could explain such a substantial cultural evolution. The appearance of hybrid forms of wheat on the flood plains of the Nile points to the development of irrigation canals permitting the explosion of Egyptian civilization, which then spread its culture across the world (Smith 1928: 20–31). Originating in Egypt, the heliolithic culture complex, bringing together sun and snake worship, megalithic monuments, the swastika symbol, skull deformations, the practice of tattooing, the divine origin of kings, and the myth of the flood were diffused from the Nile to India, from India to Malaysia, from Malaysia to Oceania, and thence to the Americas. Elliot Smith thus identifies in the existence of Australian totemic clans a degraded and modified form of the adoption of strangers practised by the Egyptians (1928: 25, 67). The skills and customs of 'savage' peoples are similarly held to be decadent relics of those of ancient Egypt. It is interesting, as G. W. **Stocking** points out (1995: 208–212), that well before hyperdiffusionism Egypt had long been the focus of theoretical speculation on the origins of culture. Despite its considerable popular success, Elliot Smith's theory, extreme in its refusal to accept any independent inventions by non-Egyptian cultures, was rejected in its entirety by professional ethnologists. He was appointed professor of anatomy at University College London in 1919.

Perry, William James (1889–1949)
The son of an Anglican clergyman, William James Perry went up to Cambridge University in 1906 to read mathematics, but switched to anthropology after hearing lectures by **Rivers** and **Haddon** (Langham, 1981: 153) and found employment as a teacher in Yorkshire in 1911. He remained in close contact with Rivers, who in 1913 suggested that he work on the distribution of megalithic monuments and sun worship in Indonesia, which was supposed to be a crossing point in the passage of the heliolithic culture complex to Oceania (Stocking, 1995: 214). *The Megalithic Culture of Indonesia* (Manchester) was published in 1918. Perry became the principal propagator of the theses of Elliot **Smith**, and was appointed reader in comparative religion at the University of Manchester, where he developed Elliot Smith's published proposi-

tions on the origins of religion in *The Children of the Sun: A Study in the Early History of Civilization* (1923). Perry's Darwinian and Mendelian argument is that only a particular combination of circumstances, occasioned by the presence of easily exploitable copper resources, the Nile floods and the natural crop of barley, can explain the rapid spread of ancient Egyptian civilization (Kuklick, 1993 (1991): 126). An Asiatic (Armenoid) population, the 'Children of the Sun', then appeared, bringing sun worship with them, and they travelled around the world in search of gold, pearls and other precious objects and thereby spread this civilization across South Asia, North America and the Pacific, where their metal tools always assured them the status of sovereigns. Perry was made a reader in cultural anthropology at University College London in 1924.

SELECT BIBLIOGRAPHY

Anonymous (1991) 'Ratzel, Friedrich', in C. Winter, pp.247–248.

Basinger, H. (1993) *Volkskunde ou l'ethnologie allemande*, Paris: MSH.

Bornemann, F. (1954) 'Wilhelm Schmidt', *Anthropos*, 49: 397–432.

——(1970) 'P.M. Gusinde. Eine biographische Skizze', *Anthropos*, 65: 737–775.

Brandewie, E. (1983) *W. Schmidt and the Origin of the Idea of God*, Lanham: University Press of America.

Breuil, L. and Breuil, H. (1936) *Frobenius*, Paris: Cahiers d'Art.

Burgmann, A. (1961) 'Professor W. Koppers, SVD', *Anthropos*, 56: 721–736.

Buxton, D. (1936) *Custom is King; Essays Presented to R.R. Marett* (articles by Seligman, Rattray, Fortes, Firth, etc.), London: Hutchinson.

Chiva, I. and Jeggle, U. (eds) (1987) *Ethnologies en miroir: la France et les pays de langue allemande*, Paris: Maison des sciences de l'homme.

Conte, E. (1988) 'Le confesseur du dernier Habsbourg et les nouveaux païens allemands. A propos de Wilhelm Schmidt', *Ethnologie Française*, vol.18, no.2: 120–130.

Conte, E. and Essner, C. (1995) *La quête de la Race. Une anthropologie du Nazisme*, Paris: Hachette.

Dawson, W.R. (ed.) (1938) *Sir Grafton Elliot Smith. A Biographical Record by his Colleagues*, London: J. Cape.

Dostal, W. and Gingrich, A. (1996) 'German and Austrian anthropology', in A. Barnard and J. Spencer, *Encyclopedia of Social and Cultural Anthropology*, London: Routledge, pp.262–265.

Dupré, W. (1968) 'Schebesta, P. J.', *AA.*, vol.70: 537–545.

Elkin, A.P. and MacIntosh, N.W.G. (eds) (1974) *Grafton Elliot Smith: The Man and His Work*, Sydney: Sydney University Press.

Evans-Pritchard, E.E. (1939) 'A. M. Hocart', *Man*, 39: 131.

Frobenius, L.V. (1904) *Das Zeitalter des Sonnengottes*, Berlin.

——(1907) *Im Schatten des Kongostaates. Bericht über den Verlauf der ersten Reisen der DJAFR von 1904–1906 und über deren Forschungen und Beobachtungen auf geographischen und kolonialwirtschaftlichem Gebiet*, Berlin.

——(1911) *Auf dem Wege nach Atlantis. Bericht über den Verlauf der Zweiten Reise-Periode der DJAFE in den Jahren 1908–1910*, Berlin.

——(1913) *Und Afrika sprach*, vol.1: *Auf den Trümmern des Klassischen Atlantis*; vol.2: *An der Schwelle des verehrungswürdigen Byzanz*; vol.3: *Unter den unsträflichen Aethiopen*, Berlin.

——(1921) *Paideuma. Umrisse einer Kultur und Seelenlehre*, München.

——(1921–1930) *Atlantis, Volksmärchen und Volkschichtungen Afrikas. ed. by Leo Frobenius*, 10 vols, Nendeln. Kraus Reprint, 1978.

——(1968) *Voice of Africa: being an account of the travels of the German Inner Africa, Expedition in the years 1910–1912*, New York: B. Blon.

——(1973) *L. Frobenius, an anthology*. With a foreword by L. Sédar Senglor. Edited by Eike. Trans. P. Crampton, Wiesbaden: F. Steiner.

Fuchs, S. (1991) 'W. Koppers', in C. Winter, pp.359–360.

Fürer-Haimendorf von, C. (1961) 'W. Koppers, 1886–1961', *Man*, 61: 140.

Galey, J-C. and Vidal, D. (1991) 'Hocart Arthur Maurice', in P. Bonte and M. Izard (eds) *Dictionnaire de l'ethnologie et de l'anthropologie*, Paris: PUF, pp.339–340.

Graebner, F.R. (1905) 'Kulturkreise und Kulturschichten in Ozeanien', *Zeitschrift für Ethnologie*, 37: 28–53.

——(1923) 'Ethnologie' in G. Schwalbe (ed.) *Kultur der Gegenwart*, Leipzig: Part 3, Section 5, pp.435–587.

——(1924) *Das Weltbild der Primitiven*, Munich.

Gusinde, M. (1917) *Publicaciones del Museo de Ethnologia y Anthropologia de Chile*, Santiago de Chile, 1917: vol.1, 1922: vol.2.

——(1924) *Einige Resultate meiner Forschungsreisen durch das Feuerland*, Vienna.

——(1931–1939) *Die Feuerlandindianer*, vol.1: *Die Sehk'nam*, vol.2: *Die Yamaná*, vol.3: *Tafelband*, Mödling: Vienna.

——(1949) *Die Twa-Pygmäen in Ruanda*, Mödling: Vienna.

——(1966a) *Von gelben und schwarzen Buschmännern. Eine untergehende Altkultur im Süden Afrikas*, Graz Akadem: Druck Verlagsanst.

——(1966b) *Verzeichnis von Beiträgen zur Anthropologie und Ethnologie, die in 50-jähriger Forschungsarbeit entstanden sind (1916–1966)*, Mödling: Missionsdruckerei St Gabriel.

Gusinde, M., Koppers, W. and Schebesta, P. (1977) *Sammelbände des Seminars für Ethnologie, ein Registerband*, Mödling: Missionsdruckerei St Gabriel.

——(1961) *The Yamana, the life and thought of the water nomads of Cape Horn*, Trans. F. Schütze, 5 vols, New Haven: Human Relation Area Files.

Haekel, J., Hohenwart-Gerlachstein, A. and Slawik, A. (1956) 'Die Geschichte des Institutes für Völkerkunde' in J. Haekel, A. Hohenwart-Gerlachstein and A. Slawik (HG.) 'Die Wiener Schule für Völkerkunde', *Festschrift zum 25-jähriger Bestand (1929–1954)*, Vienna: Horn, pp.1–6.

Harms, V. (1984) 'Das historische Verhältnis der deutschen Ethnologie zum Kolonialismus', *Zeitschrift für Kulturaustausch*, 34: 401–416.

Heine-Geldern, R. (1964) 'One hundred years of ethnological theory in the German-speaking countries: some milestones', *CA*, 5: 407–418.

Henninger, J. P. (1956) *Wilhelm Schmidt S.V.D., 1868–1954. Eine biographische Skizze*, Freiburg, Switzerland.

——(1961) 'W. Koppers', *Mitteilungen der Anthropologischen Gesellschaft in Wien*, vol.9: 1–14.

——(1987) 'Schmidt, W.', in M. Eliade (ed.) *The Encyclopedia of Religion*, New York.

Hirschberg, W. (ed.) (1988) *Wörterbuch der Völkerkunde*, Berlin: Reimer.

Hocart, A.M. (1927) *Kingship*, Oxford University Press.

——(1929) *The Lau Islands of Fiji*, Honolulu: Bishop Museum.

——(1935, 1933) *Les progrès de l'homme*, Paris: Payot.

——(1936, 1950) *Caste: a Comparative Study*, London: Methuen.

——(1952) *The Northern States of Fiji*, London: Royal Anthropological Institute.

——(1953, 1970), *The Life-giving Myth and other Essays*, Foreword by R. Needham, London: Methuen.

——(1970, 1936), *Kings and Councillors* with intro. by R. Needham, Chicago and London: University of Chicago Press.

Ita, J-M. (1972) 'Leo Frobenius in West African History', *Journal of African History*, 13: 673–688.

Izard, M. (1991) 'Frobenius, L.', in P. Bonte and M. Izard (eds) *Dictionnaire de l'ethnologie et de l'anthropologie*, Paris: PUF, pp.299–300.

Jensen, A.E. (1938) 'V. Frobenius', *Paideuma*, no.2.

Kluckhohn, C. (1936) 'Some reflections on the method and theory of the Kulturkreislehre', *AA*, 38: 157–196.

Koppers, W. (1915/16) 'Die ethnologische Wirtschaftsforschung', *Anthropos*, vol.10–11.

——(1921) *Anfänge des menschlichen Gemeinschaftslebens*, Munich, Gladbach.

——(1924) *Unter die Feuerland-Indianer*, Stuttgart.

——(1929) *Die Religion der Indogermanen*, St Gabriel.

——(1936) *Pferdopfer und Pferdekult der Indogermanen. Eine ethnologisch-religionswissenchaftliche Studie*, Wiener Beiträge, vol.IV.

——(1949) *Der Urmensch und sein Weltbild*, Vienna.

——(1956) 'Professor Pater W. Schmidt SVD. Eine Würdigung', *Anthropos*, vol.51: 61–80.

Korinham, M. (1984) 'Friedrich Ratzel, Karl Haushofer, Politische Ozeanographie', *Hérodote*, no.32.

Kuklick, H. (1991) *The Savage Within. The Social History of British Anthropology 1885–1945*, Cambridge: Cambridge University Press.

Kuper, A. J. (1973, 1996) *Anthropologists and anthropology. The British school, 1922–1972*, London: Routledge.

Langham, I. (1981) *The building of British social anthropology. W.H.R. Rivers and his Cambridge disciples in the development of kinship studies, 1898–1931*, Dordrecht, London: Reidel.

Le Roy, A. (1906) 'Le rôle scientifique des missionnaires', *Anthropos*, vol.1: 3–10.

Leger, R. (1991) 'Schebesta, Paul Joachim', in C. Winter, pp.614–615.

Leser, P. (1977) 'Fritz Graebner: eine Würdigung', *Anthropos*, vol.72: 1–55.

Lips, J. (1935) 'Fritz Graebner', *AA*, 37: 320–326.

Lonergan, D. (1991) 'Marett, R.R.', in C. Winter, pp.455–456.

Lowie, R. (1937) *The History of Ethnological Theory*, New York: Farrar, pp.156–177.

Lupton, C. (1991) 'Smith, Sir Grafton Elliot' in C. Winter, pp.644–645.

Luzbetak, L. (1961) 'Father W. Koppers, SVD', *Anthropological Quarterly*, 34: 164.

Marett, R.R. (1912) *Anthropology*, New York: Holt.

——(1932, 1972) *Faith, Hope and Charity in Primitive Religion*, New York: Blon.

——(1935) *Head, Heart and Hands in Human Evolution*, London: Hutchinson.

——(1936) *Tylor*, New York: J. Wiley.

——(1941) *A Jerseyman at Oxford*, London: Oxford University Press.

Needham, R. (1967) *A Bibliography of A.M. Hocart (1883–1939)*, Oxford: Blackwell.

——(1979), 'A. M. Hocart', in *International Encyclopedia of the Social Sciences*, D.L. Sills (ed.) vol.18: 305–307.

Penniman, T.K. (1944) 'R.R. Marett', *Man*, 44: 33–35.

Perry, W.J. (1923) *The Growth of Civilization*, New York: Dutton.

——(1935, 1973) *The Primordial Ocean : An Introductory Contribution to Social Psychology*, New York: Barnes and Noble.

Pützstück, L. (1991) 'F. Graebner', in C. Winter, pp.247–248.

Rahman, R. 'Fünfzig Jahre "Anthropos"', *Anthropos*, 51: 1–18.

——(1957) 'Vier Pioniere der Völkerkunde: den Paters Paul Arndt, Martin Gusinde, Wilhelm Koppers und Paul Schebesta zum siebzigsten Geburstag', *Anthropos*, 52: 263–276.

Roy, E. (1988) 'Persistence and change in the relationship between anthropology and human geography', *Progress in Human Geography*, 12: 229–262.

Ruel, M.J. (1968) 'Marett, R.R.' in *International Encyclopedia of the Social Sciences*, D.L. Sills (ed.) pp.565–567.

Schebesta, P.J. (1919) 'Eine Bantu-Grammatik aus dem 17. Jahhundert: Arte da Lingua de Cafre', *Anthropos*, 19: 764–787.

——(1924, 1977) *Among Congo Pigmies*, trans. G. Griffin. New York: AMS Press.

——(1938–40) *Die Bambuti-Pygmäen von Ituri*, 4 vols, Brussels: Hayez Imprimerie Royale.

——(1952–57) *Die Negrito Asiens*, 2 vols, Mödling: St. Gabriel Verlag.

——(1961) *Ursprung der Religion*. Berlin: Morus Verlag.

Schmidt, W. (1906) 'Die moderne Ethnologie', in *Anthropos*, 1: 34–163.

——(1911) 'Die kulturhistorische Methode in der Ethnologie', *Anthropos*, 6: 1010–1036.

——(1926) *Die Sprachfamilien und Sprachenkreise der Erde*, Heidelberg: C. Winter.

——(1927) *Rasse und Volk*. Munich: Kösel.

——(1935) 'F. Graebner', *Anthropos*, 30: 203–214.

——(1937, 1973) *The Culture Historical Method of Ethnology. The Scientific Approach to the Radical Question*. Trans. A. Sieber. Westport: Greenwood Press.

——(1946–1949) *Rassen und Völker in Vorgeschichte und Geschichte des Abendlandes*, 3 vols. Luzern, Stocker.

——(1952) *Die tasmanischen Sprachen*, Utrecht: Spectrum.

Smith, G.E. (1915) *The Migrations of Early Culture, a Study of the Significance of the Geographical Distribution of the Practice of Mummification as Evidence of the Migrations of Peoples and the Spread of Certain Customs and Beliefs*, Memoirs and Proceedings, Manchester Literary and Philosophical Society.

——(1919) *The Evolution of the Dragon*. Manchester, London: The University Press and Longmans.

—— (1924a) *Elephant and Ethnologist*, New York: Dutton.

—— (ed.) (1924b) *The Evolution of Man*, Humphrey Milford: London.

—— (1928) *In the Beginning. The Origin of Civilisation*, New York.

—— (1929) *Human History*, New York, Dutton.

Stocking, G. W. (1995) *After Tylor: British Social Anthropology, 1888–1951*, Madison: University of Wisconsin Press.

Straube, H. (1974) 'Frobenius L.', in *International Encyclopedia of the Social Sciences*, Sills (ed.), vol.8: 17–21.

Sylvain, R. (1996) 'L. Frobenius: from Kulturkreis to Kulturmorphologie', *Anthropos*, 91: 483–494.

Vajda, L. (1973) 'Leo Frobenius heute', *Zeitschrift fur Ethnologie*, 98: 19–29.

—— (1991) 'Frobenius, Leo', in C. Winter, pp.220–221.

Vorbichler, A. (1967) 'Prof. Dr. P. Schebesta, SVD', *Anthropos*, 62: 665–685.

—— (1983) 'Schebesta, Paul', in H. Jungraithmayr and W.J.G. Möhlig (eds) *Lexikon der Afrikanistik*, Berlin, pp.208–209.

Vorbichler, A. and Dupré, W. (1963) 'Vorwort' in *Festschrift P. J. Schebesta zum 75. Geburtstag*, Vienna: Mödling.

Wingate, T. (1937) 'The scientific influence of Sir Grafton Elliot Smith', *AA*, 39: 523–526.

Winter, J.C. (1983) 'Frobenius, L.V.', in H. Jungraithmayr and H.J.G. Möhlig (eds) *Lexikon der Afrikanistik*, Berlin, pp.86–88.

Zuckerman, S. (ed.) (1973) *The Concepts of Human Evolution: A Symposium Held to Mark the Centenary of the Birth of Sir Grafton Elliot Smith*, London: Academic Press.

Zwernemann, J. (1969) 'Leo Frobenius et la recherche scientifique sur les civilisations africaines', *Notes et Documents Voltaïques*, 2(3): 27–42.

IV

American anthropology

The stimulus for the development of American anthropology was the presence, in all their variety, of the American Indians, and the new discipline fixed as its object of study their linguistic, physical, cultural and historical-archaeological characteristics. Anthropologists took up these four fields, but without ever being able to move beyond juxtaposing them as separate areas of knowledge. So today one may be an archaeologist, an expert on lemurs or an ethnologist, but rarely two or all three at once. Nevertheless, a student in the USA is often required to gain a broad-based knowledge of the discipline, so that he may, if he wishes, keep abreast of progress in areas other than his own.

My thesis here is that, for historical reasons, anthropology in the USA has from the outset been a receptacle of protest movements and social struggle, thereby occupying a place similar to that held in France by philosophy. More than any other discipline in America, anthropology has provided a space, like the one created by philosophy in France, in which dialogue can take place between the nation and its intellectuals. At a national level, the significance of a **Mead** is only comparable with that of a Sartre, and vice versa.

LAYING THE FOUNDATIONS. THE AMERICAN ETHNOLOGICAL SOCIETY, THE AMERICAN ANTIQUARIAN SOCIETY AND THE BUREAU OF AMERICAN ETHNOLOGY

Thomas Jefferson, himself the author of a small treatise on the vocabularies of Amerindian languages, was an early patron of research and ordered the major expedition of Clark and Lewis, in which the painter G. Catlin (1774–1809) also participated. In 1842 the American Society of Ethnology was founded, and, like many others set up during this and the following decade, it pursued both scientific and ideological ends. The battle against slavery and assessments of material culture, the protection of American Indians and the classification of languages, were all on its agenda.

After eight years of debate, the Smithsonian Institution was founded by Congress in 1846 with a bequest from James Smithson to the USA Treasury, to which a clause was attached by which the US government undertook to add 6% of interest to the capital each year. At the Smithsonian's first meeting **Schoolcraft** presented a plan for the investigation of American ethnology, and in 1868 opened the American Museum of Natural History. In the same year the Smithsonian also organized a mission for the exploration of the Grand Canyon directed by J. W. **Powell**. In 1879 this mission turned into a permanent research project as the American

Geographical and Geological Information-gathering Mission for the Rocky Mountain Region, and at the same time the Bureau of American Ethnology was created within the framework of the mission. Powell emphasized the importance of fieldwork from the outset. And while evolutionism was the official doctrine of the Bureau, this did not stand in the way of its collecting large quantities of ethnographical data (as Hinsley points out, 1981). **Cushing**, **Bandelier**, **Gastschet**, J.O. **Dorsey** and **Mooney** were the Bureau's first researchers, and they were soon joined by **La Flesche**. In 1902 W. H. **Holmes** succeeded Powell as head of the Bureau.

In 1866, George Peabody set up a fund to build the Peabody Museum of Archeology and Ethnology at Harvard University, to endow a professorship, and to purchase artefacts. The archaeologist J. Wyman became the museum's first curator, to be replaced by F. W. **Putnam** in 1875. In 1877 a new museum building opened, in 1882 A. C. **Fletcher** became the first ethnologist to join the staff, and in 1897 the Museum became a fully integrated part of Harvard University, which opened its own anthropology department. R. B. **Dixon** worked as assistant curator at the museum from 1897, and continued his career at Harvard as lecturer in anthropology (1901) and then as professor (1915). He was joined in 1901 by A. Tozzer, a linguist and archaeologist of Central America, and in 1913 by the physical anthropologist E. A. Hooton.

A third focus was constituted by the anthropology department of the Field Museum of Chicago, which was curated by W. H. Holmes from 1894 until 1897, when he left to take charge of the anthropology department of the US National Museum–Smithsonian Institution. Holmes was succeeded at the Field Museum by George Amos **Dorsey**, who remained in post until 1915. An anthropology course was launched at Columbia University by F. **Boas**, who had taught at Clark University from 1889 to 1892. In 1899 Boas became a professor at Columbia, and in 1902 anthropology, which had led a joint existence there with psychology, gained its own department. And in the West, **Putnam** created an autonomous anthropology department in 1903 at the University of California at Berkeley, where **Kroeber** had already been teaching since 1901. These, then, were the headquarters of American anthropology at the turn of the century.

Hale, Horatio Emmons (1817–1896)
Born at Newport, Horatio Emmons Hale studied Oriental languages and law at Harvard University, where he began compiling an Algonquin lexicon, published in 1834. He participated as a linguist and ethnographer in the celebrated US Exploratory Expedition (also called the Wilkes Expedition), undertaken between 1838 and 1842 and focusing mainly on the South Pacific. Hale contributed to the writing of the expedition report, published in 1846, and also compiled the first Fijian grammar. In the years that followed he practised as a lawyer while still devoting himself to Amerindian linguistics. His research concentrated particularly on the Iroquois, and in the *Iroquois Book of Rites* he describes their beliefs and funeral rites. He was president of the anthropological section of the American Association for the Advancement of Science and of the American Folklore Society. Having worked for a period in the 1850s in British Columbia, he supervised **Boas**'s missions in the same area between 1888 and 1894 on behalf of the committee of the British Association for the Advancement of Science, which provided the necessary funding.

Gastschet, Albert Samuel (1832–1907)
Born in Switzerland, Albert Samuel Gastschet studied linguistics at the universities of Berne

and Berlin. In 1867 he published his first book, a description of the etymology of Swiss toponyms, and then, after a year spent in Paris and London, he emigrated to the USA. There he almost at once became one of the pioneers of Amerindian linguistics. **Powell** secured a position for him at the Bureau of American Ethnology as soon as it opened in 1879, and he worked there until his retirement in 1905. While maintaining his research into linguistics Gastschet also became a notable ethnographer with a special interest in the Klamath Indians, and was the author of a very large number of articles.

Powell, John Wesley (1834–1902)

Born at Mount Morris in New York State, John Wesley Powell studied at Indiana College and volunteered for service in the Civil War, in which he lost an arm. In 1869 he led an exploratory mission to the Colorado Grand Canyon, which turned into a permanent research project as the American Geographical and Geological Information-gathering Mission for the Rocky Mountain Region. In 1879 the Mission was combined with two others of that same type operating in other regions, with all three under the control of a new institution directed by Powell between 1880 and 1894. In 1879 the three information-gathering missions were fused, and Powell used the institution he had created to found the Bureau of American Ethnology, which he headed until 1902. For a long time the Bureau remained the most important centre for anthropological research in the USA. Powell is also remembered as the founder of several learned societies, and as one of **Darwin**'s most fervent American supporters.

Mason, Otis Tufton (1838–1908)

Born in Maine, Otis Tufton Mason studied at George Washington College (then called Columbia College). He obtained his BA in 1861 and began teaching in the following year. His early interests were in the Eastern Mediterranean, but he later turned his attention to the American Indians, and between 1874 and 1884 took an unpaid position at the Museum of the Smithsonian Institution. Finally, in 1884, he was offered the post of curator in the ethnology department of the National Museum of Washington. Mason postulated a category of human material needs which must be met by the production of artefacts, and stated that these artefacts should be catalogued in terms of families, genres and types. On this basis he organized the Museum collections following the chronological order in which individual artefacts on display were invented. In so doing he took his cue from the procedure proposed by **Klemm**, to whom he acknowledged his debt ('The Leipzig Museum of Ethnology', *Smithsonian Report*, 1973: 390–410). In 1887 **Boas** opened a polemic against this mode of presentation in an article for the journal *Nature*, in which he argued the case against such technological classification and in favour of an ethnic classification based only on the specificity of each culture (*Science*, vol.9: 485–486). Mason responded to this (*Science*, vol.9: 534–535), and then J. W. **Powell** concluded the debate (*Science*, vol.9: 612–614). Mason was the first editor of the journal *American Anthropologist* and contributed to the founding of the Anthropological Society of Washington.

Fletcher, Alice Cunningham (1838–1923)

Alice Cunningham Fletcher was born in Cuba of American parents. After a long period of travelling she settled in Boston, where, as she herself said, she decided to improve herself by becoming a regular visitor to the Peabody Museum. In 1880 she began lending small sums of money to American Indians who wished to buy land and visited their encampments in South Dakota and Nebraska. From 1881 she took a specialist research interest in the Plains cultures, especially that of the Omaha. In 1882 she joined the staff of the Peabody Museum as a volunteer, and was granted the title of assistant curator in 1886. In 1911 her classic text *The Omaha Tribe* appeared, which she wrote with the assistance of her adopted Omaha son F. **La Flesche**. During Fletcher's time with the Peabody, it was reordering its collections according to the stages set out by **Morgan**, and she herself studied the process of acculturation. However, her progressive bent did not save her from one of the ideological errors of the age. Working as a government agent allotting reservation land to individual Indians, and holding strong assimilationist views, she was convinced that parcelling reservations into small units to be farmed by family groups would lead to the establishment of private property and thus allow the Indian population to escape from its economic distress. The fruit of this policy was the General Allotment Act of 1887, which enforced a division of land and resulted in the impoverishment of the Indian tribes. A. Fletcher held several important positions of responsibility, including the presidencies of the Women's Anthropological Society and of the American Folklore Society.

Putnam, Frederic Ward (1839–1915)

Born in Salem in Massachusetts, Frederic Ward Putnam was an ornithologist before he became the 'father of American archaeology'. In 1856 he went to Harvard University, where he became a naturalist. In 1875 he was appointed curator of the Peabody Museum of American Archeology and Ethnology, which in 1897 was formally incorporated into Harvard University, and he organized its collections in terms of the ethnic periodization advocated by **Morgan**. He employed **Boas** as his principal assistant, first at the World's Columbian Exhibition at Chicago (1893), and then in the anthropology department of the American Museum of Natural History, which he organized and directed from 1894 to 1903. In 1903

Putnam became the first professor of anthropology at the University of California and the director of its Anthropological Museum. He contributed significantly to the popularization of anthropology and was the author of more than 400 articles.

Matthews, Washington (1843–1905)

Born near Dublin in Ireland, Washington Matthews emigrated with his father to the USA in 1847, where after studies in medicine at the University of Iowa he became a military surgeon. He spent time with the American Indians and soon became an expert on the Hidatsa and other Plains Indians, and also on the Navajo. He studied Indian rituals and myths, on which he wrote numerous articles, and also made anthropometric measurements.

Holmes, William Henry (1846–1933)

Born near Cadiz in Ohio in 1846, William Henry Holmes took up drawing, and in 1872 was recruited as a scientific illustrator by the American Geological Information-gathering Mission. In 1874 he became an assistant geologist, and in 1875, while working as such on a cadastral survey of the region of San Juan, Colorado, he was able to report the existence of an archaeological site of considerable importance. Between 1878 and 1880 Holmes studied art in Germany, and then he worked for a while as curator of ceramics at the National Museum before being transferred to the Geological Information-gathering Mission of the American Bureau of Ethnology in 1889. After a period running of the Field Museum of Chicago he became director of the American Museum of Natural History, and in 1902 succeeded J. W. **Powell** at the head of the Bureau of American Ethnology. He wrote approximately 200 articles.

Dorsey, James Owen (1848–1895)

Born in Baltimore, James Owen Dorsey entered theological college and became a clergyman in 1871. After studies in the classical languages he undertook research, first among the Ponkas of Dakota, to whom he was sent as a missionary, and then among the Omaha of Nebraska, where he worked under **Powell**'s direction as a linguist. He was engaged by the Bureau of American Ethnology when it was set up in 1879 and worked with the Athabaskan, the Kusan and the Takilman Indians. Dorsey's best-known works, all published by the Bureau of American Ethnology, are: 'Omaha Sociology' (*ARBE*, vol.3 (1884): 205–370), which addresses questions of so-called Omaha kinship nomenclatures and served as the basis for J. Kohler's *Zur Urgeschichte der Ehe* (Stuttgart, 1897) and continues to be discussed today (Barnes 1984); 'Osage Traditions' (*ARBE*, 1888); 'A Study of Siouan Cults' (*ARBE*, vol.11 (1894): 351–544); and 'Siouan Sociology' (*ARBE*, vol.15(1896): 205–244). These texts formed part of the inspiration behind the famous article 'Primitive Forms of Classification' by E. Durkheim and M. **Mauss**.

Bandelier, Adolph Francis Alphonse (1850–1914)

Born in Berne in Switzerland, Adolph Francis Alphonse Bandelier emigrated to the USA with his parents while still a child. He took an interest in archaeology and ethnology, read and became a follower of **Morgan**, and in 1877 travelled to Mexico and Central America. He published a succession of studies: *On the Art of War and Mode of Warfare of the Ancient Mexicans* (1877), *On the Distribution and Tenure of Lands, and the Customs with Respect to Inheritance, among the Ancient Mexicans* (1878), *On the Social Organization and Mode of Government of the Ancient Mexicans* (1879), and *On the Sources for Aboriginal History of Spanish America* (1879). In the 1880s he studied the Cholula pyramids and the festival of the Quetzacoatl, used Morgan's schema to look at Aztec Society, and made the acquaintance of **Cushing** among the Pueblo Zuni Indians (1883). With Morgan's support he obtained the directorship of an American archaeological institute which was charged with undertaking historical, ethnographical and archaeological work in the American Southwest, and in 1890 he published *Contributions to the History of the Southwestern Portion of the USA* (1890). From 1882 to 1903 he lived in Peru and Bolivia, and between 1894 and 1906 worked for the American Museum of Natural History. In 1911 he was appointed associate researcher by the Carnegie Institute of Washington with the task of studying the history of the Pueblo Indians using Spanish documents. He died in Seville on 19 March 1914.

McGee, William John (1853–1912)

Born in Iowa, William John McGee educated himself privately and then worked as a geologist, taking an interest in Amerindian archaeological remains. Before long he was given a post in the American Geological Information-gathering Mission directed by **Powell**, and in 1894 he joined the Bureau of American Ethnology. In 1903 he left to work for the Agriculture Department. The main focus of his research were the American Indians of the Mississippi Valley and of California. His importance resides in his role as one of the founders of the journal *American Anthropologist* (1898), and his having been the first president of the American Anthropological Association (AAA), founded in 1902 to succeed the Anthropological Society of Washington. At the creation of the AAA McGee clashed with **Boas**, who hoped it would be an association of not more than about forty professional anthropologists. McGee's aim was to establish a much more broadly based and open association, and it was his wishes that prevailed (R. B. Woodbury, 'American Anthropological Association', in Levinson and Ember, *Encyclopedia of Cultural Anthropology*, 1996, vol.1: 52–56).

Cushing, Frank Hamilton (1857–1900)

Born in Medina in New York State, Frank Hamilton Cushing has been described by F. **Eggan** as probably the first professional ethnologist (F. Eggan, 'One Hundred Years of Ethnology and Social Anthropology', in J. O. Brew, ed., *One Hundred Years of Anthropology*, Harvard, 1968: 125). After a brief period of study at Cornell University Cushing became an ethnological assistant at the Smithsonian Institution, and he took part in the expedition sent by the National Museum to the Zuni Pueblo Indians in 1879. The expedition itself lasted only three months, but Cushing made a stay of two and a half years, learning the language and being initiated into the 'Society of the Bow'. Under **Powell**'s protection he was then transferred to the Bureau of American Ethnology. In 1881 he wrote several articles which were the source of a paper by **Mauss** and Durkheim entitled 'On Certain Primitive Forms of Classification' (1903). In **Bandelier**'s estimation 'Cushing was the only American ethnologist who ever ' "saw beneath the surface" of the Indians, who was able to think as Indians thought' (*AA*, vol.16 (1914): 349–358, p.353). Cushing died on 2 April 1900, aged forty-two. He was the author of a number of significant articles published in the *Annual Report of the Bureau of American Ethnology*.

La Flesche, Francis (1857–1932)

Francis La Flesche was born into the Omaha community in Nebraska, where his father, himself the son of a French merchant and an Indian woman, was one of the chiefs. La Flesche attended a Presbyterian missionary school while at the same time taking part in the last great bison hunts. He was employed by the Bureau of Indian Affairs from 1879 and obtained a law degree in 1893. In 1910 he joined the Bureau of American Ethnology where he worked until his retirement in 1929, becoming the curator of the Peabody Museum. A large part of his output focuses on the Omaha, and he worked together with A. C. **Fletcher**, whom he met in 1881 and whose adoptive son he became in 1891. A second, more personal part of La Flesche's work is devoted to Osage culture.

Boas, Franz (1858–1942)

Franz Boas was born on 9 July 1858 in the German town of Minden into a family of secular Jews impregnated with the ideals of the German revolution of 1848. He first studied mathematics at Heidelberg, then moved to Bonn and Kiel, where at twenty-three he received his doctorate with a thesis on physical geography entitled *Contributions to the Understanding of the Colour of Water* (his minor thesis was entitled *On The Necessity of Condemning Contemporary Operetta on Artistic and Moral Grounds*). He performed his military service as an officer and then set off in 1883 on a voyage of geographical study in Northern Canada with the aim of drawing up maps of the region. Boas spent several months in the Arctic in extremely difficult conditions (he tells the story in 'A Journey in Cumberland Sound and on the West shore of David Strait in 1883 and 1884', *Journal of the American Geographical Society of New York*, vol.14, 1884: 242–272). It was during this stay that he came across the Inuit. G.W. **Stocking** has pointed out that this, Boas's first period in the field, took place in the year in which **Malinowski** was born, and that his last fieldwork was carried out ten years before Malinowski set off for the Trobriand Islands, which gives us a good yardstick by which to situate Boas historically. Fascinated by the human capacity to adapt and keen to understand what he saw as a common human nature with geographically determined variants, he turned to anthropology. Having become the foremost specialist on the American Indians of British Columbia, he unsuccessfully sought employment in New York during the winter of 1884–1885, and then returned to Germany, where he found work as assistant curator at the *Völkerkunde-museum*, founded by A. **Bastian**, as a colleague of R. **Virchow**.

In 1886 he began to teach geography at the University of Berlin and wrote *Baffin-land: Geographische Ergebnisse einer in den Jahren 1833 und 1884 ausgeführten Forschungsreise* (Petermanns Mitteilungen, 1885) and *The Central Eskimo* (1888). After a meeting with a group of Bella Coola Indians from British Columbia who had been brought to the Museum of Berlin, Boas suggested to Bastian the idea of carrying out fieldwork on the ethnic and racial relations between the Inuit and the American Indians; the study of migration and racial relations through linguistics and physical anthropology was a classic topos at that time (Stocking, 1974: 84). Bastian then sanctioned a trip by Boas to Vancouver Island in British Columbia. However, obtaining a position at the University of Berlin would have required Boas to disavow Judaism, which although not a practising Jew he refused to do, and so he took the opportunity offered by this second mission to renew his search for a post in the USA.

Boas found work in New York as assistant editorial director of the journal *Science*. He married Maria Krakowitzer, whom he had already known in Germany, and obtained American citizenship. In 1887 he published 'Museums of Ethnology and their Classification' (*Science*, 9: 137–141), which attracted notice by its criticisms of the then largely dominant evolutionist presentation of ethnographical collections and its advocacy of presentation in terms of culture areas. The

publication in 1888 of *The Central Eskimo*, a substantial work of ethnography, assured Boas's burgeoning reputation. In one of the very first books on the Inuit, Boas described their geographical distribution, their material culture, their mythologies, the determination of their social structures by the seasonal cycle, their religious imagery, etc.

Repudiating his German masters, he distanced himself from all finalist explanatory models, instead holding that culture and language are more weighty determining factors than natural environment. In 1888 he was able to return to British Columbia to study the Kwakiutl, Tsimshian and Chinook Indians thanks to an award granted by a committee of the British Association for the Advancement of Science. This committee, of which **Tylor** was an eminent member and which in the USA was supervised by **Hale**, was set up in 1884 to further research into the tribes of Northwest Canada. The committee gave Boas the opportunity to make five trips to the Kwakiutl, amounting to twelve months of fieldwork between 1884 and 1894 ('Boas must be understood primarily as a field researcher', **Lowie**, 1937: 131). At the end of 1895 Boas lost his position with the journal *Science*. He was then recruited by Clark University in Worcester, Massachusetts, to open a psychology department, in which anthropology was taught at the suggestion of G. S. Hall, founder of the *American Journal of Psychology*.

Boas was professor at Clark University from 1889 to 1892. He supervised the first Ph.D. in anthropology awarded in the USA[1] before resigning in 1892 in the wake of a student protest movement, soon to be

---

1 According to G.W. Stocking, Boas supervised the first anthropology Ph.D. in the USA (Stocking (1974: 58), awarded in 1892 to Alexander Francis Chamberlain for a thesis entitled 'The Language of the Mississaga Indians of Skugog: A Contribution to the Linguistics of the Algonkian Tribes of Canada' (Clark University), while Hinsley asserts that the first American anthropology Ph.D. was awarded to George A. Dorsey by Harvard University (C. Hinsley, 'From Shell-heaps to Stelae: Early Anthropology at the Peabody Museum', HAO, vol.3: 72). Stocking investigated this claim and found that Dorsey in fact obtained his Ph.D. in 1894, but, as he writes: 'Firsts, however, are always problematic, and it is not impossible (though very unlikely) that another might be discovered sometime' (e-mail of 22.02.01 to G. Gaillard).]

followed by the new doctorate-holder, A. F. Chamberlain. It was during this period at Clark University that Boas dedicated himself to linguistics and physical anthropology and acquired what he called his 'systematic self-education' (Lowie, 1934: 183).

Boas's work touched on all areas of anthropology (ethnology, linguistics, and physical anthropology). However, he followed Bastian in particular in making myths and folklore his primary interest, taking up R. Virchow's statistical method and **Herder**'s thesis that such narratives best embody *Völkergedanken* or 'popular genius'. Having fixed on skull shapes as a yardstick of the variation caused by environmental influences ('Changes in the bodily form of immigrants', *AA*, vol.14, 1912), he and thirteen assistants measured the various skull forms of 17,821 subjects, and concluded that there were differences between those of immigrants to the USA and those of their descendants who were born there.

In 1892–1893 Boas became the senior assistant in the anthropology section of the Field Museum of Chicago, and was appointed its curator in 1895. A disagreement with the management obliged him to leave his post, and at the beginning of 1896 he became a part-time lecturer in physical anthropology at Columbia University. In this year he published his first important theoretical article, in which he propounded 'historical particularism' ('The Limitations of the Comparative Method of Anthropology', *Science*, vol.4 (1896): 901–904). This was a great turning-point in American anthropology. From 1883 he rejected all evolutionist approaches, which he felt took too broad a view of human cultures. He suggested the collation of the maximum quantity of all types of data (ethnographic observation, physical measurement, languages, mythology, etc.) and the avoidance of all hypotheses based on generalizations. The essence of his method is to gather together facts and only facts, and to let them speak for themselves without being made to fit any preconceived theories. Any generalization could then only be conjectured from this body of information. What Boas proposes is a 'historical reconstruction' which rejects the deductive in favour of the inductive method. To this end, he envisages the analysis of a number of well-defined societal groups and a comparison of their processes of development. He reproaches transformists and their 'comparative method' with attributing similar social effects to identical causes, and contends that because customs, characteristics and beliefs which seem alike can have different origins it is always dangerous only to compare the results of a social development. General laws of social development cannot be identified until the developmental processes of delimited geographical regions have been thoroughly studied. Each society can only be understood in terms of its own history, which is never more than a succession of accidents producing a 'historical particularism'. In fact, Boas increasingly came to reject generalizations of a any kind, including those based in history, so that one may speak of a 'Boasian nominalism'.

In 1897 Boas published one of his most celebrated texts, *The Social Organization and the Secret Societies of the Kwakiutl Indians* (Washington, Report of the US National Museum for 1895), in which he discussed the potlatch for the first time. In the ceremony of the potlatch (a Nootka or Chinook term), the chiefs of a clan battled with one another for predominant social status by means of extravagant expenditure, either by imposing gifts on one another or even by destroying objects of value: quilts were distributed, copper badges were broken or given away, and slaves had their throats slit. Boas sees this as a classic economic institution, because the underlying principle is that of investment with interest, inasmuch as the adversary must counter gifts and invitations with even more generous offerings. R. **Benedict** writes of usury, P. **Radin** of capitalist credit. Together with Malinowski's Kula, the potlatch without doubt became one of anthropology's central terms, inspiring works such as *Essai sur le don* [*The Gift*] by M. **Mauss** (1922) and *La Part maudite* [*The Accursed Portion*] by G. Bataille (1949), and these texts would be complemented by C. **Meillassoux**'s interpretation of the same phenomenon in 1972.

In 1898 Boas was appointed professor of anthropology at Columbia University, and remained in this post until his retirement in 1936. From 1901 to 1905 he was also curator of the ethnology and somatology section of the American Museum of Natural History, and from the Museum's president, M. Jesup, he obtained funding for the Jesup Expeditions in the North Pacific. These took place over six years and comprised fourteen interdisciplinary missions, with ethnology enjoying a predominant position. One essentially geographical expedition to the Inuit of Baffin Island brought American researchers together with their Russian counterparts. The latter were former revolutionaries who had been living in exile in Siberia, where they had studied local populations and published their findings before being released by the Czar. One of them, W. **Bogoras**, went on to become a Bolshevik, and another, V. Iochelsen, emigrated to the USA.

Appointed an 'honorary philologist' by the Bureau of American Ethnology in 1901, Boas began a *Guide to the Indians of America*, a large work in three volumes. He was the editorial director of the *Journal of American Folklore* from 1909 to 1925, and continued his studies of Tsimshian, Kwakiutl and Kutenai folklore. He founded the International School of American Archeology and Ethnology in 1910 in Mexico, where he lived for one year, and in the same year he was elected to the presidency of the New York Academy of Sciences. He co-authored *Changes in the Bodily Form of Descendants of Immigrants*, which appeared in 1911. He also wrote the first volume of the *Handbook*

of American Indian Languages (4 vols, 1911–1944), entitled *The Mind of Primitive Men*. Boas's volume was a collection of articles he had published between 1894 and 1911, in which he took issue with the racist doctrines of Gobineau and Chamberlain, and also with the views of H. F. Osborn, the director of the American Museum of Natural History, and set out the general principles of modern anthropology: the independent development of race, culture and language, and the fact that they are all acquired and combined in an unstable way. In 1917 Boas founded the *Journal of American Linguistics*. His 1920 article 'Methods of Ethnology' (*AA*, vol.22: 311–322) was a turning-point because of the way he takes a favourable view of the new psychological approach, which would become the key feature of the culture and personality school, while showing little enthusiasm for diffusionism.

Anthropology and Modern Life, another collection of articles published in 1928, considers such salient questions of the time as education, eugenics and nationalism, but **White** has observed (1966: 16) that Boas's presentation of modern life ignores the gulf between labour and capital as well as the Industrial Revolution and the Russian Revolution.

Although overtly pro-German during the First World War, Boas denounced the Nazi regime well before the Second World War and was one of the first American academics to take a political position on the issue. He gave a lecture on 'race and civilization' at the University of Kiel in 1931 on being awarded an honorary doctorate (soon his books would be burnt at this same institution). In 1933 he sent a letter to Hindenburg protesting against Hitler's accession to power and resigned from the Munich Academy of Sciences. He took part in creating the Commission for Democracy and Intellectual Freedom (1938–1939), which mobilized American opinion against Nazism. In 1940 he published a selection of his major essays under the title *Race, Language and Culture* (New York: Macmillan). He had his first heart attack at the age of seventy-three in 1931, and it was of a heart attack that he died a decade later on 21 December 1942 during a lunch given in the honour of P. **Rivet** in the Professors Club of Columbia University. After giving a speech against racism he collapsed into the arms of the man sitting next to him, who was none other than C. **Lévi-Strauss**. Boas has over 600 articles to his name.

Mooney, James (1861–1921)

Born in Richmond in Indiana, James Mooney developed a passionate interest in the American Indians, and a meeting with J. W. **Powell** led to his being offered a research post at the Bureau of American Ethnology in 1885. He became a specialist in the Cherokee, the Cheyenne and the Kiowa Indians. He is remembered as the author of the classic study 'The Ghost-Dance Religion and the Sioux Outbreak of 1890' (*Fourteenth Annual Report of the Bureau of American Ethnology*, Part 1, 1896: 641–1110; repr. 1965). In this work Mooney examines the ecstatic religious movement founded on the prophecy that the dead would soon return and that White man and his culture were at the same time to be destroyed by a natural cataclysm, which he sees as an adaptive response to poverty and oppression. Mooney also became involved in American Indian–White intercultural relations and was one of the founders of the American Anthropological Association.

Dorsey, George Amos (1868–1931)

Born in Hebron in Ohio, George Amos Dorsey studied at Harvard University, where in 1894 he obtained the second Ph.D. in anthropology awarded in the USA. He was first given employment by **Putnam** at the Peabody Museum, and was curator of the Field Museum of Natural History in Chicago from 1896 to 1915. He was professor of comparative anatomy at Northwestern University and then associate professor of anthropology at the University of Chicago. He carried out research among the Plains Indians, concentrating particularly on the sun dance ceremonies of the Arapaho and the Cheyenne. From 1909 to 1912 he took unpaid leave and worked as an international journalist. Thereafter he continued in this line of work but at the same time returned to teaching by taking a post at the New School for Social Research in New York. He was a popularizer of anthropology and achieved great success with *Why We Behave Like Human Beings* (1925). He was also active as an adviser to President Wilson.

Curtis, Edward Sherriff (1868–1952)

A native of Wisconsin, Edward Sherriff Curtis accompanied his father on a preaching circuit to an Indian village near his home. These visits must have made a deep impression on him, because in 1897, at the age of twenty-nine, he began photographing the American Indians. Like all photographers of the time he made his subjects pose for the camera. Thanks to the financial assistance of J. P. **Morgan**, Curtis systematically photographed eighty tribes from 1905. His major work, *The North American Indians*, fills twenty volumes. He took more then 40,000 photographs between 1897 and 1930.

Cooper, John Montgomery (1881–1949)

Born in Rockville in Maryland, John Montgomery Cooper attended a Catholic school and then completed his studies in Rome. In 1905 he obtained a Ph.D. and was at the same time ordained a priest. He was assigned to Washington, where his interest in science and archaeology led him to become a frequent visitor to the Smithsonian Institution. He gave courses in religious studies at the Catholic University of America, and in 1923 was invited to teach anthropology in the same university's sociology department. Cooper was appointed professor of anthropology in 1928 and became the first head of the newly created anthropology department in 1935. He attended the first Indigenist Interamerican Congress, held in Patzcuaro (Mexico) in 1940, as a delegate of the US government, and he also assumed a number of other positions of responsibility. In 1941 a coronary arterial sclerosis forced him to reduce his workload. Cooper's work often shows a diffusionist influence (e.g. 'Culture Diffusion and Culture Areas in Southern South America', *Proceedings of the Twenty-First International Congress of Americanists*, pp.401–421). His central thesis is that 'marginal cultures' have hardly changed location since prehistoric times. Cooper planned and set out the theoretical framework of the much-renowned *Handbook of South American Indians*, produced between 1946 and 1959 by the Smithsonian Institution under the direction of J. **Steward**. As well as being active as a member of the committee, made up of **Nordenskjöld**, **Lowie** and **Spier** and himself, which initiated the *Handbook* project in 1932, Cooper naturally contributed numerous articles of his own to the work.

Cole, Fay-Cooper (1881–1961)
Born in Michigan but raised in California,

F.-C. Cole obtained a BA from North-western University in 1903. He joined the staff of the Field Museum of Chicago and worked under the direction of G. A. **Dorsey**. At Dorsey's suggestion he studied at Columbia University and in Berlin and then, accompanied by his wife, carried out fieldwork among the Tinguian of the Philippines. He was awarded a doctorate in 1914 for his thesis *A Study of Tinguian Folklore*. In 1924 he was engaged by the University of Chicago, where he created a department of sociology and anthropology which counted among its earliest students L. A. **White** (working on the Keresan) and R. **Redfield** (working on Tepoztlán, a Mexican village). He brought E. **Sapir** to Chicago when an independent anthropology department was created there in 1929, and then replaced him with **Radcliffe-Brown** when Sapir left for Yale University in 1931. Cole himself retired in 1947. As well as important work on Malaysia (Indonesia and the Philippines) and his wide-ranging involvement in military anthropology during the Second World War, he made a substantial contribution to American Indian archaeology.

THE GENERATION OF BOASIANS

While **Sturtevant** has called the period running from 1880 to 1920 the 'museological period' in US anthropology, he also writes that the first two decades of the twentieth century in American anthropology can be called the age of **Boas**, such was his domination of the discipline (Mead and **Bunzel**, 1960: 400). For forty years Boas taught statistical theory and Amerindian languages at the Columbia University. Although he insisted on 'an uncompromising adherence to his own values' (in the words of Kroeber), when he introduced a study programme in 1901 he was able to attract large numbers of students, who can be divided into two 'waves'. The first wave included R. **Swanton** (Ph.D. 1900), A. Kroeber (Ph.D. 1901), C. Wissler (Ph.D. 1909), R. Lowie (Ph.D. 1908), F. G. Speck (Ph.D. 1908), E. Sapir (Ph.D. 1909), P. Radin (Ph.D. 1910), A. **Goldenweiser** (Ph.D. 1910), H. **Herskovits** (Ph.D. 1923), E. C. **Parsons** (introduced to Boasian anthropology after obtaining his Ph.D. in 1899), L. **Spier** (Ph.D. 1920), T. Michelsen, Reichard, Jacobs and others. These scholars filled the first posts and university chairs at a period when professional anthropologists were still scarce.

From 1900 to 1920 Boas's influence led these researchers to make the historical reconstitution of American Indian societies their main interest. However, it would be wrong to assume that they all remained faithful to Boasian ideas. From 1906 **Wissler** began to distance himself from his master, **Radin** openly attacked the 'pseudo-scientific historicist method' and its neglect of individual initiative (P. Radin, *The Method and Theory of Ethnology*, New York, 1933: 32), **Kroeber** made the opposite criticism that Boas's relativism did not permit the constitution of a scientific historical narrative, and **Sapir** broke with him in a polemic about whether or not Amerindian languages had a common origin (see **Greenberg**). Another defector was R. **Dixon**, who, on the basis of the geographical distribution of skull shapes, constructed a racist history of mankind by interweaving race, nationality and cultural inventiveness (Dixon, 1923, 1928).

For all these deviations, Boas's students did form a school of American diffusionism, of which Wissler, Sapir and Kroeber were the three masters. Untouched by the British and German tendency to make fanciful connections between societies in two distant parts of the world merely on the strength of a few perceived common features, they were practitioners of a 'moderate diffusionism' (for example Kroeber accepted that the zero was invented independently by the Maya and the Hindus).

After his polemic with **Mason** concerning museum presentation at the end of the century, Boas's strong advocacy of the German cause during the First World War and his violent attack on anthropologists who contributed to the American war effort revived deep tensions between him and the Establishment. Under pressure from **Holmes**, the American Anthropological Association censured Boas in 1919. There was a steadily increasing hostility between Anglo-Saxon Protestants in Washington, who worked almost exclusively on the American Indians, and the New York-based Boasian school, with its large German-Jewish contingent (**Lowie**, Goldenweiser, Sapir, Kroeber, **Benedict**, etc.).

F. W. Voget writes that the work of R. Benedict (Ph.D. 1923) forms the link between the first and second waves of Boas's students (Voget, *A History of Ethnology*, 1975: 334). After initially taking a historicist approach and analysing the issues surrounding acculturation (*The Concept of the Guardian Spirit in North America*, 1923), Benedict became a leading light in the exploration of the interface between culture and personality. Sapir's evolution followed the same pattern, as to a lesser extent did that of Herskovits. This second wave of Boas's students, of whom M. **Mead** (Ph.D. 1925) is the best-known, founded the culturalist approach and the so-called culture and personality school. As Boas writes: 'Once I thought that historical methods were firmly in place, I began, in about 1910, to stress the problems of cultural dynamics, cultural integration and interaction between an individual and his society' (Boas, 'History and Science in Anthropology: A Reply' (1936), reprinted in *Race, Language and Culture*, New York, 1940: 311).

It should be noted that the second Boasian generation differs from the first not just in its theoretical approach and main interests, but also in the regions where it carried out its fieldwork. While the first generation made the American Indians its specialism, the second, which came to anthropology during or soon after the First World War when, as we have seen, Boas was on very poor terms with the Establishment, often chose to work in Pacific islands, many of which were mandated to the United States.

Wissler, Clark (1870–1947)
Born in Wayne County, Indiana, Clark

Wissler worked as a primary school teacher from 1887 to 1892, and then studied at

Indiana University, gaining a BA in 1897. He was appointed as tutor in psychology at Ohio University, obtained an MA from Indiana in 1899, and then enrolled at Columbia University, where he worked as a teaching assistant and obtained a Ph.D. in psychology in 1901. Having attended Boas's anthropology courses, he joined the staff of the American Museum of Natural History in 1902, where he worked under the direction of **Putnam** and **Boas**, replacing the latter as curator in 1906. He was assistant lecturer and then lecturer in anthropology at Columbia from 1903 until he quarrelled with Boas in 1909. In 1924 Wissler began teaching in the psychology department at Yale University, where he was appointed professor of anthropology when the department opened in 1931. He held important responsibilities as adviser to the Carnegie Foundation, president of the American Anthropological Association and president of the Academy of Sciences of New York. From 1902 he engaged in research among the Blackfoot, the Sioux and the Dakota Indians, and subsequently among other Indian populations.

Of all American anthropologists Wissler was the most consequential in his development of diffusionism. At a time when Boas was seeking to eradicate the evolutionist style of museological presentation, Wissler came up with the notion of 'culture areas', an idea he applied in *The American Indian: An Introduction to the Anthropology of the New World* (1917). In 1914 he published 'The Influence of the Horse in the Development of the Plains Culture' (*AA*, vol.16: 1–25), a major article in which he demonstrates how the use of horses transformed social organization to the point that matrilocal was succeeded by patrilocal residence. He also introduced the notions of the 'age area' and of concentric diffusion (later taken up by **Kroeber**). According to Wissler, cultural traits are diffused from a central point at a constant speed, and so traits present at the periphery of an area are the longest-established; in this way the spatial extension of given traits can be said to correspond to different temporal layers. This theory has been specifically criticized for failing to account for the possibility of innovations originating at the periphery. Wissler draws up a table setting out nine subdivisions which, when combined, allow all the world's cultures to be described. This idea would be revived in more elaborate form by **Murdock** in the constitution of his Human Relations Area Files. As well as a large number of articles, Wissler produced two important introductory guides to anthropology: *Man and Culture* (New York, 1923) and *An Introduction to Social Anthropology* (New York, 1929), and he supported the efforts of R. S. and H. M. Lynd to open a new perspective on the subject by writing an introduction to their celebrated *Middletown* (1929). He also helped M. **Mead** gain a position at the American Museum of Natural History and sent **Lowie** on his first fieldwork project.

Swanton, John Reed (1873–1958)

Born in Gardiner in Maine, John Reed Swanton was without doubt one of the most prolific scholars of the period. He studied at Harvard University and obtained a Ph.D. in 1900. Employed by the Bureau of American Ethnology, he became an expert on the Haida Indians, but also worked on the cultures of the Southwest (the Tunica, the Chitimancha and the Atakapa), the Northwest and the Southeast, often writing as a historian of their ancient migrations. Among other things, he is known for producing the first classification of kinship systems in North America in 'The Social Organization of American Tribes' (*AA*, vol.7 (1905): 663–673), which was not supplanted until the publication in 1937 of *Social Anthropology of North American Tribes* by **Radcliffe-Brown**'s students **Eggan** and **Redfield**.

Dixon, Roland Burrage (1875–1934)
Born in 1875, Roland Burrage Dixon studied at Harvard University, and after obtaining his BA in 1897 became assistant curator in anthropology at the Peabody Museum. In 1898 he took part in the famous Jesup North Pacific Expedition organized by the American Museum of Natural History, directed by **Boas**. He was also a participant in the Huntingdon Expedition to California in 1899, and afterwards he worked among the Californian Indians and gained his doctorate on the language of the Maidu in 1900. He was engaged by Harvard University as lecturer in anthropology (1901), then as assistant professor (1906–1915), and finally as professor (1915). In the early part of his career he published widely on the Californian Indians, including his substantial monograph *Northern Maidu* in 1905, and with **Kroeber** established an important typology of the Amerindian languages of California. Subsequently he devoted himself to writing vast works of synthesis aimed at the popular market, all with a diffusionist bias, of which the best-known are on the oral traditions of Oceania (*Oceanic Mythology*, 1916), the physical measurement of races (*The Racial History of Mankind*, 1923), and human migration and diffusion (*The Building of Cultures*, 1928). Regrettably, these works contain racist connotations.

Parsons, Elsie Clews (1875–1941)
Born in New York, Elsie Clews Parsons studied at Barnard College (BA 1896) and then read sociology at Columbia University, where she gained a Ph.D. in 1899 with a thesis entitled *Educational Legislation and Administration of the Colonial Governments*. She then taught at Barnard College until 1905, published *The Family: An Ethnographical and Historical Outline* (1906), and accompanied her husband, a reformist Republican Congressman, on a world tour. She then successively published *The Old-Fashioned Woman: Primitive Fancies about the Sex* (1913), *Religious Chastity: An Ethnological Study* (1913), *Fear and Conventionality* (1914), *Social Freedom* (1915), and *Social Rule* (1916). These books all adopted a feminist perspective and defended non-conformist behaviour and individual freedom. In 1915 she began twenty-five years of research on the Pueblo Indians, on whom she published an impressive series of reports, books and articles. She also took a keen interest in folklore, myths and cosmologies, and studied acculturation processes in Mexican and Ecuadorian villages. Equally noteworthy is her association with the New Republic Group and her assistance in the founding of the New School for Social Research. At her death she was president of the American Anthropological Association.

Webster, Hutton (1875–1955)
Hutton Webster was primarily a sociologist, but he was also the author of an important anthropological study entitled *Primitive Secret Societies* (1908), which contains the thesis that male secret societies grew out of initiation rites. Rather than analysing the symbolism of these rites and ceremonies, he stresses the division between the initiators and the initiated, and demonstrates that the importance of the payments and provisions pledged by the younger men, and of the services they were obliged to perform for the initiators, was founded exclusively in the need to mark differences of status.

Kroeber, Alfred Louis (1876–1960)
Alfred Louis Kroeber was born in Hoboken, New Jersey, into a Protestant family which was of German origin and still spoke German. He was admitted to Columbia University in 1892 to study English literature, and discovered anthropology by attending the lectures on linguistics which **Boas** had been giving since 1895. In 1897 he gained his MA and then switched to anthropology. He began fieldwork among the Arapaho and published his first article on their folklore in

1899. In 1901 he gained a doctorate with a thesis on the decorative arts of the Arapaho (the first Ph.D. in anthropology to be awarded by Columbia). Kroeber then secured a post in the newly opened anthropology department of the University of California at Berkeley. Although this department was initially conceived exclusively as a research institute, he provided it with a museum and a teaching programme, and he continued to teach until his retirement in 1946.

The Californian Indians had been little studied by the beginning of the twentieth century, and so Kroeber amassed a large and varied body of archaeological, ethnological and linguistic material, as well as details of physical anthropology. In 1903 he and R. **Dixon** produced the first classification of the sixteen languages of the Californian Indians, dividing them into three types, and ten years later Kroeber established their genetic filiations.

The publication in 1909 of an article entitled 'Classificatory Systems of Relationship' (*JRAI*, vol.39: 77–84) constituted Kroeber's first important theoretical contribution. In 1907 **Rivers**, adopting a perspective shared with E. B. **Tylor** and J. **Frazer**, proposed to draw together classificatory nomenclatures, principles of exogamy and marriage customs. However it had proved difficult to explain the so-called Crow terminology, by which Ego assigns his mother's brother's children's children to his own children. Using a psychological perspective, Rivers had interpreted this in terms of the fact that Ego marries the widow of the mother's brother and thereby becomes the adoptive father of his children. Kroeber attacked this interpretation and went on to denounce the ethnocentric nature of **Morgan**'s classification and its separation of classificatory kinship systems from descriptive ones. He showed that Western kinship models tend to contain fewer classes than the more classificatory Amerindian systems, and proposed a typology of nomenclatures

founded on eight criteria: distinction or non-distinction between persons of the same or different generations, the distinction between direct and collateral relationships, age distinctions within a single generation, the gender of the relative, the gender of Ego, the gender of the person through whom the relationship exists (thus between the father's brothers and the mother's brothers, who in English would both be called 'uncles'), the distinction between blood relatives and relatives by marriage, and the status of the person through whom the relationship exists (dead or alive, married or unmarried, etc.).

Between 1918 and 1920 Kroeber practised psychoanalysis, but although well-disposed to Freud's work he never sought to apply it to anthropology. He first worked on the chronology of different types of Zuni pottery under the guidance of C. **Wissler**, and then undertook research in Peru in 1922. In 1923 he published an introduction to the discipline entitled *Anthropology*, and in 1925 produced *A Sourcebook in Anthropology*, a volume of texts prepared in collaboration with T. T. Waterman. Also in 1925 came the appearance of Kroeber's *Handbook of the Indians of California*, a synthesis of all the anthropological literature on the state. From 1936 he revisited the topics examined by Wissler and investigated them in greater depth, developing the notion of the 'culture area' and associating it with a 'level of cultural integrity' (1936), thus providing a model for describing how a culture constructs and maintains its cultural level. This level is determined by the statistical accumulation of cultural elements capable of generating their own cultural models and establishing relations between cultures. Kroeber's model is applied in 1939 in his *Cultural and Natural Areas of Native North America*, in which he emphasizes the importance of ecological determinations and divides North America into six large cultural units and fifty-five regions. In 1950 he supported the Californian Indians in their battle for recognition of their land rights.

From 1917 onwards Kroeber made much of the notion of culture understood as a 'superorganism', an entity with its own rationale above and beyond particular societies and the individuals within them. *Configurations of Culture Growth*, published in 1944, describes the way civilizations succeed one another and looks into the causes of their periods of innovation and decline. In 1948 he published a collection of his major essays as *The Nature of Culture*, and issued a revised edition of his manual *Anthropology*, in which he places an even greater emphasis on the idea of culture as a 'superorganism' into which individuals are incorporated, and at the same time he rejects L. **White**'s definition of this phenomenon. Shortly afterwards Kroeber started working in association with T. Parsons (Kroeber and Parsons, 1958), and they asserted that sociology is the study of social structures while anthropology is the study of culture. The project they thereby outlined has provided the orientation for American anthropology up to the present day (**Kuper**, 1999). Kroeber was responsible for organizing a symposium entitled *Anthropology Today: An Encyclopedic Inventory* (Chicago UP, 1953), which without doubt provides the best picture of the state of anthropology after the Second World War. Kroeber died in Paris in October 1960 on returning from Austria, where he had presided at a colloquium on 'Anthropological Horizons'.

Goldenweiser, Alexander Alexandrovich (1880–1940)

Alexander Alexandrovich Goldenweiser was born in Kiev to a father of Jewish extraction, who took him on his voyages across Europe and America. Between 1900 and 1901 he studied philosophy at Harvard University, and then enrolled in the anthropology department at Columbia University, headed by **Boas**. In 1910 he obtained a Ph.D. with his thesis *Totemism: An Analytical Study*, which was published in the same year. An examination of totemism in different parts of the world, it showed that the comparative method employed most notably by **Frazer** to establish totemism as a system worked merely by extrapolating original states from end results. Goldenweiser contended that clan organization, the attribution to clans of animal and plant names and emblems, and the belief in the relatedness of the clan and its totem were reflected in one another, thus formulating a deconstruction of the favourite subject of anthropology at the turn of the century and anticipating the more radical arguments of **Lévi-Strauss** (Lévi-Strauss, 1974). Goldenweiser taught at Columbia from 1910 to 1919, at the Rand School of Social Science from 1915 to 1929, and at the New School for Social Research between 1919 and 1928. He became a professor at the University of Oregon, where he remained until his death in 1940. Goldenweiser was the editor of the first *International Encyclopaedia of the Social Sciences* (published between 1930 and 1935).

Lowie, Robert Harry (1883–1957)

Robrt Harry Lowie was born in Vienna in 1883 as the son of a Hungarian merchant and his German wife. His parents emigrated with him to New York in 1893, and he was educated at New York City College, publishing an article on Edgar Allan Poe in the *New Yorker Review* (1898) when he was only fifteen years old. In 1904 he began studies in psychology at Columbia University, where he attended lectures by **Boas** and turned his attention to anthropology. As well as Boas's course, Lowie followed lectures given by A. **Bandelier** on Central America and went on to work under C. **Wissler** as a volunteer in the anthropology department of the American Museum of Natural History. Wissler was working at the time on the Blackfoot Indians, and sent Lowie to find information he needed about their neighbours, the Shoshone. The Shoshone had been established in reservations for about thirty years and were already completely acculturated, living off rations distributed by the government after attempts to set them up as farmers had failed. Lowie perceived that the aspects of their culture which had altered the least were the 'patterns of family life and the nuances of social interaction' (**Murphy**, 1972: 17). After a summer of fieldwork he published 'The Northern Shoshone' (American Museum of Natural History paper, no.2 (1909): 165–203). An anti-evolutionist, Lowie said that the Crow had taught him that even a primitive society was culturally very diverse, and that this diversity was matched by a strong individualism. The task, as he saw it, was thus to separate culture as such from individuals and their personalities.

In 1907 Lowie was taken on as a trainee at the American Museum of Natural History, where he remained for fourteen years, becoming assistant curator in 1909 and associate curator in 1912. In the spring of 1907 Wissler sent him to gather information on a myth present among the Blackfoot and the Crow, on whom he would work for the rest of his life. As well as these peoples, Lowie studied the Hidatsa of North Dakota, the Southern Ute of Colorado, the Piaute of Southern Nevada and Utah, the Piaute of Northern Nevada, and the Hopi of Arizona. In 1908 his thesis on questions of comparative mythology was published as an article of about fifty pages in the *Journal of American Folklore*. During the First World War Boas and his disciples took up a pro-German position, and in 1914 Lowie published a short article in support of this view.

With his 'Exogamy and the Classificatory System of Relationship', published in 1915 (*AA*, vol.17: 223–239), Lowie argued against **Kroeber** in favour of the explanation of exogamy and kinship nomenclatures given in the psychologist theses of **Rivers**, but without following him in the case of non-

generational systems. According to Lowie, the particularities of these systems are fully explained by the clan element, making consideration of other possible forms of determination unnecessary. In matrilineal clans such as those of the Crow, the Hopi, and a majority of other societies with a Crow naming system, a man belongs to the same clan as his mother's brother, whom he considers as his older brother and whose children he considers as sons and daughters. Conversely, on the patrilateral side of a matrilineal society, a father and his sister are considered together as being members of the same clan. This is why 'father' and 'father's sister' must in fact be seen as meaning the male and female individuals belonging to the father's clan. This represents the principle of solidarity of lineage later given more precise definition by **Radcliffe-Brown**.

Lowie spent parts of 1916 and 1917 among the Hopi, and discerned that behind their ethic of harmony, solidarity and co-operation lay a society riven by hostility between villages and rival factions within each village. The conclusions he drew from this contradicted the Apollonian ideal which R. **Benedict** claimed to find among the Zuni and presented as characteristic of the Pueblo Indians in general.

Soon after being invited to Berkeley by Kroeber in 1917, Lowie published *Culture and Ethnology* (New York: P. Smith, republ. in 1929), in which he sought to give the term 'culture', advanced by the Boasians, an integrated signification embracing considerations of environment and psychology. In 1920 he was elected president of the American Society of Ethnology just as his post at the American Museum of Natural History was suppressed in a round of staff cuts necessitated by budgetary problems. He also became a lecturer in primitive law at Columbia University. The same year saw the appearance of *Primitive Society* (1920), one of the very earliest anthropological texts to popularize the Boasian approach, in which

Lowie is critical of **Morgan**'s idea of primitive communism and of the incoherence of the stages in his evolutionist theory (1920: 211–212), and in which, inspired by H. **Schurtz**, he lays a quite new emphasis on certain types of association which he perceives as equalling kinship in importance. In 1921 he was appointed associate professor at Berkeley, where he became a professor in 1925. As director of Berkeley's anthropology department between 1922 and 1946, his most notable students were J. **Steward**, C. **Du Bois**, H. **Driver**, T. McCown, C. Voegelin, D. Shimkin, R. Beals, R. Heizer, G. Foster, R. Spencer, as well as R. Murphy, who described his teacher as 'an assiduous attender of student parties during prohibition, at which his performances of Crow war dances were particularly appreciated' (Murphy, 1972: 34). In 1927 Lowie published *The Origin of the State* (New York: Harcourt), which takes up Schurtz's idea that, contrary to evolutionist premises, voluntary associations play a greater role than clans in determining primitive political organizations, and unties the classic triad of territory, state and legitimate use of violence. At the age of fifty, and only after the death of his mother, Lowie married Luella Cole in 1933. In 1934 he published his *Introduction to Cultural Anthropology* (New York: Farrar), which calls for a general exhibition of cultural anthropology such as it was taught in the USA. *The Crow Indians*, which appeared in 1935 (New York: Farrar and Rinehart), represents the culmination of work begun in 1907 and opens with methodological statements on questions such as observation and informants which could still be read with profit today by all researchers. Lowie describes the material culture, social organization, associations, myths and beliefs of the Crow, and shows that neither their most ancient social order nor what he observed during his first sojourn among them is in any way more authentic than what exists in the present.

In *The History of Ethnological Theory*, published in 1937 (New York: Farrar), Lowie provides a history of the discipline, which for all its personal character (his anti-Marxism was such that he did not even permit the inclusion of Marx and **Engels** in the book's index (**Harris**, 1968: 228)), was nonetheless the first work of its kind to concentrate exclusively on cultural anthropology, which in previous accounts had been all but obliterated by physical anthropology. In 1946 he resumed his anti-evolutionist crusade, this time against L. **White**, by revealing the contradictions in any closed system ('Evolution in Cultural Anthropology: A Reply to Leslie White', in *AA*, vol.48: 223–233).

In 1948 Lowie published *Social Organization*, which brought *Primitive Society* up to date with the addition of numerous ethnographical examples and a new sophistication in handling themes and concepts, but without changing the essence of the earlier work. He spent time teaching in Germany and Central Europe after the Second World War, and in 1945 produced *The German People: A Social Portrait to 1945*. In 1950–1951 he carried out six months of fieldwork in Germany to study the effect of the war on personality (*Toward Understanding Germany*, 1954). Rejecting the notion of 'national character' proposed by R. Benedict, he advanced a mosaic-like conception in which German culture is comprised of a large number of sub-cultural varieties but does not contain a specific character predisposing it to authoritarianism.

Although they sprang from the same movement, Lowie should not be seen merely as an adjunct to Kroeber, but as introducing into American anthropology a degree of specialization it had not previously known. Describing his approach as 'eclectic', Lowie wrote that the picture of human civilizations is like a harlequin's coat made of scraps of material.

He taught at Berkeley until his retirement

in 1950, and then at the universities of Columbia, Harvard, Washington and Hamburg, while continuing to hold annual seminars at Berkeley, where he died of cancer in 1957. In 1960 the University's museum was named after him.

Radin, Paul (1883–1959)

Born at Lodz in Poland to a rabbi who then emigrated with his family to the USA, Paul Radin spent his childhood in New York. He obtained a BA from New York City College in 1902 and then studied history at Columbia University. From 1905 to 1907 he spent time at the universities of Munich and Berlin and was then admitted to study anthropology with E. **Sapir** and F. **Boas**, and, after a period in the field studying the Winnebago (1908), he gained his doctorate in 1910. His fieldwork concentrated on the Wappo of California, the Zapotec of Mexico, the Ojibwa (whom he studied from 1913 to 1917 in the context of the geological survey of Canada directed by Sapir), the Fox, the Wintun and the Huave. Above all he devoted himself to the Winnebago, to whom he returned continually during his whole career and amongst whom he discovered a social organization both dualist and tripartite. The Winnebago camps were divided into two exogamous halves (highland and lowland), and this was reflected in their spatial and social organization. These halves were themselves divided into clans, with the lowland half comprising two groups of four clans (land people and water people), and the highland half comprising a single group of four clans (sky people). This apparent contradiction of a social organization both dualist and tripartite was interpreted by Radin first in diffusionist terms (immigration of new clans), and later according to the structuralist paradigm. Radin lectured at Cambridge at the invitation of **Rivers** from 1920 to 1925.

One of the central themes of Radin's work concerns the way in which the individual subject responds to his immediate social environment. In 1920 he published *The Autobiography of a Winnebago Indian* (U of California P), and in 1926 *Crashing Thunder: The Autobiography of an American Indian* (*UCPAAE*), thereby introducing a new autobiographical genre which broke with the tradition of anecdotal narratives current in the USA since the beginning of the nineteenth century (*Life of Black Hawk*, 1934). These books gave 'life stories' scientific character and set a trend followed by such works as W. Dyk's *Son of Old Man Hat: A Navaho Autobiography* (1938) and L. W. Simmons's *Sun Chief: The Autobiography of a Hopi Indian* (1942).

Radin's best-known work is undoubtedly *Primitive Man as a Philosopher* (New York: Dover, (1927) 1957), which shows that individual reflection is as prevalent in primitive societies as elsewhere, and that it is individuals who construct cultures rather than the other way round (the thesis of Kroeber and culturalism). In *Primitive Religion: Its Nature and Origin* (New York, 1937), he demonstrates that in any culture the degree of religious feeling in the individual varies from indifference to great profundity, and also that monotheism is universal and a belief in transcendence inherent in human thought. All these ideas are opposed point for point to the then dominant theses of **Lévy-Bruhl**. *The Road of Life and Death: A Ritual Drama of the American Indians*, published in 1945, describes the beliefs and rituals of the religious brotherhoods of North American Indians. Radin also wrote a book on the 'trickster', the persona of the mischievous swindler who plays a central role of demiurge and scourge, taking various animal forms and consistent only in his changeableness, including a physical instability. In his view the trickster, who is present in myths across all North American Indian territories, is also one of the oldest mythologies in Eurasia and survives in medieval buffoons and travelling acrobats. While Radin sees this phenomenon as a symbol of the passage from the animal to the human, Jung then adds the idea of the developmental stages of a child and his entry into the collective consciousness. E. Desveaux notes that this figure plays no part in the general system of transformation linking all the mythologies of the New World established by **Lévi-Strauss** in his *Mythologiques*, and explains it as a key which makes the construction of his narrative possible (Desveaux, 1991).

Rather then making teaching his main activity in his early career, Radin devoted himself to applied anthropology, working with a group of specialists who explored Canada from a geological perspective. Later he taught successively at the universities of Berkeley and Chicago, before being appointed director of the anthropology department at Brandeis University, where he stayed until the end of his career.

Gifford, Edward Winslow (1887–1959)

Born in Oakland, Edward Winslow Gifford studied natural sciences and pursued his research in this subject in numerous expeditions (Revillagigedo Island, Mexico, 1903; Galapagos Islands, 1905). He worked for a while as an ornithologist and was then appointed curator of the Museum of Anthropology at the University of California and lecturer in the university's anthropology department in 1920. In 1938 he became an assistant professor and in 1945 a full professor, and in 1947 he was appointed director of the museum. He retired in 1955. Gifford was one of the last scholars whose research interests and publications spanned archaeology (after his work in Mexico he was one of the first to practise this discipline in Oceania), physical anthropology ('California Anthropometry', *UCPAAE*, vol.22 (1926): 287–390), and social anthropology (*Tonga Society*, B. P. Bishop Museum, 1929; 'California Kinship Terminologies', *UCPAAE*, vol.18: 1–285). He is best remembered as the first to use the term 'lineage' in its current sense ('Miwok Lineages and the Political Unit in Aboriginal California', *AA*, vol.28 (1926): 389–401). In this Gifford anticipated **Evans-Pritchard** (who however did not acknowledge him).

Spier, Leslie (1893–1961)

Born in New York City, L. Spier obtained a B.Sc. in 1915 and then enrolled to study anthropology at Columbia University under **Boas**. Subsequently he worked as assistant curator at the American Museum of Natural History with C. **Wissler** and R. **Lowie**, gaining a doctorate in 1920 with a thesis entitled *The Sun Dance of the Plains Indians: Its Development and Diffusion* (*AMNH*, vol.16 (1921): 421–527). In this work he tried to discern an original form of sun dance by comparing the cultural traits of several Plains peoples. Employing historicist and diffusionist conceptions, his fieldwork examined a wide variety of American Indian populations, including the Zuni (1916), the Salish (1921–1923), the Mohave (1931–1932), but it is generally thought that his research on the Havasupai (1918–1921) constitutes his major contribution to the discipline. Among other places Spier taught at the universities of Washington (1920–1928), where he was the first anthropologist, Oklahoma (1927–1930), Chicago (1930–1932), Yale (1932–1939), and finally New Mexico (1939–1955), where he remained until his retirement. In 1944 he founded *The Southwestern Journal of Anthropology*.

Whorf, Benjamin Lee (1897–1941)

Benjamin Lee Whorf entered the chemistry department of the Massachusetts Institute of Technology in 1915 and obtained his B.Sc. there in 1918. He was then employed by an insurance company as an inspector of fire prevention precautions, and he occupied various positions in the same firm until his death.

His reading of Prescott's *The Conquest of Mexico* (1847) sparked his interest in Central

American civilizations, while his reading of A. Fabre d'Olivet's *La langue hébraïque restituée* (1817) led him to question the nature and functioning of languages. These twin stimulations soon fostered in him a fascination for Nahuatl (Aztec) and for other Central American languages. Whorf met **Sapir** at the International Congress of Americanists in 1928, by which time he already knew his works, and followed the lecture series on linguistics given by Sapir at Yale following his appointment there in 1931. In 1932 Sapir authorized Whorf to stay among the Hopi, and in the mid-1930s Whorf set out the so-called Sapir–Whorf hypothesis (thus named although the two men never wrote jointly). This hypothesis states simply that all levels of thought are dependent on language, that the structure of the language employed has an impact on the apprehension and comprehension of environment, and that each language represents and creates a distinct reality. This view has been strongly criticized by Lenneberg ('Cognition in Ethnolinguistics', *Language*, vol.26 (1953): 463–471) and by Feuer ('Sociological Aspects of the Relation between Language and Philosophy', *Philosophy of Science*, vol.20 (1953): 85–100); Lenneberg challenged Whorf's methodology and Feuer refuted his arguments on the basis that survival is predicated on correct perception of the physical world, and that this must everywhere be identical. Whorf died after a long illness on 26 July 1941 at the age of forty-four.

Kroeber-Quinn, Theodora (née Kracaw, 1897–1979)

Theodora Kroeber-Quinn was born in 1897 in Colorado to Emmett and Phebe Kracaw. At the University of California she studied clinical psychology, gaining an MA in 1920. She was married to three different men; Clifton Brown, Alfred **Kroeber** and John Harrison Quinn, two of whom died before her. In 1926 she wrote an article in collaboration proposing a method of statistical analysis of cultural relations in Polynesia. A. Kroeber and others developed this idea and applied it to American Indian cultures in California under the general rubric 'distribution of cultural data'. Also in 1926, she married Kroeber and thenceforth devoted herself to the education of her four children (of whom U. Le Guin was to become a major author of fantastic and futuristic fiction). In 1961 she published *Ishi in Two Worlds: A Biography of the Last Wild Indian in North America* (Berkeley, California UP), which met with wide success.

See also: ISHI

Bunzel, Ruth Leah (1898–1990)

Although less well-known than R. **Benedict** or M. **Mead**, R. L. Bunzel joins them to form a trio of important women in the early stages of Boasian anthropology. Born in New York, she obtained a BA from Barnard College in 1918 and then worked with **Boas**. In 1924 she accompanied Benedict on a research trip to the Zuni, and began to make a study of their ceremonies and their pottery. She was awarded a Ph.D. in 1929 for a thesis with a diffusionist orientation entitled *The Pueblo Potter*. She was appointed as a lecturer at Columbia University in 1930 and became an associate professor there in 1954. Bunzel also carried out research in Guatemala and Mexico. Turning her attention to the analysis of psychological characterizations of whole cultures, she took part in a research project led by Benedict on contemporary cultures and assisted A. **Kardiner** with his work on this topic.

Hoebel, Edward Adamson (1906–1993)

Born in Madison in 1906, Edward Adamson Hoebel studied sociology at the University of Wisconsin, graduating with a BA in 1928. He then enrolled in the sociology department of New York University, where he obtained an MA, and in the anthropology department of Columbia University, where he followed the courses of F. **Boas** and

R. **Benedict**. When Hoebel signalled his intention to write his thesis on the legal systems of the Plains Indians, Boas directed him to K. Llewellyn, a law professor at Columbia and leader of the school of 'legal realism'. On the basis of fieldwork carried out in 1933, Hoebel was awarded a Ph.D. in 1934 for a thesis which in 1940 he published as a book: *The Political Organization and Law-ways of the Comanche Indians* (Menasha: AAA). He undertook research on the Shoshone of the Northeast in 1934, on the Cheyenne in 1935–1936, and on the Pueblo Indians of New Mexico from 1945 to 1949, and he also worked in Pakistan. He taught at New York University (1929–1948), at the University of Utah (1948–1954), and then at the universities of Minnesota (1955–1972), Oxford and Nijmegen. He wrote *The Cheyenne Way* (Menasha: AAA) in collaboration with K. Llewellyn, and its appearance in 1941 opened up new perspectives for legal anthropology and attracted the attention of jurists. Hoebel died on 23 July 1993.

A biography of Hoebel and a bibliography of his work are available in a special, two-volume number of the journal *Studies in Third World Societies* entitled 'The Anthropology of Peace: Essays in Honor of E. Adamson Hoebel'. Finally, it is worth noting that Hoebel rejected **Malinowski**'s precept that any form of social control is to be seen as a law, adhering instead to the classic definition which acknowledges the existence of a law only when it can be enforced by authorized agents.

Driver, Harold Edson (1907–1992)
Born in Berkeley, Harold Edson Driver studied anthropology at the University of California (BA 1930), where he became a disciple of **Kroeber** and worked with him on the compilation of a standardized cultural element list (Driver and Kroeber, 'Quantitative Expression of Cultural Relationships', *UCPAAE vol.31 (1932): 211–256). In 1936 he obtained a Ph.D. with his thesis The Reliability of Culture Element Data* (Berkeley: University of California Anthropological Records, vol.1, 1938). Driver was unable to find employment in anthropology and so worked for many years in the family transport business. In 1948 he returned to the discipline as a research volunteer before gaining a bursary, a lectureship and finally the post of professor at Indiana University, which he held until his retirement in 1974. He worked in North American Indian societies, and his output was both historical and comparative. His major texts are *Girls' Puberty Rites in Western North America* (Berkeley, 1941), *A Comparative Study of North American Indians* (with C. Massey, Philadelphia, 1957), 'Geographical-historical vs. Psycho-functional Explanations of Kin Avoidances' (*Current Anthropology*, vol.7 (1966): 131–182), and a global analysis of 280 societies written with James L. Coffin: *Classification and Development of North American Indian Culture: A Statistical Analysis of the Driver-Massey Sample*, Philadelphia, 1975). Also worth mentioning are *The Contribution of A. L. Kroeber to Culture Area Theory and Practice* (Baltimore, 1962), and 'Correlational Analysis of Murdock's 1957 Ethnographic Sample' (with K. E. Schnessler) (*AA*, vol.69 (1967): 332).

SELECT BIBLIOGRAPHY

Abélès, M. (1991) 'Robert Lowie', in P. Bonte and M. Izard (eds) *Dictionnaire de l'ethnologie et de l'anthropologie*, Paris: Presses universitaires de France, pp.427–428.

Abélès, M. and Izard, M. (1991) 'Kroeber, A.', in P. Bonte and M. Izard (eds) *Dictionnaire de l'ethnologie et de l'anthropologie*, Paris: Presses universitaires de France, pp.405–407.

Anonymous (1902) 'J. Powell', *AA*, 4: 564–565.

Banta, R.E. (ed.) (1949) *Indiana Authors and Their Books, 1816–1916*, Crawfordsville: Wabash College.

Barnes, R.H. (1984) *Two-Crows Denies it: A History of Controversy in Omaha Sociology*, Lincoln: Nebraska University Press.

Basehart, H.W. and Hill, W.W. (1965) 'Leslie Spier', *AA*, 67: 1258–1272.

Beals, A. 'On E. Wolf and the North Berkeley gang', and E. Wolf 'Reply' *CA*, 29(2): 306.

Benedict, R. (1942) 'Franz Boas, an obituary', *Science*, 97: 60–62.

Boas, F. (1889) *Letter and Preliminary Data*, Fourth Report of the Committee on North-Western Tribes of Canada, Report of the British Association for the Advancement of Science.

——(1890) *The Indians of British Columbia*, Fifth Report of the Committee on North-Western Tribes of Canada, Report of the British Association for the Advancement of Science.

——(1891) *The Indians of British Columbia*, Sixth Report of the Committee on North-Western Tribes of Canada, Report of the British Association for the Advancement of Science.

——(1897, 1970) *The Social Organization and the Secret Societies of the Kwakiutl Indians*, (Washington, Report of the US National Museum for 1895), New York: Johnson Reprint.

——(1898, 1975) *The Mythology of the Bella Coola Indians*, (Publications of the Jesup North Pacific Expedition, vol.1), New York: AMS Press.

——(1902, 1977) *Tsimshian Texts*, St. Clair Shores: Scholarly Press.

——(1909a, 1975) *The Kwakiutl of Vancouver Island*, (Publications of the Jesup North Pacific Expedition, vol.5), New York: AMS Press.

——(ed.) (1909b) *Putnam Anniversary Volume : Anthropological Essays Presented to Frederic W. Putnam in Honor of his 70th Birthday*, New York: Stechert and Co.

——(1921) *Ethnology of the Kwakiutl*, Washington, Smithsonian Institution.

——(1940, 1982) *Race, Language and Culture*, Chicago: University of Chicago Press.

——(1945, 1969) *Race and Democratic Society*, New York: Biblo and Tanner.

——(1966) *Kwakiutl Ethnography*, ed. H. Codere, Chicago: University of Chicago Press.

——(1972) *The Professional Correspondence of Franz Boas*, Microfilm edition. Wilmington, Del.

Browman, D.L. (2002) 'The Peabody Museum, F. W. Putnam, and the Rise of US anthropology, 1866–1903', *AA*, 104(2): 508–520.

Browmann, F.L. (2002) 'Anthropological professionalization and the Virginia Indians at the turn of the century', *AA*, 104(2): 499–508.

Buckley, T. (1991) 'Kroeber, Alfred', in C. Winter (ed.), pp.364–366.

——(1996) 'The little history of pitiful events: the epistemological and moral contexts of Kroeber's Californian ethnology', in G.W. Stocking (ed.) *Volksgeist as method and ethic. essays on Boasian ethnography and the German anthropological tradition*, *HOA*, vol. 8: 257–297.

Bunzel, R. (1975) 'Spier, Leslie', in *International Encyclopedia of the Social Sciences*, D.L. Sills, vol.15: 130–131.

Bunzel, R.L. (1929, 1972) *The Pueblo Potter: A Study of Creative Imagination in Primitive Art*, New York: Dover Publication.

——(1952) *Chichicastenango, a Guatemalan Village*, New York.

——(1962) 'Introduction' to the reissue of Boas, *Anthropology and Modern Life*, New York: Norton.

Buzaljko, G.W. (1988) 'Theodora Kracaw Kroeber', in Gacs (ed.) 1988, pp.187–194.

Calhoun, M. (1991a) 'Fay-Cooper Cole', in C. Winter, pp.119–120.

——(1991b) 'Dorsey, George A.' in C. Winter, pp.153–154.

Carroll, J.B. (1956) 'Introduction' to Whorf 1956.

Codere, H. (1966) 'Introduction' to Boas 1966.

Cole, D. (1983) 'The value of a person lies in his Herzensbildung': Franz Boas's Baffin Island Letter-Diary, 1883–1884' in Stocking (ed.) *Observers Observed: Essays on Ethnographic Fieldwork*, *HOA*, vol.1: 13–53.

Cole, D. and Long, A. (1999) 'The anthropological survey tradition: the role of F. Boas in North American Anthropological Survey', in E.C. Carter, II, *Surveying the Record: North American Exploration to 1930*, Philadelphia: American Philosophical Society, pp.225–251.

Cole, F.-C. (1913) *The Wild Tribes of the Davao District*, Chicago: Mindanao Field Museum.

——(1931) 'G.A. Dorsey', *AA*, 33: 412–414.

——(1937) *Rediscovering Illinois: Archaeological explorations in and around Fulton Country*, Chicago: University of Chicago Press.

——(1945, 1968) *The Peoples of Malaysia*, Princeton: Van Nostrand.

Cushing, F.H. (1901, 1986) *Zuni Folk Tales*, Intro by M. Austin, Foreword by J.W. Powell, Tuscon: University of Arizona Press.

——(1920, 1974) *Zuni Breadstuff*, New York: Museum of American Indians.

Darnell, R. (1969) 'The development of American anthropology 1879–1920: from the Bureau of American Ethnology to Franz Boas', unpublished thesis, University of Pennsylvania.

——(1970) 'The emergence of academic anthropology at the University of Pennsylvania', *Journal of the History of the Bahavioral Sciences*, 6: 80–92.

——(1998) 'And along came Boas.' *Continuity and Revolution in Americanist Anthropology*, Amsterdam, Philadelphia: J. Benjamins.

Darnell, R. and Gleach, F.W. (eds) 'Special Centennial Issue Articles', *AA*, vol. 104(2).

DeMalli, R.J. (1988) 'James Owen Dorsey', in W. Washburn (ed.) *History of Indian-White Relations, Handbook of North American Indians*, vol. 4, Washington: Smithsonian Institution.

Deacon, D. (1997) *Elsie Clews Parsons: Inventing Modern Life*, Chicago: University of Chicago Press.

Dellenbaugh, F.S. (1918) 'Memorial to J.W. Powell', *AA*, 20: 432–436.

Desveaux, E. (1991) 'Radin, Paul', in P. Bonte and M. Izard (eds) *Dictionnaire de l'ethnologie et de l'anthropologie*, Paris: Presses universitaires de France, pp.614–615.

Dexter, R.W. (1966) 'Putnam's problems popularizing anthropology', *American Scientist*, 54: 315–332.

Diamond, S. (ed.) (1960) *Culture in History: Essays in Honor of Paul Radin*, New York: Columbia University Press.

——(1981) 'P. Radin', in S. Silverman (ed.) *Totems and Teachers: Perspectives on the History of Anthropology*, New York and Guildford: Columbia University Press, pp. 67–101.

Dixon, R. B. (1923) *The Racial History of Mankind*, New York: Scribner.

——(1928) *The Building of Cultures*, New York: Scribner.

Driver, H.E. (1962) *The Contribution of A.L. Kroeber to Culture Area Theory and Practice*, Baltimore.

Dubois, C. (1959) 'Robert H. Lowie, ethnologist: a personal record', in C. Dubois (ed.) 1960, *Lowie's Selected Papers in Anthropology*, Berkeley, CA: University of California Press.

Dundes, A (1966) *The Complete Bibliography of Robert H. Lowie*, Berkeley: The R.H. Lowie Museum of Anthropology.

Eggan, F. (1963) 'Fay Cooper-Cole', *AA*, 65: 641–648.

——(1968) 'One hundred years of ethnology and social anthropology' in J.O. Brew, *One Hundred Years of Anthropology*, Cambridge, MA: Harvard University Press, pp.119–153.

Elasser, A.B. (1980) 'Obituary, Théodora Kroeber-Quinn', *AA*, 82: 114–115.

Fawcett, D.M. and McLuhan, T. (1988) 'Ruth Leah Bunzel', in Gacs (ed.) 1988.

Fenton, W.N. (1959) 'J.R. Swanton', *AA*, 61: 633–638.

——(1991) 'Hale, H.E.', in C. Winter, pp.262–263.

——(1963; 1883) 'Introduction, Horatio Hale (1817–96)' in H. Hale, *Iroquois Book of Rites*, New York: AMS Press.

Flannery, R. (1950) 'J. M. Cooper', *AA*, 52: 64–74.

Foster, G.M. (1960) 'E. Gifford', *AA*, 62: 327–329.

Fowler, D.D. and Fowler, C. (1971) *Anthropology of the Numa: J. W. Powell's manuscripts on the Numic peoples of western North America, 1868–1880*, Washington: Smithsonian.

Fowler, Euler, R.C. and Fowler, C. (1969) *J.W. Powell and the Anthropology of the Canyon Country*, New York: Dutton.

Freed, S.A. and Freed, R.S. (1983) 'C. Wissler and the development of anthropology in the USA', *AA*, 85: 800–825.

——(1991a) 'Wissler', in C. Winter, pp.763–764.

French, D.H. (1972) 'Goldenweiser, A.', in *International Encyclopedia of the Social Sciences*, D.L. Sills, vol.6: 196–197.

——. (1991b) 'Goldenweiser, A.' in C. Winter, pp.444–445.

Friedlander, J. (1988) 'Elsie Clews Parsons', in Gacs (ed.) 1988, pp.282–290.

Gidley, M (1998) *Eward S. Curtis and the North American Indian, Incorporated*, Cambridge, New York: Cambridge University Press.

Glenn, J.R. (1991a) 'Dorsey, G.A.', in C. Winter, pp.154–155.

——(1991b) 'LaFlesche, Francis', in C. Winter, pp.375–376.

——(1991c) 'Mooney, James', in C. Winter, pp.480–481.

Glick, T. (1997) 'A. Kroeber', in Barfield, T. (ed.) *Dictionary of Anthropology*, Oxford, Cambridge MA: Blackwell, pp.270–271.

Goldenwieser, A.A. (1922, 1970) *Early Civilization*, reissued in 1937 under the title *Anthropology: An Introduction to Primitive Culture*, New York: Crofts.

——(1931) *Robot or Gods: An Essay on Craft and Mind*, New York: A. Knopf.

——(1932, 1968) *History, Psychology, and Culture*, Gloucester: P. Smith.

Goldschmidt, W. (ed.) (1959) *The Anthropology of F. Boas*, San Francisco: Chandler.

Green, J. (ed.) (1979) *Zuni: Selected Writings of Frank Hamilton Cushing*, foreword by T. Eggan, Lincoln: University of Nebraska Press.

Gruber, J.W. (1967) 'H. Hale and the development of American anthropology', *PAPS*, 111: 5–37.

Hallowell, A.I. (1960) 'The beginnings of anthropology in America' in F. de Laguna (ed.), *Selected Papers from the American Anthropologists, 1888–1920*, Evanston: AAA, pp.1–90.

Hare, P. (1985) *A Woman's Quest for Science: Portrait of the Anthropologist Elsie Clews Parsons*, New York: Prometheus Books.

Harley, B.A. (1933) 'F. La Flesche', *AA*, 35: 328–331.

Harris, M. (1968, 2001) *The Rise of Anthropological Theory*, with intro. by M.L. Mangolis, Walnut Creek: Alta Mira Press.

Heizer, R.F. (1959) 'E. Gifford', *American Antiquity*, 25: 257–259.

Herskovits, M. (1953) *F. Boas: The Science of Man in the Making*, New York: Scribner.

Herzfeld, R.F. (1991) 'Cooper, John Montgomery', in C. Winter, pp.125–126.

Hewitt, J.N. (1895) 'J.O. Dorsey', *AA*, 8: 180–183.

Hewitt, J.N.B. (1922) 'J. Mooney', *AA*, 24: 209–214.

Hinsley, C.M. (1981) *Savages and Scientist: the Smithsonian Institution and the Development of American Anthropology, 1846–1910*, Washington: Smithsonian Institution Press.

——(1985) 'From shell-heaps to steal: Early anthropology at the Peabody Museum' in G.W. Stocking (ed.) *Object and Others: Essays on Museums and Material Culture*, HOA, vol. 3: 49–74.

——(1991a) 'Powell, John Wesley', in C. Winter, pp.549–550.

——(1991b) 'Putnam, F.W.', in C. Winter, pp.555–557.

Hodge, F.W. (1914) 'Discussion and Correspondence, Adolph Bandelier', *AA*, 16: 349–358.

Hoebel, E.A. (1954) *The Laws of Primitive Man: A Study in Comparative Legal Dynamics*, Cambridge: Harvard University Press.

——(1961) *Cheyennes: Indians of the Great Plains*, New York: Holt, Rinehart and Winston.

——(1979) *Anthropology: The Human Experience*, New York: McGraw-Hill.

Holmes, F.W. (1912) 'McGee', *AA*, 14: 683–687.

Hough, W. (1923) 'Alice Fletcher', *AA*, 25: 254–257.

——. (1933) 'Holmes, W.H., *AA*, 35: 752–764.

Hyatt, M. (1990) *F. Boas, Social Activist: The Dynamics of Ethnicity*, Westport: Greenwood.

Hymes, D. (1961) 'A. L. Kroeber', *Language*, 23: 1–23.

Hyslop, J. (1991) 'Bandelier, Adolph', in C. Winter, pp.22–23.

Jacknis, I. (2002) 'The first Boasian: A. Kroeber and F. Boas, 1896–1905', *AA*, 104(2): 520–533.

Jorgensen, J.G. (1974) 'Biographical sketch and bibliography of H. E. Driver', in Jorgensen, ed., *Comparative Studies by H.E. Driver and Essays in his Honor*, New Haven, HRAF Press.

——(1991) 'Driver, Harnold E.', in C. Winter, pp.160–161.

Joseph, J. (1996) 'The immediate sources of the Sapir–Whorf hypothesis', *Historiographia Linguistica*, 23: 365–404.

Judd, N.M. (1967) *The Bureau of American Ethnology: A Partial History*, Norman: University of Oklahoma Press.

Kroeber, A.L. (1913) 'Putnam, F.W.', *AA*, 17: 712–718.

——(1917a) *Zuni Kin and Clan*, New York: American Museum of Natural History.

——(1917b) 'The Superorganic', *AA*, 19: 163–213.

——(1919, 1974) *The People of the Philippines*, Westport: Greenwood Press.

——(1931) 'Review of Growing up in New Guinea', *AA*, 33: 248–250.

——(1931) 'The culture-areas and age-area concept of C. Wissler', in S.A. Rice (ed.) *Methods in Social Science: A Case Book*, Chicago: University of Chicago Press.

——(1936) *Area and Climax*, Berkeley: University of California Press.

——(1939) *Cultural and Natural Areas of Native North America*, Berkeley: University of California Press.

——(1943) 'E.C. Parsons', *AA*, 45: 252–255.

——(1944) *Configurations of Culture Growth*, Berkeley: University of California Press.

——(1952, 1987) *The Nature of Culture*, Chicago: University of Chicago Press.

——(1956) 'The place of Boas in anthropology', *AA*, 58: 151–159.

——(1963, 1923), *Anthropology*. Foreword F. Eggan, Lincoln: University of Nebraska Press.

——(1902, 1983) *The Arapaho*, New York: Galleon.

Kroeber, A.L. *et al.* (1943) 'Franz Boas, 1853–1942' in *AA*, 45: 1–120.

Kroeber, A.L. and Parsons, T. (1958) 'The concept of culture and the social system', *American Sociological Review*, 23: 582.

Kroeber-Quinn, T. (1959) *The Inland Whale*, Bloomington: Indiana University Press.

——(1970) *Alfred Kroeber: A Personal Configuration*, Berkeley: University of California Press.

Kroeber-Quinn, T., Elsasser, A.B. and Heizer, R.F. (1977) *Drawn from Life: California Indians in Pen and Brush*. Socorro: Ballena Press.

Kroeber-Quinn, T. and Heizer, R.F. (1968) *Almost Ancestors: The First Californians*, New York: Ballantine.

Kuper, A. (1999) *Culture: The Anthropologists' Account*, Cambridge, MA: Harvard University Press.

Lange, C.H. and Riley, C.L. (1996) *Bandelier: The Life and Adventures of A. Bandelier*, Salt Lake City: Utah University Press.

Lesser, A. (1981) 'Franz Boas' in S. Silverman, (ed.) *Totems and Teachers*, pp.1–35.

Lévi-Strauss, C. (1973; 1965) 'L'oeuvre du Bureau of american anthropology et ses leçons', *Anthropologie structurale deux*, Paris, Plon, pp.63–77.

——(1991) 'F. Boas', in P. Bonte and M. Izard (eds) *Dictionnaire de l'ethnologie et de l'anthropologie*, Paris: Presses universitaires de France, pp.116–118.

Liberty, M. (1978) 'Francis LaFlesche : the Osage Odyssey' in M. Liberty (ed.) *American Indian Intellectuals*, St. Paul: American Anthropological Society, pp.44–59.

Lewis, M. and Clark, W. (1809, 2002) *Definitive Journals of Lewis and Clark*, G. Moulton (ed.), Lincoln: University of Nebraska Press.

Lonergan, D. (1991a) 'Cushing, Frank Hamilton' in C. Winter, pp.132–133.

——(1991b) 'E. Gifford' in C. Winter, p.236.

——(1991c) 'Spier, Leslie', in C. Winter, pp.657–658.

Lowie, R.H. (1920, 1947) *Primitive Society*, New York: Diveright.

——(1934) *An Introduction to Cultural Anthropology*, New York: Farrer.

——(1937) *The History of Ethnological Theory*, New York: Farrar.

——(1946) 'Professor White and anti-evolutionist schools', *Southwestern Journal of Anthropology*, 2: 240–241.

——(1951) 'C. Wissler', *AA*, 51: 527–528.

——(1961) 'A. Kroeber', *AA*, 63: 1038–1087.

Lucy, J.A. (1991) 'Whorf, Benjamin Lee' in C. Winter, pp.756–758.

Mark, J. (1980a) *4 Anthropologists: An American Science in its Early Years*, New York: Science History Publications.

——(1980b) 'William Henry Holmes' in J. Mark, *4 Anthropologists: An American Science in its Early Years*, New York, pp.131–171.

——(1982) 'F. LaFlesche: the American Indian as anthropologist', *Isis*, 73: 497–510.

——(1989) *A Stranger in Her Native Land: Alice Fletcher and the American Indians*, Lincoln: University of Nebraska Press.

——(1991) 'Fletcher, Alice', in C. Winter, pp.202–203.

Matthy, P. (1991) 'Lowie, Robert H.' in C. Winter, pp.426–427.

Maud, R. (2000) *Transmission Difficulties: F. Boas and Tsimshian mythology*, Vancouver: Talonbooks.

Mead, M. and Bunzel, R. (eds) (1960) *The Golden Age of American Anthropology*, New York: Braziller.

Meadows, P. (1952) *J. W. Powell: Frontiersman of science*, Lincoln: Nebraska University Press.

Meillassoux, C. (1972) 'Potlatch' in *Encyclopedia Universalis*, vol. 13: 423–425.

Miller, F. (1993) 'A Hoebel', *AN*, vol. 34(6): 6.

Mooney, J. (1885) *Linguistic Families of Indian Tribes North Mexico*, Washington: Bureau of American Ethnology.

——(1905) 'W. Matteys', *AA*, 7: 514–523.

——(1907) 'A.S. Gastschet', *AA*, 9: 561–570.

——(1928) *The Aboriginal Population of America North of Mexico*. Washington: Bureau of American Ethnology.

Moses, L.G. (1984, 2002) *The Indian Man: A Biography of James Mooney*, Lincoln: University of Nebraska Press.

Muller, M. (1891) 'On the work of Major J. W. Powell, director of the US. Ethnological Bureau', Report of section H, 61st Meeting of the British Association for the Advancement of Science, Cardiff, August.

Müller-Wille, L. (1998) *Franz Boas among the Inuit of Baffin Island, 1883–1884: Journals and letters*, Toronto: University of Toronto Press.

Murdock, G.P. (1950) 'Clark Wissler', *AA*, 50: 292–304.

Murphy, F. (1990) 'R.L. Bunzel', *AN*, March, 31: 5.

Murphy, R. (1972) *Robert H. Lowie*, New York: Columbia University Press.

Murra, J.V. (ed.) (1976) *American Anthropology: the Early Years*, Saint Paul: American Anthropological Society.

Murray, S.O. (1983) 'Historical inferences from ethnohistorical data', *Journal of the History of the Behavioral Sciences*, 19: 335–340.

——(1991a) 'Dixon, Roland B.' in C. Winter, pp.149–150.

——(1991b) 'Parsons, Elsie Clews', in C. Winter, p.529.

——(1991c) 'Swanton, John Reed' in C. Winter, p.680.

Nicholsen, M. (1991) 'Hoebel, E. Adamson' in C. Winter, p.297.

Oestreich Lurie, N. (1966, 1986) 'Women in Early American Anthropology' in J. Helm (ed.) *Pioneers of American Anthropology, The Uses of Biography*, New York: AMS Press, pp.31–81.

Parsons, E.C. (1936) *Mitla: Town of Souls*, Chicago: University of Chicago Press.

——(1939, 1996) *Pueblo Indian Religion*, with intro. by P. Turner Strong, Lincoln: University of Nebraska Press.

——(1945) *Peguche: Canton of Otavalo, Ecuador, a Study of Andean Indians*, University of Chicago Press.

Penn, J. (1972) *Linguistic Relativity Versus Innate Ideas: the Origins of the Sapir–Whorf Hypothesis in German Thought*, La Hague: Mouton.

Radin, P. (1923, 1970) *The Winnebago Tribe* (1915–1916), Lincoln: University of Nebraska Press.

——(1933, 1987) *The Method and Theory of Ethnology, An Essay in Criticism* with Intro. by A. Vidich, Hadley: Bergin.

——(1949) *The Culture of the Winnebago, as Described by Themselves*, Bloomington, Indiana.

——(1958) 'Robert H. Lowie', *AA*, 60: 358–375.

——(1959) 'P. Radin', *AA*, 61: 839–343.

Rollins, P. (1980) *Benjamin Lee Whorf: Lost Generation. Theories of Mind, Language and Religion*, Ann Arbor: Popular Culture Association.

Rowe, J.H. (1962) 'A. L. Kroeber', *American Antiquity*, 27: 395–415.

Sanjek, R. (1996) 'Boas, F.', in A. Barnard and J. Spencer (eds) *Encyclopedia of Social and Cultural Anthropology*, London: Routledge, pp.71–74.

Shelden, W.H. (1919) 'Dr. Goldenweiser and historical indeterminism', *Journal of Philosophy, Psychology, and Scientific Method*, 16: 327–330.

Spier, L. (1925) *The Distribution of Kinship Systems in North America*, Seattle: Washington University Press.

——(1933, 1970) *Yuma, Tribe of the Gila River*, New York: Cooper Square.

——(1935, 1979) *The Prophet Dance of the Northwest and its Derivatives: The Source of the Ghost Dance*, Menasha: American Anthropological Society .

——(1936, 1970) *Cultural Relations of the Gila River and Lower Colorado*, New Haven: Human Relations Area Files Press.

——(1943) 'Elsie Clews Parsons', *AA*, 45: 244–51.

Stanton, W. (1975) *The Great US Exploring Expedition of 1838–1842*, Berkeley: University of California Press.

Stegner, D.D.W. (1954, 1982) *Beyond the Hundredth Meridian: J. W. Powell and the Second Opening of the West*, Lincoln: University of Nebraska Press.

Steward, J. (1960) *John Reed Swanton*, New York: Columbia University Press.

Steward, J.H. (1946) 'Introduction' to vol.1 of *Handbook of South American Indians*, Smithsonian Institution, Bureau of American Ethnology, pp. 1–8.

——(1961) 'Alfred Kroeber', *AA*, 63: 1038–1060.

——(1973) *Alfred Kroeber*, New York: Columbia University Press.

Stocking, G.W. (1968) 'Franz Boas and the culture concept in historical perspective' in *Race, Culture, and Evolution: Essays in the History of Anthropology*, Chicago: University of Chicago Press, pp. 195–234.

——(1974) *The Shaping of American Anthropology 1883–1911: A Franz Boas Reader*, New York: Basic Books.

——(1980) *Anthropology at Chicago*, Chicago: The J. Regenstein Library.

——(1992) *The Ethnographer's Magic and Other Essays in the History of Anthropology*, University of Wisconsin Press.

——(ed.) (1996) *Volksgist as Method and Ethic: Essays on Boasian Ethnography and the German Anthropological Tradition*, *HOA*, vol.8, University of Wisconsin Press.

Tax, S. (1991) 'Boas, Franz', in C. Winter, pp.68–69.

Temkin, A.S. (1988) 'Alice Cunningham Fletcher', in Gacs (ed.) 1988.

Ten Kate, C. (1900) 'F. H. Cushing', *AA*, 2: 254, 768–771.

Tozzer, and Kroeber (1936) 'R.B. Dixon', *AA*, 38: 291–300.

Verdier, R. (ed.) (1988) 'Dossier E.A. Hoebel', *Droit et Cultures*, 15–16.

Wallace, A.F.C. (1965) 'Introduction' to the reprint of J. Mooney *The Ghost Dance Religion*, Chicago: University of Chicago Press.

Wallis, W.D. (1941) 'A. Goldenweiser', *AA*, 43: 250–255.

Wendling, T. (1991) 'Amérique du Nord. L'anthropologie Nord-américaine', in Bonte and Izard (eds) *Dictionnaire de l'ethnologie et de l'anthropologie*, Paris: Presses universitaires de France, pp.53–57.

White, D.R. (1975) 'Process, statistics and anthropological theory: an appreciation of H. E. Driver', *Reviews in Anthropology*, 2: 295–314.

White, L. (ed.) (1940, 1978) *The Correspondence between Bandelier and Morgan*, New York: AMS Press.

——(ed.) (1966) *Southwestern Journals of Adolph Bandelier*, Alburquerque: University of New Mexico Press.

White, L.A. (1966) *The Social Organization of Ethnologicol Theory*, Rice University Studies, vol.52.

Whorf, B.L. (1956) *Language, Thought and Reality: Selected Writings of Benjamin Lee Whorf*, Cambridge, MA: Massachusetts Institute of Technology Press.

Wissler, C. (1912, 1974) *North American Indians of the Plains*, New York: B. Franklin Reprints.

——(1913) 'Societies and dance associations of the Blackfoot Indians', *Anthropological Papers*, American Museum of Natural History, vol.11, pp.359–460.

Wolf, E.R. (1981) 'A. L. Kroeber', in S. Silverman (ed.) *Totems and Teachers: Perspectives on the History of Anthropology*, New York: Columbia University Press, pp. 35–67.

Wolf, M.S-F. E. (1991) 'Radin, Paul', in C. Winter, pp.565–566.

Woodbury, N.F.S. (1991) 'Bunzel, Ruth Leah' in C. Winter, p.86.

Woodbury, R.B. (1996) 'American Anthropological Association', in Levinson and Ember, pp.52–56.

Wright, B. (ed.) (1988) *The Mythic World of the Zuni*, Albuquerque: University of Mexico Press.

V

The French tradition and the *Institut d'ethnologie*

The accounts and testimonies of G. de Ruysbroeck (1294–1381), J. de Léry (1534–1613), A. Thevet (1502–1590), J. Thévenot (1633–1664), and Lafiteau (1681–1746); the anthropological reflections of Montaigne (1533–1592) and Enlightenment thinkers; the founding of the *Société des observateurs de l'homme*; and the publication of *Considérations sur les diverses méthodes à suivre dans l'observation des peuples sauvages* [*Reflections on the Various Methods to be Followed in the Observation of Primitive Peoples*] (1800) by J. M. de Gérando (1772–1842): all of these factors could have permitted France to make early progress with a vigorous programme of anthropological research, whereas in reality it was rather late in the day before such research got underway. **Mauss** complained of this in 1913:

> Such missions as were recognized by the state were nonetheless carried out thanks to the generosity of individual benefactors, and those led by Prince R. Bonaparte, Bourg de Bozas, Créqui-Montfort and Sénéchal de Grange, among others, yielded outstanding ethnographic results, from which institutions like the *Musée du Trocadéro* and the *Muséum* greatly profited. But ethnography as a whole led a Cinderella-like existence. Although abundantly represented in the *Commission des Missions*, it was neglected in favour of other, more established and well-endowed areas of learning: its budget for the last thirty years does not exceed what is granted to archaeological studies in a single year [. . .] in contrast to the federal government of the USA with its Bureau of American Ethnology.
>
> (Mauss, 1969 (1913): 395–435)

Anthropology was not properly institutionalized in France until the opening in 1925 of the *Institut d'ethnologie* at the University of Paris, created by Mauss, **Rivet** and **Lévy-Bruhl**; prior to that, French anthropology was practised piecemeal in a myriad of unconnected organizations. The period before the founding of the *Institut* can be seen in terms of five main currents.

The first and predominant current was physical anthropology, which would be carried forward by P. Rivet. In 1855 Quatrefages de Bréau (1810–1892) acceded to the chair of anatomy and the natural history of man at the *Musée d'histoire naturelle*, and in 1856 he transformed this into a chair of anthropology, defining its role as the illumination of the various human races from all possible perspectives. The idea contained in this project of linking culture and physical anthropology was opposed by P. Broca (1824–1880), who proposed that these two fields of knowledge be kept apart, albeit without succeeding in separating them in the institutions he himself created: the *Ecole d'anthropologie de Paris* and the *Société d'anthropologie de Paris*, or indeed in the latter's *Bulletins et Mémoires* and its journal *l'Anthropologie*. In 1878 Hamy (1842–1908), 'while working as assistant to

Quatrefages at the *Muséum*, created the *Musée d'ethnographie du Trocadéro*, partly with collections from various parts of Paris, but mainly with the material assembled for the *Exposition universelle* of 1878' (Mauss, 1969 (1913): 398). The *Musée du Trocadéro* and its management were to remain attached to the anthropology chair of the *Musée d'histoire naturelle*. Hamy was succeeded by R. Verneau (1852–1937), a specialist in the Gouaches and a cheerful popularizer of the discipline, who in turn was replaced by P. Rivet in 1928.

The second current flowed from knowledge acquired through colonialism. From the beginning of the colonial period, military men, administrators and churchmen gathered a formidable quantity of documentation. Faidherbe (1818–1889) moved to Senegal in 1852 and rapidly set about writing linguistic studies and monographs on its peoples and regions. This current gained the support of geographical societies, of which the first was founded in Paris in 1821. By combining scientific endeavour with commercial ambition, these societies acquired considerable importance by the turn of the century, and as early as 1886 the Lille society contained 1,200 members.

The third current was the *belles lettres* tradition. From Napoleon's Egyptian Expedition onwards, a tradition of highly erudite research developed in France which had its focus in the *Institut des Langues Orientales* (otherwise known as the *Ecole des langues et civilisations orientales vivantes*), the *Ecole française d'Extrême-Orient*, and the *Institut français de Damas*. This sort of research would subject archaeological inscriptions found in Cambodia to painstakingly meticulous analysis, but nothing or almost nothing would be said about the country's inhabitants.

A fourth current was made up of the extensive mass of information accumulated on French folklore and society, from which the modern *Institut d'ethnologie* has retained but little. The work of **Herder** (1744–1803) and the Brothers Grimm (*Kinder- und Hausmärchen* [*Fairy Tales for Children and the Home*], 1819, 1857) stimulated the practice of collecting tales, folklore and popular beliefs. These investigations went hand in hand with the nationalist movements which swept across the European continent and were often incorporated into the quest for ethnic origins. In France these efforts bore fruit in the works of P. Sébillot (1846–1918), who collected popular tales in Brittany from 1880 to 1908, Saint-Yves (1870–1935), and A. **van Gennep** (1873–1957). In the provinces learned societies sprang up which combined research into popular folklore, archaeology and prehistory. These societies were often drawn into the orbit of the *Société d'ethnographie* established in 1859, which published the journal *l'Ethnographie*. This journal was later joined by the *Revue de tradition populaire*, launched in 1886, and the *Revue d'ethnologie et de traditions populaires*, which appeared from 1920 to 1929.

The fifth and last current was that of the *Ecole française de sociologie*, to which Lévy-Bruhl and Mauss belonged. Often called 'primitive sociology', ethnography (and by the same token ethnology) was the application to non-literate peoples of positivist Durkheimian sociology. The importance of this area of sociological inquiry is indicated by V. Karady's finding that 45% of review articles published in *L'Année sociologique* were on ethnological or exotic subjects (Karady, 1981). This work was focused above all on questions of 'social morphology', or, in Mauss's phrase, 'social physiology', that is the study of the categories operating in collective psychologies (Mauss, 1969: 209). Promoted most strongly by Lévy-Bruhl and Mauss, this line of research was notably pursued in **Leenhardt**'s fieldwork with the Kanak and in the work of **Griaule** and his disciples, particularly their description of systems of representation.

French anthropology can thus be seen as a confluence of various currents of thinking and research, each with a distinct spirit and style. The discipline merged the colonial explorations, the anthropology of the *Musée d'histoire naturelle*, the thought of the *Ecole de Sociologie française* and the erudite *belles lettres* tradition. The *Institut d'ethnologie* awarded both arts and sciences degrees, and its founders became the discipline's sole guardians, exercising their authority by controlling the way it was taught, choosing what research to fund, and deciding what to admit for publication in the series *Travaux et mémoires de l'Institut d'ethnologie* [*Papers and Memoranda of the Institute of Ethnology*]. Van Gennep was doubtless the most high-profile victim of this hegemony, as is borne out by the rapid collapse of his own initiatives: the *Institut ethnographique international de Paris*, the *Revue d'ethnographie et de sociologie*, which he launched in 1910–1911, and his dream of a *Musée des civilisations* (promoted in a circular published by his institute's own journal in 1911). Whatever the ill effects of this concentration of power in their hands, it yet remains the case that the founders of the discipline succeeded in giving French anthropology its institutional and conceptual embodiment by anchoring its national characteristics in humanist principles. As J. Jamin has shown, the *Musée de l'Homme* and the French anthropological tradition issued from the Third Republic and the 1789 Revolution rather than from the natural sciences. Established under the jurisdiction of E. Deladier (1884–1970), Minister for the Colonies, the *Institut d'ethnologie* explicitly put itself at the service of colonialism (Lévy-Bruhl, 1926; P. Rivet, 1940). This accommodating approach was, however, only meagrely rewarded, and anthropological missions had to rely mainly on funding from the banker A. Kahn (1860–1940) and the Rockefeller Foundation. The solicitations made by ethnology to the colonial authorities were numberless, the responses extremely few. Things are hardly any different today: ethnologists endeavour to market their knowledge to development agencies, the state, local communities and even private businesses, but the interest shown falls far short of fulfilling their aspirations. With only a few exceptions, the colonial state tolerated rather than nurtured the school founded by Rivet and Mauss.

A FORERUNNER

Fustel de Coulanges, Numa Denys (1830–1889)

Numa Denys Fustel de Coulanges was a student at the ENS, and after a period spent at the French School at Athens he obtained his doctorate in 1858. He was appointed professor at the University of Strasbourg, at the Sorbonne, and finally at the ENS, where he became director and counted Durkheim among his pupils. He is known above all as the author of *La Cité antique* [*The Ancient City*] (1864). Breaking with previous approaches, he provided a comparative study of the beliefs, family life (private space), and the city (public space) in the Rome of Cicero, the Athens of Pericles, and Sparta at its zenith. The political history of Rome and lastly the advent of Christianity fill the second half of the book. Fustel de Coulanges invented a theory of segmentarity which would be developed by Durkheim and transmitted via his work to the British School.

MEMBERS OF THE FRENCH SCHOOL OF SOCIOLOGY

In a work of this size only authors held to be of major importance can be treated, and so neither H. Beuchat, co-author with **Mauss** of the celebrated article 'Sur les variations saisonnières des sociétés eskimo' ['On Seasonal Variations in Eskimo Societies'], nor V. Larock, author of *Essai sur la valeur sacrée de la valeur sociale des noms de personnes dans les sociétés inférieures* [*Essay on the Sanctity of the Social Value of Personal Names in Inferior Societies*] (1933), nor M. David are treated below. As Mauss has stated, the French School of Sociology concentrated particularly on the social history of categories of the human spirit, so it is easy to understand why it devoted considerable attention to ethnology.

Bouglé, Célestin (1870–1940)

Célestin Bouglé was one of the philosophers whom Durkheim drew into the orbit of *l'Année sociologique*. In 1890 he enrolled at the ENS, by 1909 he was an assistant professor of social economics at the Sorbonne, and in 1919 he obtained tenure there. He was appointed deputy director of the ENS in 1927 and its director in 1935. He died of cancer in 1940. Bouglé attracted a great many students into the social sciences and recruited members of the French mission in Latin America, such as **Lévi-Strauss**, **Bastide** and Braudel. Furthermore he headed the *Centre de documentation sociale*, which existed from 1920 to 1940 and awarded travel bursaries and other forms of assistance. The *Centre* was incorporated into the ENS and financed first by the banker A. Kahn and then by the Rockefeller Foundation. Of Bouglé's works the best-known today is *Les Castes en Inde* [*Castes in India*], published in 1908, and although he himself never travelled to India, his book remains one of the best introductions to its subject. Bouglé was the first to distinguish three main criteria which define castes: group hierarchization (the classification of individuals in different castes from the top to the bottom of society), hereditary specialization (professions are fixed from birth, so that for example only untouchables collect refuse), and mutual repulsion (the prohibition of certain contacts between castes on the grounds that they are contaminating – e.g. water and meals cannot be shared between members of different castes). With his *Bilan de la sociologie française* [*Survey of French Sociology*], published by Alcan in 1935, Bouglé gave one of the very first accounts of the French school and

thereby provided a useful pendant to the study of G. Davy. His *Les Sciences sociales en France: Enseignement et recherche* [*The Social Sciences in France: Teaching and Research*] of 1937, published to coincide with the *Exposition universelle*, offers an appraisal of French ethnology of the period.

Lévy-Bruhl, Lucien (1857–1939)

Lucien Lévy-Bruhl was a philosophy student at the ENS, where one of his fellow students was J. Jaurès. He shared Jaurès's convictions and during this period he wrote for the newspaper *l'Humanité*. In 1884 he successfully defended two theses: *L'Idée de responsabilité* [*The Idea of Responsibility*] and *Quid de deo Seneca senserit*, and by 1892 he occupied a place on the *agrégation* jury alongside Durkheim. In 1904 he was appointed to the chair of history of modern philosophy at the Sorbonne. Following the trail blazed by A. Comte, on whom he wrote a book (*La Philosophie d'Auguste Comte* [*The Philosophy of Auguste Comte*], 1900), Lévy-Bruhl produced works of sociological philosophy. He was a republican and socialist, and in this he followed E. Durkheim, to whom he paid heartfelt homage in the opening pages of *Les Fonctions mentales dans les sociétés inférieures* [*Mental Functions in Inferior Societies*] (1910: 2–3). With an optimism typical of the period, he endeavoured to construct a new morality which would replace religious precepts and join the ranks of the sciences. These ideas are expressed in *La Morale et la science des moeurs* [*Morality and the Science of Morals*] (1910), which Durkheim warmly praised in a review in *l'Année Sociologique* (1902–1903). At a time when the young discipline of psychology was gaining acceptance in universities, Lévy-Bruhl turned to the study of the influence of geographical and historical factors on the way thought patterns are constructed. As the philosopher Husserl would write, philosophical thought ought to be confronted 'with all the possible variants of "us" '(letter to Lévy-Bruhl, 11 March 1935, publ. in Gradhiva, 4 (1988), pp. 63–71 (p. 69)). *Les Fonctions mentales dans les sociétés inférieures* (1910) was Lévy-Bruhl's first book on ethnology, and in it he seeks to identify the specific features of the primitive mentality using the ethnographic data then available (he mainly refers to Australian societies). He presents a dichotomy between the rational cast of mind and a mystic, so-called prelogical mentality which obeys a principle of participation and is little attuned to the principle of contradiction. By the end of the second decade of the century Lévy-Bruhl had acquired a worldwide reputation, and in 1919 he gave a series of lectures at universities outside France (Berkeley, London, Brussels, etc.) which left a deep imprint on ethnology in the English-speaking world. In 1922 his *La Mentalité primitive* [*The Primitive Mentality*] returns to the general theme of the opposition between primitive and civilized thought. His *L'Ame primitive* [*The Primitive Soul*] of 1927 is a study of the representation by 'primitives' of their own individuality, and it also addresses topics such as the duality of the individual subject, reincarnation, and the status of the dead. A 'card-carrying Sorbonnard' (Karady, 1982: 18), Lévy-Bruhl contributed with P. **Rivet** and M. **Mauss** to the founding of the *Institut d'ethnologie* in 1925, and in the speech he gave at its opening in 1926 he described it as a tool at the service of colonialism. In 1927 he became editor-in-chief of the *Revue philosophique*, was elected to the *Académie des sciences morales et politiques*, and retired from his academic posts to devote himself fully to writing. *Le Surnaturel et la nature dans la mentalité primitive* [*The Supernatural and Nature in the Primitive Mentality*], published in 1931, looks at the principles of mystic experience, prelogical thought and the participatory system to explain how it was that the primitive perceived the supernatural where we would not, but did not perceive it where we might expect him to do so. This book was a turning-point because Lévy-Bruhl pays less attention to the dualism between primitive and logical mentalities than to the study of the former in their own right. The two works that followed, *Mythologie primitive* [*Primitive Mythology*] (1935) and *L'Expérience mystique et les symboles chez les primitifs* [*Symbols and Mystic Experience among Primitives*] (1938), are characterized by the same approach. It should be noted that, in Mauss's view, Lévy-Bruhl was a philosopher operating outside the tradition of the *Ecole de sociologie française*. While expressing gratitude to him for 'adding so greatly to the popularity of our work', Mauss rejects his radical opposition between the two mentalities, criticizes the application of the term 'primitive' to diverse peoples and points to his undeniable lack of historical method (Mauss, 1969 (1929), *Oeuvres*, vol.2: 131).

Although Lévy-Bruhl's *Posthumous Notebooks*, published in 1949 (in which the last entry is for 2 February 1939) contain a rejection of the idea of the primitive mentality in favour of the notion of two stable poles which delimit the human spirit, his previous use of such ideas and of terms like 'inferior' is distasteful. He tried to justify his early employment of such vocabulary by stating, for example in a preface published in 1922, that he had used expressions such as 'mentality' and 'primitive' (in the sense of 'primary') at a time when they had not yet become established in everyday language. It is certainly the case that Lévy-Bruhl's work must be read in the context of its period. By affirming that the features of social reality are interdependent and that any society will have its own collective mentality, his evolutionism linked mentality and its 'logic' to questions of environment, thereby boldly attacking the basic question of the essence of the 'other'. He thus opened up a line of inquiry in which **Leenhardt**, **Griaule** and **Lévi-Strauss** have achieved brilliant results, and which is still pursued by cognitive anthropology through the alliance of ethnological method with linguistics and the neurosciences. Finally, Lévy-Bruhl, like **Frazer**, must be seen as a synthesizer of the ethnographic material of his period, and it is for this achievement that scholars like **Evans-Pritchard** speak of 'his extraordinary brilliance' (1943: 9). (Issue 4 of the *Revue Philosophique* 1989 is entirely devoted to the world of Lévy-Bruhl.)

Hubert, Henri (1872–1927)

A student at the ENS, Henri Hubert completed an *agrégation* in history and then became interested in the sociology of religion. With M. **Mauss** he shared responsibility for the presentation of reviews on the sociology of religion in *l'Année sociologique*, and they also wrote important essays together: *Essai sur la nature et la fonction du sacrifice* [*Essay on the Nature and Function of Sacrifice*] (1904), *Esquisse d'une théorie générale de la magie* [*Sketch for a General Theory of Magic*] (1909), and *Mélanges d'histoire des religions* [*Miscellaneous Essays on the History of Religions*]. Two further works by Hubert were published posthumously: *Les Celtes depuis l'époque de la Tène et la civilisation celtique* [*The Celts and Celtic Civilization from the Age of La Tene*] (Paris: Albin Michel, 2 vols, 1974) and *Les Germains* [*The Teutons*] (Paris: Albin Michel, 1952). **Radcliffe-Brown** opened *The Andaman Islanders* with a quote from Hubert.

Mauss, Marcel (1872–1950)

Marcel Mauss was a nephew of Durkheim and fifteen years his junior; like him he was born in Epinal and formed by the Third Republic. In his youth Mauss associated with C. Péguy, P. Janet, L. **Lévy-Bruhl** and J. Jaurès. He played an important role in

founding the newspaper *L'Humanité* and was active in radical circles and as a *Dreyfusard*. After an *agrégation* in history Mauss turned to the history and sociology of religions, a discipline which gained recognition as a legitimate area of scholarly inquiry in around 1880 despite opposition from an authoritarian church. Another discipline becoming established at this time was linguistics, and Mauss immersed himself in the study of Sanskrit. In 1897 and 1898 he spent time in Great Britain, meeting J. G. **Frazer** and building a bridge with the English school. In 1898 he replaced Foucher in the chair of Indian religions in the religious studies section of the EPHE (Section V), and in 1902 was made director of studies in the religions of primitive peoples at the same institution. He also taught at the *Collège de France* from 1931 to 1941, when he was stripped of his post following the enactment of the Vichy government's anti-Semitic laws. His belief in progress having already been severely dented by the 1914–1918 war, Mauss never recovered from this new blow, and produced no more work in the years preceding his death in 1950. He was a central figure in the *Ecole de sociologie française*, and with G. Davy shared Durkheim's intellectual inheritance following his death in 1917: Davy in the field of sociology, Mauss in ethnology.

'His work is brilliant, composed of a profusion of texts which reveal a mind of limitless intellectual curiosity but resolutely turned towards concrete facts' (**Condominas**, 1972). It is therefore not surprising that, rather than large works, Mauss wrote numerous articles published mainly in *l'Année sociologique*, which Durkheim had founded in 1898. Particularly notable among these is his *Essai sur le sacrifice* [*Essay on Sacrifice*] of 1898, which describes sacrifice as a metonymy of religious phenomena. This was followed in 1902 by *De quelques formes primitives de classification* [*On Some Primitive Forms of Classification*], written in collaboration with E. Durkheim. The two authors relate the conception of space found among Australian Aborigines and American Indians to their social organization, and state that these peoples classify the natural world in terms of their own clan structures. With the *Essai sur les variations saisonnières des sociétés eskimo* [*Essay on Seasonal Variations in Eskimo Societies*], written together with Beuchat in 1905, Mauss for the first time presents a society as an integrated whole, and shows how the seasonal changes which determine group formation (gathering together and dispersing) find expression in cults, economic life, laws and morality. This integrated conception is used again in *Essai sur le don* [*The Gift*] (1924), in which Mauss states that to describe a society fully would be an infinite task unless one or several of its features could convey it in its entirety, and he develops the concept of the 'essential social phenomenon' to designate a feature which is at once religious, economic, political, mythological and juridical. He identifies such phenomena in the potlatch of the Indians of British Columbia and in the North of the USA as described by **Boas**, and in the Kula as described by **Malinowski**. These two phenomena, one antagonistic and the other pacific, work to the same goal of effecting the cohesion, harmony and integration of a whole society. Also worthy of mention is Mauss's demonstration in *Les Techniques du corps* [*Techniques of the Body*] of 1935 that swimming instruction, nursing techniques, and modes of relaxation among Australian soldiers are all culturally rooted; and also *La Notion de personne* [*The Notion of Selfhood*] of 1938, in which he examines ideas of selfhood among the Pueblo Indians, the Australians and others, and then in Western history. Lastly, D. **Paulme** has published a *Manuel d'ethnographie* [*Handbook of Ethnography*] in 1947 based on Mauss's lecture notes.

As well as devoting considerable efforts to publishing the posthumous works of friends who lost their lives in the First World War, Mauss was an important driving force behind the discipline. He was able to arouse the interest of his acquaintances in the Parisian avant-garde in ethnology, then still a young subject, and himself wrote a short *Hommage à Picasso* [*Homage to Picasso*] in 1930. He played a central role in the founding of the *Institut d'ethnologie* in 1925, and gave individual attention to the students he trained, who went on to become great figures in French anthropology (including P. **Mus**, D. Paulme, M. **Griaule**, M. **Leiris**, C. **Lévi-Strauss**, L. **Dumont**, A. **Leroi-Gourhan**, G. **Dieterlen** and J. **Soustelle**).

Hertz, Robert (1882–1915)

Born in Saint Cloud, Robert Hertz studied at the ENS, where he was taught by Durkheim, and then passed his *agrégation* in philosophy in 1904 and joined the group associated with *l'Année sociologique*. In 1905–1906 he studied in London and completed a thesis entitled 'Le crime et le péché, et comment et pourquoi la société les efface-t-elle?' ['Crime and Punishment, and how and why Society eradicates Them?']. In 1906–1907 he was a professor of philosophy at Douai and then taught part-time in the religious studies section of the EPHE (Section V) until he was mobilized. In 1907 his 'Contribution à une étude sur la représentation collective de la mort' ['Contribution to a Study of the Collective Representation of Death'] appeared in *l'Année sociologique* (vol.10: 48–137); using the ethnography of the Dayak of Borneo, he sees such representations as a sort of initiation comparable to marriage or rites of birth. In 1909 he published in *Revue philosophique* a paper entitled 'Prééminence de la main droite' ['The Pre-eminence of the Right Hand'], a phenomenon he judged to be a projection onto the human body of the dualism inherent in primitive thought. Another significant work was his 1913 study of the cult of Saint Besse, which he interpreted from a Durkheimian perspective. A collection of his texts was edited posthumously in 1928 under the title *Mélanges de sociologie religieuse et de folklore* [*Miscellanies on the Sociology of Religion and on Folklore*], and it was published in a new edition in 1970 by Presses universitaires de France with a preface by G. **Balandier**. Following the outbreak of war Hertz was called up and he fell in 1915, at the age of thirty-three, leading his men in an attack on a German machine gun position at Marchéville. He left an unfinished thesis, which M. **Mauss** published in 1922 in the *Revue de l'histoire et des religions*. This text was reprinted in 1988 as *Le Péché et l'expiation dans les sociétés primitives* [*Sin and Atonement in Primitive Societies*] with an introduction and notes by M. Mauss and a preface by J. Jamin (Paris: Jean-Michel Place). Mauss drew on Hertz's thesis for a series of lectures given from 1935 to 1938 at the *Collège de France*, and his notes for these lectures have been published in the journal *Gradhiva*, edited and annotated by J. Jamin and F. Lupu (no.2, Summer 1987).

Granet, Marcel (1884–1940)

Marcel Granet was admitted to the ENS in 1904 and passed his *agrégation* in history in 1907. Having developed interests in feudalism and then in Chinese history, he persuaded the Ministry of Public Instruction to support his mission to China of 1911–1913, which coincided with the establishment of the First Chinese Republic in 1912. On his return in 1913, he replaced E. Chavannes as director of studies in Far Eastern religions in Section V of the EPHE. Granet was wounded in the 1914–1918 War and was awarded the *Croix de guerre*. In 1920 he obtained a doctorate for his two theses *Fêtes et chansons anciennes de la Chine* [*Ancient Chinese Festivals and Songs*] (Paris: Leroux, 1919), which he dedicated to M. **Mauss**, and *La Polygénie sororale et le sororat dans la Chine féodale* [*Sororal Polygyny and the Sororate in Feudal China*] (Paris: Leroux, 1920).

Breaking with the then dominant *belles lettres* and scholarly approaches, Granet chose a sociological focus rather than concentrating on chronological history or the history of art. He drew together elements taken from different bodies of information to reconstitute ancient China in an almost ethnographical manner. He examined games, economic practices, dances, matrimonial customs, attitudes of mind and other facets of Chinese culture in an attempt to understand what made it specifically Chinese. His theory of kinship (1939) offers models of exchange which **Lévi-Strauss** was to adopt, albeit not without criticizing them (1949). From 1920 Granet lectured on Chinese civilization at the Sorbonne, and in 1926 was appointed professor at INALCO.

Cohen, Marcel (1884–1974)

Marcel Cohen gained an *agrégation* as a grammarian and graduated from INALCO and from Section V of the EPHE, where he followed courses given by M. **Mauss** in 1909. In 1910–1911 he carried out a mission to Abyssinia financed by the Ministry of Public Instruction, and on his return took a post teaching Amharic at INALCO. In 1920 he was appointed director of studies for Semitic Ethiopian languages in the EPHE (Section IV: history and philology). In 1924 he successfully defended his doctoral thesis *Le Système verbal sémitique et l'expression du temps: Couplets amhariques du choa* [*The Semitic Verbal System and its Expression of Tense: Amharic Couplets of the Choa*] and was then given a professorship at INALCO in 1926. A close associate of Mauss, Cohen took part in the founding of the *Institut d'ethnologie*, becoming its first secretary and taking responsibility for linguistics teaching. In 1934 he and A. Meillet published *Les Langues du monde* [*The Languages of the World*], the first scientific description of the world's languages and peoples, which contained contributions from practically every French ethnologist of the time.

OTHER RESEARCHERS

Aside from those whose bibliographies are given below, researchers worthy of mention include the folklorist P. Sébillot and L. Mariller, the first man to establish a study programme on the religious history of non-civilized peoples. Other, less well-known or now forgotten figures are E. Verrier, Schoebel, the sociologist C. Letourneau, the jurist R. Maunier, and Georges Montondon, a naturalized French anthropologist of Swiss origin, a eugenicist, anti-Semite and racist who in 1935 wrote *Ologénèse culturelle: Traité d'ethnologie cyclo-culturelle et d'ergologie systématique* [*Cultural Hologenesis: Treatise on Cyclo-cultural Ethnology and Systematic Ergology*] (Paris: Payot). Montondon was a professor of ethnology at the *Ecole d'anthropologie de Paris*, founded by Broca, and he launched the journal *l'Ethnie française* in 1941. During the Liberation he was executed for collaboration.

Marin, Louis (1871–1951)

After gaining a number of academic qualifications, Louis Marin turned to politics. As a deputy he secured the passage of a considerable amount of social legislation, including provisions for maternity leave and laws on parental neglect. He was a minister several times, founder of the newspaper *La Nation*, president of the *Société d'ethnographie de Paris*, and director of the *Ecole d'anthropologie de Paris*, where he succeeded Broca. He provided great assistance to French anthropology in its early days and supported the creation of the *Musée de l'Homme*, whose library is named after him. He also wrote many articles, all published in the journal *L'Ethnographie*.

van Gennep, Arnold (1873–1957)

Born in Württemberg in Germany, Arnold van Gennep studied at the EPHE and then taught in Neuchâtel, where he directed the *Musée d'ethnographie* (1912–1915). After research on totemism in Madagascar (*Tabou et totémisme à Madagascar* [*Taboo and Totemism in Madagascar*], 1904) and Australia (*Mythes et légendes d'Australie* [*Myths and Legends of Australia*], 1906), he spent a lengthy period reflecting on religion before writing *Les Rites de Passage* [*Rites of Passage*] (1909), which remains one of the great classics of ethnology. He invented the cate-gory of the 'rite of passage', which he presented according to a typology – death, withdrawal and rebirth – which has been much used since. Although van Gennep took an interest in North Africa and published a series of important articles on Algerian ethnography in the *Revue d'ethnographie et de sociologie*, which he himself founded in 1911, the main focus of his work was French folklore, on which he produced a vast investigation published from 1943 to 1958. N. Belmont (1974, 1975) has aptly written that van Gennep's work closes the period of amateur scholarship and that he is the founder of ethnography in France.

Rivet, Paul (1876–1958)

Born into a modest family in the Ardennes, Paul Rivet entered military college in Lyons as a means of improving his family's finances, and he graduated in 1897 at the age of twenty-one. In 1901 he became the physician to a French mission sent to measure a meridian in Ecuador, where he stayed for five years and amassed a collection of artefacts and observations (*Ethnologie ancienne de l'Equateur* [*The Ancient Ethnology of Ecuador*], 1912). On his return in 1906 he was seconded by the Armed Forces Ministry to the *Musée d'histoire naturelle*, and in 1909 was appointed as its deputy director. His research was devoted mainly to the American continent: its languages, pre-Columbian metallurgy and ancient populations. In 1920 a coalition of socialists and communists enabled him to defeat Colonel Delarocque of the *Croix de Feu* in an election in the fifth arrondissement of Paris and he become a deputy. As secretary general of the *Société des Americanistes* he initiated and then directed its bibliographical work. He also contributed material on Amerindian languages to the seminal work *Les Langues du monde* [*The Languages of the World*], edited by Meillet and **Cohen** and published in 1924, elaborated several theories on ancient migrations, and, most importantly, founded the *Institut d'ethnologie* at the University of Paris with **Lévy-Bruhl** and **Mauss**, becoming its first secretary general. After an election in 1928 which appeared to pit adherents of anatomical anthropology against advocates of the integration of ethnology into anthropology, Rivet became the fourth occupant of the chair of anthropology at the *Musée d'histoire naturelle*, where he succeeded R. Verneau. He renamed the post 'chair of the ethnology of contemporary and fossilized man', and secured its merger with the *Musée d'ethnographie du Trocadéro*. Following the riots of 6 February 1934, Rivet, already a member of the *Ligue contre l'oppression coloniale et l'impérialisme* (established in 1927) formed the *Comité de vigilence des intellectuels anti-fascistes* together with Alain (Emile-Auguste Chartier, 1868–1951) and Paul Langevin (1872–1946). Following the holding of the *Exposition universelle* in Paris in 1937 he won the necessary funds for the construction of the new *Musée de l'Homme* to replace the *Musée du Trocadéro* (1938). He was then forced to flee France by an order for the arrest of those belonging to the network of the *Musée de l'Homme*, directed by B. Vildé, and to this end he acquired a passport through the good offices of the Abbé Breuil. He moved to Columbia and then Mexico. After the Liberation Rivet was elected as a socialist deputy and reoccupied his old chair until his retirement in 1950. During the latter part of his career he developed a deep interest in international relations, and he particularly spoke up for French colonial rule of Algeria in South America.

Leenhardt, Maurice (1878–1954)
Born in Montauban, M. Leenhardt gained a *baccalauréat* in theology with his dissertation *Le Mouvement éthiopien au sud de l'Afrique de 1896 à 1899* [*The Ethiopian Movement in Southern Africa from 1896 to 1899*]. He was ordained a pastor and sent as a missionary to New Caledonia, where he lived for almost twenty-five years (1903–1926). In 1909 he published his first version of *La Grande Terre* [*The Great Earth*] and two articles in the *Bulletins et Mémoires de la Société d'Anthropologie de Paris*. In 1921, while in France during his second leave of absence from missionary duties, Leenhardt met **Lévy-Bruhl**, with whom he remained in contact thereafter. In 1922 he returned to New Caledonia by boat, but en route spent eighteen months in Africa and pioneered African sociology of religion. On returning again to France in 1927 he launched the journal *Propos protestants*. In 1930 the *Institut d'ethnologie* published his *Notes d'ethnologie néo-calédonienne* [*Notes on the Ethnology of New Caledonia*], and followed this in 1932 with his *Documents néo-caledoniens* [*New Caledonian Documents*]. While engaged in the translation of the Bible into Houaïlou, a language on which he was the foremost specialist (*Vocabulaire et grammaire de la langue houaïlou* [*Vocabulary and Grammar of the Houaïlou Language*], 1935), Leenhardt took an interest in the lived experience and the psychic representations of the Kanak and subsequently of other Melanesian peoples (*Langues et dialectes de l'Austro-Mélanésien* [*Austronesian Languages and Dialects*], 1946). He can be said to have established Melanesian anthropology, and he assembled a body of

documentation which is still drawn on today. From *Ethnologie de la parole* [*The Ethnology of Speech*] (1946) onwards he became increasingly absorbed by the subjective interiority of Melanesians (*La Personnalité mélanésienne* [*The Melanesian Personality*], 1942). In 1940 he was entrusted with directing the Oceanic department of the *Musée de l'Homme*. When the passing of the anti-Semitic laws of the Vichy government deprived **Mauss** of his teaching rights, he asked Leenhardt to take over his teaching. He taught in Section V of the EPHE until 1950, when he was succeeded by **Lévi-Strauss**. After the Liberation Leenhardt introduced the teaching of Houaïlou at INALCO and became president of the newly founded *Société des Oceanistes*. In 1947 he published his best-known work: *Do Kamo, la personne et le mythe dans le monde néo-calédonien* [*Do Kamo: Individual and Myth in New Caledonia*] (Paris: Gallimard, 1971). This work surveys representations of space, time, social relations and the body in New Caledonia, poses the question of the relationship between ancient and modern mentalities, and seeks to define how individuals and myths 'are supported by each other, proceed from each other and justify each other' (1971 (1947): 255). After his appointment as director of the new *Institut Français d'Océanie*, created under the auspices of ORSTOM, he travelled to Nouméa in New Caledonia for a year in 1948. In 1949 he published Lévy-Bruhl's *Carnets posthumes* [*Posthumous Notebooks*], for which he provided a preface. As a co-founder of the International Committee for Indian Ocean Territories, Leenhardt became known for his repeated efforts on behalf of indigenous populations confronting the acculturation process. He was a vigorous defender of the Kanaks against all forms of colonial spoliation and appropriation. He founded the journals *Propos protestants* (1927) and *Mondes non-chrétiens* (1947) as vehicles for scholarship and, above all, as organs promoting association among intellectuals with religious affiliations (L. Massignon, J. Poirier, J. **Guiart**, P. Métais, etc.).

THE COLONIALISTS

This section is devoted to Maurice **Delafosse**, traditionally seen as the founder of Africanism in France, and Henri **Labouret**, who followed up Delafosse's work by supervising teaching provision in languages and cultures for the *Institut des Langues Orientales Vivantes*, and whose own published work appeared in the collection of the *Institut d'ethnologie*. My aim here is to use these two names to convey the character of a considerable body of work produced contemporaneously with that of the Durkheim school, which paid careful attention to scholarship written in English and German but largely or completely ignored France's own colonial researchers. French Africa and Indochina were neglected by the academic establishment, doubtless for reasons of epistemology as well as institutional strategy. Thus Durkheim became interested in the 'primitives' of Tasmania and Australia but held back from Africanism, while Mauss's works analyse texts relating to Melanesia, the American Indians and India but contain only a few short lines on Africa and French Indochina, and this despite the uniquely rich body of source material contained in the pages of Faidherbe, Charles Monteil, Henri Gaden, Louis Tauxier, Raymond Decary, Gilbert Vieillard, Cardaire, Marc, Clozel, Vidal, Urvoy, Arcin and Father Tastevin.

Delafosse, Maurice (1870–1926)

It was after hearing an emissary of Cardinal Lavigerie denouncing the slave trade that Maurice Delafosse decided to enrol in the *Institut des Frères armés du Sahara*, whose members sought to liberate slave caravans. He was called up in 1891 and completed his military service, after which he returned to France to study Arabic under O. Houdas at INALCO, graduating in 1894. He found employment as a clerk working on indigenous affairs in the Ivory Coast, and this was followed by various positions, including a period as vice-consul in Liberia before he again returned to France in 1900. He was then engaged to give a course on Sudanese language and civilization at INALCO, the first teaching post of its sort in France. In 1901 he was appointed as head of the French section of the Anglo-French mission to fix the borders of the Ivory Coast, which involved him tramping through more than three thousand kilometres of forested country on foot. From 1904 to 1907 he was in charge of the Korhogo and Kong circles, organized the Colonial Exhibition in Marseille, married one of Houdas's daughters, and then departed again for the Ivory Coast, where he was chosen by Clozel to head the Bamako circle. Significantly, he opposed the recruitment of Black troops as advocated by Diagne. After failing to secure the governorship of the Ivory Coast he returned to France for good in 1917 and resumed teaching at INALCO. He played a part in founding the *Académie des sciences d'Outre-Mer* and the International African Institute, which was co-directed by Lord Lugard.

M. Delafosse's writings are of major importance, particularly in the field of linguistics, but he is known above all for his *Haut Sénégal–Niger* [*Upper Senegal–Niger*] in three volumes (1912), the first historical and ethnographic monograph on French Sudan. Also noteworthy is his *Broussard ou les états d'âme d'un colonial* [*Life in the Bush, or the Colonial's State of Mind*], a collection of journalistic articles and eyewitness accounts of contemporary Africa as seen through an administrator's eyes.

Labouret, Henri (1878–1958)

After joining the army at a very young age, H. Labouret became an officer-cadet on completing legal studies and then a lieutenant in fourth regiment of the Senegalese infantry in French West Africa. In 1918 he was severely wounded in the campaign against the Agba and lost the use of one hand. He was sent on secondment to the Lobi country, where he learnt Lobi, and also Mandingue and Birifor. He returned to France in 1926 and succeeded M. **Delafosse** in the Colonial School and in his chair for the Sudanese language at INALCO. He also replaced him as co-director of the International African Institute and of its journal *Africa*, and was a consistent campaigner against granting independence to the colonies. Most importantly, he was the author of important monographs on the people of Volta.

SELECT BIBLIOGRAPHY

Affergan, F. (1991) 'Participation et irrécupération. Le cas Lévy-Bruhl', *Critiques anthropologiques*, Presses de la Fondation nationale des sciences politiques, pp.68–90.

Amselle, J.-L. and Sibeuf, E. (eds) (1998) *M. Delafosse. Entre orientalisme et ethnolographie: l'itinéraire d'un africaniste (1870–1926)*, Paris: Maisonneuve et Larose.

Belmont, N. (1974, 1979) *Arnold Van Gennep: The creator of French ethnography*, trans. D. Coltmann, Chicago: Chicago University Press.

——(ed.) (1975) *Textes inédits sur le folklore français contemporain d'Arnold Van Gennep*, Archives d'ethnologie francaise. no.4, Paris. G.-P. Maisonneuve & Larose.

Cazeneuve, J. (1963, 1972) *Lucien Lévy-Bruhl*, trans. P. Rivière, Oxford: Blackwell.

——(1968) *Marcel Mauss*, Paris: Presses universitaires de France.

Centlivres, P. and Vaucher, P. (1994) 'Les tribulations d'un ethnographe en Suisse. A. van Gennep à Neuchâtel (1912–1915)', *Gradhiva*, 15: 89–101.

Chailleu, L. (1990) 'Histoire de la Société d'ethnographie. La revue orientale et américaine (1858–1879). Ethnographie, orientalisme et américanisme au XIXe siècle', *L'Ethnographie*, 86: 98–107.

Chamboredon, J-C. (1984) 'Emile Durkheim: le social, objet de science. Du moral au politique?', *Critique*, pp.460–513.

Champion, P. (1976) 'P. Rivet', Paris: Musée de l'Homme.

Clifford, J. (1982, 1992) *Person and Myth: M. Leenhardt in the Melansian World*, Durham: Duke University Press.

Condominas, G. (1972) 'Marcel Mauss, père de l'ethnographie française', *Critique*, 28(297): 118–139, (301): 487–504.

Copans, J. (1999) 'Oeuvre secrète ou oeuvre publique' (on Mauss), *L'Homme*, 1450: 217–220.

Copans, J. and Jamin, J. (1978) *aux origines de l'anthropologie française. Les mémoires de la société des observateur de l'homme en l'an viii*, Paris: le Sycomore.

Cornevin, R. (1971) 'M. Leenhardt, pionnier de la sociologie religieuse africaine et précurseur de l'Afrique latine', *France-Eurafrique*, Paris, 225: 41–45.

——(1977) 'Préface' to *Delagosse Haut Sénégal Niger*, Paris: Maisonneuve, pp.5–28.

——(ed.) *Dictionnaire biographique d'Outre-Mer. Hommes et destins*, 8 vols, Paris: Académie des Sciences d'Outre-Mer.

d'Harcourt, R. (1958) 'Paul Rivet, 1876–1958', *J. de la Société des Américanistes*, 47: 7–11.

Delafosse, L. (1976) *Le Berrichon conquis par l'Afrique*, Paris: Société d'histoire d'Outre-Mer.

Deschamps, H. (1959a) 'Nécrologie de Henri Labouret' *Africa*, vol.29.

——(1959b) 'H. Labouret', *JSA*, 29: 291–292.

Dias, N. (1991) *Le musée d'ethnographie du Trocadéro (1978–1909)*, Paris: CNRS.

Evans-Pritchard, E.E. (1943) 'Lévy-Bruhl's theory of primitive mentality', Cairo, Bulletin of the Faculty of Arts, no.2: 1–36.

——(1960) 'Introduction', to R. Hertz *Death and the Right Hand*, trans. R. Needham, Glencoe: The Free Press.

——(1965) 'Lévy-Bruhl', in *Theory of Primitive Religion*, Oxford: Oxford University Press.

Fabre, D. (1992) 'A. V. Gennep et le Manuel de folklore français contemporain', in P. Nora (ed.) *Les lieux de mémoires, Tome 3: Les Frances*, Paris: Galimard, vol.2, pp.641–675.

Fournier, M. (1994) *Marcel Mauss*, Paris: Fayard.

Garelli, J. (1995) 'La phénoménologie du jugement et la dimension "cosmomorphique" du corps chez les Canaques, selon M. Leenhardt', *Droit et Cultures*, 29: 255–274.

Geanā, G. (1983) 'Les projets roumains d'A. van Gennep', *Ethnologica*, pp.33–44.

Gluckman, M. (1962) 'Les rites de passage', in Gluckman (ed.) *The Ritual of Social Relations*, Manchester: Manchester University Press, pp.1–53.

Goldman, M. (1998) 'Raison et différence: à propos de L. Lévy-Bruhl', *Gradhiva*, 23: 1–21.

Goudineau, Y. (1991) 'Granet, Marcel', in P. Bonte and M. Izard (eds) *Dictionnaire de l'ethnologie et de l'anthropologie*, Paris: Presses universitaires de France, pp.308–309.

——(1993) 'Une vérification expérimentale dans la Chine de 1912. Marcel Granet en terrain lettré', *Gradhiva*, 14: 95–99.

Granet, M. (1922) *La religion des Chinois*, Paris: Gauthier-Villars.

——(1926, 1975) *Festivals and Songs of Ancient China*, trans. F. Edward, New York: Gordon Press.

——(1929, 1974) *Chinese Civilizations*, New York: AMS Press.

——(1939) *Catégories matrimoniales et relation de proximité dans la Chine ancienne*, Paris: Alcan.

——(1953) *Etudes sociologiques sur la Chine*, Paris: Presses universitaires de France.

Grosz-Nagaté, M. (1988) 'Power and knowledge. The representation of the Mande world in the work of Park, Caillié, Monteil and Delafosse', *CEA*, 28(3–4): 485–511.

Héran, F. (1989) 'Une question de généalogie: la théorie de la segmentation' in M. Ségalen (ed.) *Anthropologie sociale et ethnologie de la France*, Louvain-la-Neuve: Peeters, vol.1, pp.231–238.

——(1998) 'De Granet à Lévi-Strauss', *Social Anthropology*, 6(1): 1–60; 6(2): 169–201; 6(3): 309–330.

Herzt, R. (1994) *Sin and Expiation in Primitive Societies*, trans. and ed. R. Parking, Oxford: Institute of Social and Cultural Anthropology.

Karady, V. (1982) 'Le problème de la légitimité dans l'organisation historique de l'ethnologie française', *Revue française de sociologie*, 23(1): 17–35.

——(1988) 'Durkheim et les débuts de l'ethnologie universitaire', *Actes de la recherche en sciences sociales*, 74: 21–32.

Labouret, H. (1927) 'Maurice Delafosse', Académie des sciences coloniales, vol.7: 537–551.

——(1931) *Les Tribus du rameau Lobi*, Paris: Institut d'ethnologie.

——(1941) *Paysans d'Afrique Occidentale*, Paris: Gallimard.

——(1946) *Histoire des Noirs d'Afrique*, Paris: Presses universitaires de France.

Labouret, H. and Rivet, P. (1929) *Le Royaume d'Arda et son évangélisation au XVIIe siècle*, Paris: Institut d'ethnologie.

Lebovics, H. (1988) 'Le conservatisme en anthropologie et la fin de la Troisième République', *Gradhiva*, 4: 3–17.

——(1992) True France: The Wars over Cultural identity, 1900–1945, Ithaca: Cornell University Press.

Leenhardt, M. (1930) *Notes d'ethnologie néo-calédonienne*, Paris: Institut d'ethnologie.

——(1952; 1937) *Gens de la Grande Terre, Nouvelle-Calédonie*, Paris: Gallimard.

Lejeune, D. (1993) *Les Sociétés de géographie en France et l'expansion coloniale au XIXe siècle*, Paris: Albin Michel.

Lévy-Bruhl, L. (1925) 'L'institut d'ethnologie de l'Université de Paris', *Revue d'Ethnographie*, 24–25: 233–235.

——(1926) 'l'Institut d'ethnologie de l'université de Paris', *Annales de l'Université de Paris*, May.

Llobera, J.R. (1996) 'The fate of anthropology in l'Année Sociologique', *Journal of Anthropological Society of Oxford*, 27: 235–251.

Mauss, M. (1979) *Sociologie de M. Mauss*, Paris: Presses universitaires de France.

——(1969a; 1913) 'L'ethnographie en France et à l'étranger', in Mauss, *Oeuvres*, Paris: Minuit, vol.3, pp.395–435.

——(1969b; 1927) 'les divisions de la sociologie', in Mauss *Oeuvres*, Paris: Minuit, vol.3, pp.178–245.

——(1969c) 'Maîtres, compagnons et disciples' *Oeuvres* vol.3: 535–567.

——(2003) *On Prayer: Text and commentary*, New York: Berghahm Books.

Mucchielli, L. (1997) 'Sociologie versus anthropologie raciale. L'engagement décisif des durkheimiens dans le contexe "fin de siècle" (1885–1914)', *Gradhiva*, 24: 77–95.

——(1998a) 'Revue de l'histoire des religions (1898–1916): une zone d'influence méconnue', *Durkheimian Studies*, 4: 51–72.

——(1998b) *La découverte du social, Naissance de la sociologie en France (1870–1914)*, Paris: Éditions La Découverte.

Needham, R. (1978; 1973) 'Introduction' to *Right and Left: Essays on Dual Symbolic Classification* (on Hertz, Gonet . . .), Chicago: University of Chicago Press.

——(1979a) chapter 9 of *Belief, Language and Experience*, Oxford.

——(1979b) 'Hertz, R.', in *International Encyclopedia of the Social Sciences*, D. L. Sills (ed.), vol.18: 295–297.

Parkin, R. (1996) *The Dark Side of Humanity. The Work of R. Hertz and its Legacy*, Gordon and Breach.

Rivet, P. (1939) 'Lucien Lévy-Bruhl', *JSA*, 9: 214–216.

——(1940) 'L'ethnologie en France', *Bulletin du Muséum d'histoire naturelle*, series 2, vol. 12, January 1940, pp.38–52.

Sibeud, E. (1994) 'La naissance de l'ethnographie africaniste en France avant 1914', *CEA*, 34(4): 638–658.

Spinder, M. (1980) 'L'écclésiologie de Maurice Leenhardt', *JSA*, 69: 279–91.

Stocking, G.W. (1968) 'French anthropology in 1800', in Stocking *Race, Culture and Evolution*, New York: The Free Press, pp. 13–42.

Tubiana, J. (1995) 'Postface', (1936) Cohen, M. *Traité de langue amharique (Abyssinie)*, Paris: Institut d'Ethnologie.

Vallois, H. (1944) 'L'Evolution de la chaire d'ethnologie du Muséum national d'Histoire naturelle', Bulletin du Muséum, second series, vol.16(1), pp.38–55.

Van Gennep, A. (1911, 1967) *Semi-scholars*, trans. and intro. by R. Needham, London: Routledge.

——(1916) *En Savoie: du berceau à la tombe*, Chambéry: Dardel.

——(1932–1933) *Le folklore du Dauphiné, Isère*, Paris: Maisonneuve, 2 vols.

——(1943) *Manuel du folklore français contemporain*, Paris: Picard, 7 vols (reissued by Picard in 1972) *Coutumes et croyances populaires en France*, reissued by Le Chemin vert in 1980.

——(1946–1948) *Le folklore des Hautes-Alpes*, Paris: Maisonneuve, 2 vols.

——(1996, 1919) *Le traité comparatif des nationalités* (preface by J-F. Gossiaux), Paris: CTHS.

Van Hoven, (1990) 'Representing social hierarchy. Administrators-ethnographs in the French Sudan: Delafosse, Monteil et Labouret', *CEA*, 30(2): 179–190.

Verneau, R. (1910) 'Le professeur Hamy et ses prédécesseurs au Jardin des Plantes', *L'Anthropologie*, 21: 257–279.

Zerilli, F.M. (1993) 'Il terreno ecuadoriano di Paul Rivet: Anthropologia, Linguistica, Etnografia', *Annali della Facoltà di Lettere e Filosofia 2. Studi Storico-Antropologici*, 29–30: 363–396.

——(1998) *Il lato oscuro dell' etnologia: Il contributo dell'antrología naturalista al processo di instituzionalizazione degli studi etnologíci en Francia*, Rome: CISU.

Zumwalt, R. (1982) 'A. van Gennep: the hermit of Bourg-la-Reine', *AA*, 84: 299–313.

VI

The American tradition from the end of the First World War to the 1950s

FROM RESEARCH ON THE LAST PRIMITIVES TO INVESTIGATIONS INTO SOCIAL TRANSFORMATIONS

The pacification of the exotic world was completed a few years after the end of the First World War, and from this moment missionaries were to be found everywhere in the world, often providing support for ethnological research. It was at this time that American anthropology gained access to newly acquired Pacific islands, which contained 'resolutely' primitive populations unlike the acculturated American Indians who had hitherto been its sole object of study. In the words of **Lévi-Strauss**, 'Ethnology has only consciously been practised for one century and will only survive for one more century. One can predict that in the twenty-first century the human race will be all but unified [. . .] During the course of two centuries and two centuries only, one type of humanity will be succeeded by another' (*Entretiens radiophoniques avec Georges Charbonnier*, 1959). This verdict defines the origins of ethnology, and great emphasis was placed during this period on the need to study primitive societies before they disappeared (Mead, *Letters from the Field*, New York: Harper, 1977). This spirit was dominant until the eve of the Second World War, in which American anthropologists participated actively (R. L. Beals, 'Anthropology during the War and After: Memorandum Prepared by the Committee on War Service of Anthropologists, Division of Anthropology and Psychology, National Research Council', 1943). With the coming of peace, research focused increasingly on the social dynamics caused by colonization and by the acculturation process, although research on the latter had in fact already been initiated by **Linton**, **Herskovits** and **Redfield** in a memorandum of 1936.

By 1930 a number of universities possessed independent anthropology departments. Harvard's department originated from its incorporation of the Peabody Museum in 1897, and its leading figures were **Dixon** (assistant professor 1897, professor 1915–1934), the archaeologist Tozzer (assistant professor 1904, professor 1921–1948), the physical anthropologist Hooton (1913–1954), Coon (1927–1948), and **Kluckhohn** (1936). Columbia had had a department since 1902, which contained **Boas** (1898–1936), **Wissler** (assistant professor 1903–1909), **Goldenweiser** (assistant professor 1910–1919), **Lowie** (lecturer 1920–1921), **Benedict** (1924–1948), **Linton** (1936–1946), Strong (1936–1962), and Lesser (1936–1950). Berkeley's department dated from 1908, and included **Putnam** (1903–1915), **Kroeber** (1908–1946), **Gifford** (1920–1955), and **Lowie** (1921–1950). The department at Chicago opened in 1929, and among its members were **Cole** (1924–1947), **Sapir** (1925–1931), **Radcliffe-Brown** (1931–1937), **Redfield** (1930–1958), **Eggan** (assistant professor 1931, professor 1936), **Warner** (a department member from 1935, but also active in the

---

101

sociology department). Yale had a department from 1931, which contained Wissler (1924–1940), Sapir (1931–1939), **Spier** (1933–1939), and **Murdock** (assistant professor 1931, professor 1938–1960). The Catholic University of Washington's department existed as of 1935, and contained Spier (1920–1929), and **Cooper** (1923–1941). Important figures in the University of Pennsylvania's department were Speck (1908–1950), and **Hallowell** (1924–1962). Lastly, in 1928 **Steward** gave the first course in anthropology at the University of Michigan, where **White** was appointed associate professor in 1930 and then professor in 1943, remaining in post until 1970.

It has not been possible to provide an exhaustive list of anthropologists, and so some of those not treated below should at least be honoured with a brief mention: C. S. Coon, a productive scholar and popularizer; G. Gorer, who made pioneering studies of 'national character'; A. Holmberg, author of a fine best-seller dedicated to a Bolivian hunter population (*Nomads of the Long Bow*, 1950); Wolfenstein, a pioneer in the study of childhood; A. Leighton, who charted the transition of the Navajo from tradition to modernity; L. Sharp, who opened up Thailand and the Philippines to American anthropology; R. Métraux; H. Powdermaker; D. Mandelbaum; the Pacific ethnohistorian D. Oliver; and the great geographer O. Latimore.

THE AMERICAN CULTURALISTS

Between 1920 and 1930 **Boas** abandoned historicism and embraced a psychological approach (Boas, 1930), but this position was itself then jettisoned by his own students, and the second, 'culturalist' Boasian wave was influenced less by Boas himself than by his first students, especially E. **Sapir** and R. **Benedict**. The approach known as culturalism or the 'culture and personality school' was centred on the personalities of the members of a given society considered as the product of its culture. All human beings are thus products of features of the culture to which they belong, and this culture takes the form not of a sum of cultural traits but of an organic totality.

To simplify rather drastically, it is possible to identify two stages of culturalism. The first stage, under the influence of psychology, made the individual the primary object of research. Modes of education in a society are examined and its norms and social values are reconstructed on the basis of observation of individual behaviour. The work of **Mead** and **Du Bois** is typical of this approach. Reviving a view of exoticism which dates back to Montaigne and Montesquieu, the ethnographic text often serves as a sort of 'ethno-pretext' for an illumination and critique of contemporary American society, for example in Sapir's denunciation of materialism (Sapir, 1924). By means of the enormous popular success enjoyed by some anthropological studies, the discipline was able (albeit with a slight time lag) to play a central ideological role in the transformation of values and social relations (the recognition of the legitimacy of sexual desire, the emancipation of the individual from puritanical morality and from the absolute power of the church, the right to education and health provision, the struggle against racist prejudice). The teaching handbooks of Dr Spock, which in the 1950s reached sales figures in the millions, were the fruit of M. Mead's work. The figures who best represent the transition to the second stage of culturalism are doubtless **Kardiner** and Benedict, who put forward the notions of 'basic personality' and 'national character' (which both became basic cultural standards absorbed during training in the discipline), and used them to begin examining the conduct of the German, Japanese and then

Soviet peoples. The most representative works of the second stage are those of **Kluckhohn** and **Linton**, who researched into institutional behaviour (role, status, personality, etc.) and modes of social and cultural integration. The culturalist school has sometimes been associated with the work of Freud, but although the school's members certainly knew his work, they often had reservations about it. As early as 1917 Sapir expressed criticism of Freud's theoretical excesses and declared a preference for the Jungian model, which he considered more readily applicable to anthropology (Sapir, 1917, 1923), while Benedict was as inspired by Jung's work as she was by her reading of Nietzsche's *Birth of Tragedy*. Hays also notes that W. F. Ogburn's and A. **Goldenweiser**'s *Social Sciences and their Interrelations*, published in 1927, exhibits behaviourist tendencies, and that Freud's name appears only once in a footnote (Hays, (1958) 1967: 364). So while Freudian techniques left their mark on culturalism, particularly in terms of its objects of investigation (e.g. the mother–child relationship), it never incorporated Freudianism's central discovery, the presence of the unconscious, preferring instead to work with the notion of culture. In culturalist theory the social world ranks higher than the deep structures of the human mind. Furthermore, Freud's great anthropological texts (*Totem and Taboo, Moses and Monotheism*) were ignored by all except **Malinowski**, gradually becoming assimilated to the evolutionist tradition from which they were in any case largely derived. This response is hardly surprising in the case of Mead, who was not yet twenty-five years old when she wrote her first 'psychological' pages, but the case of Kardiner, who worked closely with Freud for two years only then to come under the influence of E. Fromm, requires more explanation. Ultimately, Kardiner chose the tests of H. Rorschach rather than the work of Freud for his seminar introducing ethnologists to psychoanalysis, and it was Rorschach's approach that he transmitted. There is also the question of the non-correspondence between fieldwork data and psychoanalytic categories, all too clearly demonstrated by the history of conflictual relations between psychoanalytic and fieldwork traditions. **Rivers** and **Seligman** were the first to investigate the potential application of psychology to anthropology, but both rejected the importance accorded by Freud to sexuality. Malinowski opened up the debate in earnest by looking seriously at Freud's work (at Seligman's request). He examined his own Trobriand material in the light of Freud's theories, but criticized their failure to account for sociological variables. **Roheim** was in fact the first and for a long time the only ethnologist to work with a strictly Freudian perspective. Others who should be mentioned in this connection but cannot be considered fully are W. La Barre, G. Gorer, R. A. LeVine, C. S. Coon, L. Wylie, A. F. C. Wallace, and finally D. C. Leighton, a pioneer of medical anthropology.

Sapir, Edward (1884–1939)

Edward Sapir was born in Lauenburg in Germany, and emigrated to the USA with his family. A pianist and poet, he went to Columbia University to study German, but then switched under the influence of **Boas** to anthropology and linguistics. He carried out fieldwork among the Chinook (1905), the Takelma (1906), and the Yana (1907–1908), and obtained a Ph.D. in 1909 with a thesis on the grammar of the Takelma Indians. From 1907 to 1908 he worked as assistant to **Kroeber** at the University of California, and then took up a teaching position at the University of Pennsylvania, where he researched on the Piaute Indians. In 1910 he was appointed as director of the anthropological division of the Geological Survey of Canada and as curator in the anthropology department of the Canadian National Museum in Ottawa. During his fifteen years in Canada Sapir studied Amerindian languages and criticized the shortcoming of various evolutionist theories and of diffusionism. In 1916 he published one of his best-known works, 'Time Perspective in Aboriginal American Culture: A Study in Method' (Mandelbaum, 1949: 389–463), a diffusionist study which draws up a list of obstacles to the propagation of cultural traits. In 1921 his *Language* appeared, which remains one of the best introductions to linguistics. In this work Sapir introduced his theory of linguistic drift, which states that grammatical changes are never haphazard, but adhere to systematic trends. His main example is the drift undergone by most Indo-European languages as they passed from complex declension systems to a syntactic principle based on word order. In 1925 Sapir accepted a teaching post in the newly created anthropology department at the University of Chicago, and it was at this time that his most original works appeared. In 'Sound Patterns in Language' (1925) (Mandelbaum, 1949: 33–46), he demonstrated that the sounds of language, rather than being exclusively physical phenomena, have psychological value, for in all languages each sound belongs to a discrete unified system which functions by contrasts, so that sound combinations are determined by linguistic conventions and not by physiological necessity. By emphasizing the unconscious but real structure of the phonological and grammatical features of language, he developed the thesis that cultures must be seen as individually learnt models of convention (1927) ('The Unconscious Patterning of Behavior in Society', Mandelbaum, 1949: 544–560). A culture is thus defined as a set of rules of behaviour learnt by the individual rather than as a consequence of the conventional behaviour of that individual, for it is through language, which organizes sensory experience, that a culture imposes its conceptual categories on individuals without their knowing it. This thesis inspired the work of **Benedict**, and in this way Sapir became, in La Barre's words,

'the founder of culture and personality studies' (1978: 282). Sapir also stresses that culture implies an individual psychological dimension. His first wife fell prey to a mental illness which first manifested itself in 1916 (Darnell, 1986: 166), and from this date he took a growing interest in psychiatry, which he hoped would help him design a new anthropological model. In his view the individual must form the point of departure for all social theory (1917), an approach which offered an alternative to **Kroeber**'s superorganic and to **Murdock**'s comparatism, and Sapir also differed from his colleagues in the 'culture and personality' school because of his insistence that individuals within a society realise their culture in various ways, which amounts to thinking in terms of 'personality and culture' rather than the other way around (Darnell, 1986: 166). Sapir became professor of anthropology and linguistics at Yale in 1931. In 1937 he suffered a first heart attack and he died in 1939.

Benedict, Ruth Fulton (1887–1948)

Ruth Fulton was born in New York, where her father worked as a surgeon, into an old Baptist family of rural origins. She studied English literature at Vassar College (1905–1909), and after spending a year in Europe taught English in a high school for girls. In 1914 she married the biochemist S. Benedict, and then for five years devoted herself to dance and poetry using the pseudonym Anne Singleton. From 1919 to 1922 Ruth Benedict studied anthropology at the New School for Social Research in New York, where she was taught by A. **Goldenweiser** and E. C. **Parsons**. In 1922 she enrolled at Columbia University, and while pursuing her studies she also worked as **Boas**'s assistant at Barnard College. At **Kroeber**'s instigation she gained her first fieldwork experience among the Serrano in Southern California, and then under **Lowie**'s influence she carried out comparative research into collections of visions among American Indians, and she obtained a doctorate with her work on this topic in 1923 ('The Concept of the Guardian Spirit in North America', Columbia Univ. Memoirs of the AAA, No.29: 1–97). In 1927, while working on the Pima and the Pueblo Indians of the Southwest, she conceived the theory of a 'cultural configuration' proper to each group selected from among the potentially immense variety of human possibilities. She explained this theory and its application to Amerindian cultures in a paper to the Congress of Americanists in 1928. In her best-known book, *Patterns of Culture* (1934), Benedict uses the notion of cultural personality to construct a typology based on Nietzsche's central distinction between the Apollonian and the Dionysian in *The Birth of Tragedy*. She contrasts the Apollonian cultural model of the Pueblo, their calm and balanced conduct (discreet prayers, the absence of destructive activity, etc.), with Dionysian cultures showing a preference for excessive and violent behaviour. The latter category includes the Pima, the Kwakiutl and the Dobuan, who manifested paranoiac traits and whose lives were dogged by endless rivalries and antagonisms. In 1928 Benedict founded the *Journal of American Folklore*, which she edited for the rest of her life. She taught at Columbia from 1924, and whilst increasing deafness prevented her from undertaking further fieldwork herself, she nonetheless directed the work of others on the Apaches of the Southwest (1930) and the Blackfoot of the North Plains (1938). She took a stand against racism during the Second World War (1940) and, like her colleague **Mead**, supported the entry of the USA into the war in the struggle against totalitarianism. The Army Information Bureau commissioned her to study national character in territories to which Americans did not usually have access: Germany, the Netherlands, Romania, Japan and Thailand. In 1944 the War Department charged her with writing a monograph on Japan (1946),

which aimed, among other things, to determine whether or not the Emperor should remain in place. This work achieved considerable success and made 'shame' (as opposed to blame) into an anthropological concept. After her appointment to the chair of anthropology at Columbia, Benedict set in motion an enormous comparative survey of contemporary cultures (France, Syria, China, the USSR, Eastern Europe, etc.), which drew on the efforts of 120 full-time researchers of 14 disciplines and 16 nationalities. Like a number of others, this project was driven by the idea that 'wars are born in the first instance in the minds of men' (UNESCO), and represented the adoption by cultural anthropology of the responsibility for preventing wars by assisting in the establishment of comprehensive relations between nations. Benedict visited Europe in 1948 and died one week after her return in September of that year. Although it has enjoyed great popular success, Benedict's work has been criticized by professional scholars, less for her theory of culturally determined personality and psychological normality than for the excessive simplicity of the oppositions which this theory erected (e.g. Apollonian/Dionysian).

Kardiner, Abram (1891–1981)
Born in New York, Abram Kardiner studied psychiatry at Cornell University and then spent two years working with Freud in Vienna (1921–1922). He taught at Cornell and Columbia universities, and from 1922 to 1944 directed a seminar on the study of the psychology of so-called 'primitive' societies, which sought to effect a synthesis of anthropology and psychoanalysis. This seminar was incorporated into the teaching provided by the Psychoanalytical Institute of New York (set up in 1932 as the first body to teach psychoanalysis in the USA). Kardiner played an important role in the founding of the so-called 'culture and personality' school, and with **Linton** he developed the notion of the 'basic personality'. At various times

Kardiner's seminar was co-directed by **Du Bois** and Linton, and its participants included R. **Benedict**, E. **Sapir** and R. **Bunzel**. In 1939, he published *The Individual and His Society: The Psychodynamics of Primitive Social Organization* (New York: Columbia UP, 1939). This was followed in 1945 by *The Psychological Frontiers of Society* (New York: Columbia UP), and in 1947 by *War Stress and Neurotic Illness* (New York: Norton). He is also known for his study on Black Americans written in collaboration with L. Ovesey (*The Mark of Oppression: The Psychological Study of the American Negro*, New York: Norton, 1951), and for his popular *They Studied Man*, a history of the discipline in the form of biographies of its founders, co-authored by E. Prebble. Mention should also be made of *My Analysis with Freud* (New York, 1977).

Hallowell, Alfred Irving (1892–1974)
Born in Philadelphia, Alfred Irving Hallowell obtained a BA in economics from the University of Pennsylvania in 1914 and then worked in the social sector while continuing his studies in sociology and anthropology under Speck, **Goldenweiser** and **Boas**. He was awarded a Ph.D. by Columbia University in 1924. In the 1920s he worked among the Algonquins and in the 1930s among the Cree and the Ojibwa in Canada. He used projective tests to measure the relative differences in personality accompanying various degrees of acculturation. He was appointed to a professorship at the University of Pennsylvania, where he taught until 1962, and subsequently worked in other institutions, as well as holding a number of other prestigious positions. His best-known work is *Culture and Experience* (1955), in which he offers an evaluation of the application of Rorschach tests to the Ojibwa. Inspired by the Sapir–Whorf hypothesis, Hallowell maintained that the social and physical environment is a cultural construct rather than an objective reality, and is only given meaning

by those operating within it (see **Sapir**, **Whorf**. Although close to culturalism, Hallowell's position differs from it in that it emphasizes the consciousness of self in each individual rather than the collective unconscious. Issuing from a cultural symbolic system in the process of mankind's emergence, Hallowell's 'self' is situated at the conjunction of external environment and those impulses, such as imagination, which exist within the individual. The self protects the social order by ensuring the regularity of its functioning. And because individual behaviour is dependent on metaphysical principles (other human subjects, relations with ancestors, etc.), kinship cannot be understood as the foundation of the social order.

Linton, Ralph (1893–1953)
Born into a Quaker family from Philadelphia, Ralph Linton went to a Quaker school and then entered Swarthmore College, where one of his teachers, S. Trotter, took him to visit archaeological digs in New Mexico and Colorado (1912–1916), Guatemala (1912–1913) and New Jersey (1915). Linton obtained a BA in archaeology in 1916. He served as a corporal in the US Army and saw action in France (where he suffered gas poisoning), and his wartime experience helped him in writing his first article on social anthropology, which appeared in 1924: 'Totemism and the A. E. F.' (*AA*, vol.26: 296–315). Extricating totemic phenomena from their mystical and exotic associations, he showed how signs used by aviators functioned in what can be called a totemic fashion. After the war Linton resumed his archaeological research in Colorado (1919), Ohio (1924) and Wisconsin (1929–1933). In 1920 he travelled to the Marquesas Islands (where he laid out Gauguin's tomb) as an archaeologist, but in 1922 he came away an ethnologist. He then found employment as an assistant curator in the Field Museum of Natural History in Chicago,

and from 1925 to 1927 carried out research in Madagascar. In 1927 he obtained his Ph.D. from Harvard University, and between 1928 and 1937 taught at the University of Wisconsin. In 1933 he published *The Tanala, a Hill Tribe of Madagascar*, in which he expounded the opposition between magicians and the possessed. After this he worked in the field among the Comanche of Oklahoma, and on his return published *The Study of Man: An Introduction* (New York). While **Kroeber**'s handbook of 1923 gives considerable space to historical reconstruction and diffusionism, Linton's work devotes only two chapters to these topics. Instead he endeavours to define culture as a process of psychological transmission, and advances the notions of pattern (model), status (inherited or acquired), and role, understood as status in its dynamic aspect (later sociologists such as Morton and above all Goffman would base a whole new approach on this concept of role). He also noted the universality of typical models of antisocial conduct. In 1936 Linton worked with **Redfield** and **Herskovits** on a *Memorandum for the Study of Acculturation* (Memorandum of the AAA), in which he studied the effects of acculturation on American Indians and Black Americans, and this work also bore fruit in *Acculturation in Seven American Indian Tribes* (New York, 1940). In 1937 he succeeded **Boas** as head of the anthropology department at Columbia University. In *The Individual and His Society* (New York: Columbia UP, 1939), which he wrote with A. **Kardiner**, Linton returned to his earlier description of the Tanala forest people and compared them with the Betsileo rice cultivators, concluding that social conditions determine a personality-type which itself determines secondary institutions. The cultivation of rice according to the practice of slash and burn, which is associated with property held in common, engenders a sense of security in the basic personality of the Tanala, and therefore accusations of witchcraft are rare and illnesses are attributed to human error or possession by evil spirits. Conversely, among the Betsileo, who use irrigated rice fields, the existence of private landholdings foments a psychological insecurity which explains the perceived importance of witchcraft and the view that illnesses are always caused by magic spells. In 1946 Linton joined the anthropology department of Yale University. Here he set up a seminar from which emerged *The Psychological Frontiers of Society*, written jointly by himself, Kardiner, **Du Bois**, and J. West, and *The Cultural Background of Personality*, which Linton wrote alone; both appeared in 1945. The second book examines the nexus which ties the individual to society (the entire complex of institutional relationships) and to culture (learnt behavioural models organized as status and role). The individual is seen as comprising both a basic personality, that is to say behaviour understood as normal, and a statutory (group) personality which is superimposed on the basic personality. Personality is thus an aggregate displaying subconscious responses stimulated by concrete situations, but the individual can choose between several modes of adaptation and many forms of conduct. At Linton's death the manuscript of his *Tree of Culture* lay unfinished, and it was completed and published by his wife Adelin Linton in 1955.

Mead, Margaret (1901–1978)

A specialist in Pacific cultures, an activist and public figure, Margaret Mead played an important role in increasing the familiarity of the general public with the notion of culture. She authored or co-authored forty-four books, and the diversity and importance of her work, and above all the influence it exercised, made her without doubt the major anthropologist of the American school. Mead was born in Philadelphia, where her father worked as an economics professor at the University of Pennsylvania.

Her mother was a teacher with a degree in sociology, at a time when this subject was just becoming established in university curricula and when women generally did not pursue higher education. In 1920 Mead began studies in psychology at Barnard College, where her teachers included F. **Boas** and W. Ogburn, an advocate of the works of Freud, Jung, Adler and **Rivers**. She gained a BA in 1923 and an MA in 1924, married L. Cressman, and then joined Barnard's anthropology department, directed by Boas with the help of his assistant R. **Benedict**. All her life Mead remained close to Benedict, and after her death she edited her works and wrote her biography. In 1925 a grant from the National Research Council allowed her to travel to Samoa to study the lives of adolescent girls (1925–1926), a trip which Boas sanctioned in the knowledge that a boat put in there every three weeks. In Samoa, Mead made what she believed was a new discovery, namely that adolescent girls did not experience the psychological tensions suffered by American teenagers, and that their transition to adulthood was a smooth process. On her return she wrote *Coming of Age in Samoa: A Psychological Study of Primitive Youth for Western Civilization* (1928a), and her editor requested that she add a chapter on the significance of her discoveries. This was the first of Mead's statements seeking to influence public opinion, and **Kroeber** was critical of her reflections on the education given to American children (Kroeber, 1931). It should be noted that in 1983 R. A. Goodman and D. **Freeman** both published books denouncing the superficiality of Mead's ethnography and her conclusions on cultural relativism. Freeman also made a film in 1988 which showed Mead's old informants admitting having lied to her (Shankman, 1996). While Mead's first book presents absolutely no analysis of Samoan social structures, she makes up for it in *Social Organization of Manu'a* (1930), which is entirely devoted to this topic (Honolulu:

Bishop Museum). She successfully defended her thesis in 1928 and was appointed as assistant curator in ethnology at the American Museum of Natural History. She then won a research grant which allowed her to travel to the Admiralty Islands with R. F. **Fortune**, whom she married on the boat. The couple stayed on Manus for six months in 1928–1929 (Mead was to return there six times between 1928 and 1975). In 1930 she published *Social Organization of Manu'a*, which in **Firth**'s opinion is 'one of the best systematic pieces of work on kinship then published in the whole Oceanic field' (Parking, 'An interview with Firth', *CA*, vol.29/2 (1988): 327–341), and *Growing Up in New Guinea: A Comparative Study of Primitive Education* (1930, 1975). Mead was the first anthropologist to study the education of children, and her conclusions challenged both the idea that the problems associated with adolescence are universal and the notion of a prelogical mentality (see **Lévy-Bruhl**). But her novelty also lay in her style of writing: like **Malinowski**, and in the same period, Mead produced a type of anthropology that was easy and pleasant to read. Unlike Malinowski, however, she does not speak of 'natives', but mentions individuals who recur in the study by name (Ngasu, Kawa, Ngalowen, etc.). A further notable aspect of Mead's writing is the dichotomy she proposes between the unfamiliar 'them' and the American 'us', which in most cases aims to reveal the positive, liberating and healthy aspects of the former. The comparative analysis between societies largely untouched by 'foreign commerce' and modern American society is then expanded to take in three New Guinea populations with very dissimilar cultures, the Arapesh, the Mundugumor and the Chambuli, among whom Mead and Fortune lived from 1931 to 1933. Mead published her findings in *Sex and Temperament in Three Primitive Societies* (New York: William Morrow, 1935), in which she observes how cultural differences affect the identities and personalities of women and men, and their relationships with children. This was the first anthropological study to provide a comparative examination of the situation of women. This theme emerges most clearly in Mead's dichotomy between the Arapesh and the Mundugumor: among the Arapesch, mothers and children have a prolonged relationship, young boys are not encouraged to behave aggressively, men help with childrearing tasks, and both sexes have gentle natures, whereas among the Mundugumor pregnancies are associated with devastating taboos, aggressiveness is encouraged, and women, who do all the hard physical work, are as violent as the men. As for the Chambuli, they are presented as a society in which men are nominally in charge of each collective but in reality submit to their womenfolk. Her next mission took Mead to Bali, where she stayed from 1936 to 1938 accompanied by G. **Bateson**, whom she had met while working among the Chambuli in 1933 and then married. Their shared interest in psychology led them to study trances and other forms of hypnosis, and they made extensive documentary use of photography. They took 38,000 photographs, from which they chose 759 for publication in 1942 in *Balinese Character: A Photographic Analysis* (New York: New York Academy of Sciences). In 1938 Mead returned to the Iatmul of New Guinea and in 1939 gave birth to her only child, M. C. Bateson. In 1941 R. Benedict asked her to assume control of a committee on eating habits in the army, and she also headed a national investigation into American eating habits before wartime rationing (1942). In 1944 she created the Institute for Intercultural Studies, which she financed almost entirely from her own pocket. In 1945, the year of her divorce from G. Bateson, she published *American Troops in a British Community*, a study commissioned by the Ministry of the Armed Forces which aimed to foster understanding between British and American communities. Mead joined the anthropology department of Columbia University in 1947 but was not made a professor there until 1954. In *Male and Female: A Study of the Sexes in a Changing World*, published in 1949, she returns to her comparison of Pacific and American societies by contrasting their construction of gender, and argues that American prudishness and hypocrisy prevent the possibilities of full adult sexuality from being realized. More interestingly, as the first ethnologist to describe such events as birth and lactation in detail, Mead presents the mother and child as forming a culturally defined biological and psychological system (a theme to which she would often return: 1957, 1958, 1967, 1974) and sketches out an anthropological approach to the processes of imprinting. She was appointed director of the Research Program on Contemporary Cultures after the death of Benedict and wrote a book on the Soviet national character (1951) using methods which she set out in *The Study of Culture at a Distance* (1953). In Mead's view, individuals mature in a cultural context constituted of an ideological system, the expectations of those around them, and techniques of socialization, all of which condition their responses to situations and even their psychic make-up. Mead also became associated with the analysis of forms of social and economic change as well as forms of personality change (1949). During the 1950s she worked within the framework of UNESCO on questions of social transformation and development (Mead, ed., *Cultural Patterns and Technical Change*, UNESCO, 1955). In 1953, after an absence of twenty-five years, she returned to the Peri village where the children she had known in 1929 were now leaders of a community exposed to the difficulties of transition to the modern life they all seemed to desire. She described this process in *New Lives for Old: Cultural Transformation – Manus 1928–1953* (1956). If from the 1930s

Mead's work had always been a vehicle for her preoccupation with the difficulties of adaptation experienced by American youth, in the 1960s she made this subject her exclusive concern. Her *Anthropologists and What They Do* (1965), which was aimed at students, describes her own student years and, to a lesser extent, her fieldwork. She discussed her fieldwork in more detail in 'Field Work in the Pacific Islands, 1925–1967' (in Peggy Golde, ed., *Women in the Field: Anthropological Experiences*, 1970). Above all Mead campaigned for better educational standards, greater autonomy for students and a role in decisions regarding their future. *Culture and Commitment* (1969) begins to reveal this new engagement, to which she returns in *A Way of Seeing* (1970), which addresses problems such as pollution, racism, the risk of war, overpopulation and world famine, and her commitments are revealed again in *Blackberry Winter: My Earlier Years* (1972). As well as at Columbia, Mead taught at the universities of Fordham, Cincinnati and Topeka, was a member of numerous ethics and health committees, and integrated an awareness of the importance of cultural differences into the growing anthropological element of the training given to social workers. She was also curator of the American Museum of Natural History, where she established a new Pacific section which opened in 1971. Mead died on 15 November 1978 in New York of cancer of the pancreas. It should be noted that, apart from the controversy unleashed by Freeman, she has often been criticized for her neglect of quantitative approaches in favour of a reliance on what has often been called an anecdotal approach. She has thus been accused of imposing on a collective an approach founded on individual psychology, and thereby ignoring historical and economic factors.

Du Bois, Cora (1903–1991)
Born in New York, Cora Du Bois studied at

Barnard College under **Boas** and obtained a BA in 1927. After an MA at Columbia University in 1928 she enrolled at Berkeley, where **Lowie** sent her to research the Wintu of California in 1929–1930. She was awarded a Ph.D. in 1932 for her thesis *Wintu Ethnography* (Berkeley, 1935). In 1935 she received a grant from the National Research Council Fellowship to investigate how psychiatric training might be used by professional anthropologists. She spent six months at the Boston Psychopathic Hospital, and then **Kardiner** invited her to lead a seminar with him in the summer of 1936, which brought together 'Freudian sociology' and ethnological writing under the auspices of the New York Psychoanalytic Society. The seminar was continued into the following year, and in 1938 Du Bois obtained funding from the Research Council for Social Sciences of Columbia University for a period of fieldwork (while **Linton** took her place with Kardiner in the seminar). In search of a place which presented evidence of substantial pathology, she chose Alor on the advice of **Josselin de Jong**, without however finding there the promised pathologies, known as Arctic Hysteria or Amok. She remained there until 1939, and in 1944 published *The People of Alor: A Social-Psychological Study of an East Indian Island*. The book aimed to describe the evolution of the individual from birth to adulthood, as well as treating other themes, such as the psychology of religion and biographical narratives, and presenting the results obtained from projective tests (Rorschach, free association, children's drawings). Each of Du Bois's sections was closed with a concluding chapter by A. Kardiner. During the Second World War she joined the Office of Strategic Services, working in the research and analysis branch as chief of the Indonesia section. In 1944 she moved from Washington DC to Ceylon (Sri Lanka) to head the Southeast Asia Command. She taught anthropology at Hunter College (1936) and Sarah Lawrence College

(1939–1942), and worked for the World Health Organization (1942–1954), before joining the anthropology department at Harvard (1954–1969), where she held the Zemurray-Stone Chair. At Harvard she initiated a long-term research project on the Indian temple city of Bhubaneswar. After her retirement from Harvard she taught at Cornell University between 1970 and 1975.

Kluckhohn, Clyde Kay Mayben
(1905–1960)

Born in Iowa, Clyde Kay Mayben Kluckhohn began his studies at Princeton University in 1922, but after he was diagnosed with rheumatism his family sent him to live in a dry region near a Navajo reserve. He was inspired by his observation of the Navajo to write his first book, *To the Foot of the Rainbow*, published in 1927. After Princeton he studied at Wisconsin (BA 1928) before spending 1931–1932 in Vienna, where he discovered both the school of Father Wilhelm **Schmidt** and psychoanalysis, and in Oxford, where he studied under **Marett** and obtained a Master's degree in 1932. Back in the USA he became assistant professor at the University of New Mexico (1932–1934) and was awarded a Harvard Ph.D. in 1936. He taught at Harvard from 1935 and took charge of a study project on the Navajo community of New Mexico from 1936 to 1948. He instigated a new form of long-term, interdisciplinary research presenting a detailed account of the culture of the Navajo, their view of the world and problems in adapting to modernity (1938, 1940, 1944, 1946). *Children of the People* (1947) examines the development of childhood personality using psychological tests. During the Second World War Kluckhohn worked for the US administration on Japan with R. **Benedict**, and afterwards, together with the sociologist T. Parsons, the social psychologist G. Allport, and the psychoanalyst H. Murray, he created the interdisciplinary department of social relations at Harvard (*Personality in Nature, Society and Culture*, 1949), which was to play an important role in the future of anthropology. In 1947 he organized the Russian Research Center at Harvard (Kluckhohn, Inkeles and Bauer, 1956), and he was also head of Harvard's anthropology department. He sought a synthesis of culturalism while also trying to demonstrate that there are fundamental human values shared by all cultures. He died prematurely of a heart attack in New Mexico in 1960.

Opler, Morris Edward (1907–1996)

Born in Buffalo, Morris Edward Opler gained a BA and an MA from the State University of New York at Buffalo under **White**, who then sent him to the University of Chicago to be taught by **Sapir** and **Radcliffe-Brown**. He obtained a Ph.D. from Chicago in 1933 and taught there until 1935. In 1936–1937 he worked as an anthropologist at the Bureau of Indian Affairs, and then taught at Reed College (1937–1938) and Claremont College (1938–1942). From 1930 to 1940 he spent time among the Apaches and in 1941 published his most famous work: *An Apache Life-Way: The Economic, Social and Religious Institutions of the Chiricahua Indians* (Chicago UP). Following a trail blazed by **Linton** and **Kluckhohn**, the book belongs to a group of works focusing on modes of social integration. Nonetheless, Opler opposed the notion of monolithic transcendental values by stressing that contradictory values are present at the heart of a single society. He formulated the concept of 'theme', defined as 'a postulate or a position, declared or implicit, which usually controls behavior or stimulates an activity, and which is tacitly approved or overtly advocated by a society' (Opler, 1945: 198). These themes are actuated in two ways: as existential modes, expressing the nature of the world; and as normative principles guiding social relations. Every society combines several 'themes' to form an equilibrium. An example of this in Hindu culture is the way the theme of the split between the spiritual and the temporal, leading to detachment from the self, is combined with the theme of the active and responsible involvement of the individual in his own life. A satisfactory integration is thus produced by these two complementary themes (Opler, 1948). By comparing Chiricahua Apaches with Jicarilla Apaches, and Jicarilla Apaches with Lipan Apaches, Opler endeavours to show how the combination and accentuation of themes in a culture gives it its particular complexion (1959). Opler is also noteworthy for his contributions to the *Handbook of North American Indians* (Berkeley: U of California P, 1989). Particularly well-known is his long analytical description of the longevity rites performed by young Chiricahua girls during puberty. During the Second World War, Opler worked in Japanese POW camps in California and offered his services to the League of American Citizens of Japanese Origin. He taught at Harvard University (1946–1948) and was appointed professor at Cornell University (1948–1969), where he established and directed a programme of Indian studies. After his retirement from Cornell he taught at the University of Oklahoma (1969–1977).

Voget, Frederick William (1913–1977)
Born in Salem to a father who had emigrated from Germany, F. W. Voget gained a BA from the University of Oregon and then studied anthropology at Yale, where he obtained a Ph.D. in 1947 with a thesis entitled *The Shoshoni-Crow Sun Dance* (Oklahoma UP, 1985). He wrote numerous articles and became a world expert on the Crow, with whom he spent every summer in Montana. He was a professor successively at McGill University in Montreal, the University of Arkansas, the University of Toronto, and Southern Illinois University at Edwardsville. During his teaching years he produced a *History of Ethnology* (New York: Holt, Rinehart & Winston, 1975), a very detailed work written in the style of a teaching handbook.

Opler, Marvin Kaufmann (1914–1981)
Born in Buffalo, Marvin Kaufmann Opler obtained a Ph.D. in anthropology from Columbia University in 1938. He served in the armed forces from 1943 to 1946 and then taught at various universities, including Stanford and Harvard. In 1952 he joined the department of medicine at Cornell University, where he made a study of mental illnesses in urban environments, and then moved to the anthropology department at the State University of New York at Buffalo in 1958. In 1957 he founded the *International Journal of Social Psychiatry*.

THE CHICAGO SOCIOLOGICAL SCHOOL

Frederick Starr, a self-made anthropologist, occupied the first post created in the department of sociology and anthropology in the newly founded University of Chicago and kept it until his retirement in 1923. He was replaced by Fay-Cooper **Cole**, who had gained his Ph.D. from Columbia University and worked for the Field Museum. With the financial support of the Laura Spelman Rockefeller Memorial, Cooper-Cole expanded the department by appointing **Sapir** in 1926 and **Redfield** in 1928. In 1929 he was able to create an independent anthropology department, and with Sapir's help persuaded the Rockefeller Foundation to subsidize a five-year plan for anthropological research. Sapir left for Yale in 1931 and was replaced as a linguistics specialist by one of his students, Harry Hoijer, and as a cultural anthropologist by the social anthropologist **Radcliffe-Brown**, who remained in post until 1937.

After **Boas** and his students had swept away evolutionism, American anthropology was composed of two main movements. The first saw conjunctural history and culture as the main determinant, and the second stressed the relationship between the individual and his culture; both were forms of cultural anthropology. The social anthropology Radcliffe-Brown sought to establish at Chicago differed from both in assigning the central role to the structure and functioning of society.

Shortly after his arrival at Chicago, Radcliffe-Brown embarked on a comparative study project on Amerindian kinship terminology. He trained two important anthropologists: F. **Eggan**, who worked as a research assistant, and S. **Tax**. In 1937, together with W. L. **Warner**, they published *Social Anthropology of North American Tribes* (Chicago: Chicago UP), a work which formed a pendant to Radcliffe-Brown's article distilling previous scholarship on the social organization of Australian Aborigines. Radcliffe-Brown's insistence on a strictly ahistorical scientific method was an important factor in the general reorientation of American anthropology. Under Robert Park's influence, Redfield distanced himself from Boasian historicism and moved towards a social anthropology with an evolutionist colouring. When he became the third Dean of the Social Science Division at Chicago in 1934, Redfield took the opportunity to expand the department and secured the services of Warner. Now containing Redfield, Warner and Eggan, the Chicago department became the crucible of American social anthropology. One notable example of its activity was the comparative study, instigated by Redfield with financial support from the Carnegie Institution, of four communities, of which the best-known was the Yucatan. Also significant were the investigations which Sol Tax made in Guatemala in 1944 using the department's resources. Cole, after spending long years concentrating exclusively on archaeology, took retirement in 1947.

Redfield, Robert (1897–1958)

Born in Chicago, Robert Redfield enrolled at the University of Chicago in 1915 to study law. He served as a volunteer during the First World War and then as an ambulance man before returning to Chicago and gaining a BA in 1921. While working in a law firm he followed courses offered by one of the early sociologists, R. Park (who became his father-in-law). Redfield's passion for the social sciences was intensified by a journey he made to Mexico in 1923. In 1925, he began teaching sociology at the University of Colorado, and, thanks to a grant from the National Council for Social Studies, carried out his first research in the Mexican village of Tepoztlán in 1926 and 1927. He described the internal divisions among the original Indian inhabitants of the village, the effects on them of modernization and modern medicine, and the ideological values of each group (*Tepoztlán, a Mexican Village: A Study of Folk Life*, Chicago: Chicago UP, 1930). When he returned from the field in 1927, Redfield enrolled in the anthropology department at Chicago, now all but independent of sociology. After receiving his doctorate in 1928 he became assistant professor, associate professor (1930), professor (1934), and finally head of the anthropology department (1948) at Chicago. From 1930 to 1933 he studied the Maya village of Chan Kom in Yucatan with the help of the village primary school teacher, A. Villa, and they co-authored *Chan Kom: A Maya Village* (Washington: Carnegie, 1934). Redfield's next work, *The Folk Culture of Yucatan* (Chicago: Chicago UP, 1941) compared the effects of civilization on four communities which shared the same Maya heritage.

Redfield worked as an adviser to the military authorities during the Second World War, took part in the conference which led to the creation of UNESCO, directed the

American Council for Race Relations, and was president of the Council of the American Broadcasting Company. He returned to Chan Kom in 1948 and wrote *A Village that Chose Progress: Chan Kom Revisited* (Chicago: Chicago UP, 1950), which tells of the adjustments made by the Mexican peasants to the modern world since his first visit, and observes that new features of life have not destroyed their traditional culture. The effect of technical and social change on the peasant world is also the subject of his theoretical work *The Primitive World and its Transformations* (Ithaca: Cornell UP, 1953), in which he sets out to describe the moral conflicts which accompany the spread of civilization. The subject of his last book, *The Little Community* (Chicago: Chicago UP, 1955), is the existence in India of the same generic types he had found in Mexico. Redfield set the 'greater traditions' embodied in urban cultures and complex ways of life against the 'lesser traditions' embodied in peasant cultures with local knowledge.

Warner, William Lloyd (1898–1970)
Born in Redlands in California, William Lloyd Warner first studied under **Kroeber** and **Lowie** at Berkeley (BA 1925), before moving to Chicago as a student of **Radcliffe-Brown**. He worked as an assistant professor at Harvard in 1929 and travelled to the Murngin of Northwestern Australia (Arnhem), where he stayed for three years. In 1937 he published *A Black Civilization: A Social Study of an Australian Tribe* (New York), which depicts the highly subtle Murngin kinship system. However, some scholars, such as Jean **Guiart**, have felt that the descriptive elements of the book need to be reviewed, 'which would quite simply cause the system itself to disappear' (Guiart, *Clefs pour l'ethnologie*, Paris: Seghers, 1971: 70). An investigation undertaken by W. Shapiro in Arnhem territory in 1969 ('Miwuyt Marriage: Social Structure Aspects of the Bestowal of Females in Northeast Arnhem

Land', Australian National University Ph.D.) convinced many more that 'the Murngin, as they are defined in the literature of the Murngin controversy, do not exist and have never existed' (J. A. Barnes, *Three Styles in the Study of Kinship*, Berkeley: California UP, 1971: xxiii). Appointed by the University of Chicago in 1935, Warner turned his attention to urban social anthropology. He studied Yankee City in Massachusetts and, with the help of thirty collaborators, produced records on its 17,000 adult inhabitants. The years from 1941 to 1947 saw the publication of the four volumes of results yielded by Warner's inquiry into the 'American ideal', which produced the finding that this supposedly democratic ideal was in fact founded on quite different principles. In 1945 Warner made a study of Jonesville, a Republican town of the Midwest, and then extended his research to towns in Ireland and Austria.

Eggan, Fred Russell (1906–1991)
Born in Seattle, Fred Russell Eggan studied psychology at the University of Chicago (BA 1927), where he followed courses given by **Sapir**. In 1928 he submitted his Master's thesis, *An Experimental Study of Attitudes Toward Race and Nationality*, written while he was working as a schoolteacher. In 1930 he enrolled in the anthropology department which **Cole** was in the process of setting up at Chicago. When **Radcliffe-Brown** moved to the department in 1931, Eggan became his research assistant and at his request undertook a comparative study of Amerindian social structures. He took part in a fieldwork training programme run by Leslie **White** in the summer of 1932, and in 1933 gained a doctorate with his thesis *The Kinship System and Social Organization of the Western Pueblos with Special Reference to the Hopi Indians*, which demonstrated that Hopi kinship nomenclature was the basis for the tribe's rules of social interaction. Eggan found that the principle of unity of descent

advanced by Radcliffe-Brown was applicable to the matrilineal system of the Hopi. The male Ego distinguishes his mother's brothers from his own brothers and nephews, but includes his mother's mother's brothers and his sister's daughter's sons in the same category as his immediate brothers. After his doctorate Eggan was appointed as an associate researcher by the Chicago department and examined processes of acculturation among the Choctow of Mississippi, the Cheyenne, and the Arapaho of Oklahoma. In 1934 Cole sent him to the Philippines, where he had worked himself, to study the social transformation of the Tinguin. On his return from the field in 1936, Eggan took up a teaching post at Chicago and in 1937 co-edited *Social Anthropology of North American Tribes.* He left the department during the war to occupy various research and teaching positions connected with the army. In 1948 he was appointed professor, and worked as head of department until 1952, when he became director of the Research Centre on the Philippines. In 1953 Eggan proposed a method of controlled comparison, which would compare the social structures of societies which seem nearly identical or at least resemble one another very closely. He believed that, within such a strongly homogeneous group, a meaningful attempt could conceivably be made to distinguish universal from contingent features in the formation and reproduction of societies by looking at the modalities of their transformation (Eggan, 1954).

THE SUBSTANTIVIST SCHOOL

In 1940 **Herskovits** wrote the first handbook of economic anthropology, *The Economic Life of Primitive Peoples* (New York, rev. edn 1952), although the dialogue he thereby initiated with economists was neither extensive nor particularly fruitful. It was not until after the Second World War that economists such as G. Dalton and P. **Bohannan** began to look at the economic lives of peoples from an anthropological perspective, and they thereby contributed new conceptual tools to anthropology. This new trend led to the emergence of what became known as the substantivist school, which took as its object of study the various institutions in a society which provide the framework for exchange and for the distribution of goods.

Polanyi, Karl (1886–1964)

Karl Polanyi was born into a Jewish milieu in Budapest (Hungary). He studied law and philosophy in Budapest and in 1908 created the Galilean Circle, which brought together progressive thinkers who wished to reform the semi-feudal condition of Hungary. During the First World War Polanyi served in the army and was wounded, and afterwards he became a journalist with a Viennese daily newspaper (1924–1933). In 1933 he emigrated to England, where he taught in the Workers' Educational Association. This provoked his interest in the origins of the Industrial Revolution in Great Britain, and he began writing *The Great Transformation: The Political and Economic Origins of Our Time* (New York: Rinehart, 1944), in which he studies the rise and fall of the global economy and economic liberalism from their inception in Britain to the advent of Hitler in Germany. Having given conference papers on this theme in the USA, he was appointed professor of economic history at Columbia University in 1947. As Polanyi's wife, who had been a member of the Hungarian Communist Party, was refused a US visa, the couple settled in Canada. Until 1953 Polanyi taught at Columbia, continually shuttling back and forth from his home in Canada, and during this period he co-directed a seminar with C. M. **Arensberg** and H. W. Pearson, the proceedings of which were later published as *Trade and Market in the Early Empires: Economies in History and Theory* (New York: Free Press, 1957). In 1944 he defined an economy as an institutionalized process of interaction between man and his environment, which takes the form of the provision of material goods he requires for the satisfaction of his needs, and he contrasted societies governed by economic institutions with societies shaped by institutions of other sorts. He asserts that while the aim of a capitalist market economy is profit, the institutions of exchange in primitive societies function in a quite different way. In such societies the local market has fixed prices and fulfils the function of integrating different social groups otherwise riven by permanent rivalries. Trading ports establish relations between mercantile and non-mercantile economies and answer both the military and political needs of the state. Functionaries rather than traders are in charge of commerce with foreigners, and contact with other cultures is kept to a minimum. Formal economic theory applies only to the capitalist market system in which the economy is free, whereas elsewhere it is embedded in religious or kinship structures, in which the replication of relationships and not profit is the prime motive force for individuals.

Following the sociologist Weber, Polanyi proposes a distinction between three empirically constituted models of social integration: reciprocity, redistribution and exchange. Reciprocity assumes the existence of symmetrical groups woven together by balanced relations of exchange. This involves intervention both in production (provision of services, periodical allocation of land) and in the distribution of products (gifts offered and received). Redistribution requires a centralized institutional model, in which the centre (priest, state, suzerain, notable) collects products, stores them and redistributes them in such a way that its own agents are rewarded and the social order is upheld. In the market system, the means of production, land and labour are types of merchandise subject to the laws of the market. These analyses divide the circulation of goods into distinct spheres of exchange: substance, matrimonial goods, prestigious goods, market goods (see **Bohannan**; **Barth**). It would be fair to say that Polanyi is the true founder of economic anthropology.

Arensberg, Conrad Maynadiner (1910–1997)

Born in Pittsburgh, Conrad Maynadiner Arensberg studied at Harvard University, gaining a BA in 1931 and a Ph.D. in 1934. His thesis, entitled *The Irish Countryman: An Anthropological Study*, was published in 1937. While at Harvard he also took part in William Lloyd **Warner**'s Yankee City project. After the completion of his studies, Arensberg's posts were successively as assistant professor at the Massachusetts Institute of Technology (1938–1941), associate professor in the sociology and anthropology departments of Brooklyn College (1941–1946) and Barnard College (1946–1952), and finally associate professor in the anthropology department of Columbia University (1953–1980). In his early career Arensberg was an expert on rural Ireland, and then, in addition to participating extensively in the work of UNESCO, he increasingly devoted his attention to the anthropological study of the Middle East, India and a number of other regions, as well as making a substantial contribution to the development of urban anthropology. He also joined Polanyi in running the Interdisciplinary Project on the Economic Aspects of Institutional Growth, which resulted in a study entitled *Trade and Market in the Early Empires: Economies in History and Theory* (New York: Free Press, 1957).

THE NEO-EVOLUTIONISTS

Alongside the movements of Boasian relativism and culturalism, the period after the First World War saw a renewal of evolutionism (known as neo-evolutionism), the principal characteristics of which were the revival of totalizing approaches to human history and the rejection of the psychologization of social phenomena.

Two currents can be discerned: the main protagonist of the first was G. P. **Murdock**, critic of historicist particularism and instigator of the Human Relations Area Files; the second, less clearly defined, was represented by V. G. Childe, K. **Wittfogel**, L. **White** and J. **Steward**. Childe popularized the idea that the prehistoric evolution of mankind was founded on economic production, Wittfogel advanced the hypothesis that hydraulic civilization lay at the origin of the modern state, White considered culture and its evolution from an 'energetist' perspective, and Steward developed a schema of polygenic evolution based on determination by the natural environment.

Wittfogel, Karl August (1896–1988)

Born in Germany, Karl August Wittfogel became an active member of the German Communist Party and was associated with the Institute of Social Research in Frankfurt. He was briefly imprisoned after Hitler came to power in 1933, and then fled to the USA, where he soon became a virulent anti-communist, albeit without giving up his deep admiration for Marx's work. He became an American citizen in 1941, and in 1951 he testified against the sinologist O. Latimore during the communist-hunting McCarthy trials. Wittfogel adapted the Marxist concept of mode of production (condemned in the Leningrad Congress of 1931) to develop his own notions of 'Oriental despotism' and the 'hydraulic society', whose history he traced in practice and theory from Montesquieu to Marx and Stalin. He held that large public works, such as irrigation projects in China, promote a bureaucratic state centralism which extends its power to all aspects of social life, and he sees in this dynamic, which he contrasts with the atomism of peasant societies, the origin of the modern state. Wittfogel became director of the Center for Chinese Studies at Columbia University. More information on Wittfogel can be found in *The Times* of 18 June 1988.

Murdock, George Peter (1897–1985)

George Peter Murdock was born near Meriden, Connecticut, into a family of prosperous farmers. He served in the National Guard on the Mexican border in 1916, and then in the artillery when the USA became involved in the First World War. He gained a BA in American history from Yale in 1919 and entered the law faculty in 1920. After interrupting his studies in 1922 to travel around Asia and Europe, he enrolled in the social sciences department at Yale, where he came under the influence of A. G. Keller. Keller was well known as the author of *The Science of Society* (4 vols, New Haven: Yale University Press, 1927), which, as a note written by his mentor W. G. Summer has it, 'carried forward Spencer's grandiose plan for a total picture of world evolution' (Harris, 1968: 607). Murdock obtained a Ph.D. in 1925 for his critical translation of Julius Lippert's *The Evolution of Culture*. He taught at the University of Maryland from 1926 to 1928 and then worked as Keller's research assistant at Yale from 1928 to 1931. From 1931 he occupied a post which straddled the newly created departments of sociology and anthropology at Yale. In the summers of 1932, 1934 and 1935, Murdock travelled to the Haida on the Northeastern coast and to the Tenino of Oregon, and these were the only fieldwork experiences of his career. In 1934 he published *Our Primitive Contemporaries* (New York: Macmillan), a work intended for use in teaching. It was in 1937, in a contribution to a Festschrift for Keller, that Murdock set out for the first time his ideas for a comparative methodology applicable to both sociology and anthropology (the latter eschewing all biological data). These ideas corresponded to the principles set out in the Human Relations Area Files (HRAF), which sought to identify and catalogue the salient traits of all the cultures of the world. In 1938 Murdock succeeded **Sapir** as the head of the anthropology department at Yale and published the first edition of *Outline of Cultural Materials*, which would be systematically augmented with each new edition. He was appointed professor of anthropology at Yale in 1939 and served in the US Navy during the Second World War as a lieutenant (1943–1945) and then as a captain (1945–1946). The Files project increased its scope enormously thanks to financial support from the navy, and in 1949 it became an inter-university undertaking bringing together sixteen institutions. The Files assembled details of more than 2,500 codified cultures with about one hundred variables, and they provided Murdock with material for a large number of articles (on the correlations between matrilineal and patrilineal institutions, on marital stability, on gender divisions in work etc.) and for books such as *Africa: Its Peoples and Their Cultural History* (New York: McGraw Hill, 1959). To provide ethnographical nourishment for the Files he founded the journal *Ethnology* in 1962. In 1949 he published *Social Structure*, which is his major work (New York: Macmillan). On the basis of an analysis of the functional relations between traits found in 250 societies, he attempts to discover the underlying rules for cultural change, most particularly in the area of kinship. He sees the social world as composed of layers of independent changes

and evolution as presenting a palette of possibilities. Change is adopted most readily in matters of residence, and this brings about new rules of filiation leading to modifications in kinship terminology. However, as **Harris** observes, 'if residence is the most powerful determinant of kinship terminology, why does an analysis of the coefficients show that descent and marriage forms are more "effective" in producing particular varieties of kinship terminologies?' (Harris, 1968: 620).

Murdock was an outstanding critic both of the historical particularism of **Boas** (and even of the quality of his ethnographical research (see Murdock, 1949: xiv)), and of British social anthropologists, whom in a celebrated review he reproached for their dismissal of the history of social transformations and for the absence in their work of in-depth comparative study (Murdock, 1951). In 1960 he moved from Yale to the University of Pittsburgh, and he died on 29 March 1985.

White, Leslie A. (1900–1975)
Born in Salida, Colorado, Leslie A. White first studied history and political science under T. Veblen at the State University of Louisiana, and then switched to psychology at Columbia University, where he was taught by the behaviourist J. B. Watson and gained an MA. He also attended courses given by **Goldenweiser** at the New School for Social Research. In 1925 he enrolled at the University of Chicago, where his professors were **Cole** and **Sapir**, and it was at Sapir's suggestion that he carried out research among the Acoma Pueblo Indians. White obtained a Ph.D. in 1927 and then taught anthropology at the State University of New York at Buffalo and at the Buffalo Museum of Science. He commenced work on the Seneca Indians while still maintaining his interest in the Pueblo, on whom he wrote five monographs. While studying the Seneca he reread **Morgan** (later he would edit his *Ancient Society*, his journal and his correspondence with **Bandelier**) and reoriented his own

research towards a global evolutionary perspective. A voyage to the Soviet Union in 1929 and a temporary teaching post in Beijing familiarized him with Marxism but left him unimpressed with its dialectic. In 1930 he succeeded J. H. **Steward** as associate professor at the University of Michigan, where he was given tenure in 1943. He retired in 1970.

White believed that the human race, by inventing symbols, brought into being a superorganism known as culture. This idea is already present in **Kroeber** and, to a lesser extent, in Durkheim, but it was White who invented culturology, the scientific study of culture as a 'suprapsychic' instance, symbolic in nature, with its own laws governing its functioning, reproduction and evolution, and taking the place occupied by sociology in a Comtean tree of science. In 'Energy and the Evolution of Culture', published in 1943, he put forward the idea that cultures develop in line with the growth in energy resources. 'White's Law' states that cultural evolution is dependent on the quantity of energy available per capita. *The Evolution of Culture* (New York: McGraw Hill, 1959) brought together articles published between 1938 and 1949. Apart from those mentioned already, White's most important idea is that individual human behaviour is determined entirely by the cultural superorganism, and this idealist view is allied to a materialism which sees technology as the dominant factor in any cultural system. A polemical opponent of the Boasian school (1960), White trained such cultural anthropologists as M. **Sahlins**, M. **Harris**, E. **Service**, and R. **Carneiro**, and the archaeologist L. Binford. He was elected president of the AAA in 1964, retired in 1970 and died in 1975, leaving unfinished a manuscript he had been working on for twenty years: *Modern Capitalist Culture*.

Steward, Julian H. (1902–1972)

Born in Washington into a family of Christian Scientists, Julian H. Steward studied anthropology at Berkeley under A. **Kroeber**, R. **Lowie** and E. **Gifford**. After a research trip to the Shoshone he moved to Cornell to study zoology, gaining a BA in 1925, before returning to Berkeley, where at that time C. D. **Forde** was a visiting professor. He wrote his first article, on archaeology, in 1927, and in 1929 was awarded a Ph.D. in anthropology for his thesis *The Ceremonial Buffoon of the American Indian* (published in 1931 by the Michigan Academy of Sciences, Arts and Letters). From 1928 he taught at the University of Michigan, offering its first ever anthropology course (Manners, 1973: 889), and his subsequent posts were at the University of Utah (1930–1933), where he began research on the Pueblo Indians, and then at Berkeley (1933–1934). From 1935 to 1946 Steward worked in the Bureau of American Ethnology of the Smithsonian Institution. Dissatisfied by the way cultural relativism, functionalism and historical particularism took account only of singular phenomena, he turned to comparative approaches and the search for laws of causality, and set forth a typology for the analysis of band types and of the development of societies in the Southwest from prehistoric times (1936, 1937). The publication in 1938 of his *Basin-Plateau Aboriginal Sociopolitical Groups* (Washington: Bureau of American Ethnology) founded an ecological and cultural anthropology of an evolutionist and environmentalist character. In this work he proposed the idea of a 'cultural ecology', stating that the combination of environmental resources and available technologies determines forms of production, which in turn influence the social system. Steward then carried out research in British Columbia and the Peruvian and Ecuadorian Andes, and in 1940 the Smithsonian Institution commissioned him to edit the *Handbook of South American Indians*, which he decided to arrange according to cultural rather than geographical criteria. This project, which Steward ran until his departure from the Bureau, was divided into six volumes which appeared from 1946 to 1949: 1) marginal tribes; 2) higher cultures; 3) the tropical rainforest; 4) Caribbean peoples; 5) comparative ethnology; 6) index (New York: Cooper Square). This project offered the first complete description of South American Indians, with contributions from all Americanists of the time. Steward himself wrote about a dozen of the articles, and also produced a condensed version of the handbook entitled *The Native Peoples of South America* (New York: McGraw Hill, 1959), which he wrote together with L. A. Faron. In 1943 he created the Institute for Social Anthropology within the framework of the Bureau to investigate problems of modernization and cultural change, and this gave him the opportunity to send anthropologists to Columbia, Mexico, Peru and Brazil to focus on new objects of anthropological interest in these countries. In 1946 Steward was appointed professor in the anthropology department at Columbia University, where he lectured on Latin America and cultural dynamics (though according to Wolf these courses were in fact given by David Bidney and Paul **Kirchhoff** (see E. **Wolf**, 1988, 'Reply' in *CA*, col.29(2): 307). At the same time he joined the Bureau of Indian Affairs, which allowed him to practise applied anthropology and focus particular attention on subcultures, a topic he introduced to the discipline especially through a project on Puerto Rico which he directed from 1948 to 1952 (1956). Steward was elected to the National Academy of Sciences and received the Viking Fund Medal, and in 1952 he accepted a position as senior researcher at the University of Illinois, where he took over the Project of Study in Cross-cultural Regularities financed by the Ford Foundation

(1952–1955). Dedicated to the comparative analysis of causes and modes of change, the project bore fruit in the publication of the three-volume *Contemporary Change in Traditional Societies* (vol.1: Introduction and Africa; vol.2: Asian Rural Societies; vol.3: Mexican and Peruvian Communities; Urbana: Illinois UP). The attention Steward brought to bear on modernity was amplified by another, more theoretical work on cultural evolution. He stated that borrowing does not adequately explain the passage from one culture to another, and in 1953, and again in 1955, he developed the thesis, already present in his work of 1938, of a multilineal evolution, using cross-cultural comparisons to explain the diverse patterns of development which societies may follow towards greater complexity. This draws on **White**'s approach (autobiographical statement for the National Academy of Sciences, quoted by Manners, 1973: 887), although he also criticized White for his ultimately functionalist version of history (1949). Steward's schema retains White's view of the passage from band to tribe to chiefdom to state, but departs from his generalizing tendencies by concentrating on a small number of cases, all located in similar forest or desert environments and all showing the same levels of socio-cultural integration, but sufficiently far apart from one another for resemblances not to be attributable to diffusion. It was in 1951 that Steward first advanced this idea of levels of socio-cultural integration, to which his name has become attached, and which asserts that families, rural societies and states actuate different levels of social and cultural integration. From 1940 Steward suffered from recurring stomach ulcers, and after a twenty-year illness he died in February 1972.

THE SOCIAL QUESTION AND ACCULTURATION

From 1908 to 1946, **Kroeber** taught at the University of California at Berkeley, and in 1921 he was joined by **Lowie**, at first intermittently and then permanently. At Columbia, **Boas** took retirement in 1936 and three teachers were chosen to replace him: **Linton**, **Steward** and Strong (the last two being former students of Kroeber). After the foundational work of **Cole** at the University of Chicago, **Radcliffe-Brown** taught there from 1931 to 1937, **Sapir** having moved to Yale, where he remained until 1938. During this period, American anthropology maintained its interest in the reconstruction of ancient Amerindian cultures and in the study of the last remaining primitive societies in the Pacific, but at the same time developed in its major centres new research traditions examining American rural and urban communities and the question of acculturation.

The sociologists H. Lynd and R. S. Lynd were the pioneers of the first approach. In 1925 they completed a study of a Midwest community which they named Middletown, 'rather as anthropologists approach a primitive tribe' (C. **Wissler**, 'Foreword' to *Middletown*, 1956: vi). After spending time with Australian Aborigines, W. L. **Warner** chose to study the small town of Yankee City in Massachusetts, on which he and his thirty collaborators published four volumes of research from 1941 to 1947. Lastly, J. Dollard and H. Powdermaker, the latter having previously worked on Melanesia, began researching on the town of Cottonville in Mississippi in 1936. Strict limitations of space make it impossible to look at these projects in detail, but it should be noted that urban anthropology continued to expand.

As for acculturation, it was first defined by **Graebner** in 1880 as the study of modifications resulting from contact between two populations with different cultures. A number of anthropologists, notably **Malinowski** and those of the South African school, addressed this question, but it assumed central importance only with the work of R. **Redfield** in the mid-1920s. In 1935 a sub-committee was formed by the National Council for the Social Studies to apply this new approach, and in 1936 Redfield, R. **Linton** and M. **Herskovits** published a memorandum on the study of acculturation (*AA*, vol.38: 149–152). The war precipitated these social transformations and anthropology claimed for itself the status of an applied social science. The discipline set out to enlighten the military authorities during the war and decision-makers in the peace that followed, and it soon grew into a largely anti-Establishment science by making itself the mouthpiece of the poor and of ethnic minorities, particularly in the writings of S. **Tax** and O. **Lewis**. Until the mid-1970s, funding was nevertheless provided more or less in line with the discipline's requirements, but the recession of the 1980s and 1990s and the return to dominance of economic liberalism ushered in much more difficult times.

Herskovits, Melville Jean (1895–1963)

Born in Belle-Fontaine, Ohio, Melville Jean Herskovits was a pioneer of Afro-American studies. He studied first the University of Chicago, where he was taught by E. C. **Parsons** and T. Veblen, and then at Columbia University, where his teachers were **Boas** and **Goldenweiser**. He was awarded a Ph.D. in 1923, and then worked at Northwestern University in Evanston, where in 1927 he established the first programme in African studies in the USA. Much later, in 1961, he would hold the first American chair in Afri-can studies. He was also the founder and first president of the Association of African Studies and the author of more than 500 articles. His early work focused on defining African culture areas (1924), and he introduced the notion of the cattle complex to illustrate economic irrationality in the husbandry of Eastern and Southern Africa ('The Cattle Complex in East Africa', *AA*, vol.28). This was followed in 1928 by a field investigation carried out with his wife Frances Herskovits among the Bush inhabitants and among urban dwellers in Surinam (1934, 1936). He also drew up the first ethnographic inventory of rural societies in Haiti (1937) and Trinidad (1947). But it was the publication in 1941 of *The Myth of the Negro Past* (New York: Harper) that constituted Herskovits's major contribution to the discipline. In this work he followed in the footsteps of W. E. B. Du Bois by stating not only that there were elements in Black American subculture which were properly African, but also that some of these traits had been passed on to White Americans. This thesis was attacked by white liberals and by the Black middle class, as both of these militantly anti-racist groups saw in it an ideological assertion of the inability of Black Americans to integrate into the American melting pot. However, the reclaiming by Black Americans of African culture in the 1960s and 1970s caused Herskovits's view to come very much into vogue. His ideas made him a notable opponent of absolute relativism. Herskovits worked in New Guinea, Brazil, Haiti, and West Africa, and he is known for his substantial research on the ancient kingdom of Dahomey. Another important facet of his work is its focus on economic anthropology, on which he wrote the first handbook. However, his discussions with economists on this topic failed to resolve differences of perspective.

Tax, Sol (1907–1995)
Sol Tax was introduced to anthropology by Ralph **Linton** while a student at the University of Wisconsin. He gained his BA there in 1931, submitting a dissertation entitled 'A Re-interpretation of Culture, with an Examination of Animal Behavior', and then moved to the University of Chicago. Although **Benedict** supervised his first fieldwork, carried out in 1931 as part of the Summer Ethnology Program at the Mescalero Indian Reservation, Tax was most strongly influenced at this time by **Radcliffe-Brown**, who oriented him towards the study of social structures. He was awarded a Ph.D. in 1934 and then worked at the Carnegie

Foundation under the direction of **Redfield**, who introduced him to research on the Maya of Guatemala. Tax worked for eight years in Guatemala and for four more in Mexico, and from 1940 he was an associate professor at the University of Chicago, where he became professor in 1944 and succeeded Redfield as head of the anthropology department. Towards the end of the 1940s he launched Action Anthropology, which aimed to place anthropology at the service of the people it studied. This approach, which soon became known as interventionist anthropology, aimed to shed light on the implications of decisions taken by Amerindian communities and defend their cultural identities. An advocate of political autonomy for American Indians, Tax coordinated the first National Congress of American Indians at Lurie in 1961 and directed the cultural programme of the Carnegie Foundation for the Indians of Oklahoma from 1962 to 1967. In 1958, at the request of the Wenner–Gren Foundation, he founded *Current Anthropology*, which has since become probably the world's most prestigious anthropology journal. Tax was president of the University of Extension from 1963 to 1968, and from 1968 to 1970 worked at the Center for Advanced Study in the Behavioral Sciences of Princeton University. He died on 3 January 1995 in Chicago.

Wagley, Charles (1913–1991)
Born in Texas, Charles Wagley studied at the universities of Oklahoma and Columbia (BA 1936). He belonged to the very last generation of students taught by **Boas** (who died in 1942). Wagley gained his Ph.D. in 1941 for his research in Guatemala in 1937–1938 (*Economics of a Guatemalan Village*, Menasha, AAA, 1941). As Mercier has observed in his *Histoire de l'anthropologie* (Paris: PUF, 1966: 189), Wagley, together with **Tax**, was one of the first anthropologists on the American continent to look at economic conditions. While he was an assistant professor at Columbia University, he co-

wrote the articles on the Tenetehara and the Tapirape with the Brazilian E. Galvão for the third volume of the *Handbook of South American Indians* edited by **Steward** (like Wagley a professor at Columbia). Wagley and Galvão went on to write a book together on the Tenetehara (1949).

Wagley participated in UNESCO initiatives on the race question, especially by editing a commissioned volume entitled *Race and Class in Rural Brazil* (Paris: UNESCO, 1952). In 1955, in collaboration with his student Marvin **Harris**, he set out a typology of subcultures valid for the whole of Latin America. Together they also published *Minorities in the New World* (New York, Columbia UP, 1958). He taught at Columbia from 1946 to 1971, when he took a position at Gainesville before finishing his career at the University of Florida, where he ran the Center for Latin American Studies. Wagley died on 25 November 1991. He was the author of a large number of articles, some of which have been gathered together under the title *The Latin American Tradition: Essays on the Unity and Diversity of Latin American Culture* (New York: Columbia UP, 1968).

Lewis, Oscar (1914–1970)

Born in New York to a Jewish family emigrated from Poland, Oscar Lewis (real name Yehezkiel Lekowitz) gained a BA in history from City College in New York in 1936. He enrolled at Columbia University to continue his studies in history, but turned to anthropology after meeting Ruth **Benedict**. In 1939 he spent time among the Blackfoot population of Canadian Montana with his wife R. Maslow-Lewis, who was his constant companion in the field. He was awarded a Ph.D. in 1940 for a thesis entitled *The Effects of White Contact upon Blackfoot Culture, with Special Reference to the Role of the Fur Trade*, and then worked on the Human Relations Area Files at Yale University. In 1943 Lewis was employed by the Justice Department and sent to Mexico as a repre-

sentative of the USA at the Interamerican Indian Institute, which had just been created. While in Mexico he pursued research on the problems of rural development and on the peasant community of Tepoztlán, which **Redfield** had already studied. In 1951 he published *Life in a Mexican Village: Tepoztlán Restudied*, which differed from Redfield's work in its assertion that progress was not homogeneous and that it led to social differences becoming more marked. Lewis worked for the Agriculture Department and then became an associate professor successively at the universities of Washington, St Louis (1946) and Illinois, where he set up an anthropology department in 1948. He did fieldwork in Spain in 1949 and then in India, and his Indian research yielded *Group Dynamics in a North Indian Village: A Study of Factions* (New Delhi, 1954) and *Village Life in Northern India* (Illinois UP, 1958).

In the years that followed Lewis concentrated on urban anthropology and the analysis of family biographies, and he developed the concept of the 'culture of poverty', which first appeared in his 1959 book *Five Families: Mexican Case Studies in the Culture of Poverty* (New York: Basic Books). The culture of poverty is defined as a collection of traits which statistical analysis shows to be present among the poorest groups and to constitute a common subculture. In 1963 Lewis embarked on a vast inquiry into one hundred Puerto Rican families in San Juan and New York, which allowed him continually to refine this concept. He made it clear that the culture of poverty is a feature and consequence of capitalist culture, which tends to exacerbate class distinctions, but also that it creates its own self-perpetuating mechanisms which operate regardless of external factors. In 1968 Fidel Castro invited Lewis to study Cuban society and examine how the culture of poverty had evolved in a revolutionary socialist state. He and his team collected a significant body of material there, which was published after his death. Shortly before his death from a heart attack in 1970, Lewis published his *Anthropological Essays* (New York: Random House, 1970), which provides a retrospective on his work.

SELECT BIBLIOGRAPHY

Anonymous (1991) 'Warner, Lloyd', in C. Winter (ed.), pp.739–740.

Anonymous (1981) 'Opler, M.', *AA*, 83: 617–621.

Arensberg, C.M. (1978) 'C. Arensberg, President-elect', *AN*, 19(5): 13.

Atran, S. (1991) 'Mead, Margaret', in P. Bonte and M. Izard (eds) *Dictionnaire de l'ethnologie et de l'anthropologie*, Paris: Presses universitaires de France, p.459.

Azevedo de, T. (1991) 'C.W. Wagley', in C. Winter (ed.), pp.737–738.

Barett, R.A. (1989) 'The paradoxical anthropology of L. White', *AA*, 91: 986–999.

Bashkow, I. (1991) 'The dynamics of rapport in colonial situation: David Schneider's fieldwork on the islands of Yap', in G.W. Stocking, *Essays on the Contextualization of Ethnographic Knowledge*, *HOA*, vol.7: 170–242.

Bastide, R. (1953) 'The field method and the problems of the basic personality school', *British Journal of Sociology*, 3: 1–13.

Bateson, M.C. (1984) *With a Daughter's Eye*, New York: Simon and Schuster.

Baudelot, C. (1991) 'E. Sapir', in P. Bonte and M. Izard (eds) *Dictionnaire de l'ethnologie et de l'anthropologie*, Paris: Presses universitaires de France, p.651.

Beals, R.L. (1979) 'Julian Steward: the Berkeley days', *J. Steward Anthropological Society*, vol.11: 3–15.

——(1988) 'On E. Wolf and the North Berkeley Gang', and E. Wolf, 'Reply' in *CA*, 29(2): 306–307.

Benedict, R.F. (1931; 1981) *Tales from the Cochiti Indians*, with intro. by A. Ortiz, Albuquerque: University of New Mexico Press.

——(1935; 1969) *Zuni Mythology*, New York: AMS Press.

——(1939) 'E. Sapir', *AA*, 41: 465–477.

——(1940; 1982) *Race: Science and Politics*, rev. ed. with *The Races of Mankind* by R. Benedict and G. Weltfish, Westport: Greenwood Press.

——(1946; 1989) *The Chrysanthemum and the Sword*, foreword by E. F. Vogel, Boston: Houghton Mifflin Company.

Bennett, L.A. (1991) 'Arensberg, C.M.', in C. Winter (ed.), pp.12–13.

Bock, P. K. (1988) *Rethinking Psychological Anthropology*, New York: Freeman.

Brown, J.S.H. (1991) 'Hallowell, Alfred', in C. Winter (ed.), pp.265–66.

Butterworth, D. (1972) 'Oscar Lewis', *AA*, 74: 747–757.

Caffrey, M. (1989) *Ruth Benedict: Stranger in this Land*, Austin: University of Texas Press.

——(1991) 'Benedict, R.', in C. Winter (ed.), pp.44–46.

Carneiro, R. (1973) 'The four faces of evolution', in J.J. Honigman (ed.) *Handbook of Social and Cultural Anthropology*, Chicago: Rand McNally.

——(1979) 'L. White', in *International Encyclopedia of the Social Sciences*, Sills (ed.), vol.18: 803–807.

——(1981) 'L.A. White', in S. Silverman (ed.) *Totems and Teachers: Perspectives on the History of Anthropology*, New York: Columbia University Press, pp.209–255.

——(1991) 'White, L.A.', in C. Winter (ed.), pp.753–54.

Chambers, E. (1985) *Applied Anthropology: a Practical Guide*, Englewood Cliffs: Prentice-Hall.

Chapman, A. (1991) 'Polanyi, Karl', in P. Bonte and M. Izard (eds) *Dictionnaire de l'ethnologie et de l'anthropologie*, Paris: Presses universitaires de France, pp.578–79.

Claessen, H. (1996) 'Evolution and evolutionism', in A. Barnard and J. Spencer (eds) *Encyclopedia of Social and Cultural Anthropology*, London: Routledge, pp.213–218.

Cleary, D. (1992) 'C.W. Wagley', *AT*, 8(3): 17–18.

Clemer, R.O., Myers, L.D. and M.E. Rudden (eds) (1999) *Julian Steward and the Great Bassin: The Making of an Anthropologist*, Salt Lake City: University of Utah Press.

Cole, D. (2002) 'Mrs. Landes meets Mrs. Benedict: culture pattern and individual agency in the 1930s', *AA*, 104(2): 533–544.

Collective (1967) Review of the work of O. Lewis by numerous contributors, *CA*, 8: 480–500.

Comitas, L. (1997) 'C. M. Arensberg', *AN*, 38(5): 18.

Corrêa, M. (1991) 'Interview with R. Cadoso de Oliveira', *CA*, 32(3): 335–343.

Dalton, G. (ed) (1968) *Primitive, Archaic and Modern Economies: Essays of Karl Polanyi*, New York: Anchor Books.

——(1991) 'Polanyi, Karl', in C. Winter (ed.), pp.543–545.

Dalton, G and Köcke, J. (1983) 'The work of the Polanyi Group: past, present and future', in S. Ortiz (ed.) *Economic Anthropology, Topics and Theories*, Lanham: University Press of America.

Dapsley, H. (1999) *Margaret Mead and Ruth Benedict: The Kingship of Women*, Amherst: University of Massachusetts Press.

Darnell, R. (1986) 'The fate of the sapirian alternative', in G. W. Stocking (ed.) *Romantic motives. Essays on Culture and Personality*, *HOA*, vol.6: 156–184.

——(1990) *E. Sapir: Linguist, Anthropologist, Humanist*, Berkeley: University of California Press.

——(1998a) *And Along Came Boas: Continuity and Revolution in Americanist Anthropology*, Amsterdam and Philadelphia: John Benjamins.

——(1998b) 'Camelot at Yale: the construction and dismantling of the Sapirian synthesis, 1931–39', *AA*, 100: 361–372.

Davis, E. (1991) 'Cora Dubois', *AN*, 32(6): 5.

DeMallie, R.J. (1991) 'Eggan, Fred', in C. Winter (ed.), pp.174–175.

Descola, P. (1991) 'Steward, Julian Haynes', in P. Bonte and M. Izard (eds) *Dictionnaire de l'ethnologie et de l'anthropologie*, Paris: Presses universitaires de France, pp.673–674.

Devereux, G. (1954) 'The Logical foundations of Culture and Personality Studies', *Transaction of the New York Academy of Sciences*, vol.7, pp.110–131.

Dillingham, B. and Carneiro, R. (eds) (1987) White's *Ethnological Essays*, Albuquerque: University of New Mexico Press.

Dixon, R.B. (1930) 'Anthropology, 1866–1929', in S. Morison (ed.), *The Development of Harvard University Since the Inauguration of President Eliot, 1869–1929*, Cambridge, MA: Harvard University Press, pp. 202–215.

Dole, G.E. and Carneiro, R.L. (eds) (1960) *Essays in the Science of Culture in Honor of Leslie A. White*, New York: Crowell.

Du Bois, C. (1960) 'Introduction' to *The People of Alor*, Cambridge, MA: Harvard University Press.

——(1980) 'Some anthropological insights', *Annual Review of Anthropology*, 9: 1–13.

Dumont, L. (1977) *From Mandeville to Marx. The genesis and triumph of economic ideology*, Chicago and London: University of Chicago Press.

——(1983) 'Preface' to *La Grande Transformation* (on Polanyi), Paris: Gallimard.

Eggan, F. (1974) 'Among the anthropologists', *Annual Review of Anthropology*, 3: 1–19.

Eggan, F.R. (1950) *The Kinship Systems and Social Organization of the Western Pueblos with Special Reference to the Hopi Indians*, Chicago: University of Chicago Press.

——(1954) 'Social anthropology and the method of controlled comparison', *AA*, 56: 743–763.

——(1966) *The American Indian: Perspectives for the Study of Social Change*, Chicago: Aldine.

——(1975) *Essays in Social Anthropology and Ethnology*, Chicago: Aldine.

Ember, M. (1991) 'Murdock, G.P.', in C. Winter (ed.), pp.493–94.

Fenton, W.N. (1947) *Area Studies in American Universities*, Washington, DC: American Council on Education.

Fernandez, J.W. (1990) 'Tolerance in a repugnant world: the cultural relativism of M.J. Herskovits', *Ethos*, 18: 140–164.

——(1991) 'Herskovits, Melville' in C. Winter (ed.), pp.285–87.

Freeman, D. (1983) *Margaret Mead and Samoa: The Making and Unmaking of an Anthropological Myth*. Cambridge, MA: Harvard University Press.

——(1997) *Margaret Mead and the Heretic*, New York: Penguin Putnam inc.

Freeman, D., Orans, M., Côté, J. E. (2000) 'Forum: Sex and Hoax in Samoa', *CA*, 41(4): 609–623.

Geertz, C. (1988) *Works and Lives, the Anthropologist as Author*, Stanford: Stanford University Press.

Givens, D.R. (1997) 'F. Voget', *AN*, Sept. 1997: 44.

Goldschmidt, W. (ed.) (1979) *The Uses of Anthropology*, Washington: AAA.

Goodenough, W.H. (1979) 'Murdock, G.P', in *International Encyclopedia of the Social Sciences*, Sills (ed.) vol.18: 554–559.

——(1985) 'G.P. Murdock', *AN*, 26(10): 4.

——(1988) 'G.P. Murdock's contributions to anthropology: an overview', *Behavior Science Research*, 22: 1–9.

Goldenweiser, A.A. (1941) 'Recent trends in American anthropology', *AA*, 43: 151–163.

Goldfrank, E. (1978) *Notes on an Undirected Life as One Anthropologist Tell It*, Flushing NY: Queen's College Press.

Golla, A. (ed.) (1984) *The Sapir-Kroeber Correspondence: Letters Between E. Sapir and A.L. Kroeber, 1905–1925*, Berkeley: Berkeley University Press.

Golla, V. (1991) 'Sapir, Edward', in C. Winter (ed.), pp.603–606.

Goodman, R.A. (1983) *Mead's Coming of Age in Samoa. A Dissenting View*, Oakland: Pepperine Press.

Gordan, J. (ed.) (1976) *Margaret Mead: The complete bibliography, 1925–1975*, La Hague: Mouton.

Grinager, P. (1999) *Uncommon Lives: My lifelong friendship with Margaret Mead*, Lanham: Rowman and Littlefield.

Grosskurth, P. (1989) *Margaret Mead*, London, New York: Penguin Books.

Guggenheim, S. 'Redfield, R.', in P. Bonte and M. Izard (eds) *Dictionnaire de l'ethnologie et de l'anthropologie*, Paris: Presses universitaires de France, pp.616–617.

Hallowell, A.I. (1955; 1974) *Culture and Experience*, Philadelphia: University of Pennsylvania Press.

——(1976) *Contributions to Anthropology: Selected Papers of A. Irving Hallowell*, Chicago: University of Chicago Press.

Handler, R. (1983) 'The dainty and the hungry man: literature and anthropology in the work of E. Sapir', in G.W. Stocking (ed.) *Observers Observed, HOA*, vol.1: 208–31.

——(1986) 'Vigorous male and aspiring female: Poetry, personality and culture in E. Sapir and R. Benedict', in Stocking (ed.) *Romantic motives. Essays on Culture and Personality, HOA*, vol.6: 127–155.

——(1989) 'Anti-romantic romanticism: E. Sapir and the critique of American individualism', *Anthropological Quarterly*, 62: 1–14.

Hansen, T. (1976) 'R. Redfield, the Yucatan project, and I', in J. Murra (ed.) *American Anthropology the Early Years*, St. Paul, AAA, pp.187–260.

Harris, M. (1968) *The Rise of Anthropological Theory*, London: Routledge and Kegan Paul.

Hay, J. (1991) 'Kluckhohn', in C. Winter (ed.), pp.353–354.

Helm, J. (1984) *Social Contexts of American Ethnology, 1840–1984*, Washington: AAA.

Herkovits, M.J. (1924) 'A preliminary consideration of the culture areas of Africa', *AA*, 26: 50–64.

——(1936; 1969) *Suriname Folk-Lore*, New York: AMS Press.

——(1938a; 1958) *Acculturation, the studies of Culture Contact*, Gloucester: P. Smith.

——(1938b; 1967) *Dahomey, an Ancient West African Kingdom*, Evanston: Northwestern University Press.

——(1948) *Man and his works: the science of cultural anthropology*, New York: Knopf.

——(1952) *Economic Anthropology*, New York: Knopf.

——(1962) *The Human Factor in Changing Africa*, New York: Knopf.

Herkovits, M.J., Campbell, D.T. and Segall, M.H. (1966) *The Influence of Culture on Visual Perception*, Indianapolis: Bobbs-Merrill Co.

Herzog, D. (1965) *Klassengesellschaft ohne Klassenkonflikt: eine Studie über William Lloyd Warner und die Entwicklung der neuen amerikanischen Stratifikationsforschung*, Berlin: Duncker and Humboldt.

Hinshaw, R. (ed.) (1979) *Currents in Anthropology: Essays in Honor of Sol Tax*, The Hague: Mouton.

Holmes, L. (1986) *Quest for the Real Samoa: The Mead-Freeman Controversy and Beyond*, South Hadley: Bergin & Garvey.

Howard, J. (1984) *Margaret Mead: A Life*, London: Harvill Press.

Humphreys, L.S. (1969) 'History, economics and anthropology: the work of K. Polanyi', *History and Theory*, 8.

Hunt, R. (ed.) (1967) *Personalities and Cultures: Readings in Psychological Anthropology*, New York: American Museum of Natural History Press.

Izard, M. (1991a) 'Ruth Benedict', in P. Bonte and M. Izard (eds) *Dictionnaire de l'ethnologie et de l'anthropologie*, Paris: Presses universitaires de France, pp.112–113.

——(1991b) 'Kardiner, A.', in P. Bonte and M. Izard (eds) *Dictionnaire de l'ethnologie et de l'anthropologie*, Paris: Presses universitaires de France, pp.403–404.

——(1991c) 'Linton, Ralph', in P. Bonte and M. Izard (eds) *Dictionnaire de l'ethnologie et de l'anthropologie*, Paris: Presses universitaires de France, pp.424–425.

Jamin, J. (1991) 'L. White', in P. Bonte and M. Izard (eds) *Dictionnaire de l'ethnologie et de l'anthropologie*, Paris: Presses universitaires de France, pp.745–746.

Kluckholn, C.K.M. (1942) 'Myths and rituals: a general theory', *Harvard Theological Review*, 35.

——(1947; 1969) *Children of the People: The Navaho Individual and his Development*, New York: Octagon Books.

——(1949; 1985) *Mirror for Man*, foreword by A. Montagu, Tucson: University of Arizona Press.

——(1958) *Ralph Linton*, New York: National Academy of Sciences.

——(1962) *Culture and Behavior: Collected Essays of C. Kluckhohn*, R. Kluckhohn (ed.), New York: Free Press.

Kluckholn, C.K.M. and Kroeber, A. (1952), *Culture: A Critical Review of Concepts and Definitions*, Cambridge, MA: Harvard University Press.

Kluckholm, C., Bauer, R. A. and Inkeles, A. (1956) *How the Soviet System works. Cultural, psychological, and social themes*, Cambridge, MA: Harvard University Press.

Koerner, K. *et al.* (ed.) (1984) *E. Sapir: Appraisals of his Life and Work*, Amsterdam and Philadelphia: J. Benjamins Pub.

Kroeber, A. (1931) 'Compte rendu de Growing up in New Guinea', *AA*, 33: 248–250.

——(1948) 'White's scholarly influence', *AA*, 50: 405–415.

La Barre, W. (1978) 'The clinic and the field', in G. Spindler (ed.) *The Making of Psychological Anthropology*, Berkeley: University of California Press, pp.259–299.

Legros, D. (1991) 'Eggan, Fred', in P. Bonte and M. Izard (eds) *Dictionnaire de l'ethnologie et de l'anthropologie*, Paris: Presses universitaires de France, pp.224–225.

Leslie, C. (2001) 'R. Redfield', in Carrasco, D. (ed.) *Oxford Encyclopedia of Mesoamerican Cultures*, New York: Oxford University Press.

Levinson, D. (1996) 'Human Relation Area Files', in Levinson and Ember, pp.597–598.

Lewis, O. (1948) *On the Edge of the Black Waxy: A Cultural Survey of the Bell Country, Texas*, St. Louis: Washington University Studies.

——(1961) *The Childern of Sanchez. Autobiography of a Mexican family*, New York: Random House.

——(1966) *La Vida: A Puerto Rican Family in the Culture of Poverty*, New York: Random House.

——(1968) *A Study of Slum Culture: Backgrounds for la Vida*, New York: Random House.

——(1969) *A Death in the Sánchez Family*, New York: Random House.

Lewis, O., Lewis, R. and Rigdon, S. (1977–1978) *Living the Revolution: An Oral History of Contemporary Cuba*, Urbana: University of Illinois Press, 3 vols.

Linton, A. and Wagley, C. (1971) *Ralph Linton*, New York: Columbia University Press.

Linton, R. (ed.) (1945; 1980) *The Science of Man in the World Crisis*, New York: Octagon Books.

Linton, R. (1956) *Culture and Mental Disorders* (posthumous publication), Devereux, G. (ed.) Springfield: Thomas.

Lonergan, D. (1991) 'Lewis, Oscar', in C. Winter (ed.), pp.405–406.

Lurie, N. (1961) 'The voice of the American Indian: report on the American Indian Chicago conference', *CA*, 1: 478–500.

Lynch, O.M. (ed.) (1984) *Culture and Community in Europe: Essays in Honor of Conrad M. Arensberg*, Delhi: Hindustan Pub Corp.

MacMillan, R.A. (1986) 'The Study of Anthropology, 1931–1937, at Columbia University and the University of Chicago', unpublished thesis, New York University.

Madden, D.K. (1999) 'Clio's fancy: documents to pique the historical imagination. A radical ethnographer work in the Columbia anthropology department 1936–37', *HAN*, 26 (2): 3–10.

Mandelbaum, D. G. (ed.) (1949) *Selected Writings of Edward Sapir in Language, Culture and Personality*, Berkeley and LA: Cambridge Uiversity Press.

Manners, R. (ed.) (1964) *Process and Pattern in Culture: Essays in Honor of Julian H. Steward*, Chicago: Aldine Pub.

——(1973) 'Julian Haynes Steward', *AA*, 75: 886–903.

Manson, W.C. (1986) 'Abram Kardiner and the Neo-Freudian alternative in culture and personality' in Stocking (ed.) *Malinowski, Rivers, Benedict and Others*, *HOA*, vol. 4: 72–95.

——(1988) *The Psychodynamics of Culture: Abram Kardiner and Neo-Freudian Anthropology*, New York: Greenwood Press.

——(1991) 'Kardiner, A.', in C. Winter, pp.339–440.

May, M.A. (1971) 'A retrospective view of the Institute of Human Relations at Yale', *Behavioral Sciences Notes*, 6: 141–172.

Mead, M. (1948) 'Benedict, R.', *AA*, 51: 457–468.

——(1949; 2001) Male and Female. A study of the sexes in a changing world, Victor Gollancz: London.

——(1959a) 'Search', 'Anne Singleton', 'Patterns of Culture', 'The Years as Boas' Left Hand', 'The Postwar Years' in *An Anthropologist at Work*.

——(ed.) (1959b; 1997) *An Anthropologist at Work. Writings of Ruth Benedict*, Westport: Greenwood Press.

——(1967; 2000) *And keep your powder dry: an anthropologist looks at the American character*, Intro. by H. Varenne, New York: Berghahn Books.

——(1974) *Twentieth century faith. Hope and survival*, New York: Harper and Row.

——(1975) *Ruth Benedict*, New York: Columbia University Press.

Melhuus, M. (1997) 'Exploring the work of a compassionate ethnographer: the case of Oscar Lewis', *Social Anthropology*, 5(1): 35–54.

Merriam, A.P. (1964) 'M. Herskovits', *AA*, 66: 83–109.

Métraux, R. (1991) 'Mead, Margaret', in C. Winter (ed.), pp.467–469.

Mines, M. (1991) 'Opler, Morris E.', in C. Winter (ed.), pp.523–524.

Mintz, S.W. (1981) 'R. Benedict', in S. Silverman (ed.), *Totems and Teachers: Perspectives on the History of Anthropology*, New York: Columbia University Press, pp.141–171.

Mosca, L. (1991) 'Linton, Ralph', in C. Winter, pp.413–415.

Murdock, G.P. (1931) 'The Science of Culture', *AA*, 34: 200–215.

——(1934) 'Kinship and social behaviour among the Haïda', *AA*, 36: 355–385.

——(1941) *Ethnographic Bibliography of North America*, New Haven: Human Relation Area Files Press.

——(1949; 1965) *Social Structure*, New York: Macmillan.

——(1951) 'British social anthropologists', AA, 53: 465–473.

——(1957) 'World ethnographic sample', *AA*, 59: 664–687.

——(1965) *Culture and Society, Twenty-four Essays*, Pittsburgh.

——(1966) 'Cross-cultural sampling', *Ethnology*, 4.

Murdock, G.P., Ford, C., Whiting, W.M., Hudson, A. and Simmons, L. (1982) *Outline of Cultural Materials*, 5th edn, New Haven: Human Relations Area Files Press.

Murdock, G.P. and Morrow, D.O. (1970) 'Subsistence economy and supportive practices: cross cultural codes', *Ethnology*, 12: 302–330.

Murdock, G.P. and White, D.R. (1969) 'Standard cross-cultural sample', *Ethnology*, 8: 329–369.

Murdock, G.P., *et al.* (1987) *Outline of World Cultures*, 6th edn, New Haven: Human Relations Area Files Press.

Murphy, C.M.R. (ed.) (1976) *Selected Papers from the American Anthropologist, 1946–1970*, Washington: AAA.

Murphy, R.F. (1977) 'Introduction' to J. Steward, *Evolution and Ecology: Essays on Social Transformation*, Urbana: University of Illinois Press.

——(1981) 'J. Steward', in S. Silverman (ed.) *Totems and Teachers: Perspectives on the History of Anthropology*, New York: Columbia University Press, pp.171–209.

Murphy, R. (1991) 'Steward, Julian H.', in C. Winter (ed.), pp.671–672.

Naroll, R (1964) 'On ethnic unit classification', *CA*, 5: 283–312.

Nash, D. (ed.) (1977) 'Essays in subjective culture: an appreciation of A. Irving Hallowell', *Ethos*, 5(1).

Opler, M.E. (1945) 'Themes as dynamic forces in culture', *American Journal of Sociology*, 51: 198–206.

——(1948) 'Some recently developed concepts relating to culture', *Southwestern Journal of Anthropology*, 4: 107–122.

——(1959) 'Component, assemblage, and theme in cultural integration and differentiation', *AA*, 61: 955–964.

——(1983) 'The Apachean Culture Pattern and its Origin' and 'Chiricahua Apache', Washington, *Handbook of North American Indians, South West*, vol.10. pp.368–392 and 401–418.

Opler, M.K. (1959) *Culture and Mental Health, Cross-Cultural Studies*, New York: Macmillan.

——(1963) 'The need for new diagnostic categories in psychiatry', *Journal of the National Medical Association*, 55: 133–137.

Paddock, J. (1961) 'Oscar Lewis's Mexico', *Anthropological Quarterly*, 34: 129–150.

Parsons, T. and Vogt, E.Z. (1962) 'Clyde Kay Mayben Kluckhohn, 1905–1960', *AA*, 64: 140–161. Reprinted as part of the introduction to the second edition of *Navaho Witchcraft*, 1967, Boston: Beacon Press.

Peace, W. (1998) 'Bernhard Stern, Leslie A. White, and an anthropological appraisal of the Russian Revolution', *AA*, 100: 84–93.

Polanyi, G. (1991; 1971) 'Primitive, archaic and modern economies: K. Polanyi's contribution to economic anthropology and comparative economy', G. Dalton (ed.) *Economics, Anthropology and Development: Essays on tribal and peasant economies*, New York: Basic Books.

Polanyi, K. (1966; 1991) *Dahomey and the Slave Trade*, Seattle: University of Washington Press.

Polanyi-Levitt, K. (ed.) (1990) *The Life and Work of Karl Polanyi: a celebration*, Montréal, New York: Black Rose Books.

Preston, P.R.J. (1966) 'Edward Sapir's anthropology: style, structure and method', *AA*, 68: 1105–1128.

Price, R. (1991a) 'Kluckhohn, C.', in P. Bonte and M. Izard (eds) *Dictionnaire de l'ethnologie et de l'anthropologie*, Paris: Presses universitaires de France, pp.404–405.

——(1991b) 'M.J. Herskovits', in P. Bonte and M. Izard (eds) *Dictionnaire de l'ethnologie et de l'anthropologie*, Paris: Presses universitaires de France, pp.322–323.

Redfield, R. (1962) *The Papers of Robert Redfield*, 2 vols, ed. by M. Park-Redfield, Chicago: University of Chicago Press.

——(1991; 2002) *Doing Fieldwork: the correspondence of R. Redfield and Sol Tax*, R. Rubinstein ed. and intro. Foreword by L. Redfield, New Brunswick: Transaction Pub.

Rice, E. (1979) *Margaret Mead: A Portrait*, New York: Harper & Row.

——(1980) 'In memoriam Margaret Mead', *AA*, 82 (special issue dedicated to M. Mead).

Rigdon, S.M. (1988) *The Culture Facade: Art, Science and Politics in the Work of Oscar Lewis*, Urbana: University of Illinois Press.

Rubinstein, R. (1982) 'A Conversation with S. Tax', in *CA*, 32(2): 175–183.

Rubinstein, R.A. (1991) 'Tax, Sol', in C. Winter (ed.), pp.682–684.

Sahlins, M. (1992) 'Fred Eggan', *AT*, 8: 23–25.

Sandall, R. (1999) 'Herskovits' last day in Dahomey', *AT*, 15(6): 18–20.

Sapir, E. (1915) *Noun Reduplication in Comox, a Salish Language of Vancouver Island*, Ottawa: Government Printing Bureau.

——(1917) 'A Freudian half-holiday', review of S. Freud, *Delusion and Dream*, *The Dial*, 63: 635–637.

——(1923) 'The two kinds of human beings', review of C.G. Jung, *Psychological Types or the Psychology of Individuation*, *The Freeman*, 8: 211–212.

——(1924) 'Culture, genuine and spurious' reprinted in *Selected Writings* (1949), pp.308–331.

——(1934) 'The emergence of the concept of personality in a study of cultures', *Journal of Social Psychology*, 5: 408–415.

Schachter Modell, J. (1983) *Ruth Benedict: Patterns of a Life*, Philadelphia: University of Pennsylvania Press.

Schmidt, N.J. (1991) 'Dubois, Cora', in C. Winter (ed.), pp.162–163.

Schneider, D.H. and Handler, R. (1995) *Schneider on Schneider*, Durham: Duke University Press.

Schusky, E.L. (1989) 'F. Eggan: anthropologist full circle', *American Ethnologist*, 16: 142–157.

Service, E.R. (1976) 'L.A. White 1900–1975', *AA*, 78: 612–617.

Seymour, S. (1988) 'Cora du Bois', in U. Gacs (ed.), pp.72–80.

Shankman, P. (1996) 'Mead-Freeman Controversy' in Levinson and Ember (eds) pp.757–759.

Simpson, G.E. (1973) *Melville J. Herskovits*, New York: Columbia University Press.

Singer, M.B. (1991) 'Redfield, R.', in C. Winter (ed.) pp.573–574.

Spiro, M.E. (ed.) (1965) *Context and Meaning in Cultural Anthropology*, New York: The Free Press.

——(1976) 'R. Hallowell', *AA*, 78: 608–611.

Sponsel, L. (1997) 'Steward', in T. Barfield, pp.448–450.

Steward, J.H. (1936) 'The economic and social basis of primitive bands', in R. Lowie (ed.) *Essays in Anthropology*, Berkeley: University of California Press, pp.331–350.

——(1949) 'Cultural causality and law: a trial formulation of the development of early civilizations', *AA*, 51: 1–27.

——(1950) *Area Research: Theory and Practice*, New York: Social Science Research Council.

——(1951) 'Levels of sociocultural integration: an operational concept', *Southwestern Journal of Anthropology*, 7: 374–390.

——(1953) 'Evolution and process', in A. Kroeber (ed.), *Anthropology Today*, Chicago, pp.313–325.

——(ed.) (1956) *People of Puerto Rico: A study in Social Anthropology*, Urbana: University of Illinois Press.

——(1960) 'Review of White, *The Evolution of Culture*', *AA*, 62: 144–148.

——(1973) *A. Kroeber*, New York: Columbia University Press.

——(1976; 1955), *Theory of Culture Change: The Methodology of Multilinear Evolution*, Urbana: University of Illinois Press.

——(1977) *Evolution and Ecology: Essays on Social Transformation*, Urbana: University of Illinois Press.

Stewart, C. (1996) 'Great and little traditions' in A. Barnard and J. Spencer (eds) *Encyclopedia of Social and Cultural Anthropology*, London: Routledge, pp.267–268.

Stocking, G.W. (1976) 'Ideas and institutions in American anthropology: thoughts toward a history of the Interwar Years' in G.W. Stocking (ed.) *Selected Papers from the American Anthropologist, 1921–1945*, Washington: AAA, pp.1–44.

——(1979) *Anthropology at Chicago: Tradition, Discipline, Department*, Chicago: Chicago University Press.

——(1980) 'Sapir's last testament on culture and personality', *HAN*, 7: 7–11.

——(ed) (1986) *Malinowski, Rivers, Benedict and Others: Essays on Culture and Personality*, Madison: University of Wisconsin Press.

——(2000) 'Do good, young man: Sol Tax and the world mission of liberal democratic anthropology', *HOA*, vol.9: 171–264.

Sullivan, G. (1999) *M. Mead, G. Bateson, and Highland Bali: Fieldwork Photographs of Bayung Gede 1936–1939*, Chicago: Chicago University Press.

Tarn, N. (1981) 'R. Redfield' in S. Silverman (ed.) *Totems and Teachers: Perspectives on the History of Anthropology*, New York: Columbia University Press, pp.255–289.

Tax, S. (1937a) 'The municipios of the midwestern highlands of Guatemala', *AA*, 39: 423–444.

——(1937b) 'Some problems of Social Organization' and 'From Lafitau to Radcliffe-Brown: a short history of the study of social organization', in F. Eggan (ed.) *Social Anthropology of North American Tribe*, Chicago: University of Chicago Press, pp.3–33, 445–481.

——(1952) 'Action Anthropology', *America Indigena*, 12: 103–109.

——(ed.) (1953) *An Appraisal Anthropology Today*, Chicago: University of Chicago Press.

——(ed.) (1960) *Evolution After Darwin*, 3 vols, Chicago: University of Chicago Press.

——(ed.) (1968) *The People versus the System: A Dialogue in Urban Conflict*, Chicago: University of Chicago Press.

——(1988) 'Pride and puzzlement: a retro-introspective record of 60 years of anthropology', *Annual Review of Anthropology*, 17: 1–21.

Taylor, W.W., Fischer, L.J. and Vogt, E.Z. (eds) (1973) *Culture and Life: Essays in Memory of Clyde Kluckhohn*, Carbondale: Southern Illinois University Press.

Valentine, L.P. and Darsnell, R. (eds) (1999) *Theorizing the Americanist Tradition*, Buffalo: University of Toronto Press.

Wagley, C. (1953; 1976) *Amazon Town: A Study of Man in the Tropics*, London, New York: Oxford University Press.

——(1963; 1971) *Introduction to Brazil*, New York: Columbia University Press.

——(1977) *Welcome of Tears: The Tapirapé Indians of Central Brazil*, Prospect Heights: Waveland Press.

Wagley, C. and Galvão, E. (1949) *The Tenetehara Indians of Brazil*, New York: Columbia University Press.

Warner, M. (1988) *W. Lloyd Warner: Social anthropologist*, New York.

Warner, W.L. (1930–1931) 'Morphology and function of the Australian Murngin type of kinship', *AA*, 32–33.

——(1953; 1962) *American Life: Dream and Reality*, Chicago, new revised edition in 1962.

White, L.A. (1932a; 1973) *The Acoma Indians*, Glorieta: Rio Grande Press.

——(1932b) *The Pueblo of San Felipe*, Washington: AAA.

——(1935) *The Pueblo of Santo Domingo*, New Mexico: Kraus.

——(1942) *The Pueblo of Santa Ana*, New Mexico and New York: Kraus.

——(1940) 'The symbol: the origin and basis of human behavior', *Philosophy of Science*, 7: 451–463.

——(1945) 'History, evolution, and functionnalism: three types of interpretation of culture', *Southwestern Journal of Anthropology*, 1: 221–248.

——(1947a) 'Evolutionism in cultural anthropology: a rejoinder', *AA*, 49: 400–411.

——(1947b) 'Evolutionary stages, progress and the evaluation of cultures', *South Western Journal of Anthropology*, 3: 165–192.

——(1949; 1969) *The Science of Culture: A Study of Man and Civilisation*, New York: Farrar-Straus.

——(1962) *The Pueblo of Sia*, Washington: Bureau of American Ethnology.

——(1966) *The Social Organization of Ethnological Theory*, William Marsh Rice University.

Whiting, J.M.W. (1967) 'Methods and problems in cross-cultural research', Munchison (ed.), *Handbook of Social Psychology*, New York: Russel.

——(1970) 'What have we learned from cross-cultural surveys ?', *AA*, 72: 1227–1280.

——(1986) 'G. P. Murdock', *AA*, 88: 682–886.

Williams, G.C. and Peel, C. (eds) (1977) *Essays in Anthropology in Honor of Morris E. Opler*, Norman.

Willigen, J. Van (1993) *Applied Anthropology. An Introduction*, Westport: Bergin.

Woodbury, N. (1991) 'F.R. Eggan', *AN*, 32(6): 5.

Zamora, M.D., Mahar, M. and Orenstein, H. (eds) (1971) *Themes in Culture: Essays in Honor of Morris E. Opler*, Quezon City: Kayumanggi Publishers.

VII
British functionalist anthropology

THE REFOUNDERS: RADCLIFFE-BROWN AND MALINOWSKI

The first step in the institutional development of British anthropology was taken when the study of primitive peoples gained academic status at Oxford University. This was achieved in 1883 when **Tylor**, the curator of the Pitt Rivers Museum, was made a lecturer, and was reinforced in 1896 when he was appointed, at the age of sixty-four, to a professorship. In 1895 a degree in anthropology was awarded for the first time, in 1910 Tylor's successor **Marett** was granted a readership in social anthropology, and in 1914 a small independent department was opened. At Cambridge University **Haddon**, the leader of the Torres Straits Expedition, became a lecturer on his return to Britain in 1900. From 1904 the University offered anthropology teaching consisting of courses in prehistory, sociology, ethnology, and physical and psychological anthropology. Haddon was promoted to a readership in 1909, but remained the university's only salaried teacher of anthropology (Leach, 1984: 5). In 1907 Liverpool University endowed an anthropology chair for **Frazer**, but after only half a year he gave up this post. From 1904 the London School of Economics (LSE) of London University offered an anthropology course aimed at colonial civil servants and missionaries (**Firth**, 1963: 3). Teaching was provided by Haddon, **Radcliffe-Brown** and **Seligman** (1910), who obtained a part-time professorship in anthropology in 1913, while from 1907 **Westermarck** held a new sociology chair. It was only when **Malinowski** was appointed alongside Westermarck at the LSE in 1923 that British social anthropology began to expand its scope. Malinowski soon also took charge at the International African Institute, benefiting from Rockefeller Foundation funding, and most of his students became Africanists.

   As for its theoretical development, British anthropology first concentrated on juridical institutions (**Maine**, **McLennan**, etc.), and subsequently a focus on representations, particularly religious representations, was introduced by Tylor, Frazer and Marett. A common feature of both evolutionist approaches and the diffusionist methods of Tylor, **Rivers** and Haddon which replaced them was that they examined material according to chronological schemata. Malinowski and Radcliffe-Brown, on the other hand, proposed that this temporal dimension be supplanted by an analysis in terms of organic wholes, and it was from the rupture caused by this new departure that social anthropology was born.

   As the most eminent figures in the discipline, Radcliffe-Brown and Malinowski led many students towards social anthropology in the years from 1920 to 1940, and in the 1930s these disciples began to publish their own work.

Radcliffe-Brown, Alfred R. Reginald (1881–1955)

Born near Birmingham in Warwickshire, Alfred Radcliffe-Brown studied at Trinity College, Cambridge. Fascinated by **Kropotkin**, he decided, after gaining a BA in 1904, to enrol in the university's anthropology department, where under the tutelage of **Rivers** and **Haddon** he became the first student to receive an education in anthropology. He then carried out a mission to the Andaman Islands from 1906 to 1908, one of many that took place in the wake of the Torres Straits Expedition. The report he submitted following this mission secured him a bursary paid by Trinity College from 1908 to 1914. From 1908 to 1910 Radcliffe-Brown taught intermittently at Cambridge and then at the LSE. At the suggestion of H. Ellis he read Durkheim, and in 1909 declared his conversion to Durkheimism, although it was not until 1923 that he stated clearly that ethnology and social anthropology were two separate disciplines ('The Methods of Ethnology and Social Anthropology'). R. **Lowie** places him in the chapter on French sociology in his *History of Classical Anthropology* (1937), and **Frazer**'s examiner's report on Radcliffe-Brown's thesis *The Andaman Islanders* was critical of the way it drew on the French sociological school. This thesis was not published until 1922, the year in which **Malinowski**'s *Argonauts of the Western Pacific* also appeared.

With the financial assistance of a sheep farmer who had attended one of his lectures, Radcliffe-Brown travelled to Western Australia in 1910–1911. His expedition was made up of the zoologist Grant Watson, a Swedish seaman named Olsen and Daisy Bates, an amateur ethnographer and philanthropist. Before long Miss Bates was sent back home, and the remaining team turned its attention to 'the main business of our task, which was to tabulate facts pertaining to the four-class marriage system' (E. L. Grant Watson, *But to what Purpose? The Autobiography of a Contemporary*, London, 1946: 109). This work was carried out exclusively by means of interviews with acculturated Aborigines. In 1913 Radcliffe-Brown returned home to give a lecture series in Birmingham which took 'social anthropology' as its subject, and he also provided some teaching at the LSE. Declared unfit for active service in 1916, he was appointed director of education in Tonga, a British colony in Polynesia, where he remained until he fell ill in 1919. He then travelled to South Africa in 1920. Without work, he made a plea for assistance to Haddon, who made use of his old connection with the Prime Minister of the Union to secure the establishment of a chair in social anthropology at Cape Town University in 1921. Radcliffe-Brown felt that research into the origins of institutions presented the principal obstacle to the development of a scientific theory of human societies, and so in 1924 he proposed that kinship terms should be understood in a functional manner, in other words as interpretations of forms of conduct or of norms. He developed this point in a new explanation of the avunculate; whereas **Junod**'s theory explained avuncular relationships in patrilineal societies in Mozambique as a vestige of an earlier matrilineal stage, Radcliffe-Brown employed a structural perspective, writing that the classification principle most commonly adopted in primitive society is that of the equivalence of brothers. Thus the father's brother is seen as a kind of father, while the mother's sister is seen as another mother. The mother's brother can be seen as a mother, and may even be called a 'male mother' ('The Mother's Brother in South Africa', 1965: 18–31). In his view, moreover, the study of social conduct is quite independent of considerations of psychology, and the individual as such is of no relevance to an anthropology which would seek to discover laws. It was at this time that he changed his name to Radcliffe-Brown by adding his mother's maiden name to his surname; his reason, as he wrote to Haddon, was that there were too many Browns in the world, including one at his own university.

In 1926 he left South Africa, but not before giving a last lecture in which he stated that 'South African nationalism must be a nationalism composed of both black and white' (quoted in **Kuper**, *Among the Anthropologists*, 1999: 149). He then moved to Sydney University, where he occupied the first chair in social anthropology and created an anthropology department with financial help from the Rockefeller Foundation (**Goody**, *The Expansive Moment* 1996: 13). In 1929 Radcliffe-Brown wrote a celebrated text on totemism which developed some of Durkheim's reflections on the subject. In 1931 he published 'The Social Organization of the Australian Tribes' in the first issue of the journal *Oceania*, offering no original observations but presenting the totality of information on its subject together for the first time. While the article's conclusions were rejected in the 1960s, it nonetheless gives a brilliant illustration of the application of the comparative method to a particular region. In 1931 he was succeeded in his chair, first very briefly by **Firth**, and then for a longer period by **Elkin**.

By the time Radcliffe-Brown arrived in the USA in 1931, evolutionism had been swept away by **Boas** and his students, to be replaced by two currents of thought. One was a development of historical particularism (**Kroeber**, Lowie, etc.), and the other was the 'culture and personality' school (**Mead**, **Linton**, etc.) which drew its inspiration from **Sapir**. Outside the ambit of either of these currents, Radcliffe-Brown trained three important disciples at the University of Chicago: Fred **Eggan**, Sol **Tax** and William Lloyd **Warner**, who collectively published *Social Anthropology of North American Tribes* in 1937. In the same year their teacher returned to England to become the first occupant of the newly endowed chair of anthropology at Oxford University, while

Malinowski left the London School of Economics for the USA (where he died in 1942).

In his 1940 article 'On Joking Relationships', Radcliffe-Brown examines relationships between two people which are characterized by the obligation, for either one or both parties, to make fun of and play practical jokes on each other, without any offence being taken. He relates this to avoidance obligations (for example the avoidance of the mother-in-law in an Australian society or among the Navajo) and shows that both joking relationships and avoidance serve the same purpose of maintaining peaceful relations and averting potential conflicts. In 1941 he published 'The Study of Kinship Systems', in which he defines the family as the basic cell of the social order and its polygamous variant as producing types of elementary family structure which all share a common member. Whether family relations are marked by filiation, cousinship or couples, the same kinship system is established in terms of the network of social relations (i.e. rights and duties). Radcliffe-Brown specifically stresses the structural principle of the unity of descent, already mentioned in his 1924 work, and sees in it an explanation of the levirate, the sororate, the avunculate and of the various kinship terminologies. These ideas achieved their final definition in his introduction to *Family and Matrimonial Systems in Black Africa*, a collection of essays by his students published in 1950. For Radcliffe-Brown every culture can be defined as a systematic or integrated unit in which each element has a distinct function. The aim of the researcher must be to ascertain the structure of the social order rather than that of the order of the social order. His thinking led to a divergence of British social anthropology from American cultural anthropology, a divergence illustrated by **Murdock**'s criticism 'that British anthropologists do not use the notion of culture [. . .] and so they are not anthropologists, but professionals belonging to different category' (Murdock, 'Review of African Systems of Kinship and Marriage', *AA*, vol.53(1951): 465).

With the exception of a two-year posting in Brazil, Radcliffe-Brown spent the years from 1937 to 1946 as professor of social anthropology at Oxford University. In 1946 he retired, but continued to teach at the universities of Alexandria (1947–1949), Grahamstown, Shanghai, Manchester and London (1951–1954).

Malinowski, Bronislaw Kaspar (1884–1942)

Bronislaw Malinowski was born on 7 April 1884 in Cracow, where his father was a professor of Slavonic languages. He studied at the John Sobieski Royal College and then at the Jagiellonian University, where he obtained a physics and mathematics doctorate in 1908 with his thesis 'On the Principle of the Economy of Thought', a critical survey of the positivist epistemology of Avenarius, and, more particularly, of March. After deciding on a career in research, he was forced by his susceptibility to tuberculosis to take time off work, and during this period he read **Frazer**'s *Golden Bough*, which, at least according to the legend he himself propagated, led him to anthropology (Malinowski, 1964: XVIII). With the help of a grant awarded to future university teachers, he moved to Leipzig, where he was taught by K. Bücher and W. Wundt, two masters of the evolutionist school. Bücher was an economist who had formulated a theory of the stages of economic development and took a particular interest in primitive economies. Wundt was the founder of experimental psychology and played a role in *Völkerpsychologie* or the 'psychology of peoples'. In 1910 Malinowski, who was writing a thesis on the Australian Aborigines using ethnographic documents, emigrated to Britain, where he studied at the LSE under **Seligman** and **Westermarck** (who had already rejected

the idea of an original stage of universal promiscuity in 1891 in his *History of Human Marriage*). James had introduced functionalism into psychology (*Principles*, 1890), and, according to **Leach** (1957: 121), it was from him that Malinowski drew his inspiration.

In 1912 Malinowski published 'The Economic Aspect of the Intichiuma Ceremonies', which shows how rites organize collective labour, and states that the ideas of magic and religion must be taken into consideration as coercive mental forces which serve to encourage human economic activity (Thornton and Skalnik (eds) 1993: 226). In the same year Seligman wished to send Malinowski to do four months' research on an Arab tribe in the Sudan. He applied to the director of the LSE for a small grant for this purpose, but was refused; funding was later made available, but for an ethnographical mission to New Guinea. In 1913 Malinowski gained a Ph.D. with his thesis *The Family among the Australian Aborigines: A Sociological Study*. This work, which was reviewed by **Radcliffe-Brown** for *Man*, is accompanied by an assessment of Durkheim's *Elementary Forms of Religious Life* for the journal *Folklore*. As Panoff has observed (1972: 31–33), at that time research on the Aborigines considered them in terms of their matrimonial systems and notions of 'totemism', but Malinowski chose to avoid both topics in favour of an analysis of primitive conjugal (or 'nuclear') families. As part of his investigation of the family as an economic unit he examined property rights and the division of labour, remarking that the latter is founded on gender distinctions within each household and serves to establish the unity of the social group. While examining the question of descent, he took the opportunity to assert, following **Rivers**, that consanguinity holds no legitimate interest for the ethnologist, who should focus only on sociological kinship.

Then came a crucial intervention by **Marett**, who later described what happened:

As Recorder of Section H. of the British Association, about to visit Australia in 1914, I needed a Secretary, whose travelling expenses would be found for him. Thereupon that brilliant pupil of mine Miss M. A. Czaplicka (for whom, I hope, a special niche is reserved in the Polish Temple of Fame) besought me to assist her compatriot that he might see with his own eyes peoples of the Antipodes about whom he had hitherto known from books alone; and thus began a friendship which if on my part wholly delightful, soon proved for him disastrous, at least at first sight. For as our ship was on its way from West to South Australia, the war descended upon us [4 August 1914], and Malinowski, as an Austrian subject, became technically an enemy, and who as such must be interned. Nothing, however, could have been more generous than the treatment by the Australian authorities of the young scholar, for they not only granted him a *libera custodia* so that he could explore where he chose within their vast territories, but actually supplied him with funds to do so.

(R. Marett, 'Prof. B. Malinowski: An Account', given at the memorial meeting held in London on July 13, 1942 (London, 1943), p. 7).

In fact, except for **Graebner**, all enemy scientists were allowed to return to Europe. What Malinowski did was to take an opportunity which presented itself. He may have intended to remain in any case, all the more so as he came armed with scholarships from London University and the LSE which Seligman had obtained for him. Malinowski's plan was to settle on the Island of Dobu (later studied by **Fortune**), but as this proved impracticable he instead chose Mailu, a small island in the south of New Guinea. There he took lodgings with the missionary W. J. Saville, and from September 1914 to March 1915 made daily trips to the native village to carry out his research.

The Australian Department of External Affairs assisted him financially when his funding ran out, and it was in Australia that he published *The Natives of Mailu* in 1915. His data on land ownership regimes made it clear that land rights were multiple rather than being concentrated by law in the hands of a single person. Malinowski pursued his interest in the Trobriand Islanders, whose crafts and songs were thought to have informed those of other Melanesian peoples. He stayed in the Trobriands from June 1915 until May 1916, and then from October 1917 until October 1918. Although close to a European settlement, he declined to live there, instead pitching his tent in the middle of a native village. His *Baloma: The Spirits of the Dead*, published in 1916, takes as its subject representations of the soul and the after-life. It shows that the Trobriand Islanders held, in various forms, a belief in the existence of two types of soul: *baloma*, which joined the island of the spirits, and *kosi*, which returned to frighten the living. He took issue with the Durkheimian postulate of a collective psyche as it would have forced a reductive choice on the observer from among the phenomena he had found; with two distinct groups of beliefs coexisting in the individual minds, no purpose would be served by trying to ascertain which was more ancient or traditional.

In 1919 Malinowski sought to improve his poor health by settling in the Canary Islands for a year with his wife Elsie Masson. She was the daughter of a Melbourne academic, and bore him three daughters before her death in 1935 (he would marry Anna Valetta Hayman-Joyce in 1939). During the summer of 1920 Malinowski published his first text on *kula*, and then gave a lecture series at the LSE under the title 'The Primitive Economy of the Trobriand Islands'. These lectures contain the essential points of what **Firth** has defined as Malinowski's place in the history of economic anthropology: they provide descriptions of sorcery, seen as a system whereby the magician operates as a sort of foreman, giving the signal that cultivation work is to commence and instigating its various stages (burning, clearing, harvesting, etc.), as well as establishing quality standards by his magical control over plant life through the imposition of taboos (Firth, 1957a: 216). Malinowski also suggests that sorcery and magic give those who make use of them the necessary confidence to accomplish their tasks. This last proposition has been criticized by Fortune, who has underlined sorcery's potential to create anxiety, and by Firth in *We, the Tikopia: A Sociological Study of Kinship in Primitive Polynesia* (London, 1939: 185); others too have said that magic has an inhibiting effect by hindering the search for new, alternative procedures.

The Trobriand economy does not fit the concepts of classical economics. The Islanders do not work under the pressure of necessity or to earn their living, but following the promptings of their imagination and convinced that the fruits of their labours are in fact the results of sorcery. This is a major point, because on the one hand Encyclopaedists such as Diderot had disseminated the image of a natural order whose prevailing luxuriance promoted playful insouciance in individuals (or laziness, in the racist interpretation), and on the other hand the stages of economic development set out by Bücher, like evolutionist thought in general, supposed a historical period beyond which 'savages' had not yet moved (for Bücher this is overcome when the satisfaction of needs in a world of scarce resources imposes the survival of the fittest). Malinowski refutes both of these views and shows that a pre-economic stage does not exist in any primitive people, and that far from being indolent, lazy or irresponsible, savages are capable of strenuous work, even though their rationale owes nothing to classical utilitarianism. He also shows that possession in such societies must be defined, not in terms of individual property or primitive communism, but in terms of multiple rights held by groups and individuals. Finally, exchange, far from being haphazard, is both regular and complex.

Using his Trobriand material, Malinowski wrote seven monographs, each on a particular topic. His *Argonauts of the Western Pacific*, published in 1922, presents a new conception of the discipline: 'The goal is, briefly, to grasp the native's point of view, his relation to life, to realise his vision of his world' (Malinowski, 1964 (1922): 25), and it is only by means of a full immersion in the alien culture, observing and sharing the lives of subjects, that this can be achieved. This he calls 'participatory observation'. *The Argonauts* describes the intertribal cyclical exchange known as *kula*, which covers more than 150,000 km^2 of ocean and involves thousands of partners spread over about twenty different islands in the Massim area in Southeastern New Guinea. The objects exchanged are of two types: long necklaces made of red shells or coral (*soulava*) which circulate in a clockwise direction, and armbands of white shells (*mwali*), which circulate in an anti-clockwise direction. Each object takes from two to ten years to move full circle and return to its point of departure. Two *kula* partners owe each other hospitality, protection and assistance in times of war. The *kula* exchange comprises a gift followed by another gift offered in return, and Malinowski makes the point that there is an interval between the two. He stresses that 'the whole tribal life is permeated by a constant give and take', and that the Trobriand Islanders love giving and receiving for their own sakes (Malinowski, 1964 (1922): 173). He draws up a typology of exchanges, divided into presents pure and simple (between husband and wife, parents and children) and ceremonial exchanges of deferential offerings (e.g. taro for fish) (Malinowski, 1964: 188), and observes that in an economic system of this sort exchanges create social bonds (1964: 175). As is well-known, this theme was taken up by **Mauss**.

Malinowski's work appeared after that of the evolutionists and the diffusionists, and it also followed the great geographical and ethnographic data-gathering exercises. At this time anthropology faced the need for a change in its procedures because of the sheer volume of learning that had been accumulated. Of course British anthropology could have taken a different route, but it seems logical that it should have turned to a geographically delimited approach. The missions of the second generation were supervised by the first, and completed a scientific programme in a more or less prescribed area. Moreover, because he saw no need to produce repetitive inventories, Malinowski felt he could legitimately employ a prose style drawn from novel-writing, and used this agreeable form to overcome the problem of the reification of ethnographic information.

Following the publication of *The Argonauts* Malinowski worked on psychological topics, and in 1923 published a long article on the question of fathers, to which he returned in 1927 in *Sexuality and its Repression in Primitive Societies* (London: Routledge and Kegan). His examination of the feelings of Trobriand children for their fathers, whose authority was negligible, led him to conclude that the Oedipus complex is not universal, and that, rather than a repressed desire to kill their fathers and marry their mothers, Trobriand Islanders display, and their myths attest to, a 'matrilineal complex', that is a desire to marry their sisters and kill their maternal uncles (1927: 80–81). The responses of Freud's disciple E. Jones to the two articles forming the first half of the book led Malinowski to subscribe in its third and fourth parts to the hypothesis which Jones's comments suggested to him: that the system of matrilineal filiation and the negation of the father's role in procreation are two means employed by the Islanders for transferring a child's hatred of its father onto the maternal uncle (1927: 138–139). All the same, he makes it his primary aim to refute the arguments of *Totem and Taboo* (1913), in which Freud suggests that the parricide of the tribal chief is the turning-point allowing mankind to pass from the rule of nature to the rule of culture, and that the guilty sons thereby establish the two rules – the prohibition of incest and respect for totemic animals – from which further laws flow. Malinowski objects to the reductive consideration of social phenomena in terms of individual psychology and states that, in a state of nature, young adults would have left the group very early, as is the case with anthropoids, and would therefore have had no occasion to desire women within the group or to kill an old male (1927: 182). In *The Father in Primitive Psychology* (1927), he addresses matrilineal, patrilineal and bilateral filiation, and accords them only minimal importance, stating that the relationship between parents and children is primarily a directly emotional one.

Malinowski was appointed to a readership at the LSE in 1923, and in 1927 acceded to the first chair in social anthropology to be created at the University of London (Seligman already occupied a chair in ethnology in the older sense). From 1924, he led a seminar whose participants included E. E. **Evans-Pritchard**, A. **Montagu**, R. **Firth**, U. Grant-Duff, B. Freire-Marreco, H. Powdermaker, I. **Schapera**, A. **Richards**, J. Driberg, E. Clarke and L. **Mair**.

Malinowski worked briefly among the Pueblo Indians in 1926. He then successively published *Crime and Custom in Savage Society* (London: Kegan Paul, 1926), *Myth in Primitive Psychology*, *The Sexual Life of Savages* (London: Routledge), and *Coral Gardens and their Magic* (London: Routledge, 1935), a book on landholding arrangements, vegetable gardening, farming rites and associated magical practices. He reveals the indigenous conception of the garden as a work of art (Malinowski, 1935: 80–81), and underlines the role of exchanges of food and the ostentatious practices which accompany them. Published seven years before his death, this was the last great monograph on a Trobriand subject by Malinowski, who had not been in the field since 1919.

In 1926 the International Institute for the Cultures and Languages of Africa was founded, and Malinowski soon afterwards became its scientific director, and most of his students became Africanists. He visited them in the field in 1934, and in 1938 he edited *Methods of Study of Culture Contact in Africa*. He also wrote *The Dynamics of Cultural Evolution: Research into Race Relations in Africa*, which was published posthumously in 1944 (ed. P. Kaberry, New Haven: Yale University Press). He supervised twelve or thirteen Ph.Ds at the LSE, of which the last was by the Chinese student Fei **Xiao-tong**. Having already visited once before, Malinowski returned to the USA in 1938 at the invitation of Yale University and carried out an investigation of markets in Mexican peasant communities. Then the war broke out and he remained in the USA. He became president of the Bureau of Polish Exiles in the Academy of Arts and Sciences and took an active interest in the situation of exiled Polish intellectuals. He died at New Haven at the age of fifty-eight.

In 1944 came the posthumous publication of three essays under the title *A Scientific Theory of Culture and Other Essays* (Chapel Hill: North Carolina UP), providing the most complete presentation of the Malinowski system. He has often been characterized as a great field worker but a mediocre theoretician. In the place of the Marxist idea of the primacy of the technological and economic infrastructure, he posits a psychological infrastructure seen in terms of the needs of the individual organism. These needs, which he calls 'primary', necessitate the creation of an organization responsible for satisfying them. In this way the primordial biological needs are met through the mediation of culture, which is composed of secondary needs. These two categories of needs require co-ordination and integration which are provided by tertiary needs such as religion, knowledge or magic.

STUDENTS AND DISCIPLES OF MALINOWSKI AND RADCLIFFE-BROWN

When **Malinowski** was appointed reader at the LSE in 1923 his seminar was 'composed of **Evans-Pritchard** (who had studied history at Oxford), of Ashley **Montagu** (whose main work was on the biological side), of Ursula Grand-Duff (the daughter of Lord Avebury, an important figure in the earlier history of British anthropology), of Raymond **Firth** (who had studied economics in New Zealand), and of Barbara Freire-Marreco (or Mrs Aitken, who worked among the Tewa of Hano in the South-west of the USA' (**Goody**, 1996: 15). H. Powdermaker writes that in 1925, 'During my first year at the LSE, only three graduate students were in anthropology. The other two were E. E. Evans-Pritchard and R. Firth. I. **Schapera** came in the second year and we were joined by A. **Richards**, E. Clarke, J. Driberg, C. Wedgwood and G. and E. Brown. Strong personal bonds developed between us and with Malinowski; it was a sort of family with the usual ambivalences' (Powdermaker, 1966: 36). These figures were followed by M. **Fortes**, M. **Wilson**, G. **Bateson**, S. **Nadel** and M. **Gluckman**. If one may speak of a family, then of a family divided. **Seligman** also taught at the LSE (and had a strong influence on Evans-Pritchard, who always kept his distance from Malinowski), and, as Goody writes, 'the split took a territorial form with separate High Courts being held in summer at Seligman's home at Toot Baldon and at Malinowski's residence at Sopra Bolzano, to which their respective friends were invited' (Goody, 1996: 25).

The success enjoyed by Malinowski's seminar went hand in hand with what **Leach** calls a 'politicization' of a generation of Cambridge undergraduates, which in the 1920s began to reject the stifling atmosphere and the retrograde traditions of the bastions of British learning. As Leach writes: 'At this period Cambridge had an official policy of sexual segregation [. . .] some members of the teaching staff refused to lecture if women were present [. . .] *Sex and Repression in Savage Society* (1927) [. . .] could not be read without a special authorization from a senior college official'. And worse still, 'The majority of my contemporaries, not only in my own college (Clare) but in other colleges also, had been selected from a very limited range of private schools on the basis of personal recommendation rather than any obvious merit [. . .] We thought that we could recognize the encroachment of a "fascist mentality" in every aspect of British life' (Leach, 1984: 8–9).

Malinowski's Trobriand material served as the basic study matter for those who attended his seminars, and Fortes has written that the typescript of *The Coral Garden* was discussed page by page (Fortes, 1978: 5). Soon it was joined by the writings of Firth on the Maori, Schapera on the Hottentot Bushmen, and then Evans-Pritchard on the Zande, 'but also drawn upon were the ethnographic classics of **Smith**, **Junod**, **Spencer**, **Gillen** or the more theoretical works of **Rivers**, **Lowie** . . .' (Firth, 1975: 2).

It has not been possible to include all the disciples and students of Radcliffe-Brown and Malinowski in a book of this scope. I particularly regret the need to exclude I. Hogbin, Clarke, Wedgwood, Kalervo Oberg, Gunter Wagner, Sjoerd Hofsdtra, the Dribergs and the Browns, whose work seemed to me, rightly or wrongly, to be less significant than that of those treated below.

Richards, Audrey Isabelle (1899–1984)

Born in London into an academic family, Audrey Isabelle Richards studied natural sciences and then moved to the LSE in 1927 to join **Evans-Pritchard**, **Firth** and **Schapera** as a member of the very first generation of researchers to be trained by **Malinowski**. For a long time she was his closest disciple, and came close to marrying him after the death of his first wife. She was also the first of his disciples to carry out fieldwork in Africa, undertaking a mission to Zambia (Northern Rhodesia) in 1930–1931 funded by the International African Institute. In 1932 she gained a doctorate with her thesis on the Bemba: *Hunger and Work in a Savage Tribe: A Functional Study of Nutrition Among the Southern Bantu* (London: Routledge). She returned to the Bemba in 1933–1934, but it was not until 1939 that she published *Land, Labour and Diet in Northern Rhodesia: An Economic Study of the Bemba Tribe* (Oxford UP, 1939). She devotes a chapter to the indigenous conceptualization of food, but without neglecting questions of production and property, and the result is certainly one of the finest ethnographic monographs of the British functionalist school. Richards taught at the LSE in 1937, and then in Johannesburg in 1938, and spent 1939–1940 among the Twasna of Northern Transvaal. In 1941 she was employed by the Colonial Office and in 1944 as secretary of the Colonial Council for Scientific Research, and from 1944 to 1950 she taught at the University of Witwatersrand. Between 1950 and 1955 she was the director in Uganda of the Institute of Research into Eastern Africa, founded in 1948. In 1956 she published *Chisingu: A Girl's Initiation Ceremony among the Bemba in Northern Rhodesia* (London: Faber), which offers a new approach to initiation by following its course through the eyes of a young girl. In 1956 Richards returned to England, taught at Cambridge, and founded the Centre for African Studies there in 1962.

She also carried out a study of an Essex village with **Leach**.

Firth, Sir Raymond William (1901–2002) Born near Auckland in New Zealand into a family of Methodists (Parkin, 1988: 329), Raymond William Firth was educated in Auckland and wrote *The Kauri-Gam Industry: Some Economic Aspects* (Wellington, 1924) before leaving to study economics at the LSE. There he wrote a thesis on the frozen meat industry in New Zealand and attended seminars led by the historian of economic development R. H. Tawney and by the newly appointed **Malinowski**. Both men encouraged him to work on primitive economies. In 1925 Firth published 'Economic Psychology of the Maori' (JRAI), in which, following Malinowski, he argues that the economies of traditional societies cannot be understood without consideration of psychological factors. Under Malinowski's supervision he wrote his doctoral thesis 'The Primitive Economics of the New Zealand Maori', which was based on existing published literature and gained him the first anthropology Ph.D. awarded by the LSE. He then returned to New Zealand to complete a brief period of research on the Maori before undertaking an investigation of the Tikopia of the Solomon Islands in 1928 (he would return there in 1952, 1966 and 1972). He was conveyed to the islands by the Southern Cross of the Melanesian Mission, which only returned three and then nine months later. After having spent twelve months in the field, he joined **Radcliffe-Brown** as a lecturer at Sydney University. When Radcliffe-Brown left the department in 1931, Firth became its head, but left in 1932 for the LSE to take up a lectureship (1932–1935) and then a readership (1935–1944). After a number of articles on the Tikopia he published a book on their kinship systems in 1936: *We, the Tikopia: A Sociological Study of Kinship in Primitive Polynesia* (2nd edn, New York: Barnes and Noble, 1961). This was the first

of five monographs he produced on the Tikopia. His 1939 work *Primitive Polynesian Economy* (2nd edn, London: Routledge, 1965) showed that notions of exchange and reciprocity were linked to concepts of value and scarcity. This was followed in 1940 by *The Work of the Gods in Tikopia* (2 vols, 2nd edn, London: Athlone, 1967), which approaches the religious aspect of Tikopia culture from a strictly functionalist perspective.

Firth then switched to a different geographical area by travelling in 1939 with his wife Rosemary Upcott-Firth to Malaysia, where his studies of a fishing community bore fruit in *Malay Fishermen: Their Peasant Economy* (1946). He was forced by the Japanese invasion of 1940 to leave Malaysia, and on his second journey there in 1947 he was confronted with a communist insurrection. He did not return again until 1963, and afterwards republished his 1946 book with additional material on the capitalist development of production. During the war he served in the British Admiralty and was charged with producing four documentary volumes on the Pacific islands. He then became the first secretary of the Colonial Council for Research in the Social Sciences when it was founded in 1944, and also filled the LSE chair which had been left vacant at the death of Malinowski in 1942.

In 1951 Firth published *Elements of Social Organization* (London: Watts, 1971), composed of a series of lectures given at Birmingham University in 1947. This work defines anthropology as the science of observation of small human groups, and in it Firth signals his move away from what he calls the rigidity and limitations of structural functionalism. From the first page he introduces the idea of 'social organization', as opposed to 'social structure', and argues that this new notion provides a means of grasping the diversity of basic social relations and the functioning system in action. He conceives anthropology as aiming at reasoned comparative analysis of individual conduct ignored by structural-functionalist approaches. In relation to the structural principle of the kinship complex, he asserts that Radcliffe-Brown fails to consider all the alternatives presented by real situations. What, for example, would happen if a mother has no brother and recourse must be made to a classificatory uncle who is at the same time the real uncle of other nephews? His 1959 book *Social Change in Tikopia: Re-study of a Polynesian Community after a Generation* (London: Allen and Unwin) demonstrates that between 1929 and 1952 the transformations that took place in Tikopia pertain to issues of organization, but not to the basic social structure.

The debate between formalists and substantivists led Firth the revisit the economic aspect of his work. He was convinced that the concept of scarcity alone permitted an understanding of the whole range of systems, a view he expressed in two collections of articles by a formalist team of scholars: *Essays on Social Organization and Values* (1964) and *Themes in Economic Anthropology* (1965–1967). He was also critical of **Mauss**'s position, which he saw as too attached to equivalence and to the magical qualities of performance (1967: 9–17). Following his retirement in 1968 Firth taught at the University of Hawaii and other institutions. He was knighted in 1973.

Mair, Lucy Philip (1901–1986)

Born in London as the step-daughter of Sir William Beveridge, the director of the LSE, Lucy Mair studied classics at Newnham College, Cambridge (BA 1923), and then worked as a secretary to the politician Sir Gilbert Murray. In 1927 she enrolled in the international relations department of the LSE, but she was drawn into anthropology through her exposure to seminars directed by **Malinowski**, which she attended while completing her first book *The Protection of Minorities: The Working and Scope of the Minorities Treaties under the League of Nations* (London: Christopher, 1928). From her first fieldwork experience in Uganda and Nyasaland in 1931, she specialized in problems of social transformation and change, which at the time were also Malinowski's exclusive interest (**Firth**, (ed.) 1957a: 229). In the following year she wrote a thesis on landholding regimes and agricultural activity. Immediately afterwards she was appointed to a lectureship in colonial administration at the LSE, where she became reader in applied anthropology in 1956 and professor in 1963. Her special research interest in the transformations caused by colonization informs *An African People in the Twentieth Century* (1934), *The Growth of Economic Individualism in African Society* (1935), and *Native Policies in Africa* (1936). She also investigated questions of marriage (*Free Consent in African Marriage*, 1958) and chieftaincy and autochthonous administration (*Studies in Applied Anthropology*, 1961). After the decolonization of Africa she turned her attention to recent developments in the newly independent states (*New Nations*, 1963), and was the author of several introductory works, mainly written after her retirement in 1968. She was also the first person to win the crossword competition organized by the *Times Literary Supplement*.

Evans-Pritchard, Sir Edward Evan (1902–1973)

Born in Crowborough in Sussex as the son of an Anglican clergyman, Edward Evans-Pritchard studied at Winchester College and then read modern history at Exeter College, Oxford. He then turned to anthropology, which he studied at the LSE under **Seligman** and **Malinowski**, while at the time following courses given by G. E. **Smith** and W. J. **Perry** at University College London. From 1923 to 1931 he was a teaching assistant at the LSE. Thanks to the funding provided by the Royal Society and the Laura Spelman Rockefeller Memorial Fund

Trustees, Seligman was able to send Evans-Pritchard on a mission to the Anglo-Egyptian Sudan in 1926. On his return he completed a doctoral dissertation on the Azande, submitted in 1927. Between 1926 and 1940 he spent much of his time in the field (Sudan, Congo and Kenya), and became a specialist on the peoples of the White Nile regions.

From 1932 to 1934 Evans-Pritchard occupied the sociology chair at the University of Cairo, and then from 1934 to 1940 held a research position at the Institute of Social Anthropology at Oxford University, created by **Radcliffe-Brown**. In 1940 he was employed by the British Government as an adviser on military administration with the task of organizing a revolt among the Anouk frontier people against the Italian occupation of Ethiopia (**Geertz**, 1988). Then, from 1942 to 1944, he was posted as an adviser to the military administration in Cyrenaica (Syria) to work with the Alawite Bedouins. He was appointed a reader in anthropology at Cambridge in 1945, and in 1946 succeeded Radcliffe-Brown in the anthropology chair at Oxford. In 1950 he became a professor at Chicago and in 1957 was invited to join the Center for Advanced Studies in Behavioral Sciences at Stanford. He retired from Oxford in 1970, was knighted in 1971, and died in 1973.

After writing an article entitled 'Dance' (*Africa*, 1928), Evans-Pritchard compared his Azande material with Malinowski's work on the Trobriands and showed that the functions and conceptions of magic differ according to social structures (1929). Magic and religion were his main areas of interest up to the publication in 1937 of *Witchcraft, Oracles and Magic among the Azande* (Oxford: Oxford UP), in which he seeks to follow the Azande's own conceptions by conserving their typology and not placing what they would have understood as dissimilar phenomena under a single heading. The Azande claimed to be able to use

autopsies (or indeed oracles) to discover in the small intestine of witch doctors a patrilineally transmitted substance named *mangu*. Sorcery, on the other hand, necessitated the mastery of materials and formulas. Evans-Pritchard therefore distinguishes between witchcraft, defined as an innate and often unconscious power to attack others by supernatural means, and sorcery, which is acquired and can be put to benign or malign uses. Africanists have since made use of this dichotomy to distinguish between subjects possessed by a force and subjects possessing a force.

In 1930 Evans-Pritchard travelled to the Nuer (to whom he would return in 1931, 1935, and 1936), soon after the British had suppressed their revolt. Although he would complain that he was never fully accepted by them, it was on the Nuer that he wrote one of the classic texts of anthropology: *The Nuer: A Description of the Modes of Livelihood and Political Institutions of a Nilotic People* (Oxford UP). This book was published in 1940, and in the same year he and M. **Fortes** edited *African Political Systems* (Oxford UP), a study of comparative political anthropology using the categories advanced in *The Nuer*. In *The Nuer* Evans-Pritchard presents the seasonal morphology of this population in the same way as **Mauss** had done for the Inuit (**Dumont**, 1968: 4), describing group formations and their relations to the natural world in terms of the alternation of the rainy and dry seasons. In the rainy season villagers lead withdrawn lives, separated from neighbouring settlements by the flooded plain, while in the dry season they all mingle at watering places. The study of the Nuer's movement and its determinants, their modes of subsistence, and their close relationships to their cattle constitute the first part of the work. In what follows Evans-Pritchard describes Nuer social structures, which are founded on interlocking oppositions, so that a single group defines itself entirely in terms of its differences from other groups. The permanent hostility felt by the Nuer towards their neighbours, especially the Dinka, leads them to consider the Nuer district as the highest political unit. In fact, though, the district exists only as an expression of this antagonism, being nothing more than the final stage of the interlocking of smaller units, which in declining order are groupings of villages, individual villages, clans and parts of clans. According to the structural principle, the relations between these entities are determined, not by their inherent qualities, but by the antagonisms created by situations. Groups oppose one another as wholes when operating on their own level, but unite when they are forced to confront another, larger group. In this way alliances are determined by the nature of the antagonism, so that *a* and *a′* oppose each other within *A*, but unite when *A* confronts *B*. The only political authority among the Nuer is wielded by a chief wearing a leopard skin, whose role it is to mediate between different clans. Separation from other groups makes a permanent state of hostility towards those outside a limited territory acceptable, particularly as it legitimizes raids and forays. Following Durkheim, Evans-Pritchard defines the Nuer as a segmentary society, and states that splits within such societies create an 'ordered anarchy': 'anarchy' because there is no central power base, but 'ordered' because of the principle of opposition. He thus develops a functionalism in which the concept of the function is no longer primary, and suggests an understanding of social organization which goes beyond the juridico-political approach hitherto advanced (from **Maine** to Radcliffe-Brown), in which social links are always based on vaguely contractual notions. Contradiction now becomes the principal agent of an unconscious but real structure. The first part of the study sticks closely to the fieldwork material, while the second is wholly abstract, so that Dumont (1971b) may be right in thinking that this schema occurred to Evans-Pritchard during the writing of the book. This would also explain a difference of tone between the two sections.

Evans-Pritchard takes up the questions of political organization first addressed in *The Nuer* again using the example of the Sudanese Anuak, but it is in *African Political Systems* that he and Fortes create a political model for stateless societies founded on the notion of segmentary lineage. In a comparative spirit reminiscent of Radcliffe-Brown, this work examines eight African societies in terms of the role of kinship, the problem of territorial boundaries, lifestyle and demography. By distinguishing between centralized political organizations (states) and segmentary societies (e.g. the Tallensi and Nuer), the two authors take the view that the passage from the latter to the former is a consequence of territorial conquest, and that both forms have spatial foundations.

Invited to give the Frazer Lecture in 1948, Evans-Pritchard presented his paper *The Divine Kingship of the Shilluk of the Nilotic Sudan*, in which he attacks one of **Frazer**'s principal theses. Frazer presents Shilluk royalty as godlike and describes how the acts and the very existence of a king, considered as the centre of the universe, is thought to affect the world's course and equilibrium. The king is therefore put to death when his powers decline and the ancestral spirit installs itself anew in a more vigorous body (*The Golden Bough*, 3rd edn). Evans-Pritchard radically challenges this theory by pointing out that it is not supported by any incontestable historical testimony, and asserting that in truth the throne is successively seized by rival branches of Shilluk society. The 'custom' of regicide is therefore a way of resolving group conflict rather than a consequence of the sacredness of royalty. M. Young has observed that this structural interpretation suppresses the problem of ritual sacrifice (Young, 'The Divine Kingship of the Jukan', *Africa*, vol.36 (1966): 135–153), and Adler states that 'Evans-Pritchard reduces the political process to the competition for power' (Adler, *La Mort est le masque du roi*, Paris: Payot, 1982: 265).

With *The Sanusi of Cyrenaica* (Oxford: Clarendon Press, 1949), the fruit of two years of fieldwork among the Bedouins, Evans-Pritchard introduced historical considerations into his work, and in his Marett Lecture delivered to Oxford University in 1950 ('Social Anthropology: Past and Present', *Man*, 198: 118–23) he went further by announcing his break with structural functionalism and his intention to move from the study of functions to the study of meaning.

Having addressed questions of kinship only obliquely in *The Nuer*, he collected his articles on the subject in *Kinship and Marriage among the Nuer* (Oxford: Clarendon Press, 1951), which takes a critical attitude to its topic. The ease with which the Nuer insert maternal ancestors into paternal descent led him to reconsider filiation and account for the existence of a whole range of incest prohibitions. He comes to the conclusion that while lineage can be seen as a structural group, family relations are too variable for domestic organization to be viewed in the same way.

The publication of *Nuer Religion* in 1956 opens a new period. Steering clear of Durkheimian theory, Evans-Pritchard restricts his analysis to a consideration of religion as explaining the mysteries of the world. Using the term *Weltanschauung* (1956: 315), he tries to present the religious consciousness from within, on the grounds that this is the only way to comprehend it. He also provides highly detailed studies of rituals and sacrifices. His *Theories of Primitive Religion* (Oxford UP, 1965), the fruit of his teaching in 1962, investigates the major currents of thought in research into religion, and he draws in his early work on **Tylor**, Frazer and **Lévy-Bruhl**.

For Evans-Pritchard, social anthropology is not so much a science as a humanities discipline. The anthropologist is a purveyor of culture who interprets his material using categories of concepts and values which issue from his own society: 'Social anthropology endeavours to discover structures rather than laws, it demonstrates the coherence of phenomena rather than the existence of necessary connections between social activities, which it interprets more than it explains.' (Evans-Pritchard, 1951)

Forde, Cyril Daryll (1902–1973)
Born in Tottenham in England, Cyril Forde studied geography at University College London and then became a lecturer there while at the same time writing a thesis on prehistory which was accepted in 1927. From 1928 to 1930 he filled a post at the University of California, and during his time there he researched in Arizona and New Mexico, publishing a study of agriculture and property among the Hopi Indians in 1931. In 1930 he returned to Britain and was appointed to the chair in geography and anthropology at the University of Wales. In 1934 he published a book which rapidly became a classic: *Habitat, Economy and Society: A Geographical Introduction to Ethnology* (London: Methuen), a general and theoretical work which made strong claims for the existence of connections between environment, habitat, technical practices, economy, religion and social organization. Now primarily an ethnologist, Forde travelled to Southeastern Nigeria in the following year (1935) to study the Yakö, and in these investigations he broke with the dominant archaeological and technological approaches while retaining a focus on the influence of ecology. Having spent a second period with the Yakö in 1939, he in 1941 published *Marriage and the Family among the Yakö in South-Eastern Nigeria* (London, IAI), in which he describes the functioning of double descent in their kinship system. In 1944 Forde was appointed administrator of the International African Institute (a post he would occupy until 1970), and in 1945 he filled the chair in anthropology created at

University College London. He used the ethnography of the Yakö as the basis for general reflections on anthropology (1947) and became a vigorous co-ordinator of Africanism in Europe. He was editor of the journal *Africa*, and supervised the Ethnographic Survey of Africa, which produced eighty-two monographs on questions of ethnicity. He also organized an annual Africanist seminar between 1959 and 1969, which with the assistance of the Ford Foundation yielded a series of publications and promoted new research topics ranging from African history to the role of associations in modern Africa.

Nadel, Siegfried Frederick (1903–1956)

Born in Vienna, Siegfried F. Nadel studied musical composition and conducting between 1920 and 1923, and from 1923 he followed courses in psychology given by K. Bühler, submitting his thesis *Zur Psychologie des Konsonanzerlebens* [*On the Psychology of the Experience of Consonance*] in 1925. From 1925 to 1927 he directed the orchestra of the Düsseldorf opera, and by the age of 27 he had already written two musicological treatises and a biography of the composer Ferruccio Busoni (*Ferruccio Busoni 1866–1924*, Leipzig, 1931). While an assistant conductor in Berlin he attended courses given by D. H. **Westermann**. At this time Westermann was still director of the International African Institute, and he was able to obtain for Nadel a bursary from the Rockefeller Foundation allowing him to study at the LSE under **Malinowski** and **Seligman** in 1932. With funding from the International African Institute, Nadel then carried out fieldwork among the Nupe of Nigeria from 1933 to 1935. In 1935 he was awarded a doctorate for his thesis *Political and Religious Structure of Nupe Society*, the first study of an African society organized as a state. After a second period in the field in 1935–1936 he trained to become a colonial administrator at Oxford University, and in 1938 was appointed as an anthropologist working for the Anglo-Egyptian government in Sudan, where he carried out research on the Nuba. Back in London he published *A Black Byzantium: The Kingdom of Nupe in Nigeria* (Oxford UP) in 1942. Using a large body of statistical information, Nadel reconstructs the history of the kingdom and its invasion by the Islamized Foulani, who established a feudal society with a political system in which the royal heir was selected successively from each of the three dynasties of the first Foulani conquerors. He shows that Islam did not supplant the already existing institutions, but grafted itself onto Nupe symbols and ceremony, and also gives an account of the effects of British imperial rule.

In 1943 Nadel enlisted in the British army and served as secretary of the Bureau of Native Affairs in Ethiopia and then in Tripolitania. Demobilized in 1946 after having seen extensive action on the African front (Faris, 1973), he was appointed to a lectureship at the LSE and then at Durham University. In 1947 he published *The Nuba* (Oxford UP). He became head of the anthropology department at King's College London, but left England in 1950 to take up the professorship of anthropology at the National University of Australia at Canberra. This move was followed by the publication of his first theoretical work *The Foundation of Social Anthropology* (London: Cohen and West, 1951), which moves away from rigid functionalism by replacing the notion of function with the idea of competences which exist in a more fluid relationship with individual subjects. Nadel died in 1954 soon after the appearance of his *Nupe Religion: Traditional Belief and the Influence of Islam in a West African Chiefdom* (London, 1954). In this work he looks at beliefs, divination and rituals, and views witchcraft as exercising a negative influence on social cohesion, thereby differing from **Gluckman**, who sees it as a means of conflict resolution. *The Theory of Social Structure*, published posthumously in 1957 (London and Glencoe), presents a rigorous formulation of functionalist theses. Nadel's aim in this work is to accord scientific status to concepts such as role and social relations, which he says tend to be used naïvely, and he gives a precise definition of the notion of structure as the nexus between culture and society. In his view two different levels of structuration can be observed, one of which constitutes a 'pattern' and the other a 'network'. Nadel's study of the complementary features of role and status leads him into a minute dissection of these terms.

Bateson, Gregory (1904–1980)

The son of the founder of genetics in Great Britain, Gregory Bateson was born in Cambridge into a family which for several generations had been connected to St John's College. After a period in Switzerland he returned to Cambridge to study for a B.Sc. in zoology, which he gained in 1924, and then spent a brief period in the Galapagos Islands. His interest in anthropology was aroused by a meeting with A. C. **Haddon**, who promised to send him on a mission to New Guinea, and he then became a student of **Malinowski** and **Radcliffe-Brown**.

After this training Bateson spent time with the Sulka and the Baining in New Britain in 1928–1929, and was then offered a post teaching linguistics at the University of Sydney by Radcliffe-Brown. He returned to Britain in 1930 where he gained an MA and received funds from St John's College to travel to the Iatmul of Middle Sepik in 1931, and it was here that he met R. **Fortune** and M. **Mead** and wrote his first article, published in 1932. He returned to Cambridge in 1934, and in 1935 Mead secured an invitation for him to travel to the USA and give a series of lectures at the universities of Columbia and Chicago. In 1936 Bateson published *Naven* (republished with an important epilogue in 1958), which takes what at the time was a highly unusual approach, for instead of giving a full presentation of the social structures of the Iatmul of Sepik he concentrates exclusively on the symbolism of relations between a mother's brother and a sister's son as prevalent in a ritual of male cross-dressing. He introduces the concept of *ethnos*, which by accounting for individual variations replaces the idea of 'collective representation'. In 1936 Mead and Bateson set off together for Bali and married during a stopover in Singapore. Bateson made another journey to the Iatmul with Mead in 1938, and in 1940 started work at the American Museum of Natural History in New York as a specialist in Balinese culture. In 1942 he and Mead published *Balinese Character: A Photographic Analysis*. In 1941–1942 he analysed Nazi propaganda films at the Museum of Modern Art and was then seconded to the Federal Office of Strategic Services. Subsequently he accepted a guest professorship and then a lectureship at the New School for Social Research before going on to work at Harvard in 1947–1948.

In 1948 Bateson became a research associate at the Langley Porter Neuropsychiatric Institute, and in 1950 he joined the staff of the Palo Alto Military Hospital in California, having separated from Mead in 1949. A grant from the Rockefeller Foundation in 1952 gave him the opportunity of forming a team to study the families of schizophrenics, making special use of film. This team developed the hypothesis of the double bind, which states that a child receives two contradictory instructions from the same parent. The example often given is that of a mother asking her son to embrace her only to push him away because he has ruffled her hair, and furthermore forbidding him to perceive the contradictory nature of her instructions, while the father fails to counteract this influence. The child, always in the wrong, loses faith in his own perceptions and withdraws from communication by 'choosing' to shut himself away. Bateson uses the term 'metacommunication' to designate the specific messages human beings convey by the style they use to communicate. Bateson became a naturalized American in 1956, and in 1959 established the Mental Research Institute at Palo Alto, for which he recruited Watzlawick. Bateson's aim was to gather together a basic theoretical corpus, and to this end he studied communication among dolphins and worked successively at the John Lily laboratory, at the Oceanographic Institute of the University of Hawaii and, in 1972, at the University of California at Santa Cruz. He took part in seminars at the Californian Center of Humanist Psychology at Esalen and at the Naropa Buddhist Institute in Colorado, becoming a leading figure of a sort of messianic ecological humanism.

Montagu, Ashley (1905–1999)

Born Israel Ehrenberg to Russian emigrants in London, Ashley Montagu was admitted to the LSE, where he studied anatomy, statistics and, under **Malinowski**, anthropology. After a brief period at the University of Florence he moved to the USA in 1930, and in 1937 obtained a Ph.D. at Columbia University under the supervision of **Boas** (*Coming into Being among the Australian Aborigines*). His long-held ambition was to bring biological and social factors together in a single perspective, and to achieve this he developed the concept of neotony, the idea that the human infant is by nature born premature and constructs itself biologically in its relation to its environment and its mother. Montagu was assistant professor of anatomy at New York University from 1931 to 1938 and then at the University of Philadelphia from 1938 to 1949, and finally he occupied the chair of anthropology at Rutgers University between 1949 and 1955. He strongly desired to address a broad readership and infused much of his own personality into his eighteen books and numberless articles. He took a stance successively against eugenics, against racism (especially in his work for

UNESCO: *Statement on Race*, New York, 1951), and against sexism. He is also known for his lengthy reflections on the nature of violence.

Wilson, Godfrey (1908–1944)

Godfrey Wilson's father was a Shakespeare scholar, and he himself studied English at Oxford University before M. Hunter, whom he married in 1935, awakened his interest in anthropology. Together they attended **Malinowski**'s seminars and came to belong to his second generation of students, at a time when he was turning his attention to the dynamics of acculturation and was director of the International African Institute with access to the funds of the Rockefeller Foundation. The Wilsons were sent by the Institute to Tanganyika (Tanzania) to undertake research focused exclusively on the acculturation process, and in their work they were unwilling to make distinctions between sociology, history and social anthropology. On the recommendation of Lugard and Hailey, Wilson was appointed director of the Rhodes–Livingstone Institute, the first organization of its type, in May 1938. His goal of academic independence for the Institute and his intention to engage in close studies of urban society and mining communities soon brought him into conflict with mining companies, which withdrew his permission to investigate after strikes during which miners were killed. Wilson's position as a conscientious objector during the war led to his resignation from his directorship of the Rhodes–Livingstone Institute in April 1941 (Brown, 1973: 192), to be replaced by **Gluckman**. He committed suicide in 1944.

Written together with his wife M. Wilson-Hunter, *The Analysis of Social Change Based on Observations in Central Africa* (Cambridge UP) offers a global perspective on social transformations through an examination of their effect on the Nyakyusa. The basic idea used is that of balance as a fundamental social necessity.

RESEARCHERS IN SOUTH AFRICA AND RHODESIA

Ethnology in South Africa was for a long time divided between the anthropologists of the Afrikaans-language universities on the one hand, who defined themselves as *volkekundiges*, specialists in ethnic science, and concentrated on the traditional social order and culture of African peoples, and on the other hand the disciples of British social anthropology. Of the second movement A. **Kuper** has written that 'the traffic between colony and metropolis was by no means one way. Not only were funds, jobs, even careers sometimes on offer to metropolitan anthropologists from colonial or dominion governments, but there was also a two-way traffic in ideas. Indeed, it could be argued that the institutional and intellectual origins of British social anthropology can be traced to Australia and South Africa. As late as 1920, social anthropology had barely established a foothold in British universities and it had only fugitive and peripheral connections with African colonial governments' (Kuper, 1999b: 145). But the same author also writes that the South African school 'was in reality a local branch of British social anthropology' (Kuper, 2000: 267).

While visiting South Africa in 1905, **Haddon** exhorted the government to create a research institute, but it was not until 1920, after several South African scholars had repeated the same request, that a School of African Life and Language was established at Cape Town University. In the same year a linguistics specialist was appointed at the same university, and, after consultations with a committee which included Haddon, **Frazer**, **Marett** and **Rivers** among its members, **Radcliffe-Brown** was invited to fill a new chair of social anthropology.

However, the government's official ethnologist was J. van Warmelo, a linguist with a doctorate obtained from the Colonial Institute of Hamburg. In his 1935 work *A Preliminary Survey of the Bantu Tribes of South Africa* (Pretoria: The Government Printer), van Warmelo put forward a classification of the South African Bantu based on language rather than on history or culture.

All the same, other forms of anthropological teaching soon became established. Agnes **Hoernlé** gave a course at the University of Witwatersrand in Johannesburg, and teaching was also provided at the Afrikaans-language University of Stellenbosch, where in 1932 a chair was endowed and first filled by W. W. W. Eiselen. Another chair was established at Pretoria and first held by Gérard Lestrade, who also directed the anthropological section of the government's Native Affairs Department from its creation in 1925. Both Eiselen and Lestrade repudiated popular racial prejudices, and Eiselen wrote that 'nor was any race or nation privileged to lead the world forever in civilization [. . .] the government's policy should be aimed at fostering higher Bantu culture and not producing black Europeans' (quoted by Kuper, 1999: xiii), but it was consonant with the logic of his argument that Eiselen called for the creation of reservations to reverse the effects of acculturation. When in 1948 the Afrikaner Nationalist Party took power, Eiselen held several posts and was in a strong position to advance his conception of Apartheid. Opposing him, Hoernlé, and soon after her **Schapera**, sought to demonstrate that the conditions for autonomous development were not in place and took more interest in social transformations than in culture.

When Radcliffe-Brown vacated the chair at the University of Cape Town in 1926, he was succeeded by T. T. Barnard, the scion of a distinguished family who had trained as a botanist and also attended some lectures given by Haddon and Rivers. According to **Leach**, 'he did not know any anthropology [. . .] Schapera, then a graduate student, lent Barnard his notes on Radcliffe-Brown's lectures, and Barnard used these as the basis for his own lectures for the next eight years' (Leach, 1984: 7). Barnard was succeeded by Schapera in 1935. When in 1931 the government discontinued all funding for Africanist research, the Inter-university Committee for African Studies was established, while the International Institute of African Languages and Cultures, founded in 1926 by the Rockefeller Foundation, gave subsidies for research, of which the main beneficiaries were the students of **Malinowski**. In 1934 Malinowski made a visit to South Africa himself, having already made contact with Lucy **Mair** and Audrey **Richards** in the field, the former in Uganda and the latter in Rhodesia (Zambia). Mair and Richards had carried out fieldwork in 1930 and 1931, while Schapera returned to South Africa after having been sent to England by Hoernlé to be taught by Malinowski, thus setting the precedent for a route to be followed by a number of other South Africans in the early 1930s: M. Hunter, H. Beemer-Kuper, M. **Fortes**, B. Marwick, M. **Gluckman**, E. Krige, Z. K. Matthews (a black scholar from Fort Hare and participant in the master's seminars), who all studied with Malinowski before returning to the field. Despite the opposition of the Colonial Office, the Rhodes–Livingstone Institute in Central Africa was founded in 1937 (Brown, 1973), and in 1938 G. **Wilson** was appointed its director. He designed three research programmes, on the industrial belt, migrant workers and poor rural areas. After Wilson's resignation in 1941 Richards declined the offer to succeed him, and so the post went instead to Gluckman (Goody, 1996: 69), who had arrived in 1938 fresh from research in Zululand, to which he was unable to return after 1939. Gluckman took up Wilson's plan and extended it to a seven-year project, and in 1947 he was replaced by Elisabeth Colson.

When the Afrikaner Nationalist government took office in 1948 *Volkekunde* departments and their anthropologists were expected to contribute to the theory and practice of Apartheid. P. J. Coertze, a student of Eiselen, obtained the chair in the Pretoria department in 1951, and advanced the ethnos theory, which asserted 'the primordial identity of national groups, and the enduring significance of cultural difference. The ethnos was a cultural group, but it tended to be endogamous, and so developed significant racial traits' (Kuper, 1999: 160). The department developed under Coertze's influence and his students created departments in other Afrikaner universities and participated in the Broederbond, a secret society for the defence of Apartheid. On the other hand, most of the functionalist and anti-Apartheid anthropologists emigrated, a fate shared by Schapera, Matthews, H. **Kuper**, Absolom Vilakazi, Bernard Magubane and others.

Following the pioneering studies of Lorna Marshall in the 1950s, two Americans – I. de Vore, a primatologist, and R. Lee, an ethnologist influenced by J. **Steward** – began intensive research on the Bushmen of the Kalahari in 1963. They employed an evolutionist perspective, thereby opening this region of the world to a different anthropological tradition.

As Apartheid unravelled in the 1980s, some Afrikaner anthropologists began to draw closer to their colleagues in the English-speaking universities, although the two separate South African associations of anthropologists were united only in 2001.

Hoernlé, Agnes Winifred (née Tucker, 1885–1960)
Born in Kimberly in South Africa, Agnes Winifred Hoernlé was educated at Cambridge University as a fellow student of **Rivers** and **Haddon** (1908–1910), then moved to Leipzig to study under Wundt before spending time in Bonn and finally Paris, where she attended lectures by Durkheim. In 1912 she returned to South Africa and carried out research on the Nama Khoi (Hottentots). She married a German professor of philoso-

phy in 1914, and while they were in Harvard her husband developed tuberculosis. The couple returned to South Africa, where she founded an anthropology department at the University of Witwatersrand which she intended should be weighted towards applied anthropology. Among Hoernlé's students were M. **Gluckman**, E. Krige, H. **Kuper**, and I. **Schapera**, whom she sent to study under **Malinowski** at the LSE. She contributed in 1929 to the founding of the South African Institute of Race Relations and supervised the first ethnographic studies of African urban slums, which adapted the methods of the Chicago school. In 1938 Hoernlé resigned from her academic post to devote herself to activist work on race relations and to campaigning against segregationist ideas.

Schapera, Isaac (1905–2003)

Born in a village in Namaqualand (South Africa) to a merchant father, Isaac Schapera was taught by **Radcliffe-Brown** at the University of Cape Town. He obtained an MA there in 1925 and then enrolled at the LSE, where he attended seminars held by **Seligman** and **Malinowski**. After obtaining a Ph.D. in 1929 he returned to South Africa, completed his first fieldwork on the Tswana of Botswana (whom he studied until 1950), and then worked on the Hottentots and the Bushmen. This work culminated in *The Khiosan Peoples of South Africa: Bushmen and Hottentots* (London: Routledge, 1930), in which he took up the category of the Khiosan first developed by the anthropologist L. Schulte in 1928 to designate a common ethnic line. In 1930 Schapera temporarily replaced Agnes **Hoernlé** at the University of Witwatersrand, where his students included M. **Gluckman**, E. Krige and H. **Kuper**. In 1934 he edited *Western Civilization and the Natives of South Africa* (London: Routledge), which opens with a description of traditional Bantu culture and then considers the changes it has gone through, the

poverty of its land, and its migrations, with the various contributors expressing their opposition to the segregationist arguments of the time. Schapera was appointed professor of social anthropology at the University of Cape Town in 1935, at a time when he was extending his investigations on the Tswana to take in most aspects of their social existence. This led him to contribute to the establishment of legal anthropology with the publication in 1938 of his *Handbook of Tswana Law and Custom* (Oxford UP), which soon attained classic status. He also made innovative studies of sexuality in *Married Life in an African Tribe* (Oxford UP, 1940) and of migration and work in *Migrant Labour and Tribal Life: A Study of Conditions in the Bechuanaland Protectorate* (Oxford UP, 1947).

In 1950 Schapera was appointed professor at the LSE. From then on he turned his attention to the ethnology of political power. Like **Nadel** and **Evans-Pritchard**, Schapera believed that ethnology should aim for regional comparisons rather than vast syntheses transcending regional limits. He puts forward this view in *Government and Politics in Tribal Societies* (London: Watts, 1956), a collection of articles on the study of political organization, in which political functions are presented in a comparative optic in relation to the environment, the economy and the population density of particular groups. Schapera notably rejected Gluckman's argument that rebellion operates as a factor which reinforces unity on the grounds that it often results in secession. In the final stage of his career Schapera devoted much of his time to the history of the first explorers, editing the papers and correspondence of Livingstone from 1959 to 1974. He retired in 1969.

Fortes, Meyer (1906–1983)

Born in 1906 in Bristown in Cape Province into a family of Russian-Jewish emigrants, Meyer Fortes studied at the University of

Cape Town, and after gaining an MA there moved to the LSE, where he was awarded a Ph.D. in 1930 for a psychology thesis on perception tests: *The Cross-Cultural Testing of Intelligence*. From 1931 to 1933 he worked on juvenile delinquency, and, in his own words, 'it was a chance meeting with **Malinowski** in 1931 in the home of J. C. Flugel, an eminent psychoanalyst, which eventually brought me into anthropology' (Fortes, 1978: 3). At Malinowski's invitation Fortes joined the anthropology seminar at the LSE as a psychologist, and there he struck up a friendship with **Evans-Pritchard** and **Schapera**. With the support of **Seligman** he held a post with the International African Institute from 1933 to 1937, and worked in Ghana among the Tallensi, the Ashanti and the Tswana. He published his first article on Tallensi rituals in 1936, followed by another on Tallensi marriage customs in 1937. He was a lecturer at the LSE in 1938–1939, and then a researcher in African sociology at Oxford University from 1939 to 1941. In 1940 he co-edited *African Political Systems* with Evans-Pritchard (Oxford UP). As well as an introduction by **Radcliffe-Brown**, the book contained eight contributions on African political systems explored through the role of kinship in political organization, the influence of demography, mode of life, territorial issues, organized force, and the responses of the colonial administration. Drawing on the Durkheimian paradigm of the opposition between societies with mechanical and those with organic solidarity structures, Fortes and Evans-Pritchard present a dichotomy in this book between societies with central political organization and segmentary, clan-based societies.

After service in the armed forces from 1941 to 1944, Fortes was appointed director of the sociology department of the West African Institute located in Ghana. In 1945 he published *The Dynamics of Clanship among the Tallensi: The First Part of an Analysis of the Social Structure of a Trans-Volta Tribe* (Oxford UP), which develops the idea he had advanced in his contribution to *African Political Systems* that territorial stability is the result of cultural homogeneity and an economic system based on agriculture, and that political life is structured by kinship and clan networks and above all by mystical doctrines and ritual practices which anchor the status of individuals and connect them with one another. This was followed in 1949 by *The Web of Kinship among the Tallensi: The Second Part of an Analysis of the Social Structure of a Trans-Volta Tribe* (Oxford UP). While the 1945 book treated only of patrilineage, this second work addresses the relations between the two lineage systems which come together in the domestic unit and thereby assure their continuation. While remaining faithful to the principles of Radcliffe-Brown regarding clan unity and solidarity, Fortes supplemented these with a study of conflicts and divisions, especially between generations. He also edited *Social Structure: Studies Presented to A. R. Radcliffe-Brown* (Oxford UP, 1949), which proposes that research into a structure requires investigation by induction of the prevailing norms which determine the functioning of a society, with recourse to recurring examples studied using statistical method.

Without ever losing his interest in the Tallensi, Fortes began to work on the Ashanti and their bilinear or undifferentiated filiation, which he examines in his contribution to *African Systems of Kinship and Marriage* (Oxford, 1950). Although, like Radcliffe-Brown, he rejects the history of economic conditions, he does analyse structural contradictions in 'Time and Social Structure: An Ashanti Case Study' (1949), where he shows how the arrival of missionaries throws cultural heritage into uncertainty. From 1947 to 1950 Fortes was reader in social anthropology at Oxford University, and from 1950 to 1973 professor at Cambridge University. Published in 1959, his *Oedipus and Job in West African Religions* (London: Cambridge UP) examines the cult of ancestors and reveals the double and contradictory aspects in the belief of certain population groups in an (Oedipal) principle of fatality and at the same time in a (Jobian) principle of a less deterministic supernatural justice, with each individual's perspective characterized by this contradiction. In *Kinship and the Social Order: The Legacy of Lewis Henry Morgan* (Chicago: Aldine, 1969), he defines filiation and descent as being at the heart of kinship rather than as a privilege accorded to alliances. Fortes defined himself as a 'journeyman' whose eyes are fixed 'on his material, not on higher things. His aim is to turn out a particular product at a time using the best tools at his disposal' (Fortes, 1978: 1).

Wilson, Monica (née Hunter, 1908–1982)
Born of missionary parents in Lovedale, a small South African village, Monica Hunter-Wilson studied history and then anthropology at Girton College, Cambridge, gaining a BA in 1930. She then worked among the Pondo of Cape Province, carrying out the first study of social change in Africa, before returning to Cambridge and gaining a Ph.D. under Hodson's supervision in 1934. In 1936 she published *Reaction to Conquest: Effects of Contact with Europeans on the Pondo of South Africa* (Oxford UP), in which she observes the changes experienced by the Pondo as a result of colonial rule. In 1935 she married Godfrey **Wilson**, and together they undertook a Rockefeller Foundation research programme to study the impact of European cultures on African societies, supervised by the International African Institute. In 1938 G. Wilson was appointed as the first director of the Rhodes–Livingstone Institute, but he resigned in 1941 and took his own life in 1944. Their co-authored study *The Analysis of Social Change* was published in 1945. The two authors stressed the notion of scale, arguing that it is in terms of difference of scale that acculturation must

primarily be understood. M. Wilson was then engaged as a lecturer by Fort Hare College, in 1947 she obtained the chair of anthropology at Rhodes College, and in 1952 she succeeded **Schapera** at the University of Cape Town. She immersed herself in the study of towns, the urbanization of rural communities, their patterns of solidarity, and the organization of ethnic minorities. She also worked on the Nyakyusa of Malawi, giving prominence to their rituals and age–class systems as determinants of residential communities. She saw kinship and age as the two fundamental principles of village organization and religious rituals. An opponent of Apartheid, M. Wilson nonetheless remained in South Africa, where she was director of the anthropology department of the University of Cape Town until her retirement in 1973.

Gluckman, Max Herman (1911–1975)
Born in Johannesburg, Max Herman Gluckman studied law at the University of Witwatersrand and then anthropology under Agnes **Hoernlé** (BA 1934), followed by a period at Oxford University under **Marett** and attendance at **Malinowski**'s seminars. From 1936 to 1838 he carried out research among the Zulus, and in 1938 gained a Ph.D. for *The Realm of the Supernatural Among the Southeastern Bantu*. Gluckman chose to become a British subject and was a tireless critic of Apartheid in South Africa. In 1939 he was prohibited from entering Zululand, but in the same year found employment with the Rhodes–Livingstone Institute in Zambia, allowing him to carry out research on the Lozi of Borotseland (1939–1941). In 1940 he contributed an article on the Zulus to *African Political Systems* (Oxford UP). After **Evans-Pritchard** had revealed that the structure of segmentary societies is maintained by an integrative equilibrium in which vendetta plays a role, Gluckman showed that, in the same way, rebellions and revolts threaten those in power but not the institution of monarchy

itself, which is in fact reinforced. A. **Kuper** has pointed out that Gluckman addresses the question of white racial supremacy in this text, and that he is the only anthropologist of the period to do so (Kuper, 1983: 145). He was director of the Rhodes–Livingstone Institute from 1941 to 1947, and turned it into a genuine anthropological school (Gluckman 1945). He worked on the Tonga in 1944 and the Lamba in 1946 before being appointed a lecturer at Oxford University. In 1949 he became the first professor of social anthropology at Manchester University, and created what became known as the Manchester school (F. G. Bailey, V. **Turner**, R. Frankenberg, A. **Epstein**, etc.). He contributed in 1949 to a *Festschrift* presented by M. **Fortes** to **Radcliffe-Brown**, and in 1950, with an article on the Lozi and the Zulus, to *African Kinship and Marriage Systems* (Oxford UP). He expanded on the thesis of a revitalization of order by challenges to that order with the example of a ritual battle between the sexes. In 1951 Gluckman edited *Seven Tribes of British Central Africa* (Oxford UP) with E. Colson, as well as contributing an article on the Lozi, to whom he returned in his 1955 work *The Judicial Process among the Borotse of Northern Rhodesia* (Manchester UP), and again in 1965 in *The Ideas in Borotse Jurisprudence* (Manchester UP). The two last-named books describe the techniques and legal procedures in Lozi courts and constitute a major contribution to legal anthropology. Based on his Frazer Lecture given in 1952, *Rituals of Rebellion in South-East Africa* (Manchester UP, 1954) reaffirms that rituals are the expression of conflicts but nonetheless reinforce the existing social order. His *Custom and Conflict in Africa* (Glencoe: Free Press, 1955) is devoted to rituals, the principle of authority and witchcraft, and is one of the best introductions to the major principles underlying African societies. In 1962 his work as editor of *Essays on the Ritual of Social Relation* (Manchester

UP), which gathered together lectures given by Fortes, Forde and Turner at Manchester, gave Gluckman the opportunity to read **van Gennep**'s celebrated work on rites of passage. *Order and Rebellion in Tribal Africa: Collected Essays with an Autobiographical Introduction* (London: Cohen), published in 1963, restates the broad outlines of Gluckman's thought. He asserts that individuals and groups are always located in a network of multiple allegiances by rules which are themselves often contradictory and ambiguous, and argues that rituals serve to resolve conflicts by restoring the attachment of all parties to common values. He also criticizes **Malinowski** for his ahistorical approach and declares that it is necessary to establish the structural duration of any institution. In 1963 Gluckman directed the Bernstein Israel Research Project studying immigration and industrialization in Israel. In 1965 he and **F. Eggan** edited and wrote an introduction for *The Relevance of Models for Social Anthropology* (London: Tavistock Publications), one of four volumes issuing from an Anglo-American conference entitled 'New Approaches in Social Anthropology', held in Cambridge in 1963 with the aim of building a bridge between the two national traditions. As of 1971 Gluckman was employed by the Nuffield Foundation, and he resigned as head of the Manchester department while still continuing to direct his seminar there. He died on 13 April 1975, soon after he had been invited to the University of Jerusalem.

Kuper, Hilda (née Beemer, 1911–1992)
Born in Bulawayo in Rhodesia (Zimbabwe), Hilda Kuper studied anthropology under Agnes **Hoernlé** and Isaac **Schapera**, gaining a BA in 1930. She investigated the Indians of Natal and the conduct of workers who had migrated to the city from the countryside, and from 1934 carried out research on Swaziland. She then moved to London, where she gained a Ph.D. from the LSE in

1942 and worked as Malinowski's assistant. In 1947 her thesis appeared in two separately published volumes, the International African Institute having decided to publish only the first volume, *An African Aristocracy* (Oxford UP), which gives a detailed description of Swazi social organization and claims that their grand royal ceremonies fulfil an integrative function. The second volume, *The Uniform of Color: A Study of White–Black Relationships in Swaziland*, published by Witwatersrand University Press, considers changes during the colonial period and the destructive effects of white economic domination on traditional societies, while insisting on the biological equality of races. Having accompanied **Malinowski** on a visit to King Sobhuza in 1934, Kuper was eventually appointed as the official biographer of King Sobhuza II in 1972. She taught at the universities of Witwatersrand (1940–1945) and Natal (1959–1962), and then left South Africa to take up a post at the University of California at Los Angeles (1962–1978).

AUSTRALIA AND NEW ZEALAND

From the moment they were 'discovered', the Australian Aborigines fascinated Europeans and immediately became the prototype of primitive man, or, in other words, of original man (Burridge, 1973; Hiatt, 1996). After a heroic phase of work by **Howitt**, **Fison**, **Spencer** and **Gillen** and the information-gathering efforts of numerous amateurs (Elkin, 1963), it fell to **Radcliffe-Brown** in 1926 to place ethnological research in this part of the world on a firm footing by establishing the first chair and department of anthropology at Sydney with the financial support of the Rockefeller Foundation. However, A. **Kuper** remarks that

> This post was secured for him by that distinguished Sydney alumnus, the anatomist Elliot **Smith**, whose extreme diffusionist theories Radcliffe-Brown considered so ludicrous. Once again he built up an undergraduate programme, and mounted special offerings for colonial officers and missionaries [. . .] With the help of substantial government grants he also established research projects on the Aborigines, and started a new journal, *Oceania*.
>
> Despite all this activity, Radcliffe-Brown's tenure of the Sydney chair was in the end only just short of disastrous. He began under the most promising auspices, but his overbearing ways and political maladroitness alienated his supporters. In a period of growing financial stringency he turned the state governments against his schemes, and when he left Sydney in 1931 the department and all the subsidiary activities he had initiated were on the point of collapse. Firth took over to supervise the dissolution, but he and his successor, Elkin, managed to re-establish the department and most of its programmes.
>
> (Kuper, (1983) 1996: 45)

Oceania first appeared in 1930, and in 1931 the Australian Museum founded *Mankind*. **Firth**, a New Zealander by birth, arrived in Sydney in 1930 as a lecturer before becoming professor there in the following year, and with Ian Hogbin's support he set up and became president of the Anthropology Committee of the Australian National Research Council. Firth left Sydney in 1933, to be replaced as professor by **Elkin**, with Hogbin working alongside him, and Elkin was replaced in turn by Geddes in 1956. Geddes was joined in the department by P. Lawrence (1921–1987), who became a lecturer in 1963 and then held the professorship himself beginning in 1971.

The year 1946 saw the founding of the Research School of Pacific Studies, a body with a regional focus and with anthropology as one of its priorities. In 1947 Australia's second anthropology department was created at the Australian National University at Canberra, and the new chair was offered to **Nadel**. When he died in 1956 he was replaced by J. A. Barnes, who was joined by D. **Freeman**, P. Lawrence from Cambridge, and A. L. **Epstein**, who was initially appointed reader and became professor in 1966. When Epstein left Canberra for the University of Sussex in 1974, his place was taken by Anthony Forge (1929–1981) from the LSE, who opened a new department devoted to research on Indonesia.

The University of Perth, also known as the University of Western Australia, endowed a chair in 1956 which was first filled by R. M. **Berndt**, and he was joined by P. Lawrence from the Australian National University. A new department was attached to the chair and in 1963 it launched the journal *Anthropological Forum*. Finally, while the universities of Melbourne and Adelaide did not create independent anthropology departments at that time, both soon provided teaching in the discipline.

In New Zealand fieldwork was initiated by Skinner towards the close of the nineteenth century. A second important figure was Ernest Beaglehole (1906–1965), an LSE and Yale graduate who taught at Victoria College in Wellington. In 1950 an anthropology department was opened at the University of Auckland, for which the services of R. Piddington were procured. New Zealand possessed four important museums – at Canterbury, Auckland, Wellington and Otago.

In 1961 the Australian government sought to correct the bias of the country's anthropology towards the study of the 'authentic' populations of Papua New Guinea by founding the Australian Institute of Aboriginal Studies (later renamed the Australian Institute of Aboriginal and Torres Strait Islander Studies), devoted to research on both traditional cultures and cultures in the throes of change. An Australian Anthropological Society was established in 1973, at a time when many anthropologists were taking on the role of activists campaigning for the introduction of an Aboriginal Land Rights Act (voted into law in 1976) and were also increasingly employed as experts. In 1976 the University of Western Australia created the Anthropology Research Museum, renamed the Berndt Museum of Anthropology in 1992. In 1977 the Australian National University founded the journal *Canberra Anthropology*, and the University of Adelaide launched *Social Analysis*, which was subsequently co-published with the University of Toronto. Finally, in 1990 *Mankind* was retitled the *Australian Journal of Anthropology*, and in 1996 it was transformed into the official organ of the Australian Anthropological Society, which by 1994 boasted 243 members.

A number of names omitted in this section should be given brief mention: Geddes, who filled the anthropology chair at the University of Sydney on Elkin's retirement; the Englishmen P. Lawrence, professor at Sydney from 1971 to 1987, and Anthony Forge, who succeeded J. M. Barnes at Canberra in 1974; C. W. M. Hart, who left Australia for California; and also R. Keesing, Lester Richard Hiatt and, among the younger generation, David Trigger.

Elkin, Adolphus Peter (1891–1979)
Adolphus Peter Elkin studied at the University of Sydney and was then ordained an Anglican clergyman in 1915. After completing his MA thesis on Australian religions, he obtained a Ph.D. from the University of London for a thesis entitled *Myth and Ritual of the Australian Aborigines* (1927). With the support of **Radcliffe-Brown** he succeeded **Firth** in the anthropology chair at the University of Sydney in 1933, directing what until 1945 was the only anthropology

department in Australia, and he remained in this post until 1956. Elkin is known as the author of *The Australian Aborigines* (Sydney 1938, re-edited in 1943, 1954, 1964), the first complete overview of Australian culture, examining Aboriginal archaeology, ethnology and physical anthropology. Until 1979 Elkin was editor of the journal *Oceania*, and he was also one of the first defenders of the rights of the Aboriginal peoples both in Australia and in Papua New Guinea.

Keesing, Felix Maxwell (1902–1961)

Born in Taiping in what was then British Malaysia, Felix Maxwell Keesing gained an MA from the University of New Zealand and then spent some time in the USA. He returned to New Zealand to make a study of the Maori and write his Ph.D. thesis *The Changing Maori*, which was accepted in 1928. After this he moved to Yale and then Chicago. From 1930 to 1934 he worked for the Institute of the South Pacific, and in 1933–1934 studied under **Malinowski** before creating an anthropology and sociology department at the University of Hawaii. In 1942 he joined the war effort as an instructor and adviser to the US Navy, and continued to work for the American military after the war. In 1948 he became head of the sociology and anthropology department at Stanford University, and when this department was divided into its two component parts in 1956 he became head of anthropology.

Fortune, Reo Franklin (1903–1979)

Born in New Zealand, Reo Franklin Fortune studied at Victoria College (BA 1924), at Cambridge University (MA in anthropology 1927), and then at Columbia University with fieldwork in Melanesia (1928–1929). He met Margaret **Mead** on the boat returning from Dabu and married her. They travelled together to the Omaha reservations in Nebraska in 1929, and then to New Guinea. Fortune gained his doctorate in

1931, and in 1932 co-authored *Omaha Secret Societies* (New York: Columbia UP) and his best-known work *Dobu Sorcerers: Social Anthropology of the Pacific Dobu Islanders* (New York: Dutton). He carried out further fieldwork in 1932–1933, 1935–1936 and 1951–1952. It was during the second of these periods that Mead left him after having met Gregory **Bateson**. Fortune's subsequent publications included *Manus Religion* (Philadelphia: American Philosophical Society, 1935) and *The Arapesh* (New York: Augustin, 1942). From 1936 to 1939 he held a teaching post at the University of Canton, where he edited a book on the Yao, and then taught in Ohio (1940–1941) and in Toronto (1942–1944). He served in the Canadian Army and then in the frontier administration in Burma before taking up a post at Cambridge University in 1947.

Berndt, Ronald Murray (1916–1990)

Born in Adelaide of parents who had emigrated from Germany, Ronald Murray Berndt developed a fascination for the Aborigines, and was made an honorary assistant ethnologist at Adelaide's South Australian Museum in 1939. In 1940 he began studies in social anthropology at Sydney University under **Elkin** and Hogbin. He met and married Catherine Webb, and both of them held government posts with assignments to the Northwestern Aborigines and then with the Papuans of the highlands of New Guinea. Berndt made specialisms of Papuan myths, religion and artistic traditions, all topics on which he published, and he also wrote extensively on the question of war among these peoples. The Berndts left for London in 1953 and both obtained Ph.Ds at the LSE under the supervision of **Firth** in 1955. They taught anthropology at the University of Perth-Western Australia from 1956, and established and directed an anthropology department there in 1963, as well as founding a museum. They were also active as campaigners in the struggle for Aboriginal land rights.

Berndt, Catherine Helen (née Webb, 1918–1994)

Born in Auckland in New Zealand in 1918, Catherine Helen Webb studied anthropology at Sydney University, where she met her future husband Ronald Murray **Berndt**, with whom she would share a life's work. She studied at the LSE and obtained a Ph.D. there in 1955. Her best-known work is *Women's Changing Ceremonies in Northern Australia* (Paris: Mouton, 1950), in which she describes female ceremonies and relations between the sexes. Both she and her husband fought for Aborigines' rights.

Freeman, Derek (1916–2001)

Born in New Zealand, Derek Freeman attended lectures in anthropology at Victoria College in Wellington given by Ernest Beaglehole and **Nadel**. His fieldwork in Samoa was interrupted by the Second World War in 1940, and in 1943 he served in the Royal Navy. He then enrolled at the LSE and in 1948 gained a Master's degree with a thesis on Samoan social organization under the supervision of **Leach**. He married Monica Maitland, who henceforward became his fieldwork companion. He was appointed a research officer with the colonial government and in 1949–1951 carried out work on the Iban (a Dayak population) of Sarawak (British Borneo from 1946), and then he completed a doctoral thesis under **Fortes** at Cambridge University in 1953. In 1955 he became a naturalized Australian, and in the same year published two important texts describing Iban agriculture and social organization: *Iban Agriculture: A Report on the Shifting Cultivation of Hill Rice by the Iban of Sarawak* (London: Her Majesty's Stationery Office, 1955), and

Report on the Iban (London: Athlone, 2nd edn, 1970). As a student of Leach, for whom 'ethnological description only acquires scientific value when it concerns itself with details in an almost obsessive manner' (Leach, preface to the French edition of the collection *The Unity of Mankind*; Paris: Gallimard, 1980: 15), Freeman allied ethnographic precision with reflections on the relations between society, environment and ritual. Whereas the main focus in those years was on unilinear forms of filiation, he investigated the cognate system of the Iban. He saw the social space (the long house which constitutes the village) and what he called personal kindred (personal kinship ties) as providing the structure for the reproduction of minimal family units (the *bilek*). A child may belong to his father's or mother's *bilek*, but not to both at once (1957). Freeman taught at the Australian National University in Canberra and from 1957 to 1982 was a researcher and then professor in the anthropology department of the Research School of Pacific Studies. Between 1962 and 1964 he studied psychoanalysis at the London Institute of Psychoanalysis, produced a critical reading of *Totem and Taboo* (1967), and attempted to apply its principles to his fieldwork. He became known as a controversialist for his polemical attacks on J. Rousseau concerning the nature of Iban society (1981) and for his *Margaret Mead and Samoa* (Cambridge MA: Harvard UP, 1983). The first part of the book on **Mead** contains a rejection of the culturalist position, and then goes on to refute Mead's conclusions about Samoa, especially on the questions of the value attached to the virginity of young girls, the crisis of adolescence, and the peace-loving character of the Samoans. Making use of numerous personal testimonies as well as police archives and court proceedings, Freeman unleashed a veritable scandal in anthropological circles.

SELECT BIBLIOGRAPHY

Abélès, M. and Izard, M. (1991) 'Audrey Richards', in P. Bonte and M. Izard (eds) *Dictionnaire de l'ethnologie et de l'anthropologie*, Paris: Presses universitaires de France, p.629.

Acciaioli, G., Robinson, K. and Tonkinson, R. (1999) 'Challenge for the social sciences and Australia: anthropology', *Anthropological Forum*, 9(1): 63–74.

Allen, R. and Berndt, C. (1991) 'Elkin, A.P.', in C. Winter (ed.), pp.177–178.

Anonymous (1984) 'A. Richards', *AN*, 25(Dec.): 3.

Anonymous (1986) 'Lucy Philip Mair', *AN*, November: 4.

Anonymous (1992) 'Hilda Kuper', *AT*, 8(3): 18.

Anonymous (1994) 'Catherine Berndt', *AT*, 10: 27.

Anonymous (2000) 'A. Montagu', *AT*, 16(1): 23.

Appell, G.N. (1991) 'Freeman, J. Derek' in C. Winter (ed.), p.217.

Appell, G.N. and Madan, T.N. (1988) 'D. Freeman: Notes toward an intellectual biography' in G.N. Appell and T.N. Madan (eds) *Choice and Morality in Anthropological Perspective: Essays in Honor of Derek Freeeman*, Albany: State University of New York Press.

Aronoff, M.J. (ed.) (1976) *Freedom and Constraint: A Memorial Tribute to Max Gluckman*, Amsterdam: Van Gorcum.

Asad, T. (ed.) (1973) *Anthropology and the Colonial Encounter*, London: Ithaca.

Auslander, M. (1991) 'Schapera, Isaac', in C. Winter (ed.), pp.613–614.

Australian Anthropological Society (1994) *Directory of members 1994–1995*, Sydney: Australian Anthropology Society Inc.

Barnard, A. (1991) 'Radcliffe-Brown', in C. Winter (ed.), pp.563–565.

——(1992) 'Through Radcliffe-Brown's spectacles: Reflections on the history of anthropology', *History of the Human Sciences*, 5: 1–20.

Barnes, J.A. (1971) *Three Styles in the Study of Kinship*, Berkeley, CA: University of California Press.

——(1987) 'E.E. Evans-Pritchard', *Proceeding of the British Academy*, 73: 447–489.

——(1991) 'Fortes, Meyer', in C. Winter, p.211.

Bashkow, I. (1995) 'Colonial administrators of Papua on their anthropological training', *HAN*, 12(2): 3–14.

Bateson, G. (1932) 'Social structure of the Iatmul people of the Sepik River', *Oceania*, 2(3): 245–289.

——(1972; 2000) *Steps to an Ecology of Mind*, Chicago: University of Chicago Press.

——(1979; 2002) *Mind and Nature: A Necessary Unity*, New York: Dutton.

Bateson, G. and Mead, M. (1942) *Balinese Character: A Photographic Analysis*, New York: Academy of Sciences.

Bateson, M.C. (ed.) (1977) *About Bateson*, New York: Dutton.

——(1984) *With a Daughter's Eye*, New York: Simon and Schuster.

Beidelman, T.O. (1974a) 'Sir E. Evans-Pritchard, 1902–1973, an Appreciation', *Anthropos*, 59: 553–567.

——(1974b) *A Bibliography of the Writings of E.E. Evans-Pritchard*, London: Tavistock.

——(1991) 'Evans-Pritchard', in C. Winter (ed.), pp.185–187.

Bensa, A. (1977) 'Les usages sociaux du corps à Bali', *Actes de la recherche en sciences sociales*, 14: 3–33.

Bensa, A. and Ruesch, J. (1951) *Communication: The Social Matrix of Psychiatry*, New York.

Berndt, C.H. (1993) *A World that Was: the Yaraldi of the Murray Rivers and the Lakes, South Australia*, University of Canberra Press.

Berndt, R.M. (1951) *Kunapipi: A Study of the Australian Aboriginal Religious Cult*, Melbourne: Cheshire.

——(1961) *An Adjument Movement in Arhem Land*, Paris: Mouton.

——(1962) *Excess and Restraint: Social Control among a New Guinea Mountain People*, Chicago: University of Chicago Press.

——(1974) *Australian Aboriginal Religion*, Leiden: Brill.

Berndt, R.M. and Berndt, C.H. (1964, 1996) *The World of the First Australians*, Canberra: Aboriginal Studies Press.

——(eds) (1965) *Aboriginal Man in Australia: Essays in Honour of Emeritus Professor A.P. Elkin*, Sydney: Angus and Robertson.

——(1979) 'A.P. Elkin, 1891–1979', *Oceania*, 14: 161–167.

——(1988; 1994), *The Speaking Land: Myth and Story in Aboriginal Australia*, Rochester: Inner Traditions.

Bloch, M. (2002) 'Obituaries: R. Firth', *The Guardian*, 26 February.

Brokensha, D. (1983) 'Monica Wilson 1908–1982', *Africa*, 53: 3.

Brown, R. (1973) 'Anthropology, a Colonial Rule: The Case of G. Wilson and the Rhodes–Livingstone Institute, Northern Rhodesia' in T. Asad (ed.) *Anthropology and the Colonial Encounter*, London: Ithaca, pp.173–197.

——(1979) 'Passages in the life of a white anthropologist: Max Gluckman in Northern Rhodesia', *Journal of African History*, 20: 525–41.

Burridge, K.O.L. (1973) *Encountering Aborigines*, New York: Pergamon.

Burton, J. (1992) *An Introduction to Evans-Pritchard*, Fribourg University Press.

Carstens, P. (1991) 'Hoernlé, Agnes', in C. Winter (ed.), p.298.

Castens, P. (1985a) 'Introduction', in A. Hoernlé., P. Cartens, G. Klinghardt and M. West (eds) 1987, *Trails in the Thirstland: The Anthropological Field Diaries of W. Hoernlé*, Cape Town: University of Cape Town Press.

——(1985b) *The Social Organization of the Nama and other Essays by Winifred Hoernlé*, Johannesburg: Witwatersrand University Press.

Colson, E. (1977) 'The Institute under Max Gluckman, 1942–1947', *African Social Research*, 24: 285–295.

——(1986) 'Lucy Mair', *AT*, 2: 22–24.

Comaroff, J. and Comaroff, J.L. (1988) 'On the founding fathers, fieldwork and functionalism: a conversation with Isaac Schapera', *American Ethnologist*, 15: 554–565.

David, J. (ed.) (1974) *Choice and Change: Essays in Honour of Lucy Mair*, London: Athlone.

——(1991) 'Lucy Mair', in C. Winter, (ed.), pp.437–439.

Davis, J. and Loizis, P. 'Sir R. Firth's 100th birthday', *The Times Higher Education Supplement*, 30 March 2001.

Douglas, M. (1979) 'Daryll Forde' in *International Encyclopedia of the Social Sciences*, Sills (ed.), 18: 192–194.

——(1980) *Evans-Pritchard*, London: Fontana.

——(1991) 'Forde, Daryll', in C. Winter (ed.), pp.208–209.

Druker-Brown, S. (1980) 'Notes towards a biography of M. Fortes', *American Ethnologist*, 16: 375–385.

——(1983) 'Meyer Fortes', *Rain*, 56: 15.

Druker-Brown, S. *et al.* (eds) (1983) 'In memory of M. Fortes', *Cambridge Anthropology*, 8: 1–70 (introduction by J. Goody).

Dumont, L. (1968) 'Introduction' to Evans-Pritchard *The Nuer*, Paris: Gallimard.

——(1971) 'M. Fortes' in *Introduction à deux théories d'anthropologie sociale, groupes de filiation et alliance de mariage*, Paris and The Hague: Mouton, pp.75–81.

Elkin, A.P. (1933; 1978) *Studies in Australian Totemism*, New York: AMS Press.

——(1944) *Citizenship for the Aborigines*, Sydney: Australian Publications.

——(1953) *Social Anthropology in Melanesia*, London: Oxford University Press.

——(1956) 'A.R. Radcliffe-Brown, 1881–1955', *Oceania*, vol.24.

——(1958) 'Anthropology in Australia', *Mankind*, 5(6).

——(1963) 'The development of scientific knowledge on the Aborigines', in H. Sheils (ed.), *Australian Aboriginal Studies: a Symposium of Papers presented at the 1961 research conference*, Melbourne: Oxford University Press, pp.3–28.

Evans-Pritchard, E.E. (1929) 'The morphology and function of magic: A comparative study of Trobriand and Zande ritual and spells', *AA*, 31.

——(1940; 1977) *The Political Systems of the Anuak of the Anglo-Egyptian Sudan*, New York: AMS Press.

——(1949) *The Sanusi of Cyrenaica*, Oxford: Clarendon.

——(1950) 'Social anthropology: past and present', *Man*, 198: 118–124.

——(1951) *Kinship and Marriage Among the Nuer*, Oxford: Clarendon.

——(1956) *Nuer Religion*, Oxford: Oxford University Press.

——(1962) *Essays in Social Anthropology*, London: Faber.

——(1965) *The Position of Women in Primitive Societies and other Essays in Social Anthropology*, London: Faber.

——(1967) *The Zandé Trickster*, Oxford: Clarendon.

——(1971) *The Azande: History and Political Institutions*, Oxford: Clarendon.

——(1974) *Man and Women Among the Azande*, London: Faber.

——(1981) *A History of Anthropological Thought* (intro by E. Gellner), London: Faber.

Faris, J. (1973) 'Pax Britannica and the Sudan: S.F. Nadel' in T. Asad, *Anthropology & the Colonial Encounter*, London: Ithaca, pp.153–173.

Favret-Saada, J. (1991) 'Nadel, S.F.', in P. Bonte and M. Izard (eds) *Dictionnaire de l'ethnologie et de l'anthropologie*, Paris: Presses universitaires de France, p.503.

Firth, R. (1932) 'Anthropology in Australia, 1926–1932 and after' *Oceania*, 3: 1–12.

——(1956) 'A.R. Radcliffe-Brown, 1881–1955', *Proceedings of the British Academy*, 42: 287–302.

——(ed.) (1957a; 1970) *Man and Culture: An Evaluation of the Work of Bronislaw Malinowski*, London: Routledge.

——(1957b) 'S.F. Nadel', *AA*, 59: 117–124.

——(1963) 'A brief history of the department (1913–1963)', Department of Anthropology, London: London School of Economics and Political Science.

——(1967) *Tikopia Ritual and Belief*, London: Allen.

——(1970) *Rank and Religion in Tikopia: A Study in Polynesian Paganism and Conversion to Christianity*, London: Allen.

——(1973) *Symbols: Public and Private*, Ithaca: Cornell University Press.

——(1975) 'Max Gluckman', *Proceedings of the British Academy*, 61: 479–496.

——(1983) 'Review of *Margaret Mead and Samoa*' *Rain*, 57: 12–13.

——(1985) 'Obituary of Audrey Richards', *Man*, 20: 341–343.

Forde, C.D. (1928) *Ancient Mariners: The Story of Ships and Sea Routes*, New York: Morrow.

——(1950) *The Ibo and Ibo-speaking Peoples of Southern Nigeria*, London: IAI, Oxford University Press.

——(1958) *The Context of Belief: A Consideration of Fetishism Among the Yakö (Frazer Lecture)*, Liverpool: Liverpool University Press.

——(1964) *Yakö Studies*, London: Oxford University Press.

Forde, C.D. and Kaberry, P.M. (eds) (1967) *West African Kingdoms in the Nineteenth Century*, London: IAI, Oxford University Press.

Forde, C.D. and Richenda, S. (1946), *The Native Economies of Nigeria*, London: Faber.

Fortes, M. (1953) *Social Anthropology at Cambridge since 1900*, Cambridge: Cambridge University Press.

——(1955) 'Radcliffe-Brown's contribution to the study of social organization', *British Journal of Sociology*, 6: 16–30.

——(1957) 'S.F. Nadel, 1903–1956: A memoir', in Nadel, *The Theory of Social Structure*, London and Glencoe.

——(1970) *Time and Social Structure and Other Essays*, London: Athlone Press.

——(1975) 'Isaac Schapera: An appreciation', in M. Fortes and S. Patterson (eds) *Studies in Social Anthropology*, London.

——(1976) 'Cyril Daryll Forde, 1902–1973', *Proceedings of the British Academy*, 62: 495–83.

——(1978) 'An anthropologist's apprenticeship', *Annual Review of Anthropology*, 7(1–3).

——(1983) *Rules and the Emergence of Society*, London: RAI.

——(1987) *Religion, Morality and the Person*, Cambridge: Cambridge University Press.

Fortes, M. and Dieterlen, G. (eds) (1965) *African Systems of Thought*, Oxford: Oxford University Press.

Fox, R. (2000) 'A. Montagu', *MAN*, 41(1): 61.

Freedman, M. (ed.) (1967) *Social Organization: Essays Presented to R. Firth*, Chicago: Aldine.

Freeman, D. (1956) 'S. F. Nadel', *Oceania*, 27: 1–11.

——(1957; 1971) 'The Family system of the Iban of Borneo', in J. Goody (ed.) *The Developmental Cycle in Domestic Groups*, Cambridge: Cambridge University Press.

——(1967) 'Totem and Taboo: A reappraisal', *The Psychoanalysis Study of Society*, 4: 315–344.

——(1981) *Some reflections on the nature of Iban society*, Dept. of Anthropology, Research School of Pacific Studies, Australian National University.

——(1996; 1983) *Margaret Mead and the Heretic*, Penguin.

Freilich, M. (1991) 'Nadel, S.F.', in C. Winter (ed.), pp.499–500.

Galey, J-C. (1991) 'Evans-Pritchard', in P. Bonte and M. Izard (eds) *Dictionnaire de l'ethnologie et de l'anthropologie*, Paris: Presses universitaires de France, pp.267–269.

Geertz, C. (1988) *Works and Lives: The Anthropologist as Author* (on Malinowski), Stanford: Stanford University Press.

Gluckman, M. (1944) 'G. Wilson' in *The Rhodes–Livingstone Journal*, 1.

——(1945) 'Seven-Year Research Plan of the Rhodes–Livingstone Institute' *Human Problems in British Central Africa*, vol.4: 1–32.

——(1963) 'Malinowski – fieldworker and theorist', in M. Gluckman (ed.) *Order and Rebellion in Tribal Africa*, London: Routledge, pp.24–52.

——(ed.) (1972) *The Allocation of Responsibility*, Manchester: Manchester University Press.

——(1975) 'Anthropologists and apartheid: The work of South African anthropologists', in M. Fortes and S. Patterson (eds) *Studies in African Social Anthropology*, London: Academic Press.

——(1984) Report on H. Kuper *An African Aristocracy, Africa*, 18: 63–64.

Gluckman, M. and Schapera, I. (1960) 'Dr. Winifred Hoernlé: an Appreciation', *Africa*, 30: 262–263.

Godelier, M. (1996) 'Firth, Raymond', in P. Bonte and M. Izard (eds) *Dictionnaire de l'ethnologie et de l'anthropologie*, Paris: Presses universitaires de France, pp.282–283.

Goody, J. (1996) *The Expansive Moment: Anthropology in Britain and Africa, 1918–1970*, Cambridge: Cambridge University Press.

Gordon, R. (1987) 'Remembering Agnes W. Hoernlé', *Social Dynamics*, 13: 68–72.

——(1988) 'Apartheid's anthropologists: the genealogy of Afrikaner anthropology', *American Ethnologist*, 15: 535–553.

——(1990) 'Early social anthropology in South Africa', *African Studies*, 49: 15–48.

Goslson, E. (1979) 'Gluckman, Max', in Sills (ed.) *International Encyclopedia of Social Sciences*, biographical supplement, pp.242–246.

Hammond-Tooke, W.D. (1997) *Imperfect Interpreters: South Africa's Anthropologists, 1920–1990*, Johannesburg: Witwatersrand University Press.

Hiatt, L.R. (1996) *Arguments about Aborigines: Australia and the Evolution of Social Anthropology*, Cambridge: Cambridge University Press.

Houseman, M. and Severi, C. (1991) 'Bateson, Gregory', in P. Bonte and M. Izard (eds) *Dictionnaire de l'ethnologie et de l'anthropologie*, Paris: Presses universitaires de France, pp.109–110.

——(1994) *Naven ou le donner à voir. Essai d'interprétation de l'action rituelle*, Paris: CNRS-MSH.

Huntsman, J. (2003) 'Obituary R. Firth', *AA*, vol. 105(2): 487–490.

Izard, M. (1991a) 'Gluckman, Max Herman', in Bonte and Izard (eds), p.302.

——(1991b) 'Isaac Schapera', in P. Bonte and M. Izard (eds) *Dictionnaire de l'ethnologie et de l'anthropologie*, Paris: Presses universitaires de France, pp.653–654.

Jarvie, I. (1964; 1969) *The Revolution in Anthropology*, (intro by E. Gellner), Chicago: Regnery.

Jeudy-Ballini, M. (1991) 'Malinowski, B.', in P. Bonte and M. Izard (eds) *Dictionnaire de l'ethnologie et de l'anthropologie*, Paris: Presses universitaires de France, pp.438–440.

Kaldor, S. (1988) 'Catherine Berndt', in Gacs, U. *et al. Women Anthropologists. A Biographical Dictionary*, New York, London: Greenwood: 8–17.

Karp, I. and Maynard, K. (1983) 'Reading the Nuer' (and 'Comments' and 'Reply'), *CA*, 24: 481–503.

Keesing, F.M. (1939) *Three Centuries of Contact and Culture Change among the Mimomini Indians of Wisconsin*, Philadelphia: American Philosophical Society.

——(1958) *Cultural Anthropology: the Science of Custom*, New York: Holt, Rinehart and Winston.

——(1970) 'Shrines, ancestors and cognatic descent: The kinship system of the Tallensi: a reevaluation', *AA*, 72: 755–175.

Keesing, F.M. and Keesing, M. (1956) *Elite Communication in Samoa: A Study of Leadership*, Stanford: Stanford University Press.

Kiernan, J. (1997) 'David in the path of Goliath: South African anthropology in the shadow of Apartheid', in P. MacAllister (ed.) *Culture and the Commonplace*, Johannesburg: Witwatersrand University Press, pp.53–68.

Kluckhohn, C. (1943) 'Bronislaw Malinowski, 1884–1942' *Journal of American Folklore*, 56: 221.

Kuklick, H. (1996) 'Malinowski, B.', in A. Barnard and J. Spencer (eds) *Encyclopedia of Social and Cultural Anthropology*, London: Routledge, pp.343–345.

Kuper, A. (1973; 1996), *Anthropology and Anthropologists: The Modern British School*, London: Routledge.

——(1977) 'Introduction' in *The Social Anthropology of Radcliffe-Brown*.

——(1982) 'Lineage theory: a critical retrospect', *Annual Review of Anthropology* 11: 71–95.

——(1987) *South Africa and the Anthropologists*, London: Routledge.

——(1988) 'Radcliffe-Brown and Rivers: a correspondence', *Canberra Anthropology*, 11: 49–82.

——(1991) 'Grande-Bretagne. L'anthropologie britannique', in P. Bonte and M. Izard (eds) *Dictionnaire de l'ethnologie et de l'anthropologie*, Paris: Presses universitaires de France, pp.305–308.

——(1992) 'Obituary H. Kuper' in *The Independent*, 27 April.

——(1999) *Culture: The Anthropologists' Account*, Cambridge, MA and London: Harvard University Press.

——(1999a; 1996) 'Audrey Richards: A career in anthropology' in A. Kuper, *Among the Anthropologists*, London: Athlone, pp.115–138.

——(1999b) 'South African anthropology: An inside job', in *Among the Anthropologists*, London: Athlone, pp.145–171.

——(2000) 'Comment nommer les éléments? les catégories anthropologiques en Afrique du Sud', *Revue de Synthèse*, 121(3–4): 265–290.

——(2002) 'Isaac Schapera: a conversation', *AT*, 17(6), 18(1): 14–20.

——(2003) 'Isaac Schapera', *The Independent*, 7 July.

Kuper, H. (1952) *The Swazi*, London: IAI.

——(1955) *The Shona*, London: IAI.

——(1960; 1974) *Indian People of Natal*, Westport: Greenwood Press.

——(1963) *The Swazi: a South African Kingdom*, New York: Holt.

——(ed.) (1965a) *Urbanization and Migration in West Africa*, Berkeley, CA: University of California Press.

——(1965b) *Bite of Hunger: a Novel of Africa*. New York: Harcourt.

——(1970) *A Witch in my Heart: a Play Set in Swaziland in the 1930s*, London: Oxford University Press.

——(1981) *Biography as Interpretations*, Bloomington, Indiana University Press.

——(1984) 'Function history, biography' in G.W. Stocking (ed.) *Functionalism, Historicized*, HOA, vol. 2: 192–213.

La Fontaine, J.S. (ed.) (1972) *The Interpretation of Ritual: Essays in Honour of A.I. Richards*, London: Tavistock.

——(ed.) (1985) 'Audrey Richards : in memoriam', *Cambridge Anthropology*, 10.

——(1986) 'A. Richards', *American Ethnologist*, 13: 338–362.

Leach, E. (1979) 'R. Firth', in *International Encyclopedia of the Social Sciences*, Sills, vol.18: 187–192.

Leach, E. R. (1961; 1966) *Rethinking Anthropology*, London: Athlone.

Leach, R. (1984) 'Glimpses of the unmentionable in the history of British social anthropology', *Annual Review of Anthropology*, vol. 13: 131–123.

Leclerc, G. (1972) *Anthropologie et colonialisme*, Paris: Fayard.

Levy, R.I. and Rappaport, R. (1982) 'Gregory Bateson', *AA*, 84: 379–394.

Liberski, D. (1991) 'Meyer Fortes', in P. Bonte and M. Izard (eds) *Dictionnaire de l'ethnologie et de l'anthropologie*, Paris: Presses universitaires de France, p.289.

Lienhardt, G. (1991) 'Radcliffe-Brown, A.R.', in P. Bonte and M. Izard (eds) *Dictionnaire de l'ethnologie et de l'anthropologie*, Paris: Presses universitaires de France, pp.612–614.

Lipset, D. (1980) *The Legacy of a Scientist* (on Bateson), Englewood Cliffs: Prentice-Hall.

Lombard, J. (1972) *L'anthropologie britannique contemporaine*, Paris: Presses universitaires de France.

Lonergan, D. (1991) 'Bateson, G.', in C. Winter (ed.), pp.38–39.

Maddock, K. (1996) 'Radcliffe-Brown, A.R.', in A. Barnard and J. Spencer (eds) *Encyclopedia of Social and Cultural Anthropology*, London: Routledge, pp.465–466.

Mair, L.P. (1962) *Primitive Government*, London: Penguin.

——(1965; 1985) *An Introduction to Social Anthropology*, Westport: Greenwood Press.

——(1967) *The New Africa*, London: Watts.

——(1969) *Anthropology and Social Change*, London: Athlone.

——(1971; 1977) *Marriage*, London: Scolar Press.

——(1977) *African Kingdoms*, Oxford: Clarendon.

——(1984) *Anthropology and Development*, London.

——(1922; 1984) *Argonauts of the Western Pacific*, Preface by J. Frazer, Prospect Heights: Waveland Press.

Malinowski, B.K. (1925) *The Natives of Mailu, Transactions and Proceedings of the Royal Society of South Australia*, 39: 495–706.

——(1927; 2001) *Sex and Repression in Savage Societies*, London: Routledge.

——(1935; 1978) *Coral Gardens and their Magic*, New York: Dover Publications.

——(1962) *Sex, Culture and Myth*, New York.

——(1967; 1989) *A Diary in the Strict Sense of the Term*, Trans. by N. Guterman, Pref. by V. Malinowski, Intro. by R. Firth, Stanford: Stanford University Press.

Matthey, P. (1996) 'A glimpse of Evans-Pritchard through his correspondence with Lowie and Kroeber', *Journal of the Anthropological Society of Oxford*, 27: 21–45.

Max, E. (1975) 'Anthropological studies in a centralized state: Max Gluckman and the Bernstein Israel Research Project', *Jewish Journal of Sociology*, 17: 131–150.

Montagu, A. (1943; 1997) *Man's Most Dangerous Myth: the Fallacy of Race*, Walnut Creek: Alta Mira Press.

——(1951a; 1967) *On Being Human*, New York: Hawthorn Books.

——(1951b; 1973) *On Being Intelligent*, Westport: Greenwood Press.

——(1959) *Human Heredity*, Cleveland: World Pub.

——(1969) *Sex, Man and Society*, New York: Putnam.

——(1971a, 1979) *The Elephant Man: A Study of Human Dignity*, New York: Dutton.

——(1971b; 1986) *Touching: The Human Signification of the Skin*, New York: Perennial Library.

——(1974; 1989) *The Natural Superiority of Women*, Walnut Creek: Alta Mira Press.

——(1981; 1989) *Growing Young*, Granby, Mass: Bergin Pub.

Moran, K. (1988) 'Hilda Beemer Kuper', in Gacs, U. *et al. Women Anthropologists. A Biographical Dictionary*, New York, London: Greenwood, pp.194–201.

Morphy, H. (1990) 'R.M. Berndt', *AT*, 6(3): 22–23.

Morton, J. (1996) 'Australia' in Levinson and Ember (eds), pp.116–119.

Murdock, P. (1943) 'Malinowski', *AA*, 45: 441–451.

Nadel, S.F. (1938) 'Review of *Naven*', *Man*, 37: 121–122.

Panoff, M. (1972) *Bronislaw Malinowski*, Paris: Payot.

Panofsky, H.E. (1991) 'A. Montagu' in C. Winter (ed.), p.478.

Parkin, D. (1988) 'An interview with R. Firth', *CA*, 29(2): 327–341.

Peterson, N. (1990) 'Studying man and man's nature : the history of the institutionalisation of Aboriginal anthropology', *Australian Aboriginal Studies*, 2: 3–19.

Powdermaker, H. (1966) ch. 2 in *LSE: Studying with Malinowski, 'Stranger and Friend'*, New York: Norton.

Pym, B. (1994; 1984) *A Very Private Eye: Diaries, Letters and Notebooks of B. Pym*, London: Macmillian.

Radcliffe-Brown, A.R. (1957) *A Natural Science of Society*, mimeograph of a seminar by the author in Chicago in 1937, Glencoe: The Free Press.

——(1952; 1965) *Structure and Function in Primitive Society: Essays and Addresses*, Foreword by E. Evans-Pritchard and F. Eggan, New York: Free Press.

Richards, A. (1940) *Bemba Marriage and Modern Economic Conditions*, Livingstone: Rhodes–Livingstone Institute.

——(1954) *Economic Development and Tribal Change*, Cambridge University Press.

——(1960) *East African Chiefs: A Study of Political Development in some Uganda and Tanganyika Tribe*, London: Faber.

——(1966) *The Changing Structure of a Ganda Village: Kizozi 1892–1952*, Nairobi: East African Publishing House.

Roy, E. *et al.* (eds) (1988) *Malinowski Between Two Worlds: The Polish Roots of an Anthropological Tradition*, Cambridge University Press.

Salat, J. (1983) *Reasoning As Entreprise: The Anthropology of S.F. Nadel*, trans. G. Quatember, Göttingen: Herodot.

Schapera, I. (ed.) (1937; 1974) *The Bantu-speaking Tribes of South Africa: An Ethnological Survey*, ed. by Hammond-Tooke, London: Routledge.

——(1940; 1966) *Married Life in an African Tribe*, London: Faber.

——(ed.) (1959–1963) *David Livingstone's Journals and Letters, 1841–1956*, 6 vols, London: Chatto.

——(1970) *Tribal Innovators, Tswana Chiefs and Social Change, 1795–1940*, London: Athlone.

——(1971) *Rainmaking Rites of Tswana Tribes*, Leiden: Afrika-Studiecentrum.

Schapira, I. (1989) 'A.R. Brown to Radcliffe-Brown', *Anthropology Today*, 5(5): 10–11.

Schmidt, N.J. (1991) 'Kuper, Hilda Beemer', in C. Winter (ed.), pp.369–370.

Schneider, D. (1995) *Schneider on Schneider: The Conversion of the Jews and other Anthropological Stories. D. Schneider as told to R. Handler* (on Firth), Durham: Duke University Press, pp. 129–131.

Shankman, P. (1996) 'Mead-Freeman controversy', in Levinson and Ember (eds), *Encyclopedia of Cultural Anthropology*, vol.3, pp.757–759.

Siegel, B.J. and Spindler, G. (1962) 'F. Keesing', *AA*, 64: 351–355.

Silverstein, S. (1988) 'Audrey Richards', in Gacs, U. *et al. Women Anthropologists. A Biographical Dictionary*, New York, London: Greenwood: 310–315.

Smith, M.G. *The Guardian* 4 May.

Spiegel, A. (1993) 'South African anthropology revisited', *Annual Review of Anthropology*, 22: 83–105.

——(1997) 'Continuities, culture and the common place: searching for a new ethnographic approach in South Africa', in P. MacAllister (ed.) *Culture and the Commonplace*, Johannesburg: Witwatersrand University Press.

Srinivas, M.N. (ed.) (1958) *Method in Social Anthropology: Selected Essays*, Chicago: University of Chicago Press.

Stanner, W.H. (1972) 'A.R. Radcliffe-Brown', in D.L. Sills (ed.) *International Encyclopedia of the Social Sciences*, 13: 285–290.

Stocking, G.W. (ed.) (1983) 'The ethnographer's magic: fieldwork, in British anthropology from Tylor to Malinowski', in Stocking, *Observers Observed: Essays on Ethnographic Fieldwork, HOA*, vol: 1, 70–121.

——(1984) *Functionalism Historicized: Essays on British Social Anthropology*, Madison: University of Wisconsin Press.

——(1996) *After Tylor: British Social Anthropology, 1888–1951*, London: Athlone.

Strathern, M. (2002) 'Obituaries' R. Firth, *The Independent*, 5 March.

Sullivan, G. (1999) *Margaret Mead, Gregory Bateson and Highland Bali: Fieldwork Photographs of Bayung Gede, 1936–39*, Chicago: University of Chicago Press.

Thornton, R. and Skalnik, P. (eds) (1993) *The Early Writings of Bronislaw Malinowski*, Cambridge: Cambridge University Press.

Tonkinson, R. (1991) 'Berndt, Ronald', in C. Winter (ed.), pp.51–53.

Tonkinson, R. and Howard, M. (1990) 'The Berndts: a biographical sketch' in R. Tonkinson and M. Howard (eds) *Going it Alone? Prospects for Aboriginal Autonomy: Essays in Honour of Ronald Berndt and Catherine Berndt*, Canberra: Aboriginal Studies Press.

Tuzcin, D. (2002) 'Derek Freeman (1916–2001)', *AA*, vol. 104: 1013–1015.

Vawda, S. (1995) 'The other anthropology: a response to Gordon and Spiegel's review of Southern African anthropology', *African Studies*, 53(1): 128–131.

Watson-Gegeo, K.A. (1991) 'Firth, Raymond', in C. Winter (ed.), pp.197–199.

Watson-Gegeo, K.A. and Seaton, S.L. (eds) (1978) *Adaptation and Symbolism: Essays on Social Organization, Presented to Sir Raymond Firth by his Students in the USA and Canada, 1968–1974*, Honolulu: University Press of Hawaii.

Wayne, H. (ed.) (1995) *The Story of a Marriage: The Letters of Bronislaw Malinowski and Elsie Masson*, 2 vols, London: Routledge.

Weiner, A. (1976), *Women of Value, Men of Renown: New Perspectives in Trobriand Exchange*, Austin: University of Texas Press.

——(1992) *Inalienable Possession: The Paradox of Keeping-While-Giving*, University of California Press.

Werbner, R. (1979) 'Audrey Richards', in *International Encyclopedia of the Social Sciences*, Sills (ed.) vol.18: 658–60.

West, M.E. (1988) 'Monica Hunter Wilson', in Gacs, U. *et al. Women Anthropologists. A Biographical Dictionary*, New York, London: Greenwood: 372–382.

Wilson, G. (1938) 'The Rhodes–Livingstone Institute of Central African Studies', *The Cambridge Review*, 172.

——(1940) 'Anthropology as a Public Service', *Africa*, 13.

Wilson, G. and Wilson, M. (1939), 'The Study of African Society', *Rhodes–Livingstone Papers*, 2.

——(1941–1942) 'Essay on the economics of detribalisation in Northern Rhodesia', *Rhodes–Livingstone Papers*, 5 and 6.

Wilson, M. (1951; 1983) *Good Company: A Study of Nyakyusa Age Village*, Westport: Greenwood Press.

——(1957) *Rituals of Kingship Among the Nyakyusa*, London: Oxford University Press.

——(1959a) *Communal Rituals Among the Nyakyusa*, London: Oxford University Press.

——(1959b) *Divine Kings and the Breath of Men*, Cambridge: Cambridge University Press.

——(1970) *The Thousand Years Before van Riebeeck*, Johannesburg: Witwatersrand University Press.

——(1981) *Freedom for my People. The Autobiography of Z.K. Mathews: Southern Africa 1901 to 1968*, Cape Town and London: Philip and Collings.

Wilson, M and Thompson, L. (eds) (1971) *The Oxford History of South Africa*, vol.1 and 2, Oxford: Clarendon.

Wise, T. (1985) *Self-Made Anthropologist: The Life of A.P. Elkin*, Sydney: Allen and Unwin.

Worley, P. (1956) 'The kinship system of the Tallensi: a reevaluation', *JRAI*, 86: 37–75.

Yaffe, G. (1990) 'An Anthropologist as political officer: Evans-Pritchard, the French and the Alawis' in H. Shamir (ed.) *France and Germany in an Age of Crisis 1900–1960*, Leiden, New York: Brill.

Young, M.W. (ed.) (1979) *The Ethnography of Malinowski: The Trobriand Islands 1915–1918*, London: Routledge.

——(1988) 'Editor's introduction'. *Malinowski among the Magi. The natives of Mailu*, London: Routledge, pp.1–76.

——(1991) 'Malinowski, B.', in C. Winter (ed.), pp.444–446.

——(1999) *Malinowski's Kiriwina: Fieldwork Photography 1915–1918*, Chicago: University of Chicago Press.

VIII

Mauss's students and the *Institut d'ethnologie* in the interwar years

From 1928 to 1940 the *Institut d'ethnologie* provided the framework for ethnology teaching in France. According to Denise **Paulme** (unpublished interview with G. Gaillard), at its opening the institute offered five or six presentations on physical anthropology by Paul **Rivet**, and the same number each on prehistory, by the Abbé Breuil, and linguistics, by Marcel **Cohen**, as well as seminars directed by Marcel **Mauss** twice a week. The institute's first steps were strongly characterized by what I have called the *belles lettres* spirit (see Chapter V). This is attested by the fact that the institute's first graduate, Paul **Mus**, became the director of the *Ecole Française d'Extrême Orient* (The French school of the Far East), and by the important place in research held by Abyssinia (Ethiopia), which was seen as a phantasmagorical representative of ancient classical civilizations (Cohen went to Abyssinia in 1910 and **Griaule** followed in 1928, and it took pride of place in the Dakar-Djibouti mission of 1933–1934). Between 1928 and 1935 the following scholars graduated from the institute: P. Mus, M. Griaule, A. **Métraux**, M. **Leiris**, J. **Cazeneuve**, L. S. Senghor, J. **Soustelle**, C. **Lévi-Strauss**, A. **Leroi-Gourhan**, G. **Dieterlen**, P.-E. **Victor**, D. Paulme, M. **Rodinson**. On the eve of the Second World War the courses offered were as follows: descriptive ethnography (M. Mauss), descriptive linguistics (M. Cohen), anthropology (P. Rivet); exotic prehistory (P. Wernert), African ethnography (H. **Labouret**), African linguistics (L. Homburger), linguistics and ethnography of East Asia and Oceania (J. Przyluski), zoological and biological anthropology (E. Rabaud), geology of the Quaternary and human palaeontology (A. Laquine), psycho-physiology and human beings and anthropoids (P. Guillaume), human geography (A. Demangeon), comparative racial physiognomy (J. Millot), and bibliography (Y. Oddon). After their formal training students joined missions, of which the best-known was the Dakar-Djibouti expedition, directed by M. Griaule, which crossed Africa from west to east between 1931 and 1933. From 1928 to 1940 the *Institut d'ethnologie* sponsored forty-eight such missions: ten within Europe (e.g. Estonia, Albania, Hungary), ten to Asia (e.g. Indochina, Japan), twenty-three to Africa (including ten to Maghreb countries), and five to Oceania and America. Some notable examples are Griaule's mission to Abyssinia (1928), the Franco-Belgian expedition of A. Métraux and H. Lavachéry to Easter Island (1928), the Dakar-Djibouti expedition of Griaule, **Leiris** and **Schaeffner** (1931), that of J. Soustelle to Mexico (1932), that of P.-E. Victor and R. **Gessain** to Greenland (1932), that of G. **Tillion** and Thérèse Rivet to Algeria (1934), that of C. Lévi-Strauss to the Bororo (1936), and that of Arlette and André Leroi-Gourhan to Japan (1937). Also worth mentioning are Jeanne Cuisinier's expedition to Indonesia, that of Labouret to Cameroon and Burkina, and that of Le Coeur to Chad. Griaule carried out a second mission to the Dogon at the end of which two of his team, D. Paulme and D. Lifchitz, remained behind to complete an eight-month stay in Sanga in 1934 – the first extended fieldwork by the French school. In 1928 Rivet was appointed to the anthropology chair attached to the *Musée d'histoire naturelle*, and thereby also placed in charge of the small *Musée du Trocadéro*. Rivet chose G.-H. **Rivière** as his deputy, and the two men won approval for the construction of the modernist *Palais du Trocadéro* to coincide with the holding of the International Exhibition in Paris. The new palace replaced the *Musée du Trocadéro*, which was destroyed, and became the home of the *Musée de l'Homme*, which opened its doors in 1937. It was in the *Musée de l'Homme* that the first French Resistance network was formed during the Occupation (Blumenson, 1977). The members of this network were either executed or deported (e.g. B. Vildé, A. Lewitzky, G. Tillion, Y. Oddon), while other anthropologists whose lives were in danger or who opposed the Vichy regime fled abroad, often to London (e.g. Soustelle, Lévi-Strauss, Rivet, **Callois**). After the enactment of the Vichy anti-Semitic laws on 2 June 1941, Mauss's teaching rights were withdrawn and he was replaced by M. **Leenhardt** as director of studies in primitive peoples in Section V of the EPHE. The Sorbonne finally accepted the endowment of an ethnography chair in 1942, something Mauss had long called for. This new chair was first occupied by M. Griaule, whose thesis *Masques Dogons* [*Dogon Masks*] had gained him the first French doctorate in ethnology. Griaule's successors as doctorate-holders were D. Paulme with *La communauté taisible chez les Dogon* [*The Community of the Dogon in Law*] (1942), Leroi-Gourhan with *Archéologie du Pacifique nord: Matériaux pour l'étude des relations entre les peuples riverains d'Asie et d'Amérique* [*Archaeology of the North Pacific: Materials for the Study of Relations between Riparian Peoples of Asia and America*] (1945), and Lévi-Strauss with *Les structures élémentaires de la parenté* [*Elementary Structures of Kinship*] (1948). As for the institutional organization of research, an important role was played by a state body called the *Caisse nationale des sciences* (National Science Fund), which in 1935 recruited its first ethnologists, M. Leiris and J.-P. **Lebeuf**. This Fund was the forerunner of the *Centre national de la recherche scientifique* (CNRS) (National Centre for Scientific Research), which replaced it in 1938. Other ethnology graduates became assistants at Section V of the EPHE – such as Griaule, or were put in charge of various departments of the *Musée du Trocadéro* – like Schaeffner, Leroi-Gourhan and Vildé, and the group was employed at the *Musée de l'Homme* after its opening in 1937. The thirty names dealt with in this chapter represent the majority of scholars who passed through the *Institut d'ethnologie* from 1925 to 1939, although they form an eclectic group in terms of approaches and theories.

Schaeffner, André (1895–1980)

André Schaeffner abandoned chemistry for musicology and became the pioneer of ethnomusicology in France. In 1925 he met G.-H. **Rivière** at the *Revue nègre*, which put on shows by Sydney Bechet and Josephine Baker. In the same year he wrote *Jazz*, the first book in French on its subject (Paris: Jean-Michel Place, 1986). In 1928 he helped arrange the exhibition of pre-Columbian art in the Marsan Pavilion (Museum of Decorative Arts), and P. **Rivet** then invited him join the staff of the *Musée du Trocadéro*, where he was put in charge of the musical organology section (subsequently called the section of musical ethnology and then ethnomusicology). He heard Stravinsky's *Rite of Spring* at its premiere in 1913, and in 1931 published *Stravinsky* (Paris: Riedler). He took part in the Dakar-Djibouti expedition in 1933–1934 and in **Griaule**'s Sahara-Sudan expedition in 1935. In 1936 he published *L'Origine des instruments de musique: Introduction ethnologique à l'histoire de la musique instrumentale* [*The Origins of Musical Instruments: Ethnological*

Introduction to the History of Instrumental Music] (Paris: Jean-Michel Place, 1980). He was appointed research director at the CNRS in 1941. In 1947 he travelled to the Kissi of Guinea accompanied by his wife, the ethnologist D. **Paulme**, and then carried out research among the Baga of Guinea and the Bété of the Ivory Coast. He continued as a director of his section at the *Musée du Trocadéro* until his retirement.

Rivière, Georges-Henri (1897–1985)

Georges-Henri Rivière started out as a jazz pianist at the *Boeuf sur le toit*, a cabaret in Paris frequented by artists. At the same time he acted as secretary to D. Weill, the great Parisian collector who founded *Les cahiers d'arts* and *Documents*, two important avant-garde periodicals of the day. It was through his work for these publications that Rivière met G. Bataille and A. **Métraux**, who invited him to take part in the organization of the major exhibition of pre-Columbian art held in Paris in 1928. In 1929 P. **Rivet**, appointed in the previous year as director of the *Musée d'ethnographie du Trocadéro*, took him on as his deputy even though he held no university degree. He then studied under E. **Nordenskjöld**, whose Museum of Gothenberg was considered the most modern of its kind in the world, and profited from this experience back in France when he set about the reorganization of the *Musée du Trocadéro*. He also played a role in the establishment of the *Musée de l'Homme*, which opened in 1937, and in the same year founded the *Musée des Arts et Traditions populaires* (Museum of Popular Crafts and Traditions). For the latter museum he chose not to adhere to evolutionist or strictly artistic conceptions, instead presenting the collections along the environmentalist lines set out by **Boas**. In 1966 he established the *Centre d'ethnologie française* (Centre for French Ethnology) as a CNRS laboratory, organized the fieldwork training of genera-tions of students, and directed important research on rural France, especially in the Aubrac region.

Bastide, Roger (1898–1974)

A specialist on the Black Amerindian world, R. Bastide gained an *agrégation* in philosophy in 1924 before turning to anthropology. Because of the prestige of the *Ecole de sociologie française*, it was to France that Brazil looked for assistance with its newly founded universities, and Bastide was appointed professor at São Paolo in 1938 (others who moved to Brazil include the historian F. Braudel, the geographer F. Perroux and C. **Lévi-Strauss**). Bastide exerted considerable influence on the Brazilian intellectuals among whom he lived until 1952. A specialist in religious sociology, he took a deep interest as soon as he arrived in São Paolo in problems of syncretism between Western and African civilizations on the American continent, and addressed this question in *Le Candomblé de Bahia, rite Nagô* [*The Candomblé of Bahia: A Nagô Ritual*] (Paris, The Hague: Mouton, 1958), in *Les Religions africaines au Brésil* [*African Religions in Brazil*] (Paris: PUF, 1960), and in *Les Amériques noires* [*The Black Americas*] (Paris: Payot, 1967). Bastide, interested by the specific features of pathological conditions, was among the first ethnologists to note the healing powers of trance and one of the founders of ethnopsychiatry in his *Sociologie des maladies mentales* [*Sociology of Mental Illnesses*] (Paris: Flammarion, 1965). In 1951 he was made director of social psychiatry studies in Section VI of the EPHE, and after successfully defending his thesis in 1958 he was appointed to the newly created chair of social and religious ethnology at the Sorbonne. In 1959 he took charge of the ethnography-ethnology section of the journal *l'Année Sociologique*, and in 1966 founded the *Laboratoire de sociologie de la connaissance* (Laboratory of the Sociology of Consciousness) at the CNRS.

Dumézil, Georges (1898–1987)

In creating a new approach to mythologies, G. Dumézil chose to follow the path opened up by **Fustel de Coulanges** rather than developing the ideas of Durkheim and *l'Année Sociologique*. Another enriching influence was the ushering in of comparative grammar and linguistics in France by M. Bréal, whose work was carried forward by F. de Saussure (1857–1913) and A. Meillet (1866–1936), and later by E. Benveniste (1902–1976) and Dumézil himself. Under Meillet's supervision, Dumézil gained a doctorate in 1924 with an analytical thesis on analogies between legends, using as examples the production and consumption of ambrosia in India and of beer among the Germanic peoples. The existence of family resemblances between the Greek, Persian and Sanskrit languages led Dumézil, in the late 1920s, to devote his efforts to the search for a common 'Indo-European' cultural origin which could be discovered by means of semantic comparison. In 1938 it occurred to him that rather than looking for lexical and semantic connections between languages, their structural similarities could be used to discover unchanging characteristics of apparently dissimilar phenomena. Thus the three social groups present in India – the Brahmans (priests), the Râjanya (warriors) and the Viaçya (cultivators) – are matched in ancient Rome by the priests of Jupiter (sovereign authority), Mars (war) and Quirinus (the people), with each type of priest offering a common sacrifice to his particular god. Populations migrating from India to Europe would have shared an ideology which stated that the continued existence of the world depends on the harmonious and hierarchized interaction of three functions: Mitra-Varuna, Indra and the Açvins among the Indo-Iranians; Jupiter, Mars and Quirinus among the Romans; and Odin, Thor and Freyr among the Scandinavians.

Responding to the criticism that what he purported to find was in fact a quasi-natural structure present in all human societies, Dumézil asserted that only Indo-Europeans were conscious of this and that they formed a general framework for social and religious ideology, while Asia, for example, developed a bipartite perspective. After spending some time searching for the vestiges of an earlier, really existing social organization lying behind the tripartite structure he had identified (1930), he finally chose instead to see that structure merely as a doctrine, one still present in petrified form in the Indian caste system. He introduced the notion of transformation, stating that in comparative mythology the search for a single, primitive version of a myth is always fruitless as variants would have existed at any time in its development, an insight which later influenced the work of **Lévi-Strauss**. Dumézil had a knowledge of about forty languages and made a specialism of those of the Caucasian family; among those he rediscovered were Lazes and Oubykh in Anatolia, which disappeared soon after he recorded their existence. From 1948 to 1968 he taught in the religious studies section of the EPHE and then occupied the chair in Indo-European civilization at the *Collège de France*. He also taught at North American universities, including Princeton and Chicago. In 1978 he was elected to the *Académie Française*.

Griaule, Marcel (1898–1956)

Marcel Griaule was the first professor of ethnology in France, the 'discoverer' of the Dogon, and the originator of a specific style of ethnography and ethnology. He first studied mathematics, but then interrupted his education to serve as an aeronautical volunteer in the First World War. He returned to France and obtained a *licence ès lettres* in 1929 while also attending lectures by **Mauss** and **Cohen**. In 1927 he gained a qualification in Amharic, and in 1928–1929 travelled to Ethiopia (then called Abyssinia) on his first mission. He brought back a number of articles of scientific importance and translated a scholarly work, *Le livre de recettes d'un dabtara abyssin* [*The Formula Book of an Abyssinian Dabtara*] (Institut d'ethnologie), followed in 1934 by a travelogue, *Les flambeurs d'hommes* [*The People-Burners*] (Paris: Berg International, 1991). He was appointed deputy secretary-general of the Society of Africanists when it was founded in 1931. Then **Rivet**, taking advantage of the success of the Colonial Exhibition and the holding of the first congress of the International African Institute, persuaded the *Chambre des députés* to pass a law financing the Dakar–Djibouti mission, which was to cross fifteen African countries from west to east. Griaule led the mission and was joined by E. Lutten, A. **Schaeffner**, D. Lifchitz, M. **Leiris**, J. Mouchet, Larget and P.-H. Chombart de Lauwe. It departed from Paris in May 1931 and set sail for home from Djibouti on 7 February 1933, having recorded thirty languages and amassed a collection of 300 manuscripts and 3,500 artefacts. The review *Minotaure* devoted the whole of its second issue to a major exhibition of these findings at the *Musée du Trocadéro*. In 1936 Griaule became deputy director of the *Laboratoire d'ethnologie* (Ethnology Laboratory). He published *Jeux et divertissements abyssins* [*Abyssinian Games and Entertainments*] (Paris: Institut d'ethnologie, 1934), made representations to the League of Nations in favour of Ethiopia after the Italian invasion, and wrote a militant work on the subject: *Le Peau de l'ours* [*The Bearskin*] (Paris: Grasset, 1936). However, for all his continuing interest in Abyssinia, he devoted most of his attention at this time to a study of the Dogon (who since have been investigated by five generations of ethnologists). In 1935 Griaule led the Sahara–Sudan mission, whose members included N. Gordon, S. de Ganay, D. **Paulme** and D. Lifchitz, and in 1936–1937 he was accompanied by G. **Dieterlen** and others on a Sahara–

Cameroon mission. In 1938 he obtained his doctorate with his major thesis *Masques Dogons* [*Dogon Masks*] (Paris: Institut d'ethnologie, 1938, 1983) and his minor thesis *Jeux Dogons* [*Dogon Games*] (Paris: Institut d'ethnologie, 1938). In 1938–1939 he directed the Niger–Lake No mission, in which J.-P. **Lebeuf** took part. He was called up in July 1940 and served until the following September, for which he was decorated with the *Croix de Guerre*. In late 1940 he assumed responsibility for ethnology teaching at the *Institut d'ethnologie*, and in 1941 took over at INALCO from Cohen, who was forced to resign because of the Vichy anti-Semitic laws. In 1942 he was appointed to the first ethnography chair at the Sorbonne.

In 1946–1947 Griaule directed another mission, which aimed to study Dogon and Bambarra cosmologies and Bozo and Kouroumba societies. It was during this mission that Ogotemmêli, designated as a Dogon sage, spent thirty-four days in conversation with him, passing on his knowledge of Dogon cosmology and mythology. The transcription of his narrative is published under the title *Dieu d'eau* [*The Water God*] (Paris: Fayard, 1948). Written in a popular style, the book shatters any preconceptions that African metaphysical notions are unsophisticated, demonstrating that Dogon myths equal those of the Greeks in their richness. For Griaule, it is the determining force of myths and symbols which explains the rules of social organization. Thus the basket-maker and the blacksmith reproduce primary mythic events (and thereby unify the male and female principles) in their work. He also explains the joking relations maintained by the Dogon and the Bozo in terms of their metaphysics. From earliest times a 'rule of the twin' prevailed, holding that all beings must be born in twos, and that the exchange of insults between two parties has a cathartic effect because insults cleanse the livers of each from impurities. Social reality can in this way be identified with a system of metaphysical representation which seems to function autonomously, and which illuminates the social world by refraction. What we have here is a supra-social level reminiscent of Durkheim's collective consciousness. Griaule's conception has been criticized as unscientific because it mixes scientific explanation with information properly belonging to the metalanguage he is describing, and it has also been remarked that his approach supposes a homogeneity of myths without proving that Ogotemmêli's version is the only one available. Griaule gathered around him a genuine school dedicated to studying the cosmology of the peoples of the Niger Loop (the Dogon, Bambarra, and Bozo). Today the CNRS's *Laboratoire de Systèmes de pensée en Afrique Noire* (Laboratory of Black African Systems of Thought) continues the study of mythical representations across the whole continent.

Leiris, Michel (1901–1990)

Man of letters and author of *L'Afrique fantôme* [*Phantom Africa*], Michel Leiris first studied chemistry, but a meeting with A. Masson drew him in 1924 into the Surrealist movement, with which he broke in 1929. He took an interest in early psychoanalytical work in France, and was himself in analysis with A. Borel from 1929 to 1935. He studied at the *Institut d'ethnologie* while working as a volunteer at the *Musée du Trocadéro*, accompanied G. Limbour to Egypt, and then worked for the journal *Documents* launched by G. Bataille in 1929. He took part in the Dakar–Djibouti expedition of 1931–1933 as a secretary-archivist, writing a diary of his travels which was published in 1934 as *L'Afrique fantôme* (Paris: Gallimard). This book opened up a new perspective to ethnology, for rather than dispassionate scientific observation it offered a subjective account of a period in the field. In the wake of this success, in 1935, Leiris was placed in

charge of the African section of the *Musée de l'Homme*, which became part of the *Collège de sociologie* after it was initiated by Bataille in 1937. In 1945 he completed a study mission on migration in the Ivory Coast and Ghana as part of the preparation for the abolition of forced labour. On his return to France he became a member of the editorial committee of the newly established journal *Les Temps modernes*, and, while thus continuing his involvement in current debates, he completed the writing of *La Possession et ses aspects théâtraux chez les Ethiopiens du Gondar* [*Possession and its Theatrical Aspects among the Ethiopians of Gondar*] (Paris: Plon, 1958) and of his thesis *La Langue secrète des Dogons de Sanga* [*The Secret Language of the Dogon of Sanga*] (Paris: Institut d'ethnologie, 1948). **Métraux** entrusted him with a mission to the Antilles on behalf of UNESCO, which resulted in *Contact de Civilisation en Martinique et en Guadeloupe* [*Contact between Civilizations in Martinique and Guadeloupe*] (Paris: Gallimard, 1955). From 1950 Leiris took an anti-colonialist position, for example in 'L'Ethnologie devant le colonialisme' ['Ethnology in the Face of Colonialism'], and was one of the 121 signatories of the manifesto against the Algerian War. Alongside his work as an ethnologist he pursued his vocation as a poet and novelist, and his literary work is justly characterized as the 'aestheticization of confession' (1992: 560).

Métraux, Alfred (1902–1963)

Born in Lausanne, Alfred Métraux spent his childhood in Argentina, his adolescence in Switzerland, and his university years in Paris. While still only nineteen or twenty years old he began a correspondence with J. **Cooper**. From 1922 to 1925 he studied at the *École des Chartes*, and then attended INALCO and, as a student of **Mauss**, the EPHE, graduating from both in 1927. In 1928 his doctoral thesis *La Culture matérielle des*

Tupi-Guarani [*The Material Culture of the Tupi-Guarani*] (Paris: Institut d'ethnologie) was accepted, and he moved to Sweden to study museology under E. **Nordenskjöld** at the Museum of Gothenburg, and then to Argentina to found an ethnology institute and museum at the University of Tucuman. He directed the Institute until 1934, when he left Argentina to take part in the Franco-Belgian mission to Easter Island with the archaeologist H. Lavachéry. From 1936 to 1938 Métraux was on the staff of the Museum of Honolulu and taught at the universities of Berkeley and Columbia. In 1939 he was a guest professor at the Bishop Museum of Yale University, and this was followed by periods of fieldwork in Bolivia and, again, in Argentina. In 1940 he received support from the Bishop Museum to work with J. Dollard and L. Bloomfield at the Institute of Human Relations. In 1941 he joined the Bureau of American Ethnology of the Smithsonian Institution and made a major contribution to *Handbook of South American Indians* (7 vols). Métraux returned to Europe in 1945 and worked for international organizations until 1962. He was a member of the UN Social Affairs Unit as of 1946 and a permanent member of UNESCO's Social Sciences Department (established in 1947) from 1950. In 1947–1948 he worked in the Amazon region and in 1948–1950 directed UNESCO research in Haiti, and in 1954 he began a study of the migration of the Aymara and Quechua Indians of Peru and Bolivia. On his return to France in 1961 he was made director of studies in Section VI of the EPHE, where he taught young Americanists. He committed suicide in 1963.

Mus, Paul (1902–1969)

Paul Mus was born in Bourges but spent his youth in Vietnam, where his parents were teachers. He returned to France to attend courses given by S. Lévy and M. **Granet**. He became the first graduate of the *Institut d'ethnologie* in 1925, joined the EFEO and was then appointed director of studies at the EPHE. In 1944, at the age of forty-two, he was sent by General de Gaulle to Vietnam, and parachuted himself into the country to organize its resistance against the Japanese occupation. In 1946 he published an account of his experiences in his book *Le Viêt Nam chez lui* [*Vietnam at Home*] (Paris: Le Seuil, 1946), and in the same year was made a professor at the *Collège de France*. From 1949 he campaigned for the independence of colonized peoples in the pages of *Témoignage Chrétien*, and wrote two books on this theme: *Viêt Nam: Sociologie d'une guerre* [*Vietnam: Sociology of a War*] (Paris: Le Seuil, 1952) and *Le Destin de l'Union Française: De l'Indochine à l'Afrique* [*The Destiny of the French Union: From Indochina to Africa*] (Paris: Le Seuil, 1954). Although politically active, Mus remained above all a scholar, and proved his credentials as such in *Barabudur: Esquisse d'une histoire du bouddhisme fondée sur la critique archéologique des textes* [*Barabudur: Sketch for a History of Buddhism Founded on Archaeological Textual Criticism*] (Paris, Hanoi: EFEO, 1935), and *La Lumière sur les six voies: Tableau de la transmigration bouddhique* [*Light on the Six Tracks: Tableau of Buddhistic Transmigration*] (Paris, Hanoi: EFEO, 1939). He moved closer to the sociology of G. Gurvitch in the last years of his life, as attested in his article 'La Sociologie de Georges Gurvitch et l'Asie' ['The Sociology of Georges Gurvitch and Asia'] in *Cahiers internationaux de Sociologie* (1967), based on a seminar held in 1964–1965.

Verger, Pierre (1902–1996)

Born into an upper middle-class printing family, Pierre Verger developed an interest in photography in 1932 which soon became a passion. On returning in 1933 from a visit to the USSR and Oceania he made the acquaintance of G.-H. **Rivière**. In 1934 he accompanied a *Paris-Soir* journalist on a reporting trip round the world as a photographer, and then P. **Rivet** employed him to direct the photographic laboratory at the *Musée du Trocadéro*. In 1935–1936 he took photographs in Black Africa and the Antilles, and in 1940 accepted the post of photographer for the general government of Western Africa at Dakar, where he met T. Monod, who had just established IFAN. In 1942–1943 he built up a collection of ethnographic documents in Peru and Bolivia for the Museum of Lima. As of 1946 he was engaged in research on the Candomblé and on the Orisha and Vodoun cults in Bahia in Brazil, and then on the Xango. In 1949 he was awarded a bursary by the *Ecole française d'Afrique* to fund a stay in Benin investigating the origins of African cults practised in the New World. Verger was initiated into the voodoo cult in Ketou in Benin, and became one of the high priests of Brazilian Candomblé. He was awarded a junior and then a senior research position at the CNRS in 1962 and 1972 respectively. In 1966 he completed his doctoral thesis *Flux et reflux de la traite des nègres entre le golfe du Bénin et Bahia de Todos los Santos (XVIIe au XIXe siècle)* [*Ebb and Flow in the Slave Trade between the Gulf of Benin and Bahia de Todos los Santos from the Seventeenth to the Nineteenth Centuries*] (Paris: Mouton) which studies the to-and-fro movement of Yoruba cults and traditions in depth. From 1977 to 1980 Verger was a professor at the universities of Ifé (Nigeria) and Bahia. He died on 11 February 1996 in the poor district of Salvador Bahia which he had made his home.

Dieterlen, Germaine (née Teissier du Cross, 1903–1999)

Born into a wealthy Protestant family, Germaine Dieterlen studied in Section V of the EPHE under **Mauss**. She then worked as a volunteer at the *Musée du Trocadéro*, and also took part in **Griaule**'s fourth and fifth missions in 1936–1937 and 1938–1939. Back in France she published 'Le Duge, signe historique d'alliance chez les Dogons de Sanga' ['The Duge as Historic Marriage Token among the Dogon of Sanga'] in the *Bulletin du Comité d'Etudes Historiques et Scientifiques de l'A.O.F* in 1938. In September 1940 she graduated from the EPHE after her examiners M. Mauss, L. Massignon and L. Homburger had passed her thesis *Les âmes des Dogons* [*The Souls of the Dogon*] (Paris: Institut d'ethnologie, 1941). She went on to gain a *licence ès lettres* in 1941 and qualifications in Amharic (1943) and Peul (1944). In 1946 she took part in Griaule's sixth mission, extending his research on Dogon cosmology to the Bambara and the Bozo. In 1949 she gained a doctorate with her major thesis *Essai sur la religion Bambara* [*Essay on Bambara Religion*] (Paris: PUF, 1951) and her minor thesis *Documents pour l'étude de la personne chez les Soudanais* [*Documents for the Study of the Sudanese Understanding of the Person*]. Her major thesis eschewed the ideology of the state (Ségou and Hamdallahi) and the effects of colonization to focus on her discovery of Bambara culture, an achievement comparable with Griaule's work on the Dogon. Dieterlen revealed a Bambara cosmology based on the principle of a creator-god, from whose being souls and the major deities are produced by scission. Pamda is the male principle of germination and the sun, and generates his wife, Moussa Koroni, who represents the earth. The technical arts are born of conflict between Pamda and Moussa Koroni, caused by infidelity and jealousy. Then Faro (the river) does battle with Pamda and robs him of his divine status, thereby inflicting sickness and death on the world. The book also shows that Faro, who becomes the elder deity, insinuates himself into all of life's activities – procreation, initiation, marriage, farm labour, and that the Bambara make use of a system of symbols covering all parts of the body. Dieterlen further studies rites (of birth, naming, etc.), techniques of divination, and individual and family cults, and describes the Komo brotherhoods.

Research director at the CNRS in 1950 and director of Black African religious studies at Section II of the EPHE in 1956, Dieterlen built on Griaule's research into African systems of representation after his death in 1956. In 1961 she was appointed to head the Niger Loop RCP of the CNRS, which provided a base for almost all of the younger generation of French Africanists. From 1966 to 1973 she made a film cycle with Jean **Rouch** on the Sigui ceremonial cycle of the Dogon (which takes place only every sixty years), doubtless the most important cinematic document of an African religious system ever made. From 1962 to 1972 she was head of the *Groupe de recherche sur les religions d'Afrique Noire* (Research Group on Black African Religions) at the CNRS–EPHE, which in 1974 became the *Laboratoire de systèmes de pensée en Afrique Noire* (Laboratory of Black African Systems of Thought). In 1971 she organized a seminal colloquium entitled *La Notion de personne en Afrique Noire* [*The Notion of the Person in Black Africa*] which was published by the CNRS in 1973. She was secretary-general of the Society of Africanists from 1957 to 1974 and held an important position at the International African Institute (see Lewis, 2000). Germaine Dieterlen died on 13 November 1999.

Gessain, Robert (1907–1986)

Robert Gessain qualified as a doctor of medicine in 1932, and in 1932–1933 enrolled as a student at the *Institut d'ethnologie* while working as a volunteer at the *Musée du Trocadéro*. In 1934 he completed his military service in Morocco, and brought home a number of artefacts for the museum. He took part in the 'Pourquoi pas?' mission of 1934–1935 to the Angmassalik Inuit in Greenland (photography, pathology, genetics, anthropometry) led by P.-E. **Victor**, and also in a second mission there in 1936–1937. He then founded the *Société des explorateurs et voyageurs français* (Associ-

ation of French Explorers and Voyagers) while a senior lecturer at the EPHE, and in 1937–1938 carried out research among the Tepehua in Mexico. From 1942 to 1945 Gessain was secretary-general of the 'population' team of A. Carrel's *Fondation française pour l'étude des problèmes humains* (French Foundation for the Study of Human Problems), and in 1945–1946 he was a sectional head at the INED directed by A. Sauvy. In 1945 he began to take an interest in psychoanalysis, which he later practised for a few years. He belonged to the group which broke with the International Psychoanalysis Association to found the Freudian School of Paris in 1953. Having gone to Zaire in 1955 to present J. **Rouch**'s film *Les Maîtres fous* [*Mad Masters*], he travelled on to Kedougou and Youkounkoun in Senegal, where his wife M. de Lestrange had worked immediately after the war. He too made this fieldwork territory his own and made frequent trips there between 1961 and 1978, having chosen it as one of three isolated communities for a multidisciplinary and comparative study he had in mind (the other two being Angmassalik in Greenland and Plozévet in Brittany). He obtained a science doctorate in 1957 and was made deputy director of the *Musée de l'Homme* in 1958. In 1959 he became a member of De Gaulle's newly created *Comité consultatif de la recherche scientifique* (Consultative Committee for Scientific Research), and founded the *Centre de recherche anthropologique* (Centre for Anthropological Research) at the CNRS. In 1960 he was appointed professor at the *Musée d'histoire naturelle*, and from 1968 to 1970 was also director of the *Musée de l'Homme*.

Lebeuf, Jean-Paul (1907–1994)

After attending lectures given by **Mauss**, Jean-Paul Lebeuf was recruited by the *Caisse nationale de la recherche* (National Research Fund) (which later became the CNRS) as its first ethnologist in 1935. He took part in the

Sahara–Cameroon mission of 1936–1937 and made investigations of populations in Chad, most notably the Fali. While studying the Sao, an extinct civilization bordering the River Chari, he undertook an archaeological dig which unearthed a number of artefacts. In 1938–1939 he took part in the Lebaudy–Griaule mission to Northern Cameroon and the region around Lake Iro in Chad. In 1941 he prepared and organized the *Exposition archéologique du Tschad* (Chad Archaeological Exhibition), for which he was criticized after the war. However, we know from G. Calame-Griaule that Lebeuf was part of the Le Dantec Resistance network and was imprisoned at Fresnes as a result. In 1943 he married A. Masson-Detourbet and set off with her in 1947 on an archaeological and ethnological mission which marked the beginnings of ethno-archaeology in France. He was an adviser to the World Health Organization (1953–1955), and permanent secretary of the Inter-African Committee for the Social Sciences (1956–1959). In 1959 he completed his major thesis *L'Habitation des Fali: Montagnards du Cameroun septentrional* [*Dwellings of the Fali: A Mountain People of Northern Cameroon*] (Paris: Hachette, 1961) and his minor thesis *Le Gisement Sao-Kotoko de Makari (Cameroun Septentrional): Archéologie et ethnographie* [*The Sao-Kotoko Deposits of Makari (Northern Cameroon): Archaeology and Ethnography*] (Paris: CNRS). He participated in the setting up an RCP of the CNRS on the Niger Loop, established his own team in 1965, and organized one of the first international colloquia on African archaeology in 1966. Lebeuf was also the director of the *Institut national pour les Sciences humaines* (National Institute for the Social Sciences) from its founding in Fort-Lamy (now Ndjamena) in 1961 until 1972.

Victor, Paul-Emile (1907–1995)
Born in Geneva, Paul-Emile Victor graduated from the *École Centrale* in Lyon, and then gained a science degree while also following **Mauss**'s teaching. He persuaded J.-B. Charcot to let his boat be used to convey a team, led by Victor himself and comprising F. Mattwer, M. Perez and R. **Gessain**, to the Inuit of Angmassalik in 1934 and then collect them a year later. The expedition collected 3,500 artefacts and recorded 700 legends. In 1936 Victor took charge of the French Trans-Greenland expedition, in which R. Gessain, M. Perez, E. Knuth and he crossed Greenland from east to west, and after the others returned home he spent a further fourteen months with an Inuit family. He fled France soon after the Occupation and joined the US Air Force, and in 1947 he established the *Expéditions polaires françaises* (French Polar Expeditions), which he directed until his retirement in 1976. He then settled on a small French Polynesian island which he had acquired, and it was there that he died.

Tillion, Germaine (born 1907)
Germaine Tillion graduated from the *Institut d'ethnologie* in 1932, and in 1934 undertook a mission to Algeria with T. Rivière for the *Musée de l'Homme*. With funding from the Rockefeller Foundation and then from the CNRS (1941), and on Massignon's advice, she began postgraduate research on the Aurès under **Mauss**'s supervision. In 1942 she obtained the Berber degree from INALCO, but her association with the Resistance network of the *Musée de l'Homme* led to her being denounced by the Abbé Alesch, and she was arrested and deported in 1943. She survived the war, however, and resumed her work at the museum, where she found that the Gestapo had destroyed her ethnographic papers. She moved from the ethnography section to the modern history section of the CNRS, and researched on war crimes there until 1954. Then, at Massignon's suggestion, she placed herself at the disposal of the general government of Algeria. In 1958 she was chosen as director

of studies in Maghreb ethnography in Section VI of the EPHE, and soon after took charge of the 48th RCP on the oral literature of the Maghreb. She retired in 1977. Without doubt her best-known book is *Le Harem et ses cousins* [*The Harem and its Cousins*] (Paris: Le Seuil, 1966). After completing a book-length interview with the journalist Jean Lacouture, published as *La Traversée du mal* [*Passage Across Evil*] (Paris: Arléa, 1997), she told the story of her life in *Il était une fois l'ethnographie* [*Ethnography of Yore*] (Paris: Le Seuil, 2000).

Devereux, Georges (1908–1985)

Georges Devereux was born in Romania but followed his Jewish family into exile in France. After studies of Physics in 1926–1927 he qualified in Malay at INALCO in 1931, and also graduated from the *Institut d'ethnologie*. From 1931 to 1935 he was *chargé de mission* (junior researcher) at the *Musée d'histoire naturelle*, and after his completion of a *licence ès lettres* the Rockefeller Foundation awarded him a bursary which enabled him to undertake a mission to the Hopi, Yuma, Cocopa and Mohave Indians in 1932. From 1932 to 1950 he made five journeys to the Mohave, and in 1933–1934 also visited the Roro, the Papuan Karuama Pygmies and the Moi Sedang of Vietnam. Devereux then emigrated to the USA, where he gained a Ph.D. from Berkeley in 1936. He worked as a sociologist at the Worcester State Hospital from 1939 to 1941, and in 1943 became an assistant professor of ethnology and sociology at Middlesex University and teaching assistant at the University of Wyoming. From 1945 to 1953 he was ethnologist and research director of the Winter Veterans Hospital in Kansas and lecturer at the Topeca Institute of Psychoanalysis, and between 1946 and 1952 he made several studies of American Indians hospitalized because of mental illness. In 1953–1955 he was employed as a researcher by a children's foundation in Philadelphia. He was appointed professor of ethnopsychiatry in the medicine faculty of Temple University in Philadelphia in 1956, took up a lectureship in ethnology at Columbia University in 1959, and then returned to France, where he was made director of studies in Section VI of the EPHE and also worked privately as a psychoanalyst. In 1978 he established the bilingual journal *Ethnopsychiatrica*. When he died in 1985 his wish that his ashes be scattered in the Mohave cemetery in Parker, Arizona, was honoured (Nathan, 1996: 17). A G. Devereux Fund has been deposited with the *Laboratoire d'anthropologie sociale* (Laboratory of Social Anthropology).

Lévi-Strauss, Claude (born 1908)

Born in Brussels, Claude Lévi-Strauss gained an *agrégation* in philosophy. Following a brief period of teaching in France he was appointed by the University of São Paolo on the recommendation of **Bouglé**. Before leaving France he discovered ethnography through lectures at the *Institut d'ethnologie*, and once in Brazil made several expeditions into the interior of the country. He returned to France for the 1940 campaign and was then forced into exile when France was occupied. He took a teaching post at the Free School of Higher Studies at the New School in New York, and remained there as a cultural adviser when the war ended. Lévi-Strauss related his journeys in 1955 in *Tristes tropiques*, an intellectual autobiography and one of the finest books written in the second half of the twentieth century. After having worked as a cultural adviser in New York from 1944 to 1947, he returned to France in 1948 to defend his theses: *Les Structures élémentaires de la parenté* [*The Elementary Structures of Kinship*] (Paris: Mouton, 1948, 1967) and *La Vie familiale et sociale des Indiens Nambikwara* [*Family and Social Life of the Nambikwara Indians*] (Paris: Société des Africanistes, 1948). He succeeded **Leenhardt** at the EPHE in 1950, and in 1958 was elected to the *Collège de France*, where he continued to teach until his retirement in 1983.

It was while following courses given by the linguist R. Jakobson in New York that Lévi-Strauss hit on the idea of a structural anthropology. Structural linguistics, breaking with traditional philology, showed that all languages were structured by basic binary oppositions, such as the difference between *p* and *b* in French. The principles of structural analysis are the move away from the study of conscious phenomena to that of unconscious, underlying structures; the consideration of words not as independent units but in terms of their relations with one another; the introduction of the notion of systems; and the statement of general laws. Lévi-Strauss drew inspiration from these ideas to redefine the objects of anthropological study. For example, anthropology considered the nuclear family as the basic atom of social formations and the polygamous family as an aggregate of monogamous families. As against this idea Lévi-Strauss proposed a theory of marriage founded on the exchange of women. Pointing to the inadequacy of existing hypotheses regarding incest prohibition, he demonstrated that by dint of its universality it constitutes a 'natural' feature of human life. Paradoxically, this 'nature of humanity' is realized in various ways, affecting different categories of people in different societies. Certain societies authorize and even prescribe marriage between a man and his first terminological granddaughter or between cross cousins, while other societies prohibit these practices. These differences fall within the realm of culture. This is why Lévi-Strauss describes incest prohibition as 'the fundamental step by which, through which, and above all in which the passage from nature to culture takes place [. . .] before this step, culture is not yet present, but with it nature ceases to exist'. In fact, this prohibition is not so much a negative rule which forbids something, as a positive rule obliging men to give women in their group to men outside that group, and this circulation of women between groups of men cements social relations. Lévi-Strauss devoted much effort to the description and explanation of such marriage cycles which he classified according to three models of reciprocity: elementary cycles (in which the structure designates an individual's possible spouses in a positive manner); semi-complex cycles (in which the structure forbids marriage with individuals belonging to many social groups or clans); and complex cycles (in which prohibition is defined in terms of degree of proximity).

These are the merest outlines of a huge body of work which also sets out to find solutions to a number of other problems, such as those of dualism and totemism. M. Hénaff remarks that when Lévi-Strauss wrote *Le Totémisme aujourd'hui* [*Totemism Today*] (Paris: PUF, 1961) as an introduction to *La Pensée sauvage* [*Savage Thought*] (Paris: Plon, 1962), 'the opportunity arose to develop (or dramatize) a question analogous to the one treated by grappling with the enigma of incest prohibition in the opening pages of the *Elementary Structures of Kinship*, the only difference being that incest presented a real problem, while the problem of totemism was in fact founded on an illusion' (Hénaff, 1991: 313). Following in the footsteps of **Goldenweiser** and **Linton**, Lévi-Strauss deconstructed totemic phenomena, seeing them as arising not from associations between individual clans and a supposed ancestral animal, but as representing no more than an association with the natural world based on distinctive traits and constructed by isomorphism as a way of classifying clans in a common system.

Lévi-Strauss began working on South American mythologies from 1952, and the four volumes of his *Mythologiques* [*Mythologies*] were published between 1964 and 1972. He asserts that commentary on single myths in their own right is never adequate, and that original or authentic myths have never existed. As a mode of thought, any myth is an applied manifestation of the deep structures of the human mind. Finding these structures is the task Lévi-Strauss sets for anthropology in 1950 in his 'Introduction to the Work of Marcel Mauss' (Mauss, 1950). In *Mythologiques* he analyses myths not in isolation, but in terms of their relations to one another, with the Bororo myth serving as a yardstick for the 813 myths described in the four volumes of the work. Each myth is made up of variants of basic elements which can be grouped as motifs or 'mythemes' within a larger system. The function of myths is to integrate otherwise incomprehensible problems and contradictions within a logical and intelligible structure.

Lévi-Strauss returned to the field of kinship, which he had never entirely forsaken, in his final years of teaching (1976–1982). He left aside elementary systems of marriage with unilinear filiation to concentrate on 'house societies', a term he defined during the course of a lengthy teaching programme ranging across Indonesia, Melanesia, Polynesia, Micronesia, Madagascar and Africa.

Holder of honorary doctorates from numerous universities, recipient of the Gold Medal of the CNRS, a member of the *Académie française* (1973) and of several academies outside France, Lévi-Strauss was a thinker of real intellectual distinction who was also a great organizer. With F. Braudel he founded the celebrated Section VI of the EPHE (now the EHESS), and was secretary-general of the International Council for the Social Sciences within UNESCO, a body in which he played an important role in the early 1950s. He also founded two anthropology journals, *L'Homme* and *Etudes Rurales*, and set up the *Laboratoire d'anthropologie sociale* (Laboratory of Social Anthropology), which is still one of the world's most prestigious research centres.

Lévy, Paul (born 1909)
Paul Lévy was born in Hanoi but left Indo-

china to take preparatory classes for the *Ecole coloniale* at the *Lycée Louis-le-Grand*. In 1929–1930 he studied law while at the same time beginning studies of Chinese language and Khmerian art. From 1932 he took courses in Sanskrit given by S. Lévy, as well as attending lectures by **Mauss**, **Granet** and **Leenhardt**. In 1934 he graduated from the *Institut d'ethnologie* and in 1936 gained a *licence ès lettres*. In 1937 he was employed by the EFEO, in 1938 he founded the *Institut indochinois pour l'étude de l'homme* (Indo-chinese Institute for the Study of Mankind) with P. Huard and Coèdes, and in 1939 he established the *Musée d'ethnographie d'Hanoï* (Ethnographical Museum of Hanoi). Lévy completed his theses in 1943: *Recherches préhistoriques dans la région de M'lu Prey, Cambodge* [*Research into the Prehistory of the M'lu Prey Region of Cambodia*] (major thesis, Hanoi, EFEO) and *Vocabulaire Français-Kuy* [*French-Kuy Vocabulary*] (minor thesis, Hanoi, EFEO). He was interned for a brief period during the Japanese occupation, and was director of the EFEO from 1947 to 1950. In 1948 he was elected to a lectureship on Malayo-Polynesian religions in Section V of the EPHE, and on the death of E. Mestre he took over as its director of studies for Southeast Asian religious studies. He was also president of Section V from 1971 to 1974, the year of his retirement. As well as of numerous articles, Lévy was the author of *Histoire du Laos* [*A History of Laos*] (1974).

Paulme, Denise (1909–1998)
Denise Paulme was born in Paris to parents whose work for a shipping company sometimes took them to Africa. She studied for a law degree, which included a certificate from the *Institut d'ethnologie*. She soon became enraptured by **Mauss**'s lectures at the *Institut* and developed an interest in 'primitive law'. When she made Mauss's acquaintance he suggested she join the team

of volunteers helping **Rivet** reorganize the *Musée d'ethnographie du Trocadéro*. In 1932 she graduated from the *Institut d'ethnologie* and in the same year finished her law degree. In 1935 she took part in **Griaule**'s Sahara-Sudan mission, which brought together S. de Ganay, Mme Lazareff (formerly Gordon), E. Lutten and A. **Schaeffner**. At the end of the mission the team set sail from 'Sanga', leaving behind Paulme and D. Lifchitz to begin a separate eight-month mission funded by the Rockefeller Foundation. In 1940 Paulme completed a law thesis entitled *L'Organisation sociale chez les Dogons* [*Dogon Social Organization*] (Jean-Michel Place, 1988). After the war, having written several articles on the Dogon, she travelled to Guinea to study the Kissi and the Baga (*Les Gens du riz* [*The Rice People*] (Paris: Plon, 1954)), and then became interested in the Bété of the Ivory Coast (*Une société de Côte d'Ivoire hier et aujourd'hui: les Bété* [*An Ivory Coast Society Then and Now: The Bété*] (Paris: Mouton, 1962)). She was curator of the Museum of Oceanian and African Crafts (*Les Civilisations africaines* [*African Civilizations*] (Paris: PUF, 1953); *Sculptures de l'Afrique Noire* [*Black African Sculpture*] (Paris: PUF, 1956)), and was appointed director of studies in Section VI of the EPHE in 1957. From then on Paulme's research focused on three main areas: the condition of women (she edited *Femmes d'Afrique Noire* [*Women of Black Africa*] (Paris, Mouton, 1966)); the question of age sets, on which she organized a major symposium in 1969 (*Classes et associations d'âge en Afrique de l'Ouest* [*Age Sets and Systems in West Africa*] (Paris: Plon, 1971)); and the transcription and study of African tales (*La Mère dévorante: Essai sur la morphologie des contes africains* [*The Devouring Mother: Essay on the Morphology of African Tales*] (Paris: Gallimard, 1976, 1986)). Paulme was also notable as a translator into French of works by Anglophone anthropologists.

Leroi-Gourhan, André (1911–1986)

After providing his own education and making his own preparations for the *baccalauréat*, André Leroi-Gourhan joined the group of volunteers working with **Mauss** at the *Musée du Trocadéro*, before it became the *Musée de l'Homme*. In 1931 he gained an arts degree and graduated in Russian and then in Chinese (1933) from INALCO. In 1934 he contributed several chapters (on man and nature, European man, etc.) for the seventh volume of the *Encyclopédie Française* [*French Encyclopaedia*], entitled 'The Life of the Mind'. He was then sent by the *Institut d'ethnologie* to Japan, where he lived with his wife from 1936 to 1938 before being engaged by the CNRS. He organized in 1943, a major exhibition of Chinese art and published *Documents pour l'art comparé d'Eurasie septentrionale* [*Documents for the Comparative Study of Northern Eurasian Art*] (Paris: Art et Histoire) and *L'Homme et la matière* [*Mankind and Matter*]. The latter work, a return to the study of technology, was published in two volumes: *Evolution et technique* [*Evolution and Technique*] (Paris: Albin-Michel, 1971) appeared in 1943, and *Milieu et techniques* [*Milieu and Techniques*] (Paris: Albin-Michel, 1973) in 1945. Leroi-Gourhan's starting assumption is that man differs from animals in his ability to manipulate his environment, and he proposes a classification of techniques as either primary or based on those that are primary, and then uses this distinction together with the concept of tendencies to explain how techniques come to be invented and then diffused. After the war Leroi-Gourhan was decorated with the *Croix de Guerre* and the *Médaille de la Résistance*. He applied the methods he had developed to his own material in his thesis *Archéologie du Pacifique Nord: Matériaux pour l'étude des relations entre les peuples riverains d'Asie et d'Amérique* [*Archaeology of the North Pacific: Materials for the Study of Relations between Riparian Peoples of Asia and America*]

(Institut d'ethnologie, 1946), in which he uses painstaking analysis of variations in such objects as blades and harpoons around the Baring Sea to give an account of the movement of artefacts and the exchange of techniques resulting from the migrations of Inuit and Indian populations in Asia and America. He was appointed deputy director of the *Musée de l'Homme*, and in 1947 founded the *Centre de formation à la recherche ethnologique* (CFRE) (Centre for Teaching in Ethnological Research) which for a long time remained the only place in France where ethnologists could learn their trade. While a professor at the University of Lyon Leroi-Gourhan commenced excavations in the Furtin Cavern and invented the horizontal dissection method. He reconstructed the lives of prehistoric hunter–gatherers, whereas hitherto researchers had contented themselves with gathering artefacts of manifest interest. In 1948 he began excavations at Arcy-sur-Cure, where he also started a school. In 1954 he completed a science thesis and in 1956 obtained the ethnology chair at the Sorbonne, succeeding Marcel **Griaule**. In 1964 he began work at Pincevent and published *La Geste et la parole* [*Gesture and Word*] (Paris: Albin-Michel, 1964) and then *La Mémoire et les rythmes* [*Memory and Rhythms*] (Paris: Albin-Michel, 1965). He took a global view of human development. Particularly important was his theory of the emergence of hominids, drawing on connections between the ability to stand upright and use hands freely and the position of the cranium on the vertebral column. In 1969 Leroi-Gourhan was elected to the prehistory chair at the *Collège de France*.

Haudricourt, André Georges
(1911–1996)
André Georges Haudricourt studied simultaneously at the *Faculté des lettres* (Literature Faculty) and at the *Institut national d'agronomie* (National Agricultural Institute). After

qualifying as an agricultural engineer he was put in charge of a mission to the Soviet Union of 1933–1935 on the advice of M. **Mauss** and A. Chevalier. From 1939 to 1945 he was a research assistant at Chevalier's *Laboratoire d'agronomie coloniale* (Laboratory of Colonial Agriculture). In 1943 he and L. Hédin published *L'Homme et les Plantes Cultivées* [*Mankind and Cultivated Plants*] (published in a new edition by Métailié in 1987), the first French book on ethnobotany. He qualified from INALCO in Siamese, Thai, Melanesian, Oceanian and Laotian between 1944 and 1947. In 1947 he was employed by the EFEO as a librarian based in Hanoi. In 1949 Haudricourt, in collaboration with M. Juilland, wrote his *Essai pour une histoire structurale du phonétisme français* [*Essay on the Structural History of French Phonetics*]. At the CNRS he was given a junior and then a senior research position in 1951 and 1955, and in 1960 was made a research director.

Dumont, Louis Charles Jean (1911–1998)
Born at Salonika in Greece, Louis Dumont emigrated at a young age to France, where he abandoned his studies before gaining a degree. In 1937 he found work as a secretary at the recently founded *Musée national des arts et traditions populaires* (National Museum of Popular Crafts and Traditions), directed by **Rivière**. Developing an interest in the new world he had discovered, he began attending lectures by **Mauss** and resolved to go back to university. At this time he published an article on the manufacture of clogs in Sologne. From 1939 to 1945 he was detained as a prisoner of war in Germany, working first on a farm and then in a Hamburg factory. He learnt German and acquired a Sanskrit grammar by post. An employee of Hamburg's municipal library introduced him to Professor Schubring, a specialist in Indian studies, who agreed to give him weekly Sanskrit lessons. After the Liberation he returned to his museum work, and was

appointed assistant curator in 1947 after having gained a *licence ès lettres*. He built up a section on French furniture and worked for the journal *Le mois d'ethnographie française*. He also continued his studies of G. **Dumézil**, whose work he had discovered during his captivity. Rivière sent him as an observer to the Tarasco Festival, on which he wrote his first book *La Tarasque* [*The Tarasco*] in 1951 (Paris: Gallimard). In 1948 he graduated from INALCO in Hindi and Tamil, and with a bursary secured for him by L. Renou was able to travel to India to make a structural comparison between the Aryan North and the Dravidian South. He spent eight months among the Pramalai Kallar in 1948, and then two more among the Tamils in 1949–1950. His priority was rigorous ethnographic data-gathering, but in ordering his research he drew inspiration from the chapters on India in *Structures élémentaires de la parenté* [*Elementary Structures of Kinship*], which **Lévi-Strauss** had given him to read. On his return from India in 1951 Dumont briefly returned to his museum post before obtaining a lectureship at Oxford University through the good offices of Professor von **Fürer-Haimendorf**. He adapted his approach to British social anthropology, and in 1954 gained a doctorate with his thesis *Une sous-caste de l'Inde du Sud: Organisation sociale et religion des Pramalai Kallar* [*A Sub-Caste in Southern India: Religion and Social Organization of the Pramalai Kallar*] (Paris, The Hague: Mouton, 1957). After another stay in India he was appointed director of studies at the EPHE in 1955, and set up the *Centre d'études indiennes* (Centre of Indian Studies) there in 1962, later following this up with a CNRS laboratory devoted to the Indian Subcontinent. He helped Lévi-Strauss realize his aim of establishing a teaching programme in social ethnology in Section VI of the CNRS, and then gave a series of lectures within the newly formed programme, later published as *Introduction à deux théories*

d'anthropologie sociale [*Introduction to Two Theories of Social Anthropology*] (Paris, The Hague: Mouton, 1971) and as *Dravidien et Kariera: L'alliance de mariage dans l'Inde du Sud et en Australie* [*Dravidian and Kariera: The Marriage Contract in Southern India and Australia*] (Paris, The Hague: Mouton, 1975). After the cross-cultural approach of his *La Civilisation indienne et nous* [*Indian Civilization and Our Own*] (Paris: A. Colin, 1964), he offered general reflections on the caste system in *Homo hierarchicus: Le Système des castes et ses implications* [*Homo hierarchicus: The Caste System and its Implications*] (Paris: Gallimard, 1966), which opens by rejecting existing explanations of the phenomenon. Nonetheless, as well as examining the evolution of the caste system, Dumont takes up **Bouglé**'s opposition between pure and impure within a system of graduated elements, and relates this system to a religious order perceived as a global entity encompassing politics and economics. In *Homo aequalis: Genèse et épanouissement de l'idéologie économique* [*Homo aequalis: Genesis and Expansion of Economic Ideology*] (Paris: Gallimard, 1977), he retraces the history of economic thought, seeing in it less a descriptive science than the advent of an ideology. By detaching itself from politics and general morality, economic thought sets individualism against holism, a concept used by Dumont to define an ideology which subordinates the individual to the social whole. This approach gave him the opportunity to consider Marx's work in a new light. His *Essai sur l'individualisme: Une perspective anthropologique sur l'idéologie moderne* [*Essay on Individualism: An Anthropological Perspective on a Modern Ideology*] (Paris: Le Seuil, 1983) broadens the scope of his treatment of emerging individualism to the whole of Western intellectual history. Finally, in 1991 in *Homo aequalis: L'idéologie allemande, France–Allemagne et retour* [*Homo aequalis: German Ideology, From France to Germany and Back*]

(Paris: Gallimard), Dumont uses a comparison between German and French thought as the basis for general reflections on forms of civilization seen in their relationship to the individual, an approach which reflects his conviction that only comparative perspectives permit cultural specificities to emerge.

Soustelle, Jacques (1912–1990)

Born into a working-class family in Montpellier, Jacques Soustelle won a place at the ENS, where he graduated with an *agrégation* in philosophy while following courses given by **Mauss** and **Rivet**. In 1931 he married the Tunis-born ethnologist G. Fagot. From 1932 to 1938 he carried out several missions to Central America, which resulted in the publication of *Mexique, terre indienne* [*Mexico: Land of Indians*] (Paris: Grasset, 1935), *La Famille Tomi-Pame du Mexique central* [*The Tomi-Pame Family of Central Mexico*] (Paris: Institut d'ethnologie), and 'La Culture matérielle des Lacandons' ['The Material Culture of the Lacandon'] (*Journal de la Société des Américanistes*, 1937). On resettling in France he gave lectures at the *Ecole coloniale* and at the *Collège de France*, and was made deputy director of the *Musée de l'Homme*. He was P. Rivet's favourite disciple and like him a member of the *Comité de vigilence des intellectuels antifascistes* (Antifascist Intellectuals' Vigilance Committee). The year 1940 saw the publication of his most important book *La pensée cosmologique des anciens Mexicains* [*Cosmological Thought of the Ancient Mexicans*] (Paris: Hermann), and in the same year he left France to join De Gaulle in London. After a propaganda mission to South America in 1941 he was made a representative of the *Service de l'information* in 1942 and general director of the *Services speciaux* in Algiers in 1943–1944. After the Liberation he became a Commissioner of the Republic in Bordeaux and served successively as Minister of Information (1945), as Minister of the Colonies, as a Deputy (1951–1958), as a director of

studies in Section VI of the EPHE, as Governor-General of Algeria (1955–1956), and then, after a second stint as Minister of Information (1958–1959), he became General Delegate of the *Organisation commune des régions sahariennes* (Joint Organization for the Saharan Region) (1959–1960). A supporter of French Algeria, Soustelle joined the anti-Gaullist military conspiracy in 1962 and, in danger of arrest as an enemy of state security, he fled to Mexico. He wrote on Algeria (1962, 1965) and in 1966 resumed his archaeological work. Like many others he benefited from the events of May 1968, and could return to France in October of that year after a tribunal had dismissed the case against him. He was appointed a director of studies at the EPHE in 1969, represented the Rhone as a Deputy in the National Assembly from 1973 to 1978, and was elected to the *Académie française* in 1983.

Faublée, Jacques (1912–2003)

In the early 1930s Jacques Faublée studied Malgache with J. Paulhan at INALCO while also attending lectures by **Mauss**. He became an assistant curator at the *Musée du Trocadéro* and went on expeditions to the Aurès in 1935, 1936 and 1937. He graduated from the EPHE in 1937 and then worked at the *Musée de l'Homme*. He spent the years from 1938 to 1941 in the field researching the Bara of Madagascar (*JSA*, vol. 11, 1941), and on his return took teaching positions in the ethnography of Madagascar at ENFOM and in Malgache at INALCO in 1943. In 1943 **Griaule** secured a new assistantship attached to the ethnology chair of the University of Paris and offered it to Faublée, who however refused it on the advice of the Dean. He was made a lecturer at the ENA in 1947 and then travelled to Madagascar in 1948 and Algeria in 1950. In 1950 he completed his major thesis *La Cohésion de la société Bara* [*The Cohesion of Bara Society*] and his minor thesis *Les*

Esprits de la vie à Madagascar [*The Life Spirits of Madagascar*]. After working as an assistant curator at the *Musée d'histoire naturelle* he was appointed to a professorship at INALCO in 1953. An important part of Faublée's work was for the journal *l'Année Sociologique*, where he was almost solely responsible for reviewing ethnology publications as of the 1965 issue (which was in fact published in 1967). He used this platform to oppose structuralism during the 1970s.

Callois, Roger (1913–1978)

Born in Reims, Roger Callois enrolled at the ENS and became an assiduous frequenter of Surrealist circles before joining G. Bataille at the *Collège de sociologie*. He obtained an *agrégation* in grammar in 1936 and then, his enthusiasm for ethnology awakened by the teaching of **Mauss**, graduated from the EPHE. After publishing *Les Impostures de l'Art* [*Artistic Impostures*] (1935) and *La Mante religieuse* [*The Praying Mantis*] (1937), he wrote two major works of anthropological thought which secured his reputation while he was still a very young man: *Le Mythe et l'Homme* [*Myth and Man*] (Paris: Gallimard, 1938) and *L'Homme et le sacré* [*Mankind and the Sacred*] (Paris: Gallimard, 1939). Using an evolutionist perspective, he reveals how myths express a solidarity with the universe and how rules and the sacred generally work together to impose lawful conduct, but periodically have the opposite effect of provoking an excess which serves to reinvigorate them. Callois spent the Occupation in Argentina, where he took an active role in founding the *Institut français* in Buenos Aires and edited *Lettres Françaises*. In 1945 the post-Liberation government gave him official responsibility for cultural missions to South America. He was also a senior official at UNESCO and chief editor of *Diogène*. In 1954 he mounted an attack on the structuralism and relativism of **Lévi-Strauss** ('Illusions à rebours' ['Upside Down Illusions'], *La Nouvelle revue française*, 24: 1010–1024; 25: 58–70), who responded uncompromisingly ('Diogène couché' ['Diogenes recumbent'], *Les Temps modernes*, March 1955). Callois was elected to the *Académie française* in 1972. Having progressed from grammar to sociology, he wrote a long poetic reflection on the mineral world and then concluded his oeuvre with a study of the French language, which he described as the only geometric structure he could hold on to.

Bessaignet, Pierre (1914–1989)

Born in Cannes, Pierre Bessaignet gained a philosophy degree in Paris while also following the courses of **Mauss** in Section V of the EPHE and **Leenhardt**'s instruction in Kanak at INALCO. In 1940 he moved to the universities of Yale and then Harvard, where he studied under Schumpeter. He worked on the Marshall Plan and then joined the CNRS in 1949 as a research assistant, carried out research on the Iroquois Indians in South Dakota and elsewhere, and then became a professor at Hobart University in New York State. In 1956 UNESCO gave him the task of establishing a sociology department at the University of Dhaka, where he became a professor and researched on the Bengalis. In 1959 he followed up F. **Barth**'s work in Iran for UNESCO and taught in the newly created Social Sciences Study and Research Institute of Teheran, where he established a department of anthropological studies. Bessaignet accepted a post at the University of Nice in 1965, and set up the *Centre d'étude des relations interethniques* (Study Centre for Interethnic Relations) there as well as holding the ethnology chair from 1967 to 1983.

Cazeneuve, Jean (1915–2002)

Born in Ussel, Jean Cazeneuve enrolled at the ENS in 1937. In 1938 he gained a philosophy degree and also graduated from the *Institut d'ethnologie*. He was a prisoner of war from 1940 to 1945, gained an *agrégation* in philosophy in 1946, and was a *pensionnaire* of the Thiers Foundation from 1946 to 1948. His *La Psychologie du prisonnier de guerre* [*Psychology of the Prisoner of War*] (Paris: PUF) won prizes from the *Académie française* and the *Société des gens de lettres*. He was made a senior lecturer at the University of Alexandria in 1948 and then a researcher at the CNRS in 1950. With funding from the Rockefeller Foundation he travelled to the USA, where he gained an MA from the social relations department set up by Parsons at Harvard University and, in 1954–1955, carried out research in Arizona. In 1957 he was appointed to a more senior research position at the CNRS after having completed his theses (*Les Rites et la condition humaine* [*Ritual and the Human Condition*] (Paris: PUF, 1958) and *La mentalité archaïque* [*The Archaic Mentality*] (Paris: Armand Colin)), and then took up a lectureship at the Sorbonne, before teaching a programme on the 'sociology of the dissemination of information by radio and television' in Section VI of the EPHE (1961). A specialist on the sociology of the mass media, he became professor at the Sorbonne and director-general of the French television station TF1.

Rodinson, Maxime (born 1915)
Born into a modest family 'passionately committed to communism' (1972: 455), Maxime Rodinson had to work as an adolescent, and at the same time his interest in learning and militant beliefs led him to spend time with Muslims in around 1932. He attended lectures by **Mauss** and graduated from INALCO in Turkish (1935), Amharic (1936), written Arabic (1936) and Oriental Arabic (1936). In 1937 he was engaged by the *Caisse nationale de la recherche scientifique* (National Fund for Scientific Research), and in 1939 was sent as a common soldier to the Levant (Syria–Lebanon), then under French mandate. His unit was demobilized in Beirut in 1940, and

he joined the antiquities department of the Free French. In 1943 a journal of the Lebanese-Syrian Communist Party published his first article ('Sociologie durkheimienne et sociologie marxiste' ['Durkheimian Sociology and Marxist Sociology']). In 1947 Rodinson returned to Paris, and from 1948 to 1955 worked in the *Bibliothèque nationale*. During his time there he wrote a number of articles which were published in the *Bulletin de l'IFAN*, and in 1950–1951 he produced the monthly journal *Moyen-Orient* at the request of the French Communist Party. After a period teaching in Section VI of the EPHE he was promoted to director of studies in Section IV (historical and philological sciences) on the retirement of **Cohen**. As a result of disagreements the French Communist Party suspended his membership for one year in 1958 and he subsequently never asked to be readmitted. Rodinson began a period of intense writing activity at this time, beginning with his study 'L'Arabie avant l'Islam' ['Arabia before Islam'] (in *Histoire universelle* [*Universal History*], vol. 2 of the *Pléiade* Encyclopaedia), followed by *Mahomet* [*Mohammed*] (Paris: Le Seuil, 1961, rev. edns 1968 and 1989), *Islam et capitalisme* [*Islam and Capitalism*] (Paris: Le Seuil, 1966), *Marxisme et Monde musulman* [*Marxism and the Muslim World*] (Paris: Le Seuil, 1972), *Les Arabes* [*The Arabs*] (Paris: Le Seuil, 1979), *La Fascination de l'Islam* [*Europe and the mystique of Islam*] (Paris: Le Seuil, 1980), and *De Pythagore à Lénine: Des activismes idéologiques* [*Ideological Activism from Pythagoras to Lenin*] (Paris: Fayard, 1993).

Lot-Falck, Eveline (1918–1974)
Eveline Lot-Falck was the daughter of the mediaevalist F. Lot. After her sister's marriage to the ethnologist Boris Vildé she began visiting the *Musée de l'Homme* while still quite young, and also attended some of **Mauss**'s last lectures. She developed an early interest in Madagascar, but elected to

continue Vildé's work in Central Asia after he was shot for his membership of the Resistance during the war. In 1945 she married R. Falck, who worked at the museology department of the *Musée de l'Homme*, and wrote her first articles. From 1952 she took control of the museum's Asian, Eastern European and Arctic departments. She became the foremost French specialist on shamanism, and in 1963 founded a study group for Northern Eurasia and the Arctic within Section V of the EPHE. She died after a long illness in 1974.

Her most important book was *Les Rites de chasse chez les peuples sibériens* [*Hunting Rituals among Siberian Peoples*] (Paris: Gallimard, 1953), in which she describes the myth systems of the region's various populations, and advances the thesis of a layer of ancient rituals identifying human beings with animals. She discovers a cosmology ruled by an indifferent creator-god and a multitude of spirits, each controlling a part of the natural world (e.g. the sea, mountains, monsters), whose relations with one another are like those of mortal men.

THE SACRIFICED

The Second World War had a profound impact on the development of French ethnology. It was at the *Musée de l'Homme* that the first Resistance network against the German Occupation was formed. But this network was dismantled and most of its members arrested and shot in February 1941. The deaths of Anatole Lewitzky (1902–1942) and Boris Vildé (1908–1941) set back French ethnological research on European subjects a long way. Both had fled Stalinism and found refuge in France, where Vildé became director of the Europe department of the *Musée de l'Homme*. Three important Africanists also lost their lives during the war: Bernard Maupoil (1906–1945), Déborah Lifchitz (or Lifszyc, 1907–1942) and Charles Le Coeur (1903–1944). Maupoil, a student of Mauss, was a colonial administrator in Guinea and Benin (then Dahomey), and won a secondment with IFAN as soon as it was created in 1938. He openly showed his Gaullist sympathies at the time of the attempted Free French landing at Dakar, and was punished by being transferred home to France in 1942. Once repatriated he joined the Resistance, and was arrested and taken to a labour camp in 1944, never to reappear. He is remembered for his important work *La Géomancie de l'ancienne Côte des esclaves* [*Geomancy in the Former Slave Coast*] (Paris: Institut d'ethnologie, 1946, 1988), which describes the *Fa*, a system of divination practised in Benin and related to the Yourouba *Ifa*, and also studies the formulas, legends, songs, prohibitions and prayers connected to each of the 250 signs of this system. In a daring display of diffusionism typical of the period, he presents this system as a West African version of elements of Hindu provenance transmitted via Greece and Egypt. D. Lifchitz, a Ukrainian exile who had taken refuge in France, joined the Dakar–Djibouti expedition directed by **Griaule** in Ethiopia in 1932. She was appointed to a post at the *Musée d'ethnographie du Trocadéro* in 1933, and in 1935 undertook a mission to Dogon territory with **Paulme** funded by the Rockefeller Foundation – the first extended fieldwork in French ethnology. She was arrested in February 1943 and gassed at Auschwitz. Charles Le Coeur, who had been taught by **Malinowski**, became an editor of *l'Année Sociologique* and travelled to the Teda of Tibesti at the suggestion of **Mauss**. In 1939 he completed his doctoral theses: *Le Rite et l'outil: Essai sur le rationalisme social et la pluralité des civilisations* [*The Rite and the Tool: Essay on Social Rationalism and the Plurality of Civilizations*] (Paris: PUF) and *Textes sur la sociologie et l'école au Maroc* [*Texts on the Sociology and Schools of Morocco*] (Paris: PUF, 1939). He was appointed to IFAN and

190

travelled to Dakar in 1942, and in 1944 lost his life fighting as a volunteer in the Allied forces during the Italian Campaign.

SELECT BIBLIOGRAPHY

Adler, A. (1991) 'Griaule, M.', in P. Bonte and M. Izard (eds) *Dictionnaire de l'ethnologie et de l'anthropologie*, Paris: Presses universitaires de France, pp.309–310.

Anonymous (1945) 'A. Lewitzky', *Journal de la Société des Océanistes*, 1(1).

Anonymous (1945) 'Maupoil', *JSA*, 15: 38.

Anonymous (1991) 'R. Bastide', in C. Winter, pp.37–38.

Augé, M. (1998) 'D. Paulme', *L'Homme*, 147: 7–8.

Backès-Clément, C. (1970) *Lévi-Strauss ou la structure et le malheur*, Paris: Seghers.

Balandier, G. (1955) 'France. Revue de l'Ethnologie en 1952–1954', in *Yearbook of Anthropology*, pp.525–540.

——(1959) 'Tendances de l'ethnologie française', in *Cahiers internationaux de sociologie*, 27: 11–22.

Bastide, R. (1931) *Les Problèmes de la vie mystique*, Paris: A. Colin.

——(1936; 2003) *Social Origins of Religion*, trans. M. Baker, Foreword by J.L. Peacock, Minneapolis: University of Minnesota Press.

——(1970) *Le Prochain et le lointain*, Paris: Cujas.

——(1971; 1973) *Applied Anthropology*, trans. A.L. Morton, New York: Harper.

——(ed.) (1972) *Sens et usages du terme structure dans les sciences humaines et sociales*, Paris: Mouton.

——(ed.) (1974) *Les Femmes de couleur en Amérique Latine*, Paris: Anthropos.

——(1975) *Le Sacré sauvage et autres essais*, Paris: Payot.

Bastide, R., Morin, F. and Raveau, F. (1975) *Les Haïtiens en France*, Paris: Mouton.

Bellour, R. and Clément, C. (eds) (1979) *Claude Lévi-Strauss* (includes texts by and about), Paris: Gallimard.

Bessaignet, P. (in collaboration) (1945) *La Crise française*, Paris: le Pavois.

——(1960) *Tribesman of the Chitagong Hill Tracts*, Asiatic Society of Pakistan Publication.

——(1961) *La Méthode de l'anthropologie*, Teheran: University of Teheran.

——(1961) *L'Étude sociologique des villages du Guilan par la méthode de photographie aérienne*, University of Teheran, IERSS.

——(1966) *Principes de l'ethnologie économique*, Paris: Librairie générale de droit et de jurisprudence.

——(1988) *Ethnologie et formation d'infirmière: pratique des soins et médecines différentes*, Nice: IDERIC.

Blumenson, M. (1977) *The vildé affair: beginnings of the French Resistance*, Boston: Houghton Mifflin.

Calame-Griaule, G. (1994) 'Jean-Paul Lebeuf', *JA*, 64: 91–112.

Casajus, D. (1997) 'Review of Griaule, 1996, *Descente du troisième verbe*', *JA*, 67: 186–188.

Cazeneuve, J. (1957) *Les dieux dansent à Cibola. Le Shalaïko des indiens Zuni*. Paris, Gallimard.

——(1978) *Des métiers pour un sociologue. Entretien avec A. Akoun*, Paris: Editions France-empire.

Champion, P. and Dieterlen (1956) 'Griaule, M.', in *JSA*, 21: 267–290.

Charachidzé, G. (1991) 'G. Dumézil', in P. Bonte and M. Izard (eds) *Dictionnaire de l'ethnologie et de l'anthropologie*, Paris: Presses universitaires de France, pp.203–204.

Charbonnier, G. (1961; 1969) *Conversations with C. Lévi-Strauss*, trans. J. and D. Weightman, London: Cape.

Chiva, I. (1985) 'G.H. Rivière: un demi-siècle d'ethnologie de la France', *Terrain*, 5: 76–83.

——(1987) 'Hommage de la Société d'Ethnologie française à Georges-Henri Rivière', *Ethnologie Française*, 17(1).

——(ed.) (1989) *La muséologie selon Georges Henri Rivière: cours de muséologie, textes et témoignages*, Paris: Dunod.

Clifford, J. (1983) 'Power and dialogue in ethnography: Marcel Griaule's initiation' in G.W. Stocking (ed.) *Observers Observed: Essays on Ethnographic Fieldwork*, *HOA*, vol.1: 121–157.

Condominas, G. (1970) 'Paul Mus, Sociologue', *CIS*, 19: 53–68.

Cresswell, R. (1985) 'Leroi-Gourhan', *Journal d'agriculture traditionnelle et de botanique appliquée*, 32, and 1986, *Techniques et culture*, 7, January, *La Pensée*, November–December.

——(1988) *A. Leroi-Gourhan ou les voies de l'homme. Actes du colloque du Cnrs de mars 1997*, Paris: Albin Michel.

——(1991) 'Leroi-Gourhan, André', in P. Bonte and M. Izard (eds) *Dictionnaire de l'ethnologie et de l'anthropologie*, Paris: Presses universitaires de France, pp.414–415.

Dautry, D. (1975) 'Roger Bastide. Bibliographie 1921–1974', Paris: CNRS.

Delaby, L. and Hamayon, R. (1975) 'Evelyne Lot-Falck. Son oeuvre'.

——(1977) 'Evelyne Lot-Falck' *l'Ethnographie*, 74–75.

Deluz, A. (1991a) 'Bastide, R.', in P. Bonte and M. Izard (eds) *Dictionnaire de l'ethnologie et de l'anthropologie*, Paris: Presses universitaires de France, pp.108–109.

——(1991b) 'Devereux, Georges', in P. Bonte and M. Izard (eds) *Dictionnaire de l'ethnologie et de l'anthropologie*, Paris: Presses universitaires de France, pp.198–199.

Devereux, G. (1951; 1969) *Reality and Dream Psychotherapy of a Plains Indian*, New York: New York University Press.

——(1953) *Psychoanalysis and the Occult*, New York: New York University Press.

——(1956) *Therapeutic Education*, New York: Harper Brothers.

——(1961; 1976) *Mohave Ethnopsychiatry and Suicide*, St Clair: Scholarly Press.

——(1970; 1978) *Enthnopsychoanalysis: psychoanlysis and anthropology as complementary frames of reference*, Berkeley: University of California Press.

——(1975) *Tragédie et poésie grecque*, Paris: Flammarion.

——(1967; 1968) *From Anxiety to Method in Behavioural Science*, with intro. by Weston La Barre, The Hague: Mouton.

——(1986) *AN*, 4: 3.

Dibie, P. (ed.) (1987) *Les pieds sur terre*, Paris: Métailié.

——(1996) 'A.G. Haudricourt', *Le Monde*, 23 August.

Dieterlen, G. (1951; 1988) *Essai sur la religion bambara*, 2nd edn with new introduction, Brussels: Édition de l'université de Brussels.

Dieterlen, G. and Bâ, A.H. (1961), *Koumen, texte initiatique des pasteurs Peul*, Paris and The Hague: Mouton.

Dieterlen, G. and Cissé, Y. (1972) *Les fondements de la Société d'initiation du Komo*, Paris and The Hague: Mouton.

Dieterlen, G. and Griaule, M. (1952) *Signes graphiques soudanais*, Paris: Hermann.

——(1965) *Le renard pâle, tome 1, le mythe cosmologique*, Paris: Institut d'ethnologie.

Digard, J-P. (ed.) (1982) *Hommage à Maxime Rodinson. Le cuisinier et le philosophe. Etudes d'ethnographie historique du Proche-Orient*, Paris: Maisonneuve-Larose.

Dorst, J. (1986) 'R. Gessain', *Objets et Mondes*, vol.23.

Dreyfus, S. (1991) 'Métraux, A.', in P. Bonte and M. Izard (eds) *Dictionnaire de l'ethnologie et de l'anthropologie*, Paris: Presses universitaires de France, pp.476–177.

——(1997) *Ethnologies d'A. Métraux*, Geneva: Catalogue of the Musée d'Ethnographie.

Droit, R-P. 'Dumont', *Le Monde*, 26 November 1998.

Dumézil, G. (1924) *Le Festin d'immortalité: étude de mythologie comparée indo-européenne*, Paris: Geuthner.

——(1939) *Mythes et dieux des Germains, Jupiter, Mars, Quirinus, 1941–1948*, Paris: Gallimard, 4 vols.

——(1952) *Les Dieux des Indo-Européens*, Paris: Gallimard.

——(1968–71–73) *Mythe et épopée*, Paris: Gallimard, 3 vols. (reissued in 1995).

——(1987) *Entretiens avec D. Eribon*, Paris: O. Jacob.

Dupuis, A. (1987) 'Correspondance de Déborah Lifchitz et Denise Paulme avec Michel Leiris, Sanga 1935' *Gradhiva*, 3: 44–58.

Duvignaud, J. (1974) 'Pour R. Bastide' in *CIS*, vol.57.

Éribon, D. (1992) *Faut-il brûler Dumézil? Mythologie, science et politique*, Paris: Flammarion.

Eribon, D. and Lévi-Strauss, Cl. (1988; 1991) *Conversation*, trans. P. Wissing, Chicago: University of Chicago Press.

Fabre, D. (1997) 'L'ethnologie française à la croisée des engagements 1940–1945', in J.Y. Boursier *Résistants et Résistance*, Paris: L'Harmattan.

Faublée, J. (1946a) *Ethnographie de Madagascar*, Paris: Maisonneuve.

——(1946b) *Introduction au Malgache*, Paris: Maisonneuve.

——(1947) *Récits Bara*, Paris: Institut d'ethnologie. From 1960 the reviews column: 'Description et analyse de sociétés appartenant au domaine ethnographique' in *l'Année Sociologique*.

Faure, C. (1989) *Le projet culturel de Vichy. Folklore et révolution nationale 1940–1944*, Paris: Editions du CNRS.

Ferry, M-P. (1988a) 'R. Gessain Témoignage' *Gradhiva*, 3: 67–69.

——(1988b) 'R. Gessain In Memoriam', *JA*, 56: 125–127.

Forde, D. (1956) 'Griaule, M.', *Africa*, 26.

Fournier, D. (1991) 'Soustelle, Jacques', in C. Winter, p.651.

Gaillard, G. (1988) 'Images d'une génération. Contribution à la constitution d'une histoire de l'anthropologie française (1950–1970)', (thesis) Paris: EHESS, 10 vols.

——(1989) 'Chronique de la recherche ethnologique dans son rapport au Centre national de la recherche scientifique 1925–1980', *Cahiers pour l'histoire du CNRS*, no.3: 85–127.

——(1990) *Répertoire de l'ethnologie française, 1950–1970*, Paris: Editions du CNRS, 2 vols. (on website: Guisemine).

——(2003) 'Then and Now: Teaching Anthropology in France', in Dracklé, E. and Schippers (eds), *Educational Histories of European Social Anthropology*, London: Berghahn Books, vol. 1: 156–159.

Galey, J-C. (1982) 'The Spirit of apprentices in a master craftsman' and 'A conversation with L. Dumont, Paris, le 12 décembre 1979', in T-N. Madan *Ways of Life: King Householder Renouncer. Essays in Honour of Louis Dumont*, New Dehli: Vikas Publications.

——(1991a) 'Dumont, Louis', in P. Bonte and M. Izard (eds) *Dictionnaire de l'ethnologie et de l'anthropologie*, Paris: Presses universitaires de France, pp.204–206.

——(1991b) 'Dumont, Louis', in C. Winter, pp.166–168.

——(1999) 'Dumont', *Journal de Easa*, 25: 13–17.

Ganay, S. de, Lebeuf, J.-P. and Zahan, D. (eds) (1987) *Ethnologiques. Hommages à Marcel Griaule*, (contains complete bibliography), Paris: Hermann.

Gessain, R. (1947) *Les Esquimaux, du Groènland à l'Alaska*, Paris: Bourrelier.

——(1969) *Ammassalik ou la civilisation obligatoire*, Paris: Flammarion.

——(1981) *Ovibos. La grande aventure des hommes et des boeufs musqués*, Paris: Robert Laffont.

——(1989) *Un homme marche devant*, Paris: Arthaud (introduction and commentaries by M. Gessain, J.L. Etienne, M. Perez. Journal de route tenu en 1936), Paris: Arthaud.

Ghrenassia, P. (1987) 'A. Lewitzky. De l'ethnologie à la résistance', *La Liberté de l'esprit*, 16: 237–253.

Griaule, M. (1943) *Les Sao légendaires*, Paris: Gallimard.

——(1957) *Méthode de l'ethnographie*, edited by G. Calame-Griaule, Paris: Presses universitaires de France.

Griaule, M. and Dieterlen, G. (1965) *Le renard pâle*, Paris: Institut d'ethnologie.

Groenen, M. (1996) *Leroi-Gourhan. Essence et contingence dans la destinée humaine*, Bruxelles: de Broeck University.

Haudricourt, A.G. and Brunhes Delamarre, M.J. (1954) *L'homme et la charrue*, Paris: Gallimard (reissued by La Manufacture 1987).

Haudricourt, A.G. and Hagège, C. (1978) *La phonologie panchronique*, Paris: Presses universitaires de France.

Hénaff, M. (1991) *Claude Lévi-Strauss*, Paris: Belfond.

Héritier, F. (1999) 'D. Paulme-Schaeffner ou l'histoire d'une volonté', *CEA*, 39(1): 5–12.

Herskovits, (1945) 'Anthropology during the war: France', *AA*, 47: 639–641.

Heusch, L. de (1991) 'On Griaule on trial. Answer to Van Beek', *CA*, 32(4): 434–437.

Izard, M., Rauch, J., Alder, A., Cartry, M. (eds) (1978) *Systèmes de signes. Textes réunis en hommage à Germaine Dieterlen*, Paris: Hermann.

——(1991) 'Dieterlen, Germaine', in P. Bonte and M. Izard (eds) *Dictionnaire de l'ethnologie et de l'anthropologie*, Paris: Presses universitaires de France, pp.200–201.

Jamin, J. (1980) 'A. Schaeffner (1895–1980)', *Objets et Mondes*, 20: 131–135.

——(1985) 'Les objets ethnographiques sont-ils des choses perdues. A propos de la mission Dakar-Djiouti', in J. Hainard and R. Kaehr (eds) *Temps perdu, temps retrouvé*, Neuchâtel: Musée d'ethnographie.

—— (ed.) (1988a) reissue of *Bulletin du Musée d'ethnographie du Trocadéro*, Paris: Jean-Michel Place. Preface by J. Jamin.

——(1988b) 'Le Musée d'ethnographie en 1930: l'ethnologie comme science et comme politique', in G.H. Rivière, *La Muséologie selon G.H. Rivière: cours de muséologie, textes et témoignages*, Paris: Dunod.

——(1991a) 'Leiris, Michel', in P. Bonte and M. Izard (eds) *Dictionnaire de l'ethnologie et de l'anthropologie*, Paris: Presses universitaires de France, pp.413–414.

——(1991b) 'Paulme, D.', in P. Bonte and M. Izard (eds) *Dictionnaire de l'ethnologie et de l'anthropologie*, Paris: Presses universitaires de France, p.564.

——(1991c) 'Paulme, Denise', in C. Winter, pp.530–531.

——(1991d) 'Rivière, G-H.', in P. Bonte and M. Izard (eds) *Dictionnaire de l'ethnologie et de l'anthropologie*, Paris: Presses universitaires de France, pp.413–414.

——(1991e) 'G-H. Rivière', in C. Winter, pp.586–587.

——(1991f) 'Schaeffner, A.', in P. Bonte and M. Izard (eds) *Dictionnaire de l'ethnologie et de l'anthropologie*, Paris: Presses universitaires de France, pp.652–653.

——(1991g) 'A. Schaeffner', in C. Winter, pp.612–613.

Jamin, J. and Price, S. (1988) 'Entretien avec M. Leiris', *Gradhiva*, 4: 29–56.

Johnson, C. (2003) *Claude Lévi-Strauss, the formative years*, Cambridge: Cambridge University Press.

Jolly, E. (2001) 'M. Griaule, ethnologue. La contruction d'une discipline (1925–1956)', *JA*, 71(1): 149–191.

Juliet, C. (1988) *Pour Michel Leiris*, Paris: Fourbis.

Krebs, E. (2002) 'P. Verger: Parisian Trickster', *AA*, 104(1): 307–309.

Lapointe, F. and Lapointe, C. (1977) *Cl. Lévi-Strauss and his Critics: an International Bibliography of Criticism (1950–1976)*, New York.

Lavine d'Epinay, Ch. (1975) 'R. Bastide sociologue' and J. Faublée 'R. Bastide ethnologue' in *l'Année Sociologique*, vol. 25: 13–43.

Le Coeur, C. (1950) *Dictionnaire ethnographique de la langue téda*, Paris: Larose.

Leach, E. (1970; 1974) *Lévi-Strauss*, London: Fontana.

Lebeuf, J-P. (1941) *Les Collections du Tchad – Guide pour leur exposition*, Paris: Musée de l'Homme.

——(1945) *Quand l'or était vivant*, Paris: J. Susse.

——(1948–1951) *Fouilles dans la région du Tchad*, Paris: Société des Africanistes.

——(1957) *Application de l'ethnologie à l'assistance sanitaire*, Brussels: Institut de Sociologie Solvay.

——(1976) *Etudes Kotoko*, Paris and The Hague: Mouton.

Lebeuf, J-P. and Lebeuf, A. (1950) *La civilisation du Tchad*, Paris: Payot.

Leiris, M. (1939) *L'Age d'Homme*, Paris: Gallimard.

——(1969) *Cinq études d'ethnologie. Le racisme et le tiers-monde*, Paris: Gonthier.

——*La règle du jeu*, Paris: Gallimard, 5 vols.

——(1992) *Journal 1922–1998*, edited, presented and annotated by J. Jamin, Paris: Gallimard.

——(1995) *Miroirs de l'Afrique*, Paris: Gallimard.

Lelong, Y. (1987) 'L'Heure très sévère de B. Vildé', *La Liberté de l'esprit*, 16: 329–341.

Leroi-Gourhan, A. (1936) *La civilisation du renne*, Paris: Gallimard.

——(1964) *Les religions de la préhistoire*, Paris: Presses universitaires de France.

——(1966) *Préhistoire de l'art occidental*, Paris: Mazenod.

——(1972) *Fouilles de Pincevent. Essai d'analyse ethnographique d'un habitat magdalénien*, Paris: CNRS.

——(1983a) *Les Racines du monde. Entretiens avec Claude-Henri Rocquet*, Paris: Belfond.

——(1983b) *Mécanique vivante. Le crâne des vertébrés du poisson à l'homme*, Paris: Fayard.

——(1983c) *Au fil du temps. Ethnologie et préhistoire (1935–1970)*, Paris: Fayard.

Leroi-Gourhan, A. and Leroi-Gourhan, A. (1989) *Un voyage chez les Aïnous. Hokkaïdo 1938*, Paris: Albin Michel.

Lesure, F. and Rouget, G. (eds) (1982) 'Les fantaisies du voyageur: 32 variations Schaeffner', Paris, *Revue de Musicologie* 68.

Lévi-Strauss, C. (1947; 1971) 'French Sociology', in G. Gurvitch, *Twentieth Century Sociology*, Freepost: Books for Libraries Press.

——(1952; 1968) *Race and History*, Paris: UNESCO.

——(1958; 1999) *Structural Anthropology*, trans. by C. Jacobson, New York: Basic Books.

——(1962; 1966) *The Savage Mind*, London: Weidenfeld.

——(1973; 1983) *Structural Anthropology*, trans. M. Layton, Chicago: University of Chicago Press.

——(1975; 1982) *The Way of the Masks*, Seattle: University of Washington Press.

——(1983; 1992) *The View From Afar*, trans. J. Neugoschel, Chicago: University of Chicago Press.

——(1984; 1987) *Anthology and Myth: Lectures, 1951–1952*, trans. R. Willis, Oxford: Blackwell.

——(1985; 1988) *The Jealous Potter*, trans. B. Chorier, Chicago: University of Chicago Press.

——(1991; 1995) *The Story of Lynx*, trans. C. Tihanyi, Chicago: University of Chicago Press.

——(1993; 1997) *Look, Listen, Read*, trans. B. Singer, New York: Basic Books.

Lewis, I.M. (2000) 'G. Dieterlen', *AT*, 16(2): 25–26.

Lifchitz, D. (1940) *Textes éthiopiens magico-religieux*, Paris: Institut d'ethnologie.

Littleton, C.S. (1966; 1982) *The New Comparative Mythology: An Anthropological Assessment of the Theories of Georges Dumézil*, Berkeley, CA.: University of California Press.

——(1991) 'Dumezil, G.' in C. Winter, pp.165–166.

Lyono, A.P. (1979) 'R. Bastide', *International Encyclopedia of the Social Sciences*, D. Sills (ed.) vol.18: 40–42.

Mahn-Lot, M. and Vildé, I. (1975; 1973) 'Evelyne Lot-Falck. Sa vie', *Objets et Mondes*, 15: 106–110.

Marchant, G. 'Paul Mus' in *Bulletin de l'Ecole Française d'Extrême-Orient*, vol.14: 24–42.

Mazon, B. (1988) *Aux origines de l'Ecole des Hautes Etudes en Sciences Sociales. Le rôle du mécénat américain (1920–1960)*, Paris: Le Cerf.

Métraux, A. (1928) *La religion des Tupinamba et ses rapports avec celles des autres tribus Tupi-Guarani*, Paris: Leroux.

——(1930) *Contribution à l'étude de l'archéologie du cours supérieur et moyen de l'Amazone*, Buenos Aires.

——(1951; 1957) *Easter Island*, trans. M. Bullock, London, New York: Oxford University Press.

——(1958; 1972) *Voodoo in Haiti*, trans. H. Charleti, intro by S. Mintz, New York: Schocken Books.

——(1961) *Incas: Masters of the Andes*, Pleasantville: Reader's Digest.

——(1967) *Religions et magies indiennes d'Amérique du Sud*, Paris: Gallimard.

——(1978) *Itinéraires 1 (1935–1953). Carnets de notes et journaux de voyage*, selection, introduction and notes by A-M. d'Ans, Paris: Payot.

Métraux, A. and Ploetz, H. (1931) *La civilisation matérielle et la vie sociale et religieuse des Indiens Zé du Brésil méridional et oriental*, Tucuman: Muséo de Tucuman.

Métraux, A. (1994) *Le pied à l'étrier. Correspondance entre A. Métraux et P. Verger (1946–1963)*, edited by J.P. le Bouler, Paris: Jean Michel Place.

Métraux, R. (1991) 'Métraux, A.', in C. Winter, pp.475–476.

Montaigne, V. 'Pierre Verger', *Le Monde*, 14 February 1996.

Nathan, T. (1996) 'Préface' to G. Devereux, 1996.

Pace, D. (1983) *Cl. Lévi-Strauss; the Bearer of Ashes*, London: Routledge & Kegan Paul.

Panoff, M. (1993) *Les Frères ennemis, Caillois et Lévi-Strauss*, Paris: Payot.

Paulme, D. (1979) 'Gens et paroles d'Afrique: écrits pour Denise Paulme', *CEA*, 19.

———

Piault, M. and Hauzeur, J. (eds) (2001) 'Dossier : Les empreintes du renard pâles: pour Germaine Dieterlen', *JA*, 71(1) (articles by J. Rouch, G. Calama-Griaule, M. Gessain, M.P. Ferry, E. Bernus, L. de Heusch, P. Lourdou, N. Wanono, T. Tamari, M. Izard, G. Holder, E. Jolly, S. Sakrai, M. Douglas, J. Goody).

Pivin, J.L. and Martin Saint Leon, P. (eds) (1993) *P. Verger, le messager, the go-between. Photographies 1932–1962*, Paris: Editions Revue Noire.

Pouillon, J. (1966) 'L'oeuvre de Lévi-Strauss' *Les Temps Modernes*, 126: 150–174.

——(1991) 'Lévi-Strauss, C.', in P. Bonte and M. Izard (eds) *Dictionnaire de l'ethnologie et de l'anthropologie*, Paris: Presses universitaires de France, pp.417–419.

Price, (1991) 'Leiris, M.', in C. Winter, pp.397–398.

Ravelet, C. (ed.) (1996) *Etudes sur R. Bastide. De l'acculturation à la psychiatrie sociale*, Paris: l'Harmattan.

Rivière, C. (1988) Postface to Maupoil, B. '*La géomancie à l'ancienne Côte des esclaves*', Paris: Institut d'ethnologie, pp.687–692.

Rivière, G-H. (1968) 'Musée et autres collections publiques d'ethnographie' in J. Poirier (ed.) *Ethnologie générale*, Paris: Gallimard, pp.472–493.

Robin, C. (1985) *Mélanges luiguistiques offert à M. Rodinson* (with a complete bibliography), Paris: CNRS.

Rodinson, M. (1972; 1982) *Marxism and the Muslim World*, trans. J. Matthews, New York: Monthly Review Press.

Rouget, G. (1980) 'A. Schaeffner', *JSA*, 50: 109–110.

Rousseau, H. (1957) 'G. Dumézil', *Critique*, 8: 731–756.

Saladin d'Anglure, B. (1996) 'Lévi-Strauss, C.', in A. Barnard and J. Spencer *Encyclopedia of Social and Cultural Anthropology*, pp.333–336.

Schaeffner, A. (1951) *Les Kissi; une société d'Afrique Noire et ses instruments de musique*, Paris: Hermann.

——(1957) *Introduction et notes à Nietzsche. Lettres à Peter Gast*, Monaco, 2 vols. Reissue by Ch. Bourgois, 1981.

——(1980) *Essais de musicologie et autres fantaisies*, Paris: Le Sycomore.

Simonis, Y. (1968) *Cl. Lévi-Strauss ou la passion de l'inceste. Introduction au structuralisme*, Paris: Aubier-Montaigne.

Soustelle, J. (1955; 2002) *Daily Life of the Aztecs*, trans. P. O'Brien, Mineola: Dover Publications.

——(1962) *L'espérance trahie*, Paris: Alma.

——(1967; 1971) *The Four Suns. Recollections and Reflections of an Ethnologist in Mexico*, trans. E. Ross, New York: Grossman.

——(1968) *Vingt-huit ans de gaullisme*, Paris: La Table Ronde.

——(1970) *Les Aztèques*, Paris: Presses universitaires de France.

—(1975) *La recherche française en archéologie et anthropologie*, Paris: documentation française.

——(1980) *Les Olmèques*, Paris: Gallimard.

——(1982) *Les Maya*, Paris: Gallimard.

Sperber, D. (1982; 1985) 'Claude Lévi-Strauss today', in *On Anthropological Knowledge*, Cambridge: Cambridge University Press.

Tillion, G. (1960; 1976) *France and Algeria, Complementary Enemies*, trans. R. Howard, Westport: Greenwood.

——(1961) *L'Afrique bascule vers l'avenir. L'Algérie en 1957 et d'autres textes*, Paris: Minuit (reissued with additional texts in 1999 by Tirésias).

——(1973; 1975) *Ravensbrück*, trans. G. Satterwhite, Garden City: Anchor Press.

——(2000) Il était une fois l'ethnographie, Paris: Leseuil

Toffin, G. (1999) 'L. Dumont', *l'Homme*, 150: 7–15.

Ullmann, B. (1995) *Jacques Soustelle*, Paris: Plon.

van Beek, E.A. (1991) 'Dogon restudied: a field evaluation of the work of Marcel Griaule', *CA*, 32: 139–167.

Verger, P. (1937) *South Seas Islands*, London: Routledge.

——(1957) *Notes sur le culte des Grisha et Vodun à Bahia, la baie de tous les saints au Brésil, et à l'ancienne côte des esclaves*, Dakar: IFAN.

Victor, P-E. (1938) *Boréal*, Paris: Grasset.

——(1939) *Banquise*, Paris: Grasset.

——(1952) *Expéditions polaires françaises*, Paris: La Documentation française.

——(1953) *La grande faim*, Paris: Julliard.

——*Le Monde*, 9 March 1995.

Victor, P-E. and Robert-Lamblin, J. (1989), *La civilisation du phoque*, Paris: A. Colin et Chabaud.

Vildé, B. (1988) *Journal et lettres de prison (1941–1942)*, Paris: CNRS, *Cahiers pour l'histoire du temps présent*, no.7 (introduction and notes by F. Bedarida and D. Veillon).

Wagley, C. (1964) 'Alfred Métraux', *AA*, 66: 603–613.

IX
The other European schools

ITALY

Inspired by the example of Arab scholars, Italian authors such as Pian del Carpini, Marco Polo, Vespucci, Verrazzano and Ramusio were among the earliest contributors to a pre-anthropological literature during the Middle Ages and the Renaissance in Europe. Italy also produced Ulisse Aldrovandi (1522–1605), a professor at the University of Bologna who was the first scholarly collector of Western history; Vico (1668–1744), one of the first philosophers to conceive of history in a comparative and determinist light; and Balbi, a Venetian 'pre-linguist' who made the first recorded use of the term 'ethnographic' in the title of a book in his *Ethnographic Atlas of the Globe* (Paris, 1826). But it was not until 1861 that Italy was united with Victor Emmanuel II as its king, and not until 1870 that Rome became the nation's capital, even as it remained under occupation. Moreover, the intellectuals and bourgeois who had long worked towards national unification had not been able to develop a social science tradition in a country suffocated by religious dogma and practice, and the retarding effect of religious conservatism was scarcely mitigated by the benefits of the considerable mass of documentary literature produced by Capuchin, Franciscan and Salesian missionaries.

After working in Argentina from 1855 to 1858 and further travels to Siberia and India, Paolo Mantegazza (1831–1910), a professor of pathology at the University of Pavia, was in 1869 installed in Italy's first chair of anthropology at the *Istituto di studi superiori* in Florence, then the country's temporary capital city. Also in 1869, Mantegazza founded the first national anthropology museum in Genoa, and in the following year he created the *Società Italiana di Antropologia e di Etnologia* in Florence, which organized research trips and published the journal *Archivio per l'Antropologia e la Etnologia*. Among the Society's twenty-four founder-members were the pioneer of criminology Cesare Lombroso, the naturalist and palaeontologist Pelegrino Stroble, the famous geologist and palaeontologist B. Gastaldi, and Luigi Pigorini (1842–1925), who initiated archaeological and prehistorical studies in Italy (Grottanelli, *Comments* 1977: 594). As the country lacked colonial possessions, the Society's 'foremost aim was the study of ancient and modern Italian populations' (quoted by Bodeman from Grottanelli's *Comments*, 1977: 594), and in 1895 it published the first ethnographic map of Italy. At this time anthropology was understood as exclusively concerned with ethnology and physical anthropology and with exotic peoples, while archaeology remained stuck in the *belles lettres* tradition. In 1875 Stroble and Pigorini broke away from Mantegazza to found a second journal, *Bolletino di Palentologia Italiana*, and in the following year Pigorini opened the *Museo Preistorico-Etnografico* and occupied the first Italian chair of palaeontology at the

199

University of Rome. The Sicilian physician and philosopher Giuseppe Sergi (1841–1936), who introduced Spencer's work into Italy, held the chair in physical anthropology at Bologna University from 1880 to 1884 and at Rome University from 1884 to 1916, when he was succeeded by his son Sergio. At first Sergi was an active member of Mantegazza's *Società Italiana*, but his support for the notion of the polygenic emergence of mankind led him to break with the society and its founder, and in 1893 he set up the *Società romana di Antropologia*, which defended polygenism in the pages of its journal *Revista di Antropologia*. In 1880 Naples University endowed a chair in anthropology, and in 1882 the missionary Comboni launched the journal *Nigrizia*, published in Verona.

Italy's explorers prior to the First World War are less well-known than those of Britain and France, not least because the country became a colonial power late in the day and lacked a colonial mythology. Nonetheless a number of important Italian expeditions were carried out: by Iaggia to the Azande in 1863; by Miani to the Pygmies in 1872; by Beccari and d'Albertis to the Papuans of New Guinea in 1871 and 1876 respectively; by Cerruti to Melanesia in 1881; and by Boggiani to Mato Grosso in 1888. In the same period the Sicilian physician G. Pitrè (1841–1916) published the 24 volumes of his *Biblioteca delle tradizioni popolari siciliane* and was appointed to the first Italian chair of *demo-psicologia* (folkloric studies) endowed by Palermo University in 1910. Lamberto Loria (1855–1913), a fervent evolutionist who called for an Italian colonial empire and visited the Trobriand Islands thirty years before **Malinowski**, travelled the world building up an ethnographic collection, which he donated to Italian museums. In 1910 he founded the *Società di Etnografia italiana*, which organized the first Italian folklore exhibition in 1911, and the artefacts collected for this exhibition subsequently formed the basis of the *Museo delle Arti e Tradizioni Popolari*. Also in 1911, the history of popular traditions began to find a place in university curricula, and in 1913 Loria organized the first Congress of Italian Ethnography as a forum for all contemporary folkloric research, and followed this up by launching the journal *Lares*, which exists to this day. Thus Pitrè and Loria are considered to be the fathers of Italian folklorism. The establishment of the Catholic University of Milan at the beginning of the twentieth century and the profound influence of **Schmidt**'s theory of the universality of monotheism led to a deep engagement with the diffusionist anthropology of the Viennese School in Italy.

In 1925 the Great Missionary Exhibition was held in Rome. Pope Paul XI then helped himself to the exhibits and used them as the core collection of the *Pontifico Museo Missionario Etnologico*, which he founded in the Lateran Palace in 1927. The directorship of the new museum went to W. Schmidt (Bernardini, 1990: 4), who would later say that Divine Providence had placed Ethiopia in the hands of Italy. Schmidt established the journal *Annali Lateranensi* on the tenth anniversary of the museum's opening in 1937, and then, after engaging his disciple Michael Schulien to replace him, he returned to Austria to evacuate the library of his *Anthropos-Institut* before it fell into Nazi hands. In 1925 **Pettazzoni** launched the journal *Studi e Materiali di Storia delle Religioni*, which was published until 1969 and then replaced by *Religioni e Civiltà*, of which only two issues ever appeared. In Naples an *Istituto universitario orientale* was established, with teaching provided by the Arabist F. Gabrielli, and subsequently also by Giovanni (or Giuseppe) Tucci, a specialist in Indian religions and cultures who carried out his first fieldwork in 1933, and by Raffaele Corso, a folklorist or 'demopsychologist' who was linked to the Fascist movement, as were Lidio Cirpiani and Enrico Cerulli. The institute published the journal *Revista di Etnografia*, which became *Etnologia/Antropologia Culturale* in 1974 under the editorship of Corrain, Filesi and Battista. Another course in ethnology was introduced at the University of Genoa, taught first by Giuseppe Rosso and then, from 1945 to 1969, by Pietro Scotti. The interwar years were marked by Italy's growing confidence as a colonial power; having already conquered Eritrea in 1885, Somalia in 1889, and Libya in 1911–12, it added Ethiopia to its list of possessions in 1935–36. As of 1931 allegiance to Fascism was required of university teachers. Following the foundation of the Centre for Studies on Italian East Africa within the Royal Academy in 1936 a few study expeditions were sponsored (e.g. those of G. Danielli, E. Zavattari and V. L. **Grottanelli**), but the war soon interrupted this new work. In 1940 the Florence professor Renato Biasutti, a geographer specializing in rural habitats, published the first edition of his *Razze e popoli della terra*, whose status as a work of reference is demonstrated by the numerous editions it went through until the 1970s. In 1941 the Africanists A. Mordini and C. Conti-Rossini, and the latter's disciple Grottanelli, founded the journal *Rassegna di Studi Etiopici*, while in the same year the philosopher Antonio Banfi published *Il pensiero dei primitivi*, which falls within the intellectual tradition of **Lévy-Bruhl**.

The first Italian chair in the history of religions was held from 1923 by R. Pettazzoni, who then became curator of the *Museo Pigorini* and in 1937 was appointed professor of ethnology at Rome University, where in 1947 he founded the *Scuola di Perfezionamento in Scienze Etnologiche* within the *Istituto delle Civiltà Primitive*. Pettazzoni also launched the journal *Studi e materiali di storia delle religioni* and argued for a jettisoning of evolutionism, as well as attacking the *Kulturkreis* theory of Schmidt, with whom he engaged in polemics for three decades. Among his students were Angelo Brelich, who succeeded him in his Rome chair; U. Bianchi, the author of *Storia dell'Etnologia* (Rome, 1965); V. **Lanternari**, a specialist in messianic movements who established a teaching programme at the University of Bari in 1958; Dario Sabbatucci; and E. **de Martino**. In the postwar years all of these scholars, and especially de Martino, were subject to the rather contradictory influences of the idealist philosopher B. Croce and the Marxist philosopher Gramsci. These same influences continued to exert themselves on de Martino's disciple C. Gallini and on A. M. Cirese, who in *Cultura egemonica e cultura subalterne* (Palermo, 1971) proposed that the world of the oppressed be understood using Marxian and specifically Gramscian ideas on the relationship between centre and periphery. According to **Bernardi**, there were two anthropology courses in Rome in the years until 1945: one taught at La Sapienza University by the palaeontologist Alberto Carlo Blanc; and the other taught at Urbaniana University in the Vatican by Renato Boccassino, who had attended the seminars of Malinowski and **Mauss** and researched on the Acholi of Uganda, but who seems not to have established an anthropological school himself. From 1956–1957 V. L. Grottanelli directed Rome University's *Istituto delle Civiltà Primitive*, which he renamed the *Istituto di Etnologia* and turned into the major centre of Italian ethnology; later it was absorbed by the *Dipartimento di Studi Glottoantropologici* (department of anthropology and linguistics). He also founded the journal *L'Uomo: Società Tradizione Sviluppo*, but it was not until 1967 that his professorship was upgraded into Italy's first chair in ethnology. In 1954 Grottanelli began solitary research in Ghana, and from 1961 to 1974 he led expeditions of students and Africanist colleagues there. Among those who participated in these expeditions were Giorgio Raimondo Cardona, an ethnolinguist who had established the field of ethnoscience by the time of his early death, V. Lanternari, Ernesta Cerrulli, and Italo Signorini, who took students to Mexico in Grottanelli's place from 1974 (Grottanelli, 1977). In 1955–1956 T. Sepilli founded an ethnology institute at the University of Perugia, renamed the *Istituto di Etnologia e di Antropologia Culturale* in 1958. Also in 1958, a group including G. Cantalamessa, L. Bonacini, R. Calisi, A. Signorelli and T. Seppilli was formed around T. Tentori, a specialist in family structures who had worked at the

University of Chicago, and together they presented a manifesto for a cultural anthropology to the *Congresso Nazionale di Scienze Sociali*. A new cultural anthropology section was also created alongside the existing psychology and sociology sections in the Italian branch of the International Association of Sociology. The aim of the Tentori group was to establish an all-encompassing approach to research into complex societies and depart from existing ethnological inquiry, which was perceived to be strictly descriptive and focused exclusively on primitive societies. This new line of research set about the task of analysing contemporary culture using some of its most characteristic features: television, middle class aspirations, social services in particular localities, and immigration. In 1961 Turin University organized the first *Congresso di Scienze Antropologiche, Etnologiche e di Folklore*, which published its proceedings in 1963. By 1966–1967 cultural anthropology held a place in the courses of eleven university faculties, and by 1969 there were six posts for ethno-anthropologists in Italy. In 1971 the first Italian chair in social anthropology was created at Bologna University for Bernardi, who in 1972 organized a conference at Bologna entitled *Etnologia e Antropologia Culturale*. The aim of this conference, which was inaugurated by J. **Goody**, was to initiate a dialogue between the hitherto mutually suspicious camps of traditional ethnology and social anthropology (Bernardi, 1990: 11). There ensued a period of fantastic growth in the discipline, and in 1976 alone eleven chairs were endowed in ethnology, cultural anthropology and folklore. In 1977 the existing eight chairs in physical anthropology and seven in folklore were complemented by two ethnology chairs at Rome for Bernardi and Lanternari and another two in Genoa. One of the Genoa chairs was occupied by Maroni, who worked on initiation in Uganda and then did research on the Anu of the Ivory Coast with Ernesta Cerulli, who subsequently embraced a militant Americanism demonstrated in her *Inculturazione, deculturazione: ethno-e genocidio* of 1972. Finally, the universities of Brescia and Cagliari each endowed a chair. This rapid expansion was followed by stagnation, and until 1982 'almost no new permanent faculty positions were created' (Saunders, 1984: 448). Tired of waiting for vacancies to appear, several young researchers went abroad, including Carlo Severi, Remo Guideri and Valerio Valeri. Nonetheless, Tentori places the number of folklorists and ethno-anthropologists employed in Italian universities in 1983 at 200 (quoted by Saunders, 1984: 448). In 1991 an Italian Association for Ethnological and Anthropological Sciences (AISEA) was constituted, adopting a name suggested by Cirese in 1972; the association published the journal *Etnoantropologia*, and by 1994 counted 335 members. In the same year the subject was represented in sixty public and private universities; thirty-seven of these offered teaching in folklore or ethno-anthropology given by 108 professors and associate professors, of whom forty-four were cultural anthropologists; twenty-six universities provided an ethnology component in their courses; and sixteen universities included the study of history and popular traditions. Among the other areas covered were the religions of primitive peoples, ethnography and social anthropology. The highest concentrations of positions for professors and research staff was at La Sapienza University in Rome, where the twenty-eight post-holders were divided between the cultural anthropology programme focused on complex societies and the older department of linguistic-anthropological studies which published the journal *L'Uomo: Società, Tradizioni, Sviluppo*. There were fifteen faculty members at Perugia University and thirteen at Turin, which reorganized its department to offer an American-style anthropology programme based on physical anthropology, archaeology, geography, cultural anthropology and ethnology. Palermo employed eleven ethno-anthropologists within its Institute of Anthropological and Geographical Sciences, which in 1968 began publishing the journal *Uomo e Cultura*. Cagliari also had eleven post-holders, Bologna nine and Bari eight. An important role was played, alongside the journals already mentioned, by *Africa: trimestrale di studi e documentazione dell'Istituto Italo-Africano*, which published its first issue in 1976.

Pettazzoni, Raffaele (1883–1959)

Born in a village near Bologna, Raffaele Pettazzoni studied the philosophy of religion at Bologna University and in 1923 was appointed to the first lay chair in the history of religions at Rome University. He eschewed the theological approach which prevailed exclusively in his day in favour of a contextual view of religious phenomena, and in 1925 founded the journal *Studi e materiali di storia delle religioni*. He also opposed the influential idea of a universal primitive monotheism advanced by the Viennese School and by Father W. **Schmidt**, the director of the papal museum. Pettazzoni stated that the notion of a supreme being is culturally specific and produced a classification of the forms it could take. A notable aspect of his comparative approach was his examination of the forms taken by the expulsion of impurity in rites of confession (in Christianity, among the Inuit, and in antiquity). In 1937 he resigned his chair in the history of religions in favour of a professorship of ethnology, also at Rome University. He created the *Istituto delle Civiltà Primitive* within the *Scuola di Perfezionamento in Scienze Etnologiche* in 1947. His students included Angelo Brelich, U. Bianchi, V. **Lanternari** and E. **de Martino**.

De Martino, Ernesto (1908–1965)

Born into a Protestant family in Naples, Ernesto de Martino gained a degree in classics in 1932 and became a favourite student of B. Croce. He took an interest in religious phenomena and studied under **Pettazzoni**, whose influence led him to investigate non-European civilizations and gave him a contextualist and historical perspective resistant to the mentalist approach. While in Bari he became a militant anti-Fascist, and in 1941 published his first major work, *Naturalismo e storicismo nell'ethnologia* (Bari: Laterza), devoted to the theoretical foundations of ethnology. Here de Martino advocates what could be described as a Freudian position, for instead of deriving a relativist position from ethnology he uses it to promote an awareness of the primitive in ourselves, and to combat this tendency by promoting reason over sacrilization. This work is also a frontal attack on the theories of Father W. **Schmidt** and the idea of the *Kulturkreis*, and this placed its author in the vanguard of Italian ethnology. However, despite his analytical approach, de Martino saw the need to take account of lived experience, particularly extra-sensory perception, in a Marxian-like treatment of sacrilization. His work in this area, begun in 1940–1941, resulted in a number of articles and culminated in the publication of *Il Mondo magico* in 1948 (Turin). His *Morte e pianto. Rituale nel mondo antico* (Turin, 1958) is a comparative study of funerary customs and especially lamentation rites in countries bordering the Mediterranean. Between 1949 and 1959 de Martino carried out fieldwork in Lucania and then in the Salentine Peninsula, and this bore fruit in *Sud e magia* (Milan: Feltrinelli, 1959), an inquiry into religious practices in Southern Italy with a particular stress on sorcery and the evil eye. This was followed by *La terra del rimorso* (Milan: Il Saggiatore, 1961), which presents the results of an investigation by a collective of scholars into Tarantino possession cults. A member of the Socialist Party after the war and of the Communist Party from 1950, de Martino founded an ethnography which, instead of taking the folklorist view of evidence as representing the relics of the past, concentrates on the processes experienced by the dominated classes with a view to restoring their history to them and allowing them to take control of their future. The aim is to use an engagement with ideology to promote their awareness of class issues, permitting their reappropriation of working-class identity by means of objective critical analysis. He taught at Rome University from 1953 to 1959, when he was appointed professor at the University of Cagliari in Sardinia, a post he held until his death in 1965. His posthumously published work *La fine del mondo*, edited by Clara Gallini (Turin: Einaudi, 1977), offers a comparative analysis of apocalypses. In 1966 an E. de Martino Institute was created to promote a critical awareness of the alternatives of popular and proletarian culture.

Biocca, Ettore (see Valero, Helena)

Grottanelli, Vinigi Lorenzo (1912–1993)
Born near Turin, Vinigi Lorenzo Grottanelli obtained an economics degree in 1933 and a law degree in 1935, both from Turin University, and was appointed assistant professor of political sciences at Rome University in 1937. He took part in the expedition to the Lake Tana Basin in Ethiopia funded by the Study Centre for Italian East Africa, which had been set up as part of the Royal Academy in 1936; his task was 'to study human settlements and economic conditions in general' (Grottanelli, 1976: 25). He then undertook a second mission to the Sudanese border, but this was interrupted by the outbreak of the Second World War. He was an adherent of the diffusionism of the *Kulturhistorische Schule*, and, although he rejected its thesis of an original monotheism, nevertheless described himself as an 'anthropogeographer'. He was appointed to the *Museo Preistorico-Etnografico Pigorini* in 1945, and in 1947 began teaching at the Pontifical University of Rome. In 1951–1952 he carried out research in Somalia and Kenya and from 1954 investigated the Nzema of Ghana,

where he established a permanent base which would be used by Italian Africanists until 1974. It would be fair to say that *I fondamenti della cultura*, which he edited in 1978 as the first volume of *Una società guineana: gli Nzema*, offers a good picture of the state of the discipline in Italy at the time. The second volume, *Ordine morale e salvezza terrena* (Turin: Boringhieri, 2 vols), he wrote alone. In 1956 he was appointed director of Rome University's *Istituto delle Civiltà Primitive*, established in 1947, which he renamed *Istituto di Etnologia*, and he launched the journal *L'Uomo: Società, Tradizione, Sviluppo*. After resigning his museum post he was appointed professor of ethnology at Rome University in 1967, but often delegated his responsibility there to others while he accompanied students on expeditions to such locations as Mexico, the Ivory Coast, the Americas and Asia.

Bernardi, Bernardo (born 1916)
Born near Bologna, Bernardo Bernardi studied classical literature, and, after taking priestly orders, was given responsibility by the Vatican for its relations with the occupying forces from 1944 to 1947. He continued his studies during these years, particularly in the library of the Pontifical Missionary Museum, and fell under the influence of B. Croce's historicism while also assimilating the theories of the Viennese School. Although he declared himself above all a disciple of Schulien (Bernardi, 1990: 5), he completed a bibliographically based Master's thesis in 1946 on Kikuyu kinship systems at La Sapienza University in Rome under the supervision of **Grottanelli**. His superiors in the church hierarchy intended him for a teaching post in a secondary school in Kenya, and to this end tried unsuccessfully to secure his admission to either Cambridge or Oxford. Instead he was sent to the University of Cape Town to study under I. **Schapera**, who persuaded him of the need to combine functionalism and history. At Cape Town

Bernardi also made the acquaintance of M. **Fortes**, who was a visiting professor there in 1949, and in 1952 he completed his doctoral thesis *The Social Structure of the Kraal among the Zezuru* (Cape Town, 1950). After a stay in London he then lived in Kenya for six years, where his research on the Tharaka, one of the nine Meru groups, resulted in the publication of *The Mugwe: A Failing Prophet* (Oxford: IAI, 1959), which he republished in revised form as *A Blessing Prophet* in 1989. This work investigates the *Mugwe*, also called the Queen Bee, a religious figure whose identity had hitherto been a closely guarded secret. Following his appointment as director of education in the Missionary Society of Turin in 1959 he spent a decade travelling all over Africa, but was not able to continue his anthropological research during this period. In 1970 he became professor of ethnology in the political sciences faculty of Bologna University, and in 1982 he succeeded Grottanelli in the ethnology chair at La Sapienza University. From 1950 he developed his interest in age-class systems, publishing 'The Age-System of the Nilo-Hamitic Peoples' in 1952 (*Africa*, 22). After years of ever more detailed research he led a seminar on the topic in London and Paris and then in 1985 published *I Sistemi della classi d'età*, translated into English as *Age-Class Systems: Social Institutions and Politics Based on Age* (Cambridge UP), in which he proposes the first ever general typology of age-class systems.

Lanternari, Vittorio (born 1918)
Born in the Adriatic port of Ancona, Vittorio Lanternari read agronomy at Bologna University and then religious studies at Rome University under **Pettazzoni**. He completed his thesis in 1946 and was appointed in 1951 to an assistant professorship at Rome University, which from 1959 to 1968 he combined with a teaching post at the University of Bari. Using an approach first developed by Robertson **Smith**, he analysed religion in traditional societies in Africa and Oceania and in antiquity from a global perspective encompassing social and economic as well as properly religious considerations. Subsequently Lanternari concentrated on the dynamics of religious movements under various types of colonial rule. His enormously successful book *Movimenti religiosi di libertà e di salvezza dei popoli oppressi* (Milan, 1960), translated as *The Religions of the Oppressed* (New York: Mentor, 1965), treats of messianic cults in Africa, the Americas, Melanesia and Oceania among populations conceived not as primitive but as oppressed. After demonstrating that these cults are not so much a return to authenticity as an attempt to use shared meanings to respond positively to each period of acculturation, Lanternari moves on to analyse contemporary minority religious movements in Western countries, such as the Children of God, Hare Krishna and new popular music. He was appointed professor at Rome University in 1972.

SPAIN

The great expansion of Spanish possessions beyond Europe's boundaries began with the acquisition by Castile of newly discovered territories following Columbus's first voyage in 1492. The conquest of Mexico in 1519–1525, Chile in 1536, Bolivia in 1538 and finally the Philippines in 1565 precipitated the birth of ethnography ('el imperio español produjo la etnografía'). Important early authors, all missionaries, include Diego de Landa (1525–1579), Marcos de Niza (1500–1543), José de Acosta (1540–1600), and Juan de Betanzos (1510–1576), and the best-known of all is Bernardino de Sahagún (1499–1590), author of the famous *General History of New Spain* (1547–1577) and sometimes described as the father of modern anthropology. The expulsion from Spain of the Moriscos from 1606 to 1610, two plague epidemics, countless wars, and the commercial rivalry with France, Holland and England did little to promote the new discipline, which was at best straightforwardly ethnographic in form. Spain launched some expeditions during the eighteenth century, including those of Malaspina, Mutis, Sesse and Mociño, but a period of political and social unrest in the metropole caused it to lose its grip on its colonies. Mexico gained independence from 1810 to 1820, followed by Argentina in 1816, Columbia in 1819, Bolivia in 1825, Chile from 1814 to 1821, and Peru in 1824, so that by the restitution of the monarchy in Spain in 1823 the country's American empire was dwindling rapidly. Following the enlargement of Spain's Moroccan *Presides* (trading posts), which were consolidated as direct colonial control of Morocco in 1861, hopes were revived that the state could hold on to some of its American territories. However, these hopes were dashed when a military expedition of 1862 to the Peruvian and Chilean coasts, mounted as a show of force, ended in defeat in the war of 1865–1866. Nonetheless, neither this expedition nor the one sent to the aid of the Emperor Maximilian of Mexico, also in 1862, were failures in all regards, for the troops were accompanied in both cases by a contingent of scholars – led respectively by Marcos Jiménez de la Espada and Manuel Almagro – who were able to collect large bodies of ethnographic data and artefacts, including the famous Peruvian and Bolivian mummies and the equally famous decorated Guarani skulls.

A *Museo Antropológico* containing anatomical, ethnographic and palaeontological collections was built in Madrid and opened in 1875 as a result of the efforts of Dr Pedro Gonzáles Velasco (1815–1882). These collections and those who organized them, many of whom won *catédras* (professorial chairs) and founded societies, made the *Museo Antropológico* the hub of Spanish anthropology until the 1970s. A friend and student of Broca, Velasco was one of the founder-members of Spain's first anthropological society, established in 1865. In 1874 the society began publishing the *Revista de Antropología*, whose first issue was entirely given over to a defence of Darwinian theory, and as of 1883 this was supplemented by the society's second journal *La Antropología moderna*. During the same period, the *Real Sociedad Geográfica* and the *Sociedad Española de Africanistas y Colonistas* raced to secure a Spanish presence in African territories. Their efforts to establish themselves in Cameroon came to naught when it was granted to Germany by the Treaty of Berlin in 1885, and so instead they concentrated on Spanish Morocco and the Rio de Oro protectorate (Spanish Sahara), and also on the island of Fernando Poó and Equatorial Guinea, which became the destinations of the military-scientific expeditions of Amado Ossorio e Iradier (1884, 1886, 1901), Luis Sorela (1886) and José Valero Belenguer (1890–1891). Preparations for an 1887 Madrid exhibition on the Philippines and the Mariana and Caroline Islands gave anthropologists the opportunity to examine the natives of these territories and make off with artefacts. The Spanish state acquired the Anthropology Museum in 1887, but spread its collections among various institutions. Two further important exhibitions on the Inuit of Labrador in 1890 and on the Ashanti in 1897 added further to the existing collections, which in 1910 were reunited in the *Museo de Antropología*, a section of the new *Museo de Ciencias Naturales*. The Museum's first director, from 1911 to 1929, was Manuel Antón Ferrándiz, who viewed anthropology in morphological terms as a human natural history consisting in the evolution of mankind, but also used psychological, sociological, artistic and moral perspectives. Ferrándiz, a monogenist and, although a student of the Frenchman Quatrefages, a Darwinian, held the anthropology chair in the science faculty of the University of Madrid from 1892. He himself taught Telesforo de Aranzidi, Francisco de las Barra y de Aragón and Luis de Hoyos Sáinz, all three of whom subsequently spent several years in the *Musée d'histoire naturelle* in Paris. The first anthropology society more or less disappeared after the crushing defeat suffered by Spain at the hands of the USA and the abandonment of Cuba, Puerto Rico and the Philippines in 1898. In 1921 the *Sociedad Español de Antropología, Etnografía y Prehistoria* was founded, and in the following year it began to publish *Actas* and *Memorias*. At first these works concentrated primarily on physical anthropology and archaeology, with ethnography and folklore reduced to a marginal role. However, the society was a part of the *Junta de Investigaciones Científicas de Marruecos y Colonias*, created on the initiative of Ignacio Bauer in 1927 and charged with organizing a modest programme of overseas research. Telesforo de Aranzidi and his pupil José Miguel de Barandiarán founded an ethnology of the Basque Country, and Francisco de las Barra y de Aragón replaced Manuel Antón Ferrándiz in his anthropology chair and as director of the *Museo de Antropología*, holding these posts from 1929 to 1936. Luis de Hoyos Sáinz, who was given responsibility for the museum's ethnographic section, carried out research on the ethnography and folklore of the peoples of Spain, gave the first university course on this topic from 1932 to 1936, and in 1934 persuaded the three-year-old republic to found a *Museo del Pueblo Español*. In an attempt to realign itself with Franco and his new regime, the *Sociedad Español de Antropología, Etnografía y Prehistoria* took to referring to the Republic as a criminal and barbarous regime and decided to expel 'reds and separatists' like Juan Comas Camps from its membership (*Atlantis*, vol. 15 (1936–1940), quoted by Romero, 1992: 38). However, this did nothing to diminish the devastating effect of the Caudillo's victory on the folkloric and ruralist forms of anthropology. The folkloric tradition owed much to the Enlightenment spirit (Comas and Prat, 1996), while the ruralist tradition was suspected of encouraging regional separatism (Prat, 1991). All that survived was the historical research of J. **Caro Baroja**, who had no teaching post, and instead Spain became a destination for foreign scholars such as G. G. Foster and, above all, J. Pitt-Rivers, whose *People of the Sierra* appeared in 1954. A decree of 1940 attached the ethnological section to the Institute of Geography; the anthropological collections were moved and the prehistorical collections were transferred to the National Museum of Archaeology in 1941. In 1942 the museum and the Anthropology Society separated, and soon afterwards the latter was disbanded. In 1941 the Upper Council of the *Junta de Investigaciones Científicas* founded an *Instituto Bernardino de Sahagún de Antropología y Etnología*, whose task was the anthropological and biological investigation of the Spanish and the study of the customs, crafts and beliefs of the peoples of Spain, Morocco and the other colonies. The results of the institute's work were published in the *Trabajos del Instituto Fray Bernardino de Sahagún* from 1945 and in *Antropología y etnología* from 1949. On the occasion of the first International Conference of Western Africanists, held in Dakar in 1945, Martínez Santa Olalla constituted a *Comité Español de Africa occidental* and proposed the creation of a Museum of Africa devoted to Equatorial Guinea, Morocco and the Spanish Sahara. A site was not immediately found for the new museum, but in 1948 it could open the doors of its new premises within the General Directorate for Morocco and the Colonies. In 1945 the *Instituto Bernardino de Sahagún* organized an ethnological and palaeontological expedition to Equatorial Guinea under Martínez Santa Olalla, followed in 1948 by another expedition to the same country led by Santiago Alcobe Noguer, professor of physical anthropology at Barcelona. In 1952 the anthropology chair in Madrid was separated from the anthropology museum, which came under the control of the General Directorate of the Fine Arts in 1962. In 1965 the museum's premises became the home of the *Centro Iberoamericano de Antropología* and, more importantly, of its adjunct the *Instituto de Cultura Hispánica*, whose founder and director, C. **Esteva Fabregat**, was also director of the museum. The institute, the first of its sort in Spain, provided teaching in general ethnology, social and physical anthropology, linguistics, and the history of Spain and the Americas. When it closed in 1968 Esteva Fabregat left Madrid for Barcelona University, where he was appointed to Spain's first chair in social anthropology in 1970 and founded the journal *Ethnica*, which was published from 1971 to 1984. Shortly afterwards C. Lisón Tolosana, who had studied at Oxford University, established a new anthropology course at Complutense University in Madrid, and a further course was introduced at Oviedo University by R. Valdes de Toro, who had trained in Germany. In 1973 a meeting was held in Seville by the small complement of Spanish anthropologists, and this paved the way for the first *Congreso de antropologos españoles*, held in Barcelona in 1977. In the late 1970s and early 1980s the discipline grew at an extraordinary rate, and no less than twelve university chairs were endowed (at Complutense in Madrid, the autonomous Uned University, Barcelona University, the autonomous University of Barcelona and Tarragona, the Lagunal University of Tenerife, and the Zorroaga University of San Sebastián, as well as the universities of Lerida, Seville, Santiago de Compostela, Valencia, Salamanca, Murcia, Girona and Grenada). The year 1978 saw the establishment of the *Institut catalá d'antropologia*, which published the *Quaderns de l'Institut catalá d'antropologia* from 1980. This was followed in 1979 by the founding of the *Asociación Madrileña de Antropología*, which from 1982 published *Alcavenas: Revista de Antropología* (renamed *Antropología: Revista de Pensamiento Antropológico y Estudos Etnográficos* in 1991). Finally, the *Instituto Aragonés de antropología* was founded in 1980. A *Federación de Asocianiones de Antropología del Estado Español* was founded in 1981 as an umbrella organization for the growing number of regional associations.

Caro Baroja, Julio (1916–1995)

Author of *Los pueblos de España* (Madrid, 1946), Julio Caro Baroja is Spain's most famous anthropologist. After directing the *Museo del Pueblo Español* from its reopening in Barcelona in 1944 until 1954, he devoted all his time to his own research; he never taught. A *Festschrift* published in his honour in 1978 lists forty books and 354 articles in its bibliography of his works. His *Estudios sobre la vida tradicional española* of 1968, intended as a development of his *Los Vascos: Etnología* of 1949, is a meticulous examination of the Basque culture he experienced as a child. *Los Baroja* of 1972 describes the lives of his mother and two brothers. He received international recognition for his 1961 study of sorcery, *Las Brujas y su Mondo*, which he followed up with *El Carnaval* in 1965 (Madrid: Taurus).

Esteva Fabregat, Claudio (born 1918)

Born in Marseille, C. Esteva Fabregat moved to Barcelona before being forced into exile in 1939 after having fought on the Republican side in the Civil War. He chose to settle in Mexico, where he joined a group of Spanish exiles and edited the journal *Presencia*. Following the example of a number of older anthropologists (Pedro Armillas, Pedro Carasco, José Luis Lorenzo) he enrolled in the National School of Anthropology and History, where he was taught by two other Spanish exiles, Juan Comas Camps and P. Bosch-Gimpera. The situation of Mexico as a multi-ethnic, developing country made applied anthropology seem particularly relevant, but Esteva Fabregat, who had been in analysis with Erich Fromm, was drawn by this experience to the 'culture and personality' school. He carried out research in

San Nicolás Totolapán, gained a Master's degree and returned to Madrid in 1956. He obtained a doctorate in the history of the Americas from the *Instituto de Cultura Hispánica*, in which he established the *Centro Iberoamericano de Antropolgía*, the first Spanish centre of cultural anthropology, in 1965. He left in 1968 to take up a teaching post at Barcelona University, where he was appointed to Spain's first chair in social anthropology in 1970, and from then on the main focus of his research was urban life and interethnic relations. In 1971 he launched the journal *Ethnica: Revista de antropología cultural.*

PORTUGAL

From the fifteenth to the seventeenth centuries Portugal produced a rich body of documentary literature, but the early Portuguese ethnological tradition was almost exclusively ruralist, as can be seen from works by T. Braga, A. Coelho and P. de Carvalho. This tradition survives in the more recent work of J. Leite de Vasconcelos, who published the ten-volume *Etnografia Portuguese* from 1933 to 1985. In 1875 a *Sociedade de Geografia de Lisboa* was founded with its own journal which concentrated on colonial ethnography, and a new Colonial School was formed by some of its members at the beginning of the dictatorship in 1926. The *Museu e Laboratório Antropológico* was opened at the University of Coimbra in 1885 with a focus on physical anthropology, and the same focus characterized the work directed by M. Corrêa at the University of Porto from the 1930s. In 1919 Corrêa founded the journal *Trabalhos de Antropologia e etnologia*, and he, together with J. dos Santos Junior and other assistants, became known for anthropometric investigations of colonized peoples.

A group of trustees founded a Portuguese School of Colonial Ethnography after the Second World War. The school was staffed in Angola by José Redinha, Mario Fontinha and Acacio Videira in conjunction with the Luanda Institute of Scientific Research; in Mozambique by Pegado e Silva; and in Guinea-Bissau by R. Quintino, A. Carreira and T. Da Mota (110 issues of the *Boletim cultural da Guiné Portuguesa* were published from 1946 to 1973). A museum was established in each of these territories.

A. J. **Dias**, who had studied in Germany, was employed by the Centre for Studies in Peninsular Ethnology, founded in 1945. He helped open up Portuguese anthropology to American culturalism and British social anthropology from 1950 to 1970. Dias also founded the Museum of Ethnology in Lisbon. Some of the work done in this period, for example by M. Lima and R. de Aria, was very modern, but it was not until after the Carnation Revolution of 1974 and the return to Portugal of a generation trained abroad that anthropology could really grow, and in the 1980s it grew very rapidly. As well as the universities of Coimbra and Porto, there are three universities in Lisbon currently offering complete degree courses in ethnology. These are the *Instituto Superior de Ciências Sociais e Políticas Ultra marina* (which replaced the Colonial School) and two further institutions which grew out of it: the *Universidade Nova* and the *Instituto Superior de Ciências do Trabalho e da Empresa*. The last of these began publishing the journal *Etnográfica* in 1997.

Dias, António Jorge (1907–1973)
After studies in German philology at the University of Coimbra, António Jorge Dias moved to the German town of Rostock in 1938 to work as a lecturer in Portuguese. While in Germany he was taught by

Thurnwald in Berlin and completed a thesis at the University of Munich, and then from 1944 to 1947 he worked in Spain. In 1948, while employed by the Centre for Studies in Peninsular Ethnology, he published a recast version of his German thesis in Portuguese translation, as well as a work on the origins and distribution of instruments of labour. In 1950 he travelled to the USA and in 1952 he took a teaching position at Coimbra before being appointed professor at the School of Colonial Administration (renamed the *Instituto Superior de Ciências Sociais e Politicas Ultramarina* in 1961). He worked on Africa, visiting Portuguese Guinea in 1956 and Angola and Mozambique in 1957. Most of his research was done during university vacations, but he nevertheless managed to complete a four-volume monograph on the Maconde.

BELGIUM

The Belgians have contributed to the discipline from the earliest days of its development. The Flemish Franciscan monk Guillaume Rubroeck (or Rubruquis, 1220–1293) travelled as far as Karakorum in Mongolia and was the first European to provide an objective description of elements of Tartar and Mongol culture. The plying of trade routes gave further opportunities for 'exotic' narratives, like those on Africa by Eustache de la Fosse of 1479–1480 and by P. van den Broecke of 1605–1606 and 1609–1612. While ethnology was not born of colonialism, it partook of the same process of expansion. The highly volatile history of what is now Belgium, once part of the Netherlands and later annexed by Austria and France, ruled out colonial conquest until independence and the establishment of a constitutional monarchy under Leopold I in 1831. Following his accession in 1865, Leopold II took a personal role in submitting the Congo to Belgian rule (aided by the British explorer Stanley, who was in his pay), and in the Treaty of Berlin of 1887 the territory was recognized as a Belgian colony. In 1880 a *Société d'anthropologie de Bruxelles* was founded with its own journal, and yet Belgian anthropology from that period until the 1930s consisted chiefly in voluminous ethnographical studies on Africa composed by army officers, including A. Burdo, E. Storms and T. Masui. They also assembled collections which were displayed in the Antwerp International Exhibition of 1894, and immediately afterwards the exhibition hall in Tervuren which housed them was reopened as the *Musée du Congo*, with T. Masui as its director and E. Coart as his deputy. The journal *Belgique coloniale* was launched in 1897, and in 1899 the new museum began publishing the *Annales du Musée du Congo*, with contributions from Belgian colonial administrators like Liebrechts, Costermans and Dhanis. A *Bureau international d'ethnographie* directed by C. van Overbergh was created on the occasion of the International Congress of Economic Expansion, held in Mons in 1905, and it published over ten monographs between 1907 and 1914. Two other journals, which both appeared from 1910 to 1914, were *Onze Kongo* and *Revue congolaise*. C. van Overbergh's assistant at the bureau was E. de Jonghe, who in 1908 inaugurated a course in the general ethnology and ethnography of the Congo at the Catholic University of Louvain. By then the University of Liège had already introduced an ethnography course in 1904 taught by the geographer Halkin, and this was followed in 1907 by a new programme at the University of Ghent taught by the botanist and geographer Bruyne. Finally, the Free University of Brussels introduced its course in 1910 under M. Weiller. In the same year a refurbished *Musée du Congo* was opened, curated by J. Maes, who had replaced Masui's successor Coart, and in 1920 an *Ecole coloniale supérieure*, which also provided teaching in ethnography, opened in Antwerp. F. H. Lambrecht, who worked as a missionary in the Philippines, established himself as the first major specialist on the Ifugao from 1924 onwards. In 1930 the journal *Aequatoria* first appeared, joining *Congo* (1920–1940) and *Kongo-Overzee* (1934–1959). Particularly important was the expedition of G. Smets, an academic specializing in mediaeval history, to Burundi in 1932–1933 to investigate feudal-type societies in Black Africa. Smets then replaced Weiller in his chair at the Free University of Brussels. F. M. **Olbrechts**, who after studies under **Boas** held a post in the *Musées Royaux d'Art et d'Histoire* in Brussels, undertook several African expeditions, especially to West Africa. In 1940 he opened an *Institut pour l'étude de l'art africain* at the University of Ghent, where he held a teaching post, and soon afterwards he was given a further appointment replacing the retiring Maes as director of the *Musée du Congo* at Tervuren. Among Olbrechts's students were J. **Maquet**, J. Laude, Maesen, J. P. van den Houtte and J. Weyns. He also taught Brurssens, who later combined a chair in African linguistics with a part-time directorship of the Ghent institute, where he taught van Geertryen. The early postwar years were marked by the publication of *Bantoe-filosofie* by Father Placide **Tempels** (criticized by Léon de **Sousbergh**) and by the creation in 1947 of the *Institut pour la Recherche Scientifique en Afrique Centrale* (IRSAC) with a social sciences section overseen by Olbrechts. This institute recruited a number of young scholars, whose research was published in the journal *Zaïre* (1947–1961), and its early members were J. Hiernaux, a physical anthropologist; J. Maquet, the first head of the Rwandan station; and J. Biebuyck, who researched on the Bembe and the Nyanga. They were joined by L. de **Heusch**, who worked on the Tetela; by J. **Vansina**, who worked on the Kuba; and by the linguists A. Coupez and J. Jacons. Later members included A. Doutreloux (Yombe), J. Cuypers (Shi), P. van Leynseele (Libinza), J. Theuws (Luba), E. Roosens (Yaka), F. Crinne and D. Bieck. In 1948 the Fourth International Congress of Anthropological and Ethnological Science was organized in Brussels and Tervuren by E. de Jonghe assisted by F. M. Olbrechts as secretary-general. L. Cahen succeeded F. M. Olbrechts as director of the *Musée du Congo*, and H. **Lavachéry** (1885–1972), an archaeologist and Polynesian specialist who had taken part in a Franco-Belgian mission to Easter Island with A. **Métraux** in 1934, then replaced Smets at the Free University of Brussels in 1950, but retired almost immediately afterwards. He was succeeded by Dorsinsang-Smets, the holder of a chair dedicated to the Americas, and Dorsinsang-Smets was joined for a short period by J. Maquet. From 1955 Luc de Heusch acted as Belgium's main advocate of structural analysis. When the colonial period came to an end in 1960 and the independent state of Zaïre was created, the *Musée du Congo* was renamed *Musée Royal de l'Afrique Centrale*, and in 1961 the journal *Congo-Tervuren* became *Africa Tervuren*. The years that followed saw a diversification of the areas covered by Belgian anthropologists, and Lilyan Kesteloot wrote the first thesis on Black francophone writers in 1961. J. Vansina proposed a new ethnohistory, and the universities of Ghent, Louvain and Brussels introduced courses on this topic. Luc de Heusch was made professor at the Free University of Brussels in 1960, and he and Dorsinsang-Smets, together with their assistants Louis Bastin and Robert Kaufmann, created a *Centre d'anthropologie culturelle* in 1965. It was here that E. Pollet and P. Jorion, and later J.-P. Colleyn, D. Jonckers, P. Jespers, P. Posno and M. Meuseur were trained and then held teaching positions from the 1970s onwards. The Catholic University of Louvain closed its Africanist Institute in 1964, but instead introduced teaching in social and cultural anthropology and created a *Centre d'anthropologie sociale et culturelle* in 1972. The man responsible for both of these initiatives was Eugeen Roosens, who had returned from a study trip to Zaïre (where IRSAC had become the *Institut zaïrois* in 1973), and whose later research was on the Hurons. In the new centre at Louvain medical anthropology was developed by R. Devische, and other members of the teaching staff were W. de Mahieu, and later de Boeck, M. C. Foblets and V. Necherbrouck. The Catholic University of Louvain-la-Neuve broke away from the existing university in the same town and established a course in anthropology taught by Father M. Doutreloux, who launched the journal *Culture et développement*, published from 1969 to 1985. Of those who joined Doutreloux at Louvain-la-Neuve, perhaps the best-known was the Indianist R. Deliège. It is not possible to map out all of Belgian anthropology here, and so no more than a mention can be made of the existence of a cognitive anthropology at the University of Ghent centred around R. Pinxten, a specialist on the Navajo.

Olbrechts, Frans-M. (1899–1958)

After gaining a philology doctorate in 1925 with a thesis on the Flemish magic formula, Frans-M. Olbrechts spent the years from 1926 to 1929 at Columbia University studying under **Boas** and working as an ethnographer and linguist on the Cherokee and the Onondaga. On his return to Belgium he was put in charge of the ethnographic collections of the *Musée Royal d'Art et d'Histoire* in Brussels. In 1929 he published his first book *Kunst van Vroeg en van Verre*, an examination of exotic arts, which he called 'primary' arts, and in 1932 he made his first journey to West Africa with a view to expanding the museum's collections. Later in the same year he was appointed professor of ethnology and the history of primitive arts at the *Institut supérieur d'histoire de l'art et d'archéologie* at the University of Ghent. In 1947 he was made director of the *Musée du Congo* at Tervuren. Olbrechts' importance in the history of Belgian Africanism resides in the trend he set with his focus on the anthropology of art – there are few if any Belgian anthropologists who have not published at least one book on statuary, from L. de **Sousbergh** on Pende art to L. de **Heusch** (under the pseudonym Zangrie) on Boyo statues.

Sousbergh, Léon de (born 1903)

An exile during the First World War, Léon de Sousbergh went to school in London and Paris. He then studied philosophy and law at the Catholic University of Louvain before moving to Vienna to be taught by Father W. **Schmidt**. Back in Belgium he joined the Society of Jesus in 1930 and was ordained a priest in 1936. In 1949 he moved to London to study anthropology under C. D. **Forde**, and in 1950 he published his first work, a criticism of the theses of P. **Tempels**. He spent the years from 1951 to 1953 and from 1955 to 1957 in the Congo, becoming the foremost specialist on the Pende. He paid particular attention to their kinship system, disagreeing with **Lévi-Strauss**'s assertion that it is based on alliance by marriage. De **Sousbergh** lived in Mexico from 1960 to 1962 and then taught in Lovanium (Zaïre) and in Bujumbura.

Tempels, Placide (1906–1977)

A Flemish missionary and amateur anthropologist, Placide Tempels attempted to study Bantu thought structures using their own categories. The result was *Bantoe-filosofie* (Antwerpen, De Sikkel, 1946) [*Bantu Philosophy*, 1969], which rejected the notion of Bantu primitivity and put forward the idea of a Negro philosophy with an ontology founded on the concept of vital force (where we see beings, they see forces). This forms a coherent world view whereby what reinforces life is good and what weakens it is bad, and these principles impinge on penal and land ownership law. This book can be considered to have launched ethnophilosophy, and it was hugely successful despite criticisms from Césaire, Hountondji and many others. At first Tempels's approach was tolerated by the Catholic Church, but it was not long before it aroused condemnation, and he himself was sent to a remote part of Belgium.

Maquet, Jacques Jérôme (born 1919)

Born in Brussels, Jacques Jérôme Maquet gained doctorates in law in 1946 and philosophy in 1948 from the University of Louvain before studying social anthropology at the universities of Harvard and then London, where he obtained a Ph.D. in 1952. In late 1952 he began a long period of fieldwork in Central Africa, and in the years that followed he taught in various institutions. In 1963 he was appointed a director of studies at the EPHE, and later became a professor at the universities of Brussels and Cleveland and at UCLA.

Heusch, Luc de (born 1927)

Luc de Heusch studied at the Free University of Brussels under G. Smets and then, in 1951–1952, at the Sorbonne under M. **Griaule**. From 1953 to 1955 he carried out research on the Tetela of the Kasai for the Solvay Institute. He made the acquaintance of **Lévi-Strauss** after reading his *Elementary Structures of Kinship*, and in 1955 published an article in *Zaïre* defending his theses against de **Sousbergh**'s criticisms. In this article he supported the model of generalized exchange and demonstrated the validity of Lévi-Strauss's structural distinction between matrilateral and patrilateral cross-cousin marriages. After completing his doctoral dissertation in 1955, de Heusch returned to fieldwork studies, this time for IRSAC, and in 1960 was appointed professor at the Free University of Brussels. In 1966 he was promoted to the position of director of the *Centre d'anthropologie culturelle* at the same university. From 1966 to 1968 and again from 1972 to 1975 he was director of studies in Section V of the EPHE. In *Mythes et rites bantous: Le roi ivre ou l'origine de l'Etat* (Paris: Gallimard, 1972) he proposes a structuralist reading of the myths of the Central

African kingdoms, in which he identifies a complete cosmogenesis. He worked on sacrifice during his time as director of the CNRS's *Laboratoire de systèmes de pensée en Afrique Noire* and subsequently turned his attention to Haitian voodoo and to Tzigane culture.

Vansina, Jan (1929–2001)

Jan Vansina studied at London University under C. D. **Forde** and then worked for the *Institut pour la Recherche Scientifique en Afrique Centrale*. He carried out fieldwork on the Kuba from 1953 to 1956 and obtained a doctorate from the University of Louvain in 1957 for a thesis in Dutch which was then recast and published in French translation as *De la tradition orale: Essai de méthodologie historique* (Tervuren, 1961). In this work he argues that the researcher must determine the voluntary or non-voluntary nature of his interviews with informants, the meanings these interviews yield, the genre they belong to, and the rules of their internal construction. Oral traditions are intended to justify the status quo, and so they are found mainly where authority is strong, and far less frequently where the political structure is unstable. After publishing on questions of methodology, Vansina applied his own proposed methods in *Les Anciens Royaumes de la Savane* (University of Lovanium, 1965), which describes the migrations and then the establishment of kingdoms in Central Africa in the fifteenth century, as well as the ensuing social changes. His books revolutionized approaches to African history. He then taught in Kinshasa while researching in Rwanda-Burundi, and afterwards became professor at Brussels University and also associate professor and then professor at the University of Wisconsin. Vansina's learning is synthesized in his *Paths in the Rain Forests: Toward a History of Political Tradition in Equatorial Africa* (Wisconsin UP, 1990), which traces a three-thousand year history of Equatorial Africa.

THE NETHERLANDS

In 1837 P.-F. van Siebold brought together his Japanese collection to create the Leyden Museum of Ethnology, the world's first ethnology museum. In 1851 the Royal Institute of Linguistics, Geography and Ethnology of the Dutch East Indies was founded with government support, followed in 1883 by the Rotterdam Museum of Ethnology and then by the Royal Amsterdam Institute of Tropical Regions. In 1898 the Dutch Anthropological Association established by the physical anthropologist J. Sasse held its first conference, attended by **Steinmetz**, **Nieboer** and **Wilken** under the presidency of Winkler, a psychiatrist and disciple of Lambroso, and the proceedings of the conference were published in 1904. All the same, anthropology in Dutch universities issued in the first instance from a tradition of colonial scholarship known as Indology: the philological study of the Indonesian languages and the inquiry into Indonesian Islam and the *adat* law of custom. These topics were investigated by colonial administrators and by jurists, such as C. van Vollenhoven, who were interested in non-European legal systems. Other areas examined by Indologists were tropical agriculture, economics and physical anthropology. From 1834 a course in ethnology tailored to the needs of colonial administrators was offered at Surkarta College in Java, and from 1864 teaching in colonial Indology was provided by the *Indische Instelling* (Indian Institute) of Delft (**de Josselin de Jong** and Vermeulen, 1989: 284). Finally, in 1877 a chair devoted to the geography and ethnology of the Indonesian archipelago was endowed at the University of Leyden, followed by the creation of the *Koninklijk Instituut voor Taal-, Land-, en Volkenkunde* (Royal Institute of Linguistics, Geography and Ethnology). This new institute made the Delft institute obsolete, and it closed down in 1900 (de Josselin de Jong, 1983: 4). The Leyden chair was held successively by Pieter Johannes Veth (1877–1885), George Alexander Wilken (1885–1890), J. J. M. de Groot (1890–1904), and A. W. Nieuwenhuit (1904–1935), a physician who had led several missions to the forests of Borneo, especially to study the Dayak. In 1907 the University of Amsterdam created a chair of *Volkenkunde* (ethnology) with a bias towards geography, and this was first occupied by S. R. **Steinmetz**. In 1922 Nieuwenhuit was joined at Leyden by J. P. B. de Josselin de Jong, who replaced him in the chair in 1935. In these years important studies were produced by Held, Van Wouden and Van Baal.

Cultural anthropology was in relative decline within the Dutch Anthropological Association during this period. In 1917 the first Annual Ethnological Meeting was held in Amsterdam, and in the years that followed this became the major event in the profession. The organizers of the first meeting were Steinmetz, Van Eerde, a former colonial administrator and head of the ethnological and anthropological section of the Colonial Institute founded in 1910, and Kleiweg de Zwaan (1875–1971), honorary professor of physical anthropology at Amsterdam University. As of 1924 Dutch folklorists, who until then had been counted among the anthropologists, organized their own meetings.

Following the examples of Leyden and Amsterdam, the University of Utrecht endowed an ethnology chair held by Dr Kohlbrugge (1865–1942) until his retirement in 1935. According to De Wolf, 'originally the Utrecht chair was meant for teaching geographers, but in 1925 the training of colonial administrators was added to Kohlbrugge's duties. Dissatisfied with the alleged progressive character of the courses given at Leyden University, big business firms with major colonial interests funded an alternative faculty at Utrecht with the approval of the government then in power' (De Wolf, 2001). Fischer (1901–1987) occupied the chair vacated by Kohlbrugge in 1936, having already relieved him of the teaching of the colonial ethnology course.

'Somewhat surprising', in De Wolf's view, 'is the neglect of intensive field research by professionally trained Dutch anthropologists in Indonesia during this period'. There was no government funding for this kind of research. Thus the teaching of ethnology to colonial administrators had to rely on ethnographic data which were supplied by administrators, soldiers, missionaries, explorers and collectors as well as anthropologists from other countries. The latter category included Margaret **Mead** and Gregory **Bateson**, who worked on Bali, and Cora **Du Bois**, who did research on the Alor' (De Wolf, 2001). All the same, 1924 saw the appearance of the first issue of *Mensch en Maatschappij* (*Man and Society*), which in 1936 published the proceedings of the first meeting of the Dutch Sociological Association, founded in 1936.

The first meeting of the International Anthropology Institute was held in Paris in 1920, and in 1922 Kleiweg de Zwaan created the Dutch National Bureau for Anthropology as one of the Institute's branches. The bureau's ethnography and ethnology section was run by Van Eerde, and the section on folklore, genetics, eugenics, sociology and criminology was run by Steinmetz. In the interwar period the bureau played a dominant role in the discipline and instituted the separation between social and physical anthropology. During the occupation of the Netherlands from 1940 to 1945 the folklorists adopted a pro-German position, but in Leyden the anthropology department was shut down and Fischer had to go into hiding. In 1949 the Dutch Society for Anthropology was founded, which in 1952 was divided into two sections devoted to physical and cultural anthropology. Following Indonesian independence in 1949 (Western New Guinea was not restored to Indonesia until 1962, and Surinam gained independence in 1975), Dutch anthropology entered a new phase, and 'non-Western sociology' was developed. At Leyden an institute was created which contained, alongside an Indology chair for J. P. B. de Josselin de Jong, a Latin American and Caribbean chair, held by the Surinam specialist Van Lier; a Southeast Asia and Pacific chair, to which Locher was appointed in 1953; and an African chair, successively held by Hofstra, Busia, Holleman, **Beattie** and **Kuper**. In 1956, P. E. De **Josselin de Jong** replaced his uncle in the Indology chair and turned it into a chair of cultural anthropology. The Agricultural University of Wageningen created the first chair with a technical bias in 1946 and a second, for Van Lier, in 1956 (De Wolf, 2001). Further chairs were created at the Free University of Amsterdam (1947, 1956, 1965), the University of Nijmegen (1948, 1956), the University of Groningen (1951), and the Economic University of Rotterdam (1964) (Vermeulen, 1998(1): 9).

In 1969 a far-reaching ministerial reform resulted in a geographical reconfiguration of chairs and departments: Leyden became responsible for Africa and Indonesia, Utrecht for Latin America, the Caribbean, cognitive anthropology and linguistic anthropology, Nijmegen for Oceania and economic anthropology, Amsterdam for Europe, the Mediterranean world and South Asia, and the Free University of Amsterdam for religious and urban anthropology. Another reform implemented in the early 1990s stipulated that the programmes taught by the smaller departments be regrouped in research schools. Thus Leyden created a department of non-Western languages and cultures, Utrecht and Nijmegen concentrated on development studies, and Amsterdam on a historically informed sociology.

In 1959 *Mensch en Maatschappij* became a sociology journal, but each year it published one social anthropology issue in association with the journal *Bijdrage tot de Taal*. The *International Archives of Ethnography*, launched in 1888, found itself without an editor in 1967, while *Sociologische Gids* accorded increasing space to anthropology. From 1982 the new journal *Antropologische Verkenningen* was published annually, and then from 1988 to 1996 three times a year, before folding. The journals *Focaal* (1986) and *Etnofoor* (1988) were launched by students at the universities of Nijmegen and Amsterdam respectively (De Wolf, 2001).

Wilken, George Alexander (1847–1891)

The son of a Protestant missionary working in the Minhasa region north of Sulawesi, George Alexander Wilken passed the colonial service examination in 1868 and worked as a colonial administrator for the next twelve years in the East Indies, on the Island of Buru and in different areas of Northern Sulawesi. During this period he wrote his first articles on primitive marriage, the origins of the family, and the nature of kinship and inheritance in Indonesia (1881). His interest very soon turned to notions of animism and *adatrecht* (the law of custom). He was the only Dutch ethnologist of this period to exchange ideas with celebrated contemporaries such as **Morgan**, **Tylor**, **Frazer** and Robertson **Smith**, and he is often thought to have fuelled the emergence of Dutch ethnology. He applied evolutionist theory to Indonesian societies, and between 1885 and 1890 he held the chair in the geography and ethnology of the Dutch Indies at the University of Leyden, succeeding P. J. Veth.

Steinmetz, Sebald R. (1862–1940)

After legal training at the University of Leyden, Sebald R. Steinmetz moved to Leipzig University to complete his studies, and in 1894 he published his doctoral thesis, which was reviewed by **Mauss**, on the origins and development of legal punishment. This topic betrays the influence of Steinmetz's teacher **Wilken**, who had emphasized the gains of applying ethnology to comparative jurisprudential studies. In 1907 Steinmetz was appointed to the chair in political and non-political geography, anthropology and ethnology of the Indonesian archipelago at the University of Amsterdam, and he played a vital role in early stages of the scission of

ethnology in the Netherlands. Unlike Wilken he based his method on library research, describing himself as a comparatist, and his object was the constitution of a vast catalogue of extant peoples designed to facilitate comparative studies. According to De Wolf, Steinmetz thought that the objective of ethnology is to examine the different lifestyles of primitive peoples and discover their orally communicated laws. Although recognized mainly as a sociologist, Steinmetz also enabled Dutch ethnology to develop, and he is remembered for his *History of Ethnology*, published in 1917.

Ossenbruggen, F. D. E. van (1869–1950)

F. D. E. van Ossenbruggen trained as a lawyer and then worked in the East Indies, first as a teacher in schools for native administrators, then as judge, and from 1929 as a magistrate in the Batavia Supreme Court in Jakarta. His profession brought him into contact with Indonesian juridical conceptions, and his growing interest in this topic drew him towards comparative law, the law of custom (*adatrecht*), and social anthropology. Under the influence of the work of Durkheim and **Mauss** he turned his attention increasingly to the indigenous population's understanding of its own culture. By spreading knowledge of the work of the founding fathers of social anthropology in the Netherlands, he exerted a decisive influence on the course of ethnology both there and in Indonesia.

Nieboer, J. H. (1873–1920)

An evolutionist, J. H. Nieboer concentrated his research on slavery, seen as the situation of a man who is the property or possession of another man. In his view, slavery is not to be found in situations where survival depends on material resources present in limited quantities, which is why it is a rare phenomenon among hunters and fishermen. Nieboer's thesis on this topic, submitted to the law faculty of the University of Utrecht in 1900, has been described by De Wolf (1995) as a classic of ethnology.

Rassers, Willem Huibert (1877–1973)

A close friend of J. P. B. De **Josselin de Jong**, Willem Huibert Rassers studied languages and literature at the University of Leyden, obtaining Master's degrees in both Dutch language and literature and in the languages and literatures of the Indonesian archipelago. Health problems delayed until 1922 the completion of his thesis *De Pandj-roman*, which made his name. He then worked as a curator in the Malayo-Polynesian section of the National Ethnography Museum in Leyden, becoming its director from 1937 until his retirement in 1943; it was at the museum that he met De Josselin de Jong. Although he never travelled to Indonesia, Rassers made a significant impact on the Leyden structuralist school, influencing not just its ethnologists, but also students of linguistics, history, literature, archaeology and *adatrecht* (the law of custom).

Josselin de Jong, Jan Petrus Benjamin De (1886–1964)

Born in Leyden, Jan Petrus Benjamin De Josselin de Jong studied linguistics and then worked with the linguist C. C. Uhlenbeck on the Blackfoot and the Ojibwa in 1910–1911. He was a curator of the National Ethnography Museum in Leyden from 1911 to 1935, and from 1922 also taught at the University of Leyden, where he became a professor in 1935. From 1932 to 1934 he did linguistic and then ethnological research in Indonesia, which became his area of specialism. **Lévi-Strauss** acknowledged his strong influence on his own works, and de Jong was the first to respond in print

to *Elementary Structures of Kinship* in his book *Lévi-Strauss's Theory of Kinship and Marriage* (Leyden, 1952).

Ball, Jan van (born 1909 or 1914)

After studies in Indology from 1927 to 1932 and the completion of his thesis on a population of head-hunters entitled *Godsdienst en samenleving in Nederlandsch Zuid-Nieuw-Guinea*, Jan van Ball entered the colonial service in 1934 and served in New Guinea. In 1942 he carried out research in Indonesia, where he and his wife were captured by the Japanese and interned for three months in a camp. On his return to the Netherlands he formulated his first theorization of religion as the fundamental human experience. He then went back to New Guinea provisionally to establish an Office of Native Affairs in 1951, and subsequently was appointed *Kontroleur*, or Governor, of Dutch New Guinea. His best known book is *Dema: Description and Analysis of Marind Asim Culture (South New Guinea)* (The Hague), published in 1966 after a number of his other works had already appeared. Written in collaboration with the missionary clergyman R. P. Verschuren, who spent his whole life in the region, the book describes the Marind Asim head-hunting people of Iriant Jayat, who had already became familiar through the photography of P. Wirz. Van Ball taught in the anthropology department of the University of Amsterdam's Tropical Institute from 1959, a post he combined with teaching at the University of Utrecht from 1960. He was made professor at Utrecht in 1969 and retired in 1975.

Josselin de Jong, Patrick Edward De (1922–1999)

The son of a Sinologist and born in Beijing, Patrick Edward De Josselin de Jong began studies of Indonesian languages at the University of Leyden in 1948. In 1951 he completed an anthropology thesis, supervised by his maternal uncle J. P. B. De **Josselin** de **Jong**, on socio-political resemblances between the Negri Sembilan society of Malaysia and the Minangkabau of Sumatra, a topic which remained central to his whole research career. In 1949 he became deputy curator of the National Ethnography Museum in Leyden, and from 1953 to 1956 he taught at the University of Malaya while doing research on the Negri Sembilan. In 1956 he succeeded his uncle in the Leyden anthropology chair when the latter retired, and he remained in this post until 1987. He carried out further fieldwork in Thailand, and also on the Minangkabou of Indonesia and the Sarawak of Borneo. Appearing from the years following Indonesian independence, De Josselin de Jong's published work forms a bridge between the most traditional form of Dutch ethnology and the research of the anthropologists of independence. It also went beyond Dutch structuralism by emphasizing 'The Vision of Participants in their own Culture', to quote the title of an article of 1956. He produced more than 180 publications, including nine books.

GERMANY AND AUSTRIA

Traditionally, German-language anthropology has been close to Orientalism and to geography. When the discipline re-emerged tentatively after the Second World War it was lacking in dominant theories and very inward-looking, but it developed rapidly in the 1970s and spawned a great variety of new approaches. Now almost every major German university contains an ethnology department, while Austria is the home of an important institute.

Schmidt and **Koppers** fled from Austria to Switzerland in 1938, taking with them the archives of the *Societas Verbi Divini* and the *Anthropos-Institut*. In the same year **Heine-Geldern**, a professor since 1931, went into exile in England, and so H. **Baumann**, previously of the Museum of Berlin, settled in Vienna to direct the university's abandoned *Völkerkunde* institute. After the Allied victory in 1945 Koppers returned to his post at the institute, where he was joined by Josef **Haekel**, who by 1956 had persuaded him to accept that the *Kulturkreislehre* had had its day. The institute also benefited from the teaching of W. **Hirschberg**, the curator of the African section of the museum, who in time became a *Dozent* and then a professor before directing the institute from 1962 to 1975. Hirschberg proposed that the *Kulturkreislehre* be replaced by a new form of research he called 'ethno-history', which would reconstruct the cultural history of African societies from their first moment of contact with Europeans. In the years that followed K. Wernhert, a specialist on Polynesia and later on the Caribbean, and W. **Dostal**, an expert on Yemen, joined the institute and opened it up to these culture areas. Dostal retired from the institute in 1996 and was replaced by A. Gingrich, who transformed it into an Institute of Cultural and Social Anthropology, which by 2000 had two thousand registered students.

The *Forschungsinstitut für Kulturmorphologie*, first established in Munich, moved to Frankfurt am Main in 1925, and A. E. **Jensen** became its director after the death of L. V. **Frobenius** in 1938. Jensen kept his distance from Nazi ideology, and the Frobenius Institute, as he renamed it, was fairly inactive during the war years. When Jensen retired in 1963 he was replaced by C. A. Schmitz, a specialist on New Guinea and in particular on its kinship structures, and he in turn was succeeded by Eike Haberland, an Ethiopian specialist who had previously directed the Ethnological Institute at the University of Cologne.

At the end of the nineteenth century the Americanists K. von **Steinen** and Eduard Seler had introduced anthropology teaching at the Humboldt University of Berlin. Their student M. **Schmidt** became the university's first professor of ethnology in 1921 with K. T. **Preuß** and L. **Adam** as colleagues, while the professorship of physical anthropology was held from 1909 by Felix von Luschan.

In 1933 the Humboldt University created an *Institut für Völkerkunde*, and in 1937 R. C. **Thurnwald** returned from Yale University to become its professor in place of Adam, who had emigrated to England. Thurnwald secured the appointment of **Mühlmann**, who was close to the regime, and the two of them ruled over the institute for the rest of the Nazi period. After the war Mühlmann's teaching rights were briefly suspended, while Thurnwald was selected by the American occupying forces to refound German anthropology. With the help of his wife Hilde, he established an Ethnology Institute in 1946 which became part of the Free University of Berlin in 1948. When Thurnwald died in 1954 he was replaced by one of his disciples, S. Westphal-Hellbusch, while the directorship of the Humboldt University Ethnology Institute fell to Frederick Rose. After many years of exile in the USA spent doing research on the American Indians, J. E. Lips moved to East Germany in 1948 to fill the anthropology chair at the University of Leipzig. He also became director of the *Ethnologisches Institut* which operated alongside the newly created *Institut für Vergleichende Rechtssoziologie*. When he died in January 1950 his wife Eva Lips became director of both institutes, which she then merged as the *Institut Julius Lips*. She was assisted by Lothar Stein, who subsequently became director of the *Museum für Völkerkunde*, which from 1951 published a yearbook. Baumann, who had been expelled from Vienna in 1945 and then cold-shouldered until the early 1950s, created an *Institut für Völkerkunde* in 1955 at the University of Munich, where he then held the ethnology chair until he was replaced by Mühlmann in 1967.

Alongside the institutions already mentioned, an important role is played by the sociology faculty of the University of Bielefeld, which includes many scholars working on the anthropology of development. Tübingen has a small Ethnology Institute specializing in Central American cultures and American archaeology and also an *Institut für Empirische Kulturwissenschaft* for the study of the ethnology of modern everyday life, which has been directed by U. Jeggle. At Heidelberg there is a Southeast Asian Institute, and in the 1980s a Cultural Ethnology Institute was created by J. Wassmann, while in Münster R. Schott established a department focusing on juridical anthropology in 1965. Today the Ethnology Institute of the Free University of Berlin is divided into two parts, each with its own chair: the Asian section is directed by G. Pfeffer, and the African section by G. Elwert. Alongside its anthropology department, the University of Göttingen founded an institute with a particular emphasis on ethnographic cinema. Other notable departments are those of the University of Bayreuth, which enjoys an excellent reputation in Africanist studies; the University of Bonn, reformed after the war by Hermann Triamborn; the University of Cologne, with its specialism in the culture areas of Latin America and Asia; the University of Mainz, where Mühlmann was professor from 1950 until 1960 before being succeeded by the Australian specialist H. Petri; and the universities of Hamburg, Freiburg im Breisgau, Trier and Marburg. Following the fall of the Berlin Wall the Anthropology Institute of the European University of Frankfurt an der Oder was set up under the direction of W. Schiffauer, and in 1998 a Max Planck Institute for Social Anthropology was established in Halle with Günther Schlee and Christopher Hann as its directors.

There are currently about twenty ethnology institutes in Germany with a variety of different names. One of the significant features of the German tradition is the way links between ethnology museums and university anthropology departments have been maintained to the present day, for example at Hamburg, Tübingen, Göttingen and Mainz (see Diallo, 2001). Another important feature of German ethnology is that 'except for the period 1885–1918, it is the ethnology of a society without either colonies or indigenous reserves' (Conte, 1991). Finally, Switzerland has three important centres of anthropology in Zurich, Basel and Bern.

Bastian, Adolf (1826–1905) (see Chapter 1)

Steinen, Karl von (1855–1925)
A psychiatric doctor and intrepid traveller, Karl von Steinen began working for the Berlin Ethnology Museum after making the acquaintance of A. **Bastian**, and he directed several ethnographic expeditions, most notably to Brazil. In 1890 he gained the second German post as a *Dozent* in ethnology at the University of Marburg, Bastian having obtained the first at the University of Berlin.

Ratzel, Friedrich (1844–1904)
(see Chapter 3)

Ankermann, Bernhard (1859–1943)
After studies under both A. **Bastian** and R. **Virchow**, Bernhard Ankermann was given responsibility for the African section of the Museum of Berlin. He contributed greatly to the classification of African material culture, particularly musical instruments. Together with L. **Frobenius**, and later R. F. **Graebner**, he played an important role in forming the principles of German diffusionism, especially in his remarks to the 1904 conference of the Berlin Anthropology Society. And it was in a diffusionist spirit that he expanded his research to probable migrations between Africa, Oceania and Indonesia, which he identified by means of comparative studies of cultural elements in these three areas.

Buschan, Georg (1863–1942)
Born in Frankfurt an der Oder, Georg Buschan studied medicine and then, like A. **Bastian** before him, fixed on a career as a naval physician. While travelling the world he published his medical observations and, from 1902, ethnographic texts. His *Illustrierte Völkerkunde* in several volumes (1910–1926) is addressed to a lay readership. Buschan also edited the *Zentralblatt für Anthropologie* (1886–1913) and the *Ethnologischer Anzeiger* (1926–1942).

Weule, Karl (1864–1926)
While training as a geographer Karl Weule also studied under A. **Bastian** and R. **Virchow**, and after graduating in linguistics and museology at the University of Berlin he joined the staff of the Museum of Leipzig, which he directed from 1906. From 1920 he was also the first holder of the ethnology chair at the University of Leipzig, where he had already worked as a *Dozent* for many years. A diffusionist, he examined the distribution of weaponry in Africa and inferred three culture complexes. Weule organized several expeditions, and took the original step of dropping the requirement for physical measurement of the indigenous population from their programme.

Schurtz, Heinrich (1863–1903)
Ratzel's favourite student Heinrich Schurtz had already published six books when he died prematurely: *Grundzüge einer Philosophie der Tracht* (Stuttgart, 1891), *Katechismus der Völkerkunde* (Leipzig, 1897), *Grundriß einer Entstehungsgeschichte des Geldes* (Leipzig, 1898), *Das afrikanische Gewerbe* (Leipzig, 1900), *Urgeschichte der Kultur* (Leipzig, 1900), *Altersklassen und Männerbünde* (Berlin, 1902). The last of

these works, which 'too soon became a classic' (**Mauss**, 1969: 59), earned Schurtz a reputation still undimmed today. Working on prehistoric civilizations, he became convinced that male societies had played just as important a role as the family in human history. He was the first to submit secret societies and all-male associations to anthropological analysis. The argument propounded in *Altersklassen und Männerbünde* [*Groups of Contemporaries and Male Associations*] is that women, who are fundamentally conservative and antisocial, endeavour to keep men in the closed world of the marital bond, while men, once their sexual desire has been sated, are more interested in brotherly relations with other men – hence the emergence of associations and secret societies. Such fraternities, in which men meet outside the home, then acquire the function of protecting their members from succeeding generations of men who become their rivals. On the basis of these two fundamental antagonisms against women and younger men, Schurtz constructed an evolutionist schema which took in groups of contemporaries, early associations and complex hierarchical societies. This book was the first to advance a theory of primitive political organization which did not see it exclusively in terms of family clans. **Lowie** was inspired by Schurtz in his 1912 study of Crow associations, but in *Primitive Society* (1920) reproached him for neglecting diffusional aspects and noted that the existence of numerous female associations confutes his schema.

Schmidt, Father Wilhelm (1868–1954)
(see Chapter 3)

Preuß, Konrad Theodor (1869–1939)
After gaining a doctorate from the University of Königsberg in 1894 and joining the staff of the Berlin Ethnology Museum in the following year, Konrad Theodor Preuß completed fieldwork in Mexico from 1905 to 1907 and in Columbia from 1913 to 1919. He obtained his *Habilitation* under the supervision of Eduard Seler in 1921 and was then appointed to a professorship at the University of Berlin. He co-edited the *Lehrbuch der Völkerkunde* with L. **Adam**, and when Adam lost his post as a 'non-Aryan' Preuß continued as sole editor. He worked on primitive religion and eventually became an adherent of Father W. **Schmidt**'s theory of a universal original monotheism.

Thurnwald, Richard Christian (1869–1954)
Born in Vienna, Richard Christian Thurnwald studied law, economics and oriental languages at Berlin, gained a law doctorate in 1891 and then took a government post. After initial researches in Bosnia he travelled to Egypt in 1898, and on his return to Berlin he studied Egyptology and Assyriology. He was appointed as an assistant curator in the Berlin Ethnology Museum in 1901 and began writing articles on definitions of the state and the law and on the status of women in ancient Egypt and Assyria. Assisted by the Berlin International Association for Comparative Law and Political Economy, he expanded his research with the use of an ethnological questionnaire comprising 2,500 questions. From 1906 to 1909 he carried out research in Micronesia, particularly in New Britain and the Solomon Islands, bringing back numerous artefacts for the Ethnology Museum. He then continued his investigations in New Guinea as a member of the 1912–1915 Kaiserin-Augusta-Fluß Expedition (Sépik Expedition) organized by the Ethnology Museum. Other participants in this expedition were the geographer W. Behrmann, the botanist Ledermann, the zoologist and physician Bürgers, and the ethnologist and museologist Adolf Roesicke. A few months before he was scheduled to complete his research, and just before he was due to leave New Guinea for Jakarta (then Batavia) because of the

outbreak of the First World War, Australian forces placed two Banaro informants at his disposal, and it was from them that he gleaned most of the material he published in 1916. Thurnwald's later research trips took him to East Africa in 1930, Melanesia in 1932, and finally Australia. From 1925 to 1930 he taught at the University of Berlin, and from 1931 to 1936 at the universities of California (at **Kroeber**'s invitation), Harvard and Yale. Although initially hostile to the National Socialism, he returned to Berlin to take up a professorship in 1937 and then openly declared his adherence to the regime (**Dostal**, 1994). These pronouncements did not hamper his career after the war, for in 1946 he and his wife Hilde founded the Ethnology Institute, which became part the Free University of Berlin in 1948.

Thurnwald started out from the diffusionist position of the *Kulturkreislehre* (theory of culture circles) as developed by **Graebner**, his colleague at the Museum of Berlin. Later he became increasingly interested in the psychological context of phenomena, and this led him to embrace functionalism, albeit in less rigid a form than **Malinowski**. He founded two journals: *Zeitschrift für Völkerpsychologie und Soziologie*, which he edited from 1923 to 1933; and *Forschungen zur Völkerpsychologie und Soziologie*, which he edited from 1925 to 1935 (it was renamed *Sociologus* in 1952). Published in five volumes between 1931 and 1934, *Die menschliche Gesellschaft in ihren ethnosoziologischen Grundlagen* [*The Ethno-Sociological Foundations of Human Society*] is without doubt his major work. Thurnwald was also a pioneer of economic anthropology.

Frobenius, Leo Viktor (1873–1938)
(see Chapter 3)

Schmidt, Max (1874–1950)
After legal studies and a thesis on Roman law in 1899, Max Schmidt took an unpaid position at the Museum of Berlin, where he became an assistant curator on returning from his first trip to Brazil in 1900. He studied under K. von **Steinen** and E. Seler, and then made two more visits to Brazil in 1910 and 1914. He completed a thesis at the University of Leipzig in 1916, and was appointed to a professorship at the University of Berlin in 1921. He decided to spend a further period in Brazil and other Latin American countries from 1926 to 1928. Instead of returning to Germany he first settled in Mato Grosso and then, in 1931, moved to Paraguay, where he established an Ethnography Museum and lived out the rest of his life. A jurist turned ethnologist, Schmidt first investigated aspects of economic and political anthropology and then looked at the anthropology of art. He formulated the theory that the origins of geometrical ornamentation (geometric art) derive from weaving techniques.

Westermann, Diedrich Hermann (1875–1956)
Born in Baden in 1875, Diedrich Hermann Westermann studied theology at Basel and Tübingen and then spent the years from 1901 to 1903 as a missionary in Togo. On his return he taught African languages at the University of Berlin, translated the Bible into Ewa and published his first linguistic studies. In 1925 he obtained the chair of African culture and language at Berlin, and in 1926 took a part in creating the International African Institute, becoming its first director. He edited the journal *Africa* from 1928 to 1940, retired in 1950, and died in 1956. He is best known as a co-author, with H. **Baumann**, of *The Peoples and Civilizations of Africa*, the first scholarly overview of the whole of African society.

Graebner, Robert Fritz (1877–1934)
(see Chapter 3)

Heine-Geldern, Freiherr Robert von (1885–1968)

Born in Grub in Austria, Robert von Heine-Geldern studied first at the University of Munich and then at the University of Vienna, where he read philosophy, art history and anthropology. In 1910 he travelled to the frontier between India and Burma to research the local mountain populations. He completed his thesis *Die Bergstämme des nordöstlichen Birma* [*The Mountain Tribes of Northeastern Burma*] in 1914, and after the First World War worked for the ethnography section of the Museum of Natural History in Vienna, becoming an adherent of the diffusionist school. He was a member of the Vienna faculty from 1927 and appointed to a professorship in 1931. Forced to flee Austria after its annexation by Nazi Germany in 1938, he accepted an invitation to the USA to work in the American Museum of Natural History, but returned to Vienna in 1950 to become a professor at the Ethnology Institute. He organized the Fourth International Congress of Anthropological Sciences in Vienna in 1952 and also carried out a lot of work commissioned by UNESCO.

Gusinde, Father Martin (1886–1969) (see Chapter 3)

Koppers, Father Wilhelm (1886–1961) (see Chapter 3)

Schebesta, Father Paul Joachim (1887–1967) (see Chapter 3)

Adam, Leonhard (1891–1960)

After a legal training Leonhard Adam studied ethnology and then joined the management commission for the collections of the Berlin Ethnology Museum, whilst also working as a *Dozent* for legal anthropology at the University of Berlin. He was editor-in-chief of the *Zeitschrift für vergleichende Rechtswissenschaft* (*Journal for Comparative Juris-prudence*) and, jointly, of the *Lehrbuch für Völkerkunde*, but had to resign from these positions and from his university post following the anti-Jewish laws of 1933. He went into exile in England in 1938 and then Australia in 1940. He was appointed a reader at the University of Melbourne and was the driving force behind the creation of the Melbourne Ethnographic Museum.

Baldus, Herbert (1899–1970)

After taking part in the Spartacist movement Herbert Baldus moved to Argentina in 1920 and Brazil in 1921 to teach German. In 1923 he carried out his first expedition to Chaco to film the Indian populations there and then did research on the Guarani before returning to Germany in 1928 to study in Berlin under R. C. **Thurnwald**, Walter Lehmann and K. T. **Preuß**. He obtained a doctorate in 1932 and then returned to Brazil, where he became professor of ethnology at the *Escola de Sociologia e Politica* (School of Sociology and Politics) in São Paolo, and in 1941 he adopted Brazilian nationality. In 1946 he took a position at the *Museu Paulista*, which he directed from 1952, and launched the *Revista do Museu Paulista*. Baldus was one of the main founders of Brazilian ethnology, which he tried to fashion as an applied discipline attentive to acculturation processes.

Jensen, Adolf Ellegard (1899–1965)

Born in Kiel, Adolf Ellegard Jensen first studied science subjects before becoming the pupil, and from 1923 the assistant, of L. V. **Frobenius**. He worked for the *Institut für Kulturmorphologie* located in Munich and then Frankfurt am Main, carrying out extensive fieldwork in Africa and later among the Seram of Indonesia. He succeeded Frobenius on the latter's death in 1938 and became an expert on myths in relation to ancient cultures (*Das religiöse Weltbild einer frühen Kultur* [*The Religious World Picture of an Early Culture*] 1948; *Mythos und Kultur bei* den Naturvölkern [*Myth and Culture amongst Peoples of Nature*], 1949). He always kept his distance from Nazi doctrine and was out of favour during the Third Reich. In 1946 he was appointed to the anthropology chair at the University of Frankfurt am Main and then relaunched *Paideuma*.

Kirchhof, Paul (1900–1972)

After studying theology in Berlin Paul Kirchhof turned to ethnology and gained a doctorate from the University of Leipzig in 1927 with his thesis 'Die Verwandtschafts-organisation der Urwaldstämme Südameri-kas' ['Kinship Structures of the Primeval Forest Tribes of South America'], which was published by the *Zeitschrift für Ethnologie* in 1931 and 1932. This work examines Amer-indian kinship terminology and, in its rigour, anticipates the classifications of **Lowie** and **Murdock**. Kirchhof then worked for the Berlin Ethnology Museum and organized a number of its expeditions before fleeing Nazi Germany for Paris and then emigrating to Mexico. He was stripped of his German nationality in 1939 and became a Mexican citizen in 1941. He was employed by the *Museo Nacional de Antropolgía* and played a role in the creation of the *Escuela Nacional de Antropología e Historia*, in which he taught until 1965 while at the same time holding a chair at the *Universidad Nacional Autonoma de Mexico*. During his time in Mexico Kirchhof became increasingly drawn to archaeology. He forged strong links between German and Mexican institutions and established several joint programmes in the late 1960s. The development of the con-cept of Central America as a culture complex was his achievement.

Baumann, Hermann (1902–1972)

Hermann Baumann studied in his home town of Freiburg im Breisgau under E. Fischer and then in Berlin under B. **Ankermann**. From 1921 he worked for the Berlin Ethnology Museum and in 1930 he undertook an expedition to Angola to study myths of origins. A fervent supporter of National Socialism, he was appointed professor at the University of Vienna in 1939 but suspended from this post in 1945. He completed a second mission to Angola in 1954 and in the following year became a professor at the University of Munich, where he remained until his retirement in 1967. In his work on Africa he employed the *Kulturkreis* model, giving it historical depth by connecting it with aspects of lineage, culture and race (a procedure he abandoned in the 1950s). Baumann carried out a final mission to Angola in 1972. His most important achieve-ment was his co-authorship, with D. **Wester-mann**, of *Völkerkunde von Afrika* [*Ethnology of Africa*], published in 1940 and recognized as the work of reference on all African cultures for a long time thereafter.

Hirschberg, Walter (1904–1996)

Born in Croatia, Walter Hirschberg studied at the University of Vienna and obtained his doctorate there in 1928. He then worked for the Museum of Vienna until the completion of his *Habilitation* in 1939. After serving during the Second World War he returned to Vienna to become an assistant professor in 1953 and a full professor in 1962, and he also directed the *Völkerkunde* institute between 1962 and his retirement in 1975. He specialized in technology and material culture in Africa, and his work represents a continuation of the *Kulturkreis* school. He edited the *Wörterbuch der Völkerkunde* (Berlin: Reimer, 1988), the first ever German-language dictionary of ethnology, which later appeared in a new, enlarged and updated version edited by C. F. Feest, H. Fischer and T. Schweizer (Berlin: Reimer, 1999).

Mühlmann, Wilhelm Emil (1904–1988)

Born in Düsseldorf, Wilhelm Emil Mühl-mann studied physical anthropology (under E. Fischer) and sociology, gaining a

Ph.D in 1932. From 1931 to 1933 he was editor of the *Zeitschrift für Völkerpsychologie und Soziologie* and then worked in the Museum of Berlin and the Museum of Hamburg. In 1936 he published *Rassen- und Völkerkunde* [*Races and Ethnology*] and in 1938 completed a *Habilitation* supervised at the University of Berlin by R. C. **Thurnwald**, whose disciple he became. Mühlmann worked as a *Privatdozent* at Berlin from 1939, having joined the Nazi Party in the previous year. He was not called up when war broke out, but instead spent the years from 1939 to 1945 in Berlin, where he was responsible for developing a colonial policy and worked as chief editor of the *Archiv für Anthropologie und Völkerforschung*. He was suspended from his posts in 1945, but in 1948 was elected general secretary of the *Deutsche Gesellschaft für Anthropologie, Ethnologie und Urgeschichte*. In 1950 he was made an *Außerplanmäßiger Professor* (a post without formal recognition) of *Völkerpsychologie* and sociology at the University of Mainz, where in 1957 he became a full professor of ethnology and sociology. In 1960 he was made a professor at the University of Heidelberg, but was forced to take early retirement as an Emeritus following student protests at his appointment. In his early work Mühlmann attempted to bring physical anthropology and ethnology together in a raciological perspective, but he is best known for his studies of messianic movements and aspects of nationalism and collective identity. He developed the notions of 'the community conscience' and 'the common creative will' with particular reference to ethnic minorities unwilling to assimilate. He also wrote a history of anthropology, which follows Thurnwald's approach by drawing in political science, economics and psychology (*Geschichte der Anthropologie*, Bonn, 1948; Wiesbaden, 1984), and offered anthropological readings of literary texts by such authors as A. von Droste-Hülshoff and Cervantes.

Haekel, Josef (1907–1973)
Josef Haekel studied in his home town of Vienna under W. **Koppers**. After the war he joined his former teacher at the institute and persuaded him that the *Kulturkreislehre* was no longer borne out by reality. Haekel wrote a history of the movement called *Die Wiener Schule der Völkerkunde* (1956).

Fürer-Haimendorf, Christoph von (1909–1995) (see Chapter 14)

Mayer, Philip (1910–1995)
Born near Berlin into a Jewish family of socialist intellectuals, Philip Mayer studied law at the University of Heidelberg but was prevented by Nazi thugs from taking his final exams. He left Germany for Switzerland and then settled in London, where his parents had already taken refuge. After a brief period of study at the LSE he became a Zionist and moved to Haifa in 1936. During a visit to England in 1939 the war broke out, and, unable to return to Palestine, he decided to enrol at Oxford University. In 1945 he and his wife were appointed by the British as government sociologists in Kenya, where they studied the Gusii, and in 1949 Mayer obtained the anthropology chair at Rhodes University in Grahamstown. He did research on the Xhosa population and became an expert on the processes of migration and urbanization. He wrote *Townsmen or Tribesmen: Conservatism and the Process of Urbanisation in a South African City* (Cape Town: Oxford UP, 1961). He held professorships at the universities of Witwatersrand and then Durham before returning to Grahamstown, where he remained until retiring in 1979 and settling in Oxford. An important work written late in Mayer's career is *Black Migration in South Africa* (Cape Town: Oxford UP, 1980).

Reichel-Dolmatoff, Gerardo (1912–1994)
Born in Austria-Hungary, Gerardo Reichel-

Dolmatoff studied in Paris under P. **Rivet**. Unwilling to move back to Austria after its annexation by Nazi Germany, he was invited to Colombia in 1939 through the good offices of Rivet, who went into exile there himself in 1941. In Colombia Reichel-Dolmatoff pursued a career combining anthropology, ethnology, linguistics and archaeology, teaching at the University of Bogotá and for a while running its anthropology department. He published a very large number of articles in the *Revista del Instituto Etnológico Nacional*, and in Port Hormiga in Bolivia unearthed the most ancient American Indian ceramics yet discovered (*Datos Hostorico-Culturales sobre las Tribus de la Antigua Gobernación de Santa Marta*, 1951). By reconstructing the whole complex of ancient Columbian chiefdoms he was able to establish where the exchange routes they maintained with Amazon Basin societies must have run. One of Reichel-Dolmatoff's most important works is *Desana: Symbolismo de los Indios Tukano del Vaupés* (1968), which describes the cosmology of the Tukano as expressed in their myths, rituals and graphic representation. Equally well known is *The Shaman and the Jaguar: A Study of Narcotic Drugs among the Indians of Columbia* (Philadelphia, 1975), an examination of shamanism and the use of native drugs which contains an account of how the author was affected by drugs administered to him during his participation in rituals.

Dostal, Walter (born 1927)

Walter Dostal studied anthropology and Islamic and Arab studies at the University of Vienna at a time when the previous 'culture circle' tradition, of which he became a trenchant critic, was already in decline. Throughout his academic life he sought to combine the Western mainstream anthropology of his day with historical analysis and fieldwork in Arabia. This orientation is already evident in his *Habilitation* thesis 'Die Beduinen in Saudi-Arabien' of 1967. As his career progressed he became increasingly interested in the local economies, environment, kinship and rituals of Arabia and the interface between local cultures and wider historical processes. Through his positions as full professor in Bern from 1966 to 1975 and in Vienna from 1975 to 1996 he helped shape a whole generation of anthropologists in the German-speaking lands by emphasizing the value of extended fieldwork, competence in local languages, and an understanding of current theories in international anthropology.

Fabian, Johannes (born 1937)

Born in Glogau in Germany, Johannes Fabian was the nephew of the great Austrian ethnologist Father **Schebesta**. He studied in Vienna and Bonn from 1956 to 1962, publishing his first article in 1961, and he very soon developed an interest in the messianic movement. He spent 1962–1963 at the University of Munich and then 1963 to 1968 at the University of Chicago, where in 1965 he gained an MA for a thesis, part of which he then recast as an article and published in *Anthropos* ('Kung Bushman Kinship: Componential Analysis and Alternative Interpretations', *Anthropos*, 60: 663–718). He began to consider the issue of ideology ('Ideology and Content', *Sociologus*, 16 (1965b): 1–18), and in June 1965 he travelled to Zaïre to undertake a research project on the Jamaa messianic movement, which occupied him until 1968. In 1969 he obtained a Ph.D supervised by Lloyd A. Fallers. He was successively instructor and then assistant professor in the department of anthropology at Northwestern University (1968–1974), professor in the department of sociology and anthropology at the National University of Zaïre (1973–1974), and associate professor of anthropology and then professor and chairman of the department of anthropology at Wesleyan University (1974–1982).

During the following years and until his retirement he was chair of cultural anthropology and non-Western sociology at the University of Amsterdam. In 1983 he published his most famous work *Time and the Other: How Anthropology Makes its Object* (New York: Columbia UP), an epistemology of ethnology. Fabian demonstrates how anthropologists replaced the temporal distance of historians with spatial distance while retaining the same principles of inquiry. Subsequently contemporary popular culture in Africa became his main research topic. He was visiting professor in about thirty universities of rank and the author of more than two hundred articles and other contributions. In 1998 he set up a website (http://www.pscw.uva.nl/lpca/) devoted to the preservation, presentation and study of texts that document popular culture in its many aspects as well as the use of languages such as Katanga Swahili.

SCANDINAVIA

The Anthropological Society in Stockholm was founded in 1873 by the ethnographer and archaeologist Hjalmar Stolpe (1841–1905), the archaeologists Hans Hildebrand (1842–1913) and Oscar Montelius (1843–1921), and the anatomist and craniologist Gustaf Retzius (1842–1919). Retzius, whose father Anders Retzius invented the Cephalix Index, wrote on Finnish and Lapp cultures. Also in 1873, the *Nordiska Museet* was established with folklorist and nationalist credentials. Like other Scandinavian societies, the one in Stockholm was grounded on the German version of ethnography (*Völkerkunde*), as became all the clearer when it was renamed the Swedish Society for Anthropology and Geography in 1877. The society's purpose was to study mankind on the model of the natural sciences, and before long it addressed itself to the problematics of racial classification. Denmark soon followed the Swedish lead and created an Ethnographic Museum directed by Christian Bahnson, and Stockholm replied by founding a *Statens Etnografiska Museum*. In 1910 the Finn Antti Aarne published his *Verzeichnis der Märchentypen* [*Index of Fairy Tale Types*] (Helsinki), which remains the work of reference on the topic to this day. In 1919 an ethnology chair with a ruralist and folklorist bias was attached to the *Nordiska Museet* in Sweden.

The creation of the Museum of Gothenburg and the appointment of E. N. H. **Nordenskjöld** as its director in 1913 opened up a new era for exotic ethnology in Sweden. Nordenskjöld made the new museum one of the most modern in the world, and it was enriched by the donation of his cousin G. Nordenskjöld's collections from Mesa Verde. Nordenskjöld also became the first occupant of the ethnology chair at the University of Gothenburg, where he founded a distinct school of Americanist ethnography and archaeology. He always employed his students as assistant curators in the museum and sent them all into the field from the mid-1920s onwards: notable among his students were Sven Lovén, Sigvald Linné (1899–1986), Karl Gustav Izikowitz (1903–1984), Stig Rydén (1908–1965), and S. Henry Wassén (1908–1996), a specialist in the use of drugs by American Indians and a forerunner of medical anthropology. Sigvald Linné became an assistant curator at the *Statens Etnografiska Museum* and *Docent* at the University of Stockholm in 1929, then professor at the same university in 1934, and in 1954 director of the museum, where he was joined by Rydén in 1965. K. G. Izikowitz was appointed *Docent* at the University of Gothenburg in 1936, and after the war he worked on the Lamat of Laos, introduced social anthropology to Sweden, and in 1955 was appointed to the Gothenburg ethnology chair, which he renamed the chair of social anthropology. In Denmark, the Inuit specialist William Thalbitzer (1873–1958) became the first occupant of the ethnology chair at the University of Copenhagen in 1920. He was later succeeded by K. **Birket-Smith**, who had participated in the Thulé expedition and in 1929 joined the ethnography department of the National Museum of Copenhagen, and who in 1945 realized his aim of creating an anthropology department at Copenhagen. In Norway the Missionary Society began a course in Sâme (Lapon) in 1878 taught by Just Knud Ovidstad (1853–1957), who with Ørnulv Vorren founded the Museum of Tromsø. Social anthropology was introduced to Norway by F. **Barth**, who was employed as a researcher in Oslo and then as professor at the universities of Bergen from 1961 and Oslo from 1973. Finally, anthropology owes a great debt of gratitude to the Swede Axel Wenner–Gren (1881–1961) for the creation of the foundation bearing his name.

Westermarck, Edvard Alexander
(1862–1939)

Born in Helsinki as the son of a university treasurer, Edvard Alexander Westermarck studied and then taught aesthetics and philosophy. In 1886 he spent a year in London, practically living in the British Museum, and then moved back to Finland having written the first few chapters of a history of marriage which he submitted as a doctoral thesis. He then returned to England, where **Tylor** introduced him to the publisher Macmillan, who in 1891 published his *History of Marriage* in four volumes (London). This book comprehensively disproves the myth of original sexual promiscuity by demonstrating the systematic recurrence of monogamy among primitive populations. Westermarck rejects both the precedence of matrilineality over patrilineality and **Maine**'s notion of the primitive horde. He replaces these notions with the monogamous family cell with a protective male at its head, justifying his approach with reference to anthropoid monkeys and other animals such as hippopotamuses, squirrels and seals. In his view there is a biological and functional need for this arrangement because the young of the human species are for many years unable to fend for themselves. It is only later, and for circumstantial reasons, that polyandry and polygeny emerge. Westermarck also advanced one of the first general explanations for the universality of the incest prohibition, rather naïvely asserting that living in close quarters during childhood subdued sexual desire between family members. **Lévi-Strauss** refuted this idea by alluding to the Zande proverb that 'The desire for a wife begins with the sister' (Lévi-Strauss, *The Elementary Structures of Kinship*, Boston: Beacon, 1969: 17) and asking why societies should see the need to prohibit relationships which purportedly have no appeal; however, later statistical studies corroborated Westermarck's thesis (A. Wolf, 1970, 1995). With a university grant he did research abroad and then combined teaching positions in Helsingfors and London. In 1897 he began a series of expeditions to Morocco, a country on which he wrote extensively. In 1906 he published *The Origins and Development of Moral Ideas* (London), and in 1907 he was appointed to the sociology chair at the University of London, where he subsequently taught **Malinowski**.

Nordenskjöld, Erland Nils Herbert, Baron (1877–1932)

Born as the son of the North Pole explorer A. E. Nordenskjöld in Ström in Sweden, Erland Nils Herbert Nordenskjöld studied geology and palaeontology and then in 1898 travelled to Argentina. There he became interested in the American Indians, exploring Chaco and Paraguay and working in Bolivia and Brazil as well as Argentina during stays in 1908–1909, 1913–1914 and 1927. In 1912 he published his *History of South American Indian Culture*, in which he argues that Amerindian cultures have an independent origin and have influenced Oceania rather than the other way round. Nordenskjöld gained considerable renown as an Americanist, and P. **Rivet** sent A. **Métraux** to complete his training under him. He became professor of ethnology at the University of Gothenburg in 1924, and in the years that followed he turned the Museum of Gothenburg, which he had directed from 1913, into one of the finest and most modern of its type in the world. It was this museum that provided G.-H. **Rivière** with his model for the *Musée de l'Homme* in Paris. Nordenskjöld died in 1932. His cousin, the amateur archaeologist Gustaf Nordenskjöld (1868–1895), discovered the Mesa Verde site.

Birket-Smith, Kaj (1893–1977)

Born in Copenhagen, Kaj Birket-Smith spent two brief periods in Greenland before taking part as an ethnographer in the fifth Thulé expedition directed by K. Rasmussen from 1921 to 1923. He then wrote his thesis *The Caribou Eskimo: Material and Social Life and Their Cultural Position* (2 vols, 1929), which presents the Caribou as the most ancient of the Inuit peoples. In 1929 he joined the ethnography department of the Danish National Museum, acting as its chief curator from 1946 to 1963. In 1945 he established an anthropology department at the University of Copenhagen.

Barth, Frederick (born 1928)

Born in Leipzig as the son of a geologist, Frederick Barth spent his childhood in Germany, the USA and, during the Second World War, Norway. In 1946 he accompanied his parents to Chicago, where he finished his secondary education and went to university to study palaeontology, gaining an MA in 1949. In 1951 he was invited by his archaeology professor R. Braidwood to participate in archaeological excavations in Jarmo in Iraq. When this work was finished, Barth continued living among the Iraqi Kurds and made them the subject of his first studies in cultural anthropology. As there was nowhere for him to study anthropology in Norway, he obtained a government grant on his return from Iraq to go to the LSE to be taught by R. **Firth**, and it was there that he discovered the work of E. **Leach**. In England he wrote his *Principles of Social Organization in Southern Kurdistan* (Oslo, 1953). Back in Oslo he set about learning Parse (Pashtu, Afghan) under G. Morgenstierne in 1954 and then travelled to Northern Pakistan to study the Swat. After this he spent two years at Cambridge University, gaining a Ph.D in 1957. A. **Métraux** chose Barth to undertake a UNESCO project to investigate the settling process among nomads, and sent him to study the Basseri of Iran in 1957–1958. He completed further research in China, Norway, Sudan, Papua New Guinea and Indonesia. He was a research assistant at the University of Oslo from 1953 to 1961 and then professor of social anthropology at the universities of Bergen from 1961 to 1972 and Oslo from 1973 to 1985. Thereafter he taught at Emory College in the USA while retaining his position as a researcher at the Oslo Ethnographic Museum. He first gained an international reputation with his *Leadership among Swat Pathans* (1959), an examination of a caste-based Afghan society in which he demonstrates that in relationships of dependency there is nonetheless considerable scope for personal decisions by each individual. This focus on individual choice within a structural context led him to promote the study of social change. Another of his classic works is *Nomads of South Persia: The Basseri Tribe of the Khamseh Confederacy*

(London and Oslo, 1961), which reveals the processes set in motion by animal reproduction and extends the idea of segmentation to strategies in the power struggle and to the constitution of politically founded groups. In *Ethnic Groups and Boundaries* (Oslo, 1969) Barth shows that there is no clear correspondence between ethnic identity and culture and suggests that any given cultural heritage is continually recodified to distinguish it from those of neighbouring peoples.

THE SOVIET UNION AND RUSSIA

In 1845 the Russian Geographical Society was founded in St Petersburg, with one of its divisions being devoted to ethnography (i.e. cultural anthropology). Some of the founders of the ethnographic division of the society placed great emphasis on the study of the non-Russian peoples of the Russian empire. However, at that time Russian nationalism was growing, and Nadezhin, one of the society's founders, declared that the main object of attention must be precisely the fact that Russia is Russian. As a result of this approach, the interest in non-Slavic peoples, both exotics and other non-natives, was somewhat weaker than it had been in the eighteenth century when the Russian Academy of Scientists sent its scholars to study indigenous Siberians. However, in the second half of the nineteenth century there were a number of famous expeditions, notably those of V. V. **Radlov** to the Altaï from 1859 to 1871; of N. **Miklukho-Maclay** to Oceania from 1870 to 1880; and of Sibiriakov to Siberia from 1894 to 1896. Other important ethnographic explorers of the period were P. Semenov-Tianchanski, a geographer and ethnographer, V. Barthold, an Orientalist, and M. Castren, a prominent specialist on the Ugro-Finnish peoples of Northern Russia and Northern Siberia. In 1864, under the aegis of Moscow University, a Natural History Society was founded which contained ethnography and physical anthropology sections. In 1867 it was renamed the Imperial Natural Science, Anthropology and Ethnography Society. From 1850 to 1870 the Russian Empire pushed forward into Central and Eastern Asia, swallowing up the Caucasus, Turkestan and Siberia, and these regions retained their exotic status even as they became state possessions, providing Russian anthropologists with new locations for interesting ethnographic research. Nonetheless, the influence of Slavophilism (and the Russian patriotism common among geographers and ethnographers) ensured that the discipline's main focus remained, to a significant extent, the Russian people itself. Writers like Dostoevsky saw Russian towns as islands of modernity in a mediaeval ocean which hosted a vast folkloric tradition, and in 1890 the folklorist A. N. Pypin wrote that the study of this tradition was also the study of the national consciousness and its progress. Among the most distinguished folklorists from the eighteenth century onwards were Pallas, Lepehin, I. Georgi, P. Saharov, Kavelin, V. Dahl, and, in the 1920s, D. Z. Zelenin. Saturated with German influences, Russian anthropology was thus at once a *Volkskunde* and a *Völkerkunde*. In 1867 the National Ethnographic Exhibition was opened and eventually the artefacts exhibited there were turned over to a special 'Dashkov Ethnographic Museum', a subdivision of the (Moscow Public) Rumyantzev Museum. In 1889 the journal *Ethnograficheskoe Obozrenie* (*Ethnographic Review*) was launched in Moscow by the Imperial Natural Science, Anthropology and Ethnography Society, and in 1890 the ethnographic division of the Russian Geographic Society began publishing its own journal *Zhivaia Starina* (*Living Antiquity*). Ethnography was to some degree co-opted to the policy of Russification, by which minorities were integrated into Russian society and a settled lifestyle was imposed on nomadic peoples. Those intellectuals not belonging to contingents which had the ear of those in power and pressed the Czar to modernize the country (serfdom was abolished in 1861) tended to become members of revolutionary groups and were often exiled to Siberia. Two prominent figures in this category were Waldemar Germanovich **Bogoras** (1865–1936) and Vladimir Il'ich Iochelson (or Jochelson, 1855–1937), who both took an enthusiastic interest in non-Russian peoples: Borogas became a specialist on the Chukchi and Iochelson on the Koryak. Both were invited to take part in Sibiriakov's expedition of 1895 to 1897 for the Russian Geographical Society, and in the Jesup North Pacific Expedition of 1900–1901 directed by F. **Boas** for the Museum of Natural History in New York. Iochelson was appointed curator of the Anthropology and Ethnography Museum of St Petersburg in 1912, but was forced into exile with the advent of the Soviet Union and settled in the USA in 1922, where he continued publishing his ethnographic data from Siberia. Bogoras also worked as a curator at the same museum in the early 1920s, and in this and the following decade he and his friend and colleague Lev **Shternberg** taught ethnology at several institutions of higher education in Leningrad. In addition, he was actively involved in establishing and leading the Institute of the Peoples of the North. A new and distinct ethnographic school developed around Shternberg which collected large quantities of basic ethnographic data as well as information on the socio-economic conditions of the peoples of the North and on economic relations among the Yakuts, the Kazaks, and the Tajik mountain people, who were thought to have a society devoid of class distinctions. In 1924 a Committee of the North aimed at helping the indigenous peoples of Siberia to make a smoother transition to modernity was set up by Bogoras and Shternberg, and in 1925 an ethnology faculty was established at Leningrad State University, with Shternberg serving as its first dean. Ethnology was also being taught at the time at the Moscow State University. In 1926 the journal *Etnografia* began to be published.

But this expansion was short-lived. After Stalin's victory over Trotsky in 1927 the country was submitted to a number of purges affecting every domain of national life. Ethnology (*etnologija*) was designated as a 'bourgeois substitute' (*antropologija* was the term used for physical anthropology), and as a result the Moscow ethnology department was suppressed in 1930, followed in 1931 by the ethnography section of the Geographical Society and in 1932 by the ethnography department of Leningrad University. Rather than being abolished, the journal *Etnografia* was transformed into *Sovietskaja ètnografia* in 1931, and from then until 1933 it was edited by Nikolai M. Matorin, the head of the Museum of Anthropology and Ethnography in Leningrad, the director of the Institute for the Study of Peoples within the Academy of Sciences of the USSR, and a specialist in sectarian movements and the role of religion in social life. Matorin was shot in 1936, and many other ethnographers were imprisoned, exiled and executed during the Stalinist era. The Shternberg school was eradicated (although some of his and Bogoras' students survived the Gulag and continued their research upon returning to Leningrad) and the ethnographic investigations of the 1920s, especially on traditional rural communities, declined somewhat. Most importantly, ethnographic research was now supposed to provide raw data for a Marxist study of the five successive stages of human history and the modes of production which accompany them. The passage from one mode to the next is determined by the class struggle and is characterized by the opposition between the economic base, that is the forces and relationships of production, and the superstructure of religion, law and ideology which reflects that base. According to the schema set out by F. **Engels** in *The Origins of Private Property, the Family and the State*, the whole of primitive humanity has passed from the matriarchal to the patriarchal stage, a doctrine defended by M. O. Kosven until the mid-1970s. In 1933 a new Institute of

Anthropology, Archaeology and Ethnology was established in Leningrad. However, the work of its scholars was now supposed to be guided directly by that of dogmatic Marxist historians, reflecting the principle that in the Marxist–Leninist scientific system, there can be no place for ethnography as an independent science claiming to enjoy the same status as history. The discipline's subaltern position vis-à-vis history was also not forgotten when it regained university chairs at Leningrad in 1937 and Moscow in 1939, an Institute of Ethnography having already been set up in Moscow in 1937. From 1939 to 1951 the Moscow chair was held by S. P. Tolstov, who from 1942 to 1966 was also director of the Institute of Ethnography, a body which organized the discipline at a national level and formed part of the Academy of Sciences, and which in 1947 was renamed the Miklukho-Maclay Institute of Ethnography. During this period ethnography was called upon to take up arms against cosmopolitanism, nationalism and bourgeois objectivism, and in 1938 its position was re-evaluated when the journal *Marxist Historian* declared that 'it is the enemies of the people, Trotskyites, Bakharinists and Fascist hirelings who have chased ethnography out of our universities' (4: 164, quoted by Chichlo, 1984: 255). The newly favoured but still far from autonomous subject was described by Potexin as a branch of the historical sciences responsible for studying the evolution of societies from their prehistorical and primitive states to the emergence of the class system. The aim of investigating different peoples was to assimilate them, and one of ethnography's tasks was to argue for the official nationalities policy and to take a stand against the survival of ancient rites and customs perceived to be incompatible with socialist ideology and morality. This perspective led to a particular emphasis on questions of ethnogenesis (the subject of a colloquium of the Academy of Sciences in 1938), the struggle against idealization of the epic heroes of ethnic minorities, and the fight against anti-historicism and formalism, particularly V. Propp's approach to oral literature. Aside from discussions about the discipline's orientation, there were two major debates in the period from 1930 to 1970. The first, initiated in 1928, concerned language and the question of minority nationalities. The main adversaries in this debate were the linguist and Indo-Europeanist Polivanov (1891–1938) and Marr (1864–1934), who argued that language is a superstructure, denied the existence of an original Indo-European language, and constructed the utopia of a future language born of a classless society. Marrism triumphed and remained dominant until 1950, when Stalin intervened personally in the dispute to state that language is merely a tool uninformed by class divisions. The subject of the second, more theoretical, debate was the Asiatic Mode of Production, and at issue was the nature of communist governments in general and the Chinese government in particular. First developed by Marx, the idea of an Asiatic Mode of Production was officially discarded at the Leningrad Conference of 1931, and its abandonment was confirmed by Stalin in 1938 in *Dialectical Materialism and Historical Materialism*. At the same time the German scholar **Wittfogel** published his first article on the topic, which he treated fully in 1957 in his book *Oriental Despotism*, and in 1958 the Hungarian Tökei (or Tokey) took up the same concept in his analysis of China. All these discussions resulted in a symposium held in Moscow in 1965 and in the publication of numerous articles from then until around 1970. At the Seventh Congress of Anthropological and Ethnological Sciences, which took place in Moscow in 1964, the process of de-Stalinization was ritually enacted by the restoration of East–West relations, but fundamental dogmas were not revised. The dawning of the post-Stalin period (1953–1985) brought no changes in the situation of ethnology, which, unlike other disciplines, retained its rigid Marxist–Leninist identity. From the late 1960s to the 1980s a great deal of research was done on inter-ethnic relations with the aim of contributing to the process of nation-building, but this approach had little in common with intensive fieldwork methods (even though a relatively small number of dedicated ethnographers continued to collect valuable data from around the country including its northern and other peripheral regions). Instead it relied on the notion of the 'ethnos' as developed by S. M. **Shirokogorov** before his departure for China in 1923 and then redefined by Y. N. **Bromley** after he replaced Tolstov as director of the Institute of Ethnography in the Academy of Sciences in 1966. There was much discussion and categorization of different types of ethnos; one author, Arutiunov, identified no less than sixteen. Ethnology became the science of ethnicity, but without ever criticizing the official policy towards minorities. It remained deliberately blind to changes in reality, and M. V. Kryukov later stated that in their conclusions regarding processes at work in the Soviet Union scholars claimed the desirable as real. The interlocutors chosen from among the indigenous *nomenklatura* were held to reflect their own populations as a whole, and the official doctrine held that, unlike in capitalist countries, their assimilation was voluntary and progressive. As Bromley wrote, 'ethnography as a science of ethnicities does not leave room for pessimism' (quoted by Khazanov, *Cahiers du monde russe et soviétique*, 1990: 214). During the twenty years following 1950 ethnologists distinguished between harmful and harmless traditions and played a role in the establishment of new popular rituals and holidays to replace ancient ceremonies. Some of those who composed the scenarios for these rituals were, like I. A. Kryvelev, ardent propagandists; others 'perceived the campaign for the new ritualism as an opportunity to return to classical themes in studying folk ritual', and 'to pour the old wine of ancient customs into the new wineskins of socialist ritual' (Sadomskaya, *Cahiers du monde russe et soviétique*, 1990: 247–248). From the late 1950s onwards there were various research centres devoted to Third World countries, especially those of Sub-Saharan Africa. In 1959 the Academy of Sciences established an African Institute which oversaw the research of such figures as Smirnov, Yablochkov, Ismagilova and Sharevskaia. In 1976 scholars from East and West came together at the Burg Wartenstein Conference, but the Soviet delegation acted like a monolithic bloc as on previous occasions (E. **Gellner**, *Soviet and Western Anthropology*, London: Duckworth, 1980). Furthermore, 'Y. Bromley still refused to use the term "anthropology", from *anthropos* (= man), to speak of a science exclusively focused on the study of peoples' (quoted by Chichlo, 1984: 247), and he informed Stocking that 'ethnography in the Soviet Union is an historical science' (Stocking, 1984: 8). In 1978 Bromley attended the 10th Congress of Anthropological Sciences in New Delhi together with Kulichenko of the Marxist–Leninist Institute, and from 1980 to 1986 the three volumes of *Istorija pervobytnog obscestva* (*History of Primitive Society*) appeared under his editorship. This history perpetuated the dogmas of the 1930s, and facts which contradicted them were declared non-existent or attributed to foreign influences. Similarly, *Present-Day Ethnic Processes in the USSR*, published in English in 1982, stuck to the Party line: ethnic tensions are neglected and all people of the USSR are drawing ever closer. However, despite the gulf that still divided them, Western and Soviet scholars undertook a joint research project entitled 'Directions and Tendencies in the Cultural Development of Modern Society: Interaction of National Cultures'. Moreover, in 1983 C. **Lévi-Strauss'** *Structural Anthropology* was translated into Russian (in fact, a strong interest in structuralism and semiotics developed in the USSR in the 1960s but only on the margins of the humanities and not within ethnology). However, it was not until January 1988, during the period of *perestroika*, that M. Kryukov could publish an article in *Sovietskaja ètnografia*, still the Soviet Union's only journal in the discipline, inviting his colleagues to reject the purely descriptive character of Soviet ethnography and its refusal to emancipate itself from history. Bromley then reminded Kryukov that 'the profession of ethnography does not exist, rather there are historians whose specialism is the history of ethnic relations'. Then *Sovietskaja ètnografia*, under the editorship of Krupnik, devoted a special issue to the work of the younger generation. Of the articles published in this issue the biggest stir was caused by T. Shchepanskaia's examination of the sub-cultures of urban Russia using an approach developed by V. **Turner**. In March 1989 a conference on Soviet anthropology and traditional societies was organized in Paris by W. Berelowitch of the CNRS. The Russian delegation was led by Abraham Pershits and included a number of younger scholars (Vitebsky, 1989). The conference questioned the pertinence of the 'ethnos' concept at a time when the conflict in Nagorno–Karabakh was providing incontrovertible evidence that the nationalities problem had not been successfully solved (Skalnik, *Cahiers du monde russe et soviétique*, 1990: 188). Although the conservative Bromley was appointed president of a new interdepartmental committee for the study of national processes within the Academy of Sciences, a few days earlier he had resigned his position as director of the Institute of Ethnography after a tenure of more than a third of a century. His replacement was Valery Tishkov (formerly a loyal Marxist and Bromley's right-hand man), a specialist on national questions who edited an issue of *Sovietskaja ètnografia* entirely given over to the study of nationalist movements (1989: 1). Tishkov also requested that the institute he now directed be renamed the Institute of Ethnology, but this was turned down by the Scientific Council of the Academy of Sciences. Today, however, it does bear the name of Institute of Ethnology and Anthropology. In 1992 he addressed the question of the discipline's aims in *CA* (Tishkov, 1992), and in remarks appended to his article Levin Abrahamian wrote that 'The Soviet Union disintegrated primarily because of powerful national movements within the former empire, so it is no wonder that Soviet ethnography is in a state of crisis' (Abrahamian, 'Comments', *CA*, 33/4: 382).

Radlov, Vassily Vasilevich (1837–1918)
Born in Berlin, Vassily Vasilevich Radlov completed a doctoral thesis on religious influences among the peoples of Siberia in 1858. His subsequent investigations took him to the Altaï Mountains from 1859 to 1871 and to Kazan from 1871 to 1884, and he became one of the earliest Turki specialists. Back in St Petersburg, where he had sent vast quantities of material, he was appointed director of the *Aziatskii Muzei* (Asiatic Museum) in 1885 and of the *Muzei Antropologii i Etnografii* (Museum of Anthropology and Ethnology) in 1894. He died of starvation in St. Petersburg (Petrograd) in 1918. Musicologist, museologist, ethnographer, and archaeologist, Radlov played a role in Russia equivalent to that of A. **Bastian** in Germany. He published an enormous body of work, some of it in German, for example *Ethnographische*

Übersicht der Türkenstämme Sibiriens und der Mongolei [*Ethnographic Overview of the Turk Tribes of Siberia and Mongolia*] (Leipzig, 1883) and *Aus Sibirien* [*Out of Siberia*] (2 vols, Leipzig, 1884).

Kropotkin, Pyotr Alekseevich (1842–1921) (see Chapter 2)

Miklukho-Maclay, Nikolai Nikolaevich (1846–1888) (see Chapter 2)

Shternberg, Lev Jakovlevich (1861–1927)
Born in Shitomir in the Ukraine, Lev Jakovlevich Shternberg joined the Russian revolutionary movement and was exiled to Siberia, where he took the opportunity of studying the Orok and Gilyak (Nivkh) peoples. Although he could not take part in the Jesup North Pacific Expedition led by F. **Boas**, he contributed an important

manuscript on the social organization of the Gilyak for the Jesup Expedition publication series, which did not, however, appear until 1999 (Kan 2000). (While in New York during the war **Lévi-Strauss** read it in manuscript form, praised it highly, and used its data for his 1949 monograph on the elementary structures of kinship (Kan 2000).) After the 1917 Revolution Shternberg was appointed to a professorship at Leningrad University, where he created a distinctive Leningrad school of ethnography, which included a large group of enthusiastic young ethnographers, many of whom eventually perished in the Gulag. With W. **Bogoras** he set up the Committee of the North to defend the interests of the small populations in that part of the country. He died near Leningrad in 1927.

Bogoras, Waldemar (1865–1936)

Born Nathan Mendeleevich and raised in the Ukraine, Waldemar Bogoras began legal studies at the University of St. Petersburg in 1880. As a result of his membership of a revolutionary group he was exiled to Siberia, where he wrote novels and poetry and also took an interest in the peoples of the region. In 1895 the Russian Geographical Society invited him to join Sibiriakov's expedition to Northeastern Siberia, and he profited from this experience to become the foremost expert on the Lamut and on the Chukchi, a population divided between an inland group living off reindeer and a coastal group living off cetaceans. Bogoras learnt the languages of these groups and wrote his first book in 1898 on their mythology and shamanistic practices, which he describes as the only remaining institutions of a social organization in ruins. Indeed, he thought the decline so far advanced that he told Durkheim and **Mauss**, who were searching for evidence of clans, that 'all traces of clans have disappeared' (Durkheim, *Journal sociologique*, 1969 (1912): 714; Mauss, *Oeuvres III*, 1969 (1909): 87). However, the existence of bride service indicated to him that their 'uterine' family structures had become paternal. In 1900 he and Waldemar Iochelson, another exiled revolutionary, joined the Jesup North Pacific Expedition led by F. **Boas**. Bogoras was charged with investigating the northeastern coastline of the Bering Strait, and he and his wife Sofia Konstantinovna spent two years studying the Northern Siberian peoples, amassing thousands of artefacts and texts, somatological (morphological) measurements and even sound recordings. After the 1917 Revolution Bogoras became a major force in the Institute for the Peoples of the North, which functioned as a development agency. In 1924 he created the Committee of the North with Lev Shternberg and other ethnographers and political activists to protect the rights of minorities, and he also campaigned, unsuccessfully, for their political autonomy. He died in 1936.

Shirokogorov, Sergei Mikhailovich (1887–1939)

Born in Susdal, the geographer and sinologist Sergei Mikhailovich Shirokogorov became the leading specialist on the Tungus–Manchurian peoples of Siberia, on whom he published numerous texts in Russian. He worked for the Museum of Anthropology and Ethnography in St. Petersburg under **Shternberg**, whom he considered his mentor. In 1918, during the Civil War, he was appointed to the University of Vladivostok, and remained there until 1922. His fieldwork among the Tungus took him close to the Chinese border, and he took the opportunity of escaping from the Soviet regime into China, working at the universities of Shanghai and then Beijing, where he died. He was one of the earliest writers on shamanism, most notably in his *Psychomental Complex of the Tungus* (1935), but he is best remembered for being the first to define the 'ethnos' or ethnic group in a way that emphasizes its dynamic and plastic qualities, and for his theory that the ethnic group is created in a field of inter-ethnic tension and pressure.

Bromley, Yulian N. (1921–1990)

A specialist in the history of the Southern Slavs, Yulian Bromley was appointed director of the Institute of Ethnography in the Academy of Sciences in 1966 by the Communist Party, replacing Tolstov and remaining in post until 1989. This was not a period of intensive fieldwork, and the focus of a significant part of the institute's research was the notion of the 'ethnos' as developed by S. M. **Shirokogorov** but disseminated by Bromley in his numerous publications. Bromley's stance as a supporter of the assimilation of the Soviet Union's minority populations drew criticism both as a theoretical position and for the practical policies that went with it. Nevertheless, according to *Anthropology Today*, 'he was known for the assistance and protection which he gave to some younger scholars during the Brezhnev era'. He was the author of more than 300 texts, although he never engaged in ethnographic field research himself.

A HUNGARIAN

Róheim, Geza (1891–1953)

Born in Budapest, Geza Róheim developed an enthusiastic interest in Hungarian folklore and in the works of **Tylor**, whose obituary he wrote in *Man*, and of **Frazer**. He studied at the universities of Budapest, Leipzig and Berlin, gaining a doctorate in the geography department at Berlin. Back in Budapest he took a position in the National Museum and wrote for the journal *Ethnographia*. He used Freudian concepts to analyse popular Hungarian tales and mythology, and then extended his range to take in all Slav nations and then Australia. In 1915–1916 he underwent psychoanalytic treatment with Ferenczi, who in 1918 began teaching a new course in psychoanalysis at the University of Budapest. The Bolshevik revolutionaries who briefly took power in 1919 upgraded Ferenczi's post to a chair and also created an anthropology chair for Róheim, but both men were ejected from their new positions once the revolutionary government fell. Though no longer drawing an academic salary, Róheim was able to continue his research thanks to a private income. In 1921 he published a lengthy study entitled *Das Selbst* [*The Self*], which received the Freud Prize, and in 1925 his *Australian Totemism* appeared. Then Freud, Ferenczi and Princess Marie

Bonaparte suggested he make a research trip to Australia to be funded by the Princess, and together with his wife he travelled to Somalia and then to Central Australia between 1928 and 1930. These sojourns yielded a few articles, but the main fruits of Róheim's research on Somalia and Australia only appeared in 1945 and, posthumously, in 1974. In 1931 he travelled to Normanby, one of the d'Entrecasteaux Islands which shared the same culture as the Trobriands, in order further to develop **Malinowski**'s research. He spent nearly a year on Normanby and then began the homeward journey, staying for a time en route in the USA to study the Southwestern Yuma Indians. On his return he was appointed to a professorship at the University of Budapest, and in 1932 he published *Psychoanalysis of Primitive Forms of Culture*. In the face of the Nazi threat he emigrated in 1938 to the USA, where he worked as a hospital psychoanalyst – from 1938 to 1939 in Worcester, New Jersey, and subsequently in New York, where he also taught. In the years that followed he wrote *The Origins and Function of Culture* (1943), *The Eternal Beings of Dreams* (1945), an examination of the role of the sex drive in culture, and *War, Crime and Marriage* (1945), an analysis of aggressivity.

In 1947 he received funding from the Viking Fund (later the Wenner–Gren Foundation for Anthropological Research) for a period of fieldwork among the Navajo Indians, and after this he launched and edited the journal *Psychoanalysis and the Social Sciences*. In 1950 he published his *Psychoanalysis and Anthropology*, a synthesis of the theoretical positions adopted in his previous works, followed by *The Gates of the Dream*, published on the day of his death in 1953. The latter's central thesis is the 'ontological trauma', defined as a culture's mode of intervention in the libidinal development of the child by means of the care and gratification, but also prohibitions and repression it receives from adults, with this mode varying from culture to culture. Róheim is also remembered for his idea of the necessary prematurity of the new-born child, of the incompleteness of man at his birth. He sees the resulting neoteny and immaturity as determining sexual morality and by extension culture itself. In this perspective the custom dictating that a Central Australian mother will sleep on top of her son can be seen as stimulating Oedipal desire and castration anxiety, which would explain the central role played by the penis in this culture.

SELECT BIBLIOGRAPHY

Adam, L. (1955) 'Richard Thurnwald', *Oceania*, 25(3): 145–156.

Alvarsson, J.-A. (1991) 'Nordenskjöld, Erland', in C. Winter, pp.510–512.

Anonymous (1903) 'Heinrich Schurtz', *AA*, 5: 583.

Anonymous (1961) 'Anthropological and folkloristic Institutions in the German Democratic Republic', *CA*, 2(1): 65–66.

Baldus, H. (1931) *Indianerstudien im nordöstlichen Chaco*, Leipzig: Hirschfeld.

——(1951) 'M. Schmidt', in *Zeitschrift für Ethnologie*, 71.

——(1958; 1986) *Die Jaguarzwillinge: Mythen und Heilbringergeschichten, Ursprungssagen und Märchen brasilianischer Indianer*, Leipzig: Kiepenheuer.

——(1970) *Tapirapé, tribo tupi no Brasil central*, São Paulo: Companhia Editôra Nacional.

Ball, J. van (1975) *Reciprocity and the Position of Women: Anthropological Papers*, Assen.

——(1981) *Man's Quest for Partnership, the Anthropological foundations of ethics and religion*, Assen: Van Gorcum.

Ball, J. van and van Beek, W.E.A. (1985) *Symbols for Communication: An Introduction to the Anthropological Study of Religion*, Assen: Van Gorcum.

Barnard, A. (1996) 'Dutch anthropology', in A. Barnard and J. Spencer, *Encyclopedia of Social and Cultural Anthropology*, London: Routledge, pp.167–168.

Barth, F. (1956) *Indus and Swat Kohistan. An Ethnographic Survey*, Oslo: Universitets forlaget.

——(1963; 1967) *The Role of the Entrepreneur in Social Change in Northern Norway*, Bergen: Universitets forlaget.

——(1966) *Model of Social Organization*, London: Royal Anthropological Institute.

——(1975) *Ritual and Knowledge among the Baktaman of New Guinea*, New Haven: Yale University Press.

——(1978) *Scale and Social Organization*, Oslo: Universitets forlaget.

——(1981a) *Process and Form in Social Life: Selected Essays of Frederick Barth*, vol.1, London, Routledge.

——(1981b) *Person and Society in Swat, Collected essays on Pathans: Selected essays of Frederick Barth*, vol.2, London: Routledge.

——(1985) *The Last Wali of Swat, an autobiography*, Oslo and New York: Columbia University Press.

——(1987) *Cosmologies in the Making: A Generative Approach to Cultural Variation in Inner New Guinea*, Cambridge: Cambridge University Press.

——(1993) *Balinese Worlds*, Chicago: Chicago University Press.

Baumann, H. (1935) *Lunda: Bei Bauern und Jägern in Inner-Angola*, Berlin: Würfel Verlag.

——(1936) *Schöpfung und Urzeit des Menschen im Mythus der africanischen Völker*, Berlin: Reimer.

——(1955) *Das doppelte Geschlecht*, Berlin: Reimer.

——(1975) *Die Völker Afrikas und ihre traditionelle Kulturen* 2 vols, Wiesbaden: Steiner.

Bausinger, H. (1993) *Volkskunde ou l'ethnologie allemande*, Paris: M.S.H.

Becher, H. (1972) 'H. Baldus', *AA*, 74: 1307–1312 (originally published in 1970 in *die Zeitschrift für Ethnologie*, vol.95).

Beek, W.E.A. van and Scherer, J.H. (1975) *Explorations in the Anthropology of Religion: Essays in Honor of Jan van Baal*, The Hague.

Bernardi, B. (1973) *Etnologia e antropologia culturale*, Milan: Angeli.

——(1974) *Uomo, Cultura, Società*, Milan: Angeli.

——(ed.) (1977) *The Concept and Dynamics of Culture*, The Hague: Mouton.

——(1990) 'An anthropological odyssey', *Annual Review of Anthropology*, 19: 1–15.

Birket-Smith, K. (1953) *The Chugach Eskimo*, Copenhagen: Nationalmuseets Pub.

——(1956) *An Ethnological Sketch of Rennell Island, a Polynesian Outlier in Melanesia*, Copenhagen: Nationalmuseets Pub..

——(1941; 1965) *The Paths of Culture: a General Ethnology*, trans. K. Fennow, Madison: University of Wisconsin Press.

Blok, A. and Boissevain, J. (1984) 'Anthropology in the Netherlands: Puzzles and paradoxes', *Annual Review of Anthropology*, 13: 333–344.

Boas, F. (1903) 'The Jesup North Pacific Expedition', *The American Museum Journal*, 3(5): 72–119.

——(1937) 'W. Bogoras', *AA*, 39: 314–315.

Bogoras, W. (1904) 'The Chukchee: material culture', *The Jesup North Pacific Expedition: Memoirs of the American Museum for Natural History*, vol.7, New York: Brill, pp.1–276.

——(1907) 'The Chukchee II, Religion', *The Jesup North Pacific Expedition: Memoirs of the American Museum for Natural History*, vol.7, (2), New York: Brill, pp.277–536.

——(1909) 'The Chukchee III, Social Organisation', *The Jesup North Pacific Expedition: Memoirs of the American Museum for Natural History*, vol.7, (2), New York: Brill, pp.537–737.

——(1910) 'Chukchee Mythology', *The Jesup North Pacific Expedition: Memoirs of the American Museum for Natural History*, vol.8, New York: Brill, pp.1–197.

——(1913) 'The Eskimo of Siberia', *The Jesup North Pacific Expedition: Memoirs of the American Museum for Natural History*, vol.8, New York: Brill, pp.417–456.

Brauner, S. (1999) *Afrikanistik in Leipzig (1) 1895–1945*, Köln: Rüdiger Köppe.

Bromley, Y.N. (1971) 'A propos de la définition du terme ethnie, Sciences sociales aujourd'hui. Problèmes théoriques de l'ethnographie', *Académie des sciences de l'URSS*, 3(10): 5–34.

Bromley, Y.N. and Ter-Sarkissiants, A. (1983) 'Les lignes de force des travaux des ethnographes soviétiques', *Sciences sociales en URSS* (Moscou, Académie des Sciences), 3(53): 93–113.

Bromley, Y.V. (1979) 'Problems of primitive society in Soviet Ethnology', in S. Diamond (ed.) *Towards a Marxist Anthropology*, The Hague, Paris and New York: Mouton.

——(1989) 'The theory of ethnos and ethnic process in Soviet social science', *Comparative Studies in Society and History*, July 1989.

Caravantes, V.C. (1985) 'A los veinte años de la fundacíon de la Escuela de Estudios antropológico: el renacimiento de la Antropología española', *Revista Española de Antropología Americana*, 15: 335–337.

Carreira, A. *et al.* (eds) (1978) *Homenaje a Julio Caro Baroja*, Madrid: CIS.

Cencillo, L. (1970) *Curso de antropología integral*, Madrid: Syntagma.

Chard, C. S. (1961) 'Sternberg's materials on the sexual life of the Gilyak', *Anthropological Papers of the University of Alaska*, no.10: 13–24.

Cherchi, P. (1986) 'Introduzione a V. Lanternari', in V. Lanternari, *Preistoria e folklore*, Sassari, pp.7–74.

Chichlo, B. (1984) 'L'ethnographie soviétique est-elle une anthropologie?' in Rupp-Eisenreich (ed.) *Histoires de l'anthropologie: XVI-XIX siècles*, Paris: Klincksieck, pp.247–258.

——(1985) 'L'ethnographie soviétique entre 1953 et 1983', *Revue des Etudes Slaves*, no.2: 309–324.

Collective, (1968) *VIIe congrès international des sciences anthropologiques et ethnologiques, Moscou, 1964*, Moscou: Académie des sciences, 4 vols.

Comas d'Argemir, D. and Prat, J. (1996) 'Social anthropology in Spain', *EASA Newsletter*, 18: 11–13.

Conte, E. and Essner, C. (1995) *La quête de la Race. Une anthropologie du Nazisme*, Paris: Hachette.

Dadoun, R. (1972) *Géza Róheim et l'essor de l'anthropologie psychanalytique*, Paris: Payot.

de Finis, G. (1991) 'Grottanelli, V.L.' in C. Winter, pp.252–253.

——(1991) 'Lanternari, Victorio' in C. Winter, pp.380–381.

——(1965) *A la découverte des Tsiganes*, Brussels: Université libre de Bruxelles.

——(1966) *Le Ruanda et la civilisation interlacustre. Essais d'anthropologie historique et structurale*, Université libre de Bruxelles.

——(1971; 1981) *Why Marry Her? Society and symbolic culture*, trans. J. Lloyd, Cambridge: Cambridge University Press.

——(1985) *Sacrifice in Africa: A structuralist approach*, trans. L. O'Brien, Bloomington: Indiana University Press.

——(1987) *Ecrits sur la royauté sacrée*, Brussels, editions de l'Université.

——(1997) *Posture et imposture*, Brussels: Labord.

——(1998) *Mémoire, mon beau navire*, Arles: Actes Sud.

——(1982; 2000) *Mythes et rites Bantou*, vol.3, Paris: Gallimard.

de Pina-Cabral, J. (1991a) 'Dias, A. Jorge', in P. Bonte and M. Izard (eds) *Dictionnaire de l'ethnologie et de l'anthropologie*, Paris: Presses universitaires de France, pp.199–200.

——(1991b) 'Portugal. L'anthropologie portugaise', in P. Bonte and M. Izard (eds) *Dictionnaire de l'ethnologie et de l'anthropologie*, Paris: Presses universitaires de France, pp.592–594.

——(1992) 'Anthropologie et identité nationale au Portugal', *Gradhiva*, 11: 31–46.

Devisch, E. (1991) 'Belgique. L'anthropologie belge', in P. Bonte and M. Izard (eds) *Dictionnaire de l'ethnologie et de l'anthropologie*, Paris: Presses universitaires de France, pp.110–111.

Diallo, Y. (2001) 'L'africanisme en Allemagne hier et aujourd'hui', *CEA* no.161, 41(1): 13–43.

Dias, A.J. (1948a) *Os Arados Portugueses e as suas provaveis origens*, Lisbon: Imprensa Nacional.

——(1948b) *Vilarinho da Furna. Uma aldeia comunitária*, Lisbon: Impresa Nacional.

——(1953) *Rio de Onor. Comunitarismo agro-pastoril*, Lisbon: Presença.

——(1961) *Portuguese Contribution to Cultural Anthropology*, foreword by M.G. Marwick, Johannesburg: Witwatersrand University Press.

——(1964) *Os Macondes de Moçambique. Aspectos históricos e económicos*, Lisbon: Junta de Investigações do Ultramar.

——(1970) *Os Macondes de Moçambique. Vida Social e Ritual*, Lisbon: Junta de Investigações do Ultramar.

Dias, A.J. and Dias, M. (1964) *Os Macondes de Moçambique. Cultura Material*, Lisbon: Junta de Investigações do Ultramar.

Dorsinfang-Smets, A. (1959) 'L'organisation et les tendances de l'anthropologie sociale et culturelle africaine en Belgique', *Cahiers de l'I.S.E.A.*, no.93.

Dostal, W. (1967) *Die Beduinen in Südarabien. Eine ethnologische Studie zur Entwicklung der Kamelhirtenkultur in Arabien*, Vienna: Wiener Beiträge zur Kulturkunde und Linguistik, vol.16.

——(1979) *Der Markt von San'a'*, Vienna: Österreichische Akademie der Wissenschaften, Sitzungsberichte.

——(1983) *The traditional architecture of Ras al-Khaymah (North)*, Wiesbaden: Tübinger Atlas des Vorderen Orients.

——(1990) *Eduard Glaser. Forschungen im Yemen. Eine quellenkritische Untersuchung in ethnologischer Sicht*, Vienna: Österreichische Akademie der Wissenschaften.

——(1992) *Ethnographica Jemenica. Auszüge aus den Tagebüchern Eduard Glasers mit einem Kommentar versehen*, Vienna: Österreichische Akademie der Wissenschaften.

——(1994) 'Silence in the darkness: German ethnology in the national socialist period', *Social Anthropology*, 2(3): 251–62.

Dragadze, T. (1995) 'Politics and anthropology in Russia', *AT*, 11(4): 1–3.

Dunn, S.P. (1982) *The Fall and Rise of the Asiatic Mode of Production*, London: Routledge.

Duparc, F. J. (1975) *Een eeuw strijd voor Nederlands cultureel erfgoed (1875–1975)*, Gravenhage: Staatsuitgeverij.

Dutton, L.S. (1991) 'Mühlmann, E.W.', in C. Winter, pp.491–492.

Eberhard, W. (1968) 'Richard Thurnwald', in *International Encyclopedia of the Social Sciences*, D. Sills (ed.), New York.

Eboussi-Boulaga, F. (1968; 1979) 'Le Bantou problèmatique' (on Tempel), *Présence Africaine*, no.66: 4–40.

Esteva Fabregat, C. (1965) *Función y functionalismo en las ciencias sociales*, Madrid: Instituto Balmes.

——(1973a) *Antropología industrial*, Barcelona: Edicíones Planeta.

——(1973b) *Cultura y personalidad*, Barcelona: A. Redonda.

——(1978) *Cultura, sociedad, y personalidad*, Barcelona: Promocíon cultural.

——(1988; 1995) *Mestizaje in Iberoamerica*, trans. J. Wheat, Tuscon: University of Arizona Press.

Esteva Fabregat, C. and Kanellos, N. (eds) (1993–1994) *Handbook of Hispanic Cultures in the United States*, 4 vols, Houston, Madrid: Arte Público Press, Instituto de Cooperacíon Iberoamericana.

Fabre, D. (1999) 'Un rendez-vous manqué. E de Martino et sa réception en France', *L'Homme*, no.151: 207–236.

Fischer, H. (1988) 'Ethnologie und Nationalsozialismus. Probleme bei der Untersuchung eines gemiedenen Themas', *Kölner Museums Bulletin*, vol.2: 28–39.

——(1990) *Völkerkunde im Nationalsozialismus. Aspekte der Anpassung, Affinität und Behauptung einer wissenschaftlichen Disziplin*, Berlin, Hamburg: Dietrich Reimer Verlag.

Forde, D. (1956) 'D. Westermann', *Africa*, 26: 329–331.

Fox, J. (1989) 'An Interview with P.E. de Josselin de Jong', *CA*, 29: 501–510.

Freed, S.A. Fredd, R.S. and Williamson, L. (1991) 'W. Bogoras', in C. Winter (ed.), p.72.

Freed, S.A. and Williamson, L. (1988) 'Capitalist philanthropy and Russian revolutionaries: The Jesup North Pacific Expedition (1897–1902)', *AA*, 90: 7–24.

Gagen-Torn, N.I. (1975) *Lev Iakovlevich Shternberg*, Moscow: Nauka.

Galey, J.-C. (1996) 'An interview with F. Barth', *EASA Newsletter*, no.18: 8–10.

——(1997) 'How others see us: an interview with Frederik Barth', *AN*, 38(2): 58–60.

Galini, C. and Massenzio, M. (eds) (1997) *E. de Martino nella cultura europea*, Naples: Liguori Editore.

Gellner, E. (ed.) (1980) *Soviet and Western Anthropology*, New York, Colombia: Colombia University Press.

Gallo Donato, (1988) *O Saber Português. Antropologia e Colonialismo*, Lisbon: Heptágono.

Gerholm, T. and Hannerz, U. 'Introduction: the shaping of national anthropologies', *Ethnos*, 1: 5–35.

Gerndt, H. (ed.) (1987) *Volkskunde im Nationalsozialismus. Münchner Beiträge zur Volkskunde*, Munich: Münchner Vereinigung für Volkskunde.

Gingrich, T. and Mückler, H. (1997) 'An encounter with recent trends in German-speaking anthropology', *Social Anthropology*, 5: 83–90.

Gómez, S. and Ángel, L. (1997) 'Cien años de Antropologías en España y Portugal (1870–1970)', *Etnográfica*, 1(2): 297–317.

Gräwe, K. (1999a) 'Baldus, H.', in Hirschberg, p.38.

——(1999b) 'L. Adam', in Hirschberg, p.10.

Gräwe, K. and Riese, B (1999a), 'Schmidt, Max', in Hirschberg, p.331.

——(1999b) 'W.E. Mühlmann', in Hirschberg, p. 259.

Grottanelli, V.L. (1940) *Missione etnografica nel Vollega Occidentale: I Mao*, Rome.

——(1955) *Pescatori dell'Oceano indiano*, Rome: Caemonese.

——(1961) *Principi di etnologia*, Rome: Ateneo.

——(1964) *L'etnologia e le leggi della condotta umana*, Rome: Edizioni dell'Ateneo.

——(ed.) (1965–1968) *Etnologica: L'uomo e la civiltà*, Milan: Labor.

——(1967) 'Fürer-Haimendorf. Contribution to historical ethnology', *CA*, 10: 374.

——(1976) *Gerarchie etniche e conflictto culturale*, saggi di etnologia nordest-africana, Milan: Angeli.

——(1977) 'Ethnology and/or cultural anthropology in Italy: Traditions and developments', *CA*, 18(4): 593–614.

——(1988) *The Python Killer: Stories of Nzema Life*, Chicago: University of Chicago Press.

Guerra, M. (1991) in C. Winter, pp.50–51.

Gumilev, L. N. (1990) 'Regards sur l'anthropologie soviétique', *Cahiers du Monde Russe et Soviétique*, 31: 2–3.

Guvich, I.S. and Kuzmina, L.P. (1985) 'W.G. Bogoras et W.I. Jochelson: deux éminents représentants de l'ethnographie russe 1', *Inter-Nord, Revue internationale d'études arctiques*, 17: 145–151.

Haberland, E. (1965) 'A. E. Jensen', *Paideuma*, vol.11.

——(ed.) (1978) *Paideuma, Festschrift for Vinigi Grottanelli* vol.24.

Haekel, J. (1959) 'Zur gegenwärtigen Forschungssituation der Wiener Schule der Ethnologie' in Breitinger, E., Haekel, J., Pittioni, R. (eds) *Beiträge Österreichs zur Erforschung der Vergangenheit und Kulturgeschichte der Menschheit*, Niederösterreich: F. Berger, Wender-Gven Foundation.

Hartmann, T. (1991) in 'Baldus, Herbert' C. Winter, p.22.

Hauschild, T. (ed.) (1995) *Lebenslust und Fremdenfurcht. Ethnologie im Dritten Reich.*

Hauswaldt, P., Münzel, M. and Schneider, H. (1996) *Zur Geschichte der Völkerkunde an der Philipps-Universität Marburg*, Marburg Institut für Völkerkunde.

Heine-Geldern, R. (1976) *Gesammelte Schriften*, (eds E. Stiglmayr and A. Horenwart-Gerlachstein), Vienna: Elisabeth Stiglmayr.

Henry Wassén, S. (1966–67) 'Four Swedish anthropologists in Argentina in the first decades of the twentieth century: bibliographical notes', *Folk*, 8–9.

Heusch, L. de (1958) *Essais sur le symbolisme de l'inceste royal en Afrique*, Brussels: Université libre de Bruxelles.

Hirschberg, (1938) 'Das Werk B. Ankermanns', *Zeitshrift für Ethnologie*, vol.70.

Hobsbawn, E. (1961) 'Review of Lanternari, V. *Movimenti religiosi di lebertà e di salvezza dei popoli oppressi*', in *The Times Literary Supplement*, 29 September.

Horenwart-Gerlachstein, A. (1991) 'Heine-Geldern, R.', in C. Winter, pp.279–280.

Howe, J.E. (1976) 'Pre-agricultural society in Soviet theory and method', *Arctic Anthropology*, 13(1): 84–115.

Humphrey, C. (1980) 'Soviet ethnos theory', *Rain*, 38.

Ihanus, J. (1999) *Multiple origins: Edward Westermarck in search of Mankind*, Frankfurt: Peter Lang.

Jaarsma, S.R. and de Wolf, J.J. (1991a) 'Baal, J. van' in C. Winter, p.17.

——(1991b) 'Josselin de Jong', in C. Winter, pp.330–331.

——(1991c) 'Rassers, Willem H.', in C. Winter, pp.569–570.

——(1991d) 'Steinmetz, Sebald Rudolf', in C. Winter, pp.668–669.

——(1991e) 'Wilken, J.A.', in I.D.A., pp.759–760.

Jeggle, U. (1988) 'L'ethnologie de l'Allemagne sous le régime nazi. Un regard sur la *Volkskunde* deux générations après', *Ethnologie Française*, 18: 114–119.

Jell-Bahlsen, S. (1985) 'Ethnology and fascism in Germany', *Dialectical Anthropology*, 9: 313–333.

Jones, A (ed.) (2000) *Africa in Leipzig. A City Looks at a Continent 1739–1950*, University of Leipzig, 'Papers on Africa, History and Culture', series 3.

Jong, P.E. de and Vermeulen, H.F. (1989) 'Cultural anthropology at Leiden University: From encyclopedism to structuralism' in W. Otterspeer (ed.) *Leiden Oriental Collections, 1850–1940*, Leiden, pp.280–316.

Josselin de Jong, P.E. (1956) 'De visie der participanten op hun cultuur', in *BKI*, no.112, pp.149–168.

——(1980) *Ruler and Realm: Political and Realm: Political Myths in Western Indonesia*, Noord-Hollandsche Publishing Company, Amsterdam: KNAW, no.43, 19pp.

——(1982) Symbolic Anthropology in the Netherlands (Verhandelingen van het KITLV, n°95), Nijhoff: 's-Gravenhage, 231pp.

——(1984) *Unity in diversity: Indonesia as a Field of Anthropological Study*, Dordrecht: Foris Publications.

Josselin de Jong, P.E. (ed.) 1983 (1977) *Structural Anthropology in the Netherlands: a Reader*. The Hague, Martinus.

Juillerat, B. (1993) *La révocation des Tambaran. Les Banaro et Richard Thurnwald revisités*, Paris: Cnrs editions.

Jungraithmayr, H. (1991) 'Westermann, D.H.', in C. Winter, pp.747–749.

Jungraithmayr, H. and Möhlig, W.J.G. (eds) (1983) *Lexikon der Afrikanistik*, Berlin: Dietrich Reimer.

Kagaroff, E. (1929) 'Léo Sternberg', *AA*, 31: 568–571.

Kan, S. (2000) 'The mystery of the missing monograph: or why Shternberg's "The Social Organization of the Gilyak", never appeared among the Jesup Expedition publications', *European Review of Native American Studies*, 14(2): 19–38.

——(2001) 'Franz Boas and Lev Shternberg: science, politics and friendship', paper given at the AAA annual meeting.

Kaschuba, W. (1999) *Einführung in die europäische Ethnologie*, Munich: C.H. Beck.

Kloos, P. (1991) 'Anthropology in the Netherlands: The 1980s and Beyond', in P. Kloos and H.J.M. Claessen (eds) *Contemporary anthropology in the Netherlands. The use of anthropological ideas*, Amsterdam: Uitegeverij, pp.1–29.

Kloos, P. and Claessen, H.J.M. (1981) *Current Issues in Anthropology: The Netherlands*, Amsterdam: Anthropological branch of the Netherlands Sociological and Anthropological Society.

Koentjaraningrat, R.M. (1975) *Anthropology in Indonesia: A Bibliographical Review*, The Hague: M.Nijhof.

Krader, L. (1957) 'Recent studies of the Russian peasant', *AA*, 58: 716–720.

——(1959) 'Recent trends in Soviet anthropology', *Biennial Review of Anthropology*, pp.155–184.

——(1968) 'Bogaras, V.G., Sternberg, L.Y. and V. Jochelson', in D. Sills (ed.) *International Encyclopedia of the Social Sciences*, vol.2: 116–119, New York.

Kreckel, R. (1994) 'Sociology in East German universities: decomposition and reconstruction', Journal of the *Deutsche Gesellschaft für Soziologie*, Special Edition, 3: 240–251.

Krupnik, I. (1998) 'Jesup genealogy: intellectual partnership and Russian-American cooperation in Arctic and North Pacific Anthropology, 1897–1948', *Arctic Anthropology*, 35(2): 199–226.

Lanternari, V. (1959; 1976) *La grande festa: vita rituale e sistemi di produzione nelle società tradizionali*, Milan: Saggiatore.

——(1967) *Occidente e Terzo Mondo: incontri di civiltà e religioni differenti*, Bari.

——(1974) *Antropologia e Imperialismo, e altri saggi*, Turin: Einaudi.

——(1976) *Crisi e ricerca d'identità. Folklore e dinamica culturale*, Naples: Liguori.

——(1983a) *L'incivilimento di barbari*, Bari: Dedalo.

——(1983b) *Festa, carisma, apocalipse*, Palermo: Sellerio.

——(1986) *Identità e differenza: percorsi storico-antropologici*, Naples: Lignori.

——(1988) *Dei, profeti, contadini: incontri nel Ghana*, Naples: Lignori.

——(1994) 'La parole des exclus de l'histoire. Débuts de l'anthropologie religieuse en Italie', *Ethnologue Française*, 25(3): 497–512.

——(2003) *Ecoantropologia: dall'Ingerenza ecologica alla svalta etico-cultural*, Bari: Dedalo.

Lanternari, V. and Ciminelli, M.L. (eds) (1994–1999) *Medecine, Magia, Religione, Valori*, 2 vols Naples: Ligori.

Leal, J. (1995) 'Imagens contrastadas do povo. Cultura popular e identidade nacional na antropologia portuguesa oitocentista', Conférence à l'Association Portuguaise des anthropologues published as no.13 of *Revista Lusitana*. Prefaces by J. Leal to reissues of classics of the folklore and ethnology of Portugal.

——(1999) 'The history of Portuguese Anthropology', *HAN*, 26(2): 10–18.

——(2000) *Etnographias portuguesas (1870–1970): Cultura popular e identidade nacional*, Lisbon: Dom Quizote.

Lehmann, A. (1954) 'Fünfundachtzig Jahre Museum für Völkerkunde zu Leipzig', *Jahrbuch des Museums für Völkerkunde zu Leipzig*, 12: 10–51.

Lehmann, R. (1940) 'K.T. Preuß', *Zeitschrift für Ethnologie*, 71: 145–150.

Lenclud, G. (1991a) 'Caro Baroja, Julio', in P. Bonte and M. Izard (eds) *Dictionnaire de l'ethnologie et de l'anthropologie*, Paris: Presses universitaires de France, pp.126–127.

——(1991b) 'Thurnwald, Richard', in P. Bonte and M Izard (eds) *Dictionnaire de l'ethnologie et de l'anthropologie*, Paris: Presses universitaires de France, pp.708–709.

Linimayr, W. P. (1993) *Das Institut für Völkerkunde der Universität Wien 1938–1945 unter Mitberücksichtigung des Museums für Völkerkunde Wien*, Diplomarbeit, 2 vols, University of Vienna.

Lisón Tolosana, C. (1977) *Antropología social en España*, Madrid: Akal.

Ljungström, O. (1998) 'Towards a history of Scandinavian anthropology', Uppsala Newsletter: History of Science, no.27.

Lonergan, D. 'A. E. Jensen', in C. Winter, p.326.

Lowie, R. (1933) 'E. Nordenskjöld', *AA*, 35: 158–161.

——(1954) 'Richard Thurnwald 1869–1954', *AA*, 56: 862–867.

Mancini, S. (1991) 'Le Monde magique selon de Martino', *Gradhiva*, 10: 71–84.

Maquet, J.J. (1954) *Le système des relations sociales dans le Ruanda ancien*, Tervuren.

——(1967a; 1972) *Civilization of Black Africa*, trans. J. Rayfield, New York: Oxford University Press.

——(1967b) *Africanité traditionnelle et moderne*, Paris: Présence Africaine.

——(1971) *Power and Society in Africa*, trans. J. Kupfermann, New York: McGraw Hill.

Maraña, F. (1995) *Julio Caro Baroja, el hombre necesario*, Bilbáo: Birmingham.

Marazzi, A. (ed.) (1989) *Antropologia: tendenze contemporanee: scritti in onore di Bernardo Bernardi*, Milan: Hoepli.

Maret, P. de (1993) 'Interview with Luc de Heusch', *CA*, 34: 289–298.

Marschall, Hrsg, W. (1990) *Klassiker der Kulturanthropologie: von Montaigne bis Margaret Mead*, Munich: C.H. Beck.

Melk-Koch, M. (1989) *Auf der Suche nach der menschlichen Gesellschaft: Richard Thurnwald*, Berlin: Museum für Völkerkunde.

Michel, U. (1991) 'Wilhelm Emil Mühlmann (1904–1988) – ein deutscher Professor. Amnesie und Amnestie: Zum Verhältnis von Ethnologie und Politik im Nationalsozialismus', in *Jahrbuch für Soziologiegeschichte*: 69–117.

Miller, R.R. (1983) *Por la ciencia y la gloria nacional. La expedición científica española e America, 1862–1866*, Barcelona.

Möhlig, W.J.G. (1990) 'Entwicklung und Situation der Afrikanistik in der Bundesrepublik Deutschland', in W. Prinz and P. Weingart (eds) *Die Soziologischen Geisteswissenschaften: Innenansichten*, Frankfurt am Main: Suhrkamp, pp.375–387.

Moisseeff, M. (1991) 'Róheim, Géza', in P. Bonte and M. Izard (eds) *Dictionnaire de l'ethnologie et de l'anthropologie*, Paris: Presses universitaires de France, p.636.

Mouradian, C. (1990) 'La revue Ethnographique arménienne Azgagrakan Handes', *Cahiers du Monde Russe et Soviétique*, 31(2–3): 295–315.

Muensterberger, W. (1969) *Man and his culture: Psychoanalytic anthropology after 'Totem and Taboo'*, London: Rapp.

Mühlmann, W.E. (1938) *Methodik der Völkerkunde*, Stuttgart.

——(1940) *Krieg und Frieden, ein Leitfaden der Politischen Ethnologie*, Heidelberg: Winter, Berlin.

——(1947) *Dreizehn Jahre. Aus den Tagebüchern eines Völkerpsychologen*. (Autobiography 1933–1945).

——(1955) *Arioi und Mamaia: eine ethnologische, religiös-soziologische und historische Studie über polynesische Kultbünde*, Wiesbaden: F. Steiner.

——(1959) 'L'Ethnologie contemporaine en Allemagne', *Cahiers de l'ISEA*, no.8.

——(1961) *Chiliasmus und Natavismus: Studien zur Psychologie, Soziologie und historische kasiuistik der Umsturzbewegungen*, Berlin: Reimer Verlag.

——(1964) *Rassen, Ethnien, Kulturen*, Neuwied Luchterhand.

——(1981) *Die Metamorphose der Frau: Weiblicher Schamanismus und Dichtung*, Berlin: Reimer Verlag.

——(1984) *Pfade in die Weltliteratur*, Königstein: Athnäum.

Müller, E.W. (1990) 'W.E. Mühlmann', *Zeitschrift für Ethnologie*, 114: 1–12.

Murrau, S.O. (1991) 'Leo Shternberg', in C. Winter, p.639.

Needham, R (1960) 'The left hand of the Mugwe: An analytical note on the structure of Meru symbolism', *Africa*, 30(1): 20–33.

Nicolaisen, J. (1980) 'Scandinavia: all approaches are fruitful' in S. Diamond (ed.) *Anthropology: Ancestors and Heirs*, The Hague, pp.259–273.

Nordenskjöld, E.N.H. (1910) *Indianerleben, Elgran Chaco (südaneika)*, Leipzig: A. Bonnier.

——(1919–1931) *The Comparative Ethnographical Studies*, 9 vols.

——(1929) 'Nécrologie K. von Steiner', *Journal de la Société des Américanistes*, 22: 221–227.

Oliveira, E.V. de (1974) 'António Jorge Dias', *In Memoriam A.J. Dias*, Lisbon: Junta de Investigações do Ultramar.

Ortiz, C. (1987) *Luis de Hoyos Sáinz y la antropología español*, Madrid: CSIC.

——(1996) 'J.C. Baroja, antropologo e historiador social', *Revista de dialectologia y traditiones populares*, 51: 283–301.

Ovesen, J. (1991) 'Birket-Smith, Kaj' in C. Winter, pp.60–61.

Pettazzoni, R. (1921; 1953) *La religione nelle Grecia antica fino ad Alessandro*, Turin: Einaudi.

——(1948–1966; 1978) *Miti e Leggende*, 4 vols, New York: Arno Press.

——(1954; 1967) *Essays on the History of Religions*, Leiden: J. Brill.

——(1956; 1978) *The All-Knowing God: Researches into the Early History of Religions*, New York: Arno Press.

Pitt-Rivers, J. (1996) 'A Commentary on the work and the personality of J. Caro Baroja', *AT*, 12(2): 20–22.

Plischke, H. (1929) 'K. von Steiner', *Deutsches Biographisches Jahrbuch* 1929, Berlin: Deutsche Verlags-Anstalt, pp.291–292.

Plotkin, V. and Howe, J.E. (1985) 'The unknown tradition: continuity and innovation in Soviet ethnography', *Dialectical Anthropology*, 9(1–4): 257–312.

Poncelet, M. (1995) *Sciences sociales, colonisation et développement: une histoire sociale du siècle d'africanisme belge*, 2 vol, European thesis, Lille and Liège.

Prat, J. (1991) 'Esteva Fabregat, Claudio' in C. Winter, p.183.

——(1995) 'Interview with the doyen of Catalan Anthropology', *EASA Newsletter* 16: 6–9.

Prat i Caros, J. (1991) 'Espagne. L'anthropologie espagnole', in P. Bonte and M. Izard (eds) *Dictionnaire de l'ethnologie et de l'anthropologie*, Paris: Presses universitaires de France, pp.236–238.

Preuss, K.T. (1912) *Die religion der Cora-Indianer*, Leipzig.

——(1921–1923) *Religion und Mythologie der Uitoto* 2 vols, Göttingen: Vandenhoeck.

——(1933) *Der Religiöse Gehalt der Mythen*, Tübingen.

Proctor, R. (1988) 'From *Anthropologie* to *Rassenkunde* in the German anthropological tradition', in G.W. Stocking (ed.) *Bones, Bodies, Behavior, HOA*, vol.5: 138–179.

Pusman, K. 'Die Wiener Anthropologische Gesellschaft in der ersten Hälfe des 20. Jahrhunderts', unpublished thesis, University of Vienna.

Quintens, M. (1998) 'Unité dans la diversité. Images anthropologiques du monde indonésien', master's thesis defended at the University of Lille 1.

Reichel-Dolmatoff, G. (1971) *Amazonian Cosmos. The Sexual and Religious Symbolism of the Tukano Indians*, Chicago: University of Chicago Press.

——(1978) *Beyond the Milky Way: Hallucinatory imagery of the Tukano Indians*, Los Angeles: UCLA Pub.

——(1985) *Basketry as Metaphor. Arts and Crafts of the Desana Indians of the Northwest Amazon*, Los Angeles: Musuem of Cultural History.

——(1985) *Los Kogi, una tribu indígena de la Sierra Nevada de Santa Marta*, Bogota: Procultura.

Reimann, H. (1988) 'W.E. Mühlmann', *Kölner Zeitschrift für Soziologie und Sozialpsychologie*, 40: 611–612.

Riese, B. (1991a) 'Preuß, Konrad Theodor', in C. Winter, p.550.

——(1991b) in 'Steinmetz, Sebald Rudolph' C. Winter, p.668.

——(1991c) 'Thurnwald, Richard', in C. Winter, pp.698–699.

Riviera, M. *et al.* (1978) *Perspectivas de la antropología española*, Madrid: Akal.

Róheim, G. (1919) *Spiegelzauber*, Internationale Psychoanalytische Bibliothek, Vienna.

——(1950) *Psychoanalysis and Anthropology, Culture, Personality and the Unconscious*, New York: International Universities Press.

——(1943) *The Origin and Function of Culture*, New York: Nervous and Mental Disease Monographs Pub.

——(1934; 1974) *The Riddle of the Sphinx: or Human Origins*, trans. Honey-Kyrle, Intro by W. Muensterberger, New York: Harper and Row.

——(1930; 1972) *Animism, Magic and the Divine King*, New York: International Universities Press.

Romerolde Tejada, R. (1992) *Un templo a la ciencia*. Madrid: Historia del Museo Nacional de Etnologia, Ministerio de Cultura, 79 pp.

Rüger, A. (1976) vol.25 of *Wissenschaftliche Zeitschrift der Humboldt-Universität zu Berlin* dedicated to the work of Westermann (also includes articles by W. Rusch, J. Sellnow).

Ryan, M. and Prentice, R. (1987) *Social trends in Soviet Union from 1950*, London: Macmillan.

Saunders, G. (1984) 'Contemporary Italian Cultural Anthropology', *Annual Review of Anthropology* 13: 447–466.

Saunders, G. (1991) 'De Martino, Ernesto', in C. Winter, pp.144–145

——(1993) 'Critical ethnocentrism and the ethnology of Ernesto De Martino', *AA*, 95(4): 875–893.

Schaden, E. (1991) 'Schmidt, Max', in C. Winter, pp.617–618.

Schelee, G. (1990) 'Das Fach Sozialanthropologie/Ethnologie seit dem Zweiten Weltkrieg', in W. Prinz and P. Weingart (eds) *Die soziologischen Geisteswissenschaften: Innenansichten*, Frankfurt am Main: Suhrkamp, pp.206–312.

Schmidt, M. (1905) *Indianerstudien in Zentralbrasilien: Erlebnisse und ethnologische Ergebnisse einer Reise in den Jahren 1900–1901*, Berlin: D. Reimer.

——(1923) *Die materielle Wirtschaft bei den Naturvölkern*, Leizig.

——(1929) *Kunst und Kultur von Peru*, Berlin: Propyläen-Verlag.

Schott, R. (1960) 'Das Geschichtsbild der sowjetischen Ethnographie', *Saeculum*, 1(1–2): 27–63.

——(1991) 'R. Thurnwald, le fondateur de l'ethnologie juridique en Allemagne', *Droit et Culture*, Dossier R. Thurnwald, no.21: 124–139.

Segalen, M. (1991) 'Europe du Nord. L'ethnologie de l'Europe du Nord', in P. Bonte and M. Izard (eds) *Dictionnaire de l'ethnologie et de l'anthropologie*, Paris: Presses universitaires de France, pp.263–264.

Shimkin, D.B. (1959) 'Recent trends in soviet anthropology', *AA*, 51: 621–625.

Shternberg, L.J. (1905) 'Die Religion der Giljaken', *Archiv für Religionswissenschaft*, 8: 244–274; 456–473.

——(1925) 'Divine election in primitive religion', Göteborg, Review of the XXI session of Congress of Americanists, vol.2, pp.472–512.

——(1930) 'Der Adlerkult bei den Völkern Siberiens', *Archiv für Religionswissenschaft*, 28: 125–153.

Skalnik, P. (1981) 'Community: struggle for a key concept in Soviet ethnography', *Dialectical Anthropology*, 6(2): 183–191.

——(1988) 'Union Soviétique-Afrique du Sud: les théories de l'ethnos', *CEA*, 28(2): 157–176.

Slezkin, Y. (1991) 'The fall of Soviet ethnography, 1928–1938', *CA*, 32: 476–84.

Slezkine, Y. (1994) *Arctic Mirrors: Russia and the Small Peoples of the North*, Cornell University Press.

Smet, A.J. (1976) *Le père Placide Tempels et son œuvre oubliée*, Kinshasa: Faculté de théologie catholique.

Stagl, J. (1999a) in Hirschberg, p.26.

——(1999b) 'H. Baumann', in Hirschberg, p.43.

——(1999c), 'Heine-Geldern, R.' in Hirschberg, p.168.

——(1999d) 'Jensen, Adolf Ellegard', in Hirschberg, p.195.

——(1999e) 'Preuß, Konrad Theodor', in Hirschberg, p.295.

——(1999f) 'Schutz, Heinricht', in Hirschberg, p.334.

Steinen, K. von (1886) *Durch Zentral-Brasilien*, Leipzig: Brockhaus.

——(1894; 1968) *Unter den Naturvöllkern Zentral-Brasiliens: Reiseschilderungen und Ergebnisse der Zweiten Schingú-Expedition 1887–1888*, New York: Johnson Reprint Corp.

——(1925–1928; 1969) *Die Marquesaner und ihre Kunst: Studien über die Entwicklung primitiver Südseeornamentik*, 3 vols, New York: Hacker Art Books.

Steinmetz, S.R. (1894) *Ethnologische Studien zur ersten Entwicklung der Strafe, nebst einer psychologischen Abhandlung über Grausamkeit und Rachsucht*, (2 vol.), Leiden/Leipzig: S.C. van Doesburgh/Otto Harrassowitz.

——(1930) *Gesammelte kleinere Schriften zur Ethnologie und Soziologie*, II, Groningen: P. Noordhoff.

Stocking, G.S. (1984) 'Academician Bromley on Soviet Ethnography', *HAN*, 11(2): 6–11.

Straube, H. (1972) 'H. Baumann', *Paideuma*, 18: 1–5.

Stroup, T. (ed.) (1982) *Edward Westermarck: Essays on His Life and Works*, Helsinki.

——(1991a) 'Westermarck, Edvard Alexander', in C. Winter, pp.749–750.

——(1991b) 'Westermarck, Edward', in P. Bonte and M. Izard (eds) *Dictionnaire de l'ethnologie et de l'anthropologie*, Paris: Presses universitaires de France, pp.744–745.

Tanoni, I. (1989) 'L'etnoantropologia religiosa di V. Lanternari', *Il Tetto*, 152–153: 261–280.

Tayler, D. (1994) 'Gerardo Reichel-Dolmatoff', *AT*, 10(6): 19–20.

Thurnwald, R.C. (1912) *Forschungen auf den Salomo-Inseln und dem Bismarck-Archipel*, 3 vols. Berlin: Reimer.

——(1916) *Banaro Society. Social Organization and Kinship System of a Tribe in the interior of New Guinea*, Lancaster, *AAA* memoirs 3(4): 251–391.

——(1931–1935) *Die menschliche Gesellschaft*, Berlin and Leipzig; Gruyter, 5 vols.

——(1939) *Koloniale Gestaltung*, Methoden und Probleme überseeische Ausdehnang, Hamburg: Hoffman und Campe Verlag.

Tishkov, V. (1992) 'The crises in Soviet ethnography', *CA*, 33(4): 371–82.

——(1996) 'Russian and Soviet anthropology' in A. Barnard and J. Spencer (eds) *Encyclopedia of Social and Cultural Anthropology*, London: Routledge, pp. 493–495.

Toumakine, D.D. (1962) 'L'ethnologie océaniste en URSS', *Journal de la Société des Océanistes*, 18: 1–10.

Trimborn, H. (1954) 'Richard Thurnwald', *Zeitshrift für Ethnologie*, 79: 254–255.

——(1956) 'L. Adam', *Zeitschrift für Ethnologie*, vol.81.

Vajda, L. (1991) 'H. Baumann', in C. Winter, p.40.

Valabrega, J-P. (1957) 'L'anthropologie psychanalytique', *La Psychanalyse*, no.3, Paris: Presses universitaires de France.

Vannucci, G. (1991) 'Pettazzoni, Raffaele', in C. Winter (ed.), p.537.

Vansina, J. (1954) *Les tribus bakunta et les peuplades apparentées*, Tervuren: Musée royal de l'Afrique Centrale.

——(1968) *Kingdoms of the Savanna*, Madison: University of Wisconsin Press.

——(1973) *The Tio Kingdom of the Middle Congo, 1880–1892*, London: Oxford University Press.

——(1978) *The Children of Wood: A History of the Kuba Peoples*, Madison: University of Wisconsin Press.

——(1985) *Oral Tradition as History*, Madison: University of Wisconsin Press.

——(1996) *Living with Africa*, Madison: University of Wisconsin Press.

Vansina, J. and Vansina, C. (1976; 1993), *Art History in Africa: an Introduction to Method*, London: Longman.

Verde Casanova, A. (1980) 'La primera Sociedad Antropológica de Espagaña', in *Actas del 1er Congreso Español de Antropología*, Barcelona, vol.2: 17–38.

Verebélyi, K. (1991) 'Róheim, Géza', in C. Winter (ed.), pp.590–591.

Vermeulen, H. F. (1998) 'Bibliographica Arcana. The History of Anthropology in the Netherlands', *HAN*, 25(1): 8–13; 25(2): 10–15.

——(1999) 'P.E. de Josselin de Jong' *AT*, 15(3): 18–19.

Vernau, R. (1929) 'Nécrologie. Manuel Antón Ferrándiz', *L'Anthropologie*, 39: 565–567.

Vinnikov, I. (1991) 'Lev Shternberg', in D. Sills (ed.) *International Encyclopedia of the Social Sciences,* vol.14: 388.

Vitebsky, P. (1989) 'Rethinking soviet anthropology?', *AT*, 5(5): 23–24.

Westermann, D.H. (1905–1906; 1954) *Wörterbuch der Ewe-Sprache*, 2 vols, Berlin: Akademie Verlag.

——(1912; 1970) *The Shilluk People: Their Language and Folklore*, Westport: Negro Universities Press.

——(1952) *Geschichte Afrikas: Staatenbildung südlich der Sahara*, Cologne: Greven Verlag.

Westermarck, E.A. (1914; 1972) *Marriage Ceremonies in Morocco*, London: Rowman and Littlefield.

——(1926; 1968) *Ritual and Belief in Morocco*, Foreword by B. Malinowski, New Hyde Park: University Books.

——(1929) *Memories of my Life*, trans. by A. Barwell, London: Allen.

——(1933; 1973) *Pagan Survivals in Mohammedan Civilisation*, Amsterdam: Philosophical Press.

——(1939; 1969) *Christianity and Morals*, Freeport: Books for Libraries Press.

Wilbur, G.B. and Muensterberger, W. (eds) (1951) *Psychoanalysis and Culture: Essays in Honor of Géza Róheim*, New York: International Universities Press.

Wilken, G.A. (1880) 'Over de primitieve vormen van het huwelijk en de oorsprong van het gezin, I-III', *Indische Gids*, 4(1): 601–644; 1177–1205.

——(1881) 'Over de primitieve vormen van het huwelijk en de oorsprong van het gezin, IV', *Indische Gids*, 3(2): 232–288.

——(1884) 'Het matriarcaat bij de oude Arabieren', *Indische Gids*, 4(1): 90–132.

——(1884–1885) 'Het animisme bij de volken van de Indischen archipel', *Indische Gids*, 4: 90–242.

——(1912) *De verspreide geshriften van Prof.Dr G.A. Wilken*, Verzameld door F.D.E. Van Ossenbruggen, Semarang, Soerabaia, Bandoeng, s'Gravenhage, C.G.T van Drop & co.

Winkelmann, I. (1966) 'Die bürgerliche Ethnographie im Dienste der Kolonialpolitik des Deutschen Reiches (1870–1918)', unpublished thesis, Humboldt University, Berlin.

Wolf, A.P. (1970) 'Childhood association and sexual attraction: a further test of the Westermarck hypothesis', *AA*, 72: 503–15.

——(1995) *Sexual Attraction and Childhood Association: A Chinese Brief for Edvard Westermarck*, Cambridge: Cambridge University Press.

Wolf, J. de (1995) 'Beyond evolutionism: the work of H.J. Nieboer on Slavery, 1900–1910', in H.F. Vermeulen and A.A. Roldan (eds), *Field work and Fieldnotes: Studies in the History of European Anthropology*, Routledge: London, pp.113–128.

Wolf, J.J. de (1998) *Eigenheid en samenwerking. Honderd jaar antropologisch verenigingsleven in Nederland*, Leiden: Kitlv.

Zavatti, S. (1979/1980) 'Birket-Smith, Kaj', *Archivio per l'antropologia e la etnologia*, 109–110.

Zwernemann, J. (1983) *Culture History and African Anthropology: A Century of Research in Germany and Austria*, Uppsala: Almqvist und Wiksell.

X

Latin America

BRAZIL

Research into anthropology, particularly physical anthropology, was carried out in late nineteenth and early twentieth-century Brazil by such men as S. Romero (1851–1914), N. Rodrigues (1862–1906), E. da Cunha (1866–1909) and Arthur Ramos (1903–1949). However, it was not until after the Second World War that the discipline gained a firm institutional footing in a country that did not abolish slavery until 1888. The foundational work of Brazilian social and cultural anthropology is best represented in the writings of Raimundo Rodrigues Nina (1862–1906) and later of Curt Unkel (a.k.a. **Nimuendajú**). Nina was a physician and psychiatrist who took an interest in the physical anthropology and criminology of the Afro-Brazilian population and then did pioneering research into their culture and religious practices, thereby becoming the father of Afro-Brazilian studies. Nimuendajú emigrated to Brazil in 1903 and initiated Amazonian ethnography with financial support from German and then American institutions before working for the Brazilian government in various capacities. From about 1930 to 1950 Nimuendajú's methods provided the paradigm for Brazilian anthropology, but an even more important influence on anthropology and on the humanities in general was the French *Année sociologique* school. Also, C. **Lévi-Strauss** taught in Brazil from 1935 to 1938 and R. **Bastide** from 1938 to 1952.

In 1935 the University of São Paulo endowed a chair in Brazilian ethnography and the Tupi-Guarani language which was first held by Plinio Ayrosa, an engineer, from 1935 to 1956. In 1941 the philosophy, sciences and letters faculty of the same university created an anthropology chair which was first occupied by Emilio Willems. After emigrating from Berlin in 1933, Willems, a specialist in the acculturation of migrant populations, became an assistant professor of sociology in 1937 and co-founder of the pioneering journal *Sociología* in 1939. When he left São Paulo for Vanderbilt University in 1949 his post was filled by Egon Schaden, a second-generation immigrant who translated German texts on the Amazonian Indians and, together with Nimuendajú, founded the ethnography of the Tupi-Guarani societies. In 1945 Schaden obtained the first anthropology doctorate awarded by the University of São Paulo with his thesis 'Ènsaio etno-sociológico sobre a mitologia heróica de algumas tribos indígenas do Brasi', ('Ethno-sociological Essay on the heroic mythology of several indigenous tribes of Brazil) and directed the anthropology department at São Paulo from its creation in 1945 until his retirement in 1967. He was assisted by Gioconda Mussolini (1913–1969), who graduated from the university's philosophy, sciences and letters faculty in 1937 and then taught sociology from 1938 and anthropology from 1944.

The most influential anthropologist in Brazil in the years after Nimuendajú's death in 1946

251

was without doubt Herbert **Baldus**. A former Spartacist who spent several years in South American exile, Baldus returned to Germany to study anthropology in Berlin, where he obtained a doctorate in 1932 with a thesis on the Samuko languages. After completing several fieldwork expeditions between 1933 and 1939 he was appointed professor of Brazilian ethnology at the *Escola Livre de Sociología e Política* in São Paulo, and in 1941 he took Brazilian citizenship. From 1946 he was director of the *Museu Paulista*, and in 1947 he launched the *Revista do Museu Paulista*, which he then edited. The close of this period was marked by the debate between Emilio Willems and Florestan Fernandes, the father of Brazilian sociology and a student of Baldus; Fernandes proposed that anthropological analysis be founded on class and social structure, while Willems used an approach based on social groups with a particular emphasis on culture.

In 1946 Darcy **Ribeiro** established the *Museu do Indio* as part of the *Serviço de Proteçao do Indio* in Rio de Janeiro, and created a post there for Eduardo Galvão, a culturalist and former student of C. **Wagley**. The two of them were joined in 1954 by Roberto **Cardoso de Oliveira**, and in 1955 Ribeiro began teaching an anthropology course. Cardoso de Oliveira recalls that in Brazil 'the field of ethnology had about ten professionals at the beginning of the '50s' (Corrêa 1996: 336). Alongside those already mentioned (Cardoso de Oliveira, Baldus, Ribeiro, Galvão, Schaden and Mussolini), Loureiro Fernandes taught at the Federal University of Paraná, Fernando Altenfelder da Silva at the *Escola Livre de Sociología e Política*, Estevão Pinto at the Federal University of Pernambuco, and Luis de Castro Faria and Heloísa Alberto Torres at the National Museum of the University of Brasília.

In 1949 UNESCO instigated a research programme into questions of race, and the results were published in the collection 'Races and Societies', of which the first two volumes, written by Thales de Azerodo and Wagley, were on Brazil. The 1950s were dominated by the ideas of Leslie **White** and Julian **Steward**, especially as they impinged on the social dynamic (as in 'Tappers and Trappers' by **Murphy** and Steward (1956)). In 1953 Schaden launched the *Revista de Antropologia*, published twice yearly by the University of São Paulo. In 1956 Ribeiro succeeded P. Ayrosa to the São Paulo chair in Brazilian ethnography and the Tupi-Guarani language, which in 1962 was turned into a chair in the indigenous languages of Brazil. A crisis in the *Serviço de Proteçao do Indio* in 1958 caused Ribeiro, Cardoso de Oliveira and Galvão to leave the *Museu do Indio*. Galvão returned to the *Museu Paraense Emilio Goeldi* and then joined the anthropology department at the University of Brasília, becoming its director in 1963, only to be forced from office as a result of the military coup of 1964. Ribeiro worked at the *Centro Brasileiro de Pesquisas Educacionais* (Brazilian Centre for Educational Research) and then became education minister, but he too had to flee when the military seized power.

The social sciences continued to develop despite the coup: 'At the University of São Paulo itself, the numbers studying social sciences courses grew from an average of five in the early 1950s to about three hundred in the early 1970s' (F. de Oliveira, 'Politique et sciences sociales au Brésil, 1964–1985', *Revue internationale des sciences sociales*, 111 (1987): 147–155). Research tended to take place in the context of international programmes, and UNESCO followed up its programme on racial relations with a project on areas of interethnic friction directed by Cardoso de Oliveira (*América Latina*, 5/3 (1962)). Another programme of interethnic research was assigned to the *Centro Latino Americano de Ciências Sociais* in 1962 and directed by Cardoso de Oliveira and D. H. P. **Maybury-Lewis**, assisted by Roque Laraia on the Akuawa, Roberto da Matta on the Gaviões, Julio César Melatti on the Krahó, and Marcos M. Rubinger on the Maxicali. Later came the Central Brazil Research Project of

Harvard University, which continued into the 1980s and whose first results were edited by Maybury-Lewis and published in 1979, and then a comparative project financed by the Ford Foundation in 1978 on the populations of the Northeastern and Central Eastern regions. Quite separate from these programmes were the investigations sponsored by the National Museum and the National Research Council into agriculture and the *compones*, with a particular stress on the colonization of the Amazon region. This work was begun in the mid-1960s, often on the initiative of Otávio Velho, who was supported by Moacir Palmeira and Lygia Sigaud, and a little later Schaden's assistants Ruth Cardoso and Eunice Durham developed an urban anthropology. In 1967 Schaden was replaced in the São Paulo anthropology chair by João Baptista Borges Pereira, who worked on interethnic relations. In 1968 the *Serviço de Proteçao do Indio* and the São Paulo philosophy faculty were ravaged by fire, but despite this misfortune the National Museum, which belonged to the university, launched a postgraduate course in social anthropology. At the same time **Leach**'s former student Antonio Augusto Arante began teaching anthropology in the new State University at Campinas Unicamp, and he was joined there in 1971 by Peter Fry and Verena Stolke (Martinez-Alier), who had completed doctorates under Mary **Douglas** and Peter Rivière respectively. The reforms of 1970 gave university departments the status of autonomous pedagogical entities and did away with the principle of the single *cátedra* or chair. In the same year the postgraduate course at São Paulo was redesigned, in 1972 the State University at Campinas Unicamp and the University of Brasília introduced a Master's degree (*mestrado*), and in 1973 the first volume of the *Serie antropologia* was published. In terms of 'theory', the 1970s were the years of Sol **Tax**'s 'action anthropology', that is the engagement of anthropologists in the causes of the populations they study, and the next two decades saw the rise of native Indian political organizations on a national level and the irruption of Indians onto the political scene.

Freyre, Gilberto (1900–1987)

Born in Recife in Northeastern Brazil, Gilberto Freyre went to study in the USA, where he was briefly taught by F. **Boas**, but left without a degree and travelled to Europe. In 1923 he returned to Brazil, where he fell under the influence of the ideas of the French regionalist F. Mistral and organized the traditionalist movement. In 1933 he published *Casa-grande e senzala* [*Master and Slaves*], the first book to provide a religious, economic, and historical (and even culinary) overview of what Freyre called the 'luso-tropical civilization' of Brazil. Luso-tropicalism is the defining idea of his whole oeuvre, and is set out most fully in *O Luso e o Trópico* [*The Portuguese and the Tropics*] (1961) in terms of three fundamental ideas: the Ulyssism of the Portuguese; their capacity for empathy towards other peoples, which is connected with a strong tendency towards sensualism; and a deep sense of brotherhood deriving from long-established Franciscan values. For Freyre this is why colonizers from Portugal, more than from any other country, were able to adapt to the conditions of tropical life and were predisposed to interbreeding. Slavery was domestic, with the *senzala* being reserved for sleep and the 'house' accommodating both masters and servants, and the result was the development of a quite new culture. Freyre's 'key' to Brazilian history and culture has been much criticized, not least for its culturally essentialist treatment of Black, Indian, Portuguese and Jewish 'natures', and he can be read both as expressing a national imaginary and as purveying a collection of commonplaces. And yet, for all the critics they have drawn, the two above-mentioned works are masterpieces.

Ribeiro, Darcy (1922–1997)

Born in Central Brazil, Darcy Ribeiro began medical studies at the University of São Paulo and was then persuaded by Donald Pierson to enrol at the *Escola Livre de Sociología e Política*, also in São Paulo, where he was taught by H. **Baldus**. He graduated in 1946 and worked from 1947 to 1956 for the UNESCO-sponsored *Serviço de Proteçao do Indio*, making studies of the Guarani, the Oti-Xavante, the Bororo, the Urubu-Kaaporo and especially the Kadiweu. From 1952 to 1956 he directed the *Serviço*'s research section, and drew on its resources to create the *Museu do Indio* in Rio de Janeiro in 1954. He also drew up plans for the Xingú National Indian Reservation. In 1956 Ribeiro succeeded P. Ayrosa in the chair of Brazilian ethnography and the Tupi-Guarani language at the University of São Paulo. He remained active at the *Museu do Indio* and the *Serviço* until 1958, when an internal crisis in both establishments forced him to leave, and thereafter he worked for the *Centro Brasileiro de Pesquisas Educacionais* (Brazilian Centre for Educational Research). He was appointed minister of education in Goulart's centre-left government in 1961, and made use of this position to establish five hundred new primary and secondary schools in Rio de Janeiro. Like many others, Ribeiro was forced to flee when a military coup toppled the civilian government in 1964, and in the following years he lived in several other South American countries, including the Chile of Salvador Allende and the Peru of Velasco Alvarado. In 1968 he published the first volume of his *Antropología y Civilización*, which was not completed until the appearance of the fifth volume in 1995. This work offers a sociological presentation of Latin America, an examination of Brazilian culture, and a description of the situation of American Indian societies, while also exploring the causes of inequality in the development of the Americas. On his return to Brazil in 1976 he devoted himself mainly to politics: as Vice-Governor of Rio State in 1982, minister of education and culture from 1983 to 1986, and senator from 1991 to 1994. When he died on 17 February 1997 the president F. H. Cardoso declared three days of national mourning. Ribeiro told the story of his first fieldwork expeditions of 1949 to 1951 in *Diários Índios: Urubu Kaaoir* (São Paulo: Campanhia das Letras, 1996). He was also the author of four novels, of which the best-known is *Maria*, a tale of conflicts between the Amazonian and European sections of Brazilian society (Vintage Books, 1994).

Cardoso de Oliveira, Roberto (born 1930)

Roberto Cardoso de Oliveira enrolled at the university of his home town of São Paulo to study philosophy, a discipline strongly influenced at that time by graduates of the *Ecole normale supérieure* working for the *Mission française* (see Mariza Corrêa, 1995: 38). He was introduced to Leibniz by M. Gueroult, to Marx and Weber by C. Lefort, to the social sciences by R. **Bastide**, and most importantly to epistemology by G. G. Granger and to ethnology by Florestan Fernandes, whose only fourth-year student he became (Fausto and Leite, 1992). From Fernandes he learnt that what **Freyre** called 'the warm-hearted man' (*homem cordial*) of Brazilian society had, for all his warm-heartedness, effectively exterminated the indigenous population. Cardoso de Oliveira gained a degree in 1953 and then accepted D. **Ribeiro**'s invitation to join him at the *Museu do Indio* he had just opened as part of the *Serviço de Proteçao do Indio*. He worked at the museum for a salary no larger than a student grant, and also assisted Ribeiro with the course in cultural anthropology he taught from 1955. In 1958 a crisis at the *Serviço* led him, together with Ribeiro and Galvão, to resign, and he accepted an invitation from Castro Faria to join the National Museum at the University of Brasília, where he designed a new course on social anthropology in 1960. In the same year he completed an investigation, part of a UNESCO-sponsored research programme on zones of tension, which he had begun in 1955 on the Terena of the Southern Mato Grosso and then extended to cover the Tukúna of the Solimões River. In 1966 he gained a doctorate from the University of São Paulo with a thesis supervised by Fernandes and published two years later as *Urbanização e tribalismo: A integração dos indios terena numa sociedade de classes* (Rio de Janeiro: Zahar). In the early 1960s he and D. H. P. **Maybury-Lewis** co-directed the Harvard Central Brazil Research Project, in which Roberto da Matta, Roque Laraia, Julio Cesar Melatti and M. Rubinger all participated. In 1971 he became a research associate at Harvard University, and there he began research on interethnic representations using the model elaborated by **Barth**

(1976, 1983). He was then employed by the *Instituto Nacional de Antropología e Historía*, and from 1973 also worked to preserve the culture of the Tarascan Indians of Patzcuaro. In 1979 he published a small book at Fernandes's suggestion on M. **Mauss**, a subject which drew him into a deeper engagement with epistemology. This bore fruit in his *Sobre o pensamento antropológico* (Rio de Janeiro: Tempo Brasileiro, 1988); in writings on **Lévy-Bruhl** in 1991 and **Rivers** in 1992; and in his editing of a collection of essays on the history of South American anthropology, published in 1995 after the advent of postmodernism, which he viewed as liable to pervert the proper aims of anthropology (Fauto and Leite, 1992). Finally, he created the *Anuário Antropológico* at the University of Brasília.

MEXICO

During Spanish colonial rule the Mexican population was divided for administrative reasons into castes defined according to racial and linguistic criteria. This was the first attempt at such categorization in Mexico since the early travel writings of such men as Bernardino de Sahagún, who is sometimes considered to be the father of modern anthropology. These ethnic categories were abolished in 1810, at the beginning of the war leading to Mexican independence in 1821, and the *Museo Nacional* was established by the First Republic, which was declared in 1824 after the fall of the short-lived empire. After the war of 1848 with the USA, in which Texas, California and New Mexico were lost, the country experienced a period of internal instability culminating in French intervention in 1862. The tentative beginnings of Mexican anthropology can be dated from 1865, when the Emperor Maximilian ordered that a new Anthropology Museum concentrating largely on archaeology be housed in a colonial-era building. The type of research done, which changed little during the governments of Juárez (1876) and Porfirio Días (1876–1910), involved the accumulation of linguistic, ethnographic, archaeological and other data. During this time the first specialist journal in the discipline appeared, and one of its most distinguished contributors was Zélia Nuttall (1857–1933). In 1909 Nuttall sent her student Manuel **Gamio**, who had lived with rubber plantation workers and learnt Náhuatl, to Columbia University to study under **Boas**. Back in Mexico Gamio used German and American funds to set up the *Escuela Internacional de Arqueología y Etnología* in 1910, which after a brief and intermittent existence was definitively closed in 1918 (on Boas's role in this see **Stocking**, *The Ethnographer's Magic and other Essays*, Wisconsin UP, 1992). In the 1930s ethnohistorical research into the pre-Columbian period began to outgrow the old *belles lettres* tradition and focus increasingly on questions of social organization, particularly in the works of Monzón, Olivé, and Carrasco, and in the 1940s and

1950s monographs were published based on organized research projects. In 1936 General Lázaros Cárdenas, who took power in 1934 and nationalized the petroleum industry in 1938, launched a programme of agrarian reform and created a Department of Indian Affairs which brought various existing organizations under one roof. It was at this time that the *Indigenista* movement was born. The director of the new department was Alfonso **Caso y Andrade**, professor of ethnology and archaeology at the National University since 1930, director of the National Anthropology Museum, and author of a pioneering study on the peoples of the Teotihuacan Valley. Caso founded the *Sociedad Mexicana de Antropología* in 1937 and later the anthropology department of the *Escuela Nacional de Ciencias Biologicas*, which was renamed the *Escuela Nacional de Antropología y de Historia* in 1943; the *Escuela* formed part of the *Instituto Politecnico Nacional* until 1946, when it became an autonomous body. Caso was joined there by P. **Kirchhof**, who had been stripped of his German nationality and become a Mexican citizen in 1941. From Trotsky to the Spanish Republicans, Mexico sheltered a large array of refugees during these years, including the prehistorian P. Bosch Gimpera and the physical anthropologist Juan Gomas from Spain. Both men taught at the *Escuela*, where they trained a whole generation of Mexican anthropologists, of whom the best-known are **de la Fuente**, **Aguirre Beltrán** and Villa Rojas (born 1906). Villa Rojas began his career as a schoolteacher, then worked together with **Redfield**, studied at the University of Chicago, and subsequently returned to Mexico to join the *Instituto Nacional Indigenista* (INI), which Caso had founded in 1949 to win the support of American Indian leaders for a programme of acculturation which would preserve their traditional values. The institute published *México Indígena*, but its first task was to establish Centres of Indian Coordination responsible for sanitary, educational and economic development while always remaining respectful of Amerindian culture. By 1951 such centres had been opened in the states of Chihuahua, Nayarit, Puebla, Gerrero, Veracruz, Oaxaca, Yucatán and Chiapas. The Chiapas centre, situated at San Cristobal de Las Casas among the Tzotzil Indians, was soon considered a model of applied anthropology. Departments of anthropology opened at the Ibero-American University, the University of the Americas, the University of Veracruz and the University of Yucatán, and the journals *América Indígena* and *Boletín de Antropología Americana* were published in Mexico by inter-American organizations. The Anthropology Museum, refurbished in 1964, provided a home for the *Escuela Nacional de Antropología y de Historia* from 1965 to 1979. The 1960s and 1970s were years of expansion for Mexican anthropology: the *Centro de Investigaciones y Estudios Superiores en Antropología Social* was founded, while the National Autonomous University of Mexico began publishing the *Anales de Antropología* in 1964 and also opened an anthropology department and an *Instituto de Investigaciones Antropológicas*. Meanwhile the *Escuela Nacional* opened a centre for advanced studies, anthropology departments were created at Guadalajara, Toluca and Puebla, and Michoacán College at Zamora established a Master's course. In the years that followed new journals were launched: the *Boletín de la Escuela de Ciencias Antropológicas de la Universidad de Yucatán* in 1973; *Nueva Antropología*, published by an independent group, in 1975; and *Cuicuilco de l'Escuela Nacional de Antropología y de Historia* in 1980. The INI gradually shifted its emphasis from integrating the Indians into national culture to helping them resist such integration. The politicized generation of students in the late 1960s increasingly rejected established theories in favour of neo-evolutionism or Marxism, and in 1968 a student uprising was bloodily suppressed. Research focused more and more on relations between peasant communities on the one hand and the global market and the state on the other, and the promotion of integration and acculturation was rejected in favour of critiques of the neglect by indigenist theories of the effects of internal colonization. Such critiques, which grew out of both the indigenist tradition and more classical forms of anthropology, are best represented in the work of González Casanova, G. **Bonfil Batalla** and M. **León-Portilla**. Alongside this tradition an approach based on symbolism was developed during the 1970s, and by the late 1980s Marxist theory was falling out of fashion, to be replaced by analyses of popular culture and empirically based studies of social problems, often funded on a project-by-project basis. By the mid-1990s Mexico had about ten institutions licensed to award anthropology degrees, of which three were private, as well as four institutions offering postgraduate courses.

Gamio, Manuel (1883–1960)

Manuel Gamio is thought of as the father of Mexican anthropology. He was born in Mexico City but spent part of his childhood on a rubber plantation, where he learnt Náhuatl from the seasonal workers. He was taught by Zélia Nuttall, who then sent him to Columbia University to study under **Boas** in 1909. He returned home in the following year as Mexico's revolutionary period was just beginning, and he used funding obtained from Germany and the USA to open the *Escuela Internacional de Arqueología y Etnología* (International School of Archaeology and Ethnology). Intended as a replacement for the Office of Monuments, the *Escuela* sought to promote the study of past and present Mexican culture, but its work was interrupted during the years that followed and it did not survive the end of the revolutionary period in 1918. In 1916 Gamio published *Forjando patria: pro nacionalismo* (Mexico City: Libreira de Porrúa Hermanos), which makes the case for an anthropology of American Indians of the present as well as the pre-colonial and colonial periods and tries to identify the best form of government for the Indian population. He then began excavations in the Teotihuacan Valley and advanced the idea that archaeology plays a part in the invention of the nation. In 1922 he published a revised version of his Columbia University thesis as *La población del valle de Teotihuacan*. [*The People of the Teotihuacan Valley*] Using a substantial body of quantitative data, this work shows that censuses have classified the Spanish-speaking Indians of the valley as whites and those married according to traditional rites as single. Gamio criticizes the ignorance of the Mexican elites about these communities and asks whether the new revolutionary elites will do any better. In 1925 he emigrated to the USA after denouncing corrupt practices at the Mexican education ministry, and he made studies of Mexican immigration for the Social Science Research Council which were published in 1930 and 1931. After his return to Mexico in 1930 he held various government positions, carried out sociological and applied anthropological investigations, and above all campaigned for an Inter-American Indian Institute, which he then directed from its creation in 1942 until his death. He argued that anthropology merited a strong position in the academy as the only discipline accounting for the existence of non-European culture and history. Finally, Gamio devised a well-known system for classifying the hunter–gatherers of Central America.

Caso y Andrade, Alfonso (1896–1970)

A qualified lawyer at twenty-three and a Master of Philosophy at the National University of Mexico at twenty-four, Alfonso Caso y Andrade began his career as a lecturer in the law faculty of the University of Monte Albán. He soon developed a passion for Central American architecture and then for hieroglyphic writing, and began studying under Hermann Beyer at the National Museum. From 1918 to 1940 he explored Monte Albán, a Zapotec city, and discovered treasure there. He was appointed director of the National Preparatory School in 1928, professor of ethnology at the University of Mexico City in 1930, and then director of the archaeology department of the National Museum. He founded the Mexican Anthropology Society in 1937 and the *Escuela Nacional de Antropologia y de Historia* in 1939. He became president of the University of Mexico City in 1944 and national heritage secretary in 1945, and was also appointed director of the National Anthropology Museum. In 1949 he founded the *Instituto Nacional Indigenista* to establish Centres of Indian Coordination responsible for community development, and he remained in charge there until 1970. The most important part of Caso's scholarly output concerns pre-Columbian calendars. He received the Viking Fund Prize of the Wenner–Gren Foundation in 1954.

De la Fuente, Julio (1905–1970)

Born in a village on the Veracruz seaboard, Julio de la Fuente studied chemistry for three years in Mexico City, and after taking various jobs there he spent four years in New York leading a hand-to-mouth existence. He returned to Veracruz in 1932 as an employee of the League of Agrarian Communities, and it was as such that he gained a post at the education ministry in Mexico City in 1935. In the same year he helped found the Anti-Fascist League, which survived until 1937, while his reading of **Gamio** and **Redfield** led him to decide on a career in research. His fieldwork focused particularly on the Zapotec in the mountainous territory of Northern Oaxaca, and in 1939 he published studies on the question of cooperatives and credits. In the following year he and **Malinowski** investigated the nature of the market in Oaxaca, and then after moving for a time to Yale University they co-wrote *The Economics of a Mexican Market System: An Essay in Contemporary Ethnography and Social Change in a Mexican Valley*.

Malinowski's death in 1942 delayed the publication of the book, which did not appear in Spanish until 1957 and in English until 1982, and by the publication of the Spanish edition de la Fuente had become disenchanted with its functionalist character. He later published *Yalalag*, a study of an almost entirely endogamous large village in which he demonstrates how national policies and influences are enacted and interpreted on a local level and asks the question 'what is a community?'. As research director of the *Instituto Nacional Indigenista* from 1951 to 1970 de la Fuente devoted his energies to the question of development, and his *Educación, antropología y desarrollo de la comunidad* appeared posthumously in 1973.

Aguirre Beltrán, Gonzalo (1908–1996)

It was only after completing studies in medicine and surgery in 1931 and a period of clinical practice that Gonzalo Aguirre Beltrán decided to devote himself to anthropology. He was appointed director general for indigenous affairs by the government in 1946 and helped establish the *Instituto Nacional Indigenista* (INI) in Tzetzal-Tzotzil in 1951. He persuaded **Caso y Andrade** that the regional centres of the INI should be situated not in conflict-ridden areas with large Indian populations, but in neutral locations and especially in important commercial centres known as *Centros dominicales*. Aguirre Beltrán worked on forms of indigenous government and then on Mexico's black population, publishing classic studies of these topics in 1953 and 1958 respectively. He became rector of the University of Veracruz in 1956 and a deputy in the Mexican parliament in 1961. From Caso's death in 1970 until 1977 he directed the INI, and during his tenure he was forced to defend the institute's policies against ever fiercer criticisms from the left, expressed most strikingly in *Eso que llaman antropología Mexicana* [*This that they call Mexican anthropology*], which appeared in 1970, and in contributions to the 1974 issue of *Critique of Anthropology*. He responded in print in 1976 with a history of the INI which evaluates its work positively, and then resigned his directorship at the age of 66 to become a researcher with the National University of Mexico. Aguirre Beltrán's immense body of writing, which filled fourteen volumes when it was republished in chronological order, can be seen as contributing to the struggle for the renaissance of an independent Mexican intellectual tradition and to the development of medical anthropology in Mexico.

Bonfil Batalla, Guillermo (born 1925)
Guillermo Bonfil Batalla was trained by the founders of the *Escuela Nacional de Antropología*, who believed in safeguarding authentic elements of the culture of indigenous populations while integrating them into national life. In 1962 he submitted his professorial thesis 'Diagnóstico sobre el hambre en Sudzal' ['Diagnosis of the Sudzal famine'], the product of an interdisciplinary investigation of undernourishment in a small Maya community. As a professor he was responsible for teaching a new generation, but was himself strongly influenced by student agitation culminating in the uprising of 1968. Keen to help bring about an effective democratic society, he advocated an alternative anthropology, concerned less with reproducing and refining the picture of what he called 'Imaginary Mexico' than with revealing an oppressed Mexico which, he felt, had hitherto been invisible in research publications. His *Mexico profundo: una civilización negada* [*The Real Mexico: A Civilization Denied*] (Mexico City: Grujalbo), published in 1969 while the country was mired in crisis, was an enormous success. The book is composed of three parts: a panoramic description of Mexican culture and its history until the European invasion; a study of the colonial order and an evaluation of the Revolution; and a series of reflections on the impact of the Imaginary Mexico project on Central American civilization and culture. In Bonfil Batalla's view, the Imaginary Mexico, as a product of Western civilization, encompasses only a minority of the population and configures and dominates the rest, while independence from Spain has merely led to the legal construction of a fictional state (Bonfil Batalla, 1987: 106). What Mexico therefore needs is a new development project founded on a cultural pluralism which accounts for the American Indian and practises genuine democracy (Bonfil Batalla, 1987: 232). With the work of Bonfil Batalla Mexican anthropology departed from **Gamio**'s theory of drawing the Indians into the heart of the nation and instead perceived them as claiming their right to be different.

León-Portilla, Miguel (born 1926)
Born in Mexico City as the grandson, through his father, of the founder of Mexican anthropology M. **Gamio** (E. Matos Moctezuma in Diás y de Ovando *et al.*, 1992: 15–24), M. León-Portilla completed his secondary education in Mexico and then studied philosophy at Loyola University in Los Angeles, where in 1951 he completed a Master's thesis on Bergson's *Les deux sources de la morale et de la religion* [*The Two Sources of Morality and Religion*]. On his return to Mexico in 1952 Gamio gave him the task of composing indexes for the *Boletín Indigenista* and for *América Indígena*, which he would later edit, and subsequently introduced him to Father Angel Garibay. He learnt Náhuatl from Garibay and became his disciple and later his successor in his posts. In 1956 he completed his thesis 'La filosofía náhuatl estudiata en sus fuentes' ['Náhuatl Philosophy studied through its sources'], published three years later, which describes the principal concepts of ancient Mexican thought and includes the author's own translations. In 1957 he obtained a research post at the *Instituto de Investigaciones Históricas* of the National University of Mexico, and in the same year published the first version of

his *Visión de los vencidos: Relaciones indígenas de la conquista* [*Vision of the Vanquished: Indigenous Relationships to the Conquista*]. While historiography had previously almost always adopted the *conquistador* viewpoint, León-Portilla tried to reconstruct the observations, thoughts and feelings of the vanquished people. In so doing he initiated a new and influential approach much imitated in the years that followed. In 1958 his *Ritos, sacerdotes y atavíos de los dios* [*Rites, Priests and the Finery of the Gods*] appeared, the first in a long series of Náhuatl texts in annotated editions. A member of numerous academies and a holder of honorary doctorates from about one hundred universities, León-Portilla has also served as Mexican ambassador to UNESCO.

PERU

In a development akin to that of Brazil and Mexico, Peru experienced a purely museological period, centred on the *Museo Bolivariano*, before an anthropological tradition proper was generated by reflections on Peruvian nationhood by such scholars as J.-U. Garcia, H. Castro Pozo, L.-E. Valcárcel Vizcarra and J.-C. Mariategui. Valcárcel Vizcarra, who posed the national question in the most clearly indigenist terms in the 1920s and gained a reputation as a specialist on the issue, was appointed to direct the newly created National Museum in 1931. The museum was divided into a history section on the Hispanic period and an anthropological section on the pre-Columbian period, and in 1932 it began to publish the *Revista del Museo Nacional*. In 1931 history and anthropology institutes were established at the *Universidad Nacional Mayor* at San Marcos, and by 1947 the country already employed about twenty professional anthropologists, but it was not until the decades following the Second World War that Peruvian anthropology began to expand rapidly (Doughty, 1983, 'Comments on Osterling and Martínez', *CA*, vol.24/3: 352). An important role in furthering the discipline was played by American scholars such as John Rowe, who during the war opened a research centre and an archaeology and anthropology department at the National University of San Antonio Abad de Curso. This was only the second such department in Peru (the first was in Lima), and its students included Oscar Núñez del Prado, Puerto Maldonado and Gabriel Escobar. A number of scholars from North American universities spent time in the country working on the *Handbook of South American Indians*, a project launched by **Lowie**, **Cooper** and **Spier** in 1932 and completed under the editorship of **Steward** in 1946. The second and third volumes of the *Handbook* contained contributions from the Peruvian scholars Valcárcel Vizcarra, Hildebrando Castro Pozo and Rafael Larco Hoyde. When he became minister of education in 1946, Valcárcel created the *Instituto de Estudios Históricos* and the *Instituto de Estudios Etnológicos*, the latter attached first to the National Archaeology Museum and then to the Museum of Peruvian Culture opened in 1946. Valcárcel also directed the *Instituto de Etnología y Arqueología* of the *Universidad Nacional Mayor* at San Marcos, where Jorge C. Muelle (1903–1974) began teaching anthropological theory. The institute's first wave of graduates comprised José Matos Mar, with his thesis *Tupa: Una comunidad del área del Kauke en el Perú* [*Tupi: A Community in the Kauke Area of Peru*], published in 1948; Rosalí Avalos, with *El cíclo vital en la comunidad de Tupe* [*The Life Cycle of the Tupi Community*], published in 1950; Humberto Ghersi, with *Prácticas funerarias en la comunidad de Virú* [*Funereal Practices in the Virú Community*], published in 1950; and Mario Vásquez Varela, with *La antropología cultural y nuestri problema del indio* [*Cultural Anthropology and our Indian Problem*], published in 1952. A number of monographs appeared as a result of the Smithsonian Institution's Lunahaná Project of 1949–1953, directed by Ozzie G. Simmons, and the Wenner–Gren Foundation's Huarochirí-Yauyos Project of 1953–1955. It was in this period that John Gillin, Richard Schaedel, Harry Tschopik, Fernando Cámara and Julio **de la Fuente** began contributing to Peruvian anthropology. In 1953 an anthropology seminar was established at the Riva Agüero Institute of the Catholic Pontifical University of Lima by the Frenchman Jehan Vellard, a researcher at the *Institut français d'études andines* within the French foreign ministry who had previously worked in Brazil and Chile. This seminar constituted the beginnings of classical anthropology in Peru at a time when it was already becoming dated elsewhere. In another development, the Vérano Linguistic Institute of the University of Oklahoma, with the powerful backing of the Reformed Church, sent a first group of eighteen linguists to study tropical Amazonian languages in 1946, and between 1953 and 1969 the same institute trained a large number of Peruvians as ethnolinguists. The first Inter-American Indigenist Congress, held in Mexico City in 1940, recommended the creation of national indigenist institutes, and in 1946 an *Instituto Indigenista Peruano* was set up within the ministry of justice and labour. The institute played a role in research programmes and the publication of monographic studies with the aim of assisting in the development of rural communities. At the end of the Second World War a number of development projects were launched, particularly by American institutions, which included a significant element of anthropological investigation, and these brought together foreign and Peruvian scholars, the former usually accommodated at the *Pensión Morris* (Doughty, 'Comments on Osterling and Martínez', *CA*, 24/3: 351). The most important of these projects were the Virú Valley Studies of the Smithsonian Institution in 1947, which were then subsumed by the Peru-Cornell Project of 1951 to 1966, and the Puno-Tambopata Programme of the United Nations and its subsidiary agencies, especially the International Labour Organization. Smaller-scale programmes were run by, among others, the US Peace Corps Achievements and the Chancay Valley project, while urban anthropology was pioneered in Peru by the Shantytowns Research Project directed by J. Matos Mar and financed by the National Housing Corporation. It was within the framework of such programmes that Peruvian anthropologists carried out their investigations and trained their students in the postwar period, but in 1964 a group of Peruvian scholars founded the *Instituto de Estudios Peruanos*, a private research institute, with the express purpose of securing greater national autonomy for their work. This institute, a sort of consultative group, was directed by F. Miró Quesada, then minister of education, and drew on the services of Valcárcel Vizcarra, Arguedas and Matos Mar. Alongside these developments, the courses taught at the *Universidad Nacional Mayor* at San Marcos by F. Bourricaud, Henri Favre and Juan Comas Camps offered a socio-anthropological alternative to the organized research projects and their ubiquitous North American influence. The National University at Ayacucho opened in 1959 and created an anthropology department (Gonzales Carre, 1982) where R. T. Zuidema, S. Palomino, U. Quispe, S. Catacora and J. Earls carried out important work in the mid-1960s. In 1959 the government unveiled a *Plan Nacional para la Integración de la Población Indígena* (National Plan for the Integration of the Indigenous Population), a five-year programme organized by the ministry of labour and Indian affairs and directed by Carlos Monge Medrano. In 1966 this was replaced by the *Proyecto de Integración y Desarrollo de la Población Indígena*, from which anthropologists were excluded. In the same year the *Instituto Indigenista Peruano* was taken over by the ministry of labour and Indian affairs, only to be dissolved in 1969 as a consequence of the military coup a year earlier. During its existence from 1947 to 1969, the institute had supported the work of G. Escobar, R. Galdo, H. Martinez, O. Núñez del Prado, and M. Vasquez, and published the journal *Perú Indígena*. Throughout the 1970s Peru saw the influx of a new generation of anthropologists educated abroad and strongly imbued with the then current strains of Marxism, such as H. Bonilla, J. Flores Ochoa, L. Lumbrenas, J. Matos, R. Montoya, R. Sánchez, and A. Toreno, who analysed societies in terms of their modes of production (Montoya, 1980) and power relationships. In 1969 the military government appointed M. Vasquez as director of the National Office for Peasant Communities, which in 1972 was absorbed into the *Sistema Nacional para la Mobilización Social*. This entity, whose vice-president was the anthropologist Carlos Delgado, played a leading role in organizing research and providing work for anthropologists. Its closure in 1977 left a severe shortage of openings for newly qualified anthropologists and resulted in the appearance of numerous independent research centres, such as the *Centro Amazónico de Antropología y Aplicación Práctica* at Iquitos, the *Centro de Estudios Rurales Andinos-Bartolomé de Las Casas* in Cusco, and the *Centro de Investigación y Promoción Amazónica*. Osterling and Martinez counted more than one hundred such research centres in 1983 (Osterling and Martinez, 1983), and found that, of the 91 social anthropologists in Peru in 1980, most were employed by ministries and research centres, while 'fewer than 20–30% have been engaged in traditional academic-related activities' (ibid., 1983: 355). Finally, alongside the dominant tradition of mainly applied work done in these research centres, which carried forward methods instigated in the 1940s, a smaller-scale tradition of ethnohistorical work was maintained in which the American J. V. **Murra** and his students César Fonseca and Enrique Mayer played a distinguished part.

SELECT BIBLIOGRAPHY

Aguirre, B. (1978) 'La antropología social', in Consejo Técnico de Humanidades, *Las humanidades en México, 1950–1970*, Mexico: Universidad Nacional Autónoma de México pp.545–644.

Aguirre Beltrán, G. (1952) 'La Magia del Peyoth, Universidad de Mexico', *Organo de l'universidad*, No.68.

——(1953) *Formas de gobierna indígena*, Mexico: Imprensa universitaria.

——(1957) *El Proceso de aculturación*, Mexico: UNAM.

——(1958) *Cuijila, esbozo etnográfico de un pueblo nego*, Mexico: UNAM.

——(1961) *La universidad latinoamericana y otros ensayos*, Mexico: UNAM.

——(1963) *Medecina y magía: el proceso de aculturacíon en la estructura colonial*, Mexico: INI.

——(1964) 'Introduction' to De la Fuente, 1964 and 1965.

——(1967) *Regiones de refugio. El desarrollo de la communidad y el proceso dominial en mestizoamérica*, Mexico: INI.

——(1976–1980) *Programas de salud en la situación intercultural*, Mexico: Instituto Mexicano del Seguro Social.

——(1981) *La actividad del santo oficio de la inquisicíon en Neva España, 1571–1700*, Mexico: INAH.

——(1989) Obra antropológica, 1990, *Critica antropólogica. Hombres e ideas: Contribuciones al estudio del pensamiento social en México*, México: Fondo de cultura económica.

——(1994) *El Pensar y el quehacer antropológico en Mexico*, Benemerita: Universidad autónoma de Puebla.

——(1995) *Anthropología medical: Sus desarrollos teóricos en Mexico*, Mexico: Fondo de cultura económica.

Aramburu, C. (1981) 'Aspectos del desarollo de la antropología en el Peru', in B. Podesta (ed.) *Ciencias sociales en el Perú: un balance crítico*, Lima: Universidad del Pacifico, pp.1–33.

Bazauri, C. (1940) *La población indígena de México*, 3 vols. Mexico: Secretaria de Education.

Bonfil, G.M., Nolasco, Oliveira, M. and Valencia, E. (1970) *De eso que llaman antropología mexicana*, México: Nueva Lectura.

Bonfil Batalla, G. (1973) *Cholula, la ciudad sagrada en la era industrial*, Mexico: UNAM.

——(1981) *Utopía y revolucíon: el pensamiento político contemporáneo de los Indios en América latina*, Mexico: Nueva imagen.

——(1987) *México profundo: Una civilización negada Mexico*, Mexico: Centro de Investigaciones y Estudios Superiores en Antropología Social.

——(1991) *Pensar nuestra cultura 1980, La Appropriacion y la recuperacion de las sciences sociales en el contexto de los projectos culturals endogenos*, Tokyo: Nations unies.

Cardoso de Oliveira, R. (1960) *Do indian ao bugre. O processo de assimilação do Terena*, Rio de Janeiro: Museu Nacional.

——(1964) *O indio e o mundo dos brancos*, São-Paulo: Difusão Européia do Livro.

——(1968) *Urbanização e tribalismo: A integração dos indios terena numa sociedade de classes*, Rio de Janeiro: Zahar.

——(1972) *A sociología do Brésil indígena*, Rio de Janeiro: Tempo Brasileiro.

——(1976) *Identidade, etnia e estrutura social,*, São Paulo: Biblioteca Pioneira de Ciências Sociais.

——(1979) *Marcel Mauss*, São-Paulo: Editora Atica.

——(1983) *Enigmas e soluções: exercícios de etnologia e de crítica*, Rio de Janeiro: Tempo Brasileiro.

——(1988) *A Crise do indigenismo*, Campinas: Editora da Unicamp.

——(1992) *Interpretando a antropologia de Rivers*, Campinas: Editora da Unicamp.

Caso, A. (1962) 'La Sociedad Mexicana de Antropología', in *Revista Mexicana de Estudios Antropológicos*, 28: 49–80.

Caso y Andrade, A. (1919) '¿Qué es el Derecho?', a dissertation to obtain the degree of Licentiatus Juris at the National University of Mexico.

——(1925) 'Un antiguo Juego Mexicano: El Patolli', *El Mexico Antiguo*, 2: 203–211.

——(1937) *The Religion of the Aztecs*, Mexico.

——(1948) 'Definición del indio y de lo indio', *America Indigena*, 8(4): 239–248.

——(1953) *El Pueblo del sol*, Mexico: Fondo de Culture Económica (*The Aztecs: People of the Sun*, Norman, 1958).

——(1967) *Los calendarios prehispánicos*, Mexico: Universidad Nacional Autónoma de Mexico (UNAM).

——(1969) *El tesoro de Monte Albán*, Mexico: Universidad Nacíonal Autónoma de México.

——(1972–79) *Reyes y reinos de la Mixteca*, 2 vols. Mexico: Universidad Nacíonal Autónoma de México.

Cerda Silva, Roberto de la, Rojas Gonzaléz, Francisco, et Barragán Avilés, René, (1957) *Etnografía de México. Síntesis monográfica*, Mexico, Universidad National Autónoma de México.

Colby, G. and Dennett, C. (1995) *Thy Will Be Done. The Conquest of the Amazon: Nelson Rockfeller and Evangelism in the Age of Oil*, New York: Harper Collins.

Collective (1962) *Gilberto Freyre: sua Ciência, sua filisifia, sua arte; ensaios sobre o autor de Casa-Grande e Sanzala e sua influência na moderna cultura do Brasil, comemorativos do 25e aniversário da publicacão desse seu livro*, Rio de Janeiro: J. Olympio Editora.

Collective (1988a) *Instituto Nacional Indigenista Indigenista: 40 años*, 1988, Mexico: Instituto Nacional Indigenista.

Collective (1988b) *Teoría e investigación en la antropología social mexicana*, Mexico: Centro de Investigación y Estudos Superioes en Antropología social.

Comas, J. (1964) *La antropología social aplicada en México: Trayectoria y antología*, Mexico: Instituto Indigenista Inter-americano.

Corrêa, M. (ed.) (1987) *História da antropología no Brasil (1930–1960): testemunhos*,

——(1991) 'Interview with R. Cadoso de Oliveira', *CA*, 32(3): 335–343.

——(1995) 'A Anthropologia no Brasil (1960–1980)' in S. Miceli (ed.) *História das ciências sociais no Brasil*, vol.2. São Paulo: Editora Sumaré.

Días and de Ovanda, C. (1992) 'Rostro y corazóne de Miguel' in Días *et al.*, (1992) *In Ilhiyo, in Ib lahtol Su Aliento, Su Palabra. Homenaje a Miguel León-Portilla*, Mexico, El Colegio Nacional, Instituto Nacional de Antropología e Historia, pp.15–24.

Doughty, Paul (1983) 'Comments on Osterling and Martínez', *CA* 24(3): 352.

Drucker-Brown, S. (ed.) (1985) 'Malinowski in Mexico: Malinowski and J. de la Fuente, The Economics of a Mexican Market System', *Journal des Americanistes*, 84(1): 289–291.

Fausto, C. and Leite, Y. (1992) Unpublished manuscript recast as (1993) 'Entrevista con R.C. de Oliveira. Dos filósophos europens aos Indios brasileiras', *Ciencia Hoje*, 88: 14–20.

Forthmann, H. (1957/1960) Maréchal Rondon, R. Darcy, Orlanda Villas Boas, Vídeo.

Gamio, M. (1922) *Traduction of the introduction, synthesis and conclusions of the work: The Population of the valley of Theotihuacan*, Mexico: Talleres Grafico de la Nacíon.

——(1930; 1973) *Mexican Immigration to the USA. A Study of Human Migration and Adjustment*, Chicago: Ayer Compagny.

——(1931; 1971) *The Life Story of the Mexican Immigrant. Autobiographic Documents, 1883–1960*, intro P.S. Taylor, New York: Dover Publication.

——(1948) *Consideracíones sobre el problema indigena*, Mexico: Instituto indigenista interamericano.

García, M. (ed.) (1987–1988) *La antropología en México: Panorama histórico*, Mexico: Instituto Nacional de Antropología y de Historia, 15 vols.

García Mora, C. and Medina, A. (1986) *La Quiebra política de la antropología social en Mexico*, México: Unam.

Gomes, M.P. (1997) 'Darcy Ribeiro', *AN*, 38(4): 19.

Gonzales Carre, E. (1982) 'Antropología en Ayacuchi: Informe proliminar', *Debates en antropología*, 6: 128–140.

González Gamio, A. (1987) *Manuel Gamio: una lucha sin final*, Mexico: UNAM.

Himes, J.R. (1981) 'The impact in Peru of the Vicos project', in G. Dalton (ed.) *Research in Economic Anthropology*, London, pp.141–209.

Jaúregin, J. (1997) 'La Anthropología marxista en México: sobre su inicio, auge y permanencia', *Inventario Anthropologico*, 3: 13–92

Krotz, E. (1991) 'A Panoramic view of recent Mexican anthropology', *CA*, 32(2): 183–189.

Lameiras, B.B. de (1979) 'La antropología en México: Panorama de su desarrollo en lo que va del siglo', in *Ciencias sociales en Mexico: Desarrollo y perspectivas*, Mexico: El Colegio de México, pp.107–180.

Leon-Portilla, M. (1963) *Aztec thought and culture: A Study of the ancient Nahuatl Mind*.

——(1973) 'A. Caso Obtuaries' in *AA*, 75: 877–885.

——(ed.) (1984) *Bernal Díaz del Castillo, Historia verdadera de la conquista de la Nueva España*.

Mangin, W.P. (1979) 'Thoughts on twenty-four years of work in Perú: the Vicos project and me' in Foster *et al. Long-term field research in Social Anthropology*, New York: Academic Press, pp.65–85.

Mar, M. (1949) 'Las investigaciónes antropologicas en el Peru durante el año 1949', *Revista del Museo Nacional*, 18: 173–175.

Marks Ridinger, R. (1991) 'Caso, A.' in C. Winter, p.101.

Marzal, M. (1981) *Historía de la antropología indigenista: Mexico y Perú*, Lima: Universidad Catolica del Perú.

Matos Motezuma, E. (1973) *Manuel Gamio: archeología e indigenismo*, Mexico.

Medina, A. and García, M. (1983–1986) *La quiebra politica de la antropología social en México*, 2 vols. Mexico: Universidad Nacional Autónoma de México.

Olivé, J.C. and Urteaga, A. (ed.) (1988) *INAH, Una historia*, Mexico: Instituto Nacional de Antropología.

Osterling, J. and Martinez, H. (1983) 'Notes for a history of Peruvian social anthropology, 1940–1980', *CA*, 24(3): 343–360.

Palerm, A. (1980) *Antropología y marxismo*, Mexico: Nueva Imagen.

Pásara, L. (1978) 'Política y ciencias sociales en el Perú', in B. Podesta (ed.) *Ciencias sociales en el Perú: un balance crítico*, Lima: Universidad del Pacifico.

Peirano, M. (1991) *The anthropology of anthropology: the Brazilian case*, Brasilia: Universidade de Brasilia.

Pontes, H. (1989) 'Retratos do Brasil: editores, editoras e "coleções Brasiliana" nas décadas de 30, 40, e 50', in Miceli (ed.) *História das ciências sociais no Brasil*, vol.2. São Paulo: Editora Sumaré.

Schaden, E. (1984) 'Os primeiros tempos da antropologia em São Paulo', *Anuário Antropológico*, 82: 251–258.

Show, P.V. (1957) 'G. Freyre's luso-tropicalism', *Separata de Garcia de Orta*, Porto: Centre de Estudos Políticos e sociais, pp.379–404.

Tamayo Herrera, J. (1980) *Historía del indigenismo cusqueño: Siglos XVI–XX*, Lima: Instituto Nacíonal de Cultura.

Valcarcel, L.E. (1981) *Memorias*, Lima: Instituto de Estudos Peruanos.

Villoro, L. (1979) *Los Grandes momentos del indigenismo en México*, Mexico: Edicíon de la Casa Chata.

Zappa, R. (1996) 'Entrevista', *Journal do Brasil*, 03/11/1996, p.4.

XI
Asia

JAPAN

It was with the restoration of the Meiji that the four large islands which constitute Japan began the slow process towards modernization and Westernization, and the country was opened up to Europeans in 1868. In 1886 the Englishman B. H. Chamberlain occupied the country's first chair in linguistics, and in 1896 the Japanese Society of Linguistics was founded. The American S. Morse carried out the first systematic archaeological excavations in 1887, and in 1896 a Society of Archaeology was formed. From 1884–1885 there was increasing contact between Ainu fishermen and European missionaries like John Batchelor, whose published research influenced the Japanese anthropologist Shogoro **Tsuboi** (1863–1913). Tsuboi introduced evolutionist theory into Japan and in 1884 founded the Anthropological Society of Tokyo, which aimed to study the origins and evolution of races, and which in 1941 was renamed the Japanese Anthropological Society (*Nihon Jinrui gakkai*). In 1886 the first issue of the *Journal of the Anthropological Society of Tokyo* (*Tokyo Jinrui Gakkai Zasshi*) appeared, and in 1893 Tokyo University endowed the country's first anthropology chair and simultaneously opened an anthropology department. After Tsuboi's death in 1913 his successor Ryuzo **Torii** restructured the department, whose students were initially drawn from colleges of medicine. The *Journal of the Anthropological Society of Tokyo* later became the *Journal of the Anthropological Society of Japan* (*Jinruigaku Zasshi*), and focused on physical anthropology, archaeology and linguistics. Ryuzo Torii, who undertook fieldwork among the Aboriginals of Taiwan in 1895 and the Ainu of the Kurile Islands in 1899, was without doubt the most important Japanese anthropologist at the turn of the twentieth century. He carried out research on the Miao of China from 1902, as well as on the Manchu and on Mongolian peoples from 1905. Other pioneering work was done by F. Ifa in Okinawa in 1911. In 1925 Kunio **Yanagita** defined another discipline, a form of *Volkskunde* devoted to the study of folklore and crafts, sensibilities and popular national customs, which he called *Minzokugaku*. Yanagita's most important disciple was Tsuneichi **Miyamoto**, and in the years that followed Japanese folklore split between their *Minzokugaku*, a historical and nationalist study of Japanese traditions, and *Nihonjinron*, an ethnography and social ethno-anthropology. Having invaded Formosa (Taiwan) in 1895, the Japanese established the Imperial University of Taihoku there in 1928 (the present National Taiwan University at Taipei). The new university contained an Institute of Ethnology mainly devoted to the study of the indigenous islanders. The Institute was directed by Utsurikawa, a former student of **Dixon** who worked on questions of historical reconstruction. Thus began a line of research on Formosa which culminated in the late 1930s in extensive published research by Japanese scholars, among whom a few stand out: Toichi **Mabuchi**, who looked at rituals and the clan system and then completed further work using a comparative Radcliffe-Brownian perspective; F. Masuda, a student of matrimonial customs; Y. Okada, who discerned primitive family structures in the aboriginal population; and K. Furuno, who examined aboriginal social structures during the war and then analysed Japanese social life and religion from a Durkheimian point of view. Masoa **Oka** and Eiichirou Ishida, two former students of Father Wilhelm **Schmidt**, founded the *Bulletin of the Institute of Ethnology* (*Minzoku Kenkyusyo Kiyo*). In 1927–1928 the first large-scale archaeological-ethnological survey was directed by the department of sociology and religion of the Imperial University of Keisyo (Seoul University), which was established after the Japanese annexation of Korea in 1910. From 1933 to 1938 this department led research on the Orochon, the Goldi and the Dahur, while two of its members, C. Akamatsu and T. Akiba, completed a major study of shamanism published in two volumes in 1938.

In 1928 members of the anthropology department of Tokyo University founded a study group called the APE circle (anthropology, prehistory, ethnology) on the periphery of the department. This circle, which aimed to foster a more social and psychological approach to mankind, became the Japanese Society of Ethnology (*Nihon Minzoku-gakkai*) in 1934. In the following year the society undertook research on Sakhalin, the Kurile Islands and Micronesia, and launched a new journal called *Minzokugaku Kenkyu* (a general index for 1935 to 1969 was published in 1970 in issue 34/4). In 1934 Yanagita created the Centre for Studies in Local Life (*Kyodo seikatsu kenkyu-syo*), also called the Japanese Folklore Society, which published the journal *Popular Traditions* (*Minkan densho*) devoted to material culture, ceremonies and popular crafts, and drawing on a network of schoolteachers. A more modern type of rural sociology was initiated in 1930 by E. Suzuki under the influence of the American approach. In 1940 he published *Principles of Japanese Rural Sociology*, followed by *A Study in Clan Groups*, an investigation of the Dozoko written with Kitano, Oikawa, and K. Ariga, the last two dividing their attention between sociology and folklore.

The rising tide of nationalism caused a theoretical inward turn in Japanese ethnology, paradoxically so as the occupation of territories in the Second World War created new openings for research, especially after the invasion of Indonesia and various Pacific islands in 1942. S. Izumi and Jiro Suzuki undertook fieldwork in Melanesia and New Guinea; T. Kano researched in the Philippines, French Indochina and Borneo; T. Makino analysed Chinese family structures; and K. Sugiura, later the first professor of cultural anthropology at Tokyo University, worked on Micronesia for the South Sea Islands Government Office. These new departures culminated in the creation in 1943 of an Institute of Ethnology dedicated to the populations of Southeast Asia and directed by Masao Oka.

Defeat in the war brought research to a standstill; the new institute was closed and ethnologists lost their jobs. It also caused a complete rupture between folkloristic and social ethnology. On the one hand those around Yanagita tried to salvage Japan's self-esteem by glorifying its folklore and past. Illustrious members of this group included Orikuchi Shinobu (1887–1953), most of whose work was philological; Yanagi Muneyoshi, who investigated popular crafts; and Seki Keigo, an expert on oral literature. The fruits of their labours were brought together in the publication of the enormous *Dictionary of Japanese Folk-Society and Culture* (*Nippon shakai-minzoku jiten*) (Tokyo, 1952–1960), while in the years that followed Fukutake introduced a more sociological emphasis to this tradition. On the other hand, the pioneering work of Oka, who had imbibed the Viennese concept of the culture complex, stimulated intensive research into the formation of Japanese culture by N. Egami, E. Ishida and I. Yawata. This approach was carried forward in the 1960s by T. Obyashi and K. Sasaki, the latter sometimes writing in English. Finally, the education section of the occupying American forces mounted projects, directed by Passin, Pelzl, Bennett and Ishino, which gave work to unemployed ethnologists and established an approach based on the 'culture and personality' school. Such projects followed the orientation of **Kardiner** and **Linton** in making substantial use of tests such as that of Rorschach (Benedict's *The Chrysanthemum and the Sword* was translated into Japanese in 1949).

From the 1950s there was an inrush of students into universities, and ethnologists found positions in sociology departments. The Japanese Society of Ethnology and the Japanese Society of Anthropology were merged, and in 1951–1952 research into the Ainu of Hokkaido was resumed. In 1951 Jiro Suzuki directed a major study on the outcast Buraku people within the framework of the Social Tensions Survey Project launched by UNESCO, and T. Fukutake, who had worked in China during the war, continued his studies of village life inside Japan. Funding was also provided for research in India and South America, and later also in Southeast Asia, most notably the Kyoto University Expedition to the Himalayas, J. Kawakita's mission to Nepal of 1952, and C. Nakane's research of 1953 on the Hindu Tripura Sikkim people and the Assam tribes of the Indian Himalayas. In 1955 the findings of Kawakita (Kyoto University) and Nakane (Tokyo University) were published in Japanese with an English summary in *Minzokugaku Kenkyu* (vol.19/1: 1–57 and 58–99). S. Izumi and his Tokyo University team investigated Japanese emigrants in Brazil (1952–1958), California (1953–1954), and Canada (1955–1956), and then in 1958 Izumi and E. Ishida began work in the Andes. T. Mabuchi undertook new research in the Ryukyu Islands in 1954 and then in Indonesia on his own, while a new project entitled Unified Research on Cultures of South-East Asian Countries (Laos, Cambodia, Nepal, India, Mekon in Thailand) was launched under Matsumoto in 1957. Ethnologists, botanists, archaeologists and linguists all participated in this project, and the results were published with an English summary in *Minzokugaku Kenkyu* in 1959 (vol.23/1–3). In 1961 K. Imanishi and a group from Kyoto University began a series of research trips to Africa, although this project occupied fewer than a dozen anthropologists, many of whom spent less than three months in the field (Nakane, 1974: 59). A social anthropology circle founded in 1957 published the journal *Shakai Jinruigaku*. Tokyo University opened a cultural anthropology department independent of the physical anthropology department; Tokyo Metropolitan University opened a sociology and social anthropology department in the humanities faculty; and the Catholic University of Nagoya opened an anthropology department which covered linguistics, prehistory and cultural anthropology. In 1959 there were forty-nine institutions offering anthropology teaching in departments of history, political sciences or geography. From 1960 Mabuchi directed new research in social anthropology in Okinawa and in the Ryukyu Islands. In the same year the Japanese Society of Ethnology, which sent a research group to Indonesia under Miyamoto, reportedly contained six hundred members, while the Japanese Society of Anthropology, which concentrated on prehistory and physical anthropology, contained three hundred (Takao Sofue, 1961). By 1973 the Society of Ethnology could boast a membership of one thousand, although, as Chie Nakane points out, it was less an academic association than a group of people of various professional backgrounds who had an interest in the subject, and fewer than 50 members were academic anthropologists (Nakane, 1974: 58). The economic growth of the 1970s led to a significant expansion of the discipline. The founding of a new journal *Anthropology Quarterly* (*Kikan-Jinruigaku*), edited by a group of social and cultural anthropologists from Kyoto University, was evidence of this expansion. So too was the decision by the Japanese parliament to create a National Museum of Ethnology, which was built in 1974 and opened in 1976, and which was intended to provide a National Research Institute. This Institute, directed by Tadao Umesao, operated with the notion of comparative civilization, although three quarters of its research was on Asia. Yet as Komei Sasaki points out, 'Asia makes more than half the world's population' (Knight, 1996: 18). After work in Indonesia, Mabuchi directed two-nation teams in studies on China and Korea in 1973. M. Yamaguchi of the Foreign Studies University of Tokyo researched on Africa, while K. Terada and his Tokyo University team worked on the Andes. In the 1980s Junzo Kawada launched the 'Niger Loop – Interdisciplinary Approaches' programme at the Institute for Research on Asian and African Languages and Cultures at the Foreign Studies University of Tokyo, founded in 1964. In 1986 Kyoto University founded the Centre for African Area Studies.

Today the National Museum of Ethnology, which launched two postgraduate courses in 1989, is one of the most important centres of research and teaching in Japan. Its principal characteristic is its interdisciplinarity, bringing together geographers, chemists, historians, ethnologists and other groups. Of the more strictly anthropological centres, the most significant are the departments at Tokyo University (Todai) and Kyoto University (Kyodai). The *Annual of Social Anthropology* (*Shakai jinruigaku nenpo*) first appeared in 1975, and twenty-six volumes have appeared to date. A few years later the National Museum of Japanese History was launched to promote the study of folklore, history and archaeology.

Tsuboi, Shogoro (1863–1913)

After a degree in geology at Tokyo University Shogoro Tsuboi became a practising archaeologist, and he and Arisaka Shozo unearthed the first Yayoi pottery. He then studied physical anthropology and founded the Tokyo Society of Anthropology in 1884, later the Japanese Anthropological Society (*Nihon jinrui gakkai*). After further study in Paris and London in 1892 he established Japan's first anthropology course at Tokyo University in 1893. Although a defender of the thesis that the Japanese archipelago was first inhabited by the Koropokuru (featuring in Ainu legends), he was also the main disseminator of evolutionism in Japan.

Torii, Ryuzo (1870–1953)

Ryuzo Torii became a disciple of Shogoro **Tsuboi** in 1892 despite not having completed his schooling. He worked at Tokyo University until Tsuboi sent him on expeditions to the Liao-dong peninsula of Taiwan, and then to the Yalu Basin, the Kurile Islands, Mongolia and Korea in the years from 1895 to 1910. In 1921 he was appointed assistant professor and head of the anthropology department at Beijing University, and later held professorships at the universities of Kokugakui and then Sophia. Folklorist, physical anthropologist, linguist and ethnologist, Torii made a name for himself above all as an archaeologist. He was invited to Yanjing University in Beijing in 1939 and did not return to Japan until 1953.

Yanagita, Kunio (1875–1962)

An agronomist and poet, Kunio Yanagita was required by his civil service job to travel throughout the Japanese countryside. He proposed a new agricultural policy involving the education of cultivators before leaving the civil service in 1919 to become a journalist. He then worked for the League of Nations, where he defended the Japanese policy of *manda*. After reading **Frazer** he left this position and in 1935 founded the Society for Popular Traditions (later the Japanese Folklore Society), which in its first year began publishing the journal *Popular Traditions* (*Minkan densho*). In 1947 he founded the

Centre for the Study of Local Life (*Kyodo seikatsu kenkyu-syo*), which aimed to demonstrate the singularity and unity of Japanese culture and drew on the assistance of an extensive network of volunteers. Yanagita is remembered primarily as the father of Japanese folkloric studies of disappearing rural life, but also for his vast historical inquiry into the spread of rice in Southern China and into population change in the Ryukyu Islands.

Oka, Masoa (1898–1982)
A student of Father Wilhelm **Schmidt**, Masoa Oka returned to Japan as the holder of a Ph.D from the University of Vienna, awarded in 1933 for his thesis *Kulturschichten in Altjapan* [*Cultural Strata in Ancient Japan*]. Before leaving Europe he attended the International Conference of Anthropological and Ethnological Sciences held in London in 1934. He then worked as an archaeologist and ethnologist on the Ainu and became the main champion of Viennese diffusionism. He developed a theory of the ethnogenesis of the Japanese, which states that their culture is founded on two elements: first, the so-called Tsunguis type originating from the North and introducing a patrilineal system; and second, an Austronesian type practising fishing and irrigated rice cultivation and characterized by age sets. Oka was a researcher at the Institute of Ethnology, created in 1943 to promote the study of the peoples of Southeast Asia colonized by Japan, and after the Second World War he took professorships at Tokyo University, Tokyo Metropolitan University and Meiji University.

Miyamoto, Tsuneichi (1907–1981)
A student of Shibusawa Keizo and Kunio **Yanagita**, Tsuneichi Miyamoto was a specialist in both material culture and oral traditions. When he joined the Attic Museum as a researcher in 1939 he was charged with collecting specimens of oral literature from remote fishing and mountain villages, and he became a great expert on this topic (*Research on the Inland Sea Region*, 1965).

Chiri, Mashio (1909–1961)
Mashio Chiri was one of the mere handful of Ainu half-castes of his generation to be admitted to Tokyo University. His aim from the beginning of his studies was to become the Scholar for Ainu. From 1940 to 1943 he worked at the Sakhalin Museum and then became a researcher at the Institute for the Study of North Eurasian Cultures at Hokkaido University. He began teaching at Tokyo University in 1947, completed his thesis in 1954, and became an arts faculty professor at Hokkaido University in 1958. He sought the *kotodama* (point of view or 'soul') of the Ainu language in folklore and oral literature. Chiri published more than two hundred texts, almost all devoted to the Ainu, and is particularly well-known for his *Classified Dictionaries of the Ainu Language*: 'Flora' (1953), 'Humans' (1954), and 'Animals' (1962). He also took a deep interest in ancient migrations.

Mabuchi, Toichi (1909–1988)
Toichi Mabuchi enrolled in the Institute of Ethnology at the Imperial University of Taihoku (Taipei) in 1928, the first year of its existence. He completed his first fieldwork among the Yami of the Island of Botel Tobago in 1929, concentrating particularly on the description of rituals. In 1931 he used a Radcliffe-Brownian perspective to investigate the rituals, lineage and socio-political organization of the aboriginal population of Formosa (Taiwan), and then did the same in Indonesia. Appointed assistant professor at the Imperial University of Taihoku in 1943, he worked in Java and in the Celebes (Sulawesi). He then took a teaching position at Tokyo Metropolitan University, where he became a professor in 1953 with the opening of a new department of sociology and social anthropology. He carried out numerous

research missions in Okinawa from 1959 onwards, and worked at the University of Chicago from 1961 to 1963. In 1972 he began teaching at the University of the Ryukyus, and from there moved to the Nazan University of Nagoya. In 1974 he published *Ethnology of the Southwestern Pacific* (Taiwan), a collection of his articles on the societies of the Ryukyu Islands, Taiwan, and other Southeast Asian islands, in which he classifies legends and myths, as well as all forms of social structure, with a particular focus on the way kinship organizes human groups; although parts of it were written a long time ago, this volume continues to influence research on the Malayo-Polynesian region. Mabuchi divides the societies of this region into the Oceanian type, in which sisters tend to dominate their brothers and descent is ambilineal (Okinawa, Polynesia and Micronesia), and an Indonesian type, characterized by exogamous patri-lineal groups and unilateral cross-cousin marriage (Indonesia and Formosa).

Miyata, Noboru (1936–2000)

The work of Noboru Miyata, who obtained a doctorate from the Pedagogical University of Tokyo in 1966, represents a continuation of the ethno-historical and folklorist approach of **Yanagita**. He became an assistant professor and then a full professor in the same institution, and his research on religious beliefs and cults in rural Japan yielded an immense body of published work, including many books for the general reader. He was professor in the history and anthropology department when the Pedagogical University of Tokyo became the University of Tsukuba. He then joined Amino Yoshihiko at the Centre for Research into Historical and Folkloric Documents at the University of Kanagawa and in 1994 was elected president of the Japanese Society for Folkloric Studies.

INDIA

The first travel literature about India was written by Chinese Buddhist pilgrims (Fa Hsien, 405–411; Hiuen-Thsang, 629). Srinivas is reported to have told the story that when he explained to the village chief of Rampura his purpose as an anthropologist in coming to live among the villagers, the latter replied: 'In fact you are trying to do what the early Chinese travellers in India did' (Srinivas, 2000, *CA*, vol.41/2: 164). The works of the Chinese pilgrims were followed by Arab and Persian accounts, and later by those of Europeans. Important among the early Europeans are the Englishman Oaten, the Dutchman Hyghen van Linschoten, the Frenchman Bernier, and above all Robert Knox, who spent twenty years as a prisoner in Ceylon (1681). Next came the Jesuits, who collectively wrote thirty-four volumes of edifying letters between 1702 and 1777 as well as a number of treatises, the best-known by G. L. Coeurdoux and the Abbé Dubois. In 1784 William Jones created the Asiatic Society of Bengal in Calcutta, and in the following year Wilkins published a translation of the *Bhagav-aggita*. Scholars began to study Vedic and Upanishadic texts, and soon perceived that Sanskrit must be at the source of Indo-European languages. A chair in Sanskrit endowed in Paris in 1815 was occupied first by Chézy and then by Burnouf, while in Bonn a chair in Indology was established for A. W. von Schlegel, and soon afterwards the work of F. Bopp and Max **Müller** enlarged the field. In France the *Journal Asiatique* first appeared in 1822, and the following year saw the creation of the Royal Asiatic Society of Great Britain and Ireland, which published a journal and monographs; branches of the society opened in Bombay in 1841 and Ceylon in 1845. In 1858 Queen Victoria dissolved the East India Company in favour of direct crown administration of the colony and in 1877 had herself proclaimed Empress of India.

The development of a 'classical' Orientalist scholarship has its source in the works of Müller. A different tradition, involving the objective presentation of data, was founded by the first census to establish taxable land-holdings in 1860 and by a systematic ethnic classification from 1881 onwards. This tradition became the preserve of the Survey of India, which to this day is one of the most important specialist research centres in the world and is now in the process of publishing a forty-four volume *Anthropological Survey of India* under the general editorship of K. S. Singh. Even the early censuses contained large amounts of ethnographic information. For example D. C. J. Ibbetson's *Census of the Punjab* (Calcutta: Government Printing, 1881–1883) contains several chapters on questions of race, caste and tribe, while H. H. Risley's *Census of India* (1901) includes two volumes of ethnographic appendices. Such censuses formed the basis of a number of important studies, such as *The Land Systems of British India* (Oxford, 1892, 3 vols) by B. H. Baden-Powell, and *Tribes and Castes of the North-Western Provinces and Oudh* (Calcutta, 1896, 4 vols) and *Islam in India* (1922) by W. Cooke, who in 1915 founded the journal *Folklore*. This tradition was continued until shortly after the Second World War by J. H. Hutton, who lived in India from 1909 to 1936 and then became professor of anthropology at Cambridge University, where he replaced T. C. Hodson, like Hutton a civil servant-ethnographer and the author of *India: Census Ethnography 1901–1931* (1st edn 1937; 2nd edn Usha, 1987). After writing two books on the Naga head-hunter tribes, Hutton produced his major work *Caste in India: Its Nature, Function and Origins* (Cambridge UP, 1946). Colonial researchers were aided in their efforts by Indian scholars, of whom the best-known are L. K. A. **Iyer**, S. C. **Roy**, Chanda **Ramaprasad** and Shridhar V. Ketkar, author of *The History of Caste in India* (vol.1 1909; vol.2 1911). Iyer was the first Indian to give a lecture series on the ethnology of India, held at Madras University from 1916. In 1911 the *Journal of the Anthropological Society of Bombay* was founded, followed in 1915 by the *Journal of the Bihar and Orissa Research Society*.

Towards the end of the nineteenth century a number of theoretical texts were written on the basis of existing literature. Examples include *Castes in India* (Paris: Leroux) by Sénart and *Caste in India* (Paris, 1908; Cambridge UP, 1946) by the Durkheimian E. **Bouglé**, whose holistic vision was kept alive after the Second World War by L. **Dumont**. As for fieldwork-based research, which had been pioneered for academic anthropology by the Torres Straits Expedition of 1898, an important event was a journey to India by **Rivers**, whose investigations led to the publication of *The Todas* in 1906. The first 'natives' to study in London were probably K. P. **Chattopadhyay** from 1919 to 1920, Dhirendra Nath **Majumdar** from 1922 to 1924, and Govind S. **Ghurye** from 1929 to 1932, and they were taught mainly by Hodson and **Haddon**, and also by Rivers. Ghurye moved from Sanskritism to social anthropology and was the first occupant of the sociology chair at Bombay University. In 1921 Calcutta University, which already had a department of ancient Indian history and culture, created a small anthropology department specializing largely in the study of tribal groups but also including physical anthropology. The first head of this department was the reader L. K. Ananthakrishnan Iyer, who remained in post until 1931. His colleagues were Haran Chandra Chakladar (1874–1958), Kshitish Prasad Chattopadhyay and Tarak Chandra Das (1898–1964), and they were joined in 1929 by N. K. **Bose** and D. N. Majumdar. Also in 1929, S. C. Roy launched the journal *Man in India* devoted to archaeology and prehistory but also to social and cultural anthropology and to linguistics. K. P. Chattopadhyay was the first to hold the chair of anthropology at Calcutta University, and also headed its anthropology department from 1937 to 1963. In the mid–1930s the LSE admitted Aiyappan and

P. N. Haksar, who later became Gandhi's secretary. Aiyappan's thesis on a Kerala lower caste, supervised by **Firth** and accepted in 1937, was the first functionalist monograph on an Indian community. Anthropology continued to develop in India after the Second World War and particularly after independence in 1947, with the opening of several broad-based departments combining physical anthropology, prehistory, archaeology and ethnology. One such department was created at Lucknow University by D. N. Majumdar (also founder of the journal *Eastern Anthropologist*), and both Morris **Opler** and C. von **Fürer-Haimendorf** went there to teach. On his return from Oxford M. N. **Srinivas** was appointed professor of sociology at the Maharaja Sayajirao University at Baroda in Gujarat, where he established social anthropology as an independent discipline. He began by publishing a programmatical article declaring that the diffusionist approach of G. S. Ghurye was dead and that long periods of fieldwork were needed to address issues of the here and now. Srinivas created a genuine school, made up of I. P. Desai, Arvind A. M. Shah, Ramesh Shroff and Narayan Sheth, which was then visited by a number of foreign scholars, among them F. G. Bailey, K. Marriott, A. R. Bales, B. J. Siegel, K. Gough and W. McCormack. The first Indian social anthropologists of the functionalist school were in a position to witness a rapid transformation of rural culture, which they sought to document and explain. In 1955 two books were published which proudly display this approach: *Village India: Studies in the Little Community* (Chicago UP), edited by McKim Marriott; and *India's Village* (Bombay: Publishing House, 1955), edited by Srinivas (with each editor contributing an essay to the work of his 'rival'). L. Dumont and D. Pocock, who replaced Srinivas at Oxford, founded the journal *Contributions to Indian Sociology* in 1947. When Srinivas was appointed professor at the Delhi School of Economics in 1959, he was followed there by A. Shah and Jit Singh Uberoi, and also by his doctoral students André Béteille, who worked in Bengal, and Veena Das, who was investigating voluntary associations. Among those who subsequently moved to Delhi were Ramaswamy, who studied textile syndicates in Coimbatore; Anand Chakravarti, who studied Rajasthani villages; B. S. Baviskar, who investigated the sugar co-operatives of Maharashtra; M. S. A. Rao, who studied a village on the outskirts of Delhi; and Khadija Gupta, who examined a small town in Aligarh. Although Delhi's mainly Marxist economists found such small-scale work on kinship and village life hard to take seriously (Srinivas, 1999: 9), Srinivas won the battle for the founding of the Delhi Centre for Advanced Studies in Sociology in 1968, and it partook of the enormous expansion the discipline enjoyed until well into the 1980s.

Anthropology in India is almost exclusively focused on the Indian Subcontinent, which is sufficiently diverse to nourish both the Orientalist spirit of research into great civilizations and the notion of 'otherness' informing the most traditional form of ethnology. Also well represented is the socio-functionalist approach, and A. Béteille has noted that 'more village studies have been made by anthropologists in India than probably anywhere else in the world' (Béteille, 1996: 296). A. R. Desai, S. C. **Dube**, M. N. Srinivas and other members of the first generation of Indian scholars are no longer alive, while most of those in the second generation, trained in the 1950s and 1960s, are now retiring: B. S. Baviskar, A. Béteille, D. N. Dhanagare, T. N. Madan, Satish Saberwal, A. M. Shah, Yogendra Singh and J. P. S. Uberoi (Deshpande, 2001). Their bequest is threatened despite the fact that they initiated investigations of factories and other modern sites before their Western colleagues. Srinivas describes the current difficulties as follows: 'We no longer get funding from the government or the University Grants Commission, but from foundations, which have their own agendas. They are very sharply focused on immediate returns [. . .] I don't see any future for intensive research [. . .] Moreover, like the economists, a growing number of India's ablest social science teachers and students now go abroad, especially to America' (*AT*, 1999, vol.15/5: 9).

Iyer, L. K. Ananthakrishna (1861–1937)

Born into a Brahmin family in Kerala, L. K. Ananthakrishnan Iyer obtained a BA in 1883 and then taught in various secondary schools. At the same time he took part in the State Survey of Cochin, which provided him with material for his *Cochin Tribes and Castes* (2 vols, Madras: Government Printing, 1908–1912) and gave him the opportunity to carry out research on the Malabar Coast. He presided over the anthropology section of the first Scientific Congress of India in 1914 and was a pioneer of anthropology teaching in India. In 1916 he gave a series of lectures at Madras University and then taught in the department of ancient Indian history and culture at Calcutta University, where he became a lecturer and head of the anthropology department from 1920 to 1933. A religious man and a traditionalist, he died in the village where he was born. One of his most important publications is the classic 'Naya Polyandry' (*Man*, vol.32).

Roy, Sarat Chandra (1871–1942)

Often thought of as the father of anthropology in India, Sarat Chandra Roy obtained a BA in English before studying law in 1895 and then practising as a lawyer. While defending tribes in Bihar during a territorial dispute he developed a passionate interest in their way of life, and in 1911 he began publishing texts of an anthropological character in *The Modern Review*. In 1914 his first article appeared in the *Journal of the Royal Anthropological Institute*, and he later published regularly in *Man*. He was president of the ethnology section of the 1920 Scientific Congress of India, and in the following year he launched the journal *Man in India*, the country's first anthropological organ. His work spans physical anthropology, social anthropology, kinship, folklore and archaeology, and tends to focus on the Munda, Oraon, Birhir and Chotanagpur tribes of Bihar.

Ramaprasad, Chanda (1873–1942)

The disciple of a Hindu monk in his youth, Chanda Ramaprasad then turned to science and became a teacher in a secondary school. He also took a deep interest in the history of Indian culture, and from 1901 published articles in the journals *Dawn* and *East and West*. In 1917 he was recruited to work on the Archaeological Survey of India, and in 1921 he became a lecturer in the department of ancient Indian history and culture at Calcutta University. A pioneer of Indian archaeology, he also worked and published as an ethnologist.

Ghurye, Govind Sadashiv (1893–1983)

A student of Sanskrit and then of sociology, Govind Sadashiv Ghurye taught at Bombay University from 1924. He was heir to the tradition of erudite Orientalist scholarship and also acquired a diffusionist approach during his time at Cambridge from 1929 to 1932. He then used anthropological concepts to interpret Sanskritic legal and ritual practices, especially with regard to castes and kinship, and he investigated the distribution of cultural traits as manifested in the literature and the records of oral tradition compiled by his students. Drawing on definitions of tribal identities in censuses, he argued that tribes are regressive entities impeding Hinduism, and that Islam is an alien body in India. Ghurye's great erudition and institutional status made him a central figure in the history of social science in India until his retirement in 1959.

Guha, Briaji Sankar (1894–1961)
After obtaining a philosophy MA at Calcutta University, Briaji Sankar Guha moved to Harvard University where he gained a Ph.D in anthropology. He specialized in the study of the ethnic composition of the Indian population, and his earliest published work appeared in *Man in India* in 1926. The founder-director of the Anthropological Survey of the Government of India, he also presided over the anthropological section of the Scientific Congress of India in 1928 and 1938.

Chattopadhyay, Kshitish Prasad (1897–1963)
After gaining a B.Sc in physics from Calcutta University, Kshitish Prasad Chattopadhyay was admitted to Cambridge University in 1919 to study for an M.Sc, but switched from physics to anthropology after meeting Rivers. In 1921 he published his first article in *Man in India* on kinship terminology, a topic he introduced into India and on which he became the country's foremost specialist. He was appointed to a post in the newly opened anthropology department at Calcutta, then left to work for the government before returning to Calcutta to head the department and become the first occupant of the chair of Indian anthropology from 1937 to 1963. He represented India at congresses in London in 1934, Vienna in 1952, and Paris in 1960. His main interests were in social changes following the Second World War.

Bose, Nirmal Kumar (1901–1972)
Nirmal Kumar Bose studied anthropology after having already obtained a B.Sc in geology at Calcutta University, and at the same time he was active in the non-cooperative movement. His first article appeared in 1924, and he then produced his *Cultural Anthropology*, the first introduction to the discipline written by an Indian (Calcutta, 1929). At Calcutta he worked first as a researcher, then as a lecturer from 1938 and a reader from 1946. He was a guest professor at the University of Chicago in 1959 before directing the Anthropological Survey until 1964, when he joined a team working in the Assam region. He was a political activist (for which he was imprisoned by the British) and worked as a spokesman for Gandhi, to whom he dedicated several of his texts. Alongside his political involvement he found time to write more than 700 articles and almost thirty books. For over twenty years he was editor of *Man in India*, and from 1959 to 1964 he was the government's director of anthropological research and anthropological adviser. *The Structure of Indian Society* (1949; see Indian anthropology) and *Caste in India: Data on Caste* (Orissa, 1960) are his most important books.

Elwin, Harry Verrier Holman (1902–1964)
Born in Dover, Harry Verrier Holman Elwin took a degree in English at University College, Oxford, and was then ordained an Anglican clergyman in 1927 and sent as a missionary to India. There he fell completely under the sway of Mahatma Gandhi, renounced Christianity and channelled his energies into the struggle for Indian independence. He also devoted himself to the welfare of remote tribal populations, and to this end he created health centres, craft centres and schools in their territories. His contribution to anthropology consists of a large number of articles, and above all his book *The Muria and their Ghotul*, published in 1947 (Bombay). Considered one of the classics of the discipline, this work describes the Ghotul, a common dormitory open to adolescents of both sexes who, from the onset of puberty, are initiated into physical love by older boys and girls, after which the older girls are married to young men from another Ghotul. This institution has often been adduced as proof of the relative and

culturally specific nature of sexual prohibitions, notably by **Lévi-Strauss** in his famous article 'The Family' (in *Man, Culture and Society*, ed. by L. Shapiro, Oxford UP, 1956). Elwin was deputy director of the anthropology department of the Indian government from 1946 to 1949, and took Indian nationality in 1954. He coined the word 'philanthropology' to express the idea that anthropology's essence is love.

Majumdar, Dhirendra Nath (1903–1960)

After studies at Calcutta University Dhirendra Nath Majumdar moved to Cambridge University, where from 1922 to 1924 he attended lectures by T. C. Hodson and the physical anthropologist G. M. Morant, while also taking part in **Malinowski**'s seminar. In 1923 he published his first article in *Man in India* before going back to India and gaining an MA in 1924. He accompanied S. C. **Roy** on a research trip to study the Ho of Kolhan, on whom he became an expert, and then returned to Cambridge to give a lecture series on Indian anthropology and complete his Ph.D 'Culture Change among the Ho Tribe'. On his return to India in 1928 he was appointed lecturer in 'primitive economics' at Lucknow University, where he subsequently became a professor and, after independence, created an anthropology department. In 1947 he founded the journal *Eastern Anthropologist*, which he edited until his death.

Karve, Irawati (1905–1970)

Born in Burma, Irawati Karve followed her father to India and obtained an MA in sociology from Bombay University. She then moved to Berlin, where she was awarded a Ph.D in physical anthropology under the supervision of the eugenicist Eugen Fischer. On her return she occupied various administrative posts before finally being appointed professor in the sociology and anthropology department of the Deccan Postgraduate College and Research Institute, which she also directed. She was a guest professor at SOAS from 1951 to 1953 and at UCLA in 1959–1960. Karve sought to combine the perspectives of physical and social anthropology with those of Indology and sociology in a holistic interpretation of the nature of Indian society. She is remembered for her many publications on archaeology, physical anthropology, folklore and ethnology (especially kinship), and also for a well-known interpretation of the Mahabharata.

Srinivas, M. N. (1916–1999)

Born into a Brahmin family, M. N. Srinivas enrolled at Mysore University in 1933 and took his BA in 1936. He was taught by the historian and archaeologist Krishna, a former LSE student of **Westermarck**, who had made him read **Lowie**. Krishna encouraged Srinivas to enrol as a sociology student at Bombay University under G. S. **Ghurye**. Srinivas's Bombay MA thesis *Marriage and Family in Mysore* was published in 1942 (Bombay: New Book Company), and soon after a page was devoted to it in *Nature* (Srinivas, 1996: 7–12). As against the notion of ossified caste distinctions, he introduced the idea that individuals belonging to the lower castes seek to raise their status by adopting the rituals and practices of the higher castes, a process he later called Sanskritization. He became Ghurye's assistant and carried out fieldwork among the Coorg, a people of martial traditions living in the Karnataka forests, and in 1944 he completed a largely diffusionist thesis in two volumes, which was externally examined by R. **Firth** (Srinivas, 1997). In 1945 he moved as an assistant lecturer to Oxford University, where he recast his earlier thesis and wrote another, submitted in May 1947, which was the last to be supervised by **Radcliffe-Brown** and the first by **Evans-Pritchard**. Published in 1952 as *Religion and Society among the Coorgs of South India* (Oxford: Clarendon) with a preface by Radcliffe-Brown, it immediately established itself as a great classic of structural-functionalist analysis, and it was the first monograph to show that a Great Tradition (of Sanskritic Hinduism) could be analysed within a social anthropological framework (Singer, 1972: vii). Srinivas was a reader at Oxford from 1948 to 1951 and then a professor of sociology at the MS University of Baroda in Gujarat. On his return to India he wrote an article severely critical of Indian anthropology, which he saw as stuck in a primitive state because of its lack of a theoretical framework and above all because of its reluctance to recognize the importance of fieldwork ('Social Anthropology and Sociology', *Sociological Bulletin*, vol.1, 1952). It was this critical perspective which prompted Srinivas to create a whole new school of social anthropology at Baroda. After editing a collection of texts by Radcliffe-Brown under the title *Method in Social Anthropology* (Chicago UP, 1958), he carried out a ten-month fieldwork study in Rampura in 1948, returning there for a few more months in 1952. As his criticisms of Ghurye had closed the doors of Bombay University to him and his approach bore little relation to the work of the Calcutta School, he founded a new department based on the sociology chair he occupied from 1959 at the Delhi School of Economics. In 1969–1970 he accepted a guest professorship at the Behavioral Science Center of Stanford University so as to write up a book from the fieldwork notes he had made in 1948. These hopes were dashed when radical students protesting against the Vietnam War, incensed at the arrival on campus of army recruiters, hurled Molotov cocktails which set fire to his office and burned all his notes. However, Sol **Tax** persuaded him to write what became the first monograph composed entirely from memory: *The Remembered Village* (Delhi: Oxford UP, 1976), which is often considered to be Srinivas's best book. In the latter part of his career he held professorships at the Institute of Social and Economic Change in Karnataka (1972–1979) and at the National Institute for Advanced Studies in Bangalore.

Dube, Charan Shyama (1922–1996)

Born in the state of Madhya Pradesh, Charan Shyama Dube was a student of D. N. **Majumdar** at Lucknow University in the 1950s. His earliest interest was in tribal ethnology, but he soon turned to the anthropology of rural communities, writing *Indian Village* (London: Routledge, 1955), followed by *India's Changing Villages* (London: Routledge, 1958). These books initiated a series of works on social change. Dube was professor of anthropology at Saugor University from 1957 to 1978, and during the same period he held a large number of administrative posts, including the directorships of the Institute for Advanced Studies and of the Institute for Rural Development. He was also a visiting scholar at foreign institutions such as SOAS and Cornell University.

CHINA

The travel narratives of Chinese voyagers and pilgrims from the beginning of the Christian era to the twentieth century constitute an important documentary source, but they tend to focus mainly on the picturesque features of minority populations. The earliest points of reference for a Chinese social science were a 1902 translation of *The Evolution of the Family* by the Japanese author Ariga Nagao (who had been inspired by **Morgan** and **Spencer**) and translations of works by **Westermarck** and Durkheim. At the same time, Western scholars such as the Frenchman Auguste Bonifacy (1856–1931) were writing ethnic monographs on

Chinese subjects. Cai Yuan-pei (1868–1940) studied at the universities of Leipzig and Hamburg from 1908 to 1911 and then became the first to teach anthropology at Beijing University. He represented China at the International Congress of Ethnology held in Stockholm in 1924, and then spent a period at the Museum of Ethnography in Hamburg. After his return to China in 1926, the journal *In General* (*Yiban zazhi*) published his article 'On Anthropology', in which he translates the word ethnology as *minze xue* rather than as *renzhong xue* (racial studies) and poses the question of how to create a Chinese ethnology of China (Lemoine, 1986: 89).

As its field of enquiry was China itself, the new Chinese ethnology was immediately confronted by the question of what separates sociology and ethnology (see Cai Yuan-pei, 'Relations between sociology and ethnology', 1930). Its response was to focus on 'backward' national minorities and evolutionism (Morgan's *Ancient Society* was translated in 1933). During their construction of the South Manchurian Railway, the Japanese conducted a first ethnological survey of Northern China from 1920 to 1930, while Chinese ethnologists found a home in the Institute of History and Philology created under the umbrella of the Academia Sinica established in Nanking in 1928. In the same year, as a result of the efforts of Cai Yuan-pei, a Central Research Institute of Beijing was founded to carry out research on the legal, economic and social systems of minority groups. The institute brought together a team of scholars, many of whom had studied abroad and now returned to disseminate the ideas of their various masters. Some important figures are **Yang Chengzhi**, who spent two years among the Lolo of Sichuan (1928); Yan Fuli and Shang Chengzu, who both studied the Yao of Lin Yun (1928); Lin Huixiang, whose research was on the aboriginal population of Taiwan (1929); **Ling Chun-sheng**, a student of **Mauss**, **Granet**, and Shang Chengzu who studied the Heche or Goldes of the Lower Sungari River (1930); Yong Che-Heng (Shiheng), who looked at the Miao of Hounan (1932) and the She of Zhejiang; and finally Ruey Yih-Fu. Yang Chengzhi, who had attended Mauss's seminar from 1931 to 1935, introduced anthropology teaching at Sun Yat-sen (Zhongshan) University in Guangzhou (Canton), and this was continued by his student Liang Zhaotao. Another of his students, Jiang Yingliang, established a teaching programme at Yanjing University. Li Hsien (Xian), a former student of **Haddon**, researched on the Li of Hainan in 1934, and in the same year Ling Chun-sheng and Tao Yunkui, who had returned from his training in Berlin and Hamburg, studied the Yi of Yunnan. The diffusionist approach was best represented at the Catholic Furen University of Beijing, where teaching was provided by Hans Stübel, whose research was on the Yao and the Li. During these years a number of major works appeared in Chinese translation: **Tylor**'s *Anthropology* in 1926; parts of **Frazer**'s work in 1931; **Lowie**'s *Primitive Society* in 1935; and some of Haddon's writings in 1937. Yanjing University opened a sociology department headed by Leonard Hsu (Xu Shilian), and one of its teachers was **Wu Wenzao**. R. E. Park, at the time a guest scholar in the department, gave his students some practical experience in realms hitherto unfamiliar to them: 'he led us even to the red-light district; he wanted us to see it first hand! We had read about such places in newspapers and in novels, but we had never actually seen one. It was an abstraction. Then we visited a prison. We realized that we knew little about our own society . . .' (Pasternak, 1988: 639). In 1929 the sociology journal *Shehuitxue gan* was founded. The sociology and anthropology department at the University of Qinghua (Tsinghua) offered teaching by Sergei Mikhailovich **Shirokogorov** (1887–1939), an anthropologist of Russian origin who based himself in Shanghai in 1922 and later in Beijing. From October 1935 to December 1936 **Radcliffe-Brown** taught at Ueching University, where his lectures were attended by about one hundred students (Chien Chiao,

1987). 1936 saw the launching of the new *Journal for Ethnographic Research* (*Minzuxue yanjiu jikan*), and in the first issue Ling Chun-sheng published his Mauss-inspired article 'Methods of Fieldwork Enquiry in Ethnology' (Lemoine, 1986: 92). While in China to study the Yao of Guangdong, R. F. **Fortune** began to teach in the anthropology department of the Sun Yat-sen University in Guangzhou. He remained until 1939, but seems not to have left any trace of a theoretical school. Also at Guangzhou were Lo Hsiang-Lin (Xianglin), the professor of culture Wei Houei-Lin, and Kiang (Jiang) Ying-Liang, the author of studies of the Yao, the Tai, and the Yi of the K'oumenming region. The seizure of power in 1928 by Chan Kai-Chek and the Koumintang provoked the Long March organized by Mao and the Chinese Communist Party in 1934–1935. Meanwhile the Japanese, masters of Manchuria since 1932, took Beijing and Nanking and then installed a new government in 1937 despite ongoing hostilities. The Academia Sinica left Nanking to reform in the regions of Sichuan, Guizhiou and Guangxi, and the members of Beijing University's sociology department fled with the government. In 1938 Tao Yunkui, who was engaged in research on cultural traits in border populations, took charge of sociology teaching at Yanjing University. He was accompanied by Wu Wenzao, who in 1942–1943 created the Yanjing-Yunnan Station for Sociological Research with help from the Rockefeller Foundation, as well as taking charge of the Institute of Beijing on the death of Tao Yunkui in 1944. Staff at the Yanjing-Yunnan Station applied the functionalist methods which Wu Wenzao had advocated from 1936, and also moved away from the exclusive study of minority cultures to a focus on the majority Han population (Lemoine, 1986, 1991). An early example of this new trend is *Peasant Life in China* (London, 1939) by **Fei Xiao-tong**, who had been taught by **Malinowski**. Zhang Ziyi (Tchang Tse-yi), Li Anshi (Li An-che), Li Youyi (Li Yeou-Yi), Tian Rukang (T'ien Jou-k'ang) and **Lin Yao-hua** made up the station's team, which published nine monographs on village life from 1943 to 1948. In Beijing, Cai Yuan-pei disappeared in 1940, to be replaced as the head of the sociology department by Souen Penwen (Sun Benwen), a student of **Boas** who progressed from historical particularism to culturalism and was the author of *Principles of Sociology*. Another student of Boas, Houang Wenchan (Huang Wenshan, Huang Wen-chan), introduced Kroeberian culturology into China. In 1945 the Academia Sinica returned to Nanking and Shanghai, while at Sun Yat-sen University in Guangzhou the first holder of the professorship of anthropology was Yang Chengzhi, who had returned from the USA in 1946. In 1949 **Redfield** gave a lecture series at Yanjing University before Beijing was taken by the Communist Party and the People's Republic of China was proclaimed. Sun Yat-sen University was renamed Zhong Shan (Zhongshan, Zhongda) University, and its modest anthropology department was merged with the history department, retaining just one staff member, Yang Chengzhi, a specialist in the ethno-history of the non-Han minority groups, until his post was attached to the Central Minorities Institute in Beijing. Functionalist ethnologists, who tended to be members of or sympathetic to the Democratic League, sought a reconciliation between the Kuomintang and the Communist Party, and chose not to flee continental China. They saw their role as participating in the anticipated major social transformation, and the new republic charged them with studying ethnic minorities with a view to furthering their development and attainment of a relative autonomy. A first survey launched after the liberation registered 400 ethnic groups which merited consideration as 'nationalities'. Tensions soon became apparent between political figures and some anthropologists. Martin C. K. Yang (Yang Qingkun maochun), who wrote the celebrated monograph *A Chinese Village: Taitou, Shantung Province* (London, 1948) and then continued his studies on other villages with his students, had to flee in 1951 leaving his notes behind. He became professor of sociology at the University of Pittsburgh and wrote up two studies from memory: *The Chinese Family in the Early Communist Revolution* (Cambridge, 1959) and *A Chinese Village in Early Communist Transition* (Berkeley, 1959). Francis L. K. Hsu (Xu Languang, Hsiu Lang-Koung), who had studied the populations near Tali and published 'The Problem of the Incest Taboo in a North China Village' (*AA*, vol.42/1 (1940)), was likewise driven out, and in exile he published *Under the Ancestors' Shadow: Chinese Culture and Personality* (London, 1948).

In 1951 the Central Minorities Institute was created with Fei Xiao-tong as its vice-president. Wu Wenzao, Lin Yao-hua and Quantin P'an were all transferred to the Institute, and until 1955 their task was to identify which minority groups merited official recognition. Although 'the state of nationalities in China soon after the liberation offered researchers a veritable living handbook of the history of social development' (Fei Xiao-tong, 1979; cited by Lemoine, 1986: 85) to which a Marxist understanding of primitive, slave, serf and feudal societies could be applied, sociology (the word used for functionalist anthropology) was banished from teaching courses in 1952 and many socio-ethnologists were re-educated. Nine Nationalities Colleges were opened in provincial centres from 1951 to 1961, and it was to these that ethnologists who did not join history departments became affiliated. In 1956 the Committee for Minority Languages and Ethnic Groups in the National Assembly was founded, and Fei Xiao-tong launched an intensive twelve-year social and historical study programme on each of the fifty-four officially recognized ethnic minorities with a view to achieving a 'democratic reform rooted in the masses'. The Hundred Flowers of 1957 was seen by many as transforming this programme into a litany of empty formulas imposed by the Party, which even set up a new Research Institute on Nationalities before 1958 at the time of the Great Leap Forward.

The Institute of History and Philology of the Academia Sinica was evacuated with the retreat of Nationalist forces and re-established in 1950 in Nan Kang in Taiwan, where it provided a home for the Institute of Ethnology founded by Ling Chun-sheng in 1955. Exiled scholars obtained their PhDs mainly from American and sometimes from Japanese universities: Tai Yun-Hui, Chen Chao-Lu, Chuang Yingchang, Chen Hsiang-Shui, Hsu Chi-Ming, Chen Chi-Nan, and Liu Chich-Wan (Liu Hui-Chen Wang), who wrote the influential *Traditional Chinese Clan Rules* (New York, 1959). Their methods were reinforced by the influence of research by British and American anthropologists in Hong Kong and Taiwan: I. de Beauclair's collection of articles entitled *Tribal Cultures of Southwest China* (Taipei 1970); Morton **Fried**'s *Fabric of Chinese Society: A Study of Social Life in a Chinese County Seat* (New York, 1953); W. P. Morgan's *Triad Societies in Hong Kong* (Hong Kong); Arthur A. Wolf's and Huang Chieh-shan's *Marriage and Adoption in China, 1845–1945* (Stanford, 1979); Margery Wolf's *The House of Lim: A Study of a Chinese Farm Family* (New York, 1968); B. Pasternak's *Kinship and Community in Two Chinese Villages* (Stanford, 1972); Maurice Freedman's *Chinese Family and Marriage in Singapore* (London, 1958), the same author's *Lineage Organization in Southeastern China* (London, 1958), and also his seminal work *Chinese Lineage and Society: Fukien and Kwangtung* (London, 1966). Finally, the programme of the Harvard-Yenching Institute encouraged research into both traditional Taiwanese fishing communities and the formation of lineage-based and clan-based societies.

On the mainland, the anti-right-wing purge which immediately followed the call for 'the blossoming of a Hundred Flowers' was particularly damaging to anthropologists, who were forced to confess their errors and denounce one another. Under the leadership of Yang Kun, who had studied Marxist anthropology in the USSR under Chebokosarov in the early 1950s, they regrouped and tailored their investigations to fit research programmes defined by the conceptions and typologies of historical materialism; 268 studies in accordance with such prescriptions had appeared by 1963. The Cultural Revolution of 1965 to 1974 brought with it the closing of the Central Minorities Institute in Beijing, which had been directed by Yang Kun, and during the night of 1 September 1966 anthropologists were declared 'enemies of the people'. Their houses were ransacked and Red Guards pulped their books and notes. They were interrogated and accused of holding 'seditious meetings', and then in 1969 sent to '7 May Schools' for the re-education of the bureaucratic class by manual labour, before being released in 1972 so that they could welcome a delegation of American intellectuals. Subsequently the institute was reopened and its reappointed members had to teach revolutionary workers and peasants at a time when the campaign against Confucius was getting under way. In 1975 specialization as an archaeologist again became possible within the history department in Zhongda University. In 1978 the Chinese Academy of Social Science replaced the social and philosophical sciences department of the Academy of Science. Anthropology was rehabilitated and allotted the task of reconstructing the stages of social development and debating the nature of feudalism, the relations between classes and the nature of religious superstitions. The journal *Minzu Yanjui* (*Studies of Nationality and Ethnicity*) reappeared after having been suppressed in the early days of the Cultural Revolution, while Fei Xiao-tong opened a Centre for Sociolinguistic Research which focused principally on applied anthropology. A first national symposium on ethnology was organized in October 1980 by Ts'ieou P'ou (Qiu Pu), one of the four sub-directors of the Research Centre on Nationalities of the Academy of Science. This symposium was attended by 123 delegates and resulted in the creation of a Chinese Society of Ethnology; its elected president was Ts'ieou P'ou and its vice-presidents were Lin Yao-hua, Ma Yao, Kou Pao, Liang Kient'ao, Hou Ts'ing-kiun, Tch'en Kouo-kiang and Hsiang Ling. This national society was soon joined by a number of provincial societies, and in 1984 the first issue of a new journal called *Ethnological Research* was published. In 1981 the Chinese government accepted the assistance of the American anthropologist M. Fried in the reconstitution of an anthropology department with fourteen members at the Zhong Shan University in Guangzhou. In 1982 the Association of Anthropologists held its second symposium on the theme of 'The Task of Ethnologists within the Policy of the Four Modernizations', followed in 1983 by a 'Conference on the Modernization of Chinese Culture' held at the Chinese University of Hong Kong, which brought together thirty-six ethnically Chinese academics and researchers from the People's Republic, Taiwan, Singapore and Hong Kong. In the same year, Yanjing University opened a new anthropology department. The increasingly liberal spirit of this period, reflected in the shift of research towards analysing the impact of globalization and economic reform and in the permission granted to anthropologists like Zhusheng Wang to study in the USA, did nothing to prevent the Tiananmen Square massacre of 4 June 1989.

Ling Chun-sheng (1901–1978)

Born in Jiangsu province, Ling Chun-sheng studied in Paris under **Mauss** and **Granet** and in 1929 obtained a doctorate for his thesis 'Ethnographic Research on the Yao of Southern China'. Back in China he undertook research together with Shang Chengzu on the Hezhe or Goldes fishermen-gatherers of the Lower Sungari River on behalf of the Central Research Institute of Beijing, which had been founded by Cai Yuan-pei in 1928. He then published the first ever monograph written by a Chinese anthropologist: *The Hezhe of the Lower Sungari River (Sung-hua* *chiang hsia yu ti Ho-chê-ts'u*). Lemoine describes this work as 'consonant with the Maussian ideal of meticulous description of every detail, down to the most trivial' (Lemoine, 1986: 92). After the fall of Beijing to the Japanese, Ling Chun-sheng moved west with the retreating Nationalist government and joined the Centre for Sociological Studies which Tao Yunkui directed from 1938 at Yanjing University. Together with Ruey Yih-Fu he carried out research in Western China ('Inquiry into the Miao of Western Siang' (Shanghai: Academia Sinica, 1947)). In 1949 he fled to Taiwan and founded the Institute of Ethnology of the Academia Sinica in Nan Chang – in 1955 according to Lemoine (1991), or in 1965 according to Huang Shu-min. Having undertaken comparative research on water transportation in primitive societies, he announced his intention to move towards diffusionist approaches and the investigation of cultural traits such as teknonymy, canine sacrifice, platform pyramids and the phallic cult. This led him to argue that the ancient Chinese had spread as far as Africa and the Pacific coast of America.

Wu Wenzao (1901–1985)

After attending a missionary school Wu Wenzao studied from 1923 to 1929 at Columbia University, where he was taught by **Boas** and completed a doctoral thesis supervised by MacIver on the opium problem in China. At the invitation of R. E. Park he spent 1931–1932 as a visiting professor at the University of Chicago. On his return to China he taught the history of Western thought and the sociology of the family at the universities of Yenching and Qinghua. Between 1936 and 1944 he wrote several articles on functionalism and was one of the first to disseminate European and American ethnography in China. Fleeing the advancing Japanese, he left Beijing in 1937 and joined the sociology department of Yanjing University. With funding from the Rockefeller Foundation he set up the Yanjing-Yunnan Station for Sociological Research in 1942–1943 and promoted the writing of village monographs of a functionalist type. He took over as director of the Institute of Beijing on the death of Tao Yunkui in 1944, was appointed to the Allied Council in 1945 and lived in Japan until 1951. At this time he was associated with the Democratic League, which opposed the Kuomintang and campaigned for national reconciliation. After turning down a post at Yale University he returned to mainland China in 1951 and took a position with the Central Minorities Institute. Denounced as a bourgeois element, he was persecuted in the wake of the Campaign of the Hundred Flowers in 1957, but was permitted to continue working on the programme of the institute, now directed by Yang Kun, until its closure in 1966 as a consequence of the Cultural Revolution. From 1969 to 1972 Wu Wenzao was forced to attend a '7 May School' for re-education through manual labour. In 1972 the institute was reopened for the visit of President Nixon and his American delegation, and Wu Wenzao discretely resumed his activities there, training new 'revolutionary students' who came from factories or rural areas. He was rehabilitated in the early 1980s after the death of Mao and the fall of the 'Band of Four'.

Yang Chengzhi (1902–1991)

Born in Haifeng province, Yang Chengzhi studied history at the University of Beijing, and in 1928 Cai Yuan-pei sent him to carry out research on the Lolo, a minority population in Sichuan which he was the first to investigate. He completed two years of fieldwork before moving to France to study under **Mauss** and at the French School of Sinology (Granet). He graduated from the School of Anthropology and from Section V of the EPHE, and then attended the International Congress of Anthropological and Ethnological Science held in London in

1934. On his return to China in 1935 he was appointed to an administrative post, but also taught anthropology at Sun Yat-sen (Zhongshan) University in Guangzhou (Canton). In 1944 he visited the USA, where he met and befriended **Lowie, Herskovits, Kroeber** and **Wissler**. In 1946 he occupied the first anthropology chair at Sun Yat-sen University and created a new department there. Like many others Yang Chengzhi chose to remain in mainland China after the Communist victory in 1949, when Sun Yat-sen University was renamed Zhong Shan (Zhongshan, Zhongda) University and the small anthropology department was merged with the history department. His post was then transferred to the Central Minorities Institute in Beijing. He took part in the survey of the 1950s, but was persecuted during both the purge following the Hundred Flowers and the Cultural Revolution.

Fei Xiao-tong (born 1910)

Fei Xiao-tong began medical studies at the Suzhou Middle School, but his activities as secretary to the anti-imperialist student organization and leader of the 1929 strike led to his ejection from the course. He enrolled in the sociology department of Yanjing University, where he studied under **Wu Wenzao** and met Martin C. K. Yang. He obtained a BA in 1933 with his dissertation 'An Examination of the Custom of Qin-Ying', which looks at the area of diffusion of the custom of 'The Groom Fetching the Bride'. The department had only one scholarship for study abroad, and Xiao-tong reports that he gave way to his friend Yang (who went to the University of Michigan), while he himself moved to the Qinghua anthropology department, then the only one in China. There he was taught by **Shirokogorov**, who asked him to study the diffusion of different physical types in China, and in 1935 he was awarded an MA for this work, in which he describes the spatial expansion of populations using measurements made on soldiers and prisoners and drawing on the work he had already done on matrimonial customs. He then received funding to go abroad, but on Shirokogorov's advice he first spent a fieldwork year among the Yao of the Guangxi mountains, where his wife Wang Tonghui was killed and he was seriously injured in an accident. During the six months of his convalescence he wrote *Social Organization of the Halan Yao People of Southeast Xiang, Xiang Country, Guangxi* (Shanghai, Shangwu) based on his wife's notes and published under her name. He then returned provisionally to his native province in 1936 to study the village of Kiaxiangong, where his sister was organizing a village co-operative. From 1936 to 1938 he studied at the LSE at the invitation of **Firth**, although it was **Malinowski**, on his return from a short trip to the USA, who insisted on supervising what would be the last thesis completed under his guidance at the LSE (Pasternak, 1988). This work, based on Fei Xiao-tong's Kiaxiangong material, was completed in 1938 and published as *Peasant Life in China: A Field Study in the Yangtze Valley* (London: Kegan Paul, 1939). It demonstrates how the traditional rural economy, founded both on agricultural production and local crafts, is undermined by the introduction of manufactured goods, which tempt peasants into debt and force them to sell their land to absentee town-dwellers. By 1938, when he returned home to become a member of the Yanjing-Yunnan Station for Sociological Research, the Japanese controlled most of the Chinese coast. Together he and Zhang Ziyi (Tchang Tse-yi, Chang Chih-I) carried out research on three village communities to establish different social models. Following the attack on Pearl Harbor and the American declaration of war on Japan, President Roosevelt invited ten Chinese scholars to work at American universities, and Fei Xiao-tong was among these even though he had refused Kuomintang indoctrination. He spent the first few months of his stay of

1943–1944 at Columbia University, where he met R. **Linton** and began co-writing *Earthbound China: A Study of Rural Economy in Yunna* (Chicago, 1945) with him. He then moved to Chicago and worked with R. **Redfield**, whose wife, the daughter of R. E. Park, helped him finish *Earthbound China* and write 'Peasantry and Gentry: An Interpretation of Chinese Social Structure and its Change' (*American Journal of Sociology*, vol.52/1 (1946): 1–17). He also wrote *China's Gentry: Essays in Rural–Urban Relations* (Chicago, 1953), which Redfield edited and revised. On his return to China in 1944 he joined the Democratic League founded by his former teacher Pan Guandan. The Kuomintang included him on a list of those to be suppressed after the defeat of the Japanese, but he was sheltered by the American consul and able to escape the country. At the invitation of the British consul he travelled to Britain, where he lectured and wrote articles in magazines and newspapers on the current situation in China. In 1947 he was appointed professor at the University of Qinghua, where he became an advocate of applied anthropology and campaigned in the press in favour of the development of small-scale industries (Tapp, 1996) and of a controlled transition for the land-holding class. He argued the case for these ideas in *Rural China* in 1948 and later in *Rural Reconstruction*. Although not a communist, Fei Xiao-tong remained in China after the revolution in the hope of contributing to the country's modernization. He spent two fieldwork years in Guangxi and Guizhou in 1950–1951 and also played a role in the establishment of the Central Minorities Institute, becoming its vice-president when it was created in 1951 and directing its programme of identification and recognition of nationalities from 1951 to 1956. This work is reflected in his publications from 'China's Multi-national Family' (*China Reconstructs*, May–June 1952) to 'What constitutes Regional Autonomy for Minorities?' (Hong Kong, 1956). Encouraged by Zhou Enlai (Pasternak, 1988: 647), he spoke of the problems experienced by intellectuals and defended the principle of their relative autonomy during the Hundred Flowers campaign, for example in his article 'The Early Spring for Intellectuals', written for *The People's Daily*. After being denounced as a right-wing deviationist he confessed his errors in 1957 ('I admit my guilt to the people') and was then appointed to the Chinese People's Political Consultative Congress in 1958. He was banned from publishing his own work and concentrated instead on translating history books and contributing to collective investigations. In 1966 the Central Minorities Institute, then directed by Yang Kun, was closed as a policy of the Cultural Revolution, and in the night of 1 September 1966 anthropologists were suddenly declared 'enemies of the people'. After a terrible year in 1967–1968 Fei Xiao-tong and his colleagues were sent in 1969 to a '7 May School' for re-education through manual labour; they were released in 1972 to welcome President Nixon and a delegation of American intellectuals. In 1979 he founded, within the re-opened Institute, a Centre for Sociological Research containing two teams: the first devoted to the study of the principles of Chinese, Western and Marxist sociology; and the second engaged in practical sociology, focusing particularly on urban life and the development of small towns. He was appointed professor of sociology at the University of Beijing and deputy director of its Institute of Sociology, and he was also made vice-president of the Chinese People's Political Consultative Congress. He firmly believed that 'knowing for the sake of knowing is playing games' (Pasternak, 1988: 660) and that 'true scholarship is useful knowledge' (Arkush, 1981: 56).

Lin Yao-hua (born 1910)
A native of Fujian, Lin Yao-hua studied at Yanjing and Beijing universities and

published his first article 'Investigation of Chinese Clans from an Anthropological Perspective' in Chinese in *Che Houei Hsiue* (vol.9, 1936). He then spent from 1937 to 1940 at Harvard University, where he obtained a Ph.D with his thesis 'Miao-Man Peoples of Kweichov' (*Harvard Journal of Asiatic Studies*, 3 (1940): 261–345). After his return to China in 1941 he was appointed head of the sociology department of Yanjing University in Beijing. In 1947 he published *The Lolo of Liang Shan* in Chinese (trans. New Haven, 1961), and followed this in 1948 with *The Golden Wing: A Sociological Study of Chinese Familism*, which he wrote in English (London: Kegan Paul). When the study of sociology was prohibited in 1952, Lin Yao-hua was transferred to the Central Minorities Institute, created in the previous year, where until the Sino-Soviet crisis he collaborated with Russian anthropologists on the history of primitive societies using the perspective and typology of historical materialism. The Cultural Revolution officially launched in June 1966 led to the closure of the institute, then directed by Yang Kun, and anthropologists were declared 'enemies of the people' on 1 September 1966. After a terrible year in 1967–1968 Lin Yao-hua was sent in 1969 to a '7 May School' for re-education through manual labour. On the occasion of President Nixon's visit in 1972 he was released to join the welcoming party for a delegation of American intellectuals, and he returned to the Central Minorities Institute when it was subsequently re-opened. Among his most important contributions to Chinese anthropology were founding the country's first anthropology department in 1983 and editing the first modern Chinese introduction to the discipline, *Minzu xue rumen* (*Introduction to Ethnography*, Beijing), in 1990.

Ma Xue-Liang (born 1913)

A reticent man who never studied abroad, Ma Xue-Liang continued the tradition of an ethnographic style of research on marginal populations. In the late 1930s he began investigations which he continued for the rest of his career into the Yi mountain people of the Southwest China, originally of Tibeto-Burman stock. In 1989 he published an integral study entitled *History and Culture of the Yi* (*Yi zu wen hua shi*) (Shanghai), which has a particular focus on representations among this people. He was a professor at the Central Minorities Institute of the Chinese Academy of Social Science.

Wang, Zhusheng (1945–1999)

Born in Guizhou province, Zhusheng Wang symbolized a new generation of Chinese anthropologists whose youth was marked by the Cultural Revolution and then by the gradual liberalization of the political system as it matured. He began his studies in the early 1980s and became interested in the economic life of minority groups. He undertook fieldwork on the Jingpo (Kachin) in Southern China together with American academics, and then completed a doctorate at the State University of New York. His thesis was published in English as *The Jingpo: Kachin of the Yunnan Plateau* (Arizona UP, 1997). Soon after he was appointed to head the anthropology department of the University of Yunnan, but died of cancer before his impact could really be felt there.

INDONESIA

Colonized by the Netherlands in the seventeenth century, Indonesia attracted many foreign researchers from the 1930s onwards. One of these was the Dutchman Gerrit Jan Held (1906–1955), who from 1935 worked there as a linguist for the Universal Biblical Society.

From 1920 to 1940 about twenty Indonesian students travelled each year to the metropole to study at the University of Leyden, and in 1940 the Dutch created a humanities and philosophy faculty in Indonesia, where in the following year Held introduced teaching in anthropology with the assistance of F. A. E. van Wouden. The Japanese invasion of 1942 forced the Dutch administration in Indonesia to take refuge in Australia, and although it returned in the wake of the victorious Allied forces, the colony proclaimed its independence immediately after Japan's capitulation. Forced to retreat before advancing Dutch troops, the new Indonesian government withdrew from Jakarta and founded the Gajah Mada Revolutionary University at Yogyakarta in 1947, one year before the Security Council of the United Nations drew a line of demarcation. Assisted by the Briton M. A. Jaspan, the new university opened a social and political sciences faculty in 1952, with social sciences enjoying a dominant position. The Dutch acknowledged Indonesian independence in 1949, and in 1950 they agreed to transfer ownership of the University of Indonesia. Held remained in post there until his death and was replaced in 1956 by Elizabeth Allard (born 1904), while introductory courses in the discipline were given to law students by C. H. M. Palm. In 1956 a new research organization called the *Majelis Ilmu Pengetahaun Indonesia* emerged, later renamed the *Lembaga Ilmu Pengetahaun Indonesia* (LIPI), which contained about ten specialized institutes and was attached to the Ministry of Research in 1962. The Institute of History and Anthropology (*Lembaga Sejarah dan Antropologi*) was created at the instigation of Sumarjo in 1959, but fell victim to the dictatorship in 1965. Social sciences continued to form part of the University of Indonesia's law faculty until 1968, but in 1957 an anthropology department was opened to accommodate the first two Indonesian ethnologists trained abroad: **Koentjaraningrat** (who in 1958 gained the country's first Ph.D in anthropology) and P. B. Avé. A few years later a second department was opened at the University of Pajajaran (Bandung), with Harsoyo appointed to run it. The department at the University of Indonesia offered two programmes, one on New Guinea (Irian Barat) and the other on Central Borneo, and in 1960 it initiated a general survey which from 1962 focused on the Ot Danum populations. In 1964 the *Lembaga Ilmu Pengetahaun Indonesia* (LIPI) was set up with Koentjaraningrat as its director, and it contained a Centre for Studies in Indonesian Culture (*Pusat Studi Kebudayaan Indonesia*) and a Centre for Studies in Foreign Cultures (*Pusat Studi Kebudayaan Asing*). The coup d'état of 1965 resulted in the closure of the Institute of History and Anthropology and the almost complete suspension of teaching and research activities, including those of the LIPI. Nonetheless a second Indonesian Ph.D in anthropology was awarded to Masri Singarimbun in 1966 for a thesis on the matrimonial system of the Batak Karo. In 1968 the Institute of Popular Customs and Literature (*Lembaga Adat Istiadat dan Cerita Rakyat*) was created and first directed by Marwati Djuned, and in 1975 it merged with the Institute of Dance as part of a new Centre of Historical and Cultural Studies. Bambnang Suwondo became director of the Centre in 1977 and initiated a programme to record and study provincial cultures and collect details of folklore, costume, music and games. In 1972 the country employed 141 teachers of anthropology, but only two tenured professors (Koentjaraningrat and Harsoyo). Following the appointment of Lie Tek Tjeng, a historian and Japanologist, as director of the LIPI in 1973, the Centre for Studies in Indonesian Culture was closed and its research staff distributed around various regional organizations. The LIPI itself became a research centre for global issues, and in 1980 Lie Tek Tjeng was succeeded by Alfian. Some ethnologists found work within programmes launched in collaboration with institutions in the Netherlands, such as the University of Leyden, the Free University of Amsterdam and the Catholic University of Nijmegen, while others undertook studies commissioned by the Ministry of Defence on East Timor, annexed by Indonesia in 1975. In that year there were, as well as those mentioned above, anthropology departments in the universities of Gajah Mada, Udayana (Denpasar), and Sam Ratulangi (Menado), and in the private University of Parahyangan, and a further twenty-one of the twenty-nine public universities also offered teaching in the discipline. Ethnology was also taught in the final year of secondary school. The country's third doctoral thesis in ethnology was completed by Mattulada in 1975 on the political anthropology of the Bugis, to be followed by the theses of Parsudi Suparlan on the Javanese of Surinam (1976), E. K. M. Masinambow on ethno-linguistic convergence in Halmahera (1976), Subar Boedhisantoso on a village in the Krawang region (1977), Tapi Omas Ihromi on marriage among the Toraja (1978), and James Dananjaya on the village of Bali Afa in Rrunyan (1979). Like all countries which host large development projects funded by international bodies such as UNICEF, the FAO, the World Bank and the European Union, Indonesia has seen a florescence of private research centres which employ ethnologists on a contract-by-contract basis.

Koentjaraningrat (1923–2000)

'Koentjaraningrat is not my father's name; at the time we did not yet use family names' (Visser, 1988: 749). Born into a family of senior court functionaries, Koentjaraningrat was sent by his mother to a Dutch school where he was given a Western education. He was working in the library of the National Museum when the Second World War broke out, and in 1945 he moved to Yogyakarta to join the self-proclaimed Indonesian Republic. He then taught history to the student-warriors of the Gajah Mada Revolutionary University, and in 1949 he was sent to Jakarta, where he joined the first generation of students at the National University. He chose to study anthropology because 'the only possibility of going there (the USA) was in order to study anthropology' (Visser, 1988: 749), and his hopes were realized when he was invited to Yale University in 1954 to be taught by G. P. **Murdock**. After obtaining an MA in 1956 he was recalled to Indonesia, where he introduced **Kluckhohn**'s scheme for variations in value orientation. In 1957 he established the country's first anthropology department at the University of Indonesia, and after completing his Ph.D thesis 'A Preliminary Description of the Javanese Kinship System' in the following year under the supervision of Elizabeth Allard he was appointed to a professorship. In 1964 he created the *Lembaga Ilmu Pengetahaun Indonesia* (LIPI), the first Indonesian national research centre, and also took responsibility for the development of anthropology in provincial universities. In 1966 he published his milestone study *Villages in Indonesia* (Cornell UP). Koentjaraningrat was the author of more than twenty books, many devoted to the question of ethnic variation within a single nation (he included the case of the Walloons and Flemings in Belgium). Published in 1984, his *Kebudayaan Jawal* [*Javanese Culture*] (Kuala Lumpur: Oxford UP, 1985) is a general survey containing seven parts: an introduction and chapters on the history of Javanese culture, peasant culture, urban culture, Javanese religion, and Javanese classification, as well as a hundred-page bibliography of great scholarly value.

SELECT BIBLIOGRAPHY

Arkush, D. (1981) *Hsiao-T'ong Fei and Sociology in Revolutionary China*, Cambridge.

——(1991) 'Fei, Hsiao-T'ong', in C. Winter, pp.191–192.

Assayag, J. (2000) 'M. N. Srinivas', in *L'Homme*, 156: 7–14.

Bachtiar, H.W. (1975) *Directory of Social Scientists in Indonesia*, Jakarta: LIPI.

Béteille, A. (1996) 'Indian anthropology', in A. Barnard and J. Spencer (eds) *Encyclopedia of Social and Cultural Anthropology*, London: Routledge, pp.297–298.

Bose, N.K. (1963) *Forty Years of Science in India: Progress of Anthropology and Archaeology*, Calcutta: Indian Science Congress Association.

Bremen, J. van and Akitoshi Shimizu (1999) *Anthropology and Colonialism in Asia and Oceania*, Curzon editor.

Butel, J.M. (2000) 'Miyata Noboru', in *Sbisu: Etudes japonaises*, Maison franco-japonaise, no.23.

Caillet, L. (1991) 'Japon. L'anthropologie japonaise', in P. Bonte and M. Izard (eds) *Dictionnaire de l'ethnologie et de l'anthropologie*, Paris: PUF, pp.397–398.

Chanda, C. (1908) *The People of India with Sir Herbert Risley*, Calcutta: Thacker.

——(1916; 1969) *The Indo-Aryan Races: A Study of Indian People and Institutions* with intro by N. Bhattachryya, Rajshahi, Varenda society.

Charsley, S. (1998) 'Sankritization: the career of an anthropological theory', *Contribution to Indian Sociology*, 32(2): 527–549.

Chien Chiao (1987) 'Radcliffe-Brown in China', *AT*, 3(2): 5–6.

Cooper, G. (1973) 'An interview with Chinese anthropologists', *CA*, 14(4): 480–82.

Cunningham, C.E. (2000) 'Koentjaraningrat', *AN*, 41(5): 45.

Deliège, R. (2000) 'Le Philanthropologue: Verrier Elwin et les tribus de l'Inde', *L'Homme*, 156: 233–240.

Deshpande, S. (2001) 'Re-presenting the past: the disciplinary history of Indian sociology and anthropology', *HAN*, 28(1): 3–6.

Eliyu Guldin, G. (1992) 'Yang Chengzhi', *AN*, 33(4): 5.

Elwin, V.H. (1939) *The Baiga*, foreword by J.H. Hutton, London: Murray.

——(1943) *Maria Murder and Suicide*, Bombay: Oxford University Press.

——(1944) (S. Hivale) *Folk Songs of the Maikal Hills*, Bombay: Oxford University Press.

——(1949) *Myths of Middle India*, Bombay: Oxford University Press.

——(1955) *The Religion of an Indian Tribe*, Bombay: Oxford University Press.

——(1942) 'Comment on Sarat Chandra Roy', *Man in India*, 22(4): 195–196.

——(1964; 1989) *The Tribal World of Verrier Elwin*, Delhi, New York: Oxford University Press.

Feedman, M. (1962) 'Sociology in and of China', *The British Journal of Sociology*, 14: 106–116.

Fei, Hsiao-tung (1982) 'Huxley Memorial Lecture (1981): The new outlook of rural China', *Rain*, 48: 4–8.

Fei Xiao-Tong (1981) *Towards a People's Anthropology*, Beijing: New World Press.

——(1988b) *Small Towns in China*, Beijing: New World Press.

Fujimoto, H. (1970) *The Life of a Scholar and Ainu Genius* (on Chiri), Tokyo: Keishodo.

Fujimoto, H. and Ohnuki-Tierney, E. (1973) 'M. Chiri', *AA*, 75: 868–876.

Fuller, (1999) 'An interview with M.N. Srivinas', *AT*, 15(5): 3–10.

Fürer-Haimendorf, C. von (1964) 'Verrier Elwin, 1902–1964', *Man*, 64: 114–115.

Guha, R. (1999) *Savaging the Civilized: Verrier Elwin, His Tribals, and India*, Chicago: University of Chicago Press.

Haddon, A.C. and Richard, F.J. (1937) 'Obituary L. K. Ananthakrishna Iyer (1861–1937)', *Man*.

Harrell, S. (1991) 'Anthropology and ethnology in the PRC: the Intersection of discourses', *China Exchange News*, 19(2): 3–6.

——(1996) 'China', in Levinson and Ember, vol.1, pp.199–202.

Hu Qiwang (Hou Ts'i-wang) (1981) 'Ts'ai Yuan P'ei et l'ethnologie', in *Minzuxue Yanjiu* (études ethnologiques) vol.1.

Huang Shu-min (1991) 'Ling Shun-Sheng', in C. Winter, p.411.

Indian Council of Social Science Research (1985–1986) *Survey of Research in Sociology and Social Anthropology, 1969–1979*, Delhi: Satvahan, 3 vols.

Jain, R. (1997) 'C. S. Dube', *AT*, 13(1): 22

Kawada, Minow (1997) *The Origin of Ethnography in Japan*, Kegan Paul.

Knight, J. (1996) 'Interview with Sasaki Kömei of the National Museum of Ethnology', *AT*, 12(3): 16–20.

Köbben, A.J.F. (1974) 'On former Chinese anthropologists', *CA*, 15(3): 315.

Koentjaraningrat (ed.) (1975) *The Social Sciences in Indonesia*, 2 vols. Jakarta: Lipi.

Koschmann, J.V., Keibô Oiwa and Shinji Yamashita (eds) (1985) *International Perspectives on Yanagita Kunio and Japanese Folklore Studies*, Ithaca: Cornell University Press.

Lemoine, J. (1978) 'Asie Orientale' in J. Poirier, *Ethnologie régionale*, Paris: Gallimard, pp.376–425.

——(1986) 'Ethnologists in China', *Diogènes*, January–March, 133: 82–112.

——(1991) 'Chine', in P. Bonte and M. Izard (eds) *Dictionnaire de l'ethnologie et de l'anthropologie*, Paris: Puf, pp.139–141.

Lonergan, D. (1991) 'Elwin, Verrier', in C. Winter, pp.178–179.

Ma Yin (ed.) (1989) *China's Minority Nationalities*, Beijing: Foreign Languages Press.

Madan, T.N. and Sarana, S. (eds) (1962) *Indian anthropology: Essays in Memory of Dhirendra Nath Majumdar*, Calcutta: Asia Publishing House.

Makagiansar, M. (ed.) (1965) 'Research in Indonesia, 1945–65', in *Bidang ekonomi, sosial dan budaya*, vol.IV, Jakarta.

Mandelbaum, D. (1965) 'V. Elwin', *AA*, 67: 448–452.

Menon, P. (1999) 'A Scholar remembered, M.N. Srinivas, 1916–1999', *Frontline*, 24: 112–113.

Minoto, M. (1967) 'Obituary of Masho Chiri', *Arctic Anthropology*, 4 (1): 257–261.

Morse, R.A. (1974) 'Research for Japan's National Character and Distinctiveness: Yanagita Kunio (1875–1962) and the Folklore Movement', unpublished thesis, Princeton University.

Nakane Chie (1974) 'Cultural Anthropology in Japan', *Annual Review of Anthropology*, 3: 57–72.

Nihon-minzohu-gakkai (Japan society of ethnology) 1968, *Ethnology in Japan: Historical Review*, Tokyo: Shibusawa memorial foundation for ethnology.

Padmanabhia, P. (1978) 'Indian Census and Anthropological investigations', *Xth International Congress of Anthropological and Ethnological Sciences*, India, Registrar General.

Pasternak, B. (1988) 'A conversation with Fei Xiaotung', in *CA*, 29: 637–662.

Pelras, C. (1981) *Les Sciences sociales en Indonésie*, Ambassade de France en Indonésie, no pagination (reworking of two articles originally published in *Archipel* no.22 and no.23).

Ray, S.K. (1974) *Bibliographies of Eminent Indian Anthropologists*, Calcutta: Anthropological Survey of India.

Reshetov, A.M. (1991) 'Wu Wenzao', in C. Winter, p.769.

Roy, S. (1970a) 'Short biography and bibliography of N.K. Bose', in S. Roy *Anthropologists in India*, New Delhi: Indian Anthropological Association.

——(ed.) (1970b) *Anthropology in India*, New Delhi: Indian Anthropological Association.

Roy, S.C. (1915) *The Oraons of Chotanagpur: Their History, Economic Life and Social Organisation, with an introduction by C.A. Haddon*, Ranchi: Author.

——(1966) *Studies in Indian Anthropology*, Edited with an Introduction by Nirmal Kumar Bose, Indian Studies Past and present.

Shah, A.M., Baviskar, B.S. and Ramaswamy, E.A. (eds) (1996) *Social Structure and Change, 1. Theory and Method: Evaluation of the Work of M.N. Srinivas*, 5 vols, New Delhi: Sage.

Shah, C.A.M. (1991) 'Srinivas, M.N.' in Winter, p.661.

Sieffert, R. (1952) 'Les études ethnographiques au Japon', *Bulletin de la Maison franco-japonaise*, NS. 2: 9–20.

Singer, M. (1972) *When a Great Tradition Modernizes*, New York: Praeger.

Sinha, S. (1971) 'Is there an Indian tradition in socio/cultural anthropology?: retrospect and prospects', *Journal of the Indian Anthropological Society*, 6: 1–14.

Sofue, Takao (1961), 'Anthropology in Japan, historical review and modern trends', *Biennial Review of Anthropology*, pp.173–214.

Srinivas, M.N. (1962) *Caste in Modern India and Other Essays*, Bombay: Asia Pub House.

——(1966) *Social Change in Modern India*, Bombay: Orient Longman.

——(1973) 'Itineraries of an Indian social anthropologist', *International Social Science Journal*, 25(1–2): 129–148.

——(1977) *Nation-Building in Independent India*, Delhi: Oxford University Press.

——(1978) *The Changing Position of Indian Women*, Delhi: Oxford University Press.

——(1982) *The Dominant Caste and Other Essays*, Delhi: Oxford University Press.

——(1984) *Some Reflections on Dowry*, Delhi: Oxford University Press.

——(1989) *The Cohesive Role of Sankritization and other Essays*, Delhi: Oxford University Press.

——(1992) *On Living in a Revolution and other Essays*, Delhi: Oxford University Press.

——(1996) *Indian Society through Personal Writings*, Delhi: Oxford University Press.

——(1997) 'Practicing social anthropology in India', *Annual Review of Anthropology*, 26: 1–24.

Srinivas, M.N. (2000) 'Commentary. Ex igni renascimur', *CA*, 41(2): 163–168.

Srinivas, M.N. and Panini, N.M. (1973) 'The development of sociology and social anthropology in India', *Sociological Bulletin*, 22(2): 179–215.

Srinivas, M.N. and Fuller, C. (1999) 'An Interview with M.N. Srinivas', *AT*, 15(5): 3–9.

Tapp, N. (1996) 'Chinese anthropology', in A. Barnard and J. Spencer (eds) *Encyclopedia of Social and Cultural Anthropology*, London: Routledge, pp.95–96.

Vidyarthy, L.P. (1977) 'The rise of social anthropology in India (1774–1972): A historical appraisal', in D. Kenneth (ed.) *The New Wind: Changing Identities in South Asia*, The Hague: Mouton, pp.61–82.

Visser, L. (1988) 'Interview with Koentjaraningrat', *CA*, 29: 749.

Wong, Sun-lun 1979, *Sociology and Socialism in Contemporary China*, London: Routledge.

XII

The French-speaking schools from the end of the Second World War to the 1980s

The *Institut d'ethnologie*, Section V of the EPHE, the *Musée de l'Homme*, and the EFEO were, until shortly before the Second World War, the only centres of anthropology teaching and research in France. This changed in 1938 with the creation of three new institutions: the *Centre national de recherche scientifique* (National Centre for Scientific Research) (CNRS), the *Institut français d'Afrique noire* (French Institute for Black Africa) (IFAN), the *Office de la recherche scientifique et technique d'Outre-mer* (Bureau for Overseas Scientific and Technical Research) (ORSTOM). These organizations won for anthropologists a new status, opening up possibilities not just for more expeditions, but also for lengthier periods of fieldwork in far-flung locations. To complement the teaching provided by the *Institut d'ethnologie*, A. **Leroi-Gourhan** in 1946–1947 created the *Centre de formation à la recherche ethnologique* (Training Centre for Ethnological Research) (CFRE), which admitted students with a *licence* including a certificate awarded by the *Institut d'ethnologie*. Such certificates could be obtained at the Sorbonne, where M. **Griaule** occupied the ethnography chair. Chairs and senior lectureships in ethnology were also established at Lyon (1945), Bordeaux (1953), Montpellier (1957), Strasbourg (1960), and Nice (1965).

The death of **Mauss** in 1950 coincided with the retirements of P. **Rivet** and M. **Leenhardt**. The professoriate of the *Musée d'histoire naturelle* chose the physician H. Vallois to succeed Rivet in the chair of anthropology and thus as director of the *Musée de l'Homme* (1950–1960). Meanwhile **Lévi-Strauss**'s influence gained full play in the economic and social sciences section of the EPHE (Section VI), established in 1947 with funding from the Rockefeller and Ford Foundations. Together with F. Braudel, Lévi-Strauss played the role of adviser at the EPHE and helped create other centres of teaching and research.

Under the direction of Vallois and L. Pales, the *Musée de l'Homme* reverted for a time to a focus on physical anthropology. Meanwhile, avenues of research in these post-war years were opened up by the work of Leroi-Gourhan, R. **Bastide**, G. **Devereux**, and M. Griaule, and it was during these years that Lévi-Strauss's structuralism and G. **Balandier**'s dynamism became predominant.

M. Griaule had already placed the Dogon cosmologies on a par with those of classical civilization. After his death in 1955 his disciples carried his work forward, and young Africanists, like J. Capron, R. Verdier, and Y. Cissé, were drawn to the CNRS by a team of scholars gathered there by G. **Dieterlen**, who was soon aided in her efforts by J. **Rouch**. When Lévi-Strauss succeeded Leenhardt as director of studies in primitive peoples (which he retitled 'studies in nonliterate peoples') in the religious studies section of the EPHE, he began to advance a new current of thought which won adherents among the younger generation. After devoting his attention to kinship and proposing a new approach to it in his thesis of

1948, he called for a rereading of Mauss in 1950 and set out an ambitious programme to discover the innate structures of the human mind. This was to be achieved in the first instance by using a 'ready-made' method (structuralism) for making sense of such matters as kinship, Amerindian mythology, and the dualist system. In the post-war years the CFRE produced a generation of researchers who immediately found work with ORSTOM or IFAN in the overseas territories. To this group belonged G. Balandier, P. Mercier (1922–1976), J. Lombard, J. **Guiart** and G. **Condominas**. Balandier and Mercier developed a new Africanism, which began as a sort of colonial sociology or colonial ethnology and subsequently became an anthropology of colonial independence and then a dynamic anthropology. Lombard played an important part in launching the ethnohistory of state-based African societies, which became one of the ornaments of French anthropology of the period (see the works of C. **Tardits**, M. **Izard**, A. **Adler**, C. H. Perrot, E. **Terray** and Lombard himself). Guiart relaunched the ethnology of contemporary Oceania, while Condominas freed the study of Asia from the straitjacket of the *belles lettres* approach, as did L. **Dumont** for India and J. Berque (1910–1995) and M. **Rodinson** for the Arab world and the Orient. Most of these men found employment in the new Section VI of the EPHE, in which they set up research centres (e.g. on Africa, India and Southeast Asia) which soon became affiliated to CNRS laboratories under their own control. With the creation in the 1960s of these laboratories, and of research co-operatives pursuing particular programmes, the CNRS was in a position to employ practically all those who had completed a course of study in anthropology. Meanwhile new journals and collections of essays mushroomed. At the very end of the 1960s, the ethnology departments of the universities of Nanterre (Paris X), Jussieu (Paris VII) and Vincennes (Paris VIII) designed teaching programmes in ethnology. This trend to expand the discipline was followed at provincial institutions such as Nice, Montpellier, Strasbourg and Lyon, which established ethnology departments or at least teaching programmes in anthropology as alternatives to similar programmes offered by the Sorbonne (Paris V) and the religious studies section of the EPHE (Section V). H. Vallois' successor in the anthropology chair at the *Musée d'histoire naturelle* and the management of the *Musée de l'Homme* was J. Millot (1897–1980), a physician who reinvigorated French ethnological research in Afghanistan, Iran and in the Himalayan region. Millot was followed first by R. **Gessain** from 1968 to 1970, and then by J. Guiart from 1970 to 1990. As of 1968 the *Institut d'ethnologie* ceased to co-ordinate anthropology teaching in France, leaving it instead in the hands of individual universities. As a result the organic link between courses in different institutions was lost, although all were entirely dependent on the Ministry of National Education, as indeed are all teaching programmes in French universities.

ANTHROPOLOGISTS OF COLONIAL INDEPENDENCE

We may use this title to designate a generation of anthropologists whose careers began after the Second World War, when it was clear that it was only a matter of time before France's colonies would achieve independence. 'Exotic' French ethnology flourished during this period and continued to do so until the mid-1970s. On becoming professors these scholars often created research centres and laboratories still in existence today, and also trained the next generation of researchers whose careers began after the colonies became independent and were marked by the Algerian War, May 1968, 'dynamic anthropology', structuralism, and Marxism. I have divided this chapter into four sections: on the group associated with the

CFRE, on the group around M. **Griaule**, on figures who defy categorization, and on the students of **Lévi-Strauss** and **Balandier**.

THE COLONIAL SCHOOL AND THE NATIONAL SCHOOL FOR FRENCH OVERSEAS TERRITORIES: ADMINISTRATORS AND SOLDIERS

Following the example of Great Britain and the Netherlands, the French state founded a Colonial School on 21 November 1889, but it was not until after the First World War that it gradually grew in importance. In 1934 it became the *Ecole Nationale de la France d'Ou-tre-mer* (School for French Overseas Territories) (ENFOM). In the 1921 entrance competition a total of 147 candidates fought for 17 places. The school's teachers included P. **Mus**, R. Delavignette, J. Dresch, M. **Leiris**, L. S. Senghor and J. **Faublée**. At a later stage it was again renamed, becoming the *Centre des hautes études sur l'Afrique et l'Asie Modernes* (Centre for Advanced Studies on Modern Africa and Asia). More information on the Colonial School can be gained from 'Centenaire de l'Ecole nationale de la France d'Outre-Mer' (*Mondes et Culture*, XLVI: 1, 1986). Regrettably, limitations of space make it impossible to treat all of the numerous figures in the 'anthropology of colonialism'. Among those excluded are H. Delavignette (1897–1976), H. Deschamps (1900-), Jean Chapelle (1905–1986), L. Pales (1905–1988), Vincent Monteil (born 1913), Jean-Claude Froelich (born 1914), R. Cornevin (1919–1988), P. Alexandre (1922–1994), Alexander MacDonald (born 1923), P.-F. Lacroix (1924–1977), R. Pageard (born 1927), and Yves Person (1925–1982).

Berque, Jacques (1910–1995)

Jacques Berque spent his childhood and youth in Algeria, where his father held an administrative post. After completing his studies and spending a brief period in France, he obtained a position as a civil inspector in Morocco. His efforts to set up community of agricultural co-operatives were met with resistance from the *colons*, and in 1947 he was transferred to the faraway province of Upper Atlas as a district administrator. He stayed there until 1953, and it was during this time that he carried out the research for his thesis *Les Structures sociales du Haut-Atlas* [*The Social Structures of the Upper Atlas Region*] (PUF, 1955, 2nd edn including 'Retour aux Seksawa' ('Return to the Seksawa'), 1978), which immediately on its publication established itself as the great classic on this part of the world. In this work Berque shows how the society in question is structured by its irrigation arrangements, and considers the adjustments it made following the encounter with Islamic law. After finishing this thesis in 1955, Berque was appointed director of studies in Section VI of the EPHE, and in 1956 he became a professor at the *Collège de France*. He also wrote a great work on the condition of the colonial subject entitled *Dépossession du monde* [*The Dispossession of the World*] (Le Seuil, 1964).

Poirier, Jean (born 1921)

After studying law and graduating from the *Ecole nationale d'administration* (ENA), Jean Poirier joined the CNRS as M. **Leenhardt**'s assistant and then created the *Institut de recherche scientifique de Madras* (Madras Institute for Scientific Research), as well as holding a senior lectureship at the University of Tananarive. After a period teaching at ENA he was appointed to the ethnology chair of the University of Lyon in 1957 to succeed **Leroi-Gourhan**. In 1961 he settled in Madagascar, where he founded the social sciences department of the University of Tananarive. In 1970 he was appointed professor at the University of Nice, where he remained until his retirement. Poirier's published work has two aspects: on the one hand is the personal work of the researcher, for example in *Les Beanzano: Contribution à l'étude des structures sociales d'une population malgache* [*The Beanzano: Contribution to the Study of Social Structures in a Malagasy Population*] (2 vols); and on the other hand is the assembler and disseminator of

knowledge initiating and supervising large scholarly projects. *Ethnologie de l'Union Française* [*Ethnology of the French Union*] (2 vols), co-written in 1953 by himself, A. Leroi-Gourhan, A. **Haudricourt** and G. **Condominas**, was the first book of this second type. It was followed by *Ethnologie générale* [*General Ethnology*] (1968), by the two volumes of *Ethnologie régionale* [*Regional Ethnology*] (1972, 1978), by the three volumes of *Histoire des Moeurs* [*A History of Customs*], which appeared in the celebrated Pléiade Library published by Gallimard, and by his 'Traditional Societies' sections in the *Encyclopédie philosophique universelle* [*Universal Philosophical Encyclopaedia*], published by PUF in 1994.

THE *CENTRE DE FORMATION A LA RECHERCHE ETHNOLOGIQUE*

A. **Leroi-Gourhan** set up the CFRE under the joint auspices of the *Musée de l'Homme*, ORSTOM and the CNRS. This new institution accepted students with law, science or arts degrees on the basis of an interview. After two years of teaching at the CFRE, they became research trainees with ORSTOM or the CNRS and at this point would begin work on their theses. In 1948–1949 the CFRE contained eight students, of whom four satisfied the examiners; in 1968 it was abolished and responsibility for teaching passed on to individual universities. More information on the CFRE can be found in the *Bulletin du CFRE*, which first appeared in January 1951. It is not possible to treat all those whose work merits attention in a book of these dimensions, and a list of names which would feature in a fuller treatment includes the following: Luc Mollet (1915–1993), Gilbert Rouget (born 1916), Joseph Tubiana (born 1919), Monique Brandily-Trolle (born 1921), Monique Gessain-de Lestrange (born 1921), Hélène Balfet (1922–2000), P. Mercier (1922–1976), Ichon (born 1922), Guy de Moal (born 1924), Jacques Lombard (born 1926), H. Lavondès (1926–1988), Suzanne Bernus-Vianès (1928–1990), Jean Capron (born 1929), Corneil Jest (born 1930), Charles Pelras (born 1934) and Nicole Echard (1937–1994).

Bernot, Lucien (1919–1993)

Born into a peasant family, Lucien Bernot obtained an arts degree and then studied Chinese at INALCO, graduating in 1947, while also taking courses in 1946–1947 at the CFRE. During his time as a trainee researcher he joined R. Blanchard for a UNESCO-commissioned investigation

into a rural community in France under the supervision of C. **Lévi-Strauss** in 1948–1949, thereby making a contribution to the renaissance in the ethnology of France. After being given a research position at the CNRS, he travelled to East Pakistan, and then produced a report on peasant communities in Haiti, again for UNESCO. He played a role in planning the *Bibliographie internationale d'anthropologie socio-culturelle* [*International Bibliography of Socio-Cultural Anthropology*] in 1955–1956, and in 1959–1960 returned to South Asia. In 1961 he was promoted to a more senior research position at the CNRS, and also taught part of the introductory course in cultural anthropology established by Lévi-Strauss in Section VI of the EPHE. When he became a director of studies there in 1964 he encouraged his students to specialize in technological questions, on which he was one of the foremost experts. In 1967 Bernot completed his major thesis *Les Paysans du Pakistan oriental: L'Histoire, le monde végétal et l'organisation sociale des refugiés marmo (mog)* [*The Peasants of East Pakistan: History, the Vegetable World and the Social Organization of the Marmo (Mog) Refugees*] (Paris: Mouton, 1967, 2 vols) and his minor thesis *Les Caks: Contribution à l'étude ethnographique d'une population de langue moï* [*The Cak: Contribution to the Ethnographic Study of a Moi-speaking Population*] (Paris: CNRS, 1967). He helped create the social ethnology department at the University of Nanterre, and in 1971–1972 took responsibility for the Atlas of the *Centre de documentation et de recherche sur l'Asie du Sud-Est et le monde insulindien* (Documentation and Research Centre on South East Asia and the Indian Subcontinent) (Laboratory 183 of the CNRS). In 1979 he was elected to the professorship of Southeast Asian sociology at the *Collège de France*. Bernot always took a very ethnographic approach to his work, aiming to grasp all aspects – linguistic, technological, social and historical – of the community he was studying.

Balandier, Georges (born 1920)

After completing an arts degree in 1942 which included a certificate from the *Institut d'ethnologie*, G. Balandier became a provincial schoolteacher. He refused compulsory wartime labour and joined the Resistance. Back in Paris after the war, he attended lectures given by M. **Leenhardt**, worked at the *Musée de l'Homme* in a 'workshop for unemployed intellectuals', and wrote a novel entitled *Tout compte fait* [*When All Is Said and Done*] (Paris: Pavois, 1946). After briefly attending a training course at the CFRE, he was engaged by ORSTOM to carry out an assignment with IFAN. Together with P. Mercier he carried out research in Mauritania and then on the Lebou near Dakar. Their co-authored work *Particularisme et évolution: Les pêcheurs Lébou* [*Particularism and Evolution: The Lebou Fishermen*] (Dakar: IFAN, 1952) reveals the influence of the American 'culture and personality' school.

In 1947 Balandier founded the *Centrifan de Conakry* and the *Bulletin d'Etudes Guinéennes*, and then joined ORSTOM in Brazzaville. He worked on the situation of the Fang, the messianic movements of the Bakongo and on the town of Brazzaville. His numerous articles and memoranda paved the way for his doctoral theses *Sociologie des Brazzavilles Noires* [*The Sociology of the Black Brazzavilles*] (Paris: Armand Colin) and *Sociologie actuelle de l'Afrique Noire: Dynamiques des changements sociaux en Afrique Centrale* [*The Sociology of Contemporary Black Africa: Dynamics of Social Change in Central Africa*] (Paris: PUF, 1955). The first book was one of the earliest studies of a newly developed town, and Balandier stresses the importance of the connections maintained between urban dwellers and the peasantry. The appearance of the second book had, in P. Alexandre's words, the effect of 'a crash of thunder across the sky of French Africanism'. From 1948 he spoke of an ethnology of the 'colonial situation' rather than emphasizing manifestations of acculturation, and his approach spurned integrationist ideas by stressing heterogeneity and movement. Balandier compares the patrilineal, segmentary and only slightly hierarchical Fang with the matrilineal Bakongo, a society of territorial chiefdoms, in terms of their responses to the crisis provoked by colonialism. He demonstrates that the differences between their two reactions derive from internal factors in each tribe, and that any society lives according to its own dynamic. These themes were developed in a course Balandier began teaching at the *Institut d'études politiques* in 1952, in which he described development using the image of a 'sprint'. He rejected the culturalist tendency to perceive an integrative totality, instead focusing on the structure of social dynamics, which is always most visible at times of crisis when what is normally excluded reappears. The notion of contradiction is fundamental to this view, but it owes nothing to Hegelian or Marxist teleology, for contradictions are retrospectively determined and any society is open to limitless possibilities. In 1951 Balandier returned to France to join the *Centre d'études sociologiques* at the CNRS, and he also taught at the *Institut de sciences politiques* before being appointed director of studies in Black African sociology in Section VI of the EPHE. He became closely associated with Gurvitch, whom he succeeded as editor-in-chief of the *Cahiers Internationaux de Sociologie*, and also with **Lévi-Strauss**, at least until they quarrelled in 1959. In 1956 he published *Tiers-Monde: Sous-développement et développement* [*The Third World: Underdevelopment and Development*] (Paris: PUF), followed in 1957 by *Afrique Ambiguë* [*Ambiguous Africa*] (Paris: Plon), which gave a fictionalized account of his activities for a broad readership. After holding an official post in charge of expeditions with the State Secretariat for Scientific Research in 1954 and directing UNESCO's International Bureau for Research into the Social Implications of Technical Progress in Developing Countries, Balandier joined Cornut-Gentille's ministry for France's overseas territories. Apparently he cut his political career short with an ill-considered prediction of Guinea's future.

In 1958 Balandier founded the *Centre d'études africaines* (Centre for African Studies) (CEA), where his students included C. **Meillassoux**, E. **Terray**, D. Sperber, J. Copans and P.-P. Rey. From him they assimilated a socio-ethnology in which the encounter with the contemporary takes precedence over nostalgia for the Neolithic era and the observation of moribund cultures. This conceptual revolution was accompanied both by repeated denunciation of the effects of Westernization and colonial rule (e.g. economic misery and the creation of a deracinated proletariat), and by views recalling those of Marx on the British colonization of India and the resulting emancipation of younger brothers from older brothers, of women from men, and even of the living from the dead. In 1960 Balandier launched the *Cahiers d'études africaines*, and from 1960 to 1966 held a post-*agrégation* seminar at the ENS. In 1962 he took over sociology and ethnology teaching at the *Centre de recherches africaines* (Centre for African Research) (CRA), which H. Deschamps had founded at the Sorbonne, and in 1965 he was appointed to the university's chair of sociology. He endeavoured to constitute a political anthropology which would integrate the idea of movement and confront the structuralist enterprise. From *Anthropologie politique* [*Political Anthropology*] (1969) to *Pouvoir sur scènes* [*The Scenes of Power*] (1980), this approach produced a series of books emphasizing the relations between power and the sacred. *Anthropo-logiques* [*Anthropo-logics*] (Paris: PUF, 1974) advances the idea that every social order is in a permanent state of disequilibrium caused by the unequal distribution of resources, conflicts between generations, and the battle between the sexes, with inequality between the sexes providing the paradigm for all other inequalities. These three antagonisms pervade all societies, so that the split between ethnology and sociology is meaningless. In this way Balandier brings anthropological inquiry to bear on France and other modern societies.

Condominas, Georges (born 1921)
Georges Condominas was born in Haiphong and as a child followed his father from posting to posting before taking his *baccalauréat* in France. In 1940 he enrolled at the law faculty of Hanoi University, where he gained his law degree in 1943, and during his studies he attended lectures by men such as G. Coedès, P. Huard and P. **Lévy** at the *Institut indochinois pour l'étude de l'homme* (Indochinese Institute for the Study of Mankind). In 1945–1946 he received a bursary from ORSTOM with which he travelled to Paris to be taught by M. **Leenhardt**, M. **Griaule** and A. **Leroi-Gourhan**. He became a trainee researcher at the CFRE, and in 1947 was sent by ORSTOM on secondment to the EFEO to study the Mnong Gar of Vietnam. As well as making the first discovery of a stone lithophone (now on display in the *Musée de l'Homme*), he wrote two of the finest works French ethnology has ever produced (1957, 1965). The first, *Nous avons mangé la forêt de la pierre-génie Göo: Chronique de Sar Luk, village Mnong Gar* [*We have Eaten the Forest of the Göo Stone Genius: Chronicle of Sar Luk, a Mnong Gar Village*] (Paris: Mercure de France, 1957; new edn 1974), reconstructs the daily life of a village and sees it in terms of **Mauss**'s notion of the total social phenomenon, while also obliquely addressing **Lévi-Strauss**'s interpretation of Mauss's theory of exchange. Condominas's pronouncements on the war in Indochina were not appreciated by the *colons* and he was recalled to France in 1950, then to be posted to Togo, where he carried out research on the Mina. From 1955 to 1959 he worked on the High Plains of Madagascar, studying the functioning of autonomous rural communities in relation to the *Fokon'olona*, a traditional form of village organization. He was appointed director of studies in Section

VI of the EPHE in 1960, and set up the *Centre de documentation et de recherche sur l'Asie du Sud-Est et le monde insulindien* (Centre for Documentation and Research on South East Asia and the Indian Subcontinent) there in 1961. He also set up the Atlas of the Southeast Asia RCP and an associated laboratory at the CNRS in 1971.

Tardits, Claude (born 1921)
Claude Tardits graduated from the HEC (Haute Ecole Commerciale) in 1942, and in the following year enlisted in the US Air Force. In 1949 he gained an arts degree and in 1949–1950 completed a training programme at the CFRE. Then, with a bursary from its cultural relations division, he moved to the USA to pursue his studies at Northwestern, Chicago and Columbia universities (1950–1953) and spend time with the Fox Indians. On returning to France he took a research position with the CNRS and travelled to Benin (Dahomey) to study landholding problems (1954) and the effects of the provision of schooling in the country (1954–1955). Tardits worked for ORSTOM in 1955 before becoming a *chargé de mission* (junior researcher) at the CNRS. In 1957–1958 he began an investigation of the Bamileke which he continued until the mid-1960s, when he turned his attention to the Bamoun societies of Central Cameroon. He was appointed to a lectureship at the EPHE in 1963 and taught part of the introductory course in ethnology designed by **Lévi-Strauss**. In 1964 he became director of studies in Section V of the EPHE, and held the presidency of the section from 1975 to 1979 and again in 1983, but then relinquished this post to become president of three sections of the EPHE (earth sciences, philological and historical sciences, and religious studies). With Eric de **Dampierre** he founded the *Classiques africains* collection. Tardits is known for his exemplary studies of African political anthropology based on impressive ethnohistorical investigations.

Cresswell, Robert (born 1922)

Born in New York, Robert Cresswell enlisted in the US Army in 1942 and took part in the French, Belgian and German campaigns, for which he was decorated with the Silver Medal. After the war he settled in France, gaining an arts degree in 1950 and enrolling at the CFRE in 1951–1952. In 1955 he began investigations in Ireland after taking a research position at the CNRS, and in 1960 he stayed in two Maronite villages in Lebanon, where he started to make comparative studies of these two fieldwork terrains ('Expériences d'ethnologie comparative: Liban et Irlande' ['Experiments in Comparative Ethnology: Lebanon and Ireland'], *Travaux et jours*, 18, Jan–Mar 1966). In 1969 Cresswell obtained his doctorate with his major thesis *Une communauté rurale d'Irlande* [*A Rural Irish Community*] (Paris: Institut d'ethnologie). His minor thesis was surplus to requirement as these were abolished before he submitted it, but it later appeared as 'Kinship and Landholding in a Lebanese Village' in the pages of *Etudes rurales*. After this he carried out fieldwork in Morocco, and from 1967 held teaching posts at the universities of Lille and then Paris V. In 1981 he was appointed a research director at the CNRS. He founded the journal *Techniques et cultures* in 1983 and set up a CNRS laboratory with the same name in 1974.

Guiart, Jean (born 1925)

Born in Lyon, Jean Guiart was a member and then director of a 'workshop of unemployed intellectuals' attached to the Oceania section of the *Musée de l'Homme* from 1944 to 1946. At the same time he attended the Protestant Theology Faculty, the *Institut d'ethnologie*, Section V of the EPHE and INALCO, where he graduated as an Oceanian in 1946. He then enrolled at the newly created CFRE and, in 1948, won a bursary from ORSTOM. At the ORSTOM centre in Nouméa he was researcher and then senior researcher between 1948 and 1956. In 1957 he joined the EPHE as a director of studies in Oceanian religions, and in 1962 set up the *Centre documentaire pour l'Océanie* (Documentary Centre for Oceania). In 1963 Guiart completed his thesis *Structures de la chefferie en Mélanésie du sud* [*Chiefdom Structures in Southern Melanesia*] (Paris: Institut d'ethnologie), which takes its place as the magnum opus on the forms and variants of power structures in Melanesia. In the same year he set up the 27th RCP of the CNRS to focus on Oceania. He held the ethnology chair first at the Sorbonne and then at the *Musée d'histoire naturelle*, also becoming director of the *Musée de l'Homme*. A disciple of **Leenhardt** and particularly of **Lévi-Strauss**, Guiart was instrumental in modernizing the study of Oceania in France.

Ottino, Paul (1930–2001)

Born in Nice, Paul Ottino gained a law degree in 1956 and then graduated from the CFRE. In 1958 he joined ORSTOM and in 1962 submitted an economics thesis entitled *Les Economies paysannes malgaches du Bas-Mangoky* [*Malagasy Peasant Economies of Lower Mangoky*] (Paris: Berger-Levrault, 1963). At the same time he worked on his doctoral thesis *Les changements dans les campagnes malgaches* [*Changes in the Malagasy Countryside*], which was followed in 1969 by a postdoctoral thesis entitled *Rangiroa: Parenté étendue, résidence et terres dans un atoll polynésien* [*Rangiroa: Extended Kinship, Dwellings and Land on a Polynesian Atoll*]. Successively Ottino became senior lecturer at the University of Nanterre (1971), professor at the universities of Tananarive and Réunion (1974), and director of studies at the EHESS (1975–1982). He was the guest of the Bishop Museum in 1966–1967, the University of Pittsburgh in 1972–1973, and the Research School for Pacific and Asian Studies at Canberra University in 1987–1988 and from 1992 to 1994. He is considered to have been one of France's foremost specialists on Oceania.

Garine, Igor de (born 1931)

Igor de Garine won a scholarship to study at the University of California at Santa Barbara before gaining an arts degree at the Sorbonne and graduating in 1953 from the CFRE, where he was taught by **Leroi-Gourhan**. During his studies he also attended courses given by **Leenhardt** and **Lévi-Strauss** at the EPHE. After military service from 1955 to 1957 he held a scholarship at the International African Institute and carried out research on the Massa of Cameroon from 1957 to 1959. In 1959 he joined the CNRS and made his first film, which would be followed by about fifteen more. In 1961 he won the Liotard Prize and in 1962 completed his thesis *Les Massa du Cameroun: Vie économique et sociale* [*The Massa of Cameroon: Economic and Social Life*], published by PUF in 1964. As of 1963 he combined his work at the CNRS with involvement in FAO missions on questions of nutrition, becoming the leading expert on this field and contributing to it with over 200 articles.

Panoff, Michel (born 1931)

After graduating from the HEC, an elite commercial school, Michel Panoff enrolled at the CFRE while also attending lectures by **Lévi-Strauss** and J. **Guiart**. In 1958–1959 he was responsible for book reviews in the social sciences for the important literary journal *Lettres nouvelles*. In 1960 he travelled to French Polynesia for ORSTOM, and a few years later joined the CNRS, where he remained for the rest of his career. As well as fieldwork studies, particularly on land tenure (*La Terre et l'organisation sociale en Polynésie* [*Land and Social Organization in Polynesia*] (Payot, 1970)), he is known for his small book on **Malinowski** (*B. Malinowski* (Payot, 1972)), which was the first general study of the man and his work. He also co-wrote the first French ethnological dictionary with M. Perrin (*Dictionnaire de l'ethnologie* [*Dictionary of Ethnology*] (Payot, 1973)), and published his thoughts on the nature and aims of anthropology (*l'Ethnologue et son ombre* [*The Ethnologist and his Shadow*] (Payot, 1978); *Ethnologie: deuxième souffle* [*Ethnology: The Second Wind*] (Payot, 1977)).

THE GRIAULIANS

For our purposes Griaulians are not only those scholars who were taught by **Griaule**, but also those whose work, for all the variety of its approaches, draws its primary inspiration from him. Significant figures in this group without individual entries below include H.H. Bâ (1901–1991), Solange de Ganay (born 1902), Jean Servier (1918–2000), Viviana Pâques-Stiatti (born 1920) and Michel Cartry (born 1931).

Zahan, Dominique (1915–1991)

Born in Romania, Dominique Zahan studied at the Sorbonne and graduated in 1942 with an arts degree before being appointed head of the immigration section of Ségou's Niger Office (in Mali). He participated in **Griaule**'s expedition of 1948 and then continued to work alongside him while also publishing numerous articles and continuing his work for the Niger Office until 1958. He completed his major and minor theses in 1960 and became the first professor of ethnology at the University of Strasbourg, a post he left in 1969 to occupy the chair in African sociology at the Sorbonne. Zahan is best known for his major thesis *Sociétés d'initiation Bambara: Le N'domo, le Koré* [*Bambarra Initiation Societies: The N'domo, the*

Koré] (Paris, The Hague: Mouton, 1960), which long remained the fullest study of the symbolism of initiation rites in West Africa.

Rouch, Jean (1917–2004)

Jean Rouch graduated as an engineer from the *École des Ponts et Chaussées* in 1941, but took a much livelier interest in the seminars of M. **Griaule** and in visits to the *Cinémathèque*. He joined the civil service and was sent to Niger, where he made himself conspicuous as a Gaullist. In 1942 he was transferred to IFAN at Dakar directed by T. Monod, and published an article on the cult of genius among the Songhay (*JSA*, 15 (1945)). He fought during the liberation of France and then returned to Dakar to persuade T. Monod of the merits of his plan to navigate the 4,000 kilometres of the Niger in a dugout canoe. He realized his plan together with J. Sauvy and P. Ponty, and their adventure provided the subject of Rouch's first two films: *La Chasse à l'hippopotame* [*The Hippopotamus Hunt*] and *Au pays des mages noirs* [*In the Land of the Black Magi*]. He was then given responsibility for audio-visual teaching at the CNRS by A. **Leroi-Gourhan**.

In 1948 Rouch commenced a series of investigations on the Songhay (1954–1960), and made the films *Circoncision* [*Circumcision*] (Misguich prize, 1949) and *Initiation à la danse des possédés* [*Initiation into the Dance of the Possessed*] (prize of the Biarritz 'films maudits' Festival, 1949). From 1950 to 1953 he continued to make important films and then began research on migrations in Ivory Coast, Ghana and Togo for the International African Institute. At the same time he made a further series of films which won him numerous prizes: *Jaguar, Mamy Water, Les Maîtres fous* [*The Mad Masters*] (first prize for a documentary, Venice Festival, 1957), *Moi, un Noir* [*I, a Black Man*] (Delluc prize, 1959), and *Chronique d'un été* [*Chronicle of a Summer*] (international critics' prize, Cannes Festival, 1961). In 1951 he set up the Committee for Ethnographic Cinema within the *Musée de l'Homme*. In 1959 he took charge of the IFAN in Niger and then of the 11th RCP of the CNRS, and in 1967 he became a research director in Section V of the EPHE, where he opened an audio-visual laboratory. He carried out research on the Bregbo community of the Ivory Coast, and from 1967 to 1974 collected footage of the Sigui ceremony of the Dogon. By the end of his career Rouch, appointed director of the French Film Archives, had 120 films to his credit.

Calame-Griaule, Geneviève (née Griaule, born 1924)

The daughter of M. **Griaule**, Geneviève Calame-Griaule successively obtained a DES in classical languages (1945), a diploma in Arabic from INALCO (1947), a degree in written Arabic (1948), and an *agrégation* in grammar in which she gained first place (1949). Her first fieldwork took her to the Dogon in Mali in 1946 as a member of Griaule's sixth expedition, and she returned to the region in 1954, 1956, 1957, 1958, 1960, and many times thereafter. In 1951 she joined the CNRS, where in 1966 she was made a research director after completing her major thesis *La Parole chez les Dogon* [*Speech among the Dogon*] (Paris: Gallimard, 1966) and her minor thesis *Dictionnaire Dogon: Dialecte Toro – langue et civilisation* [*A Dogon Dictionary: The Toro Dialect – Language and Civilization*] (Paris: Klincksieck, 1968). In 1977 she headed the CNRS's 'West African Language and Culture' group, founded by P. F. Lacroix in 1968, and launched the journal *Cahiers de littérature orale* with Jacques Dournes. She was also secretary-general of the *Société des africanistes* (Society of Africanists). *La Parole chez les Dogon* [*Speech among the Dogon*], which was published in a second edition in 1987 by the *Institut d'ethnologie*, is a model study of the notion of speech in Black Africa.

Rather than limiting itself to the ethnographic study of verbal behaviour, it shows how the physical aspects of Dogon speech are linked to Dogon mythology, to notions of the person and to the body of the human individual. Calame-Griaule must be credited with developing French ethnolinguistics and training a generation of scholars.

INDEPENDENT RESEARCHERS

This group comprises researchers whose initial training was not as ethnologists, and who subsequently chose not to situate themselves in the train of a mentor, unlike those with a philosophy training who became students or disciples of **Balandier** and **Lévi-Strauss**. These independents nonetheless either left their mark on the discipline, like **Mannoni** and **Ortigues**, or else influenced its development, like C. A. Diop and M. **Foucault**. Limitations of space make it impossible to include Montserrat Palau-Marti (born 1916), Joseph Chelhod (born 1919), Julian Pitt-Rivers (born 1919), J. Suret-Canale (born 1921), Solange Thierry (born 1921), Jacques Dournes (born 1922), Cheik Anta Diop (1923–1986), Jean-Louis Boutillier (born 1926), Marceau Gast (born 1927), Claude-Hélène Perrot (born 1928), René Bureau (born 1929), Camille Lacoste (born 1929), Edmond Bernus (born 1929), Jacqueline Thomas (born 1930) and Pierre Erny (born 1933).

Mannoni, Octavio (1913–1990)
Place must be found here for this psychoanalyst who, while teaching at a *lycée* in Tananarive in Madagascar, wrote a book which had a considerable influence on the youngest of the French post-war schools: *Psychologie de la colonisation* [*Psychology of Colonization*], which was published in 1950 by Le Seuil after having appeared in instalments in *Esprit*. In this work Octavio Mannoni attempts to describe the transition from traditional to modern Malagary society, with an emphasis on the psychological effects of colonial dependence and the guilt and inferiority complexes it engenders. The 1947 revolution then permitted the construction of a new reality by freeing the Malagary from their dependency complex.

Ortigues, Edmond (born 1917)
After gaining doctorates in philosophy and theology, Edmond Ortigues taught briefly in a secondary school in Lyon before joining the CNRS in 1952. In 1961 he was sent on secondment to the University of Dakar and undertook research at the *Centre hospitalier de Fann* together with the psychoanalyst M.-C. Ortigues, with whom he wrote *Oedipe africain* [*African Oedipus*] (Paris: Plon, 1966; 2nd edn UGE, 1973; 3rd edn L'Harmattan). Using evidence from 178 cases, the authors transposed Oedipal themes into the Wolof, Lebou and Serer contexts, and found that conflict was transferred onto brothers, and that guilt and anal forms of defence were rather undeveloped. Ortigues was made professor at the University of Rennes in 1966 and retired in 1983. His *Religions du livre et religions de la coutume* [*Religions of the Book and Religions of Custom*] (Paris: Le Sycomore, 1981) opposes religions of ancestral custom with salvationist religions, and compares their transmission using a collection of texts on Tallensi individuality, the importance of the twin among the Bambarra and the Dogon, and Augustinian belief.

Malaurie, Jean (born 1922)
Born in Mainz, Jean Malaurie was recruited

by the CNRS in 1948 as a geographer to join P.-E. **Victor**'s expedition to the Inuit of 1948–1949. After returning to France in 1949, he travelled to the Hoggar (*Hoggar, Touareg: Derniers Seigneurs* [*Hoggar, Tuareg: The Last Overlords*] (Paris: Nathan, 1954)), and then to the Arctic as a member of the Thulé French geographical mission. He was back in Paris in October 1951, and two years later presented the maps he had drawn up. He founded the collection *Terre Humaine*, which was established by Plon in 1955 and published the 'ethnobiographies' of **Lévi-Strauss**, **Condominas** and **Balandier**, but also of a Hopi Indian, a locksmith and a miner. In 1957 Malaurie was appointed director of studies in Arctic geography and ecology in Section VI of the EPHE, where he founded the *Centre d'études arctiques* [Centre of Arctic Studies] in 1958. As well as by his own publications, he contributed to the discipline by setting up the journal *Inter-Nord* in 1963. In 1965 he published *Les Derniers rois de Thulé* [*The Last Kings of Thule*] (Paris: Plon), which appeared in twenty-eight languages.

Thomas, Louis-Vincent (1922–1994)
After studies in philosophy and a period teaching in France, Louis-Vincent Thomas was appointed to the *lycée* of Dakar in 1948. The geographer P. Pélissier took him on a journey across Casamance and he began to consider writing a thesis on the Dyola people. He wrote several articles for the *Bulletin de l'Institut d'Afrique Noire* and for the journal *Notes Africaines*, and in 1959 he completed his major thesis *Les Diola: Essai d'analyse fonctionelle sur une population de Basse-Casamance* [*The Dyola: Essay in the Functional Analysis of a Population of Lower Casamance*] (Dakar: IFAN, 2 vols), and his minor thesis *Étude technique de la personnalité Diola* [*Technical Study of Dyola Personality*]. He was appointed professor of sociology in the newly opened arts faculty

of the University of Dakar, and in 1965 he succeeded V. Montiel as dean of the university. In the years following the independence of Senegal he became an enthusiastic supporter of the construction of a new Africa, as he demonstrated in his books *Les Idéologies négro-africaines d'aujourd'hui* [*Contemporary Black African Ideologies*] (Nizet, 1961; Dakar: 1965), *Le Socialisme et l'Afrique* [*Socialism and Africa*] (Paris: Le Livre africain, 2 vols, 1966–1967), and *Dakar en devenir* [*Emerging Dakar*] (Paris: Présence africaine, 1968). In 1967 he published 'La Place des morts dans la société africaine traditionelle: le culte des ancêtres' ['The Place of the Dead in Traditional African Society: The Cult of Ancestors'] in *Notes Africaines*, and this was the first of what became a long series of titles on death and human society: *Cinq essais sur la mort africaine* [*Five Essays on Death in Africa*] (Dakar: Faculté des lettres), *L'Anthropologie de la mort* [*The Anthropology of Death*] (Paris: Payot, 1975; 2nd edn 1980), *Mort et pouvoir* [*Death and Power*] (Paris: Payot, 1978), *Le Cadavre* [*The Corpse*] (Brussels, 1980), *La Mort africaine* [*Death in Africa*] (Paris: Payot, 1982), *Rites de mort* [*Death Rites*] (Paris: Fayard, 1985). In 1968 he became a professor at the Sorbonne.

Foucault, Michel (1926–1984)
Born in Poitiers into a family of doctors, Michel Foucault was admitted to the ENS in 1946, and after gaining an *agrégation* in philosophy in 1951 worked as an assistant lecturer at the University of Lille from 1952 to 1954. The passionate interest he developed in psychology and psychiatry resulted in the publication of *Maladie mentale et personnalité* [*Mental Illness and Personality*] (Paris: PUF, 1954) and *Maladie mentale et psychologie* (Paris: PUF, 1962) [*Mental Illness and Psychology* (New York: Harper & Row, 1976)]. As of 1955 he held a number of posts in Sweden, Poland, and

Germany, and in 1960 he was appointed to the University of Clermont-Ferrand. In 1961 he completed his thesis *Folie et déraison: Histoire de la folie à l'âge classique* (Paris: Plon) [*Madness and Civilization: A History of Insanity in the Age of Reason* (New York: Pantheon, 1965)], which describes madness as the result of a specific form of knowledge in a particular culture (that of the Enlightenment), which sets reason against unreason and constructs the madman out of the latter. This was followed by *Les Mots et les choses* (Paris: Gallimard, 1966) [*The Order of Things: An Archaeology of the Human Sciences* (New York: Pantheon, 1970)], which examines the emergence of anthropological reason succeeding classic forms of representation by means of the nascent discourses of economics, natural science and linguistics. After a period at the University of Tunis from 1966 to 1968, Foucault created a philosophy department at the University of Vincennes in 1968, where he taught until his election to the *Collège de France* in 1970. In *L'Archéologie du savoir* (Paris: Gallimard, 1969) [*The Archaeology of Knowledge* (New York: Pantheon, 1972)], he makes a striking methodological statement by demonstrating his technique of identifying caesuras in Western thought, thereby also offering new conceptualizations of archaeology, discursive forms and systems, and epistemology. Then in 1975 came *Surveiller et punir* (Paris: Gallimard) [*Discipline and Punish: The Birth of the Prison* (New York: Pantheon 1977)], an archaeology of the constitution of the 'delinquent subject' which seeks, through an examination of instances of repression, to explore the possibility of a power structure without a centralizing organ. In 'L'Ordre du discours' ['The Discourse on Language'], Foucault's inaugural lecture at the *Collège de France* (published in English as an appendix to *The Archaeology of Knowledge*), he outlines the project of a history of the 'will to truth'. This line of thought is then pursued in the first volume of *Histoire de la sexualité* [*A*

History of Sexuality (New York: Pantheon, 1978)], entitled 'La Volonté de savoir' ['An Introduction'], which attempts to describe the production of the modern sexual subject for whom sexuality is a site of secrecy. As against the idea of a guilty subjectivization of the flesh, Foucault shows that sexuality and desire are not oppressed and suppressed but constructed and signposted by the discursive order, particularly when this order is repressive. *L'Usage des plaisirs* (Paris: Gallimard, 1984) [*The Use of Pleasure* (New York: Pantheon, 1985)] and *Le Souci de soi* (Paris: Gallimard, 1984) [*The Care of the Self* (New York: Pantheon, 1986)] – the second and third parts of *The History of Sexuality* – present an archaeology of the constitution of the subject's relationship with its own selfhood in terms of asceticism, self-mastery and other techniques for gaining power over body and mind. Foucault's work was a quest, undertaken through study of knowledge, language, repressive institutions and sexual morality, to define the configurations and foundations of power and the dense network of multiple constraints issuing from it, as well as a search for figures who irredeemably transgress this power. He also wrote a great deal on deviants of all sorts, especially on particular artists, while his increasing preoccupation with the possibility of collective resistance to the mechanisms of power led him from 1968 to take a number of public stances. In 1971 he founded the *Groupe d'information sur les prisons* (Information Group on Prisons), supported the 'popular cause' of the Maoists, homosexual movements, and the Solidarity trades union in Poland. He was a regular fixture on American campuses, particularly at Berkeley, where through the good offices of Herbert Dreyfus and Paul Rabinow he was made a guest professor in 1979. Foucault died of AIDS in 1984, but the renewal of anthropology and of our general categories of thought stimulated by his work has hardly begun.

Bourdieu, Pierre (1930–2002)

Born in a village in the Béarn in 1930, Bourdieu was admitted to the ENS in 1951, gained an *agrégation* in philosophy in 1955, and then worked as an assistant to R. Aron. He completed his military service as a member of France's overseas development agency at the University of Algiers from 1958 to 1961, and then worked as a sociologist on social transformation (1961, 1962), and as an ethnographer on the question of social norms among the Kabylie (1972). From 1961 to 1964 he was a senior lecturer at the University of Lille, where he directed investigations on students, on photography and on museum attendance. He demonstrated how cultural heritage determines academic results in *Les Héritiers: les étudiants et la culture* [*The Heirs: Students and Culture*], written with J. C. Passeron (Paris: Minuit, 1964), and that school functions as a means of reproducing social relations in *La Reproduction: Elements pour une théorie du système d'enseignement* [*Reproduction: Elements of a Theory of the School System*], also co-authored by Passeron (Paris: Minuit, 1970). Arguing against 'the myth of innate taste', his *L'Amour de l'art: Les Musées d'art européens et leur public* [*The Love of Art: European Art Museums and their Visitors*], written with A. Darbel and D. Schnapper (Paris: Minuit), identifies the social conditions which make the appreciation of art possible and shows that the mastery of a system of codes allows members of the cultivated classes to display a spontaneous familiarity with art, while the perception of the lower classes is structured by categories of everyday experience. Bourdieu was appointed director of studies at the EPHE in 1964 and head of the Centre for European Sociology in 1968, and after establishing a new monograph series he founded the journal *Actes de la Recherche en Sciences sociales* in 1975. Bourdieu continued his studies of taste – as the most visible part of the 'habitus' – in *La Distinction: Critique sociale du jugement* [*Distinction: A Social Critique of Judgement*] (Paris: Minuit, 1979), which analyses judgements on artistic matters, leisure and consumption. In his 1981 inaugural lecture as newly elected professor of sociology at the *Collège de France* he stated that the role of the sociologist is to unmask what is going on behind the scenes of social life (*Leçon sur la Leçon* [*Lesson on the Lesson*] (Paris: Minuit, 1982)). In *Les Règles de l'art: Genèse et structure du champ littéraire* [*The Rules of Art: Origins and Structure of the Literary Field*] (Paris: Le Seuil, 1992), he studies the emergence in the second half of the nineteenth century of the idea of art for art's sake, and with it of the modern writer independent of the laws of the market place and recognizing only the judgement of his peers. He sees this as the culmination of the trend initiated in the Renaissance of making the production of cultural goods an ever more autonomous process. *La Misère du monde* [*The World's Misery*], published by Le Seuil in 1993, is a team effort which aims to let those interviewed speak for themselves. Now at the height of his fame, Bourdieu launched a European journal called *Liber* and an association called *Raisons d'agir*. He denounced media manipulation (*Sur la télévision* [*On Television*] (Liber-Raisons d'agir, 1996)), supported strikers, championed a European welfare state, and in a general way was an advocate of what became known as the 'social movement'.

Although his approach was fundamentally empirical, Bourdieu in actuality founded a conceptual system whose usefulness is now amply proven. He extended the notion of capital to social, symbolic and cultural domains, perceiving that they, like financial capital, can be subdivided ('cultural capital is divisible by cultural capital' (*The Love of Art*: 109)) and interchanged (symbolic capital can become economic capital). The state is like a central bank which guarantees the value of the currency, both in monetary terms and in terms of perceptual categories authorized by the state's agents. This amounts to a symbolic violence, in which the democratization of the education system both masks and legitimizes the reproduction of dominant ideologies by means of the norms which that system transmits. The opposition between individual and society is transcended because objective social structures correspond to the agents' mental structures. By maintaining an 'an ontological complicity with the world', the habitus forms the objective structure of the social world inscribed in the very body of the individual subject. Practices are derived from social categories, and tastes and preferences are merely the reflection of the individual's position in social space. The habitus controls the representations and practical meaning of social agents. This meaning or practical reason 'allows the future to be anticipated without being addressed as such' (*Choses dites*: 22). Social agents compete for the distinction lying at the heart of the social game, because in this field 'to be is to be different'. In its emergence and even its disappearance, a field is a site of domination and conflict with its own history. Thus social agents act according to their respective positions in fields which each have a relative autonomy and their own norms (e.g. the literary field in nineteenth-century France). This is why, ultimately, 'the true subject of the most accomplished human works is none other than the field in which – that is to say by which and against which – they are accomplished' (*Méditations pascaliennes* [*Pascalian Meditations*]: 137).

STUDENTS OF BALANDIER AND LÉVI-STRAUSS

The following section contains such students of these two masters as were not educated at the CFRE and therefore had to choose another route. They differ substantially in the degree to which their work stayed within the parameters set by these two mentors, and a number of them may seem less properly to belong under this heading than some of those considered in terms of their role in the CFRE. All the same, the researchers considered here can generally be said to have owed at least the early development of their careers to **Lévi-Strauss** or **Balandier**, or to their earliest protégés – **Condominas**, **Dumont** and **Guiart**. Other figures who belong to this category are Arlette Frigout (born 1929), Claude Rivière (born 1932), Philippe Laburthe-Tolra (born 1929), Nicole Belmont (born 1931), Araine Deluz (born 1931), Lucien Sebag (1933–1965), Jeanne-Françoise Vincent-Mulliez (born 1935), Marc Piault (born 1933), Olivier Herrenschmidt (born 1934), Georges Dupré (1938), Jean-Marie Gibbal (1938–1993), Pierre Smith (1939–2001), Jean Bazin (1941–2001), and of course numerous researchers too young for inclusion here.

Chiva, Isaac (born 1925)
Isaac Chiva was born in Romania, where he took his *baccalauréat* and began studies in textiles before moving to Paris in 1947 to continue his studies and qualify with an *Arts et Métiers* diploma in 1949. In 1950 he gained an arts degree which included an ethnology component, and from 1951 to 1953 he was a trainee researcher in the *Laboratoire d'ethnologie française* (Laboratory of French Ethnology) of the CNRS. From 1955 to 1960 he was employed by the *Musée des arts et traditions populaires* (Museum of Popular Crafts and Traditions), and in 1960 he took responsibility for the journal *Etudes Rurales*. At the same time he began working for **Lévi-Strauss** at the EPHE, where he became deputy director of studies in 1962

and director of studies in 1971. Chiva's main contribution was to train an entire generation in the ethnology of France, no longer defined as the collection of ancient traditions or the observation of a small, preferably rural social group, but looking specifically at contemporary France and its procedures of production and manipulation. He was for many years a lieutenant of Lévi-Strauss, and took the leading role in creating the ethnological heritage mission of the Ministry of Culture.

Gamelon, Simone (née Dreyfus, born 1925)

Simone Dreyfus-Gamelon joined the CFRE and in 1946 was detached to the ethnomusicology department of the *Musée de l'Homme*. After gaining an arts degree in 1951 she was recruited by the CNRS, where she joined the Laboratory of Social Anthropology on its establishment in 1961–1962. In 1963 she completed her Ph.D. thesis *Les Kayapo du Nord: Etat de Para, Brésil – Contribution à l'étude des indiens Gé* [*The Northern Kayapo, Pará State, Brazil: Contribution to the Study of the Ge Indians*] (Paris-The Hague: Mouton). She was a lecturer at the *Institut des hautes études d'Amérique Latine* [Institute of Higher Latin American Studies], *maître-assistante* in ethnology at the Sorbonne (1965), and director of studies in Section VI of the EPHE (1969). Dreyfus-Gamelon was the leading figure in French Americanism after the death of A. **Métraux**, and it was due to her efforts that Survival International was established in France. She was also responsible, with G. **Condominas**, for organizing the important symposium *L'Anthropologie en France: Situation actuelle et avenir* [*Anthropology in France: Current Situation and Future*] in Paris on 18–22 April 1977 (CNRS, 1979).

Meillassoux, Claude (born 1925)

Born into a bourgeois textile family in Roubaix, Claude Meillassoux graduated from the *Institut d'études politiques* (Institute of Political Studies) in 1947 and then studied economics and political science at the University of Michigan, gaining an MA in 1949. From 1950 to 1952 he was an interpreter at the French Production Mission in the USA, and then back in France he worked in advertising before entering political life. In 1955 **Balandier** engaged him to work in UNESCO's International Research Bureau on the Social Implications of Technical Development. It was there that Meillassoux discovered anthropology, and after following courses at Section VI of the EPHE he began to write review articles. In 1958 Balandier sent him and A. Deluz to carry out research on the Guro of Ivory Coast, and on his return he wrote his 'Essai d'interprétation du phénomène économique dans les sociétés d'autosubsistance' ['Essay on the Interpretation of Economic Phenomena in Subsistence Societies'] (*Cahiers d'Etudes Africaines*, 1: 38–67), which caused a major epistemological revolution. In this essay Meillassoux, drawing his inspiration from the substantivist school, shows how older siblings dominate younger siblings through the mechanism for the management of dowries. Completed in 1962 and published in 1964, his doctoral thesis *Anthropologie économique des Gouro de Côte d'Ivoire: De l'économie d'autosubsistance à l'agriculture commerciale* [*Economic Anthropology of the Guro of Ivory Coast: From Subsistence Economy to Commercial Agriculture*] (Paris: Mouton, 1964) opens up economic anthropology to Marxist analysis. Meillassoux entered the CNRS in 1963 and remained there for the rest of his career. He researched in Mali and Senegal, first working on the role of Soninke society in the history of Black Africa. He was then asked by the International African Institute to take part in a vast inquiry into voluntary associations in urban Africa (*Urbanization of an African Community: Voluntary Association in Bamako*, Washington, 1968). Using the platform provided by his role in organizing a symposium, he repeated his view that the notion of ethnic groups must be embedded in the socio-historical and cultural context (ed., *L'Evolution du commerce africain depuis le XIXème siècle en Afrique de l'Ouest* [*The Evolution of African Commerce from the Nineteenth Century in Western Africa*] (Oxford UP)). Meillassoux expanded the theoretical model he had developed in 1960 to analyse the encounter between the domestic community and capitalism (1975a). This work was highly influential, and its success encouraged him to examine South African systems of exploitation (1969) and to direct a CNRS team dedicated to Southern Africa (1988, 1991). Published in 1986, his *Anthropologie de l'esclavage: Le Ventre de fer et d'argent* [*Anthropology of Slavery: The Belly of Iron and Silver*] (Paris: PUF), mixes historical research and conceptualization. Because slavery is defined not in terms of loss of liberty, but by its non-generative mode of reproduction, it determines the economic and military organization of the societies which practise it. From the 1990s Meillassoux, particularly in his articles on Inuit kinship, denounced structuralist treatments of kinship as naturalist in their approach. Together with **Lévi-Strauss**, he is certainly the author who has left the strongest theoretical mark on the discipline in France.

Cuisenier, Jean (born 1927)

After taking an *agrégation* in philosophy in 1954, Jean Cuisenier worked as an assistant at the *Institut des hautes études* (Institute of Higher Studies) in Tunis and became an *assistant de recherche* (research assistant), *maître de recherche* (junior researcher) and then *directeur de recherche* (senior researcher) at the CNRS. In 1968 he succeeded G.-H. **Rivière** as head curator at the *Musée des arts et traditions populaires* (Museum of Popular Crafts and Traditions) and was also appointed director of the *Centre d'ethnologie française* (Centre for French Ethnology). In

1971 he completed his thesis *Economie et parenté: Essai sur les affinités de structures entre système économique et système de parenté* [*Economics and Kinship: Essay on Structural Affinities Between Economic Systems and Kinship Systems*] (Paris, The Hague: Mouton, 1975). Using models taken from game theory, he insists that marriage of parallel patrilinear cousins must be understood with reference to the strategies of social agents. Cuisenier wrote a large number of books on the rural and architectural anthropology of France and on the societies of Eastern Europe.

Dampierre, Eric de (1928–1998)

Eric de Dampierre obtained an arts degree, a diploma from Section VI of the EPHE (1946), a law degree (1947), and a diploma from the *Institut d'études des sciences politiques* [Institute of Studies in Political Sciences] (1948). He performed his military service in the air force in Casablanca in 1948–1949 and then held a temporary contract at the *Centre d'études sociologiques* [Centre of Sociological Studies] of the CNRS, where contributed to a research programme on the formation of worker elites alongside A. Touraine and E. Morin. From 1950 to 1952 he was a guest lecturer at the University of Chicago, and in 1954 he was given responsibility for a mission to Ubangi-Shari by ORSTOM. This project, carried out in Nzakara territory, concentrated mainly on demographic questions while also looking at kinship and client relations and at the political organization of the sultanates of Upper Ubangi (a second mission followed in 1957–1958). Back in Paris, Dampierre worked for UNESCO and founded the collection *Classiques africains*. He was appointed deputy director of studies in Section VI of the EPHE in 1961 and then senior lecturer in ethnology at the opening of the University of Nanterre in 1967. In 1969 he occupied the chair at Nanterre, where he founded the *Laboratoire d'ethnologie et de sociologie comparative* [Laboratory of Comparative Ethnology and Sociology]. He is known as a founder of the collection *Recherches en sciences humaines,* which published important titles of German and American sociology as well as works of an ethnological character.

Jaulin, Robert (1928–1996)

Robert Jaulin obtained a DES in aesthetics with his thesis *L'Opposition du magique et du religieux, est-elle valable en esthétique?* [*The Opposition Between Magic and Religion: Is it Valid in Aesthetics?*] (1950), and after a degree in philosophy in 1951 he was recruited by the CNRS in 1953. In 1955 he completed his doctoral theses: *Quelques corréspondances des structures filmiques et archaïques* [*Some Correspondences between Filmic and Archaic Structures*] and *Langage filmique et structure des Houailou* [*Filmic Language and Structure of the Houailou*]. In 1956 he became interested in psychoanalysis, and after attending the seminars of **Balandier** and **Lévi-Strauss** he travelled to the Sara territory of central Shari in Chad in 1958 to investigate economic organization of space and kinship in the Mara clan, and later also their initiation practices (Jaulin, 1965). After his appointment as a *chargé de recherches* at the CNRS he turned his attention to Americanism, carrying out his first mission to the Bari territory in 1959. He soon became a defender of the rights of American Indian minorities and a vocal critic of 'death-bringing' Western civilization. In 1967 he was given a joint appointment as professor of ethnology and director of the newly created ethnology department at the University of Jussieu. He launched the *Cahiers de Jussieu,* a paperback collection which published a large number of anthropological texts.

Izard, Michel (born 1931)

After obtaining an arts degree and a DES in philosophy in 1956, Michel Izard was able to begin a study mission on the human problems posed by the construction of a dam in Burkina-Faso thanks to a recommendation by **Lévi-Strauss**. He completed his military service in 1959–1960 and then joined a team in the *Délégation générale à la recherche scientifique* (General Delegation for Scientific Research) working on the isolated community of Plozévet. The CNRS engaged him in 1963 and he spent the rest of his career with the organization. He lived for many years in Ouagadougou (Burkina Faso) and became the foremost specialist on the Mossi, on whom he wrote extensively. He is also known as the co-editor, with P. Bonte, of a *Dictionnaire de l'ethnologie et de l'anthropologie* [*Dictionary of Ethnology and Anthropology*] (Paris: PUF, 1991).

Héritier, Françoise (later Izard and then Héritier-Augé, born 1933)

After a degree in history and geography in 1957 Françoise Héritier was given responsibility for a study mission by the *Institut des sciences humaines appliquées* (Institute of Applied Social Sciences) at Bordeaux University on behalf of the hydraulic service of Burkina-Faso (then Upper Volta). This resulted in three memoranda which she co-authored with M. **Izard**. On her return she joined the *Bureau d'analyse de l'Institut national d'etudes démographiques* (Bureau of Analysis of the National Institute for Demographic Studies), and then, in 1960, J.-C. Gardin's *Centre d'analyse documentaire* (Centre for Documentary Analysis). She was made a *chef de travaux* at the EPHE with special responsibility for the application of data processing to African ethnographic documentation. After travelling to a number of American institutions and universities in this capacity, she carried out her first mission to the Samo under the supervision of D. **Paulme** in 1963. Here she gathered material for her post-doctoral thesis *Parenté et mariage chez les Samo de langue*

Matya [*Kinship and Marriage among the Matya-speaking Samo*]. In 1967 Héritier was engaged by the CNRS, in 1980 she became *directeur d'études* at the EHESS, and in 1982 (1983) she occupied the chair in comparative studies of African societies at the *Collège de France*. She also succeeded **Lévi-Strauss** at the head of the *Laboratoire d'anthropologie sociale* (Laboratory of Social Anthropology). Her *L'Exercice de la parenté* [*Practice of Kinship*], published in 1981 (Paris: Gallimard-Le Seuil), discovers order and regularity in what Lévi-Strauss had called semi-complex marriage structures, hitherto considered haphazard, by using computer-generated data on the Crow-Omaha prohibition nomenclatures. While continuing her work on matrimony through research seminars in 1990, 1991, 1992, and 1994, she became president of the National AIDS Council and developed her interest in bodily essences and the ways in which human societies have constructed theories to explain how the bodily humours (blood, sperm, milk) are mixed, circulated and exchanged (her teaching at the *Collège de France* focuses on the symbolic anthropology of the body). These representations determine concepts both of individual identity and of 'inscription' in lines of filiation and the choice of partner (1994). Héritier extended this line of thought in her thesis that human beings, in conceptualizing their dissociation from the animal world, took as their matter for reflection that which was closest to them, namely their own bodily essences, and that this caused the difference between the sexes to assume a central importance in human thought. This absolute sexual 'otherness' underlies the dichotomy between idendicality and difference which pervades all early thought. Thus the primary matter of the symbolic order is the body. A discreet campaigner for women's causes, Héritier sought to identify and challenge the fundamental premises of male domination. She retired in 1999.

Adler, Alfred (born 1934)

After gaining a DES in philosophy in 1955, Alfred Adler began to teach the subject at secondary level while at the same time attending seminars held by the Hellenist J.-P. Vernant. He completed a period of training in the centre run by J.-C. Gardin in 1961 and then wrote 'Etudes sur les problèmes de la documentation automatique' ['Study of Problems in Automatic Documentation']. Under **Balandier**'s supervision he also produced 'Attitudes towards Time in Sub-Saharan Africa' (1961–1962), which involved him in his first fieldwork among the Yoruba in Nigeria. In 1965 he entered the CNRS, where he became a research director after completing a long investigation of the Moundang. He succeeded C. **Tardits** in the chair for African religious systems in Section V of the EPHE in 1985, and took his retirement in 2001. Adler searched for elementary forms of royalty behind the diversity of structures and institutions, and in this way his approach took up a theme of *The Golden Bough* while divesting it of its teleological import. His work is devoted to examining the fundamental questions of rites (especially of enthronement), power, representation and religion.

Clastres, Pierre (1934–1977)

Pierre Clastres studied philosophy, gaining a *licence* in 1957 and a DESS in 1958, and he also attended seminars held by **Lévi-Strauss** and **Métraux**. After joining the *Laboratoire d'anthropologie sociale* (Laboratory of Social Anthropology) of the CNRS, he carried out fieldwork on the American Indians in the company of L. Sebag in 1962. In 1965 he completed his doctoral thesis *La Vie sociale d'une tribu nomade: Les Indiens Guayaki du Paraguay* [*Social Life of a Nomadic Tribe: The Guayaki Indians of Paraguay*], and in 1973 he published *Chronique des indiens Guayaki: Ce que savent les Aché chasseurs nomades du Paraguay* [*Chronicle of the Guayaki Indians: The Knowledge of the Aché*

Hunter Nomads of Paraguay] (Paris: Plon). In 1974 he published *Le Grand Parler: Mythes et chants sacrés des indiens Guarani* [*The Oral Treasury: Myths and Sacred Song of the Guarani Indians*] (Paris: Le Seuil) and his major work *La Société contre l'Etat* [*Society against the State*] (Paris: Le Seuil). The posthumously published *Recherches d'anthropologie politique* [*Researches in Political Anthropology*] (Paris: Minuit) is a collection of earlier writings. Clastres makes a distinction between state societies and stateless societies and posits a logic underlying primitive societies. Taking a stand against ethnocentrism, he takes a positive view of the 'lack of a state', as it is described in much of the literature, seeing this as the result of a conscious rejection of centralization and its consequences, namely the separation between the dominant and the dominated. Instead social and political life are interwoven, so that 'primitive society manifests a rejection of the concentration of power, because the society itself, not its leader, is the real site of power' (1974: 136). Clastres joined the editorial committee of the newly founded journal *Libre*, which saw itself as filling the role in the 1970s that *Argument* had filled in the 1950s and 1960s. He died in a road accident. By asking the questions 'what is order?' and 'what is a law?', Clastres moved beyond Marxism in its triumphal stage, which always located the issue of the social order in discussions of alienation and modes of production.

Godelier, Maurice (born 1934)

Born into a modest family in Cambrai, Maurice Godelier completed his secondary education at the *Lycée Henri IV* in Paris, and was a member of the school's communist association. In 1952 he became the leader of this group, which met at the *Maison de lettres* to debate with intellectuals like Vernant, **Haudricourt**, Althusser and **Foucault**. In 1955 he entered the *Ecole normale supérieure* (ENS) at Saint Cloud,

and in 1958 graduated with an *agrégation* in philosophy. He was made a trainee researcher at the CNRS in 1959 and then held posts as assistant to F. Braudel (1960–1962) and then to C. **Lévi-Strauss** at the EPHE. With the support of senior party members, Godelier gained an early reputation as a thinker, especially among the circle of the *Centre d'études et de recherches marxistes* (Centre for Marxist Study and Research) (CERM), whose creation in 1960 marked a transformation of the French Communist Party. His first publications addressed major questions in contemporary Marxist thought, not least his essays on the structural analysis of *Capital* (which were published together in 1966 after he had sent them to Lévi-Strauss handwritten in a notebook). Godelier also examined Marx's writings on precapitalist societies, firstly in lengthy treatments – appearing between 1963 and 1969 – of the concept of the mode of production (which Lenin had subsumed to the concept of stage of production), and more particularly in his studies of Asiatic modes of production (1970, 1972). Through his introduction of the notion of 'system' Godelier produces a thesis compatible with structuralism, for he presents the modes of production as comprising two structures. On the basis of this reading he proposes a redefinition of the notion of 'economic rationality', seen no longer in terms of human or social finality, but in terms of the very structure of the system. He defines this as the maximum potential for realizing axiomatically the necessary social and economic transformations (1966: 194), and also as a state measure for the alignment of the two structures within a single system. While Lévi-Strauss, pointing to the substantivist school, had already called for the constitution of an economic anthropology (*Annuaire de l'Ephe*, 1961: 7), it was Godelier's 'Objet et méthode de l'anthropologie économique' ['Object and Method of Economic Anthropology'], published in

L'Homme in 1965, which, by presenting its themes and schools of thought in a systematic way, was the first text to establish this field of inquiry in France. He became a *maître de conférence* (senior lecturer) in the new subject of economic anthropology at the EHESS in 1962, and in 1974 published a collection of the classic texts in this area. Then, in what started as a review of a small book by **Métraux** on the Incas, Godelier used John **Murra**'s material as a basis for an investigation of the economic and social development of the Inca empire, looking at how new modes of production were grafted onto ancient communitarian ones. From 1967 to 1969 he worked on a CNRS assignment to study the Baruya in the highlands of the New Guinean interior, a people 'discovered' in 1951, and he focused his attention on relations between kinship and the soil. His 1969 article 'La Monnaie de sel des Baruya de Nouvelle-Guinée' ['Salt as a Currency among the Baruya of New Guinea'] (*L'Homme*, XI: 5–37) examines the Baruya notion of surplus in the light of the recent replacement of stone axes by iron axes, and their notion of the foundation of value (work or scarcity) on the exchange of salt for stones and cloaks made of bark. In the early 1970s Godelier drew on the Marxist category of fetishism to address questions pertaining to ideology and to what he called the ideal part of reality, while also attempting to illuminate the workings of multifunctional structures. This led him to suggest that the analytical distinction between infrastructure and superstructure be transcended (kinship is both infrastructure and superstructure), because ideology informs the totality of ideal realities through which individuals act in relation to themselves and their environment. Godelier then found a new focus for his research in the question of male domination over women, writing on the initiations which legitimize and institute that domination. He became deputy director of studies in Section VI of the EPHE in 1971, and

was the founder of the collection *Bibliothèque d'anthropologie*, which was published by Maspero from 1970 to 1980 and became a vehicle for the introduction of such writers as **Fortune**, **Douglas**, **Leach** and **Wolf** to a wider readership in France. He was appointed director of studies in 1975 and was head of the social sciences department of the CNRS from 1982 to 1986. On his retirement he was given responsibility for the scientific section of the planned *Musée des arts premiers* (Museum of Early Arts) by President Chirac. He filled this post until 2001, when he passed the baton on to his student Emmanuel Desveaux.

Terray, Emmanuel (born 1934)

Emmanuel Terray enrolled at the ENS in 1956 and gained an *agrégation* in philosophy in 1960. He was a very politically active student and co-founded the socialist student section. He had already discovered anthropology through his reading of **Lévi-Strauss**'s *Tristes Tropiques* and *Elementary Structures of Kinship*, when a post-*agrégation* course taught by **Balandier**, which outlined a form of anthropology with an 'interest in history, conflicts, contradictions and crises' (1995: 16), stimulated him to make connections between anthropology and politics. In 1962 he completed his military service in Dakar, where he was expected to teach and research, and where he worked under the auspices of the *Centre de psychiatrie transculturelle* (Transcultural Psychiatry Centre) founded by H. Collomb. With Balandier's support he was engaged in 1963 by the International Relations Centre of the *Institut des sciences politiques* (Institute of Political Sciences), and in 1964 took up an appointment at the University of Abidjan, established the previous year, where he and F. Lafargue later set up an ethnosociological institute. Having already worked on trades unionism in Senegal, Terray produced a classically composed doctoral thesis on the Dida, a population neighbouring the Guro in the

Centre-West of Ivory Coast, which he defended in 1966 and published in 1969 as *L'Organisation sociale des Dida de Côte d'Ivoire* [*The Social Organization of the Dida of Ivory Coast*] (Annales de l'Université d'Abidjan). In 1967 he began research towards a postdoctoral thesis on the Abron, but by putting his name to a manifesto in favour of arrested students he caused his contract to be annulled, and so he returned to France in 1968. He was recruited as a senior lecturer by the University of Paris VIII-Vincennes and published *Le Marxisme devant les sociétés 'primitives': Deux études* [*Marxism and 'Primitive' Societies: Two Studies*] (Paris: Maspero, 1969), which very soon gained him worldwide recognition. Both studies, recast versions of teaching materials, propose Marxist and Althusserian rereadings of **Morgan**'s *Ancient Society* (which Terray sees as surmounting the distinction between the diachronic and the synchronic) and **Meillassoux**'s *Anthropologie économique des Guoro de Côte d'Ivoire* [*Economic Anthropology of the Guro of Ivory Coast*]; in both cases he develops and brings to bear the concepts of social formation and mode of production. After defending his postdoctoral thesis in 1984, Terray was appointed director of studies at the EHESS, and in 1986 he replaced Balandier at the head of the *Centre d'études africaines* (Centre of African Studies) and of the *Laboratoire de sociologie et géographie africaines* (Laboratory of African Sociology and Geography). After the publication of his autobiographical narrative *Lettres à la fugitive* [*Letters to a Fugitive Woman*] (Paris: Odile Jacob, 1988), he was prompted by his long-held interest in Germany and Central and Eastern Europe to work at the University of Berlin for a lengthy period, during which he wrote three books (1994, 1996, 1999). Back in France, he resumed his teaching at the EHESS, and spent a large amount of time co-ordinating and campaigning for illegal immigrants.

Augé, Marc (born 1935)

Marc Augé entered the ENS in 1957 and gained an *agrégation* in classical literature there in 1960, while at the same time attending seminars given by **Balandier**. After his military service and a brief period as a teacher in secondary education, he was recruited as a *chef de travaux* in Section VI of the EPHE. His appointment by ORSTOM in 1964 led to a period in Ivory Coast, where he taught at the ENA and carried out research on the Alladian, on whom he wrote his doctoral thesis in 1969: *Le rivage alladian: Organisation et évolution des villages alladian* [*The Alladian Shore: Organization and Evolution of Alladian Villages*] (Paris: ORSTOM). This is a very classically composed ethnic monograph, and its originality resides in its demonstration that the matrimonial strategies of the Ebrie, Avikam and Alladian, all matrilocal and matrilinear lagoon peoples, include marriage with women from the patrilocal, patrilinear Dida society, which assures that children stay with them; the same three lagoon peoples formed the subject of his postdoctoral thesis. In 1970 Augé was appointed deputy director of studies at the EHESS, and together with J. Copans he founded the collection *Dossiers africains*, which was published by Maspero as of 1973. At this point in the development of the Marxist Africanist school in France it made less sense to think in terms of infrastructures and the articulation of modes of production than to return to the problem of ideology. It is ideology which legitimizes the social order – in particular by constant reference to the supernatural – and determines social practices. Augé's *Théorie des pouvoirs et idéologie: Etude de cas en Côte d'Ivoire* [*Theory of Centres of Power and Ideology: A Case Study in Ivory Coast*] (Paris: Herman, 1975) analyses such phenomena as belief in witchcraft, religious syncretism and prophecy, and sketches an anthropological theory of the relations between symbolism and ideology. At the core of the group there is a strong upsurge in witchcraft, which is no longer a bastion of the social order but a factor in competitive society. An extended study of the prophet Atcho, whose confession of witch doctors revealed the notion of remorse and thus the feeling of guilt, thereby opening up the possibility of a newly constructed 'self' precipitating the crumbling of traditional forms of conscience. After research in Southeast Togo, Augé published *Pouvoirs de vie, pouvoir de mort: Introduction à une anthropologie de la répression* [*Powers of Life, Power of Death: Introduction to an Anthropology of Repression*] (Paris: Flammarion, 1977), in which he attacks the ideas of **Clastres** and, by seeking a homology of the structures of power informing discourses and practices in all societies, advances the notion of 'non-state totalitarianism'. Power must be understood not as identifying itself with a single political institution, but as an all-encompassing logic which situates individuals in relation to one another in multiple and differential ways; not as present only in the different institutional forms of a society, but also in its intellectual, moral and metaphysical manifestations. The 'ideo-logical' defined as a site of 'virtual coherence' of representations constitutes this all-encompassing logic (Augé, ed., *La Construction du monde* [*The Construction of the World*] (Maspero, 1974)). This logic conveys the domination of the dominant, but informs the discourse and practice of all; it constitutes both the expression and the effectiveness of domination. *Symbole, fonction, histoire: Les Interrogations de l'anthropologie* [*Symbol, Function, History: The Questioning of Anthropology*] (Paris: Hachette, 1979) is a reflection on the nature of the discipline, particularly in its relation to history. After publishing a collection of his articles under the title *Génie du paganisme* [*The Genius of Paganism*] (Paris: Gallimard, 1982), Augé was instrumental in the construction and dissemination of medical anthropology

(1984), a new field of enquiry in France to which he directed many of his students. Then followed *La Traversée du Luxembourg* [*Crossing the Luxembourg*] (Paris: Hachette, 1985) and *Un ethnologue dans le Métro* [*An Ethnologist in the Métro*] (Paris: Hachette, 1986), setting the tone for a series of publications (1989, 1992, 1998) of a far less academic nature, in which the ethnologist offers observations and remarks on various subjects (the historical journeys re-embodied in the names of *Métro* stations resemble latent (or unconscious) respects paid to ancestors). Augé was elected president of the EHESS in 1987 and retired in 2000.

Geffray, Christian (1954–2001)

After completing a *licence* in philosophy Christian Geffray enrolled for a Master's degree in ethnology at the University of Nanterre and then for a DEA at the EHESS. From 1982 to 1985 he researched on the domestic economy and kinship structures of Makhuwa societies in Mozambique for the anthropology and archaeology department of the University of Eduardo Mondlane (*Ni père, ni mère: Critique de la parenté chez les Makhuwa* [*Neither Father nor Mother: Critique of Kinship among the Makhuwa*] (Paris: Le Seuil, 1991)). He then took an anthropological look at the question of war from 1987 to 1990 (*La Cause des armes en Mozambique* [*The Cause of Arms in Mozambique*] (Paris: Karthala, 1991)). He was engaged by ORSTOM in 1989 and began fresh fieldwork in Brazil, working on the forest frontier and what he called the paternalist question (*Chroniques de la servitude en Amazonie brésilienne* [*Chronicles of Servitude in the Brazilian Amazon*] (Paris: Karthala, 1995)). At the same time he pursued purely theoretical reflections inspired by Lacan's teaching (*Le Nom du maître: Contribution à l'anthropologie analytique* [*The Master's Name: Contribution to Analytical Anthropology*] (Paris: Arcanes, 1997); *Trésor: Anthropologie analytique de la valeur* [*Treasure: An Analytical Anthropology of Value*] (Paris: Arcanes, 2001)). Geffray also co-directed an international research programme on cocaine for UNESCO and in 1997 made a film with Frédéric Letang called *La Terre de la peine* [*Land of Suffering*]. He died of a heart attack in March 2001.

SELECT BIBLIOGRAPHY

Abensour, M. (ed.) (1987) *L'Esprit des lois sauvages* (on Clastres), Paris: Le Seuil.

Adler, A. (1982) *La mort et le masque du roi: la royauté sacrée des Moundang du Tchad*, Paris: Payot.

——(2000) *Le pouvoir et l'interdit. Royauté et religion en Afrique noire. Essais d'ethnologie comparative*, Paris: Albin Michel.

Adler, A. and Zempleni, A. (1972) *Le bâton de l'aveugle. Divination, maladie et pouvoir chez les Moundang du Tchad*, Paris: Herman.

Augé, M. (1988) *Le dieu objet*, Paris: Flammarion.

——(1992; 1995) *Non-Places: Introduction to an Anthropology of Super-Modernity*, trans. J. Howe, New York: Verso.

——(1994a; 1998) *A Sense for the Other: The Timelines and the Relevance of Anthropology*, trans. A. Jacob, Stanford: Stanford University Press.

——(1994b; 1999) *An Anthropology for the Contemporaneous World*, Stanford: Stanford University Press.

——(2000) *Fictions, fin de siècle. suivi de: Que se passe-t-il? 29 février, 31 mars, 30 avril*, Paris: Fayard.

Augé, M. and Baudrillard, J. (1998) *Diana Crash*, Paris: Descartes et cie.

Augé, M. and Colleyn, J-P. (1990) *N'Kpiti. La rancune et le prophète*, Paris: EHESS.

Augé, M. and Herzlich, C. (eds) (1984; 1996) *The Meaning of Illness: The Anthropology, History and Sociology of Illness*, trans. K. Durnin, London: Routledge.

Augé, M., Revel, J. and Wachtel, N (eds) (1996) *Une école pour les sciences sociales: L'Ecole des hautes études en sciences sociales*, Paris: Le Cerf.

Aurégan, P. (2001) *Des récits et des hommes. Terre Humaine, un autre regard sur les sciences de l'homme*, Paris: Nathan/Plon.

Balandier, G. (1965; 1968) *Daily Life in the Kingdom of the Kongo from the Sixteenth to the Eighteenth Century*, trans. H. Weaver, New York: Pantheon Books.

——(1971) *Sens et puissance. Les dynamiques sociales*, Paris: Presses universitaires de France.

——(1977) *Histoire d'Autres*, Paris: Stock.

——(1985) *Le Détour, pouvoir et modernité*, Paris: Fayard.

——(1988) *Le Désordre. Eloge du mouvement*, Paris: Fayard.

——(1994) *Le Dédale*, Paris: Fayard.

——(1997) *Conjugaisons*, Paris: Fayard.

Baudy, P. (1984) 'L.V. Thomas', *Sociétés*, 1: 34–37.

Baudry, P. and Fougeyrollas, P. 'La mort de L-V. Thomas', *Le Monde*, 25 January 1994.

Bekombo, M. "Celui qui va là-bas, ne parle pas (on E. de Darryiere)", *L'Homme*, 148: 7–14.

Benoist, J., Epelboin, A., Ferry, M-P. and Paulme, D. (1983) *JSA*, 53: 197–203.

Bernot , L. and Bernot, D. (1958), *Les Khyang des collines de Chittagong (Pakistan Oriental). Matériaux pour l'étude linguistique des Chin*, Paris: Mouton.

Bernot, L. and Blancard, R. (1953; 2000) *Nouville, un village français*, Paris: Institut d'ethnologie (reissued with a preface by Lévi-Strauss and a postface by F. Zonabend, by Editions des Archives contemporaines).

Berque, J. (1936) *Les pactes pastoraux Beni Meskine: Contribution à l'étude des contacts nord-africains*, Alger.

——(1949) *Aperçu sur l'histoire de l'Ecole de Fès*, Paris: Sirey.

——(1957) *Histoire sociale d'un village égyptien au XXe siècle*, Paris and The Hague: Mouton.

——(1960; 1964) *The Arabs: Their History and Future*, trans. J. Stewart, New York: Praeger.

——(1964) *Dépossession du monde*, Paris: Le Seuil.

——(1970) *L'Orient second*, Paris: Gallimard.

——(1980) *L'Islam au défi*, Paris: Gallimard.

——(1989) *Mémoires des deux rives*, Paris: Le Seuil.

——(1991) *Le Coran. Traduction exégétique*, Paris: Sindbad.

——(1993) *Il reste un avenir: Entretiens, Jean Suret Jacques Berque*, Paris: Arlea.

——(1995) 'Obituary J. Berque' *Le Monde* (1995) 29 June and 7 July.

Bouchard, D.F. (ed.) (1977) Michel Foucault, *Language, Counter-memory, practice. Selected Essays and Interviews*, New York: Cornell University Press.

Bourdieu, P. (1961) *Sociologie de l'Algérie*, Paris: Presses universitaires de France.

——(1962) *The Algerian*, Boston: Beacon Press.

——(1970) *Zur Soziologie der symbolischen Formen*, Frankfurt-am-Main: Suhrkamp.

——(1972; 1977) *Outline of a Theory of Practice*, trans. R. Nice, Cambridge: Cambridge University Press.

——(1980a; 1993) *Sociology in Question*, trans. R. Nice, London: Thousand Oaks.

——(1980b; 1992) *The Logic of Practice*, trans. R. Nice, Cambridge: Polity Press.

——(1982; 1991) *Ce que parler veut dire. L'économie des échanges linguistiques*, Paris: Fayard.

——(1984; 1988) *Homo Academicus*, trans. P. Collier, Stanford, Stanford University Press.

——(1989; 1996) *The State Nobility: elite schools in the field of power*, trans. C. Clough, Stanford: Stanford University Press.

——(1988; 1991) *The Political Ontology of Martin Heidegger*, trans. P. Collier, Stanford: Stanford University Press.

——(1991) *Language and Symbolic Power*, Cambridge: Polity Press.

——(1994; 1998) *Practical Reason: On the theory of action*, Stanford: Stanford University Press.

——(1997a; 2000) *Pascalian Meditations*, trans. R. Nice, Cambridge: Polity Press.

——(1997b) *Les usages sociaux de la science*, Paris: INRA.

——(1998a; 2001) *Masculine Domination*, trans. R. Nice, Stanford: Stanford University Press.

——(1998b) *Acts of Resistance: Against the new myths of our time*, Cambridge: Polity Press.

——(2000a) *Propos sur le champ politique*, Lyon: Presses universitaires de Lyon.

——(2000b) *Les structures sociales de l'économie*, Paris: Le Seuil.

Bourdieu, P., Boltanski, L., Castel, R. and Chamboredon, J.C. (1964; 1990) *Photography, a middle-brow art*, trans. S. Whiteside, Stanford: Stanford University Press.

Bourdieu, P. and Haacke, H. (1994; 1995), *Free Exchange*, Cambridge: Polity Press.

Bourdieu, P and Passeron, J.C. (1968; 1991) *Le métier de sociologue*, trans. R. Nice, Berlin, New York: Walter de Gruyter.

Bourdieu, P., Rivet, J.P. and Seibel, C. (1963) *Travail et travailleurs en Algérie*, Paris: Mouton.

Bourdieu, P. and Sayad, A. (1964), *Le déracinement* Paris: Minuit.

Bourdieu, P. and Wacquant, L.J.D. (1992) *Réponses. Pour une anthropologie réflexive*, Paris: Le Seuil.

Calame-Griaule, G. (1958) *Le Lièvre et le tambour, fable Dogon*, Paris: Présence africaine.

——(ed.) (1977) *Langage et cultures africaines: Essais d'ethnolinguistique*, Paris: Maspéro.

——(1987) *Des cauris au marché. Essai sur des contes africains*, Paris: Société des africanistes.

——(1989) *Graine de Parole. Puissance du verbe et traditions orales. Textes offerts à G. Calame-Griaule*, Paris: CNRS.

Cartry, M. (1978) 'Pierre Clastres', tribute publication as part of *Annuaire de la Ve section de l'Ecole des Hautes Etudes*, vol.85, and *Libre* 4: 55.

Champion, B. *L'Etranger intime. Mélanges offerts à Paul Ottino, Madagascar, Tahiti, Insulinde, Monde Swahili, Comores, Réunion.* Paris.

Chiva, I. (1958) *Rural Communities: Problems, Methods and Types of Research*, Paris: UNESCO.

——(1994) *Une politique pour le patrimoine*, report to J. Toubon, Minister for Culture and the French-speaking world (la francophonie).

Chiva, I. and Goy, J. (eds) (1981–1985) *Les Baronnies des Pyrénéens. Anthropologie et histoire, permanences et changements*, Paris: EHESS, 2 vols.

Chiva, I. and Jeggle, U. (eds) (1987) *Ethnologie en miroir. La France et les pays de langue allemande*, Paris: EMSH.

Chiva, I. and Rambaud, P. (eds) (1972) *Les Études rurales en France: tendances et organisation de la recherche*, Paris: Mouton

Clastres, P. (1974) Le Grand Parler: Mythes et chants sacrés des indiens Guarani, Paris: Le Seuil.

——(1992) *Mythologie des indiens Chulupi*, Louvain and Paris: Peeters.

Collective, (1990) *Pour J. Malaurie. 102 témoignages en hommage à quarante ans d'études arctiques*, Paris: Plon.

——(1989) *Singularités. Les voies d'émergence individuelle. Textes pour Éric de Dampierre, présentés par le laboratoire d'ethnologie et de sociologie comparative*, Paris: Plon.

Condominas, G. (1960) *Fokon'olona et collectivités rurales en Imerina*, Paris: Berger-Levrault.

——(1965) *L'Exotique est quotidien, Sar Luk, Vietnam Central*, Paris: Plon.

——(1978) *L'Espace social, à propos de l'Asie du sud-est*, Paris: Flammarion.

Cresswell, R. (ed.) (1975) *Eléments d'ethnologie*, Paris, Armand Colin, 2 vols.

——(1998) *Prométhée ou Pandore? Propos de technologie culturelle*, Paris: Kimé.

Cresswell, R and Godelier, M. (eds) (1976,) *Outils d'enquête et d'analyse anthropologiques*, Paris: Maspéro

Cuisenier, J. (1979) *Récits et contes populaires de Normandie*, Paris: Gallimard.

——(1990) *Ethnologie de l'Europe*, Paris: Presses universitaires de France.

——(1996) *Le Feu vivant et ses rituels dans les Carpates*, Paris: Presses universitaires de France.

Cuisenier, J., Raulin, H. *et al.* (eds) (1979) *Les Sources régionales de la Savoie: une approche ethnologique*, Paris: Fayard.

Cuisenier, J. and Ségalen, M. (1987) *Ethnologie de la France*, Paris: Presses universitaires de France.

Dawod, H. (1999) 'M. Godelier, introspection, rétrospection, projections. Un entretien', *Gradhiva*, 26: 1–25.

De Dampierre, E. (1948) 'Juin 1948. De l'enthousiasme à la déception et au massacre' in *La révolution prolétarienne*, XVII: 508–1912.

——(1963) *Poètes nzakara*, Paris: Juillard.

——(1967) *Un ancien royaume Bandia du Haut-Oubangui*, Paris: Plon.

De Garine, I. and Harrison, G.A. (eds) (1988) *Coping with Uncertainty in Food Supply*, Oxford: Clarendon.

——(1994) 'Diet and nutrition in human populations', in T. Ingold (ed.), *Companion Encyclopedia of Anthropology*, London: Routledge, pp.226–265.

Desanti, J-T. 'R. Jaulin. Un ethnologue engagé', *Le Monde* 26 November 1996, p.12.

Dobyns, H., Holmberg, A.R., Opler, M.R., and Sharp, L. (1967) *Strategic Intervention in the Cultural Change Process*, Ithaca.

Erny, P. and Stamm, A. (eds) (1996) *Mort et vie. Hommages au professeur D. Zahan*, Paris: L'Harmattan.

Fabre, D. (1997) 'L'ethnologie française à la croisée des engagements 1940–1945', *in* J. Y. Boursier, *Résistants et Résistance*, Paris: L'Harmattan.

Gaillard, G. (1988a) *Elements pour servir à la constitution d'une histoire de l'ethnologie française de ces trente dernières années*, (thesis) Paris: EHESS.

——(1988b) 'Le Centre d'études africaines, Cl. Meillassoux', chap.11 and 12 in *Images d'une génération. Eléments pour servir à la constitution d'une histoire de l'anthropologie française de ces trente dernières années*, (thesis) Paris: EHESS.

——(1989) 'Chronique de la recherche ethnologique dans son rapport au Centre national de la recherche scientifique 1925–1980', *Cahiers pour l'histoire du CNRS*, no.3: 85–127.

——(1990) *Répertoire de l'anthropologie française 1950–1970*, Paris: CNRS, 2 vols.

Gauchet, M. (1977) 'P. Clastres' *Libération* 10 and 11 October, and *Libre*, 4: 55–68.

——(1978) 'Une pensée contre l'état: hommage à Pierre Clastres', *Autogestion et socialisme*, 40.

Godelier, M. (1966a) *La notion de mode de production asiatique et les schémas marxistes d'évolution des sociétés*, Paris: Cerm.

——(1966; 1980) *Rationality and Irrationality in Economics*, trans. Brian Pearce, London: NLB.

——(1973; 1977) *Perspectives in Marxist Anthropology*, Cambridge: Cambridge University Press.

——(ed.) (1974) *Un domaine contesté: l'anthropologie économique*, Paris, Mouton.

——(1977) 'Anthropologie, histoire, idéologie. Entretien avec C. Lévi-Strauss, Maurice Godelier et M. Augé', in *Critique of Anthropology*, 2(6): 44–55.

——(1982a; 1986) *The Making of the Great Men: Male Domination and Power among, the New Guinea Baruya*, Cambridge: Cambridge University Press.

——(1982b), *Les Sciences de l'homme et de la société. Analyse et propositions pour une politique nouvelle*, Paris: la Documentation française, 2 vols.

——(1984; 1988) *The Mental and the Material Thought: Thought, economy and society*, trans. M. Thorn, London, New York: Verso.

——(1998) 'Entretien avec M. Godelier par N. Journet', *Sciences Humaines*, 'Un musée pour les cultures', no.23.

——(ed.) (1991) *Transitions et subordinations au capitalisme*, Paris: Msh.

——(1993) 'A propos de l'incidence du sexe dans la pratique de terrain', *Journal des anthropologues*, no.52: 63–75.

——(1993) 'De la philosophie à l'anthropologie. Entretien avec M. Godelier', *Société française*, no.44: 59–64.

——(1996; 1999) *The Enigma of the Gift*, Chicago: University of Chicago Press.

——(1999) 'Introspection, rétrospections, projections', in P. Descola, J. Hamel and P. Lemonnier (eds) *La production du social*, Colloque de Cerisy, Paris: Fayard.

Godelier, M. and Bettelheim, C.H. (eds) (1963) *Choix et efficience des investissements*, Paris: Mouton.

Godelier, M. and Bonte, P. (eds) (1976) *Le problème des formes et des fondements de la domination masculine: deux exemples, les Baruya de Nouvelle-Guinée, les Bahima d'Ankole*, Paris: Cerm.

Godelier, M., Copans, J., Torney, S. and Bakes, C. (eds) (1971) *L'Anthropologie, sciences des sociétés primitives?*, Paris: Denoël.

Godelier, M. and Cresswell, R. (eds) (1976) *Outils d'enquête et d'analyse anthropologique*, Paris: Maspero.

Godelier, M. and Hassoun, J. (eds) (1996) *Meurtre du père, sacrifice de la sexualité: approches anthropologiques et psychanalytique*, Paris: Arcanes.

Godelier, M. and Panoff, M. (eds) (1998a) *La production du corps*, Paris: Archives contemporaines.

——(eds) (1998b) *Le corps human, supplicié, possédé, canibalisé*, Paris: Archives contemporaines.

Godelier, M. and Strathern, M. (eds) (1991) *Big Men and Great Men: Personification of Power in Melanesia*, Cambridge University Press.

Godelier, M., Trautmann T. and Tjon Sie Fat, F. (eds) (1998) *Transformation of Kinship Systems*, Smithsonian Institution.

Gordon, C. (1980) Michel Foucault, *Power, Knowledge: Selected interviews and other writings 1972–1977*, New York: Pantheon.

Guiart, J. (1956a) *Un siècle et demi de contacts culturels à Tanna*, Paris: ORSTOM.

——(1956b) *Contes et légendes de la grande terre*, Nouméa.

——(1963a) *Les religions de l'Océanie*, Paris: Presses universitaires de France.

——(1963b) *L'Océanie*, Paris: Gallimard.

——(1966) *Mythologie du masque en Nouvelle-Calédonie*, Paris: Société des Océanistes.

Guiart, J., Espirat, J., Lagrange, M-S. and Renaud, M. (1973) *Système des titres, électifs ou héréditaires, dans les Nouvelles-Hébrides centrales, d'Efate aux îles Shepherds*, Paris: Institut d'ethnologie.

——(1983) *La terre est le sang des morts, la confrontation entre Blancs et Noirs dans le Pacifique Sud français*, Paris: Anthropos.

Habart, M (1984) 'Michel Foucault and anthropology: a murderous fascination', *RAIN*, 65: 4–5.

Héritier, F. (1983) *Leçon inaugurale*, Paris: Collège de France.

——(1994a) *Masculin/féminin. La pensée de la différence*, Paris: Odile Jacob.

——(1994b; 1999) *Two Sisters and their Mother: The Anthropology of Incest*, trans. J. Herman, New York: Zone Books.

——(ed) (1996) *De la violence*, vol.1 Paris: O. Jacob.

——(ed) (1999) *De la violence*, vol.2, Paris: O. Jacob.

Héritier, F. and Copet-Rougier, E. (eds) (1990) *Les complexités de l'alliance, vol.1: Les systèmes semi-complexes*, Paris: Archives contemporaines.

——(1991) *Les complexités de l'alliance, vol.2: Les systèmes complexes d'alliance matrimoniale*, Paris: Archives contemporaines.

——(1992) *Les complexités de l'alliance, vol.3: Economie politique et fondements symboliques (Afrique)*, Paris: Archives contemporaine.

——(eds) (1994) *Les complexités de l'alliance, vol.4: Economie, politique et fondements symboliques*, Paris: Archives contemporaine.

Izard, M. (1970) *Introduction à l'histoire des royaumes mossi*, 2 vols, Ougadougou: Recherches Voltaïques.

——(1985) *Gens du pouvoir, gens de la terre. Les institutions politiques de l'ancien royaume du Yatenga*, Paris: MSH

Izard, M. and Smith, P. (eds) (1979) *La fonction symbolique. Essais d'anthropologie*, Paris: Gallimard.

Jaulin, R. (1965a) *La mort Sara*, Paris: Plon.

——(1965b) *La géomancie, essai d'analyse formelle*, Paris and The Hague: Mouton.

——(1966) 'La maison bari', *Journal de la Société des Américanistes*, 55: 111–153.

——(1970) *La paix blanche*, Paris: Le Seuil.

——(1974) *Gens de soi, gens de l'autre*, Paris: UGE, 10/18.

——(1977) *Les chemins du vide*, Paris: Bourgois.

——(1979) *Jeux et jouets, essai d'ethnotechnologie*, Paris: Aubier.

——(1995) *L'Univers des totalitarismes*, Paris.

Jaulin, R. and Richard, R. (eds) (1972) *Anthropologie et calcul*, Paris: UGE, 10/18.

Kuper, A. (1999) *Culture: The Anthropologists' Account*, Cambridge, MA and London: Harvard University Press.

Lefort, C. (1978) 'Pierre Clastres', *Encyclopaedia universalis*, and *Libre*, 4: 50–54.

Malaurie, J. (1999) *Hummocks: relief de mémoire*, 2 vols. Paris: Plon.

Meillassoux, C. (1975a; 1981) *Maidens, Meals and Money: Capitalism and the Domestic Community*, Cambridge: Cambridge University Press.

——(ed.) (1975b) *L'esclavage en Afrique précoloniale*, Paris: Maspéro.

——(1977) *Terrain et théories*, (collection of articles), Paris: Anthropos.

——(1979) *Les derniers blancs, le modèle sud-africain*, Paris: Maspéro.

——(ed.) (1988) *Verrouillage ethnique en Afrique du Sud*, Paris: UNESCO.

——(2001) *Mythes et limites de l'anthropologie. Le sang et les mots*, Lausanne.

Meillassoux, C., Doucoure, L. and Simagha, D. (1967) *Légende de la dispersion des Kusa (épopée Soninké)*, Dakar: IFAN.

Meillassoux, C. and Messiant, C. (1991), *Génie social et manipulation culturelle en Afrique de l'apartheid*, Paris, Arcantère.

Mendras, H. (1998) 'E. de Dampierre' and M. Bekombo, 'Celui qui va là-bas, ne parle pas', *L'Homme*, no.148: 7–14.

Nuit (de la Sibérie au Groènland) (7 films, Antenne 2, 1980).

Ortigues E. (1954) *Le Temps de la parole*, Paris: Delachaux et Niestlé.

——(1962) *Le Discours et le symbole*, Paris: Aubier.

Ortigues E. and Ortigues, M-C. (1986) *Comment se décide une psychothérapie d'enfant?*, Paris: Denoël (reissued in 1993).

Ottino, P. (1965) *Ethno-histoire de Rangiroa (archipel des Tuamotu)*, Papeete: ORSTOM.

——(1972) *Rangiroa: Parenté étendue, résidence et terres dans un atoll polynésien*, Paris: Cujas.

——(1986) *L'étrangère intime: Essai d'anthropologie de civilisation de l'ancien Madagascar*, Paris: Editions des Archives contemporaines, 2 vols.

——(1996) *Les champs de l'ancestralité, parenté, alliances et patrimoine à Madagascar*, Paris: Karthala.

Ottino, P., Bonneau, P.H. and Tatard, J.C. (1977) *La promotion du milieu rural réunionnais,* Saint Denis: Service de l'Agriculture.

Panoff, M. (1977) 'Cl. Meillassoux et le mode de production domestique' *La Revue française de sociologie,* 18(1).

Retel, A. (1960) *Le niveau de santé au Sénégal. Perspectives de développement des services sanitaires. Etude statistique de l'état nutritionnel et sanitaire de 10140 enfants de 0 à 14 ans.* Dakar: Ministère de la santé.

——(1974a) *Sorcellerie et ordalies. L'épreuve du poison en Afrique Noire. Essai sur le concept de négritude,* Paris: Anthropos.

——(1974b) *Infécondité en Afrique Noire. Maladies et conséquence sociales,* Paris: Masson.

——(1975) *Infécondité et maladies. Les Nzakara de République Centrafricaine,* INSEE.

——(1979) *Un pays à la dérive. Histoire et évolution sociale d'une population en régression démographique,* Paris: J-P. Delage.

Rouch, J. (1954) *Les Songhay,* Paris: Presses universitaires de France.

——(1960) *La Religion et la magie Songhay,* Paris: Presses universitaires de France, (reissued by Univeristy of Brussels in 1989).

——(1979) 'Le renard fou et le maître pâle' in *Systèmes de signes: Textes réunis en hommage à G. Dieterlen,* Paris: Herman.

Schlemmer, B. (ed.) (1989) *Sur les terrains de C. Meillassoux,* Paris: l'Harmattan.

Schneider, D. as told to Handler, R. (1995) *Schneider on Schneider: The Conversion of the Jews and other Anthropological Stories,* Durham: Duke University Press.

Tardits, C. (1958) *Porto-Novo, les nouvelles générations africaines entre leurs traditions et l'Occident,* Paris: Mouton.

——(1960) *Les Bamiléké de l'Ouest Cameroun,* Paris: Berger-Levrault.

——(1980) *Le Royaume Bamoun,* Paris: Armand Colin.

——(1981) *Contribution de la recherche ethnologique à l'histoire des civilisations du Cameroun,* Paris: CNRS, 2 vols.

Tardits, C., Adam, P. and Clerc, J. (1956) *Société paysanne et problèmes fonciers de la palmeraie dahoméenne,* ORSTOM.

Terray, E. (1989) 'Une nouvelle anthropologie politique', *L'Homme,* 110: 5–29.

——(1990) *La Politique dans la caverne,* Paris: Le Seuil.

——(1992) *Le troisième jour du communisme,* Paris: Actes Sud.

——(1994) *Une passion allemande,* Paris: le Seuil.

——(1996) *Ombres berlinoises. Voyage dans une autre Allemagne,* Paris: Odile Jacob.

——(1999) *Clausewitz,* Paris: Fayard.

Terray, E. and Bazin, J. (eds) (1982) *Guerres de lignages et guerres d'Etats en Afrique,* Paris: Les Archives contemporaines.

Thomas, L-V. (1974) *Civilisation et divagation,* Paris: Payot.

——(1984) *Fantasme au quotidien,* Paris: le Méridien.

Thomas, L-V. and Luneau, R. (1975) *La terre africaine et ses religions,* Paris: Larousse, (reissued by l'Harmattan in 1980).

——(1977) *Les sages dépossédés,* Paris: Laffont.

Zahan, D. (1969) *La viande et la graine, mythologie Dogon,* Paris: Présence africaine.

——(1970; 1979) *The Religion, Spirituality, and Thought of Traditional Africa,* trans. K. and L. Martin, Chicago: University of Chicago Press.

——(1995) *Le feu en Afrique,* Paris: l'Harmattan.

XIII
The American schools
Third and fourth generations

Before charting the evolution of the major institutions and currents of anthropology in the USA following the Second World War, it needs to be said that the American university scene was transformed by the passing of the GI Bill, which provided study bursaries for demobilized GIs. Kissinger took advantage of this to study anthropology, as did **Geertz**, **Wolf**, **Murphy**, Milton Barnett (1916–1994), Robert Manners (1913–1996), and many more. The GI Bill caused a sudden inflation in student numbers and opened up prestigious universities to those from modest social backgrounds. As **Schneider** writes: 'with the GI Bill of Rights a large number of people came into the academic system who would not have been able to get in earlier' (Schneider, 1995: 198). Geertz said that 'without the GI Bill [I] probably wouldn't have gone to college at all' (quoted by **Kuper**, 1999: 76). A fuller testimony is provided by Murphy:

'I arrived on the campus [of Columbia College] seven months after being discharged from the Navy [. . .] Higher education had always been an ultimate aspiration but a financial impossibility for me – and for millions of other products of the Depression. The GI Bill opened college education to us, and we entered the universities like a horde of barbarians. For the first time in the history of this country, higher education became available to the excluded, the unwashed, the outsiders, the undesirables. College was not longer a middle class monopoly, and with this breaching of class barriers, ethnic and racial walls also began to crumble. Out of this came the most remarkable spurt of class mobility ever experienced anywhere [. . .]. As for anthropology, the first time I ever heard of the subject was in 1947, when I asked a friend to recommend a course that would be easy yet interesting'
(Murphy, *The Body Silent*, London: Dent, 1987, pp. 129–30).

Several universities had introduced courses in anthropology in the inter-war years, such as Wisconsin, where **Linton** taught from 1928 to 1937, and Michigan, where **Steward** taught from 1928 and was succeeded by **White** in 1930. However, it was not until after 1946 that anthropology was systematically expanded. Charting the growth of the discipline at such universities as Pennsylvania, Texas, Philadelphia, Arizona, CUNY, Florida, Indiana, Johns Hopkins, Stanford and UCLA would easily fill another book, and so I shall restrict myself to the departments at Columbia, Harvard, Chicago and Yale.

Boas retired in 1936, although he continued to teach at Columbia after this date. His vacant chair was divided into three parts, filled by the archaeologist W. D. Strong, the Americanist A. Lesser, and R. Linton, who came from the University of Wisconsin to head the department. The teaching staff also included **Benedict**, while **Kardiner** and **Du Bois** participated in some of the seminars. Notable students at Columbia before and during the war included J. **Greenberg**, M. **Opler** (Ph.D. 1938), O. **Lewis** (Ph.D. 1940), I. Goldman (Ph.D. 1941) and C. **Wagley** (Ph.D. 1941). When Linton left Columbia in 1946 he was replaced by Steward, who headed the department until 1952 and taught on Latin America and cultural dynamism. **Mead** joined the department in 1947, but was not made a professor until 1954. Benedict died in 1948 and Lesser withdrew from academia between 1950 and 1960. W. D. Strong was responsible for teaching in archaeology until his death in 1962, while linguistics was taught by G. Herzog and Asiatic cultures by M. Smith. Charles Wagley taught social organization as of 1946, **Service** was employed in the department from 1949 to 1953, and **Arensberg**, who had been an associate professor at Barnard College from 1946 to 1952, was recruited in 1953. From 1940 Steward was mainly occupied with editing the *Handbook of South American Indians*, which had been initiated by **Lowie**, **Cooper** and **Spier** in 1932, and which bulked large among the anthropological projects of the post-war years. Within the Bureau of American Ethnology at the Smithsonian Institution, Steward in 1943 founded the Institute for Social Anthropology, which sent professional scholars and students into the field in Colombia, Mexico, Peru and Brazil. He also directed the 'Puerto Rico Project', which was undertaken in 1946–1947 and provided a context for the maiden fieldwork expeditions of Wolf, **Mintz**, Elena Padilla, Raymond Scheele and R. Manners. The fruits of their research were gathered together in 1956 in *People of Puerto Rico*, one of the earliest attempts to describe a modern nation from an anthropological perspective. These young anthropologists also studied the cultural transformations taking place in various Latin American countries, and made a profound impact on the anthropology practised in those countries through their collaboration with local institutions.

During the 1960s there were considerable changes of personnel in the Columbia department. **Harris**, who had taught there from 1959, became a professor and replaced Wagley as departmental head from 1963 to 1966. His successors were Morton **Fried** in 1968 and Robert Murphy in 1972, the latter having moved to Columbia from the University of California in 1963. Andrew Vayda and Elliott Skinner also became professors, and they were joined by, among others, Alexander Alland and Joan Vincent, who became an assistant professor in 1968.

The Harvard anthropology department was headed by R. B. **Dixon** and then, from 1927 to 1948, by Carleton S. Coon, who advocated an anthropology concerned more with questions of evolution, particularly physical evolution, than with social structure. C. **Kluckhohn** contributed his culturalist form of anthropology when he became a member of the teaching staff in 1936. He was joined after the war by Cora Du Bois (1947–1970), by the Pacific islands specialist and ethnohistorian Douglas L. Oliver (1948–1973), and by Evon Z. Vogt, an expert on contemporary Maya societies. Kluckhohn was close to Parsons in the 1930s (Kuper notes 'his name as one of the scholars who read and commented on the manuscript of *The Structure of Social Action*' (Kuper, 1999: 54)), and he became associated with Parsons' plan to create an interdisciplinary department of social sciences. This department was established in 1946 thanks to Parsons' efforts, bringing together anthropology, clinical psychology, social psychology and sociology. Students in the new department, who included Geertz, Schneider and **Fox**, followed courses in all of these disciplines, but specialized in only one of them. Sociology focused on social structure, on laws and norms, while anthropology looked at extended culture as a 'set of symbols and meanings'. From 1949 to 1955 Kluckhohn directed a project in New Mexico entitled 'Comparative Study of Values in Five Cultures', which aimed to demonstrate how everyday life is organized by values. At the same time, 'there was the idea that the time had come for anthropology to turn away from its nearly exclusive focus on primitives and begin to investigate large-scale societies directly in the stream of contemporary history' (Geertz, *After the Fact*, 1995: 103). Several programmes reflecting this thinking were established at other universities. At Cornell a department of sociology and anthropology was created in 1940 by L. H. Cottrell, R. Lauriston Sharp (1907–1993) and A. H. Leighton, and in 1946 they obtained funding from the Carnegie Foundation for a comparative study of cultural change in communities in five locations: Bang Chan in Thailand, Senapur in India, Nova Scotia in Canada, the Navajo reserves in the USA, and lastly Vicos in Peru, on which Allan Holmberg of Cornell was already leading a project. This research programme, which was named 'Culture and Applied Social Science', won for the previously almost non-existent Cornell department an international reputation on questions of applied anthropology and cultural change (see Dobyns *et al.* 1967). M. E. Opler joined the department in 1948.

When Linton left Columbia for Yale in 1946, his new colleagues were C. Osgood, G. P. **Murdock**, C. S. Ford, W. C. Bennett, Irving Rouse, John Embree, and Paul Fejos, and in 1950 they were joined by S. Mintz and F. **Loundsbury**. Murdock had succeeded **Sapir** in 1936, and with the assistance of C. S. Ford worked on establishing the Human Relations Area Files (HRAF), which today contain more than one million indexed pages. He also encouraged the cross-cultural study of human culture, society and behaviour, which led to the founding of a scientific anthropology free of subjectivism. Through the connections he built up in the US Navy during and after the Second World War, Murdock was able to secure the establishment of the Coordinated Investigation of Micronesian Anthropology (CIMA), with himself as director. The project drew on the work of twenty-one institutions and forty-two researchers, including Schneider, **Goodenough**, Bernett, and Emory, and allowed American anthropology of the Pacific to make great forward strides. From 1949 the HRAF was an inter-university project, initially involving the universities of Yale, Harvard, Pennsylvania, Oklahoma and Washington, and later including about twenty institutions, including the University of Vienna and the *Collège de France*. The material gathered formed the basis of several books, and the Files appeared to hold out the hope of a positivist anthropology. However, by the mid-1960s this hope seemed lost, and meanwhile in 1956 Goodenough and Loundsbury proposed a new, 'rigorously scientific' approach called componential analysis. The fruits of this did not live up to expectations, but it did pave the way for the cognitivist ethnoscience championed first by the Yale scholar H. **Conklin** and later by **Kay** and **Andrade**. Colleagues of Conklin at Yale during this period included Irving Rouse (Ph.D., Yale 1938) and L. J. Pospisil (Ph.D., Yale 1956).

Important figures at Chicago in 1946 included the linguist McQuown, the physical anthropologists S. Washburn and A. Dahlberg, and the archaeologist R. Braidwood. The social anthropologists at Chicago were **Tax**, **Eggan**, **Redfield** and **Warner**, the last-named a convinced Radcliffe-Brownian whose post straddled the anthropology and sociology departments. In 1950 Redfield launched the 'Program in Intercultural Studies' and Eggan launched the 'Philippine Studies Program', while Tax initiated both the 'Fox Project' on the Fox Indians and 'Action Anthropology', which culminated in a meeting of representatives from ninety tribes (see N. Oestreich Lurie, 'Voice of the American Indian', *CA*, vol.2 (1961): 478–500). Also at Chicago, the sociologist Edward Shills put anthropologists in his debt by setting up the 'Committee for the Comparative Study of New Nations', whose members included L. Fallers and C. Geertz. Furthermore, Tax created the new international journal *Current Anthropology* in 1959 at the request of the Wenner–Gren Foundation. During this period the Chicago department recruited Milton Singer (1912–1994) and then Manning

Nash, and in 1959 Eggan engineered the mass defection of Schneider, Lloyd Fallers and Geertz from Berkeley (where E. Wolf taught for a while), while Sherwood Washburn made the opposite transition. The social anthropologists reached an understanding with the physical anthropologists and archaeologists that two courses would be offered in parallel. The typically Parsonian programme designed by the social anthropologists entailed social, cultural and psychological studies. Of those who joined the Chicago department in the years that followed, mention should be made of Nur Yalman, Mel Spiro, Fogelson, G.W. **Stocking**, S. Tambiah, Terry and Victor **Turner**, and Jean and John Comaroff.

As for the department at the University of California at Berkeley, neither **Kroeber** nor Lowie, who retired in 1946 and 1950 respectively, had been able or willing to expand the discipline in the post-war years, though both men remained active in retirement. As Eggan writes, 'By the time of the Wenner–Gren symposium "Anthropology Today" in 1952 it was apparent that ethnology in its traditional sense was rapidly losing ground' (Eggan, *One Hundred Years of Anthropology*, 1968: 141). Kroeber, the organizer of what was doubtless the most important symposium in the discipline, was obviously a part of this traditional anthropology. Despite containing such figures as D. Mandelbaum, J. Howland Rowe, Ann Gayton, T. McCown and R. F. Heizer, as well as numerous visiting academics such as D. **Forde** and M. **Herskovits**, the Berkeley department continued to decline. Kroeber perceived this and resolved to reconstruct the department with the help of Kluckhohn, and he secured the services of Schneider in 1955, followed later by Geertz and Fallers. Schneider recollects: 'the department was really screwed up. Two of my colleagues had gotten into a furious fight. One was failing all of the other's students. The other guy retaliated by failing all of the first guy's students (. . .) no cooperation of any kind. There was another guy who used to check if everyone was in his office by nine o'clock (. . .) It was an awful place!' (Schneider, 1995: 30–33). He explained his departure to Kroeber: 'It's a split department, they're fighting with each other, they hate each other' (Schneider, 1995: 171). I have said that Schneider, Geertz and Fallers all left Berkeley in 1958–1959 to join the University of Chicago.

Turning now to currents of ideas: post-war American anthropology was characterized by a debate setting the neo-evolutionism of White (1945, 1947) against the anti-evolutionism of Lowie (1946, 1946). White and Steward contributed a strain of thinking both evolutionist and universalist, and although not household names they attracted a large following among young anthropologists who preferred their methods to the cultural relativism of Mead and Benedict. Steward taught at Columbia from 1946 to 1952, and a number of his students there founded the facetiously named Mundial Upheaval Society, whose members included E. Wolf, S. Mintz E. R. Service, S. **Diamond**, D. McCall and R. Manners. As Mintz has explained to me, the Society met to discuss Marxism and new trends in anthropology. A few years later Wolf, Mintz, Diamond and Manners would be working from a Marxist perspective, while Service, together with M. **Sahlins**, R. Rappaport and M. Harris, continued with the evolutionist approaches first developed by White and Steward and edited *Evolution and Culture* (Michigan UP, 1960). This periodical, the manifesto of the neo-evolutionist school, submits that culture prolongs the process of evolution, and that within this process specific, local and adaptive histories must be distinguished from the broad and slow evolution of humanity as a whole, which is objectively measurable by levels of energy consumption. In the mid-1960s this generation of scholars wrote a series of introductions to the discipline which immediately became core student texts, such as E. Wolf's *Anthropology* (Princeton UP, 1964) and *Peasants* (New Jersey: Eaglewood Cliffs, 1966), E. R. Service's *The Hunters*

(New Jersey: Englewood Cliffs, 1966), and M. Sahlins's *Tribesmen* (New Jersey: Englewood Cliffs, 1968). In the view of some, neo-evolutionism was taking the form of a 'cultural materialism', with M. Harris becoming its spokesman in 1967–1968, and encompassing such scholars as R. **Carneiro**, M. Harner and M. Fried. By associating systems of thought with ecosystems through the intermediary of adaptive modes, they pushed the idea of ecological determinism to its logical extreme. At the same time a Marxist approach (and spirit) was gaining ground, often allied with feminism and finding expression in the writings of E. Wolf, S. Diamond, E. **Leacock**, Louise Lamphere, M. Zimbalist **Rosaldo**, R. Rapp and W. Roseberry. This orientation was represented in two journals: *Critique of Anthropology*, edited in London by B. Scholte; and *Dialectical Anthropology*, edited by S. Diamond, who in 1970 also founded a new department of anthropology at the New School of Social Research in New York.

Other than in the worst days of McCarthyism and during the Korean War, Americans in the years from 1945 to 1960 were convinced that they were leading the way to a better world. They successively financed the reconstruction of Europe, pushed for the independence of African and Asian colonies, disseminated a new popular culture which focused on contentment and/in consumption. It was generally accepted that the social sciences had the technical role of helping to define and explain what stood in the way of this wonderful programme.

The assassination in 1963 of J. F. Kennedy, who had promised a new America; the long struggle for racial equality during the 1960s; the protests against the war in Vietnam, in which the USA became directly engaged in 1962 (with intensive bombardments beginning in 1963–1964): all these contributed to a new mood. University campuses rose up against an America perceived as oppressive and imperialist. Glenn Miller was superseded by Jimmy Hendrix. In search of values different from those on offer in their own society, many young Americans were drawn to a discipline which opened a window to another world: anthropology. University departments grew rapidly and even the smallest colleges began to teach the subject.

The republication of large numbers of major anthropological texts during this period testifies to the role played by purely academic work in this dynamism. A collection called 'American Museum Sourcebooks in Anthropology' was launched, and in 1967 it produced no less than six large volumes, including *Law and Welfare, Gods and Rituals, Comparative Political Systems*, and *Personalities and Cultures*. Another series, entitled *Peoples and Cultures* (of the Pacific, of the Middle East, etc.), was initiated in 1968 and described populations by culture area in an easily accessible way. Finally, the series 'Case Studies in Cultural Anthropology', created by George and Louise Spinder, contained small, previously unpublished monographs.

And yet the purely intellectual aspect of this new sensibility was accompanied by a desire to break with existing scholarly traditions. In 1966, in the middle of the Vietnam War, Wolf published a work on the peasant wars of the twentieth century in which they were glorified as struggles against imperialism. In 1967 Horowitz edited 'The Rise and Fall of Project Camelot' (MIT Press), which denounced the collusion between American social science and this same imperialism. More radical still was Kathleen Gough's call for a new anthropology in 'Anthropology, Child of Imperialism' (*Monthly Review*, 19 (1968): 12–27). In 1969 the linguist Dell Hymes, who five years before had edited a very traditional collection of texts in *Language, Culture and Society* (Harper and Row), set a milestone in this development towards radicalism as the editor of *Reinventing Anthropology* (Random House).

With the end of direct American engagement in Vietnam in 1973, followed by the flight of the Boat People and the massacres which disfigured the new state of Cambodia in 1976, the dream of a new world was crushed, and revolutionary discourse fell silent. Traditional monographs no longer held much interest, analyses of 'culture changes' became routinized and funds became scarce, as reported on the front pages of *Anthropology Newsletter* ('Reagan Cuts Hit Social Sciences Hard', *AN*, vol.22/3 (1981)).

It was while anthropology was thus on the back foot that sociobiology made its appearance. Its founder was the ethologist E. O. Wilson, who proposed that social and biological data be considered together because human customs and cultural practices are adaptive in a Darwinian sense. R. Fox, N. Chagnon and A. Alexander were among the best-known advocates of this current of thought. In the same period the hitherto rather neglected area of ethnomedicine, now renamed medical anthropology, gained autonomous status thanks to the seminal works of John Janzen (*The Quest for Therapy*, California UP, 1978) and Arthur Kleinmann (*Patients and Healers in the Concept of Culture*, California UP, 1980). Many scholars moved into this field in an effort secure new funding.

In the early 1980s a new 'interpretive' school followed on from two developments in the previous decade: a series of books which stressed the importance of the anthropologist's own presence in his work, from the very fine *Never in Anger* by J. L. Briggs (Harvard UP, 1970) to J.-P. Dumont's *The Headman and I* (1978); and the critical reflections of such works as E. Said's *Orientalism* (1978). The early members of this new school were J. Clifford, P. Rabinow and G. Marcus, and they were later joined by Stephen Tyler, Vincent Crapanzano, Bernard Cohn, Renato Rosaldo and others. These thinkers, sometimes called 'post-modern', had imbibed the ideas of the French philosophers M. **Foucault** and J. Derrida and sought to deconstruct the ethnographic narrative, to refute all totalizing systems and claims to scientific validity, and to consign ethnology to the status of one fiction among others. In this view the ethnographic text reflects the position of the ethnographer imprisoned by the subjectivity of his experiences. The grand narratives and total systems must be replaced by polyphony and dialogue. Two books in particular are manifestos of this school: G. Marcus and J. Fischer, eds, *Anthropology as Cultural Critique: An Experimental Moment in the Human Sciences* (Chicago, 1986); and above all G. Marcus and J. Clifford, eds, *Writing Culture: The Poetics and Politics of Ethnography* (Berkeley: California UP, 1986).

Finally, to bring the account of intellectual currents up to date, the process of globalization has generated a considerable amount of new thinking in anthropological circles from the 1990s onwards, which can be found in the works of Appadurai, Phillips, Steiner and others.

Alongside those already mentioned, whose consideration in terms of schools is not intended to minimize the individual style and character of each author's work, researchers with entries below include those pursuing ideas and methods discussed in earlier chapters (such as **Bohannan** with substantivism), and those whose work is difficult to classify. Deciding who should have an entry in this chapter has been very difficult, and some important figures I should have liked to include are omitted: among others L. Lamphere, M. J. Meggitt, R. B. Lee, D. Hymes, I. Devore, D. Mandelbaum, R. Rappaport, R. d'Andrade, B. Scholte, C. G. Homans, E. Colson, B. Berlin, W. Roseberry and P. Riesman.

Loundsbury, Floyd Glenn (1914–1998)
Born at Steven Point, Wisconsin, Floyd Glenn Loundsbury gained a BA in mathematics in 1941. His studies were inter-

rupted by the Second World War, and from 1942 to 1946 he was posted by the Air Force to Brazil as a meteorologist. After his demobilization he obtained an MA in anthropology from the University of Wisconsin in 1946, and then enrolled at Yale University, where he was awarded a Ph.D. in 1949 for a thesis on the phonology and morphology of the language of the Oneida, a population he had become acquainted with during his war service. He then became an assistant professor at Yale, where he worked until his retirement in 1979. From 1946 onwards, Loundsbury considered himself as much a linguist as an anthropologist, and founded comparative Iroquois linguistics. He later took an interest in Maya pictograms and astronomy, and, drawing on the work of Soviet scholars then rejected in the USA for ideological reasons, made considerable advances towards their decipherment. He is also known for his semantic propositions regarding the analysis of kinship systems. Adapting the phonological models of the Prague Circle to the case of kinship, he and his colleague Goodenough argued for a componential analysis of terms, in other words the analysis of contrasts between each term and the structure on which the total system is based. Loundsbury was elected to the American Academy of Arts and Sciences in 1976.

Service, Elman R. (1915–1996)

Elman R. Service gained a place at the University of Michigan, but interrupted his studies to fight with the Republicans in the Spanish Civil War. On returning to Michigan he obtained a BA, but before long returned to military life in the Second World War. After the war he studied at the University of Chicago and then obtained a Ph.D. from Columbia University in 1950 with his thesis 'Spanish-Guarani Acculturation in Early Colonial Paraguay: The Encomienda from 1537 to 1620'. He then taught at Columbia from 1949 to 1953 and at Michigan from 1953 to 1968, before holding a professorship at California-Santa Barbara from 1968 to 1985. He carried out research among the Havasupai of the Grand Canyon and then

in Paraguay and Mexico, and wrote *Tobati: Paraguayan Town* (Chicago: Chicago UP, 1954) and *Spanish-Guarani Relations in Early Colonial Paraguay* (Greenwood, 1954). He also edited a number of texts: *Readings in Introductory Anthropology* (Ann Arbor: Michigan UP, 1956), *A Profile of Primitive Culture* (New York, 1958) and, with M. **Sahlins**, *Evolution and Culture* (Ann Arbor: Michigan UP, 1960). The last of these works aims to formulate a neo-evolutionist manifesto and proposes a typology, taken up by archaeologists, which distinguishes between local, diversified evolution and the global evolution of mankind. Service classifies the stages in bands, tribes, chiefdoms and states.

Greenberg, Joseph Harold (1915–2002)

Born in Brooklyn, Joseph Harold Greenberg learnt Greek, Arabic and Hebrew, and discovered anthropology at Columbia University under A. Lesser and **Boas**. With funding from the Social Science Research Council, he spent 1937–1938 at Yale University to deepen his knowledge of linguistics, and from there he moved to Northwestern University, which awarded him a Ph.D. in 1940 for a thesis based on ethnographic research among the Hausa of Nigeria under the supervision of M. J. **Herskovits**. He taught successively at the universities of Minnesota (1946), Columbia (1948) and Stanford (1962–1985). With the exception of *The Influence of Islam on a Sudanese Religion* (Washington UP, 1946), a revised version of his doctoral thesis, Greenberg's work all falls within linguistics. From 1948 he worked on the elaboration of a genealogical classification of African languages, thereby opening up this field to scientific analysis, and the research documented in *The Languages of Africa* (1963) is still considered more or less definitive in this area. From 1960 he extended his linguistic research to other regions, and also wrote

Anthropological Linguistics: An Introduction (New York: Random House, 1968). His *Language in the Americas* (1987) caused controversy by dividing American Indian languages into three groupings. He was the author of a large number of theoretical articles and the editor of the four-volume *Universals of Human Language* (Stanford UP, 1966, 1978).

Murra, John V. (born 1916)

John V. Murra was born in Odessa in the Ukraine and emigrated to the USA with his parents. He began his studies at the University of Chicago, but like E. R. **Service** left to enlist in the Spanish Republican army at the age of twenty, serving from 1937 to 1939. Back in the USA he was the only applicant for a post for a Spanish-speaking student advertised on the Chicago anthropology department notice board. This involved travel to the Equatorial Andes to work under D. Collier, with whom he later published *Survey and Excavations in Southern Ecuador* (Chicago: Field Museum of Natural History, 1943). From 1943 to 1947 he taught at Chicago, and on the recommendation of W. C. Bennet and A. **Métraux** was asked to write the section on the peoples of pre-Columbian Ecuador for the *Handbook of South American Indians* edited by J. **Steward**. His application for US citizenship was refused in 1946, but he secured a reversal of this decision in court in 1950, although it was not until 1956 that he was issued with an American passport. Until this date it was impossible for him to travel abroad to do fieldwork, and so he spent his time in the Library of Congress using secondary sources to research his thesis *The Economic Organization of the Inka State*, written under the theoretical influence of K. **Polanyi** and passed in 1956. In it he analyses Inca modes of production, demonstrating how ancient *ayllu* social ties are situated at the heart of Inca society and how different Andean ecological layers have been

systematically exploited. He also coined the phrase 'vertical archipelago' to describe Andean civilizations. Murra taught successively at the universities of Vassar, Yale, Johns Hopkins and Cornell, where he stayed longest and became professor in 1968 following his participation in the Peru-Cornell Project from 1951 to 1966. He was a guest professor at the National University of San Marco in Peru in 1958–1959 and again in 1963 and 1965, and there he trained many anthropologists, including Victoria Castro, Carlos Aldunate and Jorge Hidalgo, who later edited a book of conversations with him (2000).

Schneider, David M. (1918–1995)

Born in Brooklyn into a family of communist, Russian-Jewish immigrants ruined by the Depression, D. M. Schneider attended a boarding school in Connecticut from the ages of nine to eighteen. He then studied industrial bacteriology at Cornell New York State College of Agriculture, where he and his contemporary **Goodenough** attended lectures on rural sociology given by R. L. Sharp. In 1940 Sharp set up a department of sociology and anthropology at the college which awarded its first MA to Schneider. His thesis analysed 148 Australian Yir Yorent dreams which Sharp had collected (Schneider and Sharp, 1969). On Sharp's advice Schneider then enrolled in the anthropology department of Yale University, but his disaffection with **Murdock**'s positivism and inability to get on with Murdock himself caused him to leave only six months later. Married and short of money, he took a position in the Ministry of Agriculture in 1940. In 1942 he was recruited by the army and served as a social worker, and it was during this time that he was contacted by the anthropologist Geoffrey Gorer, who was directing a research programme on national character for the Office of War Information. With Gorer's encouragement Schneider wrote his first two articles: 'The Social

Dynamics of Physical Disability in Army Basic Training' (*Psychiatry* (1946): 123–29); and 'The Culture of the Army Clerk' (*Psychiatry*, 10 (1947): 323–333). After failing to gain a GI demobilization bursary, Schneider followed M. **Mead**'s advice to get in touch with **Kluckhohn**, who secured a post for him in the new department of social relations at Harvard University, directed by Parsons (who took up the idea of the 'sick role' he had found in Schneider's articles). The Coordinated Investigation of Micronesian Anthropology (CIMA), directed by Murdock, assigned to Harvard the study of the Island of Yap, which was under American army occupation. The team which set out to analyse the problem of depopulation on the island was made up of four scholars, of whom Schneider, who had been in the Harvard department for only six months, and Bill Stevens were ethnographers. Schneider lived on Yap from September 1947 to June 1949, and his six-month stay on a small island to the north of Yap inhabited by 130 people made a particular impression on him; few fieldwork experiences have been as well documented as this one (see his narrative in Schneider, 1995: 102–119; and the study of Ira Bashkow, 1991). His initial aim was to compile a report and, above all, to gather material for a thesis with a psychological slant to be supervised by Kluckhohn, but he soon switched his focus from psychology to social structure. His thesis, *Kinship and Village Organization of Yap, West Caroline Islands, Micronesia: A Structural and Functional Account*, which was passed by the examiners Kluckhohn, Parsons and Douglas Oliver in 1949, reveals a bilinear system using a hitherto unknown terminology. While still writing up his thesis he met A. **Richards** and R. **Firth** during their visit to Harvard, and they helped him obtain funding from the Peabody Museum to teach for two years at the LSE, where he disseminated the ideas of the 'culture and personality' school. Back in Harvard in September 1952, Schneider pub-

lished a first essay on Yapese terminologies (*AA*, vol.55) and co-edited *Personality in Nature, Society and Culture* with Kluckhohn and H. Murry (New York, 1953). He also worked with G. C. Homans on the American kinship system (*AA*, vol.57, 1955), and together they wrote *Marriage, Authority and Final Causes* (Glencoe: Free Press, 1955), which attacks **Lévi-Strauss**'s view of preferential marriage. In 1954 he co-directed a celebrated seminar held by the Social Science Research Council on matrilineal kinship, bringing together D. Aberle, K. Gough, E. Colson and many more, the proceedings of which were published in 1961. Schneider spent a year at the Center for Advanced Studies in the Behavioral Sciences and then taught kinship and Parsonian theory at the University of California at Berkeley at the invitation of R. McCown, a physical anthropologist and head of the Berkeley department. Wishing to undertake more fieldwork in a location he could visit with his family during university vacations, he chose to work on the Mescalero Apaches after consulting Evan Z. Vogt in 1954. His intention was to examine transformations in their kinship system and use a psychoanalytical approach to elucidate their culture. Despite finding Berkeley uncongenial, he stayed there until 1959, and in the summer of 1960 joined the department at the University of Chicago. He was invited by Firth to participate in the first symposium of the British Association of Social Anthropologists in 1963, and used this occasion to question *ad hoc* categories of kinship study and criticize the approaches of Murdock and **Radcliffe-Brown**, which defined contemporary understanding of this question (1965: 29). In his *American Kinship: A Cultural Account* (Chicago UP, first edn 1968; second edn 1980), he defines kinship as a system of symbols and meanings. Using empirical studies Schneider posits sexual relations, love and blood as the categories of American culture on which the ideological constructions of kinship are based

(1980: 91, 115). In 1969 he and L. **Dumont** organized a colloquium with the title 'Kinship and Locality', which was supported by the Wenner–Gren Foundation and brought together H. Lavondès, S. Tambiah, E. **Leach**, M. Meggitt, D. **Maybury-Lewis** and C. **Geertz**. Appearing in 1984, his *Critique of the Study of Kinship* (Ann Arbor, Michigan UP) dismisses the feasibility of comparative kinship study and provides a critical history of the field. In 1985 Schneider joined the University of California at Santa Cruz, where he taught until 1988. He had a first heart attack in 1970, and a second in 1993. He died in California on 30 October 1995 after having co-written an autobiography with Richard Handler, which is an excellent document on professional anthropology in the USA (Schneider, 1995).

Goodenough, Ward Hunt (born 1919)

Born in Cambridge, Massachusetts, in 1919 as the son of a professor of religious studies, Ward Hunt Goodenough in 1940 completed a BA at Cornell University, where he struck up a friendship with D. M. **Schneider**. His interest in anthropology was first sparked by R. L. Sharp, and it was on Sharp's advice that he studied at Yale University from 1940 to 1942, becoming one of **Murdock**'s favourite students. From 1941 to 1946 he served in the army, and during this period wrote his first article (1944). After demobilization he finished his studies at Yale and then travelled to Chuuk (Truk) in 1947 to carry out research within the Coordinated Investigation of Micronesian Anthropology (CIMA), which was directed by Murdock. After his return Goodenough taught at the University of Wisconsin while simultaneously completing his Ph.D. in 1948–1949. Published in 1951 as *Property, Kin, and Community on Truk* (rev. ed., Archon Books, 1978), this work brought him to the attention of his peers. In 1956 he published 'Componential Analysis and the Study of Meaning' in the journal *Language* (vol.32 (1956): 195–216),

and this is probably his most original contribution to the discipline. He proposes that componential analysis be applied to kinship studies, as did **Loundsbury** in the same year, and his approach consists in specifying, within a unified linguistic field, the minimal bundle of distinctive criteria permitting the separate identification of each term. Thus a centre can be located in which each term is positioned and from which it can be defined according to its so-called componential characteristics. With this model Goodenough opened up one possible path for cognitive anthropology. In 1964–1965 he returned to Truk, and his career also included research in the Gilbert Islands in 1951, in Papua New Guinea from 1951 to 1954, and in New Britain in 1954. In 1949 he was recruited as an assistant professor by the University of Pennsylvania, becoming a full professor there in 1954, and he also worked for the University museum. Goodenough became a member of the Academy of Sciences of the USA in 1971.

Bohannan, Paul (born 1920)

Paul Bohannan studied at Oxford University and then carried out research on the Tiv of Nigeria in 1949. He was awarded an Oxford D.Phil. in 1951 and returned to the Tiv in 1953 before switching his attention to the Wanga of Kenya in 1954–1955. Subsequently he taught at the universities of Oxford (1951–1956), Princeton (1956–1959), Northwestern (1959–1976) and California-Santa Barbara, where he became head of department. Having initially concentrated on legal issues in traditional African societies, Bohannan began to take an interest in the economic field. Following in the footsteps of **Polanyi** and the substantivists, he showed how the market economy in Africa developed not under its own steam, but for extraneous reasons connected with the constraints imposed by colonization. His best-known writings in this field are to be found in *Markets in Africa*, which he co-edited with George Dalton (Northwestern UP, 1962), and which relaunched economic anthropology in the 1960s. Bohannan next turned to anthropological questions in American society, exploring divorce in the San Francisco Bay Area in 1963–1964, relationships of couples with their parents-in-law in San Diego in 1974–1975, and San Diego bachelors living in lodging houses in 1975–1977. He also worked together with J. **Middleton** on editing collections of major texts.

Leacock, Eleanor Burke (1922–1987)
Born into an intellectual and artistic milieu in New York, Eleanor Burke Leacock studied at Radcliffe and Barnard colleges, gaining a BA from the latter in 1944. She then enrolled at Columbia University, where she came under the influence of W. D. Strong and G. Weltfish. After obtaining her MA in 1946, she gained the support of R. **Benedict** for a trip to Europe, accompanied by her husband, to make film footage on the comparative socialization of Italian- and German-speaking Swiss children. She also immersed herself in literature on the origins of the fur trade among the Montagnais Indians of Labrador, whom she visited in 1951. Back in 1915 F. Speck had used ancient narratives to show that in this population of hunter–gatherers each individual owned a patrilineally inherited plot of family land, and on the basis of this evidence he and **Lowie** had rejected the idea of primitive communism. The whole body of evidence on this subject is re-examined in Leacock's thesis 'The Montagnais "Hunting Territory" and the Fur Trade' ('American Anthropologist Memoir', 78), published in 1954. She concludes that the family hunting territories, rather than collectively owned, were a by-product of Indian adaptation to the fur trade, trapping being more effective as an individual than as a collective pursuit and tending therefore to lead to the breakdown of shared property ownership. In 1963 Leacock

republished **Morgan**'s *Ancient Society* with an important new introduction (New York: Meridian Books). Leacock's second marriage was to a trades union leader, and in the latter part of her career she took up arms against **Lewis**'s theory of 'culture and poverty' (*Culture and Poverty: A Critique*, New York: Simon and Schuster, 1971), travelled to Zambia, republished **Engels**'s *The Origins of the Family, Private Property and the State*, and became one of the founders of feminist anthropology. In 1972 she joined the staff of New York College, and she directed its anthropology department until her death in Samoa in 1987.

Diamond, Stanley (1922–1991)
Born into a family of Jewish immigrants, Stanley Diamond showed promise as a writer of prose and verse at a very young age. He studied at the universities of North Carolina and New York, emerging with degrees in English and philosophy. He then took various jobs, including journalism with the *New Yorker* and the *Long Island Daily Press*. During the Second World War he joined the British Army, serving in a company of volunteers in North Africa. After reading P. **Radin** he decided to enrol on his return as a postgraduate in the anthropology department of Columbia University, where his fellow students included S. **Mintz**, M. **Fried** and E. **Wolf**. He was awarded a Ph.D. in 1951 for his thesis *Dahomey: A Proto-State in West Africa*, and then spent time in an Israeli kibbutz and an Arab village. In 1953 Diamond took a public stance against McCarthyism while teaching at the University of California at Los Angeles (UCLA). As a result, he was unemployed for three years before being offered a job by Brandeis University in 1956. In 1957 he travelled to Nigeria to carry out fieldwork, and on his return in 1959 he worked at the National Institute of Mental Health. He taught at Syracuse University from 1963 to 1966 and then joined the New School for

Social Research in New York, where in 1970 he created what he hoped would become the first critical anthropology department in the USA, and in 1975 he founded the journal *Dialectical Anthropology*. The politically militant Diamond was enlisted by the Iroquois Seneca in their struggle against the decision to construct a dam which would have devastated their reserve. He was also a champion of Black causes, publishing a series of virulent articles including 'The Death of Malcolm X' and 'Black Farce, White Lies: Sonny Liston and Cassius Clay'. He emerged as one of the leaders of the anti-Vietnam War campaign in the 1960s, and became and ardent defender of Biafran independence. Diamond also wrote poetry.

Mintz, Sidney (born 1922)
Sidney Mintz studied psychology at Brooklyn College, gaining a BA in 1943. After the war he became R. **Benedict**'s assistant in a research project on contemporary cultures in 1947–1948 and carried out research in Puerto Rico in 1948–1949. He then studied at New York and Columbia universities, gaining a Ph.D. from the latter in 1951. As well as in Puerto Rico, he carried out fieldwork in Jamaica (1952), Haiti (1958–1959), Iran (1966–1967) and Hong Kong (1996). He taught at Yale University from 1951 to 1975 and subsequently at Johns Hopkins University, and also gave classes at the Massachusetts Institute of Technology, the *Ecole des Hautes Etudes* and the *Collège de France*. It is worth noting that being invited to give the Sidney Mintz lecture, an annual event in the Johns Hopkins anthropology department, is one of the most honorific distinctions in the profession. E. **Wolf** won this honour in 1992, and M. **Sahlins** in 1995. A specialist on the Caribbean, Mintz took up arms against the exploitative conditions imposed on plantation workers there. He is known as the author, with E. Wolf, of the first complete study of godparenthood (1950), and also for *Worker in the Cane: A*

Puerto Rican Life History (New Haven: Yale UP, 1960). Fourteen years later he published *Caribbean Transformation* (Chicago: Aldine, 1974), where he paints a portrait of Caribbean society in terms not of culture, but of the system of social classes bequeathed by slavery. In 1976 he and R. Price published *An Anthropological Approach to the Afro-American Past: A Caribbean Perspective* (Philadelphia: Ishi, 1976), which presents Black American culture as the product of the present and of the recent past. *Sweetness and Power*, published in 1985, offers a complete history of the exploitation and consumption of sugar. Particularly well-known are the sections of the book in which Mintz examines the transformation of sugar from sumptuary item to basic ingredient caused by the growth in Great Britain of a new industrial proletariat, which, unable to feed itself properly, alleviated its hunger with sugared tea.

Fried, Morton (1923–1986)
Morton Fried obtained a B.Sc. from the City College of New York in 1942. After war service he studied Chinese at the Harvard University Military School and then became a postgraduate anthropology student at Columbia University, gaining a Ph.D. in 1951. His *Fabric of Chinese Society* (New York: Octagon, 1953) was based on his fieldwork in Taiwan. From 1950 he taught at Columbia, where he became professor in 1961. In 1959 he edited *Readings in Anthropology* (New York: Crowell, 1959, 1968), a selection of texts by celebrated anthropologists, which served as a handbook for one or two generations of American anthropologists before being superseded by **Harris**'s collection and then that of Keesing and Konrad. Published in 1967, Fried's *Evolution of Political Society: An Essay in Political Anthropology* (New York: Random House) advances the idea of an evolution of political systems from the 'egalitarian society' to the state, initially set in motion by

demographic pressures. From 1981 onwards he played a part in the reconstruction of an anthropology department in mainland China.

Wolf, Eric (1923–1999)

Eric Wolf was born in Vienna, but was living in the Sudetenland when it was invaded by Hitler, and in 1939 he made his way as a refugee to England. Here he was briefly detained as an enemy alien in 1940, and on his release he departed for the USA. He began a degree in biochemistry at Queens College, New York, but interrupted his studies to enlist in the army. He served until the end of the war, winning the Silver Star, and then completed a BA in sociology and anthropology at Queens College in 1946. This was followed by postgraduate study at Columbia University, where he was awarded a Ph.D. in 1951. Wolf carried out research in Puerto Rico in 1948–1949, and in 1950 he travelled to Mexico, returning to the USA in 1952. He became **Steward**'s assistant at the University of Illinois, and in 1959 published *Sons of the Shaking Earth* (Chicago UP), which examines the continuum of social transformation in Guatemala and from pre-Hispanic to Hispanic Mexico. The novelty of Wolf's approach lies in his focus on continuities rather than distinctions between the two Mexicos. He campaigned for left-wing causes and against the Vietnam War, and in 1965 he and **Sahlins** organized the first teach-in against the war. His political concerns fed into his *Peasant Wars in the Twentieth Century*, published in 1966, which examined peasant guerrillas in Vietnam, Algeria, Russia and China. After filling teaching posts at various institutions – Virginia, Yale and Chicago – he became professor of anthropology at the University of Michigan. He also joined the staff of Lehmann College, part of the City University of New York, in 1971. In 1960 he initiated a comparative study between Austrian and Italian Alpine villages, and together with J. W. Cole published *The Hidden Frontier: Ecology and Ethnicity in an Alpine Valley* (New York: Academic Press, 1974). In 1982 he published *Europe and the People without History* (Berkeley: California UP) which traces the expansion of European commerce viewed from the perspective of its victims. In 1995 Wolf became a member of the Academy of Sciences. His signal achievement is to have demonstrated how processes experienced by peasant societies are embedded in national and international developments.

Murphy, Robert F. (1924–1990)

Born into modest circumstances, Robert F. Murphy went straight into employment on leaving school, and then served for three years in the Marines during the Second World War. Thanks to the GI Bill, which funded the higher education of war veterans, he enrolled at Columbia University in 1946, and it was here that he discovered anthropology. In 1950 he met Yolanda, his future wife, and they travelled together to the Brazilian Amazon in 1952–1953 to study the Mundurucú, on whom they co-wrote two books: *Headhunter's Heritage: Social and Economic Change among the Mundurucú* (Berkeley: California UP, 1960); and *Mundurucú Religion* (Berkeley: California UP, 1958). In 1959–1960 Murphy researched on the Tuareg, and his two articles on their kinship and their preferential patrilateral cross-cousin marriage have remained famous: 'Tuareg Kinship' (*AA*, vol.69 (1964): 163–170); and (with L. Kasdan) 'The Structure of Parallel Cousin Marriage' (*AA*, vol.61 (1959): 17–29). He taught at the University of California at Berkeley and then in 1963 became a professor at Columbia, where he headed the anthropology department from 1969 to 1972. In 1971 he published *The Dialectics of Social Life* (New York: Columbia UP), in which he questions theories of the social world from **Lévi-Strauss** to Marcuse. In 1974 he and Yolanda Murphy published *Women of the Forest* (New York: Columbia UP), a study of antagonisms between the sexes in which the authors showed that masculine domination among the Mundurucú was more a matter of symbolism than reality. After contracting a neurological illness in 1976, Murphy launched himself into a research programme entitled 'social relations and micro-ecology of paraplegics'. During his illness, Murphy wrote *The Body Silent* (1987), a book which aimed at being 'not an autobiography but a narrative of the repercussions of his infirmity on his status as a member of society'. This is a magnificent testimony of the life of a terminally ill man gradually debilitated by quadriplegia, but who refused to give in to his condition. The following recollection from Janet Chernela is revealing: 'In Murphy's last stays in hospital, after his debilitating and terminal illness, he told me that he would be dying when the tumor in his spine reached his seventh vertebra. I asked to which point it had reached. His response: "The seventh". His timing was always impeccable' (Janet Chernela, *Anthropology News*, vol.43/4, April 2002: 25).

Turnbull, Colin (1924–1994)

Colin Turnbull was British, but most of his career took place in the USA. He served in the Royal Navy in the Second World War and then read anthropology at Oxford University under **Evans-Pritchard**, gaining an MA in 1949. From 1949 to 1951 he investigated religious issues in India and then from 1951 to 1954 worked on the Mbuti Pygmies in the Congo, and in 1964 he was awarded an Oxford D.Phil. After falling in love with the African American Joseph Towles, Turnbull moved to New York, where from 1959 to 1969 he was assistant and then associate curator at the Museum of Natural History. His research on the Mbuti of the Ituris Forest and on the Iks of Uganda resulted in the publication of *The Forest People* in 1961 and *The Iks* in 1972, which both enjoyed wide success with a general readership. In the first work, the Pygmies are idealized as living

in perfect harmony, while the second presents the Iks as a people all of whose values have degenerated as a result of territorial losses, and who now exhibit no more than a mechanical survival instinct ('a good man is one whose stomach is full'). This book was strongly criticized and unleashed a heated controversy. Turnbull was professor of anthropology at the universities of Hofstra (1969–1972), Virginia Commonwealth (1972–1975) and Washington (1976–1985), and subsequently he lived in Hawaii and Samoa. He set up a foundation to grant financial assistance to young Black American students. After Towles died of AIDS in 1988, Turnbull returned to India, where he lived as a Buddhist monk under the name Lobsong Rigdol until his own death of the same disease in 1994. In 1976 Peter Brook and Turnbull together directed the Royal Shakespeare Company in a play called *The Ik*, which after opening in January of that year became a worldwide success. As well as with the two books cited above, he achieved success with *The Human Cycle* (New York: Schuster, 1983), which looks at how different cultures organize the major phases of life. The scale of the polemics caused by his works and their success with the reading public make the inclusion of Turnbull in this dictionary a necessity.

Castaneda, Carlos (1926–1998)

As his UCLA Master's dissertation Carlos Castaneda wrote an account of his journey through the Arizona desert in Mexico, during which he encountered a shaman who initiated him into the Peyote cult and acted as his guide. This dissertation was published in 1968 as *The Teachings of Don Juan: A Yaqui Way of Knowledge*, and gradually became an international success. Castaneda renewed his visits to Juan Matus (Don Juan) for several years, and published ten volumes, some of them translated into seventeen languages, retracing his adventures of the mind in strange worlds together with his mentor. While professional anthropologists unanimously rejected this oeuvre as a concoction of falsehoods, its popularity with the reading public doubtless led a great many young people into careers in anthropology in the 1980s, and in this way Castaneda can be said to have played a role rather similar to that of **Mead** in the 1950s.

Conklin, Harold C. (born 1926)

Born into a cultivated family in Pennsylvania, Harold C. Conklin accompanied his great uncle, a naturalist, to American Indian reserves while still a child. He struck up friendships with the Indians, and in 1939 was adopted by the Mahawk clan under the name Ionkwatahron (our friend). In 1940 he made the acquaintance of C. **Wissler** and from 1941 to 1943 worked as a volunteer in the anthropology section of the American Museum of Natural History. There he classified artefacts, read **Morgan** and other classic texts, and met **Bateson**, **Mead**, William Fenton and others. He enrolled at the University of California at Berkeley in 1943 and attended lectures by **Lowie**, **Kroeber**, Gifford and Ronald Olson, who at that time made up the full strength of the Berkeley anthropology department. Conklin was recruited into the army in the summer of 1944 and sent to the Philippines, where he learnt Tagalog, and in 1945 was made a military instructor. After demobilization in 1946 he made arrangements to stay in the Philippines, where he recorded a large quantity of information. In 1947 he spent four months among the Hanunoo of Mindora, and established relationships with local researchers and foreign scholars, including the botanist H. Bartlett, who assigned him the task of gathering an ethnobotanical collection for the National Museum of the Philippines. In 1948 he travelled to Europe, spending time in Great Britain and meeting **Firth** and **Leach** at the LSE, and then returned to Berkeley to finish his BA in 1950. Conklin's first articles appeared in 1949, and he also compiled a Hanunoo–English dictionary, which was finished in 1951 and published in 1953 (Berkeley: California UP). In 1950 he enrolled at Yale University, where he became a disciple of **Loundsbury**, and then spent a second period in the Philippines from 1952 to 1954. During this stay he sought an understanding of Hanunoo culture in terms of the ideas of **Sapir** and **Whorf** and of Loundsbury, and also used K. Pike's opposition between 'emic' and 'etic' points of view. His aim was an ethnographic transcription of the knowledge, representations and classifications which the Hanunoo extrapolate from the natural world. Completed in 1954, Conklin's thesis *The Relation of Hanunoo Culture to their Plant World* (New Haven: Microfilm, 1954) is a renewal of ethnoscience which he then published in a series of articles. The first of these, 'Hanunoo Color Categories' (*Southwestern Journal of Anthropology*, 11 (1995): 339–44) attempts a description of the principles by which the three-dimensional lexis of Hanunoo colours in structured. In 1954 he began to teach at Columbia University, and in 1962 accepted a professorship at Yale University. In 1980 he published *Ethnographic Atlas of Ifugao: A Study of Environment, Culture and Society in Northern Luzon* (New Haven: Yale UP). Using satellite and aerial photography, which he defined as a cartographical reference concerning land use, this book examines the organization of space and habitat, and offers a complete ethnography of its subject. Conklin shows that Ifugao culture 'emphasizes adaptation to the environment and the conservation of resources' (p.1), and that this culture and the agricultural practices associated with it have at least a 400-year history.

Geertz, Clifford (born 1926)

Born in San Francisco in 1926, Clifford Geertz served in the Second World War and thereby became a beneficiary of the GI Bill. He obtained a BA from Antioch College, and then in 1949, after a meeting with M. **Mead**, enrolled in Harvard University's department of social relations, founded by T. Parsons. According to Parsons' design, anthropology was assigned the study of 'culture'. Weber's concept of *Verstehen* was reinterpreted by Geertz as 'webs of significance in which individuals are caught'. Clifford and Hildred Geertz spent 1952 to 1954 in Indonesia with a multidisciplinary team, but soon began working independently on kinship and religion in a small town called Pare. After returning to the USA and completing his Ph.D. in 1956, Geertz spent a second period in Indonesia in 1957–1958, concentrating this time on Bali, which he and his wife would visit periodically over a number of years. Back home he took a post as assistant professor at Berkeley before moving to Chicago as a professor in 1960, and in the same year he published a recast version of his thesis as *The Religion of Java* (Glencoe: Free Press). This very Weberian work establishes connections between religious ideas and socio-political transformations in Indonesia by isolating three ideal types of religion: that of the village (syncretic), that of the merchants (orthodox Islam), and that of the bureaucratic elite (Hindu ritual). This was followed in 1963 by *Agricultural Involution: The Processes of Ecological Change in Indonesia* (Berkeley: California UP) and *Peddlers and Princes: Social Change and Economic Modernization in two Indonesian Towns* (Chicago: Chicago UP). Based on a report written in 1956, *Agricultural Involution* provides a historical examination of Indonesian agriculture from 1619 to 1942, and it was warmly welcomed by development specialists, economists and political scientists alike. In it Geertz reveals the foundations of the contrast between two forms of agri-culture: that of outer Indonesia, reliant on slash-and-burn farming and characterized by individual cultivation of tobacco, coffee and rubber, and thus in the process of modernizing; and the intensive irrigation farming of inner Indonesia, which was expanding statically to feed a growing population and was in a process of involution. *Peddlers and Princes* investigates the likelihood that the new class of entrepreneurs will be successful and examines the opposition between the networks of Islamic merchants and the old Balinese aristocracy with its manipulation of traditional ethics. Harassed by the Indonesian authorities in 1957 and relatively pessimistic about the country's future (1965), Geertz looked for a new country to study. He lighted on Morocco, and his researches there from 1965 to 1971 bore fruit in a number of articles, and above all in *Islam Observed: Religious Development in Morocco and Indonesia* (Chicago UP, 1968). After a brief introduction to the two countries, Geertz pursues a historical approach, and most of this small book is devoted to the evolution of two types of Islam: in Morocco the Islamic conception of life involves an individual moralism and activism, while in Indonesia Islam signifies a dissolution of personality into a religious aesthetic. The book closes with general theoretical observations and the idea that individual lives are structured by symbols. In 1970 Geertz was invited by the Institute for Advanced Studies of Princeton University to found a School of Social Sciences, and from that point onwards his work is characterized not by theoretical constructions but by a series of ethnographic *tableaux*.

Published in 1973, *The Interpretation of Cultures* (New York: Basic Books) is Geertz's first collection of essays in what he calls interpretative anthropology, and the best-known of these is 'Deep Play: Notes on the Balinese Cockfight' (1972). The main working concept here is 'thick description', a form of analysis which emphasizes the 'emic' signification underlying social action. Geertz's radicalism resides in his intention to eschew all explicit reference to conceptual frameworks extraneous to the culture under consideration. He sees each culture as unique, and the job of the anthropologist as to impress its uniqueness on the reader. A second collection of essays followed in 1983: *Local Knowledge: Further Essays in Interpretative Anthropology* (New York: Basic Books). Then, in *Works and Lives: The Anthropologist as Author* (Oxford: Blackwell) he offered critical readings of some of the great classics of the discipline from a position within postmodernist thinking. Geertz retraces his own steps in *After the Fact* (Harvard UP, 1995). Although there is no mention of this in the book, one may surmise that Suharto's CIA-backed coup of 1965, which toppled the Sukarno regime and led to the massacre of up to one million 'communists', must have devastated a researcher who a few years previously had thought his studies were contributing to the strengthening of stable and progressive democracy. This, possibly combined with a vague sense of guilt, prompted Geertz to search for a different reality. The aestheticization of life, like relativism and even cynicism, are the refuge of those whose youthful dreams have been shattered. Aside from his ability to treat a wide range of topics (Balinese theatre, Islam, agriculture, kinship, etc.) with equal virtuosity, Geertz's main strength was his style, which became increasingly literary and encompassed an erudition and breadth of reference not generally encountered in anthropological writing. These qualities make his work agreeable reading and accessible to non-specialists, and in the decade from 1990 to 2000 he overtook **Lévi-Strauss** as the most publicly esteemed anthropologist.

Sturtevant, William (born 1926)
Born in New Jersey, William Sturtevant took an anthropology degree at the University of California at Berkeley. His studies were interrupted by war service in 1945–1946, and he completed his BA in 1949, having already been made a reader in the previous year. He then moved to Yale University for his Ph.D., which he obtained in 1955, and in 1954 he became an assistant curator at the Peabody Museum. In 1956 he joined the Smithsonian Institution, where he remained for the rest of his career, while also teaching at Johns Hopkins University. Sturtevant had a knowledge of several Amerindian languages and was the author or editor of twenty-one books and published about two hundred articles. His main research subjects were the Seminole Indians of Florida, the Seneca of New York, and the people of Burma. He is also known as a museologist and, as of 1966, as the general editor of the *Handbook of North American Indians* (Washington: Smithsonian Institution). A formidable undertaking, the handbook is a systematic encyclopaedia, and by 2001 it comprised fifteen volumes.

Carneiro, Robert (born 1927)
Born in New York, Robert Carneiro studied at the University of Michigan, obtaining a political sciences BA in 1949, an MA in 1952, and a Ph.D., based on his fieldwork with the Kuikuru of Brazil, in 1957. He was then engaged by the American Museum of Natural History, where he spent his whole working life – as assistant curator from 1957 to 1963, associate curator from 1963 to 1969, and curator from 1969 onwards. He has also taught in several institutions, including Hunter College, UCLA, and the University of Pennsylvania, and he was appointed adjunct professor of anthropology at Columbia University in 1992. Carneiro is a specialist on American Indian societies and slash-and-burn cultivators, and his work takes its place in the tradition of cultural materialism. He suggests that states were born of military struggle for the cultivable land required when a population exceeds a

particular density, and he uses the example of the steep valleys of Peru to support his case. But physical environment is not the only factor, because the same phenomenon can be observed at the centre of thickly populated areas. Carneiro is the author of about two hundred articles.

Harris, Marvin (1927–2002)

While a student at Columbia University Marvin Harris joined the little group centred on **Stewart** and then on **Wagley**, and he worked with Wagley in Latin America. After his thesis was accepted in 1953 he took a teaching post at Columbia, and in 1958 he travelled to Mozambique, but was expelled after having published his first article on the country in 1959. Subsequent locations of his highly varied fieldwork were Brazil, India and the USA. He is known above all as the creator of cultural materialism: adopting a neo-evolutionism which treats of human history in its entirety and from all angles; he argues that demographic pressure is the primary historical determinant, to which diverse cultural strategies can be seen as responding. Social and cultural transformations result from the exhaustion of environmental resources caused by population growth; for example the Aztec flower war meets the population's need for proteins. Harris's theory is most fully developed in his *Cultural Materialism: The Struggle for a Science of Culture* (New York: Vintage Books, 1979). In *The Rise of Anthropological Theory: A History of Theories of Culture*, published in 1968 (New York: Crowell), he provides a polemical (and exciting) history of anthropology as an epic combat between the evolutionist tradition and its anti-scientific, relativist opponents. He also wrote a handbook entitled *Culture, People, Nature: An Introduction to General Anthropology* (New York: Harper & Row, 1971, 1980), which went through many reprintings. In 1980 he left Columbia for the University of Florida.

Stocking, George W. (born 1928)

The son of an economics professor, George W. Stocking became a historian of education with a doctorate in American civilization from the University of Pennsylvania. He first made a name for himself in 1968 as the author of *Race, Culture and Evolution: Essays in the History of Anthropology* (New York: Free Press, 2nd edn 1982). This extremely precise and well-documented book advocates more stringent standards for histories of the discipline, and includes the classic article 'On the Limits of "Presentism" and "Historicism" in the Historiography of the Behavioral Sciences'. First published in 1965, this article distinguishes between anachronistic decontextualization, which by focusing on the present day causes tunnel vision, and the more respectable historicist approach, which studies information without preconceptions. This amounts to a break with the way the discipline's history had hitherto been presented, as a slow, cumulative progression towards scientific status, with regressions glossed over and authors reified. Stocking taught in the history department at Berkeley and then became associate professor in the anthropology department at the University of Chicago in 1968. Later he was appointed director of the Morris Fishbein Center for the Study of the History of Science and Medicine, and he also founded the 'History of Anthropology' collection, published by the University of Wisconsin, and the *History of Anthropology Newsletter*. Together his two books *Victorian Anthropology* (New York: Free Press, 1987) and *After Tylor: British Social Anthropology (1888–1951)* (London: Athlone, 1995) constitute a monumental and probably unsurpassable history of British anthropology. Stocking also edited **Tylor**'s complete works.

Maybury-Lewis, David (born 1929)

David Maybury-Lewis studied at Trinity Hall, Cambridge, gaining a BA in Modern Languages in 1952. He then switched to anthropology and moved to Brazil to attend the *Escola Livre de Sociología e Política* in São Paolo, where he obtained an M.Sc. in 1956 under the supervision of M. **Baldus** with a dissertation on the Xarente Indians. In 1960 he gained a D.Phil. at Oxford University, where the influence of Needham's thought led him to join the structuralist–cognitivist current against environmentalist functionalism. Taking up questions raised by **Lévi-Strauss**, he first examined theories of matrimonial alliance and then looked at prescriptive marriage (1965, 1967), and he was instrumental in introducing this approach into American anthropology. In his career at Harvard University he was a teaching assistant from 1960 to 1961, an assistant professor from 1962 to 1966, an associate professor from 1966 to 1969, and a full professor from 1969 until 2000, when he was invited to fill the University's Edward C. Henderson chair. In collaboration with Brazilian anthropologists such as **Cardoso de Oliveira**, he in 1962 founded the Harvard-Central Brazil Research Project, a major research programme on the social structures of the Gê people (which includes the Bororo, who had served as a model for Lévi-Strauss). While a guest professor at the Center for Advanced Studies in the Behavioral Sciences at Palo Alto in 1964–1965, Maybury-Lewis wrote *The Savage and the Innocent* (London: Evans, 1965; Beacon Press, 1988), an important text on his fieldwork experiences, and then began a long struggle for the protection of the Amazonian Indians and other minority groups. One outcome of this activism was his founding in 1972 of an association called Cultural Survival, which published two journals: *Cultural Survival Quarterly* and *State of the People*. He co-founded undergraduate and postgraduate programmes at the universities of Rio de Janeiro (1968) and Pernambuco (1970), and was one of the first to provide a complete picture of the lowland South American Indians, especially in his contribution to the *Cambridge History of*

the Native Peoples of America. He won the Grand Cross of the Brazilian Scientific Order, held honorary doctorates from numerous universities, was a member of American and Danish academies of sciences, arts and letters, and was awarded the Retzius Gold Medal by the Court of Sweden.

Sahlins, Marshall (born 1930)
Marshall Sahlins studied at the University of Michigan, gaining a BA under **White** in 1951, and then moved to Columbia University to be taught by **Steward**. Although his first fieldwork took him to Turkey, his interest soon shifted to Oceania, and in 1954 he completed his thesis *Social Stratification in Polynesia* (Ann Arbor: Michigan UP, 1959). In this work he examines how stages of evolution are realized in Pacific communities, proposing a progression from small Melanesian societies to the social organization present in Fiji, and from there to states like Tahiti and Hawaii. In 1953–1954 he was secretary to the Social Sciences Research Council's famous seminar on matrilinearity, but refused to contribute to the published proceedings out of loyalty to White's evolutionism (Schneider, 1995: 28). He carried out fieldwork in Fiji in 1954–1955 and then took posts at the University of Washington and, in 1957, at Michigan. Together with **Service** he edited *Evolution and Culture* (Ann Arbor: Michigan UP, 1960), the manifesto of the neo-evolutionist group, which states the principle of an 'evolution: specific and general'. However his own fieldwork produced a conventional functionalist monograph entitled *Moala: Culture and Nature on a Fijian Island* (Ann Arbor: Michigan UP, 1962). This was accompanied by two articles which now enjoy classic status: 'Segmentary Lineage: An Organization of Predatory Expansion' (*AA*, vol.63 (1961): 322–345); and 'Poor Man, Rich Man, Big Man, Chief: Political Types in Melanesia and Polynesia' (*Comparative Studies in Society and History*, vol.5 (1963): 285–303). Sahlins was a very

vocal opponent of the American intervention in Vietnam, and was chosen by a group of his colleagues to travel there, after which he published 'The Destruction of Conscience in Vietnam' (*New York Times*, repr. in Sahlins 2001). He was based in Paris from 1967 to 1969 at the invitation of the ethnology laboratory of the University of Nanterre. In 1972 he published a collection of his articles under the title *Stone Age Economics* (Hawthorne: Aldine), which immediately became a classic and compulsory reading for students. The ideological import of this book is located in its opposition between abundance in societies based around the domestic group, which is the unit of both production and consumption, and the capitalist economics of scarcity, in which the desires of individuals can never be satisfied. The book's scientific yield is its demonstration of abundance in primitive societies using measurements of labour time and production. Working far beneath its objective potential and allied to an immanent autocratic ideal, the domestic mode of production refuses to allow economic activity to become a sphere independent of social structures. Sahlins left Michigan in 1973 to become professor at the University of Chicago. In 1976 he published *Culture and Practical Reason* (Chicago UP), which presents culture as a symbolic system which impinges on the interpretations placed on events by actors. In Western cultures the economic sphere is the principal site of symbolic production, with social relations being generated by goods in the same way as they are generated by symbols in tribal societies. Commenced in the years from 1975 to 1977, Sahlins' work on the cult of Captain Cook and his death was not complete until 1995. Based on the example of Cook, he supports the idea of absolute relativism and argues that the behaviour of Hawaiians is determined by their myths (1985, 1995). This thesis has been strongly criticized by Obeyesekere (1992), and

Sahlins' response is to state that cultural models function like grammatical systems: grammar imposes rules on speakers, but this is not to say that grammar determines what is said. Similarly, while history remains irredeemably chaotic, culture can be defined as 'The Return of the Event' (2000).

Weiner, Annette B. (1933–1977)

A specialist on the Trobriand Islands, Annette B. Weiner took up **Hallowell**'s idea that cosmology and metaphysical principles form the foundations of the social world, and created the notion of 'authenticity', a veritably Kantian axiom or *a priori* of behaviour (1992). From 1970 she carried out research on the Trobriands, and was awarded a Ph.D. by the University of Bryn Mawr in 1974. Her thesis *Women of Value, Men of Renown: New Perspectives in Trobriand Exchange* is a critique of **Malinowski**'s ethnographic work, demonstrating that he neglects the feminine aspect of funerary ceremonies, during which the accumulated 'wealth of women', in the form of ornate skirts and garlands, is distributed by and among matrilineal kin. Furthermore, Malinowski's interpretation of *kula* neglects the social benefit of keeping back the most prestigious objects of exchange for as long as possible. Weiner taught at the universities of Texas at Austin, Princeton and New York, and was president of the AAA.

Fox, Robin (born 1934)

Born in 1934, Robin Fox spent his childhood in India, where his father was in the army, and developed an early interest in politics. He was admitted to the LSE to study economics, sociology and social anthropology, gaining a BA in 1953, and then he spent two years in Harvard University's social relations department, which had been created by T. Parsons. During this time he studied the Pueblo Indians, on whom he wrote his LSE doctoral thesis *The Keresn*

Bridge: The Problem of Pueblo Ethnology (1967). Fox taught for many years in Britain before returning to the USA to found an anthropology department at Rutgers University. After the publication in 1967 of *Kinship and Marriage* (London: Penguin Books) he concentrated increasingly on ethnological research and took part in the sociobiological current. For fourteen years he and L. Tiger directed a Guggenheim Foundation research programme on violence and aggression, and together they published *The Imperial Animal* (London: Holt, Rinehart and Winston, 1971), an interactionist vision of nature and human culture which earned Fox violent attacks from feminists and left-wing (but not truly radical) colleagues. His *Red Lamp of Incest*, which appeared in 1983 (Notre Dame: Notre Dame UP), looks at the origins of society in the context of the emergence of mankind and places the avunculate at the core of the social world, while also addressing the Durkheimian problem of the relationship between collective and individual thought.

Kay, Paul (born 1934)

Paul Kay obtained a Ph.D. in social anthropology at Harvard University in 1963, and in the same year published his first article 'Tahitian Fosterage and the Form of Ethnological Models' (*AA*, vol.65). He spent a period at Stanford University with the aid of a postdoctoral grant and taught for a year at MIT before moving in 1966 to the anthropology department at the University of California at Berkeley. He published several more articles on kinship terminology, but devoted most of his time to research on the perception of colour in different cultures. He collaborated on this project with the anthropologist Brent Berlin, a specialist on Tzeltal and the contemporary Maya, and in 1969 they jointly published *Basic Color Terms: Their Universality and Evolution* (Berkeley: California UP, 2nd edn 1990), which soon became a model for cognitivist anthro-pology. This book takes up a position against the Sapir–Whorf hypothesis, which states that each culture establishes its own unique colour code, by submitting that there are universals and evolutionary sequences. Berlin and Kay present colours as forming a continuum and use a chart containing 320 boxes divided into forty columns covering the whole spectrum, supplemented by a column for the neutral colours (black and white). Their conclusion is that there are shared mental structures underlying the linguistic diversity of systems of representation, because the semantic centres of fundamental colour terms are similar in all languages. They show that all languages possess terms for black and white, and that where there is a third term, it signifies red. A fourth term designates either green or yellow, the one excluding the other, while both of these colours are accounted for in languages with five terms. Blue is covered where there are six terms and brown where there are seven. Languages with eight or more terms also add purple, pink, orange or grey, or a combination of these colours. The two authors further correlate the number of terms used in a language with levels of cultural complexity. Critics have pointed out that these conclusions are reached on the basis of a few languages and a paltry number of informants (many of them acculturated), so that their evolutionism is ethnocentric. A second edition of the book responds, in part, to these objections by increasing the number of sample languages from twenty to over one hundred. Like Chomsky, Kay assumes that children are equipped with an innate structure of linguistic competence, and has engaged in extensive research on the taxonomical structures of ethnobiological classifications and on the logical foundations of kinship semantics. He remained at Berkeley, but moved from the anthropology to the linguistics department in 1972. He became a member of the American Academy of Sciences in 1997.

Said, Edward W. (1935–2003)
Born in Jerusalem, Edward W. Said studied first in Cairo and then at Princeton and Harvard universities. In 1964 he completed his Harvard thesis 'The Letters and Short Fiction of Joseph Conrad', which was published in modified form in 1966. From 1963 he taught at Columbia University, where he later became professor of comparative literature. In 1967 he published a review of **Lévi-Strauss**'s *The Savage Mind* (*Kenyon Review*, vol.29/2: 256–268), and this was followed by assessments of the works of L. Goldman, R. Barthes and M. **Foucault**. In 1970 he published his first article on the Israeli–Palestinian conflict, on which he has since written extensively (he also became a member of the Palestinian National Council). Said's seminal *Orientalism* (New York: Random House, 1978) was inspired both by the deconstruction of the object inaugurated with Lévi-Strauss's writings on totemism, and, inversely, by Foucault's construction of objects through his archaeological readings. It offers a history of the conceptual construction of the Orient generated by the Western mind and in particular by Western ethnology. The observation of rites of passage or markets is not a neutral scholarly activity, but produces the fantasy of a homogeneous and unchanging Orient against which the Occident can measure its development. Said shows that there are not one, but many Orients, and that Orientalism is an ideology serving to justify the imperial project. This work immediately took its place among the classics of anthropology. In the thirty or so works that followed Said repeatedly attacked the static notion of 'identity'. Within the constant exchange which has taken place between Europeans and their colonial subjects for half a millennium, the only idea which has altered very little is that of the difference between 'us' and 'them', both firmly established in watertight categories. Said asserts that, contrary to this vision, culture is always multicultural.

Fox, Richard (born 1939)
After obtaining a BA from Columbia University in 1960 and then taking part in a summer programme in Ecuador, Richard Fox enrolled in the anthropology department of the University of Michigan, which awarded him an MA in 1961. He studied Hindi and carried out his first fieldwork in India in 1963, and then gained a Ph.D. in 1965. He was employed as an assistant professor by Brandeis University from 1965 to 1968, then accepted a professorship at Duke University in 1972, and finally moved to the anthropology department of the University of Washington at Saint Louis. The author of eleven books, Fox is the spokesman for a global approach at a national level, an approach which has reached maturity as the initial enthusiasm following colonial independence has been followed by a more sober assessment. After a period editing the journal *American Ethnologist*, he followed Sol **Tax**, Cyril Belshaw and Adam **Kuper** to become the fourth editor of the prestigious journal *Current Anthropology* from 1994 to 2000. He has since been appointed president of the Wenner–Gren Foundation to replace Sydel Sylverman, and the editorship of *Current Anthropology* has been taken over by S. Orlove.

Rosaldo, Michelle Zimbalist (1944–1981)
While a student at Harvard University Michelle Zimbalist Rosaldo carried out research on a group of slash-and-burn cultivators in the Philippines from 1967 to 1969. After gaining a Ph.D. in 1972 she became an assistant professor at Stanford University. She was an ethnographer of the Ifugo of the Philippines, and her classic *Knowledge and Passion: Ilongot Notions of Self and Social Life* (1980) draws on the ideas of **Foucault** in seeking the thread which connects consciousness and experience of the world (1980: 21). A pioneer of gender studies, she organized the first feminist anthropology conference in the USA and, with Louise

Lamphere, edited and published the proceedings as *Women, Culture and Society* (Stanford UP, 1974). In her preface to this volume she declares her intention to capture the universality of gender asymmetry. She subsequently turned away from the structuralism inherent in such an approach and replaced it with a primary focus on what she called the dynamics of experience. It was during her third stint of fieldwork that she fell down a precipice and killed herself while seeking help for her stricken husband Renato Rosaldo. To help himself come to terms with her death, he later wrote a remarkable and introspective text which is both a profound epistemological reflection and a very beautiful tribute to his wife: entitled 'Grief and a Headhunter's Rage', it forms the introduction of his *Culture and Truth* (Beacon Press, 1993 (1989): 1–21).

SELECT BIBLIOGRAPHY

Asad, T. (1982) 'Anthropological conceptions of religion: reflections on Geertz', *Man*, 18: 237–259.

Anonymous (1994) 'Colin Turnbull', *AT*, 10(5): 24–5.

Ashcroft, P.B. and Ahluwalia, P. (1999) *Edward Said: The Paradox of Identity*, London: Routledge.

Bashkow, I. (1991a) 'Schneider, David M.', in C. Winter, pp.621–622.

——(1991b) 'The dynamics of rapport in colonial situation: David Schneider's fieldwork on the islands of Yap', in G.W. Stocking (ed.) *HOA*, vol.7: 170–242.

Baumann, G. (1999) 'Interview with E. Wolf', *EASA- Newsletter*, March 25: 8–12.

Blanckaert, C. (1988) 'Story et history de l'ethnologie', *Revue de Synthèse*, 4th series, no.3–4: 451–467.

Bohannan, P. (1956) *Justice and Judgment Among the Tiv*, Oxford Univeristy Press.

——(1963) *Social Anthropology*, New York: Holt, Rinehart and Winston.

——(1978) *The Evolution of Sex and the Future of the Family*, Santa Barbara: Center for the Study of Democratic Institutions.

——(1995a) *We, The Alien: An Introduction to Cultural Anthropology*, Prospect Heights: Waveland Press.

——(1995b) *How Culture Works*, New York: Macmillan.

Bottomore, T. *et al.* (eds) (1983) *A Dictionary of Marxist Thought*, Cambridge, MA: Harvard University Press.

Bouquet, M. (1995) 'D. M. Schneider', *AT*, 12 (1): 20–21.

Carrithers, M. (1988) 'The anthropologist as author (on Geertz)', *AT*, 4 (4): 19–22.

Castro, V., Aldunate, C. and Hidalgo, J. (2000) *Nispa Ninchis/ Decimos Deciendo: Conversaciones con John Murra*, Lima: Instituto de Estudios Peruanos.

Caughey, J-L. and Marshall, M. (1989) 'Introduction', in Caughey and M. Marshall (eds) *Culture, Kin and Cognition in Oceania: Essays in Honor of Ward H. Goodenough*, Washington: AAA.

Chamberlain, L. and Hoebel, E.A. (1942) 'Anthropology offerings in American undergraduate colleges', *AA*, 44: 527–530.

Collier, J., Wolf, M. and Yanagisako, S. (1982) 'Michelle Zimbalist Rosaldo', *Rain*, 48: 15.

Conklin, H.C. (1962) 'Lexicographical treatment of folk taxonomies' in S.A. Tyler (ed.) *Cognitive Anthropology*, Essays in honor of G.P. Murdock, New York: Holt and Rinehart, pp.14–59.

——(1964) 'Ethnogenealogical method', in W.H.A. Goodenough (ed.) *Explorations in Cultural Anthropology*, New York: McGraw Hill, pp.25–55.

Conklin, H.C. and Sturtevant, W.C. (1998) 'F. G. Lounsbury', *AN*, Sept. 39(6): 29.

David, J. (1997) 'C. Geertz', in Barfield, pp.214–216.

Di Brizio, M.B. (1995) 'Présentisme et historicisme dans l'historiographie de G.W. Stocking', *Gradhiva*, 18: 77–89.

Diamond, S. (ed.) (1960) *Culture in History: Essay in Honor of Paul Radin*, New York: Columbia University Press.

——(1964) *Primitive Views of the World*, New York: Columbia University Press.

——(1974) *In Search of the Primitive*, New Brunswick: Transaction Books.

——(ed.) (1979) *Towards a Marxist Anthropology*, The Hague and Paris: Mouton.

——(ed.) (1980a) *Anthropology: Ancestors and Heirs*, The Hague and Paris: Mouton.

——(ed.) (1980b) *Theory and Practice: Essays Presented to Gene Weltfish*, The Hague and Paris: Mouton.

Dil, A.S. (1971) 'Introduction' to Greenberg *Language, Culture and Communication*, Stanford University Press.

Englis, F. (2000) *Clifford Geertz: Culture, Custom and Ethics*, Cambridge: Cambridge University Press.

Fox, Richard (1969) *From Zamindar to Ballot Box: Community Change in a North Indian Market Town*, Ithaca: Cornell University Press.

——(1971) *Kin, Clan, Raja, and Rule: Stade-Hinterland Relations in Pre-Industrial India*, Berkeley, CA.: University of California Press.

——(1977) *Urban Anthropology: Cities in Their Cultural Settings*, Englewood Cliffs: Prentice Hall.

——(1985) *Lions of the Punjab: Culture in the Making*, Berkeley, CA.: University of California Press.

——(1989) *Gandhian Utopia: Experiments With Culture*, Boston: Beacon Press.

——(ed.) (1991) *Recapturing Anthropology, Working in the Present*, Santa Fe: School of American Research.

Fox, Richard and Starn, O. (eds) (1997) *Between Revolution and Resistance: Dissent and Cultural Protest*, New Brunswick: Rutgers University Press.

Fox, Robin (ed.) (1975) *Biosocial Anthropology*, London: Malaby Press.

——(1978b) *The Tory Islanders: A People of the Celtic Fringe*, Cambridge University Press.

——(1989a) *The Violent Imagination*, New Brunswick: Rutgers University Press.

——(1989b) *The Search for Society: Quest for a Biosocial Science and Morality*, New Brunswick: Rutgers University Press.

——(1993) *Reproduction and Succession: Studies in Anthropology, Law and Society*, New Brunswick: Transaction Publishers.

——(1994) *The Challenge of Anthropology: Old Encounters and New Excursions*, New Brunswick: Transaction Publishers.

Fox, Robin and Mehler, J. (eds) (1985) *Neonate Cognition*, Hillsdale: Erlbaum.

Friedman, J. (1987) 'An interview with Eric Wolf' *CA*, 27: 107–118.

Galey, J-C. (1991) 'Sahlins, Marshall', in P. Bonte and M. Izard (eds.) *Dictionnaire de l'ethnologie et de l'anthropologie*, Paris: Presses universitaires de France, pp.648–649.

Geertz, C. (1965) *The Social History of an Indonesian Town*, Cambridge, MA: MIT Press.

——(1980) *Negara: the Theatre State in Nineteenth-Century Bali*, Princeton: Princeton University Press.

——(1995) *After the Fact: Two Countries, Four Decades, One Anthropologist*, Cambridge, MA: Harvard University Press.

——(2000) *Available Light: Anthropological Reflections on Philosophical Topics*, Princeton: Princeton University Press.

Geertz, C., Geertz, H. and Rosen, L. (1979) *Meaning and Order in Moroccan Society: Three Essays in Cultural Analysis*, Cambridge: Cambridge University Press.

Goodenough, W.H. (1953) *Native Astronomy in the Central Carolines*, Philadelphia: University of Pennsylvania Museum.

——(1963a) *Cooperation in Change: An Anthropological Approach to Community Development*, New York: Russell Sage Foundation.

——(ed.) (1964) *Explorations in Cultural Anthropology: Essays in Honor of G.P. Murdock*, New York: McGraw Hill.

——(1970) *Description and Comparison in Cultural Anthropology Culture, Language and Society*, Chicago: Aldine.

——(1971) *Culture, Language, and Society*, Reading, MA: Addison-Wesley Publications.

——(ed.) (1996) *Prehistoric Settlement of the Pacific*, American Philosophical Society.

Goodenough, W.H. and Sugita, H. (1980; 1990) *Trukese-English Dictionary*, 2 vols Philadelphia: American Philosophical Society.

Grinker, R.R. (2000) *In the Arms of Africa: The Life of C. M. Turnbull*, New York: St. Martin Press.

Handler, R. (ed.) (2000) *Excluded Ancestors, Inventible Traditions. Essays toward a more inclusive history of anthropology*.

Handler, R. and McKinnon, S. (1995) 'D. M. Schneider', *AN*, 36(9): 39.

Harding, T. (1997) 'E. Service', *AN*, February, p.24.

Harris, M. (1959) 'Labour emigration among the Mozambique Thonga: culture and political factors' in *Africa*, 29: 50–66.

——(1974) *Cows, Pigs, Wars and Witches: the Riddles of Culture* London: Hutchinson.

——(1977) *Cannibals And Kings: The Origins of Cultures*, New York: Random House.

——(1999) *Theories of Cultures in Postmodern Times*, Walltun Creek: Altamira Press.

Harris, M. and Brown, B.J. (2000; 2001) 'Introduction' to the new edition of *The Rise of Anthropological Theory*, (with intro. by M.L. Margolis), Walnut Creek: Altamira Press.

Harris, M. and Wagley, C. (1958) *Minorities in the New World: Six Cases Studies*, New York: Columbia University Press.

Hart, W.D. (2000) *Edward Said and the Religious Effects of Culture*, Cambridge: Cambridge University Press.

Heine, B. (1985) 'The mountain people: some notes on the Ik of North-Eastern Uganda', *Africa*, 55(1): 3–16.

Houseman M. (1991) 'Schneider, David', in P. Bonte and M. Izard (eds.) *Dictionnaire de l'ethnologie et de l'anthropologie*, Paris: Presses universitaires de France, pp.645–655.

Hussein, A. (2002) *Edward Said*, London, New York: Verso.

Inglis, F. (2000) *Clifford Geertz: Culture, Custom and Ethics*, Cambridge, Malden: Polity Press.

Jablonko, A. (1991) 'Three Days', *AN*, 32(5): 19–20.

Kay, P. (ed.) (1971) *Explorations in Mathematical Anthropology*, Cambridge, MA: MIT Press.

——(1997) *Words and the Grammar of Context*, Stanford: Stanford University Press.

Kuper, A. (1999a) *Culture: The Anthropologists' Account*, Cambridge, MA: Harvard University Press.

——(1999b) 'E. Wolf', *EASA Newsletter*, June, 26: 13–14.

Leacock, E.B. (1969) *Teaching and Learning in City Schools*, New York: Basic Books.

——(1981) *Myths of Male Dominance: Collected Articles on Women Cross-Culturally*, New York: Monthly Review.

Leacock, E.B. and Lee, R. (eds) (1982) *Politics and History in Band Societies*, Paris: MSH.

Leavitt, J. (1991) 'Geertz, Clifford', in P. Bonte and M. Izard (eds.) *Dictionnaire de l'ethnologie et de l'anthropologie*, Paris: Presses universitaires de France, p.301.

Loundsbury, F.G. (1946) 'Stray number systems among certain Indian tribes', *AA*, 48: 672–645.

——(1953) 'Field methods and techniques in linguistics', in Kroeber (ed.) *Anthropology Today*, University of Chicago Press, pp.401–410.

——(1966) 'Analyse structurale des termes de parenté', *Langage*, 75–99.

——(1968) 'One hundred years of anthropological linguistics' in J.O. Brew (ed.) *One Hundred Years of Anthropology*, Cambridge, MA: Harvard University Press, pp.153–225.

——(1971) 'Étude formelle des terminologies de la parenté Crow et Omaha', in R. Jaulin and P. Richard (ed.) *Anthropologie et calcul*, Paris: UGE, 10/18, pp.60–125.

——(1982) 'Astronomical knowledge and its uses at Bonampak, Mexico', in A.F. Aveni (ed.) *Archaeo-astronomy in the New World*, Cambridge, Cambridge University Press, pp.143–168.

Loundsbury, F.G. and Scheffler, H.W. (1971) *A Study in Structural Semantics: the Siriono Kinship System*, Englewood Cliffs: Prentice Hall.

Marcus, G. (1998) 'That damn book: ten years after writing culture', *Etnográfica*, 2(1): 5–14.

Marcus, G. and Cushman, D. (1983) 'Ethnographies as texts', *Annual Review of Anthropology*, 11: 25–69.

Maybury-Lewis, D. (1965) 'Prescriptive marriage systems', *Southwestern Journal of Anthropology*, 2: 207–230.

——(1967) *Awe-Shavante Society*, Oxford University Press.

——(1979) *Dialectical Societies* Cambridge, MA: Harvard University Press.

——(1980) *The Indian Peoples of Paraguay*, Cambridge: Cultural Survival.

——(1984a) *The Prospects for Plural Societies*, Washington: American Ethnological Society.

——(1984b) *A Sociedade Xavante*, Rio de Janeiro: Francisco Alves.

——(1984c) *The Prospects for Plural Societies*, Washington DC: American Ethnological Society.

——(1986) 'A special sort of pleading: anthropology at the service of ethnic groups' in Paine (ed.) *Advocacy and Anthropology*, St. John's: Memorial University of Newfoundland Press.

——(1992) *Millennium: Tribal Wisdom and the Modern World*, New York: Viking.

——(1999) *Cultural Pluralism: Problem or Solution in the Next Century?*, Tokyo: Sophia University Press.

Maybury-Lewis, D. and Almagor, U. (eds) (1988) *The Attraction of Opposites: Thought and Society in the Dualistic Mode*, Ann Arbor: University of Michigan Press.

Mintz, S. (1996a) *Tasting Food, Tasting Freedom: Excursions into Eating, Culture and the Past*, Boston: Beacon Press.

——(1996b) 'Food for thought: an interview with Sidney Mintz', *AN*, 37(8): 1 and 4.

Mintz, S. and Price, R. (1976; 1992) *The Birth of African-American Culture*, Boston: Beacon Press.

Munson, H. (1986) 'Geertz on religion: the theory and the practice', *Religion*, 16: 19–32.

Murphy, R. (1987) *The Body Silent*, New York: Henry Holt.

Murphy, R.F. (1976) 'A quarter century of American anthropology', in Murphy (ed.) *Selected Papers from the American Anthropologist, 1946–1970*, Washington DC: AAA.

Murra, J.V. (1980; 1956) *The Economic Organization of the Inka State*, Greenwich, Conn.: JAI Press.

Murra, J., Revel, J.N. and Wachtel (1978; 1986) *Anthropological History of Andean Polities*, Cambridge, Paris: Cambridge University Press, M.S.H.

Myers, F. and Beidelman, T.O. (1998) 'A.B. Weiner', *AN*, 39(2): 27.

Newman, P. (1991) 'Interview with Joseph Greenberg', *CA*, 32: 453.

Obeyesekere, G. (1992) *The Apotheosis of Captain Cook: European Mythmaking in the Pacific*, Princeton: Princeton University Press.

Ortner, S. (ed.) (1999) *The Fate of Culture: Geertz and Beyond*, Berkeley, CA.: University of California Press.

Parsons, T. (1956) 'The department and laboratory of social relations at Harvard. Report of the chairman on the first decade 1946–1956', Cambridge, Mass.

Rapp, R. (1999) 'E. Wolf', *AT*, 15(3): 17–18.

Revel, N. (1991) 'H.C. Conklin', in P. Bonte and M. Izard (eds.) *Dictionnaire de l'ethnologie et de l'anthropologie*, Paris: Presses universitaires de France, pp.171–172.

Roseberry, W. (1982) 'Balinese cockfights and the seduction of anthropology', *Social Research*, 49: 1013–1028.

Sahlins, M. (1977) *The Use and Abuse of Biology: An Anthropological Critique of Sociobiology*, London: Tavistock.

——(1978) 'Culture as protein and profit', *The New York Review of Books*, 25: 45–53.

——(1985) *Islands of History*, Chicago: University of Chicago Press.

——(1995) *How 'Natives' think about Captain Cook for example*, Chicago: Chicago University Press.

——(2000) *Culture in Practice, Selected Essays*, New York: Zone.

Sahlins, M. and Kirch, P. (1992) *Anuhalu: The Anthropology of History*, Chicago: University of Chicago Press.

Said, E.W. (1966) *Joseph Conrad and the Fiction of Autobiography*, Oxford University Press.

——(1975) *Beginnings: Intention and Method*, New York: Columbia University Press.

——(1979) *The Question of Palestine*, New York: Times Books.

——(1994a) *The Pen and the Sword: Conversations with David Barsamian*, Monroe: Common Courage.

——(1994b) *Representations of the Intellectual*, New York: Pantheon Books.

——(1995) *Peace and Its Discontents: Gaza-Jericho 1993–1995*, London: Vintage Books.

——(2000a) *The End of the Peace Process, Oslo and After*, New York: Pantheon Books.

——(2000b) *Reflexions on Exile and Other Essays*, Cambridge, MA: Harvard University Press.

Schneider, D. as told to Handler, R. (1995) *Schneider on Schneider: The Conversion of the Jews and other Anthropological Stories*, Durham: Duke University Press.

Schneider, D.M. (1965) 'Some muddles in the models' in M. Banton (ed.), *The Relevance of Models for Social Anthropology*, London: Tavistock, pp.25–85.

Schneider, D.M. and Gough, K. (eds) (1961) *Matrilineal Kinship*, Berkeley, CA.: University of California Press.

Schneider, D.M., Hunt, E.E., Kidder, N. and Stevens, W.D. (1949) *The Micronesians of Yap and Their Depopulation*. Coordinated investigation of Micronesian anthropology, Report vol.24, Washington DC: Pacific Science Board.

Schneider, D.M. and Sharp, L. (1969) *The Dream Life of a Primitive People, The Dreams of the Yir Yoront of Australia*, Ann Arbor: Michigan University Press.

Schneider, D.M. and Smith, R. (1973) *Class Differences and Sex Roles in American Kinship and Family Structure*, Englewood Cliffs: Prentice-Hall.

Schneider, J. (1998) 'A. B. Weiner', *AT*, 14(2): 22.

Service, E.R. (1962; 1971) *Primitive Social Organization: An Evolutionary Perspective*, New York: Random.

——(1963) *Profile in Ethnology: A Revision of a Profile of Primitive Culture*, New York: Harper and Row.

——(1966) *The Hunters*, New York: Prentice-Hall.

——(ed.) (1975) *Origins of the State and Civilization: The Process of Cultural Evolution*, New York: Norton.

——(1985) *A Century of Controversy, Ethnological issues from 1860 to 1960*, Orlando: Academic Press.

Service, E.R. and Cohen, R. (1978) *Origins of the State: the Anthropology of Political Evolution*, Philadelphia.

Shankman, P. (1984) 'The thick and the thin: on the interpretative theoretical program of Clifford Geertz', *CA*, 25: 261–279.

Spencer, J. (1996) 'Scandals, anthropological', in A. Barnard and J. Spencer (eds) *Encyclopedia of Social and Cultural Anthropology*, London: Routledge, pp.501–503.

Spinker, M. (ed.) (1992) *E. Said: A Critical Reader*, London: Basil Blackwell.

Steward, J., Mintz, S. *et al.* (1956) *The People of Puerto Rico*, Urbana: University of Illinois Press.

Stocking, G.W. (1979) *Anthropology at Chicago: Tradition, Discipline, Department*, Chicago: J. Regenstein Library.

——(1992) *The Ethnographer's Magic and Other Essays in the History of Anthropology*, Madison: University of Wisconsin Press.

——(2001) *Delimiting Anthropology: Occasional Enquires and Reflections*, Madison: University of Wisconsin Press.

——(ed.) (1983–1996) *History of Anthropology*, vol. 1–9, Madison: University of Wisconsin Press.

——(ed.) (1973–2001) *History of Anthropology Newsletters*, Chicago: University of Chicago, Dept of Anthropology.

Sturtevant, W. (1960) 'The significance of ethnological similarities between Southeastern North America and the Antille', *Yale University Publications in Anthropology*, no.64.

——(1974) *Boxes and Bowls: Decorated Containers by Nineteenth-Century Haida, Tlingit, Bella Bella and Tsimshian Indian Artists*, Washington: Smithsonian Institute.

——(ed.) (1987) *A Seminole Source Book*, London: Garland.

——(ed.) (1992) *The Christopher Columbus Encyclopedia*, New York: Schuster.

Sutton, C. (1998) *From Labrador to Samoa: The Theory and Practice of E. Burke Leacock*, Washington: AAA.

Turnbull, C. (1962) *The Lonely African*, New York: Simon and Schuster.

——(1965; 1976) *Wayward Servants: The Two worlds of the African Pygmies*, Westport: Greenwood.

——(1976) *Man in Africa*, New York: Doubleday.

Varadharahan, A. (1995) *Exotic Parodies: Subjectivity in Adorno, Said and Spivak*, Minneapolis: Minnesota University Press.

Vincent, J. (1990) *Anthropology and Politics: Visions, traditions and trends*, Tuscon: University of Arizona Press.

Vincent, J. (1996) 'American anthropology', in A. Barnard and J. Spencer (eds) *Encyclopedia of Social and Cultural Anthropology*, London: Routledge, pp.25–28.

Walter, A. (1993) 'An Interview with Robin Fox', *CA*, 34: 441–452.

Ward Gailey, C. (1975) 'Eleanor Leacock', *AN*, 16(5): 17.

——(1988) 'Eleanor Burke Leacock', in U. Gacs (ed.), pp.215–221.

——(1992) *Essays in Honor of Stanley Diamond: Dialectical Anthropology*, 2 vols. Gainesville: Florida University Press.

Weiner, A.B. (1992) *Inalienable Possessions: The Paradox of Keeping-While-Giving*, Berkeley, CA.: University of California Press.

——(1989) 'Candidates for President-elect', *AN*, May: 19.

Winkin, Y. (1986) 'George W. Stocking, jr. et l'histoire de l'anthropologie', *Actes de la recherche en sciences sociales*, 64: 81–84.

Wolf, E. (1964) *Anthropology*, Englewood Cliffs: Prentice-Hall.

Wolf, E., Koster, A., Meijers, D. (eds) (1991) *Religious Regimes and State Formation Perspectives from European Ethnology*, Albany: SUNY Press.

——(1998) *Envisioning Power: Ideologies of Dominance and Crisis*, Berkeley, CA.: University of California Press.

Wolf, E. and Hansen, E.C. (1972) *The Human Condition in Latin America*, New York: Oxford.

XIV

The British schools since 1945

In the years leading up to the Second World War, anthropology in Great Britain was taught at the LSE, Oxford University, Cambridge University and UCL. **Radcliffe-Brown** was appointed as the first professor of social anthropology at Oxford in 1937 (**Marett** having been a reader there at his retirement). At Cambridge a friend of **Frazer** endowed the William Wyse chair, which was first held by T. C. Hodson, a retired colonial administrator in India who had been made a reader in 1926. In 1936 Hodson was succeeded by J. Hutton (1885–1968), who during his time in the Indian Civil Service from 1909 to 1936 had made a population census of and written two books on the head-hunting Naga populations (see Indian Anthropology pp. 271–277). Hutton was joined by J. Driberg (1888–1946), who had left the Colonial Service to study anthropology under **Seligman** and **Malinowski** before teaching the subject from 1932 to 1942. **Evans-Pritchard** also gave a number of lectures at Cambridge. The founders of anthropology in Britain died in a span of years from shortly before to shortly after the Second World War: G. Elliot **Smith** in 1937; J. G. Frazer in 1939; A. C. **Haddon** and Seligman in 1940; R. R. Marett in 1943; and J. Driberg in 1946.

For this reason the years immediately following the war saw the emergence of a new generation, which established the dominance of social anthropology and presided over the British tradition until the early 1970s. **Malinowski** died in 1942, and was replaced at the LSE by **Firth** in 1944. In 1945 UCL created an anthropology department with its own chair, which was first held by **Forde**. After returning from São Paolo, Radcliffe-Brown resumed his teaching at Oxford in 1945 but retired the following year, to be succeeded by Evans-Pritchard. **Fortes**, a reader at Oxford from 1947, filled the William Wyse chair at Cambridge in 1950 after the removal of A. **Richards** by seeing off his rival C. von **Fürer-Haimendorf** (his election is described by Stocking, 1995: 431). In 1949 M. **Gluckman**, who had taught at Oxford from 1947, established the chair in social anthropology at Manchester University. Finally, F. **Nadel**, C. von Fürer-Haimendorf and K. Little were appointed to readerships, respectively at Durham University in 1948, SOAS in 1949, and Edinburgh University in 1950; all three established new departments in their institutions.

In 1946, on the initiative of Evans-Pritchard and following a meeting held at the LSE, the Association of Social Anthropologists of the UK and the Commonwealth (ASA) was set up as a counterweight to the Royal Anthropological Institute, which remained attached to evolutionism and brought together seasoned professionals and wealthy amateurs. Membership of the Association was conditional on proposal by an existing member and on holding, or having held, a teaching or research appointment in social anthropology. **Leach** much later specified that 'The ASA was started as a "professional trade union" . . . [that] the original role of the ASA was to prevent the Universities from employing unqualified refugees from the disappearing Colonial service to teach "applied anthropology" ' (quoted by Spencer, 2000; from Grillo, 1994: 310).

British universities counted about thirty social anthropologists at the beginning of the 1950s. Evans-Pritchard, who held the Oxford chair, supported the candidacy of the replacements for Fortes and Gluckman, who were both readers from 1947 to 1949: Fortes was succeeded by F. B. Steiner, a Czech poet of Jewish origin who had studied under Radcliffe-Brown and who died in the mid–1950s; and Gluckman's successor was J. G. Peristiany, a Cypriot doctor of law who had qualified from the Institute of Political Sciences in Paris in 1937 and gained a Cambridge Ph.D. under Marett in 1938 after fieldwork in East Africa. Evans-Pritchard also engaged G. **Lienhardt** as a lecturer in 1949; M. N. **Srinivas** as an assistant in 1945 and then as a lecturer dedicated to Indian studies from 1948 to 1951; L. **Dumont** as a lecturer from 1952 to 1954; and D. Pocock from 1955 to 1960. Staff strength was bolstered by former students such as M. **Douglas**, who taught from 1949 to 1951, and her replacement P. **Bohannan**, a lecturer from 1951 to 1956. Students at Oxford during this period included Laura Bohannan, J. **Goody**, John Barnes, Emrys Peters, P. Stirling, J. **Beattie**, J. **Middleton**, P. Baxter, D. Brokensha. I. Cunnison, R. Needham, J. Pitt-Rivers, K. Burridge, W. Newell and D. Pocock.

The chair at the LSE was held by R. Firth, and his colleagues were the lecturers Nadel (1946–1947) and E. **Leach** (1947–1953), and the professor I. **Schapera** (1950–1969). A. Richards, formerly professor at the University of Witwatersrand, also taught at the LSE, as did two Americans, E. Bott and D. **Schneider** (1949–1952). Shortly afterwards the department was joined by two more lecturers, M. Freedman and P. Stirling, and from 1956 by L. **Mair**, the new reader in colonial administration.

At Cambridge M. Fortes was at first a solitary figure before gaining teaching assistance from **Fortune** in 1947. They were joined in 1953 by a new lecturer, E. Leach, and in 1956 by A. Richards, and the staff was rounded out by J. Goody, S. Tambiah, and a number of other former students.

At UCL Forde engaged Phyllis Mary Kaberry as reader and Mary Douglas as lecturer. They were joined by M. G. Smith, P. Morton-Williams and Ray Bradbury, and later by Robin Horton and J. Middleton. At Manchester, Gluckman successively found positions for E. Colson, John Barnes, Ian Cunnison and A. L. **Epstein**. Meanwhile, Fürer-Haimendorf's appointment of Adrian Meyer and F. G. Bailey at SOAS assured its status as the headquarters of Indian studies.

Alongside those with entries below, mention should be made of, among others, K. Little, D. Tait, K. Gough, P. Stirling, P. C. Lloyd, J. La Fontaine, J. Benthall, A. Gell, D. F. Pocock, J. Pitt-Rivers, L. Fallers, P. M. Kaberry. E. Goody, P. Rivière and I. M. Lewis, who all left their mark on British anthropology.

THE THIRD GENERATION: THE IMMEDIATE POST-WAR PERIOD

'Looking back, it is apparent that as a distinctive intellectual movement, British social anthropology lasted for just fifty years, from the early 1920s to the early 1970s' (**Kuper**, 1996: 176). In what follows I shall divide what I call the third generation into three distinct groupings. The first contains those whose writings on lineage structures carried forward the functionalist project, and who sometimes sought to contribute to a resolution of the social and political problems of modern Africa. This aim was more pronounced in the Manchester School, the second grouping, which used analyses of indigenous legal systems as a basis for an examination of the antagonistic forces of cohesion and rupture. The third grouping contains those who, from the early 1960s, fell under the influence of **Lévi-Strauss**, even though their work is otherwise highly diverse.

FILIATION, SEGMENTATION, LINEAGE AND STATE

Rejecting the arguments and problematics of diffusionism and evolutionism as well as the explanatory models of culturalist psychology, this third generation of British ethnologists concentrated on empirical fieldwork study of social phenomena understood as total organized entities. Their approach consisted in restoring any phenomenon they observed to its social context and then interpreting it in terms of its position within a totality and its role in the reproduction of that totality. Leaving aside the case of **Firth** and later that of **Leach**, it is worth determining the extent to which this form of anthropology, which the British called social anthropology to distinguish it from the cultural anthropology of the Americans, was focused on Black Africa. From the 1940s university courses concentrated on kinship, marriage, forms of residence, political organization, economic life, religion, and symbolism on the one hand, and on what were then considered to be the less 'academic' fields of secret societies, urbanization and voluntary associations on the other.

Fürer-Haimendorf, Christoph von (1909–1995)

Born in Central Europe, Christoph von Fürer-Haimendorf studied at the University of Vienna and then at the LSE, where he attended **Malinowski**'s lectures, before undertaking research on the Naga in India. He obtained a doctorate in 1931 and was given a teaching assistantship at Vienna in 1934. He returned to India in 1939, where he was briefly imprisoned by the British authorities at the outbreak of the Second World War, and then worked for ten years as an adviser to the colonial administration, and during this period he published a series of ethnic monographs. He settled in England in 1949, becoming a reader and then, in 1951, a professor at SOAS, which he transformed into a major centre of meticulous ethnographic anthropology. As well as his in-depth ethnographic studies, he is known for his comparative work and his research into social change (1967). Fürer-

Haimendorf was one of the first to exploit the potential of visual documentation, collecting more than ten thousand photographs and more than one hundred hours of film. He was president of the Royal Anthropological Institute from 1975 to 1977.

Southall, Aidan William (born 1911)

Born into a religious family in Warwickshire, Aidan William Southall became interested in anthropology after studying classics. As a conscientious objector during the war he was ineligible to join the Rhodes–Livingstone Institute on obtaining his BA in 1944, but A. **Richards** found him a position in Makerere, Uganda, where he taught social sciences. There he took the opportunity to carry out fieldwork on the Luo and, in 1947, on the Alur. Three years later he returned to Britain, where he became acquainted with **Firth** and in 1948 began postgraduate research at the LSE. The colonial administration then entrusted him with an investigation into migrant workers among the Alur. In his Ph.D. thesis, which he wrote up on his return to London in 1950 and submitted the following year, Southall refines the categories of **Radcliffe-Brown** and **Evans-Pritchard** in his examination of the possible compatibility between state segmentation and formation among the Alur, advancing the notion of the 'segmentary state' (*Alur Society*, Cambridge: Heffer & Sons, 1953). In response to **Leach**'s criticisms (1961), he defended his typologies, describing them as inevitable steps towards generalization (1965). He worked at the East African Institute of Social Research and then won a UNESCO grant for a period of study in the social relations department established by T. Parsons at Harvard University. He subsequently undertook a vast research project on the position of educated women in Black Africa. He taught at the universities of Syracuse (1964–1971) and Makerere, and completed further research in Madagascar and then South Africa before taking up a professorship at the University of Wisconsin. In 1968 he wrote his classic 'Stateless Societies' for the *International Encyclopedia of the Social Sciences*, in which he asserts that in such societies political activity takes place at all levels of the social structure. In the final part of his career, Southall became one of the pioneers of urban anthropology, looking first at East Africa and then at other areas, particularly China.

Beattie, John Hugh Marshall (1915–1990)
Born in Liverpool, John Hugh Marshall Beattie studied philosophy in Dublin and then anthropology at Oxford, after which he carried out intensive research on the Bunyoro Kingdom in Uganda. He was successively an administrator in Tanganyika (now Tanzania) from 1940 to 1949, a lecturer in social anthropology at Oxford from 1953 (gaining a D.Phil. under **Evans-Pritchard** in 1956), a senior lecturer there

from 1953 to 1971, and finally a professor of African cultural anthropology and sociology at the University of Leyden from 1971. In 1974 he retired to Oxford, where he died on 13 April 1990. The Bunyoro Kingdom was the subject of three major works by Beattie: *Bunyoro: An African Kingdom* (1960), *Understanding an African Kingdom* (1965), and *The Nyoro State* (1965), which all take their place among the early classics on African kingdoms. He is also remembered for his highly popular introduction to cultural anthropology: *Other Cultures: Aims, Methods and Achievements in Social Anthropology* (1964).

Goody, Jack John Rankine (born 1919)
Born in London, Jack John Rankine Goody began a degree course at Cambridge University and then served in the armed forces during the Second World War. In 1942 he was taken prisoner by the Germans and spent nearly three years in POW camps, and he later wrote that this experience aroused his passionate interest in his fellow human beings (1996). After his release he completed his degree at Cambridge in 1946 and then enrolled in the university's archaeology and anthropology faculty, where he was soon engrossed by a lecture series on tribal warfare given by the visiting professor **Evans-Pritchard** in 1946–1947. Almost immediately on becoming a graduate student in 1950 he was sent by M. **Fortes** to the DoDagaba (Dagara or Lobi), who at **Firth**'s suggestion had been classified as a study priority by the Colonial Social Science Research Council. On his return to Britain in 1952 Goody wrote *The Social Organization of the LoWiili* (Oxford UP, 1956), and in 1956–1957 he returned to the field. His aim was to study the interpersonal relations between patrilineal and matrilineal clans, and his efforts yielded an original treatment of the question of the avunculate (1959), work on systems of descent, and a new understanding of the function of mortuary

rites which linked them to the social structure, and more particularly to the status of the deceased and of his relatives (1962). During a further period he spent in the field from 1964 to 1966 to analyse religion Goody encountered an outcast who recounted to him his version of the Bagre ceremony, which was unknown at the time (Goody, 1991: 7). In their subsequent work on the Gonja Kingdom of Northern Ghana, he and Esther Goody studied the process of the succession to power, which as in other West African cases is lateral rather than intergenerational (1996). Goody then examined the conditions of the emergence of the Gonja state (1971). In 1972 he published *The Myth of the Bagre* (Oxford UP), his first book on Bagre initiation, and this was followed in 1980 by an edition of the texts recited at initiations. As well as being an ethnographer of West Africa, Goody looked at cognitive processes and their modes of social functioning. He examined the impact of writing on 'primitive' societies (1968), and then demonstrated that the organization of information made possible by writing (the compilation of lists, systems of dating, etc.) entails the construction of a new logic independent of the context in which words and sentences are articulated (1977). *The Logic of Writing and the Organization of Society* (1986) considers the effects that the introduction of writing has on the organization of social action, such as the subjectivization and diffusion of religious discourse, the emergence of a literate class and the codification of law. This line of enquiry was taken further in 1987 in *The Interface Between the Oral and the Written* (Cambridge UP). In parallel with this research Goody wrote studies on the evolution of social structures using a method akin to that of **Murdock**. The first of these was *Production and Reproduction: A Comparative Study of the Domestic Domain* (1977), which seeks to trace the historical connection between the fields of kinship and economics, and this was followed by works of

comparative research on modes of reproduction in social structures dominated by kinship ties (1982, 1983, 1990). These comparative and evolutionist analyses sometimes focus on minor or neglected subjects like cuisine (1982) or flowers (1993), and here Goody is at his very best. He held a readership at Cambridge and then, from 1973 to 1984, was M. Fortes' successor in the William Wyse chair and head of the anthropology department.

Lienhardt, Godfrey (1921–1993)

Born in Bradford in Yorkshire, Godfrey Lienhardt took his degree at Oxford University and then carried out research among the Dinka, neighbours of the Nuer, from 1947 to 1950 at the suggestion of **Evans-Pritchard**. He produced various studies of the social organization and thought of the populations of East Africa and contributed 'The Western Dinka' to *Tribes without Rulers*, edited by J. **Middleton** and D. Tait (1958). Published in 1961, his thesis *Divinity and Experience: The Religion of the Dinka* was his major work. In it Lienhardt gives an account of Dinka cosmology and underscores the fact that individual lives are transcended by sacrificial ritual in Durkheimian fashion, while also addressing the question of what an ethnologist can perceive of the experience of others. This led him, more than any other ethnologist of the period, to approach this experience from an indigenous perspective, rather along the lines of Evans-Pritchard's *Nuer Religion* (1956). Lienhardt also made studies of the Anuak of Sudan, and in 1964 he published a small handbook entitled *Social Anthropology* (Oxford UP). He was a lecturer at Oxford from 1949, and became a reader there in 1972.

Middleton, John (born 1921)

John Middleton studied anthropology at the universities of London and then Oxford. From 1949 to 1953 he carried out fieldwork on the Lugbara of Uganda, gaining a D.Phil.

in 1953. He held teaching posts successively at London, Cape Town and Northwestern universities before directing the anthropology department at New York University until 1972. He worked in Nigeria from 1964, Ghana in 1976, and Kenya from 1986 to 1991. In 1958 he co-edited *Tribes without Rulers* with D. Tait. The two authors construct a detailed taxonomy of stateless societies by examining decentralized, so-called 'cognatic' societies and distinguishing between three types of segmentary societies: Central African societies without incorporated descent; East African societies in which age sets play an important role; and Nigerian societies where the same role is played by village councils and their associations. In his work on the Lugbara of Uganda, Middleton examined the process of lineage fission and showed how leaders manipulate rituals so as to maintain their privileges (1960). He and P. **Bohannan** co-wrote numerous books on the classic topics of anthropology, and here too he made significant contributions to the discipline. He was a professor at SOAS in London from 1972 to 1981, and then at other universities including Yale. He also edited a compendious encyclopaedia devoted to Sub-Saharan Africa (1997).

Ardener, Edwin (1927–1987)
A student at the LSE in the immediate postwar years, Edwin Ardener was also one of the youngest researchers of the wave going into the field from 1945 to 1950. He spent thirteen months among the Ibo of Nigeria, which resulted in *A Socio-Economic Survey of the Mba-Ise*, and was subsequently appointed to a research fellowship at the West African (later Nigerian) Institute of Social and Economic Research. He then worked in Cameroon for eleven years accompanied by his wife Shirley, undertaking a variety of ethnographic work, including demographic studies, which were a rarity at the time. In 1963 he was appointed to a lectureship at Oxford University, where he took an interest in the relations between anthropology and linguistics and then in the position of women. He also contributed to the creation of an anthropology of Europe and published a large number of articles.

THE MANCHESTER SCHOOL

After directing the Rhodes–Livingstone Institute from 1941 to 1947, **Gluckman** created an anthropology department at Manchester University in 1949. Thus he was the founder of what became known as the Manchester School, which contained such figures as **Mitchell**, Barnes, Bailey, **Turner**, Frankenberg and **Epstein**. Focusing its attention on Southern Africa, this school carried forward the 'extended-case' method already developed in fieldwork. This method requires that research be continued over a lengthy period of years or even decades, and that the cases studied permit the examination of carefully delimited questions. The School took a particular interest in the legal field and in social conflicts, and then in migrations and network analysis. Statistical method was used to facilitate demonstration of the cyclical nature of accusations of witchcraft and their correspondence with the various stages in the development and fission of villages. The research of the School's members diversified rapidly, and so Spencer is right to say that 'the distinctive strand of work pioneered by Gluckman and his followers in Manchester did not survive Gluckman's own retirement in the early 1970s' (Spencer 2000: 10). Turner followed a very individual path in his work at American universities, while others, such as T. S. Epstein, A. L. Epstein and A. Rew, became involved in an anthropology of development, especially in their work at the Institute of Development Studies at Sussex University.

Mitchell, J. Clyde (1918–1995)

Born in South Africa, J. Clyde Mitchell gained a BA in social sciences in 1942 and then volunteered for service in the navy. After the war he researched on the Lamba of Zambia under the supervision of **Gluckman**, and from 1947 to 1949 worked on the Yao of Malawi with the support of the Rhodes–Livingstone Institute. In 1950 he was awarded a D.Phil. by Oxford University for his thesis *The Yao Village*, which was published in 1956. Here he demonstrates how accusations of witchcraft play an important role of ideological legitimation during the process of village fission and how rituals are manipulated by village leaders. Mitchell's subsequent work focused on urban life and made use of statistical information. He was director of the Rhodes–Livingstone Institute from 1952 to 1955 and then professor of African studies at Rhodesia College from 1954 to 1964. He resigned this post in opposition to the policy of Apartheid and in 1966 became professor of urban anthropology at Manchester University. He left Manchester in 1973 to take up a fellowship at Nuffield College, Oxford, which he held until 1985. In his investigations into urban anthropology Mitchell developed network analysis.

Turner, Victor Witter (1920–1983)

Born in Glasgow, Victor Witter Turner studied English literature and then anthropology at Manchester University, the latter under **Gluckman**. He had a position with the Rhodes–Livingstone Institute from 1950 to 1954 and carried out research on the Ndembu, a Bantu population in Zambia. After gaining an appointment at Manchester he wrote his first book *Schism and Continuity in an African Society: A Study of a Ndembu Village* (Manchester UP). Published in 1957, this book treats of the contradictions at the heart of the principles of social organization, particularly the considerable marital instability caused when matrilineage is confronted with virilocal residence. Turner's application of statistical analysis to genealogical data relating to village fission reveals the regularity of the larger system of social relations (1957: 232). He also demonstrates that cases of fission are counterbalanced by the forces of cohesion, such as rituals, which reinforce solidarity in inter-village relations. He then turned to the study of divination and its symbolism in *Ndembu Divination: Its Symbolism and Techniques* (Manchester UP, 1961). After taking a position at Cornell University, he published a collection of his essays written between 1958 and 1964 on the subject of the symbolism of the Ndembu, seen particularly through their rituals: *The Forest of Symbols: Aspects of Ndembu Ritual* (Ithaca: Cornell UP, 1967). The parts of the book on colour symbolism (dating from 1963) and on rites of passage (dating from 1964) in particular have had a lasting influence on scholarship. Taking up **van Gennep**'s three-sequence schema, Turner then addressed the question of intervals known as liminal periods. In 1968 he published *The Drums of Affliction: A Study of Religious Processes among the Ndembu of Zambia* (Oxford: Clarendon Press), and in 1969 *The Ritual Process: Structure and Anti-Structure* (Chicago: Aldine), in which he refines the concept of liminality to designate the whole period of transition between two structured social states. This moment he calls an anti-structure because the individual is immersed in one of a number of *communitas* which Turner typologizes. The balance between structure and anti-structure is a constant feature of any society, and the latter reinforces the former through the replacement of celebration of social participation by a human link which transcends the statutory order and is therefore a source of stability. This Durkheim-inspired thinking is further developed in *Dramas, Fields and Metaphors: Symbolic Action in Human Society* (Cornell UP, 1974), in which he seeks to define the rituals and categories of symbolic thought and to demonstrate their symbolic and social effectiveness; this line of enquiry exerted an influence on other fields, notably literary criticism. He was engaged by the University of Chicago in 1968 and by the University of Virginia in 1977. After Turner's death his wife published his *On the Edge of the Bush: Anthropology as Experience* (Tucson: Arizona UP, 1985).

Epstein, Arnold Leonard (1924–1999)

Born in Liverpool, Arnold Leonard 'Bill' Epstein took a BA in law at the Queens University of Belfast in 1944 and then served in the Royal Navy before studying anthropology at the LSE from 1947 to 1949. He worked for the Rhodes–Livingstone Institute from 1950 to 1956 and became interested in the evolution of traditional law in the mining region of Northern Rhodesia. He showed how the constitution of an urban personality and the gradual disappearance of tribal models and traditional relationships manifest themselves in the emigrant worker (*Juridical Techniques and the Judicial Process*, Rhodes–Livingstone Paper, 1954). Prohibited by the authorities from entering the mine compounds, he was nevertheless able to gather enough material for his *Politics in an Urban African Community* (Manchester UP, 1958), one of the essential texts on the emerging Africa. He married the anthropologist T. Scarlett Epstein and held a research post at Manchester University from 1956 to 1958 before moving to the University of Canberra, where he became professor in 1966 and head of the anthropology department in 1970. At Canberra he used a Kleinian perspective to investigate such topics as identity and the emotions. He was then appointed to

a professorship at Sussex University, where he remained until his retirement in 1981. While always continuing to publish on Africa, Epstein also became a noted specialist on Papua New Guinea.

Worsley, Peter M. (born 1924)

Peter M. Worsley studied at Cambridge University, gaining a BA in anthropology and archaeology in 1947, and was then appointed to a readership at Manchester University, where he obtained an MA under **Gluckman**. His membership of the Communist Party from 1942 until the invasion of Hungary by the Soviet Union in 1956 made it impossible for him to work for the Rhodes–Livingstone Institute. On Gluckman's advice he moved to Australia, where he researched Melanesian cults and gained a Ph.D. from the Australian National University. In 1955 he returned to Britain, where he combined teaching in the sociology department of the University of Hull with work as Gluckman's assistant until his appointment to the sociology chair of Manchester University in 1964. Published in 1957, his best-known book *The Trumpet Shall Sound: A Study of Cargo Cults in Melanesia* (2nd rev. edn, New York: Schocken) gives an account of Melanesian messianic movements and the celebrated cargo cult. The disparity between White men's possessions and their own is attributed by the Papuans to the support Whites gain from their ancestors, so that they feel they must make contact not with the Whites themselves, but with the ancestors who send them cargo aeroplanes. The parachuting of goods during the Second World War did much to reinforce such beliefs.

THE 'STRUCTURALISTS'

It would be fair to say that **Leach**'s analysis of the Jingpaw–Kachin terminological system in the 1950s opened the doors to structuralism in Britain. But a definitive break with the past was only made at the **Malinowski** Memorial Lecture in 1959. Consigning functionalist works to the status of the typological obsessions of butterfly collectors, Leach argued that social phenomena should not be considered in terms of an implicitly biological finality, but as mathematical arrangements. From then on a structuralist movement could be said to exist in Britain, for, whatever differences existed between its main exponents, some of whom were in fact critical of **Lévi-Strauss**, they all held to the radical view that meaning is not yielded by functions or to be sought behind them by means of hermeneutic enquiry, but derives from the structure itself. In other words, on the analogy of the system of opposing pairs such as 'p' and 'b' in phonology, the green traffic light only makes sense in contrast to the red traffic light, and in a pack of cards the jack of spades only has a value through being different from fifty-one other cards. The task is therefore to isolate the fields of transformation and examine the variation in their elements, the logic of exclusion and inclusion, of compatibility and incompatibility, and to deduce the laws of association which explain the human world far better than the notion of functions.

Leach, Sir Edmund Ronald (1910–1989)
Edmund Ronald Leach was born in Sidmouth into a very well-to-do 'family of mill-owners with interests in the Argentine' (Goody, 1991: 2), and his great uncle was president of the Royal Archaeological Institute and a Member of Parliament (Leach, 1984: 2). Between 1929 and 1932 Leach studied mathematics and qualified as an engineer from Cambridge University. He then spent several years in the Far East, working as an engineer in Shanghai from 1932 to 1937. In 1937 he met **Malinowski** and was 'converted' to anthropology (Leach, 1984). He carried out his first fieldwork in Thailand in 1937 and in Kurdistan in 1938, and then returned to Britain to study under Malinowski and **Firth** in 1939–1940. His first book, published in 1940, was *Social and Economic Organization of the Rawanduz Kurds* (London: Athlone). During the Second World War he was conscripted into the colonial army in Burma, where he was able to gather a significant body of ethnographical material. In 1945 Leach published 'Jingpaw Kinship Terminology' with the subtitle 'An Experiment in Ethnographic Algebra' (*JRAI*, vol.75). The article was written in Calcutta in 1943 'at a time when I had never heard of structuralism', but for all its adherence to the Malinowskian dogma of the universality of the nuclear family it pre-sented a structural approach to kinship data. In 1947 Leach went on a mission to Borneo, and on his return became a lecturer at the LSE and then, in 1953, at Cambridge. One of the few British anthropologists with a reading knowledge of French, he discovered **Lévi-Strauss**'s *Elementary Structures of Kinship* shortly after its appearance in 1948, and in 1951 published 'The Structural Implications of Matrilateral Cross-Cousin Marriage', the first critical commentary on Lévi-Strauss's work. This was followed in 1954 by *Political Systems of Highland Burma: A Study of Kachin Social Structure* (Cambridge UP), which identified a political whole determined by two opposing poles. The Kachin political system is seen as constantly oscillating between the *gumlao* model, which is egalitarian and democratic, and the *gumsa* model, in which lineages are classed in a hierarchy. There is thus a constant ebb and flow between these two models in Kachin systems. Importantly, the two main Shan and the Kachin groups are not isolated communities, and the fact that the same group can fundamentally change its organization points to the purely conventional nature of the concept of unitary cultures. The oscillation of the Kachin entity can only be understood when repositioned in the context of a larger entity encompassing the Shan kingdoms of the neighbouring

plains and the influence of the Chinese empire, and so the idea of an ethnic entity is irrelevant. Responding to Leach's denial of the existence of stable systems, **Gluckman** asserted that the dynamic movements in the Kachin structure are motivated from within that structure. Leach countered that the transformation of a political system based on egalitarian lineage segments into a hierarchized and feudal system amounts to a change in the very form of the structure. This book marks anthropology's move away from the question of the birth of the state, which had haunted the discipline from its origins, in favour of a reading of historical dynamics as a process without origin, centralizing communities or pushing them to the periphery.

Leach spent the years from 1954 to 1956 on an expedition to Ceylon, and then after several articles he published *Pul Eliya: A Village in Ceylon – A Study of Land Tenure and Kinship* (Cambridge UP). Using Pul Eliya as the basis for reflections on the question of lineage, he argues that kinship structures are merely property relationships. He criticizes **Fortes**'s employment of the term 'complementary filiation' and the pre-eminence accorded by the British School to the study of the rules of descent at the expense of forms of matrimonial exchange. He also states that statistical norms and data should be treated separately, and that the latter should be privileged. He was appointed to a readership at Cambridge in 1957 and in the same year published *Rethinking Anthropology* (London: Athlone). The book's first essay, which gives it its title, is an attack on the principle of comparative analysis of social structures as advanced by **Radcliffe-Brown**. For Leach, this principle is little more than a taxonomical method comparable with that of a 'butterfly collector', a way of classifying types and sub-types according to generally arbitrary criteria which are in fact ethnocentric. He is also critical of functionalism, and challenges the idea that societies are integrated and stable systems. This collection also

contains an essay, first published in 1951, which was one of the first texts devoted to *Elementary Structures of Kinship* by Lévi-Strauss, on whom Leach would eventually write a whole book. At first a close follower of Lévi-Strauss, he later condemned as 'metaphysical' his wont to appeal to notions of the human spirit to explain structural regularities. In *Culture and Communication* (1976), he concentrated on the study of indigenous cultural categories. He was appointed to the chair at Cambridge University in 1972, and was also Provost of King's College from 1966 to 1979.

Douglas, Mary (née Tew, born 1921)
Born in San Remo in Italy as the daughter of an Indian Civil Servant, Mary Douglas spent her childhood years in the Sacred Heart Convent School, a Catholic boarding school staffed by nuns. She graduated in French civilization at the Sorbonne in 1938 and then, from 1939 to 1942, studied for a politics, philosophy and economics degree at Oxford University. She discovered anthropology while working for the Colonial Office from 1943 until 1947, and then went to the Pitt Rivers Museum wishing to be registered for the Oxford Diploma in Anthropology. The museum's curator M. Penniman told her to read and reflect on Henry Balfour's 1937 Frazer Lecture and return the next day to be questioned. But very soon afterwards A. **Richards** (1930) and **Evans-Pritchard** (1940) became her staple reading. At the time the teaching at Oxford's Institute of Social Anthropology led either to a BSc or a BA, and Douglas obtained the former with a dissertation on marriage influenced by her tutorials with Evans-Pritchard and **Fortes**. With a research bursary from the International African Institute she carried out an expedition among the Lele of the Kasai in Zaire (then Belgian Congo) in 1949–1950. Her choice of the 'untouched' and matrilineal Lele within the Institute's programme was made at the suggestion of Georges

Bruach, a Belgian colonial officer whom Douglas met at the International Congress of Anthropological and Ethnological Sciences held in Brussels in 1948, after she had already rejected two patrilineal societies as subjects. In 1950 she married J. A. T. Douglas, an economist with the Conservative Party Research Department, which he directed from 1970 and which was suppressed during the Thatcher years. A lecturer in social anthropology from 1950 to 1952, Douglas obtained a D.Phil. in 1953 with her thesis 'A Study of the Social Organization of the Lele of the Kasai'. She then moved to the department at UCL and undertook further work among the Lele, as well as giving birth to three children between 1951 and 1956. A prolific writer, she contributed to *African Worlds*, a book on African cosmologies edited by **Forde**, to *Men, Culture and Society*, edited by Shapiro, and to *Markets in Africa*, edited by **Bohannan** and Dalton. In 1961 she and the Belgian D. Biebuyck co-wrote *Congo Tribes and Parties* (London, RAI). In 1959 further travel to Congo-Zaire became impossible, and so she took extended sabbatical leave from 1960 to 1963 to write *The Lele of the Kasai* (Oxford UP, 1963). This work opens with a long, classical description of the human and geographical environment of the Lele, and then concentrates on the economic sphere, concluding that the political anarchy of the Lele explains their lack of enthusiasm for cultivating, and hence their poverty. Shifting her attention to social organization, to the significance of village wives, and to the reciprocity of matrimonial exchanges over two generations, Douglas rejects a perspective based on roles to focus on negotiations in which people are continually engaged. She was appointed reader in 1963, and with R. **Needham** and E. R. **Leach** was one of the champions of structuralism in the English-speaking world. While unable to research in the field she reflected on the status accorded by the Lele to pangolins in the light of **Lévy-Bruhl**'s idea of 'primitive thought'. Then a bout of measles suffered by her children led her to consider questions of contagion and taboos and to come to some original conclusions (interview with the French radio programme *France-Culture*, June 2001). In 1964 Douglas wrote an article entitled 'Taboo' for the journal *New Society*, an organ of the Conservative Party, and then expanded her material into a book which appeared in 1966 and became a great classic of anthropology: *Purity and Danger: An Analysis of the Concepts of Pollution and Taboo* (London: Routledge, 1996). Moving away from utilitarian explanatory models (e.g. the Islamic ban on pork can be explained by the health risks it poses in hot climates), she demonstrates how taxonomies inversely define prohibition. A common feature of eating restrictions described in Leviticus is that they all straddle distinct taxonomical definitions (e.g. that animals which can fly must all have two wings and two feet). For this reason pigs, which have cloven hooves but which do not chew the cud, or camels, which chew the cud but do not have cloven hooves, and also crustaceans, are all prohibited, as are taboo animals such as the Lele pangolin, the nightjar and the owl. With these arguments Douglas establishes a universal theory which gains further definition in her 1969 work *Natural Symbols: Explorations in Cosmology* (New York: Random House, rev. edn, 1970), which seeks to explore a form of social experience which transcends the socio-economic context. In contrast to 'modernist' approaches, she reasserts the structuring importance of rituals for the individual whose rebellions against authority (e.g. non-differentiation, anti-ritualism, messianic movements and even the Second Vatican Council) lead to greater misery and oppression. Both of these books appeared in about ten languages and were followed by appearances by their author on BBC television. While Douglas drew inspiration from structuralism, she nonetheless completely rejected

Lévi-Strauss's analysis of myths: 'somewhere between phrenology and the Piltdown man is where history will probably rank *The Raw and the Cooked*' (Douglas, 1970: 78, quoted by Fardon, 1998: 78). After obtaining the chair at UCL in 1970 she undertook an examination of the ritual aspects of eating habits, which she then broadened to include other forms of consumption. A grant from the Social Science Research Council enabled her to take a long sabbatical, during which she worked on *The World of Goods: An Anthropological Approach to the Theory of Consumption* (London: Routledge, 1996), written together with the econometrist Baron Isherwood and first published in 1978. This work proposes the foundation of a new economic anthropology which takes full account of welfare economics and of the necessary measures to combat poverty. When her hopes of obtaining a professorship at the University of Chicago were not realized she worked as a researcher at the Russel Sage Foundation from 1977 to 1981. Together she and the Foundation's director Aaron Wildavsky wrote *Risk and Culture: An Essay on the Selection of Technological and Environmental Dangers* (Berkeley: California UP, 1982), which argues that risk and the perception of risk are socially selected, that they generate accusations against authority which resemble accusations of witchcraft in African villages, and that confidence in the centre of power would be more beneficial. Douglas renewed her interest in the study of the Old Testament after her appointment as Avalon Professor of Humanities at Northwestern University in Illinois.

Needham, Rodney (born 1923)
Born in Kenten, Rodney Needham studied at SOAS in 1947–1948, at Oxford from 1948 to 1953 and then at Leyden. He spent time among the Penan of Borneo in 1951–1952 and in 1958, and among the Sunba and the Siwang of Malaysia from 1953 to 1955. With his appointment to a lectureship at Oxford's social anthropology department he joined **Leach** and **Douglas** as one of the main propagators of **Lévi-Strauss**'s thought. After producing a structural analysis of Purum kinship terminology in 1958 he devoted his first book, *Structure and Sentiment: A Test Case in Social Anthropology* (Chicago UP, 1962), to the topic of matrilateral cross-cousin marriage. Here he challenges the way Homans and **Schneider** use **Radcliffe-Brown**'s concept of 'the extension of sentiment' to assert that preferred cross-cousin marriages are contracted without the sanction of legal authority. Needham takes the opposing view, supporting Lévi-Strauss's thesis that matrilateral cross-cousin marriage brings greater group integration than does marriage with a patrilateral cousin. In his *Rethinking Kinship and Marriage* of 1971 (London) and his *Remarks and Inventions: Sceptical Essays about Kinship* of 1974 (London: Tavistock), Needham addresses the ethnographic aptness of such notions as 'marriage' and 'filiation', while in *Belief, Language and Experience* (Oxford: Blackwell, 1972) he makes a case for discarding the word 'belief', which he sees as covering too broad a semantic field (1973). From 1976 to 1990 he was professor at Oxford. As well as with his own works, Needham served the discipline by restoring some of its fundamental texts to circulation, for example A. M. **Hocart**'s *Kings and Councillors*, which he published in a new edition with a one hundred-page introduction.

THE FOURTH GENERATION

In 1963 about fifty anthropologists held university posts in Britain, but 'these were all to be found in the same few departments as in the early 1950s' (Spencer, 2000: 10). A good description of the Cambridge department in the early 1960s is provided by **Kuper**:

> I fetched up at King's College (Cambridge) in 1962, at the age of twenty as a research student (...). There were only perhaps a dozen research students, of whom four or five would be away in the field at any one time. (...) There were only seven or eight members of the academic staff, the dominant figures being the professor, M. **Fortes**, and the reader, E. **Leach**. J. **Goody** and S. Tambiah were their respective lieutenants. For very different reasons, A. **Richards** and Reo **Fortune**, famous anthropologists, were marginal figures in the department. (...) In my first week Leach invited me to lunch (...). A few days later, M. Fortes had me to lunch at King's (...). The most important thing I learnt from my lunches was that there was a serious rift between the two leading Cambridge anthropologists (...). The fact was that a new research student had to commit himself or herself to one camp or the other (...). In general, Fortes and Goody directed the Africanists, while those travelling east of Suez worked with Leach or Tambiah. But this initial choice entailed an intellectual orientation (...). There was no instruction in the methods of fieldwork by participant observation. This provoked a certain nervousness as the moment approached to depart for the field (...). At least J. Goody consented to talk to us (...). He explained that there was no real method, nothing that could be taught.
>
> [(Kuper, 1999 (1992): 20)]

The same policy seems to have characterized the Oxford department: 'fieldwork itself, in **Evans-Pritchard**'s Oxford, simply could not be taught, it could only be learned by doing' (quoted by Spencer, 2000: 19). Apart from the master himself, the departmental staff in Oxford in the early 1960s consisted of Godfrey **Lienhardt**, who became a reader in 1972; John **Beattie**, a lecturer from 1953 to 1971; Rodney **Needham**, a lecturer as of 1956; and Edwin **Ardener**, a lecturer from 1963 to 1987. All these men held Oxford D.Phils. J. G. Peristiany, a reader from 1949, switched his attention from Africa to the Mediterranean (*Honour and Shame: The Values of Mediterranean Society*, London, 1966), and in 1963 he left Oxford's Institute of Social Anthropology for UNESCO before joining the diplomatic corps. Supported by Colonial Development and Welfare funds (Goody, 1995: 82), the department had an Africanist bias in the 1950s, although L. **Dumont** and D. Pocock published the first issue of *Contributions to Indian Sociology* there in 1947. This remained true in the 1960s until Needham broadened its focus.

The immediate post-war years were the great period of the Evans-Pritchard seminar, held on Fridays and followed by discussion in the King's Arms, but by the end of the 1950s this tradition had spent itself (see Fardon, *Mary Douglas*, Routledge, 1999: 32–33). Evans-Pritchard, who had become a practising Roman Catholic in 1944, gradually reorientated his approach towards a hermeneutic understanding of cultures. In so doing he won support from Lienhardt (a recent convert to Catholicism) and the former colonial administrator Beattie, who both espoused this approach, but not from more fiery personalities such as **Gluckman**, the American **Bohannan** or **Middleton**, or indeed Fortes, whom he either could not or would not keep in the department – 'Max did not like leaving Oxford, but Evans-Pritchard persuaded him to go to Manchester to spread the discipline' (**Srinivas**, 'Interview', *AT*, 15

(1999): 7). After years of vain strivings to secure for anthropology the prestige enjoyed at Oxford by Orientalism, and failing even to get an anthropology honours course adopted (Srinivas, 1986: 7; Kuper, (1973) 1996: 126), Evans-Pritchard, who boycotted the first ASA conference in 1963 (Schneider, 1995: 132), devoted himself to revisions of his own earlier works, such as *Theories of Primitive Religion* (1965) and *The Position of Women in Primitive Societies* (1965), and to editing popular encyclopaedias such as the very handsome *People of the Earth* (20 vols). The Oxford department rested on its laurels during this period, and the publication in 1958 of *Tribes without Rulers*, a collection of texts edited by Middleton and Tait, was indicative of this as well as representing one of the group's last achievements. The situation was much more dynamic in Cambridge, where Goody edited *The Developmental Cycle in Domestic Groups*, the fruit of Fortes's Friday seminars and the first title in the series 'Cambridge Studies in Social Anthropology'.

However, the most important seminar in the 1960s seems not to have been that of Fortes, but that of the doyen of the discipline, R. **Firth**, who unassumingly filled the role vacated by **Malinowski** at the LSE. This seminar is described by **Schneider** (1995: 1925–1929) and by J. Davis (2001) as the central recurring event of British social anthropology in these years. Firth's sober distinction did not prevent him taking part in the great debates of the 1960s, unlike Evans-Pritchard. At the same time as refining his depiction of the Tikopia in several successive books, he engaged with substantivism in the first half of this decade and Marxism in the second. As well as Firth, the LSE department contained I. **Schapera**, M. Freedman, L. **Mair**, who was appointed professor in 1963, Anthony Forge (1929–1991), who arrived in 1961 and stayed until 1974, and finally Paul Stirling, who left to found a department at the University of Kent in 1964. Firth and Schapera retired in 1968 and 1969 respectively and were replaced by M. Freedman and Ioan M. Lewis, who was chosen in preference to M. **Douglas**. Jean La Fontaine arrived as a reader in 1968, and M. **Bloch** as a lecturer in 1969. With Bloch working on Madagascar (the first British scholar to do so), La Fontaine on Central Africa, Firth on Oceania, Lewis on the Horn of Africa, Freedman on China, and Schapera on South Africa, the department boasted an unusual diversity, and from 1940 was also producing one of the main collections of anthropological texts: 'The London School of Economics Monographs on Social Anthropology'.

Finally, at UCL **Forde** took retirement in 1970 and was replaced by M. G. Smith. Despite being awarded a chair, M. Douglas left the university in 1977, and P. M. Kaberry died in the same year. In the 1960s 'The academic staff and students were splitting into factions descended from the sociological trinity: Weberians headed by Smith, youthful neo-Marxists and a scattering of Durkheimians led by M. Douglas. Personality clashes fuelled intellectual differences, so that the department seemed a close analogy of the central African village riven by accusations of witchcraft' (Fardon, *Mary Douglas*, Routledge, 1999: 128). As of 1977 an overall dominance was enjoyed by the younger researchers with Marxist leanings, such as J. Gledhill, O. Harris and M. Rowlands, who together published *Critique of Anthropology* from 1974 to 1981.

Oxford, Cambridge, Manchester and the LSE were the main centres of the discipline in 1960, but anthropology developed rapidly in other universities too as a result of the expansion of higher education which took place in Britain as elsewhere. Some of the new departments created in the 1950s, such as those at Durham, St Andrews and Queen's, Belfast, grew rapidly, while the mid–1960s saw the establishment of new universities and also of a new sort of higher education institution, the Polytechnic. Many of these new foundations opened joint anthropology and sociology departments, for example the universities of Kent,

East Anglia and Sussex, where Pocock joined forces with F. G. Bailey and P. Lloyd in 1960. Moreover a number of older universities set up departments during this period, such as Hull and Swansea. At the end of the 1960s there were eighteen anthropology departments, and in 1973 these contained about ninety post-holders. In the same year the Social Science Research Council, established by the government in 1965 to support research projects and postgraduate students, attained the summit of its munificence by offering eighty-four studentships in social anthropology.

In 1963 the Association of Social Anthropologists held the first of its decennial conferences with the aim of representing the current state of the discipline. It was co-ordinated by M. Gluckman and F. **Eggan** and its proceedings were published in four volumes. The second conference of 1973, entitled 'New Directions', produced no less than six volumes (see Spencer, 2000). However, the third conference of 1983 only yielded a single volume, reflecting the fact that 'the massive expansion of the profession in the 1960s was then followed by savage cuts in the academy's resources twenty years later' (La Fontaine, 1996: 252). A very subdued period began in the mid-1970s and culminated with the government of Margaret Thatcher, who became leader of the Conservative Party in 1975 and who believed, and I quote, that 'there is no such thing as society'. The Social Science Research Council was consequently suppressed, and the Royal Anthropological Institute abandoned its Bedford Square offices and donated its library to the Museum of Mankind (Kuper, 1996 (1973): 180). Some anthropologists found refuge in sociology departments (such as Peter **Worsley**, Max Marwick and Ronald Frankenberg), while others left the UK for the USA (notably V. **Turner**, M. Douglas, P. Gulliver, F. G. Bailey, S. Tambiah, J. Middleton, R. **Fox** and T. Asad).

There were a number of changes of personnel in institutions during this period. At Oxford Peter Rivière joined the department, while Evans-Pritchard retired in 1970, to be replaced by M. Freedman from the LSE, who died in 1976. **Needham** then occupied the chair until he was succeeded in 1990 by John **Davis**, who was himself replaced in 1995 by David Parkin on becoming a fellow of All Souls College. At the LSE Jean La Fontaine was professor from 1978 to 1983, when she was replaced by Maurice Bloch. Important members of the LSE department included Henrietta Moore, amongst other things a champion of feminist anthropology, and Jonathan Parry and Chris Fuller, who both vigorously promoted Indianist studies. At Cambridge Fortes was replaced in 1973 by Goody, whose rival Tambiah left the UK for the universities of Chicago and then Harvard (1982). Goody was succeeded by **Gellner** in 1984, who was followed by Marilyn **Strathern** in 1995. Another significant figure at Cambridge was Caroline Humphrey, who contributed energetically to the creation of a Marxist and feminist anthropology. At Manchester Gluckman retired as head of department in 1971, to be replaced by Emrys Peters, who was succeeded by Marilyn Strathern in 1984. Strathern departed for Cambridge in 1995 and was replaced by Tim Ingold, who then left Manchester for Aberdeen in 2000.

Let us conclude with a quick sketch of currents of thought in anthropology during this period. The early 1960s were dominated by structural functionalism as renewed by Firth, Leach and the Manchester School. During the 1970s the influence of **Lévi-Strauss** grew continually, generating a Marxist surge which first manifested itself in the pages of *Critique of Anthropology*. Marxism then receded amid accusations that anthropology was itself imperialist, to be replaced by feminist anthropology, by medical anthropology as an autonomous area of inquiry, and by a number of other new fields – mass media, youth, arts and business – which most frequently involved fieldwork in the UK itself. At a time when the end of grand narratives and grand theories is being proclaimed, these new topics are now investigated using a meticulous empiricism, to which only the tentatively evolutionist approach of Tim Ingold offers an alternative. Finally, mention should be made of Nigel Barley's successful attempts in the 1980s to provide the general public with ironic insights into how fieldwork is done (*The Innocent Anthropologist*, 1983).

As with previous sections, there are numerous authors who have regrettably not been given entries due to limitations of space. The two criteria for inclusion are age – thus Tim Ingold and Christina Toren are too young, and academic position – hence a focus on holders of the major chairs at Oxford, Cambridge and the LSE. Also included is A. Kuper, who was behind the creation of the European Association of Social Anthropologists and editor of *CA* for about fifteen years. I must at least mention the names of some of those whom, unfortunately, I cannot treat here: J. Benthall, Jean La Fontaine, A. Gell, Ruth Finnegan, Pat Caplan, Caroline Humphrey, Penny Harvey, Karin Barber, Richard Fardon, Keith Hart and Ronnie Frankenberg.

Gellner, Ernest (1926–1995)

Born in Paris according to T. Dragadze (1995), or Prague according to J. **Davis** (1992), Ernest Gellner and his Jewish family took refuge in London in 1939. At the age of seventeen he enlisted in a Czech unit fighting in France, and then won a scholarship to study philosophy at Oxford. He taught at Edinburgh University and the LSE, where he wrote up his thesis under the supervision of P. Stirling. In 1959 he published *Words and Things* (London: Gollancz, 1959), in which he condemns philosophies of language as ideological constructs and investigates rationalism by examining ways of understanding time and progress, a line of enquiry he further developed in *Thought and Change* (Chicago UP, 1964). In *The Psychoanalytic Moment* (1985) he effects a concrete historical reconstruction of the circumstances which permitted the emergence and subsequent success of psychoanalysis, considered as an epistemology and a system of beliefs. In 1984 he was appointed to the chair of social anthropology at Cambridge University. After the fall of communism he founded the Centre for the Study of Nationalisms in Prague in 1993 at the Central European University established by George Soros, a Romanian-born American financier. Gellner is known for his studies of nationalism and Islam. After research in Morocco in the late 1950s, he published *Saints of the Atlas* in 1969 (London: Weidenfeld & Nicolson). Inspired by the segmentarism of **Evans-Pritchard**, this work describes the importance of the tradition of saints in a Berber society of Upper Atlas, and opens with a long discussion of political life and the relationship between religion and politics in Muslim societies. This discussion is taken up again in *Muslim Society* (Cambridge UP, 1981), in which Gellner contrasts this relationship with the process of secularization in European Christian societies. In *Nations and Nationalism* (1983) he defines the nation as a political unit corresponding to a specific culture, and nationalism as a political principle which affirms that political and national unity must be congruent. His central idea is that, far from being an archaism, nationalism is the necessary product of industrial modernity, whose social organization is founded upon a high culture which is itself predicated on education and on a deeply internalized conception of the protective role of the state. He also predicted the revival of nationalism in the post-Cold War world. Gellner was president of the Royal Anthropological Institute from 1991 to 1994, and died on 5 November 1995.

Davis, John (born 1938)

After studying for a BA at Oxford University from 1958 to 1961, John Davis began postgraduate studies at the LSE which led to a Ph.D. in 1969. He was successively lecturer, reader and professor at the University of Kent from 1968 to 1990, and then he held a professorship at Oxford University from 1990 to 1995 before becoming a fellow of All Souls College. His early work was on the connection between land ownership and kinship in Italy (1964–1966), and he then made a series of studies of politics in Libya (1974–1979). Over a long period he researched on exchange, publishing his first results in 1972 ('Gifts and the UK Economy', *Man*, 7: 408–429) and completing this project with the writing of *Exchange* (Buckingham, Open UP, 1992). Above all he is known for his still unique synthesis of the whole Mediterranean region, including Southern Europe, Northern Africa and the Levant. Davis stressed the importance of in-depth historical analysis in his examination of contrasts and connections among all the societies living around the Mediterranean.

Bloch, Maurice E. F. (born 1939)

Born in Caen, Maurice E. F. Bloch spent his childhood in both France and England, and then completed a BA in anthropology at the LSE in 1961, before beginning postgraduate research at Cambridge University. He was one of the first British scholars to work in Madagascar, where he lived from 1964 to 1966. In 1967 he completed his Ph.D. thesis 'The Significance of Tombs and Ancestral Villages for Merina Social Organization', which was later published under the title *Placing the Dead: Tombs, Ancestral Villages and Kinship in Madagascar* (London: Seminar Press, 1971, 2nd edn 1993). Using the cases of two villages to examine societies in the Imerina Highlands, this study focuses on the connection between land ownership and ancestors, which is metonymically represented by the custom of the 'return' of the body. The book also considers modalities for resolving the contradiction between the closed world, including the world of matrimony, and inevitable openness. Bloch was a lecturer at the University of Wales at Swansea in 1967–1968 and at the LSE from 1968 to 1976. He became a reader at the LSE in 1976 and a professor there in 1983. Drawn to Marxist thought, he organized a session of the 1973 decennial conference of the Association of Social Anthropologists in which E. **Terray**, M. **Godelier** and J. Friedman discussed Marxism with R. **Firth** (Bloch, ed., *Marxist Analyses and Social Anthropology*, Malaby Press, 1975). In 1974–1975 he worked at Berkeley, where he discovered cognitive anthropology through Lakoff and P. **Kay**, and it was in this direction that his research subsequently progressed. He was an associate research fellow at the Centre for Applied Epistemology of the *Ecole Polytéchnique* in Paris from 1994 until 1997 and a director of studies at the EPHE in 1996.

Parkin, David (born 1940)

David Parkin studied at London University, which awarded him a Ph.D. in 1965. He became professor of anthropology at SOAS in 1981 and then professor of social anthropology at Oxford University in 1995. A specialist on East African societies, he researched on kinship among the Giriama and the Lou in 1966–1967 and on the Swahili in 1977–1978. His approach went beyond the classical ethnic concerns of ethnography to incorporate connections between descent, marriage and politics (1978). Sociolinguists and French intellectuals such as Ricoeur, **Foucault** and Derrida were the main influence behind a second phase of Parkin's research, in which he developed an anthropology of symbolism and communication. He approached these topics through a consideration of people with positions of power, the performative nature of that power, and its continual recreation by those who wield it (1982).

Kuper, Adam (born 1941)
Born in Johannesburg, Adam Kuper studied at the universities of Witwatersrand (BA 1961) and Cambridge (Ph.D. 1966), and his fieldwork took him to Botswana (Kgalagadi) and Jamaica. He taught at the universities of Makerere (Uganda) (1967–1970) and Kampala, at UCL (1970–1976), and at the universities of Leyden (1976–1985), California at Santa Barbara, and Gothenburg, before becoming a professor at Brunel University and establishing and directing its social sciences department. Kuper was also instrumental in the creation of the European Association of Social Anthropologists and became its first president. He succeeded Sol **Tax** and Cyril Belshaw to become the third editor of the journal *Current Anthropology* from 1985 to 1994. The author of over one hundred articles, Kuper is known both for his ethnographic work (1970, 1976, 1982) and for his important contributions to the history of anthropology (1973, 1988, 1999).

Strathern, Ann Marilyn (née Evans, born 1941)
After completing a BA at Cambridge University in 1963 Ann Marilyn Strathern spent sixteen months in Western Papua New Guinea with her anthropologist husband Andrew Strathern in 1964–1965. While pursuing her own work classifying stone implements and investigating male–female relations and land-owning practices, she also worked with him on a book about the body as the principal aesthetic site of Papuan culture: *Self-Decoration in Mount Hagen* (Toronto UP, 1971 (1983)). On her return to Britain she became assistant curator at the Cambridge Museum (1966–1968), and gained an MA in 1967 and a Ph.D. in 1968. She made a study of the position of the Melpa women of Mount Hagen, who through their marriages enter a social group

defined by their husbands' social relationships (1972, 1995). *Nature, Culture and Gender*, a collection of essays edited by Carol MacCormack and Strathern in 1980 (Cambridge UP), demonstrates that feminist authors, in claiming that the oppression of women is determined by social structures rather than a natural order, use the categories of public/private and culture/nature without asking why the first term in each pair is considered masculine and more highly valued. For MacCormack and Strathern these categories are not universal, and they make the point that, in Hagen culture, terms relating to the domestic sphere do not have specific gender associations and do not convey any idea of subordination, so that while it is true that the personal realm is considered feminine and public exchange is considered masculine, this does not constrain individual conduct. Published in 1988, *The Gender of the Gift: Problems with Women and Problems with Society in Melanesia* (Berkeley: California UP) synthesizes knowledge on gender relations, economics and power in Melanesia, where the gift economy (pearls, pigs, etc.) among and between men and women plays as important a role in defining relationships as gender. Unlike the Western, individualistic economic system which establishes a relationship between individuals and items already objectivized, in Melanesia the construction of personal identity follows rather than precedes the act of exchange. Together with M. **Godelier** Strathern also wrote on distinctions between Melanesian societies with 'Great Men' and those with 'Big Men', and they concluded that the former are to be found where masculine rites of initiation take precedence over ceremonial exchanges (1991). Strathern developed her thinking on the conceptualization of kinship and nature in the light of new techniques of artificial insemination in a number of texts (1992), and then turned her attention to questions of institutional assessment, especially in universities (2000). In the years before 1984 she held research fellowships at Canberra University (1970–1972, 1983–1984) and Girton College, Cambridge (1976–1983), an administrative post in Papua New Guinea (1973–1984), a guest professorship at Berkeley and a lectureship at Trinity College, Cambridge. In 1985 she became professor at Manchester University and head of its anthropology department, and from there she moved to Cambridge, where she occupied the anthropology department's William Wyse chair in 1993 and became Mistress of Girton College in 1998. Strathern has also carried out research on an Essex village at the suggestion of Audrey **Richards**, exploring the nexus between kinship and the construction of social and local identities: *Kinship at the Core: An Anthropology of Elmdon, Essex* (Cambridge UP, 1981).

SELECT BIBLIOGRAPHY

Adrian, A. and Mayer, C. (1991) 'Fürer-Haimendorf, C. von', in C. Winter, pp.221–222.

Al-Shahi, A. and Coote, J. (eds) (1997) 'Special issue in memory of Godfrey Lienhardt', *Journal of the Anthropological Society of Oxford*, 28(1).

Ardener, E.S. (1965) 'A directory study of social anthropologists', *British Journal of Sociology*, pp.300–302.

Ashley, K. (ed.) (1990) *Victor Turner and the Construction of Cultural Criticism: Between Literature and Anthropology*, Bloomington: Indiana University Press.

Back, B.A. and Magaloon, J-J. (1987) 'Victor Turner (1920–1983)', *Sémiotica*, 65: 1–27.

Beattie, J.H.M. and Lenhardt, R.G. (eds) (1975) *Studies in Social Anthropology: Essays in Memory of E.E. Evans-Pritchard by his Former Oxford Colleagues*, Oxford: Clarendon.

Beattie, J.H.M. and Middleton, J. (eds) (1969) *Spirit Mediumship and Society in Africa*, London: Routledge.

Bloch, M.E.F. (1983) *Marxism and Anthropology: The History of a Relationship*, Oxford: Clarendon Press.

——(1986) *From Blessing to Violence: History and Ideology in the Circumcision Ritual of the Merina of Madagascar*, Cambridge: Cambridge University Press.

——(1989) *Ritual, History and Power. Selected Papers in Anthropology*, London: Athlone Press.

——(1992) *Prey into Hunter: The Politics of Religious Experience*, Cambridge: Cambridge University Press.

——(1998) *How We Think They Think: Anthropological Studies in Cognition, Memory and Literacy*, Boulder: Westview Press.

Bloch, M.E.F. and Parry, J. (ed.) (1989) *Money and the Morality of Exchange*, Cambridge: Cambridge University Press.

Boyer, P. (1990) 'Needham, Rodney', in P. Bonte and M. Izard (eds.) *Dictionnaire de l'ethnologie et de l'anthropologie*, Paris: Presses universitaires de France, p.505.

Brass, T. (2000) 'On Bill Epstein', *AT*, 16 (3): 26.

Burton, J.W. (1992) 'An Interview with A. Southall', *CA*, 33: 67–83.

Casajus, D. (1991) 'Lienhardt, Godfrey', in P. Bonte and M. Izard (eds.) *Dictionnaire de l'ethnologie et de l'anthropologie*, Paris: Presses universitaires de France, p.421.

Chapman, M. and MacDonald, M. (1987) 'E. Ardener', *AT*, 3(6): 21–22.

Davis, J. (1973) *Land and Family in Pisticci*, London: Athlone.

——(1977) *People of the Mediterranean: An Essay in Comparative Social Anthropology*, London: Routledge.

——(ed.) (1982) *Religious Organization and Religious Experience*, London: Academic Press.

——(1987) *Libyan Politics: Tribe and Revolution*, London: Tauris.

——(1992) 'Interview with Ernest Gellner', *CA*, 32(1): 63–72.

——(2001) 'R. Firth's 100th birthday', *The Times Higher Education Supplement*, 30 March.

de Soto, H. (ed.) (1992) *Culture and Contradiction: Dialectics of Wealth, Power and Symbol. Essais en l'honneur de Aidan Southall*, San Francisco: EmText.

Deflem, M. (1991) 'Ritual anti-structure, and religion: a discussion of Victor Turner's processual analysis', *Journal of the Scientific Study of Religion*, 39(1): 1–25.

Douglas, M. (1970a) 'Smothering the differences. M. Douglas in a savage mind about Lévi-Strauss', *Listener*, 13 September, 84: 313–314.

——(ed.) (1970b) *Witchcraft, Confessions and Accusation*, London: Tavistock.

——(1975) *Implicit Meanings, Essays in Anthropology*, London: Routledge.

——(1978) *Cultural Bias*, London: Royal Anthropological Institute.

——(1980) *Evans-Pritchard*, London: Fontana.

——(1982) *In the Active Voice: Essays in the Sociology of Perception*, London: Routledge.

——(1986) *Risk, Acceptability According to the Social Sciences*, Berkeley, CA.: University of California Press.

——(1987) *How Institutions Think*, London: Routledge.

——(1992a) *Risk and Blame: Essays in Cultural Theory*, London: Routledge.

——(1992b) *Objects and Objections*, Toronto: Victoria College.

——(1993) *In the Wilderness: The Doctrine of Defilement in the Book of Numbers*, Sheffield Academic Press.

——(1994a) 'But why do we have to use the American Language?, Interview', *EASA Newsletter*, 13: 4–5.

——(1994b) 'Godfrey Lienhardt', *AT*, 10(1): 15–17.

——(1996) *Thought Styles, Critical Essays on Good Taste*, London: Sage.

Douglas, M. and Ney, S. (1998) *Missing Persons: A Critique of Personhood in the Social Sciences*, Berkeley, CA.: University of California Press.

Dragadze, T. (1995) 'E. Gellner', *AT*, 11(6): 19–21.

Epstein, A.L. (1969) *Matupit: Land, Politics and Change among the Tolai of New Britain*, Berkeley, CA.: University of California Press.

——(1978) *Ethos and Identity: Three Studies in Ethnicity*, London: Tavistock.

——(1981) *Urbanization and Kinship: The Domestic Domain on the Copperbelt of Zambia*, London: Academic Press.

——(1984) *The Experience of Shame in Melanesia*, London: RAI Paper.

——(1992a) *Scenes from African Urban Life*, Edinburgh: Edinburgh University Press.

——(1992b) *In the Midst of Life: Affect and Idealisation in the World of the Tolai*, Berkeley, CA.: University of California Press.

——(1999) *Guantuna, Aspects of the Person, the Self and the Individual among the Tolai*, Berkeley, CA.: University of California Press.

Fardon, R. (1998) *Mary Douglas: An Intellectual Biography*, London: Routledge.

Fausto, C. and Neiburg, F. (2000) 'An interview with Adam Kuper', *CA*, 43(2): 305–13.

Fortes, M. (1975) 'An anthropologist's apprenticeship', *Annual Review of Anthropology*, 7: 1–30.

Fürer-Haimendorf, C. von (1943) *The Chenchus, jungle folk of the Deccan*, London: Macmillan.

——(1945a) *Tribal-Hyderabad; 4 reports. With a foreword by W.V. Grigson*, Hyderabad: Dept. Govt. the Nizam.

——(1945b) *The Reddis of the Bison Hills: A Study in Acculturation*, London: Macmillan.

——(1948) *The Raj Gonds of Adilabad: A Peasant culture of the Deccan*, London: Macmillan.

——(1964) *Les Sherpas du Népal: Montagnards Bouddhistes*, Evreux: Imp. Hervisey.

——(1975) *Himalayan Trader*, New York: St. Martin's Press.

——(1979) *The Gonds of Andhra Pradesh: Tradition and Change in an Indian Tribe*, London: Allen.

——(1980) *A Himalayan Tribe: From Cattle to Cash*, Berkeley, CA.: University of California Press.

——(1990) *Life among Indian tribes: the autobiography of an anthropologist*, Delhi, New York: Oxford: Oxford University Press.

Gellner, E. (1974a) *Contemporary Thought and Politics*, London: Routledge.

——(1974b) *The Devil in Modern Philosophy*, London: Routledge.

——(1974c) *Legitimation of Belief*, Cambridge: Cambridge University Press.

——(1979) *Spectacles and Predicaments*, Cambridge: Cambridge University Press.

——(ed.) (1980) *Soviet and Western Anthropology*, New York: Columbia University Press.

——(1981) *Muslim Society*, Cambridge: Cambridge University Press.

——(1985a) *Relativism in the Social Movement*, Cambridge: Cambridge University Press.

——(1985b) *Relativism and the Social Sciences*, New York, Cambridge: Cambridge University Press.

——(1987) *The Concept of Kingship and other essays on anthropological method and explanation*, New York: Blackwell.

——(1987) *Culture, Identity and Politics*, Cambridge: Cambridge University Press.

——(1988a) *Plough, Sword and Book*, University of Chicago Press.

——(1988b) *State and Society in Soviet Thought*, New York: Blackwell.

——(1994) *Encounters with Nationalism*, Cambridge: Blackwell.

——(1994) *Conditions of Liberty, Civil Society and its Rivals*, New York: Allen Lane.

——(1995) *Anthropology and Politics: Revolutions in the Sacred Grove*, Cambridge: Blackwell.

Gingrich, A. (1996) 'Christoph von Fürer-Haimendorf', *Anthropos*, 91: 238.

Goody, J.J.R. (1959) 'The mother's brother and the sister's son in West Africa', *JRAI*, 89: 61–88.

——(1962) *Death, Property and the Ancestors: A Study of the Mortuary Customs of the LoDagaba of West Africa*, London: Tavistock.

——(ed.) (1966) *Succession to High Office*, Cambridge University Press.

——(ed.) (1968) *Literacy in Traditional Societies*, Cambridge University Press.

——(1969) *Comparative Studies in Kinship*, London: Penguin.

——(1971) *Technology, Tradition and the State in Africa*, Oxford University Press.

——(1972) *The Myth of the Bagre*, Oxford: Clarendon Press.

——(1980) *Une récitation du Bagré*, Paris: Armand Colin.

——(1982) *Cooking, Cuisine and Class*, Cambridge: Cambridge University Press.

——(1983) *The Development of Family and Marriage in Europe*, Cambridge: Cambridge University Press.

——(1990) *The Oriental, the Ancient, and the Primitive*, Cambridge: Cambridge University Press.

——(1991) 'Towards a room with a view: A personal account of contributions to local knowledge, theory and research in fieldwork and comparative studies', *Annual Review of Anthropology*, 20: 1–23.

——(1993) *The Culture of Flowers*, Cambridge: Cambridge University Press.

——(1995) *The Expansive Moment: Anthropology in Britain and Africa 1918–1970*, Cambridge: Cambridge University Press.

——(1996) *L'homme, l'écriture et la mort. Entretiens avec Pierre-Emmanuel Dauzat*, Paris: Les Belles Lettres.

Goody, J.J.R. and Tambiah, S.J. (1973) *Bride-Wealth and Dowry*, Cambridge University Press.

Grillo, R. (1994) 'The application of anthropology in Britain, 1983–1993', in C. Hann (ed.) *When History Accelerates*, London: Athlone, pp.300–316.

——(2000) 'A. L. Epstein', *AT*, 16(1): 22–23.

Hann, C. (1995) *Independent*, 8 November.

Houtman, G. (1990) 'Interview with M. Bloch', *AT*, 4(1): 18–22.

Hugh-Jones, S. (1989) 'E. Leach', *AT*, 5(2): 16–17.

——(1989–1990) 'Special issue: Sir Edmund Leach', *Cambridge Anthropology*, 13(3).

Izard, M. and de Sales, A. (1991) 'Goody, Jack John Rankine', in P. Bonte and M. Izard (eds.) *Dictionnaire de l'ethnologie et de l'anthropologie*, Paris: Presses universitaires de France, p.302.

Kuklick, H. (1991) *The Savage Within: The Social History of British Anthropology 1885–1945*, Cambridge University Press.

Kuper, A. (1970) *Kalahari Village Politics: An African Democracy*, Cambridge University Press.

——(1973) expanded new edn, 1996, *Anthropology and Anthropologists: The Modern British School*, London: Routledge.

——(1976) *Changing Jamaica*, London: Routledge.

——(ed.) (1977) *The Social Anthropology of Radcliffe-Brown*, London: Routledge.

——(1982) *Wives for Cattle: Bridewealth and Marriage in Southern Africa*, London: Routledge.

——(1986) 'An interview with E. Leach', *CA*, 27: 375–383.

——(1987) *South Africa and the Anthropologists*, London: Routledge.

——(1994) *The Chosen Primate*, Cambridge, MA: Harvard University Press.

——(1999) *Culture: The Anthropologists' Account*, Cambridge, MA: Harvard University Press.

——(1999) *Among the anthropologists. History and Context in Anthropology*, London: Athlone Press.

Kuper, A. and Kuper, J. (eds) (1985) *The Social Science Encyclopedia*, London: Routledge.

Kuper, A. and Richards, A. (eds) (1971) *Councils in Action*, Cambridge: Cambridge University Press.

Leach, E.R. (1967) *A Runaway World? The Reight Lectures 1967*, London: British Broadcasting Corporation.

——(1970) *Lévi-Strauss*, London: Fontana.

——(1976) *Culture and Communication*, Cambridge University Press.

——(1982) *Social Anthropology*, London: Fontana.

——(1984) 'Glimpses of the unmentionable in the history of British social anthropology', in *Annual Review of Anthropology*, 13: 1–23.

Lombard, J. (1972) *L'Anthropologie britannique contemporaine*, Paris: Presses universitaires de France

MacFarlane, A. (1996) 'Christoph von Fürer-Haimendorf', *AT*, 11(4): 21–23.

MacIntyre, M. (1991) 'E. Leach', in C. Winter, pp.385–386.

MacIntyre, M. (Film) 'Interview with E. Leach', Canberra: Departmental Archives, Research School of Pacific Studies.

Manning, F. (1984) 'Victor Turner: a tribute', *Recherches sémiotiques*, 4(2): 195–201.

Middleton, J. (1953) *The Kikuyu and Kamba of Kenya*, London: Oxford-IAI.

——(1960) *Lugbara Religion*, Oxford University Press.

——(1965) *The Lugbara of Uganda*, New York: Holt, Rinehart and Winston.

——(ed.) (1967) *Magic, Witchcraft and Curing*, New York: AMNHP.

——(1990) John Beattie', *AT*, 6(3): 20.

——(1992) *The World of the Swahili*, New Haven: Yale University Press.

——(ed.) (1997a) *Encyclopaedia of Sub-Saharan Africa*, New York: Scribner, 4 vols.

Middleton, J. and Beattie, J. (eds) (1969) *Spirit Mediumship and Society in Africa*, London: Routledge.

Middleton, J. and Bohannan, P. (eds) (1968) *Marriage, Family and Residence*, New York: AMNHP.

——(eds) (1974) *Kinship and Social Organization*. New York: AMNHP.

Middleton, J. and Cohen, R. (1967) *Comparative Political Systems*, New York: AMNHP.

Middleton, J. and Fellow, D. (1999) 'An interview with John Middleton', *CA*, 40(2): 217–230.

Middleton, J. and Winter, E. (eds) (1963) *Witchcraft and Sorcery in East Africa*, London: Routledge.

Mitchell, J.C. (1956a) *The Kalela Danse: Aspects of social relationships among urban Africans in Northern Rhodesia*, Manchester: Manchester University Press.

——(1956b) *The Yao Village: A Study in the Social Structure of a Malawian People*, Manchester: Manchester University Press.

——(ed.) (1969) *Social Networks in Urban Situations: Analysis of Personal Relationship in Central African Towns*, Manchester: Manchester University Press.

——(1974) 'Social networks', *Annual Review of Anthropology*, 3: 279–301.

Mitchell, J.C. and Boisserain, J. (ed.) (1973) *Network Analysis: Studies in Human Interaction*, The Hague: Mouton.

Needham, R. (1958) 'A Structural analysis of Purum society', *AA*, 60: 75–101.

——(1970) *The Future of Social Anthropology: Disintegration or Metamorphosis?, Anniversary Contribution to Anthropology*, Leiden: Leiden University Press.

——(1987a) *Mamboru: History and Structure in a Domain of Northwestern Sumba*, Oxford: Clarendon.

Parkin, D. (1978) *The Cultural Definition of Political Response: Lineal Destiny among the Luo*, London: Academic Press.

——(ed.) (1982a) *Semantic Anthropology*, London: Academic Press.

——(1982b) 'Political language', *Annual Review of Anthropology*, 13: 346–365.

——(1991) *Sacred Void: Spacial Images of Work and Ritual among the Giriama of Kenya*, Cambridge: Cambridge University Press.

——(ed.) (1995) *The Anthropology of Evil*, Oxford: Blackwell.

Parkin, D. and Croll, E. (ed.) (1992) *Bush Base: Forest Farm. Culture, Environment and Development*, London: Routledge.

Rodgers, D. and Viveiro de Castro, E. (1999) 'No Limite de uma certa linguagem', interview with M. Strathern in *Mana: Estudos de Antropologia Social*, 5: 157–175.

Sathyamurthy, T.V., Beattie, H. and Coote, J. (1991) 'J.H.M. Beattie', *Journal of the Anthropology Society of Oxford*, 22: 65–73.

Southall, A.W. (1952) *Lineage formation among the Luo*, London: Oxford-IAI.

——(1965) 'A Critique of the typology of states and political system' in M. Banton (ed.), *Political System and the Distribution of Powers*, London: Tavistock.

——(1984) *The Three Worlds: Culture and World Development*, London: Weidenfeld and Nicolson.

——(1998) *The City in Time and Space*, Cambridge: Cambridge University Press.

Southall, A.W. and Gulden, G. (eds) (1993) *Urban Anthropology in China*, Leiden and New York: E.J. Brill.

Spencer, J. (2000) 'British social anthropology: a retrospective', *Annual Review of Anthropology*, 29: 1–24.

Sperber, D. (1991) 'E. Leach', in P .Bonte and M. Izard (eds.) *Dictionnaire de l'ethnologie et de l'anthropologie*, Paris: Presses universitaires de France, pp.411–412.

Srinivas, M.N. and Fuller, C. (1999) 'An interview with M.N. Srinivas', *AT*, 15(5): 3–9.

Stocking, G. (1995) *After Tylor, British Social Anthropology (1888–1951)*, London: Athlone.

Strathern, M. (1987) *Dealing with Inequality: Analysis Gender Relations in Melanesia and Beyond*, Cambridge: Cambridge University Press.

—— (ed.) (1995; 1972) *Women in Between: Female Roles in a Male World. Mt Hagen, New Guinea*, Lanham: Rowman and Littlefield.

——(1991) *Partial Connection*, Lanham: Rowman and Littlefield.

——(1992a) *After Nature. English Kinship in the Late Twentieth Century*, Cambridge: Cambridge University Press.

——(1992b) *Reproducing the Future: Essays on Anthropology, Kinship and the New Reproductive Technologies*, New York: Routledge.

——(ed.) (1995) *Shifting Contexts: Transformations in Anthropological Knowledge*, London: Routledge.

——(1999) *Property, Substance and Effect: Anthropological Essays on Persons and Things*, London: Athlone.

——(ed.) (2000) *Audit Cultures: Anthropological Studies in Accountability, Ethics and the Academy*, London: Routledge.

Strathern, M., Edwards, J., Franklin, S., Hirsch, E. and Price, F. (1999; 1993) *Technologies of Procreation: Kinship in the Age of Assisted Conception*, London: Routledge.

Strathern, M. and Godelier, M. (ed.) (1991) *Big Men and Great Men. Personifications of Power in Melanesia*, Cambridge University Press.

Tambiah, S.J. (2002) *Edmund Leach: an anthropological life*, Cambridge: Cambridge University Press.

Turner, V.W. (1957) *Schism and Continuity in an African Society: A Study of a Ndembu Village*, Manchester University Press.

——(1961) *Ndembu Divination: Its Symbolism and Techniques*, Lusaka: Rhodes–Livingstone Institute (republished in 1969 by Oxford University Press, then in 1975 as *Revelation and Divination in Ndembu Ritual*, Cornell University Press).

——(1979) *Process, Performance and Pilgrimage*, New Delhi: Concept Publishing Company.

——(1982a) *From Ritual to Theater: The Human Seriousness of Play*, New York: Performing Arts Journal Publication.

——(ed.) (1982b) *Celebration: Studies in Festivity and Ritual*, Washington: Smithsonian Institution.

Turner, V.W. and Brun, E. (eds) (1985) *The Anthropology of Experience*, Champaign: University of Illinois Press.

Turner, V.W. and Turner, E. (1978) *Image and Pilgrimage in Christian Culture*, New York: Columbia University Press.

Valeri, V. (1985) *Kingship and Sacrifice, Rituals and Society in Ancient Hawaii*.

Werbner, R. (1984) 'The Manchester School in South-Central Africa', *Annual Review of Anthropology*, 13: 157–185.

——(1990) 'South-Central Africa: the Manchester School and after', in R. Fardon (ed.) *Localizing Strategies: Regional Traditions of Ethnographic Writing*, Edinburgh: Scottish Academic Press.

Wolanin, A. (1978) *Rites, Rituals, Symbols and their Interpretation in the Writings of Victor W. Turner: A Phenomenological-Theological Study*, Rome: Facultas Theologiae Pontifica Universitas.

Worsley, P.M. (1967; 1964) *The Third World*, London: Weidenfeld and Nicolson.

——(1970) *Introducing Sociology*, Harmondsworth: Penguin.

——(1982) *Marx and Marxism*, London: Tavistock

——(1984) *The Three Worlds: Culture and World Development*, University of Chicago Press.

——(ed.) (1987) *New Introduction Sociology*, London: Penguin.

Yelvington, K.A. (1997) 'An interview with A. L. Epstein', *CA*, 38: 299–389.

Index

NOTE: Bold page numbers show the dictionary entry for an anthropologist.

Index

Baden-Powell, B.H. 272
Baer, Karl von 31
Bahnson, Christian 227
Bailey, F.G. 156, 273, 352, 356, 365
Balandier, Georges 92, 292, 293, **296–8**, 302; students of 306, 307, 309, 312–14
Balbi 199
Baldus, Herbert **223**, 252
Bales, A.R. 273
Balfet, Hélène 295
Ball, Jan van **217**
Bandelier, Adolph Francis Alphonse 56, **59**, 60, 70
Banfi, Antonio 201
Barandiarán, José Miguel de 207
Barber, Karin 366
Barker, Pat 36
Barley, Nigel 366
Barnard, T.T. 151–2
Barnes J.A. 158
Barnes, John 352, 356
Barnett, Milton 322
Barra y de Aragón, Francisco de las 207
Barth, Frederick 228, **229–30**, 255
Barthold, V. 230
Bartlett, H. 336
'basic personality' 102–3, 105–6
Bastian, Adolf 2, 5, 6, 7, 41, 61, 62, 220
Bastide, Roger 88, **173**, 251, 254, 292
Bastin, Louis 211
Bataille, Georges 63, 173, 176
Batchelor, John 266
Bates, Daisy 135
Bateson, Gregory 109, 141, **149–50**, 215
Battista 200
Baudin, Nicolas Thomas 28
Bauer, Ignacio 207
Baumann, Hermann 41, 218, 219, 222, **224**
Baviskar, B.S. 273
Baxter, P. 352
Bazin, Jean 306
Beaglehole, Ernest 158
Beals, R. 72
Beattie, John Hugh Marshall 215, 352, **354**, 363
Beaufort, L. de 9
Beccari 200
Beemer-Kuper, H. 152, 156–7; *see* Kuper, Hilda
behaviourism 103
Belenguer, José Valero 206
Belgian anthropology 210–13; Africanism 210, 211, 212, 213, 361; museums 6, 210, 211, 212

Belmont, Nicole 306
Belshaw, Cyril 343
Benedict, Ruth Fulton 62–3, 66, 72, 75, **104–5**, 323; academic career 101, 105, 108, 109, 122, 322, 325, 333; Apollonian ideal 71, 105; culturalism 102–3, 106; national character studies 72, 102–3, 105
Bennett 268
Bennett, W.C. 324, 329
Benthall, J. 352, 366
Bentham, Jeremy 10, 11
Benveniste, Emile 174
Berelowitch, W. 234
Berlin, Brent 327, 342
Bernardi, Bernardo 201, 202, **204–5**
Bernatzik, A. 44
Berndt, Catherine Helen **160**
Berndt, Ronald Murray 158, **159–60**
Bernett 324
Bernier 271
Bernot, Lucien **295–6**
Bernus, Edmond 302
Bernus-Vianès, Suzanne 295
Berque, Jacques 293, **294**
Bessaignet, Pierre **188**
Betanzos, Juan de 205
Béteille, André 273
Beuchat, H. 87–8
Bianchi, U. 201
Biasutti, Renato 201
Biebuyck, D. 361
Biebuyck, J. 211
Bieck, D. 211
Binford, L. 119
Biocca, Ettore 33
Birket-Smith, Kaj 228, **229**
Blanc, Alberto Carlo 201
Blanchard, R. 295
Bloch, Maurice E.F. 364, 365, **367**
Bloomfield, L. 177
Boas, Franz 15, 41, 45, **60–4**, 108; American Anthropological Association 59; American Indian collaborators 31; Columbia professorship 56, 63, 65–6, 101, 120–1, 322; culturalism 102; historical particularism 40, 62, 118, 136; influences on 2, 5, 7, 220; Jesup Expeditions 63, 231, 234–5; legacy to American anthropology 65–76; museum career and classification debate 5, 57, 58, 61, 62, 67
Boccassino, Renato 201
Boeck, de 212